Studies in Early Medieval Britain

General Editor: Nicholas Brooks

About the series:

The early Middle Ages, between the withdrawal of Roman authority at the start of the fifth century and the establishment of French-speaking aristocracies in the eleventh and twelfth centuries, was a key period in the history of the island of Britain. For it was then that the English, Welsh and Scots defined and distinguished themselves in language, customs and territory; it was then that successive conquests and settlements lent distinctive Irish, Anglo-Saxon, Scandinavian and Norman elements to the British ethnic mix; it was then that royal dynasties were established, that most of the surviving rural and urban settlements of Britain were created and named, and the landscape took a form that can still be recognised today; it was then too that Christian churches were established with lasting consequences for our cultural, moral, legal and intellectual perspectives.

The *Studies in Early Medieval Britain* will illuminate the history of Britain during this defining period and reveal its roots. Books in the series will be written, individually or in collaboration, by historians, archaeologists, philologists and literary and cultural scholars and are aimed at a wide readership of scholars, students and lay people.

About this volume:

The Anglo-Saxon influence on the Carolingian world has long been recognised by historians of the early medieval period. Wilhelm Levison, in particular, has drawn attention to the importance of the Anglo-Saxon contribution to the cultural and ecclesiastical development of Carolingian Francia in the central decades of the eighth century. What is much less familiar is the reverse process, by which Francia and Carolingian concepts came to influence contemporary Anglo-Saxon culture.

In this book Dr Story offers a major contribution to the subject of medieval cultural exchanges, focusing on the degree to which Frankish ideas and concepts were adopted by Anglo-Saxon rulers. Furthermore, by concentrating on the secular context and concepts of secular government as opposed to the more familiar ecclesiastical and missionary focus of Levison's work, this book offers a counterweight to the prevailing scholarship, providing a much more balanced overview of the subject. Through this reassessment, based on a close analysis of contemporary manuscripts – particularly the Northumbrian sources – Dr Story offers a fresh insight into the world of early medieval Europe.

About the author/editor:

Joanna Story is Lecturer in Early Medieval History, University of Leicester.

Nicholas Brooks is the Professor and Head of the Department of Medieval History, University of Birmingham.

Carolingian Connections

Carolingian Connections

Anglo-Saxon England and Carolingian Francia,
c. 750–870

Joanna Story

ASHGATE

Published by

Ashgate Publishing Limited
Gower House, Croft Road
Aldershot, Hants
GU11 3HR
England

Ashgate Publishing Company
Suite 420
101 Cherry Street
Burlington, VT 05401–4405
USA

Ashgate website: http://www.ashgate.com

British Library Cataloguing in Publication Data
Story, Joanna
     Carolingian connections: Anglo-Saxon England and Carolingian
     Francia, c. 750–870. – (Studies in early medieval Britain)
     1. Franks–England–History. 2. Carolingians. 3. Great Britain–
     History–Anglo-Saxon period, 449–1066. 4. England–Foreign
     relations–Europe. 5. Europe–Foreign relations–England.
     6. England–Civilization–To 1066. I. Title
     942' .015

Library of Congress Cataloging-in-Publication Data
Story, Joanna, 1970–
     Carolingian connections: Anglo-Saxon England and Carolingian
     Francia, c. 750–870 / Joanna Story.
     p.cm. – (Studies in early medieval Britain).
     Includes bibliographical references (p.) and index.
     1. Great Britain–History–Anglo-Saxon period, 449–1066. 2. Great
     Britain–Civilization–French influences. 3. England–Civilization–To 1066.
     4. England–Relations–France. 5. France–Relations–England. 6. France–
     History–To 987. 7. Carolingians. I. Title. II. Series.
     DA152.2. S76 2002
     942.01'5–dc21   2002016498

ISBN 0 7546 0124 2

This book is printed on acid-free paper

Typeset by Manton Typesetters, Louth, Lincolnshire, UK.
Printed by MPG Books Ltd, Bodmin, Cornwall.

STUDIES IN EARLY MEDIEVAL BRITAIN – 2

Contents

List of Maps and Figures

Maps

Figures

Abbreviations

AB	*The Annals of St. Bertin*
Alcuin, *Ep.*	Alcuin, *Epistolae*
ASChron.	*The Anglo-Saxon Chronicle* (cited by manuscript reference, A–F); *Two Saxon Chronicles Parallel*, ed. J. Earle and C. Plummer, 2 vols (Oxford, 1899); *The Anglo-Saxon Chronicle. A Collaborative Edition*, 17 vols (Cambridge, 1984–)
ASE	*Anglo-Saxon England*
ASSAH	*Anglo-Saxon Studies in Archaeology and History*
ARF	*Annales regni Francorum: Annales Regni Francorum inde ab a. 741 usque ad a. 829, qui dicuntur Annales Laurissenses Maiores et Einhardi*, ed. F. Kurze, MGH SS rer. Germ. 6 (Hanover and Leipzig, 1895)
BAR Bri. Ser.	British Archaeological Reports, British Series
BAV	Biblioteca Apostolica Vaticana, Vatican City
BCRFM	H. Mordek, *Bibliotheca capitularium regum Francorum manuscripta*, MGH Hilfsmittel 15 (Munich, 1995)
BCS	*Cartularium Saxonicum: A Collection of Charters Relating to Anglo-Saxon History*, ed. W. de Gray Birch, 3 vols (London, 1885–93)
Bede, *HAB*	Bede's *Historia Abbatum, Lives of the Abbots of Wearmouth Jarrow*, ed. C. Plummer, Venerabilis Bedae Opera Historica (Oxford, 1896); trans. J. F. Webb and D. H. Farmer, *The Age of Bede* (Harmondsworth, 1988), 185–210
Bede, *HE*	Bede's *Historia Ecclesiastica Gentis Anglorum*, ed. and trans. R.A.B. Mynors and B. Colgrave (Oxford, 1969)
BL MS	London, British Library manuscript
BNJ	*British Numismatic Journal*
BNJ/CR	*British Numismatic Journal, Coin Register*

CB	*Continuatio Bedae*
CBA Res. Rpt.	Council for British Archaeology Research Report
CC	*Codex Carolinus*
CCCC MS	Cambridge, Corpus Christi College manuscript
CCSL	Corpus Christianorum Series Latina
ChLa	*Chartae Latinae Antiquiores*, ed. A. Bruckner, facsimile edition of the Latin charters prior to the ninth century I-, (Olten and Lausanne, 1954–)
CLA	E. A. Lowe, *Codices Latini Antiquiores: A Palaeographical Guide to Latin Manuscripts Prior to the Ninth Century* I–XI plus Supplement (1934–72)
DA	*Deutsches Archiv für Erforschung des Mittelalters*
DCL MS	Durham, Dean and Chapter Library manuscript
EcHR	*Economic History Review*
EEMF	Early English Manuscripts in Facsimile (Copenhagen, 1951–)
EETS	Early English Text Society
EHD 1	D. Whitelock (ed. and trans.) *English Historical Documents I, c. 550–1042* (2nd edn.) (London, 1979)
EHR	*English Historical Review*
Einhard, *VK*	Einhard, *Vita Karoli Magni*, ed. G. Waitz, MGH SS rer. Germ. 25 (Hanover and Leipzig, 1911)
EMC	*Corpus of Early Medieval Coins*, Fitzwilliam Museum, Cambridge at http://www-cm.fitzmuseum.cam.ac.uk/emc
EME	*Early Medieval Europe*
Haddan and Stubbs, *Councils*	A.W. Haddan and W. Stubbs (eds), *Councils and Ecclesiastical Documents,* 3 vols (Oxford, 1869–78).
HAA	*Historia Abbatum Anonymo*; *The Anonymous History of the Abbots or the Life of the Abbot Ceolfrid*, ed. and trans. D. S. Boutflower, *Life of Ceolfrid, abbot of the monastery at Wearmouth and Jarrow by an unknown author of the eighth century* (Sunderland and London, 1912)

HpB	*Historia post Bedam*
Historia regum (*York Annals*)	*Symeonis Dunelmensis Opera et Collectanea*, ed. J. Hinde, Surtees Society 51 (Durham and London, 1868), 11–40; *Symeonis Monachis Opera Omnia*, ed. T. Arnold, RS 75, 2 vols (London, 1885), II, 30–66
JBAA	*Journal of the British Archaeological Association*
JEH	*Journal of Ecclesiastical History*
JMH	*Journal of Medieval History*
JMP	*Jaarboek Voor Munt- en Penningkunde*
LP	*Le Liber Pontificalis. Texte, introduction et commentaire*, ed. L. Duchesne, 2 vols (Paris, 1886–92)
MEC 1	P. Grierson and M.A.S. Blackburn, *Medieval European Coinage, with a Catalogue of the Coins in the Fitzwilliam Museum, Cambridge. Vol. 1: The Early Middle Ages, 5th–10th Centuries* (Cambridge, 1986)
MGH	Monumenta Germaniae Historica
AA	*Auctores antiquissimi*, 15 vols. (Berlin, 1877–1919)
Capit.	*Capitularia legum Sectio* II, *Capitularia Regum Francorum*, ed. A Boretius and V. Krause, 2 vols (Hanover, 1883–97)
Conc.	*Concilia. Legum Sectio III, Concilia II*, ed. A. Werminghoff (Hanover, 1906–8); III, ed. W. Hartmann (Hanover, 1984)
Dipl.	*Diplomatum Karolinorum* 1: *Pippini, Carlomanni, Carolo Magni Diplomata. Die Urkunden der Karolinger* ed. A. Dopsch, J. Lechner, M. Tangl and E. Mühlbacher (Hanover, 1906)
Epp.	*Epistolae* III–VIII, *Epistolae Merowingici et Karolini Aevi* (Hanover, 1892–1939)
Epp. Sel.	*Epistolae Selectae in usum scholarum*, 5 vols (Hanover, 1887–91)
Fontes	*Fontes iuris germanici Antiqui in usum scholarum ex Monumentis Germaniae Historicis separatim editi*, 13 vols (Hanover, 1909–86)
Poet.	*Poetae Latini Aevi Carolini*, ed. E. Dummler, L. Traube, P. von Winterfeld and K. Strecker, 4 vols (Hanover, 1881–99)

SS rer. Germ.	*Scriptores Rerum Germanicarum in usum scholarum separatim editi*, 63 vols (Hanover, 1871–1987)
SS rer. Merov.	*Scriptores Rerum Merovingicarum*, ed. B. Krusche and W. Levison, 7 vols (Hanover, 1885–1920)
SS	*Scriptores in folio*, 30 vols. (Hanover, 1824–1924)
MS(S)	manuscript(s)
NA	*Neues Archiv der Gesellschaft für ältere deutsche Geschichtskunde*
NCMH 2	*New Cambridge Medieval History. Vol. 2: c. 700–c.900,* ed. R. McKitterick (Cambridge, 1995)
NLR	National Library of Russia
PL	*Patrologia Cursus Completus, seu bibliotheca universalis omnium ss. patrum doctorum, scriptorumque ecclesiasticorum*, Series Latina, 221 vols (Paris, 1841–64)
RS	Rolls Series. *Rerum Britanniarum Medii Aevi Scriptores*, 99 vols (London, 1858–96)
S.	P. H. Sawyer, *Anglo-Saxon Charters: An annotated list and Bibliography*, Royal Historical Society Handbooks, 8 (London, 1968)
s.	saeculum
s.a.	sub anno
SCH	*Studies in Church History*
Sharpe, *Handlist*	R. Sharpe, *A Handlist of the Latin Writers of Great Britain and Ireland before 1540* (Turnhout, 1997)
TRHS	*Transactions of the Royal Historical Society*

Foreword

It is a privilege to edit the *Studies in Early Medieval Britain*, a series intended to illuminate the history of the island of Britain and its various regions between the fifth and the twelfth centuries. Volumes will be devoted to different aspects and phases of this long period, between the collapse of Roman imperial authority and the establishment of French-speaking aristocracies in different areas in the eleventh and twelfth centuries. It is planned that the series will be a focus for interdisciplinary collaboration between historians, archaeologists, philologists, and literary and cultural scholars. It will respect the differences between their disciplines, but facilitate communication between them. A very substantial body of evidence survives from the early Middle Ages, but much of it is fragmentary and difficult to understand. The task of early medievalists is to master the necessary technical skills without weakening the fascination of their subject. There is a large public, lay and academic, whose interest in the origins of our society, culture and institutions has been whetted at school, college or university, by local studies in adult education or by popular television programmes. The *Studies in Early Medieval Britain* will therefore seek to reach this public by eschewing inaccessible jargon, and by explaining the early medieval past with the help of good illustrations and diagrams. The objective is to maintain the highest standards of scholarship, but also of exposition. It will therefore be open both to works of general synthesis and to monographs by specialists in particular disciplines attempting to reach a wider readership. It will also include collaborative studies by groups of scholars.

I am delighted to welcome to the series Dr Joanna Story's *Carolingian Connections*, which concentrates on the relations of England and the Frankish kingdoms and Empire between the mid-eighth and the later ninth century. The importance of her theme has been well known to scholars ever since 1946 when Dr Wilhelm Levison repaid so richly his debt to the country that had given him shelter from racial persecution. The publication of his masterpiece, *England and the Continent in the Eighth Century* – a book that has delighted, daunted and intrigued its readers ever since – displayed the superb scholarship that he had honed in editing annals, laws, histories and saints' lives for the *Monumenta Germanicae Historiae*. Only a bold scholar, therefore, would dare to revisit some of Levison's ground, despite the help of two generations of subsequent work in many new areas of Anglo-Saxon studies. Dr Story's concern, however, is less with Levison's wish to explain to the post-war English how much continental Europe had already owed to Anglo-Saxons who had crossed the Channel in the eighth century. By contrast, her principal focus is on the Franks who worked in England and on Frankish influence on English politics, culture and society. It is exciting to see not only her command of different forms of evidence – archaeological and numismatic above all – that were not available to Levison, but also her very Levisonian delight in textual and manuscript history that is so fundamental to a proper understanding of her subject. Other scholars are taking the story on – to the late ninth century, the court of King Alfred of the West Saxons and beyond. Here is a volume on a theme of central importance in English history, which richly fulfils the purposes and ideals for which this series has been established.

Nicholas Brooks
University of Birmingham
October 2001

Preface

In the early spring of 1942 Wilhelm Levison was invited to give the Ford
Lectures at the University of Oxford and chose to lecture on the subject of
'England and the Continent in the Eighth Century'. His analysis was written
during the depths of the Second World War, and the combination of his own
experiences as a German-speaking Jewish intellectual in Nazi Germany and his
exile to England in 1939 provided an emotional and political framework for his
reflections on the eighth-century evidence. Mindful of his own fate, in his
preface he repeated Goethe's question 'whether a foreign country can become to
anyone a fatherland?'. Levison's measured response to that question was one of
gratitude and humility for the reception he had received in Durham, tempered
with regret for his distant friends 'who did not bow the knee to Baal, but
remained faithful until the hour of parting could no longer be avoided'. In the
twilight of his voluntary exile, Alcuin's Northumbrian patriotism was similarly
tempered with pragmatism and gratitude. After his retirement to Tours he wrote
to Charlemagne, 'In the morning, at the height of my powers, I sowed the seed
[of wisdom] in Britain, now in the evening, when my blood is growing cold I am
still sowing in Francia, hoping both will grow, by the grace of God'. Suitably
adapted, Alcuin's words are a fitting tribute to Levison's achievements.

It is a cliché to claim that, in writing this book, I have stood on the
shoulders of giants, but it happens to be true. Levison's masterful work inspired
many to follow in his footsteps, and his subject has attracted the attention of
some of the most significant scholars of early medieval Europe since the war,
many of whom have clarified and elaborated (but rarely corrected) Levison's
observations and conclusions. I do not make any such claims for myself or for
the book which follows. My objective here has been to examine the place of
England in post-Roman Europe from a different perspective to that taken by
Levison. Whereas his emphasis was on the influence and contribution of Anglo-
Saxons to continental culture during the century 700–800AD, mine focuses on
the period of Carolingian hegemony in Western Europe – that is, *c.* 750–*c.* 870AD
– and (with deference to the spirit of *my* age) of the influence which Carolingian
Francia had on the kingdoms of the English. In telling this story, I have covered
much familiar ground and, in so doing, have found some fresh shoots (and
undoubtedly missed others). The story is a rich one and, I think, enriches with
retelling. As such, I have tried to make this an accessible read for newcomers to
the subject – I've cited easily available translations wherever possible – as well
as providing detail for those to whom much is familiar. Equally, the footnotes
and bibliographic references are not as full as they might have been and may be

criticized for what they omit; but that has been an editorial decision with which I am happy to comply on grounds of style and comprehensibility.

My debts of gratitude are many; this project has provided an excuse to make many friends and to visit many libraries, and to librarians worldwide (and throughout time) I am immensely grateful. Of particular importance to me has been the library of the Dean and Chapter at Durham Cathedral; the opportunities given to me there as an undergraduate by the deputy librarian, Roger Norris, were rare and precious, and set me on my way. In Durham also, David Rollason was, and remains, an inspirational teacher. My work has benefited immeasurably from the scrutiny of many scholars and friends, especially Janet Nelson and Simon Keynes (who read the doctoral thesis on which parts of this book are based), as well as Michael Lapidge, Elaine Treharne, Mark Blackburn and Charles Insley, all of whom have read or commented on sections of the book. There are many, many others who have helped me in ways they cannot tell. Gareth Williams, Mark Blackburn, Ian Meadows, Gill Woolrich and Debbie Miles-Williams have assisted with plates and maps, and formal acknowledgments of thanks for permission to reproduce images are owed to the following institutions: The British Library; The British Museum; The Warburg Institute; Northamptonshire County Council; Sheffield Galleries and Museums Trust; the Herzog-August-Bibliothek in Wolfenbüttel; the National Library of Russia; the Istituto Suore Benedettine Di Priscilla, Rome. My editor, Nicholas Brooks, having waited very patiently, has read the entire volume and has made many valuable comments; the book is much the better for his critique, although any errors that remain are, naturally, my own. Finally, I would mention my colleagues at the University of Leicester, especially the students of my special subject on the Age of Bede and Alcuin; through teaching them I have learned an immense amount.

Despite the circumstance of composition, Levison's analysis of the Anglo-Saxon mission to Germany, of Alcuin's friendship with Charlemagne, of the centrality of the Anglo-Saxon contribution to Carolingian cultural experiment is inherently optimistic, one which understood the commonality and complementarity of the Anglo-Saxon and Carolingian experience. Levison would undoubtedly have been interested by the post-war trends to recast Charlemagne as the father of Europe, as a king who could be claimed by both France and Germany as a common ancestor, and more recently to present the Franks as 'pioneers of Europe'. History is a potent force with which to shape contemporary opinions, and the place of England/Britain within (or without) Europe remains a hotly debated political and economic topic. This does not validate an analysis of history a thousand years old, but it should serve as a reminder of its importance.

11 September 2001
Leicester

Map 1 Carolingian Europe

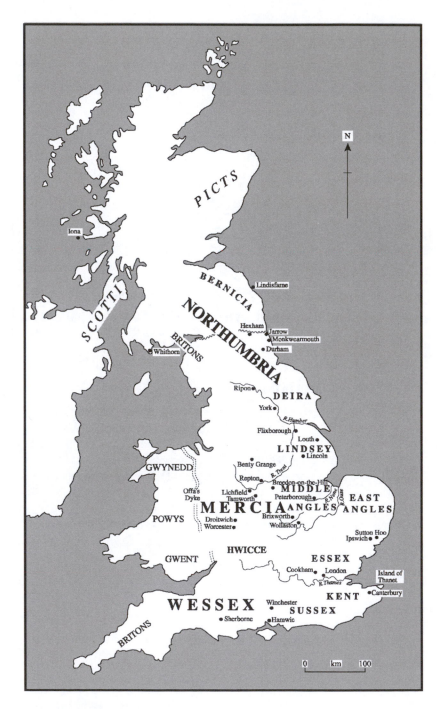

Map 2 Anglo-Saxon England

Chapter 1

Introduction: Evidence and Interpretation

Levison and the Anglo-Saxons

> The English stream flowed into the greater river that is usually called
> the 'Carolingian Renaissance'. The stream gave the river its direction,
> other tributaries reinforced the movement. … But the facts adduced
> show that the current of the eighth century was reversed at its end.[1]

These words encapsulate Wilhelm Levison's thesis on Anglo-Saxon contacts
with the Continent in the eighth century. Levison's book, published shortly
before his death in January 1947, represents the distillation of a lifetime of study
in the libraries and archives of Europe before the Second World War and, with
his meticulous scholarship and intimate knowledge of the manuscript sources, it
remains the starting point for all subsequent work on the subject.[2] His seminal
study established the importance of the Anglo-Saxon contribution to the cultural
and political development of Carolingian Francia in the central decades of the
eighth century; but he also observed the beginnings of a counterflow during the
last years of Charlemagne, of the influence which an increasingly mature
Carolingian polity had on the kingdoms of England in the closing decades of the
eighth century and the early years of the ninth. Levison was writing in 1942–43,
and his thoughts on the symbiosis of this ancient relationship would certainly
have struck a resonant chord in the minds of his audience; under his pen, the
history of England and Francia in the eighth century became a tale of close links
and cooperation, particularly in the campaigns against the 'darkness of continental heathenism'.[3] Levison described a time, over a thousand years ago, when
missionaries from England had been in the vanguard of Charlemagne's campaigns to destroy the Germanic pagan tribes which flourished to the east of his
kingdom, and to bring those regions into the light of Christian salvation by
means of military force and cultural conquest, as well as missionary endeavour.
Underlying Levison's analysis flows a feeling that, in the dark years of the
1940s, the heartlands of Charlemagne's empire (from where he had fled in April

---

[1] W. Levison, *England and the Continent in the Eighth Century* (Oxford, 1946), 107, 151.

[2] W. Levison, *Wilhelm Levison, 1876–1947. A Bibliography* (Oxford, 1948); T. Schieffer
(ed.), *In Memoriam Wilhelm Levison (1876–1947). Reden und Grußbotschaften bei der Gedenkfeier
der Universität [Bonn] zum 100. Geburtstag am 31. Mai 1976* (Cologne and Bonn, 1977); W. E.
Mosse et al. (eds), *Second Chance: Two Centuries of German-speaking Jews in the United Kingdom* (Tübingen, 1991), 162. Although he didn't leave Germany until April 1939, Levison had been
unable to continue in his lecturing post as *Ordinarius* at the University of Bonn after 1935.

[3] Levison, *England and the Continent in the Eighth Century*, 96.

1939 as a refugee from the Nazi regime) had seldom been so much in need of a renewal of the ancient bonds with the English that he had perceived in the history of the eighth century. In his preface, Levison wrote that he hoped his works would 'in their small way, contribute to join again broken links, when the works of peace have resumed their place lost in the turmoil of war'.[4]

Levison's particular interest was in the activities of Anglo-Saxon missionaries in pagan Germany during the first half of the eighth century, the same period that witnessed the rise of the Carolingian family from noble faction to royal dynasty. He demonstrated the symbiosis of these two phenomena, showing how Anglo-Saxon missionaries came into direct contact with the Carolingians (whose familial estates lay in eastern Austrasia) through their vocation to evangelize the pagan peoples whom they regarded as ancestral cousins of the English. Carolingian sponsorship of Anglo-Saxon missionary activity and their monastic foundations on both sides of the Rhine had political and cultural consequences. Through their involvement in the missionary enterprises, several Anglo-Saxons attained prominent positions within the Frankish ecclesiastical hierarchy and, as a consequence, some of them, such as Willibrord, Boniface, and Burchard, became closely involved with the dynastic and territorial ambitions of the Carolingian family. In cultural terms, the presence of Anglo-Saxon churchmen and churchwomen in Francia contributed to an insular infusion into Frankish intellectual and artistic culture that was lasting and influential, and added to the older, Irish influence which had been generated by the followers of Columbanus in Merovingian Francia.[5]

This insular influence is demonstrated, for example, by the persistence of Anglo-Saxon features in the codicology of manuscripts produced in 'insular centres' on the Continent in the second half of the eighth century, most obviously in the use of distinctive insular scripts, but also in the use of parchment produced in the insular fashion, or in characteristic punctuation, spelling and quire structure. Writing about the career of Boniface, the priest Willibald recalled that 'an extremely large number of holy men from Britain came to his aid, among them readers, scribes, and men learned in other arts'.[6] Occasionally, the names of Anglo-Saxon scribes are revealed, such as the inscription that identi-

---

[4] Ibid., vi.

[5] On the Irish influence see, in particular, the collected essays in H. Lowe (ed.), *Die Iren und Europa im früheren Mittelalter*, 2 vols (Stuttgart, 1982) and in J. M. Picard (ed.), *Ireland and Northern France, AD 600–850* (Dublin, 1991); a brief summary is given by I. N. Wood, *The Merovingian Kingdoms, 450–751* (London, 1994), 184–89. See also J. Backhouse, 'England and the Continent', in L. Webster and J. Backhouse (eds), *The Making of England. Anglo-Saxon Art and Culture AD 600–900* (London, 1991), 157–92; E. Wamers, 'Insular Art in Carolingian Europe – The Reception of Old Ideas in a New Empire', in J. Higgitt and R. M. Spearman (eds), *The Age of Migrating Ideas. Early Medieval Art in Britain and Ireland* (Edinburgh, 1993), 35–44; G. Henderson, 'Emulation and Invention in Carolingian Art', in R. McKitterick (ed.), *Carolingian Culture: Emulation and Innovation* (Cambridge, 1994), 248–73, at 251–55.

[6] Willibald, *Vita Bonifatii*, ed. W. Levison, MGH SS rer. Germ. LVII (Hanover and Leipzig, 1905), c. 6; *The Anglo-Saxon Missionaries in Germany*, trans. C. H. Talbot (London, 1954), 47.

fies Cutbercht as the scribe of a copy of the Gospels from Salzburg made in the late eighth century,[7] or the Freising manuscripts that were copied in the 780s by a scribe who called himself Peregrinus and who wrote an expert insular minuscule script.[8] Where these peculiarly insular features are combined with continental characteristics in the same manuscript we may be looking at second-generation insular influence in a continental centre, where a scribe or craftsman had been taught his craft by an Anglo-Saxon master within a Frankish environment.[9] Equally, the presence in Francia of metalworkers, trained in the insular style but working for foreign patrons, is illustrated by the splendid gilt chalice from Kremsmünster, Austria, made for Duke Tassilo of Bavaria between 777 and 788, the metal cover of the Lindau Gospels, or by the standing cross from Bischofshofen that was possibly made during the episcopacy of Virgil, the Iona-trained bishop of Salzburg (746–84).[10] Such traces of an Anglo-Saxon aesthetic within the surviving corpus of continental manuscripts and metalwork provides the anonymous, background noise to the clear voices of individuals whose names are known to us through extant sources. The names of many Anglo-Saxons who lived and worked on the Continent are known, but these names must represent only a limited proportion of the women and men from Britain who travelled to Carolingian Europe. And, although the impetus generated by the mission remained an important pull-factor well into the ninth century, Francia under Charlemagne held many additional attractions for ambitious Anglo-Saxons.

Scholars are inclined to attribute to Charlemagne himself the initiative behind the renaissance, or *renovatio*, of learning that characterized the cultural achievements of his reign.[11] The capitulary known as *Admonitio Generalis* of

---

[7] Vienna, Österreichische Nationalbibliothek Cod. 1124, fo. 4*v; *CLA* X, no. 1500; J. J. G. Alexander, *A Survey of Manuscripts Illuminated in the British Isles. Vol. 1: Insular Manuscripts, 6th to 9th Century* (London, 1978), no. 37; S. E. von Daum Tholl, 'The Cutbercht Gospels and the Earliest Writing Centre at Salzburg', in L. L. Brownrigg (ed.), *The Making of the Medieval Book: Techniques of Production* (Los Altos, 1995), 17–33. See also K. Bierbrauer, 'Der Einfluß insulare Handschriften auf die kontinentale Buchmalerei', in C. Stiegemann and M. Wemhoff (eds), *799, Kunst und Kultur in der Karolingerzeit* (Mainz, 1999), III, 465–81.

[8] Munich, Bayerische Staatsbibliothek Clm 6237, 6297, 6299, 6433; *CLA* IX, no. 1253, 1263, 1265, 1283. See also R. McKitterick, 'The Anglo-Saxon Missionaries in Germany: Reflections on the Manuscript Evidence', *Transactions of the Cambridge Bibliographical Society*, 9 (1989), 291–329.

[9] T. J. Brown, 'The Distribution and Significance of Membrane Prepared in the Insular Manner', in *La Paléographie Hébraïque*, Colloques Internationaux du Centre National de la Recherche Scientifique, 547 (Paris, 1972), 127–35, and reprinted in J. Batley, M. P. Brown and J. Roberts (eds), *A Palaeographer's View. The Selected Writings of Julian Brown* (London, 1993), 125–39; R. McKitterick, 'The Diffusion of Insular Culture in Neustria between 650 and 850: the Implications of the Manuscript Evidence', in H. Atsma and K.-F. Werner (eds), *La Neustrie*, Beihefte der Francia 16 (Sigmaringen, 1989), 395–432, and reprinted as Chapter 3 in R. McKitterick, *Books, Scribes and Learning in the Frankish Kingdoms, 6th–9th Centuries* (Aldershot, 1994).

[10] Backhouse and Webster, *The Making of England*, nos 131–33; E. Wamers, 'Insulare Kunst im Reich Karls des Großen', in Stiegemann and Wemhoff, *799, Kunst und Kultur*, III, 452–64.

[11] A useful introduction to the subject is G. Brown, 'The Carolingian Renaissance', in R. McKitterick (ed.), *Carolingian Culture: Emulation and Innovation* (Cambridge, 1994), 1–51.

789 is the document that articulates most clearly the ambitions of this movement, but it is clear that scholars had been gathering at the court for more than a decade before it was issued, probably since the fall of the Lombard kingdom to Charlemagne's armies in 774. Certainly Lombard scholars such as Paulinus (later Patriarch of Aquileia), Peter of Pisa, and Paul the Deacon were among the earliest scholars to taste the wealth of Charlemagne's patronage.[12] Insular scholars were also among those attracted to court circles during the 770s; one of them, Cathwulf, wrote an important letter to Charlemagne extolling the virtues of his kingship in the immediate aftermath of the Lombard defeat. The context of the preservation of Cathwulf's letter suggests that he was associated with the highly politicized abbey of St Denis, near Paris.[13] Others, like the Irishmen Clemens Scottus and the unidentified *Hibernicus Exul* were also early arrivals in Francia. Where they led, others followed: Beornred (later abbot of Echternach, then archbishop of Sens), Joseph 'Scottus', Candidus (Hwita/Witto), Fridugisius, Clemens 'Peregrinus', Dungal (who specialized in astronomy, a favourite subject of the king), and Dicuil (an expert on geography), to name but the most prominent, also came within the orbit of Charlemagne's court and have left ephemeral records of their activities there.[14] And as Charlemagne's status grew, his court played host to other Anglo-Saxon visitors too; travelling bishops, exiled noblemen and deposed kings came to his court, en route to Rome, seeking hospitality at the court and a sympathetic hearing for their grievances. What is interesting is that Charlemagne was often moved to act on their behalf (see Chapter 5).

Alcuin of York

The most important and well known of the Anglo-Saxon scholars linked to Charlemagne's court was, of course, Alcuin of York, 'the most learned man in the entire world'.[15] 'You invited lovers of wisdom from different parts of the world to help in your plans', wrote Alcuin to Charlemagne in 801, 'among them

---

[12] Einhard, *VK*, c. 25.

[13] Paris, Bibliothèque nationale, MS Lat. 2777, on which see J. Story, 'Cathwulf, Kingship, and the Royal Abbey of Saint-Denis', *Speculum*, 74 (1999), 1–20.

[14] On the composition of the court before 794 see D. A. Bullough, '*Aula Renovata*: The Carolingian Court before the Aachen Palace', *Proceedings of the British Academy*, 71 (1985), 267–301, reprinted in his *Carolingian Renewal* (Manchester, 1991), 123–60. See also J. Marenbon, *From the Circle of Alcuin to the School of Auxerre* (Cambridge, 1981). The evidence for the insular émigrés to Francia is usefully summarized by M. Garrison, 'The English and the Irish at the Court of Charlemagne', in P. L. Butzer, M. Kerner and W. Oberschelp (eds), *Karl der Grosse und sein Nachwirken. 1200 Jahre Kultur und Wissenschaft in Europa. Vol. 1: Wissen und Weltbild* (Turnhout, 1997), 97–124. See also Einhard's report of the miracle performed on an English pilgrim in his account of the *Translation and Miracles of Marcellinus and Peter*; trans. P. E. Dutton, *Charlemagne's Courtier: The Complete Einhard* (Peterborough, Ontario, 1998), 94.

[15] Einhard, *VK*, c. 25.

you brought me, the least of the servants of wisdom from the remotest parts of Britain.'[16] Alcuin's fame and intellectual legacy was secured because of this close association with the great Carolingian king, but he was far from being 'the least of the servants of wisdom' when he arrived in Francia; the Frankish period of his career flourished because of the reputation he had built as a teacher and scholar of renown in the distant kingdom of Northumbria.

Alcuin was born during the second quarter of the eighth century, and a date of birth that dovetails (suspiciously) with the death of Bede in 735 is generally favoured.[17] His family came from the southern Northumbrian province of Deira and seems to have been of moderate social rank, controlling land and monastic estates to the east of York, on the north bank of the River Humber towards Spurn Head.[18] Alcuin entered the community of Archbishop Ecgberht in his youth and, although he was never ordained above the rank of deacon, his organizational and intellectual talents were reason enough for him to earn promotion to master of the York school and keeper of the library. As a young man, Alcuin had travelled to the Continent with his master and teacher, Ælberht, seeking learning and rare texts for inclusion in the York library.[19] If we can judge by the wide range of Alcuin's own erudition, and from a booklist incorporated into his poem *On The Bishops, Kings and Saints of York*, the York library under Ælberht's inspiration had become one of the most extensive and important in western Europe.[20] Ælberht was widely praised for his wisdom and (in re-

---

[16] Alcuin, *Ep.* no. 229; *Alcuin of York c. A.D.732 to 804: His Life and Letters*, trans. S. Allott (York, 1974), no. 67.

[17] E. Dümmler, 'Zur Lebensgeschichte Alchuins', *NA*, 18 (1893), 51–70, at 53–54 which gives the grounds for the 'traditional' date of *c.* 735; C. J. B. Gaskoin, *Alcuin: His Life and Work* (London, 1904), 41, n. 1 arguing for an earlier date; Levison, *England and the Continent*, 153 (*c.* 730); P. Godman (ed. and trans.), *Alcuin: The Bishops, Kings and Saints of York* (Oxford, 1982), xxxvi, 133 (which gives grounds for proposing a later date than that traditionally accepted). 'An unknown year close to 740', is preferred by D. A. Bullough, 'Alcuin before Frankfort', in R. Berndt (ed.), *Das Frankforter Konzil von 794* (Mainz, 1997), 571–85, at 573.

[18] Alcuin, *Vita Willibrordi*, ed. W. Levison, MGH SS rer. Merov. VII (Berlin, 1920), c. 1. See also his letter to Archbishop Beornred of Sens who commissioned the work in which Alcuin refers to his prose *Vita* of his relative Willibrord and to a metrical version, to which he had attached a shorter elegy on Wigils, Willibrord's father, who had bequeathed the monastery in which he was buried to Alcuin; Alcuin, *Ep.* no. 120; *Alcuin of York*, trans. Allott, no. 159.

[19] Alcuin, *Ep.* no. 271 to the monks of Murbach, and no. 172 to Charlemagne; *Alcuin of York*, trans. Allott, no. 75, both of which refer to his travels abroad as an *adolescens* with Ælberht. On the latter letter see D. A. Bullough, 'Reminiscence and Reality: Text, Transmission and Testimony of an Alcuin Letter', *Journal of Medieval Latin*, 5 (1995), 174–201. See also the verse-letter written for acquaintances abroad, probably composed before 781, Alcuin, *Alcuini Carmina*, MGH PLAC I (Berlin, 1881), no. 4; H. Waddell (trans.), *More Latin Lyrics from Vergil to Milton* (London, 1976), 150–55.

[20] Alcuin, *York Poem*, lines 1531–62. P. Hunter-Blair, 'From Bede to Alcuin', in G. Bonner (ed.), *Famulus Christi* (London, 1976), 239–66; M. Lapidge, 'Aediluulf and the School of York', in A. Lehner and W. Berschin (eds), *Lateinische Kultur im VIII. Jahrhundert: Traube-Gedenkschrift* (St Ottilien, 1990), 161–78, reprinted in his *Anglo-Latin Literature. Vol. 1: 600–899* (London and Rio Grande 1996), 161–78, and 'Latin Learning in Ninth-Century England', ibid., 409–54.

hearsal of Alcuin's own destiny) was fêted by foreign kings and nobles to join their courts. He declined these invitations and, returning home, was elevated in 767 to the archbishopric of York. There, with the help of Alcuin and Eanbald, he sponsored the construction of a magnificent new church dedicated, appropriately, to *Alma Sophia*, or Holy Wisdom.[21]

As *magister* in his own right, Alcuin built a considerable reputation in York, attracting students from Northumbria and beyond. We know that at least one student came from Frisia to study with Alcuin; Liudger returned in 773 after three years in York, taking with him copies of a great many books.[22] But, despite Alcuin's central importance in the York community, the most influential part of his career lay ahead of him in Francia. On his retirement from the archbishopric, Ælberht bequeathed control of the library and of his scholarly legacy to Alcuin, passing control of the metropolitan see to Alcuin's friend, Eanbald.[23] Alcuin was sent to Rome in 780–81 to collect the pallium for Eanbald from Pope Hadrian, and it was on his return journey that he met Charlemagne at Parma. Invited by Charlemagne to join his court, Alcuin moved to Francia where he struck up a close working relationship and robust friendship with the king.[24] Differing dates have been proposed for his move from York to Francia; he may have gone as early as 782, although we have little proof of his presence there until after the legates' mission to Britain of 786.[25] He returned to Northumbria in 790, charged with the task of restoring diplomatic and trade links with Offa of Mercia, and went back to Francia late in 792 or early 793, having fulfilled a commission from Charlemagne to compose a rebuttal to an Iconodule treatise sent from Constantinople.[26] He was back in Francia when news came of the disastrous raid by Viking pirates on St Cuthbert's community in Lindisfarne in June 793.[27]

[21] Alcuin, *York Poem*, lines 1507–20; R. K. Morris, 'Alcuin, York and the *Alma Sophia*', in L. A. S. Butler and R. K. Morris (eds), *The Anglo-Saxon Church, Papers on History, Architecture and Archaeology in Honour of Dr H. M. Taylor*, CBA Res Rpt, 60 (London, 1986), 80–89.

[22] Altfrid, *Vita Liudgeri*, ed. G. H. Pertz, MGH SS 11 (Berlin, 1829), c. 12; *EHD* 1, trans. Whitelock, no. 160. D. A. Bullough, '*Albuinus deliciosus Karoli regis*. Alcuin of York and the Shaping of the Early Carolingian Court', in L. Fenske, W. Rösener, and T. Zotz (eds), *Institutionen, Kultur und Gesellschaft im Mittelalter* (Sigmaringen, 1984), 73–92, at 78.

[23] The date of Ælberht's retirement is ambiguous, and it is possible that Alcuin and Eanbald received their 'inheritance' some time before their master died: Alcuin, *York Poem*, lines 1519–35.

[24] Anon., *Vita Alcuini*, ed. W. Arndt, MGH SS rer. Merov. VII (Hanover and Leipzig, 1913), c. 9.

[25] His presence is not mentioned by Paul the Deacon whose writings are the most important sources for the court before 786; D. A. Bullough, 'Alcuin and the Kingdom of Heaven: Liturgy, Theology and the Carolingian Age', in U.-R. Blumenthal (ed.), *Carolingian Essays* (Washington, DC, 1983), 1–69, reprinted in his *Carolingian Renewal*, 161–240 at 175; *idem*, '*Aula Renovata*', at 136, and 'Alcuin before Frankfort', 578.

[26] Alcuin, *Ep.* nos 7, 8, 9, 30, 82; *Alcuin of York*, trans. Allott, nos 31, 9, 10, 11, 39; *Historia regum* (*York Annals*), 792; see below 131–32. Alcuin's letter does not survive but reflections of it may be discernible in the tract countering image worship composed by Theodulf of Orléans, known as the *Libri Carolini*; see Bullough, 'Alcuin before Frankfort', 581–82.

[27] Alcuin, *Ep.* nos 16, 17, 18, 19, 20, 21, 22; *Alcuin of York*, trans. Allott, nos 12, 48, 13, 29, 26, 27, 28.

Alcuin remained with the Frankish court when it settled at the new palace in Aachen the following year. While there he introduced the king to the liberal arts and, according to Einhard, took charge of the education of the royal children; in a later letter he remembers debating numerology with the king while bathing in the hot springs at Aachen which Charlemagne so favoured.[28] Charlemagne rewarded Alcuin's service with the command of several abbacies, St Lupus at Troyes and the abbey at Ferrières, as well as the prestigious monastery of St Martin at Tours. Alcuin moved to St Martin's in 796, acting as its abbot until 801 when the deterioration in his health was sufficient to permit his retirement from active service.[29] But, even in retirement, Alcuin still continued to attract compatriots to service overseas; one Anglo-Saxon student called Aigulf overheard four Frankish brothers of St Martin's muttering ungenerously about the number of foreigners who gathered around Alcuin, 'That Brit [*iste Britto*] has come to visit the other Brit lying inside. O God, free this monastery from these Brits; for just as bees return to their queen they all swarm to this man'.[30] Alcuin died on 19 May 804 having written his own epitaph: '... Alcuin was my name, I always loved wisdom. Pray for me as you read this'.[31]

The maximum possible duration of Alcuin's association with the Frankish court was therefore little more than two decades; the time he spent in the king's company, however, was considerably less given the military campaigning and peripatetic nature of the court before 794, and the periods which Alcuin spent in England in (and before) 786 and between 790 and 792–93. His retirement to Tours in 796 meant that he would have spent barely two years with the court newly settled at Aachen. His decision to withdraw from court was precipitated in part by a series of political and emotional disasters in England, linked to people he knew well and which clearly caused him considerable distress. On 18 April King Æthelred of Northumbria was assassinated and the usurper, the *patricius* Osbald, survived a reign of only 27 days before being expelled via Lindisfarne to Pictland.[32] Alcuin wrote to him in exile, urging him to repent of his presumption and to take holy orders.[33] Osbald's successor, Eardwulf, succeeded on 14 May and 12 days later was made king in York amid considerable ecclesiastical pomp, but within months he was accused of moral turpitude and became the

---

[28] Einhard, *VK*, c. 22; Alcuin, *Ep*. no. 262; *Alcuin of York*, trans. Allott, no. 73.

[29] Alcuin, *Ep*. nos 229, 238; *Alcuin of York*, trans. Allott, nos 67, 68.

[30] Anon., *Vita Alcuini*, c. 18; G. H. Brown, 'The Preservation and Transmission of Northumbrian Culture on the Continent: Alcuin's Debt to Bede', in P. E. Szarmach and J. T. Rosenthal (eds), *The Preservation and Transmission of Anglo-Saxon Culture* (Kalamazoo, 1997), 159–76, at 162.

[31] Alcuin, *Alcuini Carmina*, no. 123, lines 23–24; Anon., *Vita Alcuini*, c. 26.

[32] *Historia regum* (*York Annals*), 796, *ASChron*. DE, 796; Alcuin, *Ep*. nos 18, 102, 105, 106, 109; *Alcuin of York*, trans. Allott, nos 13, 102, 14, 15, 17.

[33] Alcuin, *Ep*. no. 109; *Alcuin of York*, trans. Allott, no. 17. Osbald is named as a *patricius* of Æthelred in an earlier letter (Alcuin, *Ep*. no. 18; *Alcuin of York*, trans. Allott, no. 13), he seems to have followed Alcuin's advice and died as an abbot in 799 and, according to the *Historia regum* (*York Annals*) for that year, was buried in York; see D. Rollason, *Sources for York History to AD1100* (York, 1998), 54, 148.

target of domestic rebellions and foreign invasion.[34] Furthermore, Alcuin's child-
hood friend Archbishop Eanbald I of York died on 10 August and was swiftly
succeeded by one of his own students, also named Eanbald.[35] But the new
archbishop quickly became embroiled in opposition to Eardwulf and was accused of harbouring the king's enemies and of living a luxurious and militaristic
lifestyle inappropriate for a man of his ecclesiastical rank.[36] Mercia, too, was
rocked by political instability; King Offa died on 29 July and his only son
Ecgfrith barely five months later on 17 December. Nothing Alcuin says suggests
that Ecgfrith had been assassinated, but in letters to a Mercian nobleman and to
King Coenwulf, he interpreted Ecgfrith's death in biblical dimensions, as the
sins of the father visited on the son; 'you know how much blood the father shed
to secure the kingdom for his son. It proved the undoing, not the making' of his
dynasty.[37] The rebellion led by Eadberht Præn in Kent, which ousted the Mercian-
appointed archbishop of Canterbury, further destabilized the Mercian hegemony.
All this, in combination with the recent death of Pope Hadrian and election of
the controversial Pope Leo III, reconfigured the familiar landmarks of Alcuin's
world and precipitated his retreat from Aachen in 796.

But much as he wanted to retire, claiming world-weariness and broken
health, Alcuin's role as adviser and teacher to the king was a job for life, and he
remained 'on call' even though he was not at court.[38] Many letters after 796
respond to lists of questions from the king who was in the habit of sending
messengers, hot-foot from the palace, to find Alcuin wherever he might be. 'An
envoy came at speed with a sheet of questions from your Majesty', starts one
letter 'but', complained Alcuin (with more than a hint of exasperation), 'as I am
on a journey I do not have the books to hand in which these matters are dealt
with.' In an attempt to respond to these questions from the king concerning
planetary movements, Alcuin referred Charlemagne to Bede's writings and asked
him to send a copy of Pliny's *Natural History* so that he could provide a more
detailed answer.[39] Another letter from the king wanted an explanation for the
unusual size of the moon on a particular day in March 799; it reached Alcuin as
he was travelling across the 'broad dry plains of Belgium'.[40] On 24 May 802
Alcuin recorded the arrival of a messenger from the king at 9 o'clock in the

---

[34] Alcuin, *Ep.* nos 108, 122; *Alcuin of York*, trans. Allott, nos 16, 46.

[35] He was consecrated in York on Sunday 14 August 796; *Historia regum* (*York Annals*), 796;
ASChron. DE, 796; Alcuin, *Ep.* no. 114; *Alcuin of York*, trans. Allott, no. 6; Rollason, *Sources for
York History*, 54, 145.

[36] Alcuin, *Ep.* nos 116, 209, 232, 233; *Alcuin of York*, trans. Allott, nos 7, 22, 20, 21, and
below Chapter 5.

[37] Alcuin, *Ep.* nos. 122, 123; *Alcuin of York*, trans. Allott, nos 46, 47. On the identification of the
Mercian nobleman as the *patricius* Brorda, see A. Thacker, 'Some Terms for Noblemen in Anglo-
Saxon England, *c.* 650–900', in *ASSAH*, 1, ed. D. Brown, BAR Bri. Ser. 92 (Oxford, 1981), 201–36.

[38] Alcuin, *Ep.* no. 229; *Alcuin of York*, trans. Allott, no. 67.

[39] Alcuin, *Ep.* no. 155; *Alcuin of York*, trans. Allott, no. 76.

[40] Alcuin, *Ep.* no. 170; *Alcuin of York*, trans. Allott, no. 77; see also Alcuin, *Ep.* no. 148;
Alcuin of York, trans. Allott, no. 79.

morning who arrived with gifts and instructions to return to the king at 3 o'clock the same day.[41] One gets the impression of a master who placed a high value on precise information and immediate answers, who relished and encouraged vigorous intellectual debate at court, seeking all the while to reconcile the reality of his life as a warlord with his ambitions for scholarship and learning. In a letter to Charlemagne dated *c.* 800 Alcuin quotes the king's words: 'Dear teacher in Christ', wrote the king, 'I must tell you the question about the Gospel put to us not by a cleric but by a layman. We [Charles] have delayed answering him for the present, but not because we could not answer his point.' The layman's question concerned the enigmatic passage in the Gospel of Luke in which Christ instructed the disciples to buy a sword. On being told that they already had two swords, Christ had simply said, 'it is enough'. But, asked the king, 'if the sword is the word of God and the Lord meant the word of God when he told them to buy a sword, how is it reasonable that all who receive the word of God should perish by the word of God?' Value the man who asked this question, remarked Alcuin, 'though he has a soldier's hands, he is wise in heart'.[42] Friendship with Charlemagne was demanding; he expected results as much from his scholars as from the commanders of his armies. 'I thank you, good lord, for having the book which I sent you on your instructions read in your hearing and its errors noted and sent back for correction', said Alcuin in response to a message from the king '... [however] your letter hints that you do not approve of all that you read, since you have ordered a defence of the work to be sent to you.' In the same letter Alcuin says that he had sent a messenger to Bishop Leidrad of Lyons in search of a copy of a text that Charlemagne wanted, and enclosed some mathematical problems for the king's amusement, noting that Einhard would help him work out the answers.[43]

This robust and energetic friendship between king and scholar is, fundamentally, the reason for the survival of so much information about Alcuin. It is doubtful whether anything much more than an echo of Alcuin's legacy would have reached our ears today had he (like Ælberht before him) refused the invitation to serve in the court of a foreign king. It was his association with Charlemagne that made Alcuin a 'recognisable scholar-personality' whose writings were collected and copied after his death.[44] Even a voice as strong as Alcuin's is audible through the centuries primarily because of his proximity to the renowned Frankish king. Some contemporary Carolingian scholars such as Theodulf of Orléans and Einhard talked of Alcuin in their works on the king and his court, of his liking for porridge, and his influence with Charlemagne, and a biography was written between 823 and 829 with the assistance of one of

---

[41] Alcuin, *Ep.* no. 254; *Alcuin of York*, trans. Allott, no. 149.

[42] Alcuin, *Ep.* no. 136; *Alcuin of York*, trans. Allott, no. 66.

[43] Alcuin, *Ep.* no. 172; *Alcuin of York*, trans. Allott, no. 75.

[44] D. A. Bullough, 'Alcuin's Cultural Influence: the Evidence of the Manuscripts', in L. A. J. R. Houwen and A. A. MacDonald (eds), *Alcuin of York. Scholar at the Carolingian Court*, Germania Latina 3 (Groningen, 1998), 1–26, esp. at 25.

Alcuin's Anglo-Saxon students, Sigulf, by then his successor as abbot of Ferrières.[45] But the great majority of what is known about Alcuin is autobiographical in origin. In addition to his letters (of which more than 280 survive), his poetry and his hagiographical works contain occasional references to his own past as well as insights into his personality and intellect. With few exceptions, however, all these sources from Alcuin or his contemporaries date from, and reflect, the Frankish years of Alcuin's career; we can pin little with certainty to his time in York before he left to work with Charlemagne. One epistle-poem to friends abroad almost certainly pre-dates 781, likewise an epitaph to Archbishop Ælberht, and it is possible that his poem on *the Bishops, Kings and Saints of York* was conceived during his time in York, but in its extant form it is close generically to much Carolingian court poetry and may have been revised and 'published' only after Alcuin reached Francia.[46] Certainly his other poems on English themes were written from abroad.[47] Furthermore, the vast majority of his surviving letters post-date the year 790, for in that year he returned to England and, distant from his Frankish friends, started systematically to build a register of his letters.[48] It is because of this decision to collect his letters, and that of subsequent scholars to preserve those collections, that so much is known not only about Alcuin, but also about Anglo-Saxon England and Charlemagne's Francia in the 790s, making it one of the best documented decades in the early Middle Ages.

Chronicles and coinage: Anglo-Saxon sources *c.* 750–870

The 790s are, however, atypical for the period covered here; the years 750–870 are challenging ones for the Anglo-Saxonist used to the monumental coherence of Bede's *Historia Ecclesiastica* or the wide-ranging coverage of the *Anglo-Saxon Chronicle*. The period follows the death of Bede in 735 and precedes the Alfredian *renovatio* of the late ninth century. Bede's scholarship and the revival

---

[45] Theodulf, *On the Court*; trans. P. Godman, *Poetry of the Carolingian Renaissance* (Oxford, 1985), 150–63; Einhard, *VK*, c. 25; Anon., *Vita Alcuini*, preface and c. 10.

[46] The manuscript transmission of Alcuin's poems is scattered and patchy; *Alcuin: On the Bishops, Kings, and Saints of York*, ed. and trans. P. Godman (Oxford, 1982), xxxix–xlvii, lxxxviii–xciii; *idem*, *Poetry of the Carolingian Renaissance*, 16–17; Bullough, 'Alcuin before Frankfort', 574 where he gives a date of 'the 780s (probably)' for the York Poem. The letter-poem is edited by E. Dümmler, ed. *Carmina*, MGH *PLAC* I, no. 4, and the epitaph is no. 2.

[47] For example, his poem *On the Destruction of Lindisfarne*; *Alcuini Carmina*, ed. E. Dümmler, MGH *PLAC* I, no. 9; *Poetry of the Carolingian Renaissance*, trans. P. Godman (Oxford, 1985), 17, 126–37.

[48] Bullough has argued that this collection was left behind when Alcuin returned to Francia, and is essentially that preserved in the two closely related eleventh-century manuscripts, London, B. L. Cotton, MS Tiberius A.xv and Cotton, MS Vespasian A.xiv: Bullough, 'Alcuin's Cultural Influence' 24. On the Vespasian manuscript, which belonged to Wulfstan of York and Worcester, see C. Chase (ed.), *Two Alcuin Letter-Books* (Toronto, 1975). On the evidence for letters predating 790 see Bullough, 'Alcuin before Frankfort', 578–80.

of learning under Alfred are high peaks in the literary output of Anglo-Saxon England; the sources of the intervening period are very different. If we are to believe Alfred's famous claim that, when he came to the throne of Wessex in 871, learning had declined to such an extent that few men south of the Humber could translate a word of Latin into English (and he knew of none south of the Thames), the earlier ninth century marked a nadir in the fortunes of intellectual endeavour in southern England.[49] The spotlight shone on England in the 790s by Alcuin's letters is, therefore, remarkably useful and remarkably frustrating since it throws into even deeper shadow the history of the decades that follow.

Historians of early England are spoiled by Bede. Although he was by no means the only significant scholar of his day, the convenient coherence and monumentality of his most famous work, the *Historia Ecclesiastica Gentis Anglorum*, not only dictates the interpretation of the period it most closely describes – that is, the seventh century – but also creates a vivid contrast with the sources that are its immediate successors. After the completion of the *Historia Ecclesiastica* in 731 (with some evidence of revision by 734), there is a change in the nature of the texts that provide historians with their information about Anglo-Saxon England. No longer is there a single, monolithic literary text, rather a profusion of annals, chronicles and letters that tell related, but not identical, stories of the events of their time. Bede's own work presaged this change. The last chapter of his *Historia Ecclesiastica* incorporates a chronicle which functions as a recapitulation of the entire work, even though it contains references to events not included in the main body of the text.[50] Bede had written chronicles before; two of his earlier works on the *computus*, the *De Temporibus* ('On Time') completed by 703, and the longer *De Temporum Ratione* ('On the Reckoning of Time') completed by 725, included world chronicles known as the *Chronica minora* and the *Chronica maiora* respectively.[51] The *De Temporum Ratione* was very popular in the Carolingian schools, and extant manuscripts indicate that it acted as a stimulus for the keeping of chronicles in a number of Frankish monasteries.[52] The chronicle at the end of the *Historia Ecclesiastica* also attracted additions; in the earliest copy of the text extra annals are added for the years 731–34, and a separate group of manuscripts contain a

---

[49] H. Sweet (ed.), *King Alfred's West-Saxon Version of Gregory's Pastoral Care*, EETS o.s. 45 (Oxford, 1871); *Alfred the Great: Asser's Life of King Alfred and other Contemporary Sources*, trans. S. Keynes and M. Lapidge (Harmondsworth, 1983), 25.

[50] Bede, *HE* V.24; the information in the annals for 540, 547, 675 and 711 is not included in the main body of the text.

[51] The best discussion of Bede's treatises on time is now F. Wallis (trans.), *Bede: The Reckoning of Time* (Liverpool, 1999), especially lxvii–lxxi, 353–66. See also, C. W. Jones (ed.), *Bedae Opera de Temporibus* (Cambridge, MA, 1943).

[52] 245 manuscripts of all or part of the text survive, making it the most popular of Bede's writings: ibid., lxxxv–xcii. See also W. Stevens, *Bede's Scientific Achievement*, Jarrow Lecture (Jarrow, 1985), 39–42 for a handlist of the 82 eighth- and ninth-century copies made on the Continent; D. Whitelock, *After Bede*, Jarrow Lecture (Jarrow, 1960), 7–8; Levison, *England and the Continent,* 270–73, 277, and below, Chapter 2, 32–33.

longer addition for the years 732–66, forming a text commonly known as the *Continuatio Bedae*.[53] This *Continuation* (the textual history of which remains poorly understood) is closely related to the eighth-century Latin annals embedded in the *Historia regum* and to the vernacular annals in the Northern Recension of the *Anglo-Saxon Chronicle* (Manuscripts D, E, and F) for the same period. It is generally assumed that a common set of 'Northern Annals' compiled in Northumbria in the later eighth century lies behind these texts, but the relationship of these lost annals to Bede's chronicles, and the context for the creation and transmission of the annals in the second half of the eighth century, is not fully understood, with the picture being considerably complicated by the late date of many of the manuscript witnesses.[54] Chapter 4 of this book builds on the argument that the scholarly activity in Alcuin's York in the later eighth century constituted an important episode in this process, and draws attention to the quality of the information about Charlemagne's Francia available in that place.

One of the most striking features of these northern sources is the way in which the density of the annals changes dramatically in the first decade of the ninth century. Only a few later compilations dating from the twelfth and thirteenth centuries preserve fragments of detail about Northumbrian history in the period between the exile of King Eardwulf in 806 and the arrival of Viking armies in the 860s. Thus the political instability described in the chronicles seems to be dramatically reinforced by the cessation of the chronicles themselves; the physical absence of the texts that tell of Northumbrian troubles in the last decade of the eighth century becomes a telling metaphor for the continuation of those troubles into the textual vacuum of the early ninth century.

South of the Humber, historians are faced with similar problems for this period, although here (unlike Northumbria) many charters survive to illuminate Mercian and West Saxon lordship.[55] One of the anomalies of eighth-century Mercia (discussed in Chapter 6) is the lack of a native history or chronicle to chart the history of the kingdom at its most powerful. Most of the sources about the 'Mercian supremacy' come from the kingdoms that were the victims of Mercian aggression. This comparative absence of Mercian sources could be a

---

[53] On the additions to the Moore Manuscript (Cambridge, UL MS Kk.5.16; *CLA* II, no. 139) see P. Hunter-Blair, 'The Moore Memoranda on Northumbrian History', in C. Fox and B. Dickins (eds), *The Early Cultures of North West Europe* (Cambridge, 1950), 245–57, and *idem, The Moore Bede*, EEMF 9 (Copenhagen, 1959). On the *Continuatio Bedae* (to which the additions in the Moore Manuscript are related but not identical) see *Bede's Ecclesiastical History of the English People*, ed. and trans. B. Colgrave and R. A. B. Mynors (Oxford, 1968), lxvii–lxix, 572–77.

[54] The relevant manuscripts of the *Anglo-Saxon Chronicle*, all the copies of the *Continuatio*, and the unique copy of the *Historia regum* are post-conquest in date; *Symeon of Durham: Libellus de exordio atque procursu istius, hoc est Dunelmensis, ecclesiae. Tract on the Origins and Progress of this Church of Durham*, ed. and trans. D. W. Rollason (Oxford, 2000), lxxi; *idem, Sources for York History*, 17–18.

[55] P. H. Sawyer, *Anglo-Saxon Charters: An annotated List and Bibliography* (London, 1968). For the few forged charters for Northumbria see C. R. Hart, *The Early Charters of Northern England* (Leicester, 1975).

reflection of differential source survival, but it could also suggest that social authority and power in the kingdom of Mercia was expressed in ways that were less likely to have been preserved in the textual record. Despite Alcuin's panegyric of praise for Offa's sponsorship of learning and encouragement of reading, it may be that much greater importance was attached to oral authority in Mercia than elsewhere and that, outside the Church, Mercian kingship had little use for the written word.[56] Aspects of Anglo-Saxon Mercia are virtually proto-historic, and in some ways (not least the construction of Offa's Dyke) the kingdom has closer analogies with the Iron Age communities of Roman Britain than with contemporary Wessex or Northumbria.

Canterbury, however, provides a welcome oasis of historical data, and some measure of continuity with the age of Bede.[57] The city was home to Augustine's monastery of Saints Peter and Paul, as well as to the cathedral community, and from the time of Archbishop Theodore (668–90) and Abbot Hadrian (670–709/10) had been a major centre of learning as well as the spiritual focus of Anglo-Saxon Christianity. The location of Canterbury within the kingdom of Kent means that contacts with the Continent feature in the surviving archive. Alcuin frequently wrote to the Canterbury community, and to Archbishop Æthelheard in particular, concerning the problems generated by the new metropolitan see at Lichfield as well as the crisis in the Kent see that had been precipitated by the death of Offa in 796.[58] Additionally, a significant number of original single-leaf charters survive from Canterbury for the period before 870; these permit a valuable insight into the problems to which Alfred alluded in the preface of his translation of the *Pastoral Care*. Commentators have noted that the scribes of ninth-century Canterbury (Archbishop Wulfred included) could write an accomplished pointed minuscule script; however, the quality of Latin which these scribes wrote was formulaic and poor, condemned as 'incompetent' and 'ignorant' in the 830s and 840s and 'wretched' or 'gibberish' by the 870s.[59]

The ninth century is a fallow period for insular palaeographers; a recent survey of dated and datable manuscripts from ninth-century England has produced a list of no more than 23 surviving books for the whole of the century.[60]

---

[56] Alcuin, *Ep.* no. 64; *Alcuin of York*, trans. Allott, no. 38. Alcuin's description of Offa as the 'glory of Britain' (*decus Britanniae*) is repeated in an original charter of AD 799 by Coenwulf to Canterbury (S 155, *BCS* 293). On the continuing importance of oral transmission of the *verbum regis* in Charlemagne's Francia (despite the revolution in literacy which he encouraged) see J. L. Nelson, 'Literacy in Carolingian Government', in R. McKitterick (ed.), *The Uses of Literacy in the Early Middle Ages* (Cambridge, 1990), 258–96, at 266–67. On literacy in Anglo-Saxon England see S. E. Kelly, 'Anglo-Saxon Lay Society and the Written Word', in ibid., 36–62.

[57] N. P. Brooks, *The Early History of the Church of Canterbury* (Leicester, 1984).

[58] Alcuin, *Ep.* nos 17, 128, 129, 230, 255, 290; *Alcuin of York*, trans. Allott, nos 48, 49, 50, 51, 53, 54.

[59] Brooks, *The Early History*, 167–74; M. Lapidge, 'Latin Learning in Ninth-Century England', in his *Anglo-Latin Literature. Vol. 1*, 446–54.

[60] J. Morrish, 'Dated and Datable Manuscripts Copied in England During the Ninth Century: A Preliminary List', *Mediaeval Studies*, 50 (1988), 512–38.

Nor is it clear that books were ever produced in great quantities in England during this period; drawing on the authority of Alfred himself, it has been argued that centres of learning, under increasing pressure from the Vikings, were in terminal decline. The contrast with Carolingian Francia could not be more striking. There, the estimated number of manuscripts surviving from the ninth century is in excess of 7000; for each English ninth-century codex, more than 300 Carolingian manuscripts still sit on library shelves. Even allowing for the random and unpredictable effects of losses over time, the difference seems likely to be a matter of scale of production rather than differential survival. In the one place we see the fruits of Charlemagne's *renovatio* and his emphasis on the written word and, in the other, the shuddering collapse of Latin education in southern England (to take the most pessimistic view) or else (rather more optimistically) the stuttering survival of a tradition of Latin learning which linked the eighth century with the age of Alfred.[61] Does this incongruity mean that Charlemagne's *renovatio* with its revolutionary emphasis on the written word had no impact on contemporary Anglo-Saxon practices? Is it fair to heap blame on Viking assaults, and to assume that they were more devastating in Anglo-Saxon England than in Francia?

Coinage and the historian

The study of coinage has always been an important tool for any historian of this period.[62] The varying designs, weight and fineness of the metal used by moneyers reveals important information about the ideology of kingship as well as the economic resources available to the royal patrons of the coinage. The number and distribution of mint sites around early medieval kingdoms is important for obtaining a sense of the extent of money use as well as reflecting the extent of political control of the money supply. Thus the reduction in the number of mint sites under Pippin and Charlemagne can be interpreted as a reflection of increasing royal control over the output of coinage in Carolingian Francia. Equally, the location of the main mints in contemporary Anglo-Saxon England may have been a factor in Offa's strategy to bring London, Kent and East Anglia under Mercian hegemony. In ninth-century Southumbria the surviving coinage reflects the transfer of political hegemony from Mercia to Wessex, and in contemporary Northumbria, where written sources are so sparse, analysis of the styca coinage

---

61 The pessimistic view is articulated best by Lapidge, 'Latin Learning'; see also N. P. Brooks, 'England in the Ninth Century: The Crucible of Defeat', *TRHS* 5th ser., 29 (1979), 1–20. For a more optimistic opinion see J. Morrish, 'King Alfred's Letter as a Source on Learning in England', in P. E. Szarmach (ed.), *Studies in Earlier Old English Prose* (Albany, NY, 1986), 87–107.

62 F. M. Stenton, 'Anglo-Saxon Coinage and the Historian', in *idem* (ed.), *Preparatory to Anglo-Saxon England* (Oxford, 1970), 371–82; P. Grierson and M. A. S. Blackburn, *Medieval European Coinage, with a Catalogue of the Coins in the Fitzwilliam Museum, Cambridge. Vol. 1: The Early Middle Ages, 5th–10th Centuries* (Cambridge, 1986).

provides the crucial tool for working out the regnal chronology of the period before the establishment of the Viking kingdom in York.[63]

However, our understanding of the range of coin types and extent of coin use has been transformed in the last 20 years with the development of sophisticated metal-detecting technology. Systematic use of metal detectors by archaeologists working on controlled excavations has often led to the recovery of coins in stratified contexts which might otherwise have been missed during excavation. This has been particularly important for the recovery of ninth-century Northumbrian brass stycas which are small and dark and are otherwise rarely found in reliable excavated contexts.[64] Even more important has been the increase in the recovery and reporting of coin finds by amateur metal-detectorists. These single finds have already made a tremendous impact on our understanding of the geographical distribution and chronological use of coins in the British Isles, complementing the knowledge gained from the more well-established study of coin-hoards.[65] Hoards are vitally important for establishing the relative chronology of variant coin types; single finds, on the other hand, provide evidence for the maximum geographical range of coin use, as well as chronological variations in that range. And, whereas the deliberate deposition of hoards is often assumed to be a symptom of social stress (or social ritual), the deposition of single coins is thought more likely to represent the accidental loss of coins in every day use.

Our understanding of the availability and use of Carolingian coins in Anglo-Saxon England is a good example of the changed picture produced by newly recorded single finds (see Chapter 7). In 1963 Dolley and Morrison examined the hoards which included Carolingian coins and concluded that, from Offa's day onwards, continental coinage was specifically and systematically excluded from circulation alongside Anglo-Saxon issues in Wessex, Mercia and Kent. They argued, therefore, that the very great majority of the Carolingian coins which did reach Britain were brought in by Vikings, and in that context circulated as bullion rather than coin currency.[66] Since Dolley and Morrison

---

[63] M. A. S. Blackburn and D. N. Dumville (eds), *Kings, Currency, and Alliances: History and Coinage of Southern England in the Ninth Century* (Woodbridge, 1998); H. E. Pagan, 'Northumbrian Numismatic Chronology in the Ninth Century', BNJ, 38 (1969), 1–15; D. M. Metcalf (ed.), *Coinage in Ninth-Century Northumbria*, BAR Bri. Ser. 80 (Oxford, 1987).

[64] E. J. E. Pirie, *Coins of the Kingdom of Northumbria c. 700–867 in the Yorkshire Collection* (Llanfyllin, 1996).

[65] On the systematic collection of information on single finds, see M. A. S. Blackburn and M. J. Bonser, 'Single Finds of Anglo-Saxon and Norman Coins I–III', *BNJ*, 55–57 (1984–86) superseded by the 'Coin Register', *BNJ*, 57– (1987–), and by *The Early Medieval Corpus Project: Coin Finds in Britain 410–1180*, a website run by the Fitzwilliam Museum, Cambridge; D. M. Metcalf, 'The Monetary Economy of Ninth-century England South of the Humber: A Topographical Analysis', in Blackburn and Dumville (eds), *Kings, Currency, and Alliances*, 167–98; P. J. Casey and R. Reece (eds), *Coins and the Archaeologist* (2nd edn) (London, 1988).

[66] R. H. M. Dolley and K. F. Morrison, 'Finds of Carolingian Coins from Great Britain and Ireland', *BNJ*, 32 (1963), 75–87.

wrote, more than 70 single finds of Carolingian coins minted between 751 and *c.* 900 have been reported from Britain. The geographical and chronological picture presented by their distribution presents very different conclusions – namely, that the concentration of single finds of Carolingian coins dating from the mid-eighth century in relatively discrete geographical zones points to the existence of long-lived routes of exchange that were established well before the Vikings became a seriously destabilizing factor in north-western Europe, and – more controversially still – to the notion that Carolingian coinage played a bigger part in the Anglo-Saxon monetary economies of the later eighth and ninth centuries than has been previously assumed.

A note of caution must, however, be raised with regard to any analysis of single finds. A distribution map of single finds of coins, like any other archaeological distribution map, is potentially subject to biases generated by unequal recovery and recording. It is possible that clusters of coin finds in particular areas represent the quality of contacts between local metal-detectorists and a nearby museum. A pessimist might argue that the clusters of coins on Map 3 (for example) reflects the strength of links generated by museums and archaeological units in East Anglia, Yorkshire and Lincolnshire, rather than representing any real pattern of coin use during the period 750–900. Such an attitude presumes that the gaps in the East and West Midlands are (equally and oppositely) the result of poor contacts between metal-detectorist groups and archaeological professionals in those areas, and necessarily assumes that coins are equally likely to exist in those areas but that they are either not being found or are not being reported – in short, that the absence of evidence is not evidence of absence.[67]

A detailed analysis of the material, though, suggests that not all the gaps in the coverage are of the same type. For example, the scarcity of Carolingian coins minted during the reigns of Charlemagne or Louis the Pious from London and the south-east contrasts with the relative frequency of finds of contemporary Anglo-Saxon issues from the same area. This pattern is likely to be explained along the lines of Dolley and Morrison's arguments, that the major eighth-century mints at Canterbury and London absorbed imported silver coin for reminting – a hypothesis supported by analysis of the metal alloys used in coins produced on both sides of the Channel for Offa and Charlemagne.[68] In contrast, however, the paucity of Carolingian finds in the Midlands mirrors the relative scarcity of contemporary native coins from that area: the historian of Offa's Mercia must ask whether this pattern reflects modern distortions in the rate of recovery and reporting, or whether contemporary coin use in the heartlands of

---

[67] For a useful discussion of the problems of using single finds for systematic analysis of ancient coin use see D. M. Metcalf, *An Atlas of Anglo-Saxon and Norman Coin Finds, c. 973–1086* (London and Oxford, 1998); also K. Ulmschneider, *Markets, Minsters, and Metal-detectors: the Archaeology of Middle Saxon Lincolnshire and Hampshire Compared*, BAR Bri. Ser. 307 (Oxford, 2000).

[68] D. M. Metcalf and J. P. Northover, 'Coinage Alloys from the Time of Offa and Charlemagne to c. 864', *Numismatic Chronicle*, 149 (1989), 101–20.

the Mercian kingdom was somehow fundamentally different from regions annexed by its king. More fundamental 'gaps' are evident in the countries which once formed part of the Carolingian Empire; Anglo-Saxon coins are almost never reported outside coin hoards in modern France, Germany or Italy and, mimicking Dolley and Morrison arguments, this absence is usually interpreted as proof that foreign coinage was not allowed to circulate in Charlemagne's kingdom. However, the lack of recorded single finds in these countries is a reflection of the legal obstacles to the use of metal detectors and the absence of mechanisms and incentives for reporting artefacts found outside official archaeological excavations. Until continental finds of coins can be reported in a manner similar to that developed in Britain, some aspects of the study of the circulation of coinage in early medieval Europe will remain closed.[69]

Levison's focus was on the eighth century and on the Anglo-Saxon influence on Francia. The slant of this volume, which owes so much to Levison's lead, leans towards analysis of the reverse influence, of that which Carolingian Francia had on the kingdoms of the English. It also pursues the evidence beyond the boundaries set in the earlier work, to consider the evidence for the continuity (or otherwise) of Frankish interests in Anglo-Saxon England in the ninth century during the reigns of Charlemagne's son, Louis the Pious (814–40) and his grandson, Charles the Bald (840–77). The time period thus covered, c. 750–c. 870, has a convenient coherence in terms of both Anglo-Saxon and Frankish political history. The period spans the key phase of Carolingian hegemony in Western Europe and brings the Anglo-Saxon story from the height of the Mercian hegemony to the threshold of the reign of Alfred, under whom (as another notable commentator on Anglo-Frankish affairs remarked), 'the full force of Frankish example hit England'.[70] The complex source-base of the pre-Alfredian period hides much which is useful to our subject. Close analysis reveals not just

---

[69] This issue of recovery and recording non-excavated evidence is, of course, not restricted to early medieval coinage. On single finds in Germany and the Netherlands see M. Blackburn, 'Coin Circulation in Germany during the Early Middle Ages. The Evidence of the Single Finds', in B. Kluge (ed.), *Fernhandel und Geldwirtschaft. Beiträge zum deutschen Münzwesen in sächsischer und salischer Zeit* (Sigmaringen, 1993), 37–54. On Italy see A. Rovelli, 'Some Consideration of the Carolingian Coinage of Lombard and Carolingian Italy', in I. L. Hansen and C. Wickham (eds), *The Long Eighth Century: Production, Distribution and Demand* (Leiden, 2000), 194–223, at 211–12 and on the Italian hoards containing Anglo-Saxon coinage, see C. E. Blunt, 'Anglo-Saxon Coins Found in Italy', in M. A. S. Blackburn (ed.), *Anglo-Saxon Monetary History* (Leicester, 1986), 159–69. For the situation regarding single finds in France, see S. Suchodolski, 'Der Geldumlauf in der karolingischen Epoche', *Deutscher Numismatikertag München 1981* (Augsburg, 1983) 43–53; J. C. Moesgaard, 'Stray Finds of Carolingian Coins in Upper Normandy, France', *Studia Numismatica. Festschrift Arkadi Molvogin*, 65 (Tallinn, 1995), 87–102; O. Jeanne-Rose, 'Trouvailles isolées de monnaies carolingiennes en Poitu', *Revue Numismatique*, 151 (1996), 241–84. Generally, see S. Suchodolski, 'Remarques sur la circulation monétaire dans l'Europe du haut Moyen Age', *Quaderni Ticinesi di Numismatica e antichità classiche*, 22 (1993), 249–56.

[70] J. M. Wallace-Hadrill, 'The Franks and the English in the Ninth Century: Some Common Historical Interests', *History*, 35 (1950), 202–18, at 209, reprinted in his *Early Medieval History* (Oxford, 1975), 201–16.

the degree of Carolingian influence on Anglo-Saxon England, but also the active interest of the Franks' greatest king in contemporary English affairs, and something of the continuity of that interest in subsequent generations.

Chapter 2

Pippin, England and the Merovingian Legacy

Symeon of Durham

> [News of] Eadberht's excellent fame and virtuous works spread far
> and wide, and even reached Pippin, king of the Franks, who, because
> of the bond of friendship [*amicitia iunctus*] between them, sent him
> many and varied royal gifts.[1]

Cross-Channel influence and the world of the Franks was a tangible and political
reality for Symeon who, early in the twelfth century, had been commissioned to
write the history of his monastic community. From his perspective as a Norman-
trained monk living in post-Conquest Durham,[2] it was right and proper that
diplomatic and political contacts had existed in the middle of the eighth century
between the Northumbrian king Eadberht (737–58) and Pippin III, the first
Carolingian king of the Franks (751–68). The gift exchange, mutual respect, and
bonds of *amicitia* between these kings which he described in his *Libellus* were
an entirely appropriate reflection of Northumbrian power at its zenith. To Symeon,
Frankish interest in the Anglo-Saxon kingdom which had nurtured Bede and St
Cuthbert – both, of course, buried in his new Norman cathedral – was only to
have been expected. But this historical detail which Symeon provides about
contacts between the kings of Northumbria and Francia in the 750s is unique;
nothing comparable is found elsewhere. What lies behind Symeon's comment?
A cautious reader might disregard his words as late and anachronistic, but an
examination of comparative evidence repays attention and supports Symeon's
statement that high-level, diplomatic contacts had existed between the kings of
Francia and distant Northumbria in the mid-eighth century.

Symeon knew his Anglo-Saxon history, and he was also deeply interested in
the Frankish past. Throughout his career as historian and chronicler of the Anglo-

---

[1] Symeon of Durham, *Libellus de exordio*, II.3; *Symeon of Durham: Libellus de exordio
atque procursu istius, hoc est Dunelmensis, ecclesiae. Tract on the Origins and Progress of this
Church of Durham*, ed. and trans. D. W. Rollason (Oxford, 2000), 80–83.

[2] Aspects of Symeon's own handwriting suggest that he may in fact have been of Norman or
northern French origin; M. Gullick, 'The Scribes of the Durham Cantor's Book (Durham, Dean and
Chapter Library, MS B.IV.24) and the Durham Martyrology Scribe', in D. Rollason, et al. (eds),
Anglo-Norman Durham (Woodbridge, 1994), 93–109 at 97; *idem*, 'The Hand of Symeon of Durham: Further Observations on the Durham Martyrology Scribe', in *Symeon of Durham, Historian
of Durham and the North*, ed. D. W. Rollason (Stamford, 1998), 14–31 at 18–22; R. Sharpe, *A
Handlist of the Latin Writers of Great Britain and Ireland before 1540* (Turnhout, 1997), no. 1625.

Norman north, he was at pains to correlate what he knew of Frankish history with his information about the Anglo-Saxon past. Two short chronicles, which were copied and compiled by Symeon himself, are extant evidence of his attempts to cross-reference the histories of Francia and England in the period before the Norman Conquest.[3] Very little of the information in either of these short compilations adds anything new to our knowledge of Frankish or Anglo-Saxon history, and neither contains any direct reference to the type of contacts between Pippin and Eadberht which Symeon described in his *Libellus*. But these short chronicle compilations have an historiographical value not only because they show a twelfth-century historian at work but also because they demonstrate that historical information about the Frankish past was freely available in twelfth-century Durham and was of interest to the monks working there.[4] We can add to these notational and largely derivative compilations the witness of the *Historia regum* which contains a set of Frankish annals concerning events of the later eighth century and which certainly passed through Symeon's editorial control at Durham in the earlier part of the twelfth century.[5] It is possible also that an early twelfth-century copy of the *Annales Mettenses Priores* was at Durham in Symeon's day; a record of it exists in the inventory of books drawn up there in the late fourteenth century, and marginal annotations indicate that the manuscript was used in Durham as an exemplar in the second half of the twelfth century.[6] This set of annals,

---

[3] Durham, Dean and Chapter Library MS B.IV.22 and Glasgow, University Library MS Hunterian 85 (the so-called Annals of Lindisfarne and Durham). On these texts see W. Levison, 'Die *Annales Lindisfarneses et Dunelmenses*: kritisch untersucht und neu herausgegeben', *DA*, 17 (1961), 447–506; J. E. Story, 'Symeon as Annalist', in Rollason, *Symeon of Durham*, 202–13.

[4] A comparable interest is visible in the writing of Symeon's contemporary William of Malmesbury; see R. Thomson, *William of Malmesbury* (Woodbridge, 1987), 140–47, 159–73.

[5] *Symeonis Monachi Opera Omnia*, ed. T. Arnold, RS 75.ii (London, 1885), 3–283. The Frankish component of the text is discussed in detail below, Chapter 4, 95–115. See also P. Hunter-Blair, 'Some Observations on the "Historia Regum" attributed to Symeon of Durham', in N. K. Chadwick (ed.), *Celt and Saxon. Studies in the Early British Border* (Cambridge, 1963), 63–118 and M. Lapidge, 'Byrhtferth of Ramsey and the early sections of the "Historia Regum" attributed to Symeon of Durham', *ASE*, 10 (1982), 97–122.

[6] The *Annales Mettenses Priores* are found in Durham, DCL MS C.IV.15 (s.xii[in]) which is referred to as the *Cronica Pippini* in the late fourteenth-century catalogue of books from the Durham library. The copy of Regino in the same manuscript was marked up for copying; the precise extracts are found in Cambridge, Corpus Christi College Cambridge MS 139,19r-37v (s.xii[2]): see B. Meehan, 'Durham Twelfth-century Manuscripts in Cistercian Houses', in Rollason et al., *Anglo-Norman Durham* (1994), 439–50 at 442, and below Chapter 5, 117, 120. Durham, DCL C.IV.15 is a likely candidate for the *Liber de Gestis Francorum* which is listed in the mid-twelfth-century catalogue incorporated into Durham, DCL MS B.IV.24, on which see B. Botfield (ed.), *Catalogi veteres librorum Ecclesiae Cathedralis Dunelm.*, Surtees Society, 7 (London, 1838), 3, 30, 107; A. J. Piper, 'The Libraries of the Monks of Durham', in M. B. Parkes and A. G. Watson (eds), *Medieval Scribes, Manuscripts and Libraries: Essays presented to N.R. Ker* (London, 1978), 213–49 at 218–20. See also N. R. Ker and A. G. Watson (eds), *Medieval Libraries of Great Britain: A List of Surviving Books. Supplement to the Second Edition*, Royal Historical Society Guides and Handbooks, 15 (London, 1987), 25, 27 and R. A. B. Mynors, *Durham Cathedral Manuscripts to the End of the Twelfth Century* (Durham, 1939), no. 81.

originally compiled in the first years of the ninth century at Chelles, St Denis, or perhaps at Metz itself, is well known as a source of Carolingian propaganda concerning the closing decades of the Merovingian hegemony and the gradual takeover of authority by the Arnulfing dynasty from which the Carolingians claimed direct descent.[7] These *Earlier Annals of Metz* are found in the Durham manuscript alongside a copy of Regino of Prüm's *Libellus de temporibus dominicae incarnationis* which takes the history of the Franks to 906. Symeon also supervised the copying of a more recent history, the *Gesta Normannorum ducum* by William of Jumièges[8] and himself copied the mid-ninth-century martyrology of Usuard, a monk of St Germain des Près.[9] The Durham brethren, therefore, had access to considerable quantities of high-quality Frankish history which told of the rise to royalty of the Carolingian dynasty and of the consolidation of their powers in the Frankish homelands and far beyond.[10]

In the tense political climate of the late eleventh and early twelfth centuries which saw the building of Durham Cathedral – itself a potent symbol of new Norman influence in northern England – Symeon, as an historian of the north, had a pragmatic, contemporary motive for wishing to establish the mutuality of the Anglo-Saxon and Frankish past.[11] Given the quality of the Frankish historical material which we can show was at Symeon's disposal, it is possible that his information about contacts between Pippin and Eadberht came from another source, now lost; we need not assume that he fabricated this piece of evidence, despite the fact that it appears first in his hands. Indeed, an examination of contemporary eighth-century sources reveals that there were good historical grounds for regarding his comment about links between the Frankish and Northumbrian courts in the 750s as a reflection of real diplomatic and political contact at that date and, furthermore, that this contact was both a product of the shared history of both kingdoms and a precursor of future contacts between Anglo-Saxon and Carolingian kings.

---

[7] *Annales Mettenses Priores*, MGH SS rer. Germ. 10; partially trans. P. Fouracre and R. A. Gerberding, *Late Merovingian France: History and Hagiography 640–720* (1996), 330–70.

[8] London, BL MS Harley 491. On Symeon's role in the copying of this volume with two other continental scribes see Gullick, 'The Hand of Symeon', 18–19. This manuscript is almost certainly the *Liber de Gestis Normannorum* listed in Durham DCL, B.IV.24 (note 6 *supra*).

[9] Usuard's martyrology (amplified with additional information from the Loire region) is part of the so-called Durham Cantor's Book, Durham DCL MS B.IV.24, fos 12r–39v; A. J. Piper, 'The Durham Cantor's Book', in Rollason et al., *Anglo-Norman Durham*, 79–92 at 82–84 and Gullick, 'The Hand of Symeon', 25.

[10] A. J. Piper, 'The Historical Interests of the Monks of Durham', in Rollason, *Symeon of Durham*, 301–32. Another relevant Durham manuscript is Oxford, St John's College MS 154, an early eleventh-century copy of Ælfric's Grammar which was in Durham s. xii/xiii. The fifth and final item in the manuscript is a copy by a late eleventh-century scribe of part of Abbo of St Germain's poem on the siege of Paris by Vikings, and is provided with a continuous OE gloss by the same scribe. The provenance to Durham is established by the press mark E.II.7 and by the reference to the manuscript in the 1391 catalogue; Botfield, *Cat. Vet.*, 33; see N. R. Ker, *Catalogue of Manuscripts Containing Anglo-Saxon* (Oxford, 1957), 436–37.

[11] W. Aird, *St. Cuthbert and the Normans* (Woodbridge, 1998).

Although the kingdoms of Eadberht and Pippin were geographically distant, there is much about their style and circumstance of rulership which bears comparison.[12] Both men were regarded by contemporaries as strong, competent military leaders. Pippin had fought successful campaigns in Aquitaine, Bavaria and Saxony before he became king, and more in Italy after his accession in 751. The Northumbrian chronicles also show Eadberht as a successful warrior, crushing internal dissent, fighting the Picts to the north of his kingdom, and challenging the Mercians to the south.[13] The strength of each king was heightened by the fact that both had come to power after a period of vacillating royal authority, which had been perceived by contemporaries as weak. Both had also gained power over a king who had been forced by opponents to take the monastic tonsure and resign from secular life. It was in this way that Pippin had ensured the removal of the last Merovingian monarch, Childeric III, *qui false rex vocabatur*.[14] Similarly, in the closing chapters of his *Ecclesiastical History*, Bede had expressed concerns about the strength of Ceolwulf's authority, Eadberht's cousin and predecessor in Northumbria. Bede's fears were confirmed soon after when, in 732, Ceolwulf was forcibly tonsured and made to resign his kingdom.[15] However, unlike Childeric, Ceolwulf's enforced abdication was not permanent, and he was able to regain power within a short space of time. But he eventually resigned the kingship in 737, this time *sua voluntate*, and retired to the monastery of Lindisfarne where he lived until his death in 764.[16] At Lindisfarne, Ceolwulf would have witnessed Eadberht's vigorous campaign to repress the type of internal dissent which had destabilized his own reign. In 756 Eadberht attacked the island monastery, capturing Bishop Cynewulf and a Northumbrian æthling named Offa, son of Aldfrith, who was dragged 'almost dead with hunger' from sanctuary in the island's church of St Peter.[17]

This episode demonstrates that Eadberht was not afraid of confronting episcopal authority in Northumbria when it came into conflict with his own dynastic interests. But he was careful, too, to cultivate compatible ties with other Northumbrian churchmen, and to nurture those links to the mutual benefit of Church and State. Eadberht's brother, Ecgberht, was made Archbishop of York in 735, thereby creating a blood alliance between secular and

---

[12] J. M. Wallace-Hadrill, 'Charlemagne and Offa', in *idem, Early Germanic Kingship in England and on the Continent* (Oxford, 1971), 98–123 at 109–10; J. Campbell, 'The First Century of Christianity', *Ampleforth Journal*, 76 (1971), 12–29, reprinted in his *Essays in Anglo-Saxon History* (London, 1986) 49–67 at 55.

[13] *Continuatio Bedae*, 740 and 750; *Historia regum* (*York Annals*), 750 and 756.

[14] *Annales regni Francorum*, 750.

[15] Bede, *HE* V.23; *Historia regum* (*York Annals*), 732; *Annals from the Moore Manuscript*, Cambridge, University Library MS Kk.5.16, 731; *Bede's Ecclesiastical History of the English People*, ed. and trans. R. A. B. Mynors and B. Colgrave (Oxford, 1969), 572–73. On these events see D. P. Kirby, *Bede's Historia Ecclesiastica: Its Contemporary Setting*, Jarrow Lecture (Jarrow, 1992).

[16] *Historia regum* (*York Annals*), 737, 764.

[17] Ibid., 756.

ecclesiastical powers, unprecedented in any Anglo-Saxon kingdom and which Alcuin later celebrated as a model of temporal government.[18] When Eadberht decided to resign the kingdom in 758 in favour of his son Oswulf, he retired to his brother's monastery at York and, after his death a decade later, he was buried there in a *porticus* of the church of St Peter alongside his brother who had died two years before.[19] Likewise, when Pippin realized that his own death was approaching, he returned to the monastery of St Denis in Paris where he had been educated as a young man. He died there, also in 768, having asked (according to later tradition) to be buried face down in front of the portal of the church as a measure of his humility and as a mark of respect towards the saint who was regarded as the founder of Christianity in Gaul and the special protector of Frankish kings.[20] Both Eadberht and Pippin, therefore, had close familial ties with arguably the most important churches of their respective kingdoms – St Peter's in York and St Denis near Paris – the churches where their respective ancestral *gentes* to which their own kingships laid claim had been first baptized to the faith of Christ. In life and in death both kings sustained a physical link with the symbolic locus of the Christian genesis of their people – a powerful and tangible statement about the connection between king and Church, the significance of which would not have been lost on contemporaries in Northumbria or Francia.

There is another piece of comparative evidence which links Eadberht's and Pippin's kingdoms, and which points to possible contacts between the two. Both kings were responsible for the introduction of a reformed coinage into their respective kingdoms – reforms which demonstrated their own royal authority and control of the mints. The inception of Eadberht's new coinage is difficult to date closely, but the longevity and widespread distribution of his reformed coins suggest that they were introduced soon after his accession in 737, and certainly by the 740s. Seven distinct stylistic groups are known, which, it has been suggested, necessitated the use of an estimated 400–500

---

[18] *Alcuin: On the Bishops, Kings and Saints of York*, ed. and trans. P. Godman (Oxford, 1982), 98–101, lines 1251–87. Northumbrian sceattas were issued jointly by the brothers, establishing a precedent for all archiepiscopal coinages produced up to 867 in York and 923 in Canterbury; C. C. S. Lyon, 'A Reappraisal of the Sceatta and Styca Coinage of Northumbria', *BNJ*, 28 (1955–57), 227–42 at 228; P. Grierson and M. A. S. Blackburn, *Medieval European Coinage, with a Catalogue of the Coins in the Fitzwilliam Museum, Cambridge. Vol. 1: The Early Middle Ages, 5th–10th Centuries* (Cambridge, 1986), 173, 277–78, hereafter referred to as *MEC* 1.

[19] *Historia regum (York Annals)*, 758 and 768; *ASChron*. 738; *Chronicle of Æthelweard*, 738. D. W. Rollason, *Sources for York History to AD 1100* (York, 1998), 52, 60, 147. On his burial at St Peter's see K. H. Krüger, *Königsgrabkirchen der Franken, Angelsachsen und Langobarden bis zur Mitte des 8. Jahrhunderts: Ein Historische Katalog*, Münster Mittelalter-schriften 4 (Munich, 1971), 290–99.

[20] Krüger, *Königsgrabkirchen der Franken*, 171–89, 493–96. The earliest reference to Pippin's burial *ad limina basilicae* is in a letter from Louis the Pious to Abbot Hilduin (*Epistolae variorum*, no. 19; MGH *Epp*. V); the earliest to the king's burial face-down at the portal is in c. 2 of Abbot Suger's *de Administratione*; *Suger: Œuvres* 1, ed. and trans. F. Gasparri, *Les classiques de l'histoire de France au Moyen Âge*, 37 (Paris, 1996), 113.

obverse dies over an extended period during his reign.[21] The alloy used by his moneyers was of variable quality but could reach 90 per cent purity and, as such, was in marked contrast to the seriously declining standards of silver coinage being produced in the southern Anglo-Saxon kingdoms of the day.[22] Most notably, however, Eadberht's coins reintroduced the name of the ruler inscribed as part of the obverse design – a feature which graphically symbolized royal control of the kingdom's coinage. The king's name had first been used (somewhat precociously) on Northumbrian coins by King Aldfrith *c.* 700 but the practice had been allowed to lapse after his time until Eadberht's reforms.[23] Although, the king's name had been an intermittent feature of Frankish gold coinage in the sixth and seventh centuries (and copied by the Kentish king, Eadbald (616–40)), the creation of an explicitly royal coinage was, by the 740s, a practice not employed by any other Anglo-Saxon kingdom nor, indeed, by that of the Franks.[24]

In this context, Pippin's coinage bears comparison. Shortly after his accession, and as a means of affirming his newly elevated authority, Pippin reformed and reissued the Frankish coinage in large quantities to a new standard weight and size. An early 'capitulary', issued at Ver and dated 755, provides details of the weights of the new issue which were to be minted to a standard of not more than 22 solidi (or 264 deniers) to a pound. This reform produced coinage which was heavier than the silver coinage produced by the outgoing Merovingian kings and, indeed, heavier than that normally produced in Anglo-Saxon England,

---

[21] D. M. Metcalf, 'Monetary Expansion and Recession: Interpreting the Distribution pattern of Seventh- and Eighth-century Coins', in P. J. Casey and R. Reece (eds), *Coins and the Archaeologist* (London, 1988), 237–39.

[22] J. Booth, 'Sceattas in Northumbria', in D. H. Hill and D. M. Metcalf (eds), *Sceattas in England and on the Continent*, BAR Bri. Ser. 128 (Oxford, 1984) 71–111; D. M. Metcalf, 'Estimation of the Volume of Northumbrian Coinage, c. 738–88', ibid., 113–16; Grierson and Blackburn, *MEC* 1, 173, 182–83, 187–89. The near-contemporary East Anglian coinage of Beonna is an exception to this trend in southern England, and seems to have been modelled on Northumbrian designs and weight standards; Grierson and Blackburn, *MEC* 1, 158, 277–78; M. M. Archibald, 'The Coinage of Beonna in the light of the Middle Harling Hoard', *BNJ* 55 (1985), 10–54. M. M. Archibald, 'A Sceat of Ethelbert I of East Anglia and Recent Finds of Coins of Beonna', *BNJ*, 65 (1995), 1–19.

[23] The attribution of these silver Type 1 sceattas to Aldfrith of Northumbria has been doubted with suggestions that they may date from after Offa's reforms and are perhaps attributable to Ealdfrith of Lindsey; C. S. S. Lyon, 'A Reappraisal of the Sceatta and Styca Coinage of Northumbria', *BNJ*, 28 (1956), 227–42 at 229 and Booth, 'Sceattas in Northumbria', 72. However, excavations in Southampton uncovered an Aldfrith sceatta in an early eighth-century context, that date being supported independently by dendrochronological analysis of the wooden surround of a contemporary well; see M. Brisbane, 'Hamwic (Saxon Southampton): An Eighth-century Port and Production Centre', in R. Hodges and B. Hobley (eds), *The Rebirth of Towns in the West AD 400–1050*, CBA Research Report No. 68 (London, 1988), 102–8, at 103; P. Andrews (ed.), *The Coins and Pottery from Hamwic*, Southampton Finds 1 (Southampton, 1988), 51–52; *EMC* 1998.9125.

[24] Grierson and Blackburn, *MEC* 1, 116–17, 128–31, 158; J. J. North, *English Hammered Coinage. Vol. 1: Early Anglo-Saxon to Henry III, c. 600–1272* (London, 1980), 22, 70, nos 176–78.

including Northumbria.[25] Like Eadberht, though, Pippin also demanded that his new coins carry a legend or monogram of his name and rank; just as in Northumbria, this innovation should be interpreted as a political move to emphasize the control which the new king and the new dynasty had over the supply of coinage.[26] The physical, literal stamp of royal authority on the coins of both Northumbria and newly Carolingian Francia must, in each case, have considerably enhanced the impression of dynastic change and royal strength.

The coincidence of timing between these two monetary reforms has led some to argue that the use of the royal style on Northumbrian and Frankish coin in the mid-eighth century may have been more than a coincidence of dynastic and political expedience, and it could be that the addition of Pippin's name to the currency of the new Frankish regime was influenced by aspects of the slightly earlier Northumbrian reforms.[27] Much has been made of Offa's coin reforms in the 790s, which followed the Frankish precedent of a higher silver content and wider flan than had previously been used, and of the failure of the Northumbrian coinage to follow suit.[28] The numismatic evidence can be interpreted to show that Northumbrian and Frankish coins of the 750s also shared aspects of their design, and that politically significant changes in the former may have prefigured a similar reform in the latter.[29] Though tentative, this numismatic evidence may be

---

[25] MGH Capit. I, no. 14; Mordek, *BCRFM* (1995), no. 14 at 1081. Resulting deniers should have weighed approximately 1.24g each (in contrast to the lighter Merovingian standard of *c.* 1.1g). The weights of Pippin's coins (as given by Grierson and Blackburn, *MEC* 1, nos 719–20) are between 1.15–1.17 grams in their present corroded state. Eadberht's coins (of which more are known) attain this weight but range between 0.8–1.17 grams in their present condition; see J. Booth and I. Blower, 'Finds of Sceattas and Stycas from Sancton', *Numismatic Chronicle*, 143 (1983), 139–45. Metcalf, 'Monetary Expansion', 241. On the date and nature of Pippin's reform see, D. M. Metcalf and H. A. Miskimin, 'The Carolingian Pound: A Discussion', *Numismatic Circular*, 76 (1968), 296–98, 333–34; Grierson and Blackburn, *MEC* 1, 108, 204. Although they are rare finds, there are as yet no known die-links between any examples of Pippin's coinage; see D. M. Metcalf, 'The Prosperity of Northwestern Europe in the Eighth and Ninth Centuries', *EcHR* 2nd ser. 20 (1967), 344–57.

[26] *R[ex] P[ipin]* or *R[ex] F[rancorum] Pipi;* Grierson and Blackburn, *MEC* 1, 204, pl. 33, no. 719.

[27] Booth, 'Sceattas in Northumbria', 71.

[28] Metcalf, 'Monetary Expansion', 239–45; F. M. Stenton, 'Anglo-Saxon Coinage and the Historian', in D. M. Stenton (ed.), *Preparatory to Anglo-Saxon England. Being the Collected Papers of Frank Merry Stenton* (Oxford, 1970), 371–82. See further, below 190–95, 244–55.

[29] Five coins of Pippin have been found and recorded in England, none from Northumbria: a Verdun denier (751–68) from Repton (*EMC*: 1986.0392; M. Biddle et al., 'Coins of the Anglo-Saxon period from Repton', in M. A. S. Blackburn (ed.), *Anglo-Saxon Monetary History* (Leicester, 1986), 111–32, 127–30 and *idem*, 'Coins of the Anglo-Saxon Period from Repton, Derbyshire, II', *BNJ*, 56 (1986), 16–35 at 32–33); a Dorestad denier from Richborough (*EMC*: 1986.8719; D. M. Metcalf, 'Artistic Borrowing, Imitation and Forgery in the Eighth Century', *Hamburger Beiträge zur Numismatik*, 20 (1966), 379–92 at 384–87 and Grierson and Blackburn, *MEC* 1, pl. 33, no. 719); an Angers denier from Bere Regis, Dorset (*EMC*: 1986.0405); a Dorestad denier from West Hythe, Kent (*EMC*: 1998.0028; 'Coin Register', *BNJ*, 68 (1998)); and an (as yet unpublished) find recently recovered by metal detector from Flixborough, Lincolnshire (pers. comm. K. Leahy). On these coins see further below, 192, 248–52.

proposed as corroborative evidence of Symeon of Durham's comments made some three and a half centuries later concerning cross-Channel contacts in the mid-eighth century, and we may indulge in the speculation that Eadberht's new coins were among the *multa ac diversa dona regalia* exchanged by the two kings.

Context: Anglo-Frankish contacts before 750

These diplomatic contacts and dynastic parallels between Northumbria and Francia at the dawn of the Carolingian age were in part a mutual, pragmatic recognition of the contemporary status of each king and kingdom. But these contacts were also a development and extension of political and cultural connections which had existed in previous decades. The scholarship of cross-Channel contact in the period prior to 750 focuses on three periods and themes: primarily, on the phases of Germanic settlement in Britain in the fifth and sixth centuries; secondly, on the circumstances leading up to, and resulting from, the conversion of the kingdom of Kent by Augustine's missionaries at the turn of the seventh century; and, thirdly, on the reciprocal mission by Anglo-Saxon Christians to areas of the near Continent that were still pagan in the latter part of the seventh and earlier eighth centuries. In each of these three phases, interaction between the inhabitants of Britain and neighbouring communities across the sea is regarded as the norm; in times of considerable social transition and cultural change, interaction with the Continent provides a strand of continuity with the dynamics of the Roman world and before.[30]

Questions of ethnicity and, within that, of the contribution of the Franks to the process of the settlement of post-Roman Britain have been fundamental to the development of Anglo-Saxon scholarship. Ever since eighteenth-century antiquarians began to recognize excavated artefacts as belonging to the period between the Roman and Viking invasions,[31] scholars have been guided (and sometimes misled) by Bede's famous statement on the arrival and settlement in Britain of representatives from the tribes of the Angles, Saxons and Jutes.[32]

---

[30] The bibliography is extensive, pioneered by E. T. Leeds, *The Archaeology of the Anglo-Saxon Settlements* (Oxford, 1913),126–38. See also, W. Levison, *England and the Continent in the Eighth Century* (1946); V. I. Evison, *The Fifth-Century Invasions South of the Thames* (London, 1965); M. Welch, 'Contacts across the Channel Between the Fifth and Seventh Centuries: A Review of the Archaeological Evidence', *Studien zur Sachsenforschung*, 7 (1991), 261–69; D. M. Wilson, 'England and the Continent in the Eighth Century – An Archaeological Viewpoint', *Angli e Sassoni al di qua e al di là del mare*, Settimane di Studio, 32.1 (Spoleto, 1986), 219–44; J. Haywood, *Dark-Age Naval Power: A Reassessment of Frankish and Anglo-Saxon Seafaring Activity* (London, 1991); S. Lebecq, 'England and the Continent in the Sixth and Seventh Centuries: The Question of Logistics', in R. Gameson (ed.), *St. Augustine and the Conversion of England* (Stroud, 1999), 50–67.

[31] J. Douglas, *Nenia Britannica* (London, 1793); B. Faussett, *Inventorium Sepulchrale* (London, 1856).

[32] Bede, *HE* I.15. For the most explicit equation of the archaeological evidence with this chapter of the *HE* see Leeds, *The Archaeology of the Anglo-Saxon Settlements*, 37–39 and Fig. 4.

Modern scholarship argues that the ethnic palimpsest of early Anglo-Saxon England was far more complex and multi-phased than the eighth-century perspective preserved in the *Ecclesiastical History* suggests; the nuances of the archaeological evidence permit subtle interpretations of chronology, ethnicity and mechanisms of exchange, and within this it is clear that Francia made an important contribution to the social and cultural texture of early Anglo-Saxon England.[33] Nowhere is this more clear than in Kent where the archaeology of the period leading up to the arrival of Augustine's mission unequivocally registers influences, particularly in female dress ornament, from across the Frankish domains in the first half of the sixth century.[34]

Neustria, Austrasia and the Anglo-Saxon kingdoms

In searching the written record for evidence of high-status contact between England and Francia prior to 750, scholars of text are largely at the mercy of Bede's narrative agenda. Bede talked of Francia only when it formed part of the story of the conversion and Christianization of the *gens Anglorum* by missionaries sent from Rome; he had no particular interest in Francia for its own sake. But, given the nature of the English conversion (and Bede's personal emphasis on its origins abroad as opposed to conversion by native, Romano-British Christians),[35] Bede does occasionally provide his reader with tangential references to

Eric John has pointed to the stylistic incongruity of the key passage in this chapter of Bede's work and has suggested that it was not in fact composed by Bede; E. John, 'The Point of Woden', *ASSAH*, 5 (1992), 127–34. See also J. Hines, 'The Becoming of the English: Identity, Material Culture and Language in Early Anglo-Saxon England', *ASSAH*, 7 (1994), 49–59; H. Vollrath, 'Die Landnahme der Angelsachsen nach dem Zeugnis de erzählenden Quellen', in M. Müller-Wille and R. Schneider (eds), *Ausgewählte Probleme der europäischen Landnahmen des Früh- und Hochmittelalters. Methodische Grundlagendiskussion im Grenzbereich zwischen Archäologie und Geschichte*, Vorträge und Forschungen 41 (Sigmaringen, 1993), 317–37; and N. P. Brooks, *Bede and the English*, Jarrow Lecture (Jarrow, 1999).

[33] See, for example, J. Hines (ed.), *The Anglo-Saxons from the Migration Period to the Eighth Century. An Ethnographic Perspective* (San Marino, 1997); J. Hines, K. Høilund Nielsen and F. Siegmund (eds), *The Pace of Change: Studies in Early Medieval Chronology* (Oxford, 1999), 37–92. A useful synopsis of the development of the subject is H. Hamerow, 'Migration Theory and the Migration Period', in B. Vyner (ed.), *Building on the Past. Papers Celebrating 150 years of the Royal Archaeological Institute* (London, 1994), 164–77

[34] The earliest analysis of this Frankish component in Kentish archaeology is in E. T. Leeds, *The Archaeology of the Anglo-Saxon Settlements* and *idem, Early Anglo-Saxon Art and Archaeology* (Oxford, 1936). More recently see V. I. Evison, *Dover, Buckland Anglo-Saxon Cemetery* (London, 1987) with details of subsequent excavations given in *Current Archaeology*, 144 (1995), 459–64; B. Brugmann, 'The role of Continental Artefact-types in Sixth-century Kentish Chronology', in Hines et al., *The Pace of Change*, 37–64. For an emphasis on the Jutish contribution to Kent see C. Behr, 'The Origins of Kingship in Early Medieval Kent', *EME*, 9.i (2000), 25–52.

[35] For the contribution of British Christians to the process see R. Meens, 'A Background to Augustine's Mission to Anglo-Saxon England', *Anglo-Saxon England*, 22 (1994), 5–17; C. Stancliffe, 'The British Church and the mission of Augustine', in Gameson (ed.), *St. Augustine*, 107–51; N. P.

the Frankish nobility and monastic communities which Anglo-Saxons and others had encountered on the route to and from Rome. However, in his enthusiasm for the Roman mission, he obscures the Frankish contribution to the missionary process and the extent to which Franks were directly involved in the evangelization of the Anglo-Saxons. Bede's narrative makes it clear that, by the mid-seventh century, Frankish churchmen were playing a vital role in the consolidation of the faith in Anglo-Saxon kingdoms beyond Kent. Frankish bishops such as Agilbert, Leuthere, Birinus, and Felix played important roles in the Christianization of Wessex, East Anglia and even Northumbria in the middle decades of the century.[36] But Bede is almost silent on the subject of Frankish involvement in Augustine's primary mission to the English in the 590s and does not explore the extent to which that Roman mission was prompted (or even pre-empted) by the activities of Frankish Christians already resident in Kent.[37] Was Bede's silence due to ignorance, or rather to a wish to present the story of the conversion as an undiluted papal achievement? Attempts to unravel the politics behind the conversion have encouraged historians to attribute the speedy acceptance of the papal mission in Kent in good part to the desire of its king, Æthelberht, to liberate himself and his kingdom from the threat of Frankish domination, implying that he tolerated the papal missionaries in order to preserve Kent from the prospect of subordination to a Merovingian church.[38] Alternatively, as Wood has stressed, Frankish churchmen and the Merovingian aristocracy in fact played a crucial supporting role in the papal mission, and Pope Gregory's objectives could only have been achieved through the manipulation of the longstanding cultural and political links which existed between Kent and Merovingian Francia.[39]

Both arguments hinge on the interpretation of hints in the historical record of Frankish hegemony in Kent in the second half of the sixth century. For the earliest decades of the conversion in the late sixth and earlier seventh centuries, as Bede's sources grow more distant from his own time, we can turn to various continental sources which, in passing, mention England and the attitude of the Franks to their northern neighbours. Most remarkable and challenging in this respect is the comment made by the Byzantine historian Procopius who gave an account of a claim put to the Emperor Justinian in Constantinople sometime in

---

Brooks, 'Canterbury, Rome, and the construction of English Identity', in J. M. H. Smith (ed.), *Early Medieval Rome and the Christian West: Essays in Honour of D.A. Bullough* (Leiden, 2000), 221–46 at 232–43.

[36] Bede, *HE*.II.25; III.7; III.25; IV.5

[37] I. N. Wood, 'The Mission of Augustine of Canterbury to the English', *Speculum* (1994), 1–17 at 16; *idem*, 'Augustine and Gaul', in Gameson (ed.), *St. Augustine*, 68–82.

[38] Wallace-Hadrill, *Early Germanic Kingship*, 29, 31, 45; H. Mayr-Harting, *The Coming of Christianity to Anglo-Saxon England* (London, 1991), 63; B. A. E. Yorke, *Kings and Kingdoms of Early Anglo-Saxon England* (London, 1990), 28–29; D. P. Kirby, *The Earliest English Kings* (London, 1991), 34–36.

[39] See Wood, 'The Mission of Augustine of Canterbury', 10, where he suggests that, 'it was Frankish recalcitrance not fear of the Franks' which ensured that Kent was converted by a papal rather than a Merovingian mission.

the 550s by the messengers of a Merovingian king (possibly Childebert I) that the Franks held authority over some of the *Angloi* in *Britta*.[40] This statement may simply have been self-aggrandizement by a Merovingian for the benefit of the Imperial court, or else it may have been that the real nature of relations between Francia and England in the 550s had become obscured in Procopius' translation of the envoys' message. But other evidence, both historical and archaeological, points to close links between southern England (especially Kent) and northern Francia at this date. The perception of Merovingian hegemonic interest in the English (and the importance of the Franks to the success of the mission) pervades the language and letters of Gregory the Great. In the letter of introduction written for Augustine's benefit in July 596 and addressed to Kings Theuderic II and Theudebert II, Gregory commends the kings for the constancy of their faith and of their desire that 'those subject to you be completely converted to that faith'.[41] Whether the evidence is sufficient to prove political hegemony or economic dominance by the Franks over the Kentish kingdom in the later sixth century, as has been claimed, is a matter still open to debate. But it has been noted that these Merovingian appeals to authority in England, 'seem to have much in common' with the better attested Frankish hegemony which was exercised across the Rhine in the same period, and, coupled with Bede's otherwise enigmatic statement that the eastern Frankish tribe of the *Broctuari* had been among the Germanic peoples who had settled in Britain in the fifth and sixth centuries, we should take the implications of these comments seriously.[42]

Corroborative evidence is perhaps provided by the naming patterns of the Kentish dynasty and by marriage contracts which are known to have existed between various members of the Merovingian nobility and people from 'parts beyond the sea'. The literary contexts of some of these stories – such as Basina's motives for deserting her Thuringian husband in favour of King Childeric[43] – have an anecdotal quality, but others are better attested. Bertha, the daughter of Charibert I and Ingoberga, was married *c*. 580 to Æthelberht of Kent.[44] Her

---

[40] Procopius, *Gothic Wars* VIII.20.10; A. Cameron, *Procopius and the Sixth century* (London, 1985), 214; A. R. Burn, 'Procopius and the Island of Ghosts', *EHR* 70 (1955), 258–61; E. James, *The Franks* (Oxford, 1988), 103; I. N. Wood, 'Frankish Hegemony in England', in M. O. H. Carver (ed.), *The Age of Sutton Hoo: The Seventh Century and North-western Europe* (Woodbridge, 1992), 235–41; *idem, The Merovingian North Sea*, Occasional Papers on Medieval Topics 1 (Alingsås, 1983); *idem*, 'Before and after the Migration to Britain', in Hines, *The Anglo-Saxons from the Migration Period to the Eighth Century*, 41–51. The same claim is implicit in a poem of Venantius Fortunatus addressed to Chilperic; MGH, AA IV, *Carmina Liber* IX.i, 201–5, at lines 73–75.

[41] Gregory I, *Register*, no. VI.49; trans. Whitelock, *EHD* 1, no. 162. See also *Register* no. II.47, 48, 50, 51; and Wood, 'The Mission of Augustine of Canterbury', 8.

[42] Bede, *HE* V.9. Wood, *The Merovingian Kingdoms 450–751* (London, 1994), 176; cf. S. Burnell and E. James, 'The Archaeology of Conversion on the Continent in the Sixth and Seventh Centuries', in Gameson (ed.), *St. Augustine*, 83–106.

[43] Gregory of Tours, *Decem libri historiarum*, II.12; MGH *SS rer. Merov.* I, at 80.

[44] Brooks, *The Early History*, 5–7; *idem*, 'The Creation and Early Structure of the Kingdom of Kent', in S. R. Bassett (ed.), *The Origins of Anglo-Saxon Kingdoms* (London, 1988), 55–74,

marriage was undoubtedly of great importance for the introduction and ultimate acceptance of Christianity among the Kentish nobility, accompanied as she was by a Frankish bishop named Liudhard.[45] His presence implies activity by literate, Christian Franks in Kent for at least 20 years before Augustine's arrival. The continued existence in Canterbury of a church said by Bede to have been built in Roman times and dedicated to Martin, the patron saint of Tours, in which Bertha chose to worship reinforces the evidence for a pre-Augustinian community of Frankish Christians in the Kentish capital.[46] Furthermore, Æthelberht's father, Irminric, bore a name which is rare in Anglo-Saxon sources but common in Frankish ones, suggesting that the Merovingian link with the Kentish dynasty may have gone back a generation before Æthelberht's marriage to Bertha, and possibly even earlier, to those who gave a continental Germanic name to Irminric.[47]

Given this background, it is possible that the choice of a Frankish bride by Æthelberht had been a decisive factor in the acceptance of his royal authority in Kent.[48] Gregory of Tours, when describing the match of Charibert's and Ingoberga's daughter, describes her prospective husband in modest terms, as either 'a man from Kent' (*Canthia virum*) or as 'a son of the king of Kent' (*Canthia regis cuiusdam filius*). Both are phrases which seem to suggest that, although Æthelberht was recognized as a man of rank, he was not yet established as king at the time of his marriage.[49] The links between the Merovingian and Kentish courts created by marriage alliances may account for echoes of the *Pactus Legis Salicae* and Merovingian legal traditions in Æthelberht's own law

---

reprinted in his *Anglo-Saxon Myths: State and Church 400–1066* (London, 2000), 33–60, at 49–51; Kirby, *The Earliest English Kings*, 32–33; Wood, 'The Mission of Augustine of Canterbury', 10–11.

[45] A 'medalet' inscribed LEVDARDVS EP[ISCOPU]S is extant evidence for the Frankish bishop's presence in Kent. It was found somewhere in Canterbury early in the nineteenth century, traditionally at St Martin's. The first recorded references to the find, however, refer to St Augustine's as the probable find site; see L. Webster and J. Backhouse (eds), *The Making of England: Anglo-Saxon Art and Culture, AD 600–900* (London, 1991), 23–24, no. 5b. It was found with a collection of other precious artefacts, imperial and Merovingian medalet-coins, a brooch and a Roman intaglio, probably from a number of female graves rather than as a single hoard, and seems likely to have been produced by a Frankish craftsman, perhaps working in Kent; see North, *English Hammered Coinage*, 19; P. Grierson, 'The Canterbury (St. Martin) Hoard of Frankish and Anglo-Saxon Coin-ornaments', *BNJ* 27 (1952), 39–51; M. Werner, 'The Luidhard Medalet', *ASE*, 20 (1991), 27–41.

[46] Bede, *HE* I.26; N. P. Brooks, 'The Ecclesiastical Topography of Early Medieval Canterbury', in M. W. Barley (ed.), *European Towns: Their Archaeology and Early History* (London, 1977), 487–98, reprinted in his *Anglo-Saxon Myths*, 91–100, at 94–96; *idem, The Early History of the Church of Canterbury* (Leicester, 1984), 17; F. Jenkins, 'St. Martin's Church at Canterbury', *Medieval Archaeology*, 9 (1965), 11–15.

[47] Brooks, 'The creation and early structure of the Kingdom of Kent', 64–65.

[48] Kirby, *The Earliest English Kings*, 34–35.

[49] Gregory of Tours, *Decem libri historiarum*, ed. B. Krusch, MGH SS rer. Merov. I (Hanover, 1885), IV.26 and IX.26. On the implications of these extracts for the dating of Æthelberht's marriage, see Kirby, *The Earliest English Kings*, 34–35.

code, and also for the presence of the Kentish churchmen, Peter (abbot of Canterbury) and Justus (bishop of Rochester) at the Council of Paris in 614.[50]

Merovingian blood-ties with Anglo-Saxon royalty were maintained in the next generation; Bertha's daughter, Æthelburh, was married (like her mother) to a pagan king, Edwin of Northumbria, and her son Eadbald was eventually married to Ymme, another high-ranking Frankish woman who seems to have been the daughter of Erchinoald, the Neustrian mayor of the palace.[51] If this interpretation of Ymme's background is correct, she was not strictly of royal descent but was evidently of sufficient noble standing to have been considered a suitable bride for a Kentish king, albeit a pagan one at the time of his accession. Indeed Eadbald may only have been converted to Christianity (like his father, Æthelberht) when betrothed to a Frankish princess.[52] Ymme's Frankish pedigree is reflected and preserved in the names of her son Eorcenberht (king of Kent 640–64), her grandson Hlothere (king of Kent 673–85), and her granddaughter Eorcengota who eventually entered the Neustrian monastery of Faremoûtiers-en-Brie near Paris, where her saintliness was commemorated after her death.[53] Eorcengota foresaw her own death in a vision which encapsulates symbols of her dual Franco-Kentish descent. She saw, so Bede tells us, a group of men dressed in white enter the monastery seeking, they said, 'to take back with them the golden coin (*aureum nomisma*) which had been brought thither from Kent'.[54] Gold coin was struck in seventh-century England only in the kingdom of Kent using designs based on Roman or Merovingian prototypes and metal obtained

---

[50] C. de Clercq (ed.), *Conciliae Galliae, a 511–695*, CCSL 148A (Turnhout, 1963), 282. On the legal parallels see Wallace-Hadrill, *Early Germanic Kingship*, 36–39 and P. H. Sawyer, *From Roman Britain to Norman England* (New York, 1978), 173. Note especially the provisions in the *Lex Salicae* (Pactus 39.ii) relating to the retrieval of slaves who had been taken across the sea; also K. F. Drew (trans.), *The Laws of the Salian Franks* (Philadelphia, 1991), 101. See also, Wood, *Merovingian North Sea*, 5, 12–13; idem, *Merovingian Kingdoms*, 108–12; idem, 'Before and after the Migration to Britain', 47; P. Wormald, *The Making of English Law: King Alfred to the Twelfth Century* (Oxford, 1999), 100.

[51] K.–F. Werner, 'Les rouages de l'administration', in P. Perin and L. Feffer (eds), *La Neustrie: Les pays au nord de la Loire de Dagobert à Charles le Chauve (vii-ix siècles)* (Créteil, 1985), 41–46, at 42. For the Kentish tradition of Ymme as a Frankish princess (*filia regis Francorum*) see D. W. Rollason, *The Mildrith Legend: A Study in Early Medieval Hagiography in England* (Leicester, 1982).

[52] Kirby, *The Earliest English Kings*, 41. For the suggestion that baptism was deliberately withheld from the eldest son of a king as 'insurance' against future religious fluctuations, see A. Angenendt, 'The Conversion of the Anglo-Saxons Considered against the Background of the Early Medieval Mission', in *Angli e Sassoni cal di qua e al di là del mare*, Settimane di Studio 32 (Spoleto, 1986), 747–81.

[53] F. M. Stenton, *Anglo-Saxon England* (3rd edn) (Oxford, 1971), 61. Erchinoald's name would have been spelt Earconwald in OE. Bishop Eorcenwald of London (675–93) also bears the name of the Neustrian *maior domus*, possibly reflecting a continuation of this Frankish influence, and spread of Kentish influence over the East Saxons; see B. A. E. Yorke, 'The Kingdom of the East Saxons', *ASE*, 14 (1985), 1–36 at 15; P. Fouracre and R. A. Gerberding (trans.), *Late Merovingian France: History and Hagiography 640–720* (1996), 102–4. On Eorcenwald's claim to have visited Rome see A. Scharer, 'The Gregorian Tradition in early England', in Gameson (ed.), *St. Augustine*, at 191.

[54] Bede, *HE* III.8.

from Merovingian issues.[55] A gold coin was, therefore, an appropriate metaphor for a treasured Kentish princess who had gained spiritual inspiration in Francia. Eadbald's Frankish ties are reflected also in the coinage of his reign. Despite his initial apostasy, his rule was sufficiently strong (perhaps through his maternal Frankish connections) to mint a gold coinage which displayed his own name – in Merovingian fashion – and used Frankish gold.[56] The links between the Kentish and Neustrian courts in this period are such that it is even possible that Erchinoald's gift of an English slave-girl as a bedfellow for Clovis II in *c.* 648 may have had as much to do with fluctuations in Anglo-Saxon politics as the alleged beauty of the girl, Balthildis.[57]

Notorious too was the flight of Æthelburh, queen of the Northumbrian king Edwin and daughter of Bertha, the Frankish princess who had married Æthelberht of Kent. After Edwin's death in 633 at the hands of the Christian Briton Cadwallon and Penda, the pagan king of the Mercians, Æthelburh was forced to flee Northumbria fearing the wrath, so Bede says, not so much of her husband's killers but of his Bernician rivals who succeeded him to the Northumbrian throne, the brothers Eanfrith and Oswald.[58] She sent her children, the heirs to Edwin's kingdom, to Francia to the comparative safety of the court of King Dagobert I, who was her second cousin.[59] There they were to be brought up and educated, hopefully one day to return to Northumbria. Unfortunately for the Deiran dynasty, both children died *in infantia* shortly after arriving in Francia, and Oswald's Bernician dynasty maintained firm control of the kingdom of Northumbria for many decades to come. Despite this, the incident indicates that the Deiran royal family in the 630s was sufficiently mindful of the continental ancestry of its Kentish queen (and of the contacts between her brother's wife, Ymme and the Neustrian court) that, when facing exile, Francia was considered the proper place for the Northumbrian royal children to live.

Given these close blood-ties between the Kentish and Merovingian courts in the first half of the seventh century it may be no coincidence that some manuscript evidence survives to illustrate a continued interest in the seventh-century kings of Kent within some Frankish monastic circles of later decades. A

---

[55] Grierson and Blackburn, *MEC* 1, 159–64; S. C. Hawkes, J. M. Merrick and D. M. Metcalf, 'X-ray Fluorescent Analysis of Some Dark Age Coins and Jewellery', *Archaeometry*, 9 (1966), 98–138.

[56] AVDVARLD REGES; Grierson and Blackburn, *MEC* 1, 161–62; Kirby, *The Earliest English Kings,* 43.

[57] Fouracre and Gerberding, *Late Merovingian France*, 103–4; J. L. Nelson, 'Queens as Jezebels: the careers of Brunhild and Balthild in Merovingian History', in D. Baker (ed.), *Medieval Women* (1978), 31–77. A double-sided gold seal ring which has been associated with the queen, bearing the legend *Baldehildis* + around a frontal female face on one side, and with an image of two lovers under a cross on the reverse, was recently found by a metal detectorist in Norfolk; on which see *British Archaeology*, April 2001, 26.

[58] Bede, *HE* II.20.

[59] Her maternal grandfather Charibert I and his paternal grandfather Chilperic I were brothers; see Wood, *The Merovingian Kingdoms*, 345, 348.

set of Kentish annals which provides a detailed king-list of Kentish kings from Æthelberht to Eadric (with dates of death accurate to the day of the week) is preserved in three Frankish manuscripts of the ninth century.[60] These Kentish annals circulated alongside another contemporary series from Lindisfarne and, significantly, were independent of data used by Bede. The Kentish annals provide factual details not given in any of Bede's chronological compositions, although they are clearly representative of the type of Kentish king-list which was available to Bede in Jarrow when he was writing his *Ecclesiastical History*.[61] Some of the factual details which these annals supply are unique – the dates of the deaths of kings Irminric, Eadbald, Ecgberht and Eadric, for example.[62] They suggest that a proto-annalistic king-list was being kept in Kent during the seventh century at a centre which maintained a high appreciation of chronology and record-keeping. The manuscript transmission of both these sets of annals suggests that they arrived in Francia only in the mid-eighth century as marginalia to Easter tables included with copies of Bede's treatise, 'On The Reckoning of Time'. The recopying of the Kentish annals by Frankish scribes in the ninth century catches echoes of the time when the Kentish royal dynasty, with its Frankish-sounding names, had been closely related to Frankish royalty.[63]

One further piece of historical evidence indicates that, linguistically at least, the two regions were compatible. Describing St Augustine's arrival in Kent in 597, Bede states that the Roman bishop acquired the assistance of interpreters *de gente Francorum* in order to establish the Roman mission in Kent.[64] This linguistic compatibility between Kentish and northern Frankish speakers implies a certain depth of familiarity, and supports the view that inhabitants of the two regions had previously established and maintained close contacts. The normality of this mutual understanding contrasts with Bede's comments concerning the experience of the Frankish bishop Agilbert in Wessex who was removed from his see by King Cenwealh some 60 years later, *c.* 664. The reason given by Bede

---

[60] Paris, Bibliothèque nationale MS lat. 13013 (St Germain, Corbie s.ix); Paris, Bibliothèque nationale MS n.a.l. 1615 (Fleury, Auxerre? s.ix); Würzburg, Universitätsbibliothek MS M.p.th.f.46 (St. Amand, Salzburg, s.ix[1]). D. Whitelock, *After Bede*, Jarrow Lecture (Jarrow, 1960), 7–8; J. Prinz, *Der Corveyer Annalen* (Münster, 1982); Levison, *England and the Continent,* 270–73, 277; Brooks, 'The Creation and Early Structure of the Kingdom of Kent', 55. For a related text and manuscript see C. Stiegmann and M. Wemhoff (eds), *799 Kunst und Kultur der Karolingerzeit. Karl der Große und Papst Leo III in Paderborn,* 3 vols (Mainz, 1999), Vol. 1, 41–42, no. II.4.

[61] For example, Bede (*HE* IV.26) gives date of death of Hlothere, as *viii idus Februarias* which is one day different from date in the St Germain manuscript, *s.a.* 685.

[62] E. B. Fryde, et al. (eds), *Handbook of British Chronology*, Royal Historical Society Handbooks (3rd edn) (London, 1986), 12–13; S. Keynes, 'Rulers of the English, *c.* 450–1066', in *The Blackwell Encyclopaedia of Anglo-Saxon England*, ed. M. Lapidge (Oxford, 1999), 501–2.

[63] This material is explored in greater detail in J. Story, 'The Frankish Annals of Lindisfarne and Kent', (in prep.).

[64] Bede, *HE* I.25; S. Kelly, 'Anglo-Saxon Lay Society and the Written Word', in R. McKitterick (ed.), *The Uses of Literacy in Early Medieval Europe* (Cambridge, 1990), 36–62 at 58. On the relationship between Kentish and Frankish see A. Campbell, *Old English Grammar* (Oxford, 1959), 4.

for Agilbert's dismissal was that the West Saxon king – who knew only the 'Saxon' tongue – could not understand the Frankish bishop's *barbarae loquellae*.[65] The regional variation implied here between Kentish comprehension and West Saxon incomprehension of Frankish speech matches other aspects of Bede's ethnic terminology and may reflect real dialectical differences.[66]

Outside Kent, the Frankish connections in this period are subtly different. Whereas Kentish political contacts had been with the Neustrian heartlands of the Seine basin, the archaeological evidence for the eastern seaboard of England points rather to enhanced contacts with the Rhineland.[67] This is particularly apparent in the excavated evidence from the mercantile settlements of York, Ipswich and London all of which display a large proportion of Frisian and Rhenish finds from their assemblages.[68] Recent work in the Buttermarket cemetery in Ipswich has revealed early to mid-seventh-century male graves, containing Rhenish buckle-sets and, in one case, a multiple assemblage of Rhenish artefacts (including weaponry and glass vessels) comparable with continental grave assemblages dated 640–70.[69] The explicit cultural resonance of these items suggests that the communities to which these men belonged maintained contact and familiarity with the Frankish Rhineland. Of course, the grave assemblages in themselves cannot reveal the ethnic origins of the dead men but these rich burials with their 'foreign' grave furniture present a challenge to long-held

---

[65] Bede, *HE* III.7. This is dismissed by Richter who argues that the efforts of the king to have Agilbert recalled and the eventual acceptance of Leuthere as bishop of the West Saxons, mitigates against a linguistic barrier. He argues that Agilbert 'moved effortlessly' between countries and languages; see M. Richter, 'The English Link in Hiberno Frankish relations', in J. M. Picard (ed.), *Ireland and Northern France, AD 600–850* (Dublin, 1991), 95–118 at 112, n. 42. Contrary to this view run Bede's comments in his description of the Synod of Whitby in which he says that Agilbert asked Wilfrid to expound the Romanist views on his behalf because *ille melius ac manifestius ipsa lingua Anglorum, quam ego per interpretem, potest explanare quae sentimus*; Bede, *HE* III.25.

[66] Brooks, *Bede and the English*, 9.

[67] R. Hodges, *Dark Age Economics: The Origins of Towns and Trade A.D. 600–1000* (London, 1982), 35–36; *idem*, *The Anglo-Saxon Achievement: Archaeology and the Beginnings of English Society* (London, 1989), 69–114; *idem*, *Towns and Trade in the Age of Charlemagne* (London, 2000); J. Huggett, 'Imported Grave Goods and the Early Anglo-Saxon Economy', *Medieval Archaeology*, 32 (1988), 63–96; Lebecq, 'England and the Continent in the Sixth and Seventh Centuries', at 59.

[68] On York see, for example, the excavations at Fishergate; R. Hall, 'York (700–1050)', in R. Hobley and R. Hodges (eds), *The Rebirth of Towns in the West* (London, 1988), 125–32 and R. Kemp, *Anglian Settlement at 46–54 Fishergate*, The Archaeology of York, 7. Anglian York, 1 (York, 1996). On Ipswich see K. Wade, 'Ipswich', in Hobley and Hodges, *The Rebirth of Towns*, 93–100 and *idem*, 'The Urbanization of East Anglia: The Ipswich Perspective', in J. Gardiner (ed.), *Flatlands and Wetlands: Current Themes in East Anglian Archaeology*, East Anglian Archaeology 50 (1993), 144–51. On finds from Saxon London see, for example, L. Blackmore, 'Aspects of Trade and Exchange Evidenced by Recent Work on Saxon and Medieval Pottery from London', *Transactions of the London and Middlesex Archaeological Society*, 50 (1999), 38–54.

[69] C. Scull and A. Bayliss, 'Radiocarbon Dating and Anglo-Saxon Graves', in U. von Freeden, U. Koch and A. Wieczorek (eds), *Völker an Nord- und Ostsee und die Franken* (Bonn, 1999), 39–50 and *idem*, 'Dating Burials of the Seventh and Eighth Centuries: A Case Study from Ipswich, Suffolk', in Hines et al., *The Pace of Change*, 80–92.

assumptions about the role of nearby Sutton Hoo in the development of the
contemporary trading site at Ipswich and of Anglo-Saxon kingship in this part of
East Anglia, and provide something of an alternative focus for those processes.[70]

The remarkable set of 37 Merovingian coins found in Mound One at
Sutton Hoo – traditionally associated with Rædwald (c. 616–c. 627) – are testimony to the export of valuable Frankish artefacts to East Anglia in this period.[71]
The suggestion that the coins were struck at different mints indicates deliberate
collection and gift exchange rather than more haphazard collection as a byproduct
of trading contacts. The mints concerned were spread throughout Francia pointing to a date of collection when both Neustria and Austrasia were in the hands of
a single ruler – that is, either Clothar II's rule (613–22) or the period before the
selection of Sigebert III as king of Austrasia (630–33). These dates are significant for the dating of the entire assemblage at Sutton Hoo, and may suggest a
date of deposition after the accession of Rædwald's successor to the East Anglian
throne in 630/31. That Rædwald's successor, Sigebert, shared a name with the
Austrasian king of the day may also be important, especially since there are
explicit references which connect him with Francia. Sigebert fled abroad in fear
of Rædwald sometime before 630, possibly as early as 616, and remained there
in exile until it was safe for him to return and claim his kingdom.[72] While in
Francia, he received Christian baptism and, Bede adds, was sufficiently inspired
by the Frankish example to found a school for boys in the Frankish manner when
he returned to East Anglia. Given his years of exile abroad, his return to his
native land and subsequent bid for the kingship is likely to have been made with
Frankish help; it may be (as Wood has suggested) that the Sutton Hoo coins are
remnants of the treasure which helped to restore him.[73]

Sigebert's efforts to Christianize East Anglia throw a spotlight on the role
of Frankish clergy in this process throughout England in the mid-seventh century, and emphasize the importance of Frankish churchmen in sustaining

---

[70] M. O. H. Carver, *Sutton Hoo: Burial Ground of Kings?* (London, 1998). Interestingly,
graves with a similar 'Frankish' profile have very recently been uncovered in Southampton at the
site of the new football stadium, and these present similar challenges to assumptions about the
place of Winchester in the development of Hamwic.

[71] S. Rigold, 'The Sutton Hoo Coins in the Light of the Contemporary Background of
Coinage in England', in R. S. L. Bruce-Mitford, *The Sutton Hoo Ship Burial* (London, 1975), Vol.
1, 653–77; Metcalf, 'Monetary Expansion', 232. For the connection of Redwald with Mound 1 at
Sutton Hoo see, R. S. L. Bruce-Mitford, 'The Sutton Hoo Ship Burial; Some Foreign Connections',
in *Angli e Sassoni al di qua e al di là del mare*, Settimane di Studio, 32.i (Spoleto, 1986), 143–218.
The counter argument that the mound and its treasure might relate better to the reigns of Sigebert
(acc. 630–61) and Eorpwald (d. 627–28) is presented by I. N. Wood, 'The Franks and Sutton Hoo',
in I. N. Wood and N. Lund (eds), *People and Places in Northern Europe 500–1600* (Woodbridge,
1991), 1–14, though the religious pluralism implicit within the grave assemblage points away from
the pious Sigebert.

[72] Bede, *HE* III.18; Fouracre and Gerberding, *Late Merovingian France*, 102–4; Wood, *The
Merovingian Kingdoms*, 177, 360–61; *idem*, 'The Franks and Sutton Hoo', 3–6.

[73] Wood, *The Merovingian Kingdoms*, 177; *idem*, 'The Franks and Sutton Hoo', 10–11

Christianity in southern England in the generation after the enthusiasm for the Roman mission had waned.[74] Sigebert was aided in his work by a Burgundian Frank named Felix who had been, 'born and consecrated in Burgundy' but who had been working for some time in Kent.[75] Felix was one of several Franks who crossed the Channel to assist with missionary work, following in the footsteps of Bishop Liudhard who had accompanied Queen Bertha to Canterbury. Gregory the Great's letters written in 596 to Theuderic and Theudebert, and to their mother Brunhild refer to requests for priests to be taken to England, 'from the vicinity' – apparently, that is, from Francia.[76] There seems to have been a renewed impetus to Frankish activity in the mid-seventh century possibly, as Wood has suggested, because the powerful Merovingian king Dagobert I had belatedly recognized that an opportunity to increase Frankish influence in England had been lost when the initiative for conversion of the Anglo-Saxons was taken, not by Luidhard's Franks, but by St Augustine and his missionaries from Rome.[77] Dagobert I (623–39) commanded the respect of his neighbours and drew obedience from the leaders of the Bretons, Gascons and Burgundians, as well as wielding powerful influence among the Visigoths and Lombards. The renewed Frankish interest in the mission to the English during and after his reign may partly reflect the strength of his rule but also perhaps a desire to reinforce ties with southern English courts at a time when the balance of power within England was shifting northwards to the kingdoms of Mercia and Northumbria.[78] The monastic founder Richarius is also said to have worked in England at this time and another Frank, Agilbert, who came to England from Ireland *c*. 650, became bishop of the West Saxons under King Cenwealh.[79] Agilbert was from a leading Frankish family, almost certainly connected with the family of St Audoin and possibly also related to the Merovingian dynasty itself. Frustrated with Agilbert's inability to learn the West Saxon tongue, Cenwealh divided the diocese, giving half to a different bishop named Wine who had also been consecrated in Gaul. In a fit of umbrage Agilbert returned to Francia and to the bishopric of Paris (as well as the patronage of Ebroin, the notorious Neustrian mayor of the

---

[74] Campbell, 'The First Century of Christianity', 55.

[75] Bede, *HE* II.15 and III.19; Wood, *Merovingian Kingdoms*, 314.

[76] Gregory, *Register* VI 49, XI 48; Wood, 'The Mission of Augustine of Canterbury', 8; C. Stancliffe, 'The British Church and the Mission of Augustine', in Gameson (ed.), *St Augustine*, 107–51.

[77] I. N. Wood 'The Channel from the 4th to the 7th centuries AD', in S. McGrail (ed.), *Maritime Celts, Frisians, and Saxons*, CBA Research Report 71 (London, 1990), 93–97. The work of Franks such as Felix in England was contemporaneous with the missions of Amandus to Frisia which were directly sponsored by Dagobert; see Wood, *The Merovingian Kingdoms*, 178, 314–15.

[78] Wood, *The Merovingian Kingdoms*, 159–60, 180; Fouracre and Gerberding, *Late Merovingian France*, 14–15.

[79] *Vita Richarii*, c. 7; see also Alcuin's *Vita S. Richarii*, ed. B. Krusch, MGH SS rer. Merov. III (Berlin, 1986), c. 8 in which he broadens the definition of Richarius's activity to Britain; Wood, *The Merovingian Kingdoms*, 178–79, 314. For Agilbert's appointment to the see at Dorchester-on-Thames see Bede, *HE* III.7.

palace) but not before he had travelled to Northumbria, where he consecrated Wilfrid as priest and played a decisive role at the Synod of Whitby in 664.[80] Cenwealh later regretted his action against Agilbert and sent messengers to Paris to persuade him to return. Agilbert refused but sent in his stead his nephew Leuthere (Hlothere), also a Frank, who was duly consecrated bishop of the West Saxons by Archbishop Theodore in 670.[81]

Theodore had met Agilbert in Paris on his journey to England from Rome in 669. He, and his travelling companions, Abbot Hadrian and Benedict Biscop, were warmly welcomed and entertained by Agilbert, the bishops of Sens and Meaux, and by the archbishop of Marseilles.[82] With his recent experience in England, Agilbert was well placed to brief the new archbishop of Canterbury on the state of the English Church, though perhaps from a rather jaded point of view.[83] In an interesting gloss on the nature of Anglo-Frankish links in the 660s and 670s, Bede tells us that both Theodore and Hadrian were temporarily prevented from travelling on to Canterbury by Ebroin. Apparently Ebroin was suspicious of the two Greek-speaking travellers from Rome, fearing that they might also have been bearers of an anti-Frankish plot, hatched by the Emperor Constans II, and being transmitted through them *ad Brittanniae reges*. But the Kentish king Ecgberht, hearing that Theodore was resident in Francia, sent his *praefectus* Rædfrith there to collect his new archbishop. Once Ebroin had granted permission for them to leave, Theodore travelled to Quentovic and thence to Canterbury. Hadrian, however, was kept in Francia by Ebroin a while longer until he was satisfied that no secret conspiracy was being planned by the Byzantine emperor with the kings of Britain. The incident reflects a certain reality (albeit a rather paranoid one) in the mind of the most powerful man of the day in Neustria that the kingdoms of Anglo-Saxon England had the capacity to be involved in large-scale plots against his authority in Francia. Anglo-Saxon involvement in the machinations of pan-European politics was evidently plausible.

Francia and seventh-century Anglo-Saxon monasticism

Frankish practice and precedent also had an important influence on Anglo-Saxon monasticism as it was established in the seventh century. Bede admired northern Frankish nunneries such as Faremoutiers-en-Brie, Chelles and Andelys-sur-Seine which gave hospitality to Anglo-Saxon women such as Eorcengota and her aunts Sæthryth and Æthelburh of the East Anglian royal dynasty, both of

---

[80] Bede, *HE* III.25 and III.28; Stephanus, *Vita Wilfridi*, c. 9.

[81] Bede, *HE* III.7.

[82] Bede, *HE* IV.1; Bede, *Historia Abbatum*, c. 3.

[83] P. Sims-Williams, 'Continental Influence at Bath Monastery in the Seventh Century', *ASE*, 4 (1975), 1–10 at 8, n. 7 (with reference to G. A. de Maillé, *Les Cryptes des Jouarre. Plans et relevés de P. Rousseau* (Paris, 1971)) speculates that this contact between Theodore and Agilbert may have been the critical channel of influence.

whom became abbesses at Brie.[84] Chelles had been refounded and enlarged in 657–64 by Clovis II's Anglo-Saxon queen, Balthildis, and her presence there in retirement from *c.* 665 until *c.* 677 may account for the increased English orientation of that monastery.[85] These monasteries provided inspiration and training as well as manuscripts for new nunneries founded in England in the Frankish style. Abbess Bertila of Jouarre (and later of Chelles) is recorded as having sent help to England in the form of books, relics and teachers. The new monastery at Bath which was founded during Leuthere's episcopacy, may well have been one of the recipients of Bertila's generosity in that it had at least two Frankish women, named Berta and Folcburg, in its community.[86] The Northumbrian noblewoman Hild, unable to join her sister Hereswith at Chelles, subsequently founded another such monastery at Streanæshalch.[87] And the influence was not just one way; hints in the hagiographical and epistolary sources, as well as extant manuscripts, imply an extensive movement of books and people between Anglo-Saxon and Frankish monasteries in the later seventh and earlier eighth centuries.[88]

The influence of Frankish monasticism was also acknowledged by Northumbrian clergymen who owed their ecclesiastical allegiance to the ways of Rome and who looked primarily to the Continent for spiritual inspiration. Between them, Benedict Biscop, Ceolfrid, and Wilfrid travelled to the Continent 12 times en route to Rome. Each time, even when Wilfrid was in danger of his life from Ebroin, the Neustrian mayor of the palace, the three clerics travelled into Francia bringing back treasures from their travels as well as observations on the practice of continental monasticism. Biscop spent two years at the monastery on the island of Lérins which had recently changed from an eremitic to coenobitic lifestyle, and in doing so embraced the rule of St Benedict. He duly introduced St Benedict's rule in his new foundation at

---

[84] Bede, *HE* III.8. P. Wormald, 'Bede and Benedict Biscop', in G. Bonner (ed.), *Famulus Christi: Essays in Commemoration of the Thirteenth-Centenary of the Birth of the Venerable Bede* (London, 1976), 141–69; I. N. Wood, 'Ripon, Francia and the Franks' Casket in the Early Middle Ages', *Northern History*, 26 (1990), 1–19; B. A. E. Yorke, 'The Reception of Christianity at the Anglo-Saxon Royal Courts', in Gameson (ed.), *St. Augustine*, 152–73 at 161.

[85] McKitterick, 'The Diffusion of Insular Culture' in Neustria between 650 and 850: The Implications of the Manuscript Evidence', in H. Atsma and K.-F. Werner (eds), *La Neustrie*, Beihefte der Francia 16 (Sigmaringen, 1989), 408–9; Nelson, 'Queens as Jezebels', 22.

[86] *Vita Bertilae abbatissae Calensis*; MGH SS rer. Merov. VI, at 101–9. R. McKitterick, 'Nuns' Scriptoria in England and Francia in the Early Middle Ages', *Francia* 19 (1992), 1–35; R. Gameson, 'The Earliest Books of Christian Kent', in Gameson (ed.), *St. Augustine*, at 357. The Frankish bishop of Wessex, Leuthere, is named in the foundation charter granted by the sub-king Osric to Berta (BCS43/S51); see Sims-Williams, 'Continental Influence', 2–5.

[87] Bede, *HE* IV.23.

[88] See, for example, the Life of Geretrude which says that the nunnery at Nivelles was receiving manuscripts from 'across the sea'; *Vita Geretrudis*, c.2; MGH SS rer. Merov. II; trans. Fouracre and Gerberding, *Late Merovingian France*, 322. On the insular features of manuscripts from Chelles and Jouarre see McKitterick, 'The Diffusion of Insular Culture in Neustria', at 406–13.

Wearmouth and Jarrow, employing his own combination of the rules of 17 monasteries which he had visited on his travels through Francia and Italy.[89] As well as manuscripts, ornaments and images from Francia, Biscop also brought back to Northumbria Frankish craftsmen skilled in stoneworking and glass-making in order to build and adorn his new foundations *in more Romanorum*.[90] On one occasion Biscop brought back to Northumbria Abbot John, the arch-cantor of St Peter's in Rome, in order that his new community might learn to sing the most correct and most up-to-date form of the liturgy as practised in Rome. John, who was abbot of the monastery of St Martin in Rome, went to England via St Martin's at Tours and continued his journey accompanied by men from that house who were 'to accompany him on his journey and to assist him in his appointed task'.[91] This task included not just the musical education of the Northumbrian monks but also an investigation into the canonical propriety of the English Church.

Wilfrid similarly spent several formative years in a Frankish community although, in accordance with his subsequent career, he chose to learn from an episcopal rather than a monastic community. He stayed at least three years with Annemundus, Archbishop of Lyons, and nearly suffered martyrdom alongside his Frankish master.[92] Like Biscop he was tempted to stay in Francia but he decided to return to Northumbria, taking with him grandiose attitudes and ideas about episcopal authority which find their closest parallels in the Gallo-Roman sees of Francia and which were to cause him considerable trouble throughout the rest of his career as an Anglo-Saxon bishop. Most symbolic of his debt and affection for Frankish episcopal grandeur is the account of his elevation to the rank of bishop at the royal city of Compiègne in 664–65. Bede notes Wilfrid's consecration, 'in great splendour in the presence of a number of bishops'. The author of his *Vita* describes the ceremony in the presence of 'at least twelve catholic bishops' in somewhat greater detail:

> ... having received his profession of faith, they consecrated him before all the people with great satisfaction and no less pomp. As their traditions demanded, he was borne into the oratory aloft on a golden throne by the bishops alone, to the accompaniment of songs and canticles from the choir.[93]

---

[89] Bede, *Historia Abbatum*, c. 2, 11.

[90] Ibid., c. 4–6; R. J. Cramp, 'Wearmouth and Jarrow in their Continental Context', in K. Painter (ed.), *'Churches Built in Ancient Times': Recent Studies in Early Christian Archeology* (London, 1994), 279–94; E. Fletcher, 'The Influence of Merovingian Gaul on Northumbria in the Seventh Century', *Medieval Archaeology*, 20 (1980), 69–81. See also the letter of Abbot Cuthbert of Wearmouth Jarrow to Lul requesting a glass-vessel maker dated 764; M. Tangl (ed.), *Die Briefe des heiligen Bonifatius und Lullus*, MGH *Epp Sel.* (Berlin, 1916), no. 116; *EHD* 1, trans. Whitelock, no. 185.

[91] Bede, *HE* V.18, V.24. It is John's involvement in the Council of Hatfield which is recalled in Bede's recapitulation at the end of his *History*.

[92] Bede, *HE* V.19; Stephanus, *Vita Wilfridi* , c. 4.

[93] Stephanus, *Vita Wilfridi*, c. 12.

While it is true that Wilfrid needed to go abroad in order to ensure canonical ordination by Catholic (as opposed to Irish) bishops, the elaborate induction ceremony fits with what else we know of Wilfrid's Gallic pretensions and taste for *romanitas*.

Wilfrid stands out as one of the most colourful personalities in the history of the seventh-century Church. Notwithstanding his prominence in the sources, we must attribute to him an important and high-profile role in the shaping of Anglo-Frankish relations in the later decades of the seventh century since he involved himself in Merovingian as well as Anglo-Saxon dynastic politics. Wilfrid's Frankish training and frequent trips to Rome provided him with powerful friends and contacts abroad, and with enemies too. In particular, he attracted the vengeance of Ebroin to the extent that another Anglo-Saxon bishop on a journey through Francia, who went by the name of Winfrith, was accidentally roughed up by some of Ebroin's henchmen, having been misled (as Stephanus says) by, 'a mistake in one syllable' of their victim's name.[94]

On one journey to Rome in 679 Wilfrid stayed with the Lombard king Perctarit and the Austrasian king, Dagobert II.[95] The latter was particularly indebted to the Northumbrian bishop. Stephanus relates a remarkable story of this Frankish prince in exile: having been expelled from his kingdom by Pippinid magnates in the late 650s after the death of his father Sigebert III, Dagobert was exiled to Ireland where he remained in safety for several years. His kinsmen and allies in Francia, hearing that he was still alive, sent messengers to Wilfrid to ask him to invite Dagobert *de Scottia et Hibernia* and to send him safely back to Francia as king. To this Wilfrid evidently agreed, and Dagobert was sent *de arma ditatum et viribus sociorum elevatum magnifice ad suam regionem* and was duly made king of Austrasia in 676.[96] So grateful was Dagobert for Wilfrid's role in his reinstatement to royal office that he offered the Northumbrian bishop the metropolitan see of Strasbourg on the next occasion that Wilfrid travelled through Francia in exile from his homeland. Despite the obviously partisan nature of Stephanus's account, Wilfrid's role in the reinstatement of this Frankish prince appears to have been central to the success of the venture. What is notable is that Wilfrid, as bishop of York, was specifically sought by the Austrasian faction as a suitable person to intervene in issues of their domestic politics. It is true that we only know the story from the hagiographical biography of Wilfrid, yet his involvement in high-level politics in Francia is perfectly plausible given what is known of his Frankish training earlier in his career, his stormy relationship with various Anglo-Saxon kings, and of his several journeys to Rome to clear his

---

[94] Ibid., c. 25; Bede, *HE* IV.6.

[95] Stephanus, *Vita Wilfridi*, c. 28 and 33. On Dagobert see also Levison, *England and the Continent*, 49–51; I. Wood, *The Merovingian Kingdoms,* 221–26, 231–34; J. M. Picard, 'Church and Politics in the Seventh Century: The Irish Exile of King Dagobert II', in Picard, *Ireland and Northern France,* 27–52; Fouracre and Gerberding, *Late Merovingian France,* 18–19, 22–24.

[96] Stephanus, *Vita Wilfridi*, c. 28.

name and to seek restoration to his bishopric.[97] Also important (in view of the relationship that was to develop subsequently) was that the leader of the Austrasian faction which sought to restore Dagobert to his throne was none other than Pippin II, Charlemagne's great grandfather. Despite the eventual brevity of Dagobert II's reign (he was murdered later in 679 before Wilfrid had returned from Rome),[98] the action taken by Pippin to restore Dagobert in collaboration with Wilfrid marked an early flexing of Carolingian political muscles and was an important step on the road to the dominance of the Carolingian dynasty in Austrasia and beyond.

Patronage and politics: the Anglo-Saxon mission to the Continent

Wilfrid's support of Dagobert II and the antagonism of Ebroin points to another trend in Anglo-Saxon relations with Francia which becomes increasingly marked in the latter part of the seventh century, that of alliances with Austrasian rather than Neustrian magnates as had characterized Kentish connections. This trend becomes more pronounced with the advent of the Anglo-Saxon mission to the pagan regions which lay to the north and east of the Austrasian *regnum*. The Anglo-Saxon missionaries travelled to the Continent primarily, as Bede noted, to fulfil their vocation of bringing their ancestral kindred to Christ,[99] but, in so

---

[97] For the debate over the bias of Wilfrid's biographer Stephanus and thus the reliability of his work in contrast with Bede's treatment of Wilfrid in the *Historia Ecclesiastica*, see R. L. Poole, 'St. Wilfrid and the See of Ripon', *EHR*, 34 (1919), 1–24; J. Campbell, 'Bede I', in his *Essays in Anglo-Saxon History* at 20–22; D. P. Kirby, 'Bede, Eddius Stephanus and the Life of Wilfrid', *EHR*, 98 (1983), 101–14; W. Goffart, 'Bede and the Ghost of Wilfrid', in *Narrators of Barbarian History (A.D. 550–800): Jordanes, Gregory of Tours, Bede, and Paul the Deacon* (Princeton, NJ, 1988), 235–328.

[98] Stephanus, *Vita Wilfridi*, c. 33; blaming Wilfrid for his role in the elevation of that 'tyrant' king, Dagobert's assassins threatened the lives of the bishop and his retinue, wanting to take Wilfrid before Ebroin for judgement. Wilfrid's defence of his actions, according to his biographer, is an interesting early reflection on the inherent rights of royal exiles to assistance when abroad: *quid aliud habuisti facere, si exul de genere nostro ex semine regio ad sanctitatem tuam perveniret quam quod ego in Domino feci?* See Picard, 'Church and Politics in the Seventh Century', 43 n. 36, where the author dismisses Wilfrid's role in the affair but simultaneously notes a deeper influence of the Continent on insular culture which has causes and implications beyond that of Dagobert's sojourn in Ireland. Dagobert II was eventually canonized, and his cult burgeoned at his burial site at Stenay during the eleventh century: see Krüger, *Königsgrabkirchen der Franken*, 190–93; also the *Vita Dagoberti III regis Francorum*; MGH SS rer. Merov. II, 509–24.

[99] Bede, *HE* IV.9 and V.9, and Boniface's letter to the bishops of the English; Tangl, *Die Briefes des heiligen Bonifatius und Lullus*, no. 46; *The Letters of Saint Boniface*, trans., E. Emerton, (New York, 1940) no. 36. Compare J. M. Wallace-Hadrill, 'A Background to St Boniface's Mission', in P. Clemoes and K. Hughes (eds), *England before the Conquest* (1971), 35–48 for a discussion of parallel Frankish interest in the conversion of their ancestral homelands to the east of the Rhine, and R. McKitterick, 'England and the Continent', in R. McKitterick (ed.), *NCMH* 2, (1995), 64–84 at 66. On the mission more generally see, Stiegemann and Wemhoff, *799 Kunst und Kultur*, Vol. 2, 434–91.

doing, they inevitably came into contact with the secular rulers of the Austrasian kingdom who, while offering the missionaries protection, were simultaneously able to employ them as part of their ecclesiastical armoury in pursuit of their own territorial and political ambitions. However, after the assassination of Dagobert II in 679, Austrasia never again had an independent Merovingian king. Thereafter, it was the leaders of the Carolingian family who, as mayors of the palace, were *de facto* rulers of the kingdom and who used the power of that office gradually to extend and deepen their family's hold over greater swathes of eastern Francia.[100] The monasteries and bishoprics which the Anglo-Saxon missionaries founded in the areas which bordered their homelands were an important part of this gradual acquisition of power by the Carolingians. Thus, well before they had acquired royal status in Francia, Carolingian magnates were in close contact with Anglo-Saxons working in the eastern marchlands of Francia. These missionaries were active assistants of Pippin II and his son Charles Martel in their campaigns to extend both Christianity and the influence of the Franks further to the north and east, in a process which simultaneously extended the powerbase of the nascent Carolingian dynasty.[101]

The first region to be targeted in this manner was Frisia, largely because its continued paganism and stubborn independence under Kings Adalgisl and Radbod represented a constant challenge to, and defiance of, Frankish hegemonic authority. Frankish interest was doubtless also stimulated by the mercantile wealth and coastal resources of Frisia which controlled the mouth of the Rhine.[102] For all these reasons Frisia had been an early target of Frankish evangelism. Dagobert I had made early attempts to take Frankish ecclesiastical authority there when he gave the bishop of Cologne permission to use the old Roman fort at Utrecht as a base for a mission to evangelize the Frisians.[103] Merovingian efforts continued in the region, but it took the arrival of the Francophile bishop Wilfrid to bring new impetus to the process. He initiated Anglo-Saxon activity in the region in the late 670s almost by accident. En route to Rome in 678, he preferred to risk travel through potentially hostile pagan territory rather than to run the gauntlet past Ebroin's henchmen in Francia who were eager to avenge the part which Wilfrid had played in the

---

[100] On the importance of marriage alliances for land acquisition, see R. A. Gerberding, *The Rise of the Carolingians and the Liber Historiae Francorum* (Oxford, 1987), 119–30 and references therein. On the gradual (but not inexorable) accumulation of landed power see Wood, *The Merovingian Kingdoms*, 264–66.

[101] On the relationship between the Carolingian family and the English missionaries, see P. Fouracre, *The Age of Charles Martel* (Harlow, 2000), 126–37.

[102] S. Lebecq, *Marchands et navigateurs frisons du haut Moyen*, 2 vols (Lille, 1983); *idem*, 'Routes of Change: Production and Distribution in the West (5th–8th Centuries)', in Webster and Brown (eds), *The Transformation of the Roman World*, 67–78; D. Ellmers, 'The Frisian Monopoly of Coastal Transport in the 6th–8th Centuries AD', in S. McGrail (ed.), *Maritime Celts, Frisians and Saxons*, CBA Research Report 71 (London, 1990), 91–92.

[103] *Die Briefe des heiligen Bonifatius und Lullus*, ed. M. Tangl MGH Epp. Sel. (Berlin, 1916), no. 109; *The Letters of Saint Boniface*, trans. E. Emerton (New York, 1940), no. 89.

reinstatement of Dagobert II a couple of years earlier. Ebroin had tried to bribe Adalgisl with a bushel of gold solidi in exchange for the bishop's head, but the Frisian king had nobly refused and Wilfrid had been permitted to travel on to Rome, having first impressed a group of Frisian fishermen with the power of Christ to be a fisher of men.[104]

Wilfrid's early evangelism in Frisia provided a precedent which was swiftly followed by other Anglo-Saxons such as Suidbert, Ecgberht, and Willibrord.[105] Willibrord was the most important of Ecgberht's students from the Irish monastery of Rath Melsigi, yet having been brought up at Ripon he was a churchman very much in the mould of Wilfrid, the founder of that monastery.[106] Late in 690 he left Ireland with 11 companions on a mission to tackle the stubborn heathenism of the Frisians who were at that time under the rule of King Radbod.[107] The mission was well timed, coming in the aftermath of Pippin II's important victory over his Neustrian enemies at Tertry in 687, and coincided with a renewed campaign by Pippin to impose Frankish dominance over Frisia by military might.[108] Radbod, the pagan ruler of the Frisians, comes across in the sources as a complex but not entirely unsympathetic figure. His relations with his Frankish neighbours were pragmatic, fluctuating between open hostility and alliance, even to the extent of allowing his daughter, Theudesinda, to marry Pippin's son Grimoald in 711.[109] Radbod was well able to play off one Frankish faction against another, as he subsequently proved when he allied against Charles Martel with the Neustrian king Chilperic II and his mayor Raganfred. His attitude to Christianity was equally ambivalent. Although he never actually converted, one later source goes so far as to portray him with one foot in the baptismal font.[110] On discovering that, after baptism, he would be permitted to enter heaven rather

---

[104] Stephanus, *Vita Wilfridi*, c. 26.

[105] Bede, *HE*, V.9–11; Levison, *England and the Continent*, 45–69; Wood, *The Merovingian Kingdoms*, 317–21 D. Parsons, 'England and the Low Countries at the time of St Willibord', in E. de Bièvre (eds), *Utrecht, Britain and the Continent: Archaeology, Art and Architecture*, British Archaeological Association Conference Transactions 18 (London, 1996), 30–48.

[106] On Willibrord's career see W. Levison, 'St Willibrord and his Place in History', *The Durham University Journal*, 32 (1940), 23–41. On the Irish aspects of the manuscripts associated with Willibrord's monastery at Echternach see D. Ó Cróinín, 'Rath Melsigi, Wilibrord and the Earliest Echternach Manuscripts', *Peritia*, 3 (1984), 17–42 and the comments by McKitterick, 'The Diffusion of Insular Culture', 422–27.

[107] The date comes from a marginal note on fol. 39 verso in Willibrord's own calendar; see H. A. Wilson (ed.), *The Calendar of St Willibrord* (London, 1918).

[108] The battle is presented as a dramatic and pivotal episode in the pro-Carolingian *Annales Mettenses Priores*, 687; see Fouracre and Gerberding, *Late Merovingian France*, 339–40, 356–59, Wood, *The Merovingian Kingdoms*, 261.

[109] *Liber Historiae Francorum*, c. 50; *Annales Mettenses Priores*, 711. R. A. Gerberding, '716: A crucial year for Charles Martel', in J. Jarnut, U. Nonn and M. Richter (eds), *Karl Martell in seiner Zeit*, Beihefte der Francia, 37 (Sigmaringen, 1994), 205–16 at 209–10.

[110] *Vita Vulframni*, c. 9, MGH *SS rer. Merov.* V; I. N. Wood, 'St. Wandrille and its hagiography' in I. N. Wood and G. A. Loud (eds), *Church and Chronicle in the Middle Ages: Essays Presented to John Taylor* (Hambleton, 1991), 1–14 at 13–14.

than spending eternity in hell with his pagan ancestors, he chose family and damnation over Christ and eternal salvation. The story obviously has an anecdotal air but it gives colour to the task of the missionaries as well as illustrating the importance of ancestors to pagan belief systems.

The Anglo-Saxon mission led by Willibrord at the turn of the eighth century added another dimension to these complex fluctuations in Frisian relations with their ever-more powerful Frankish neighbours. Willibrord's authority to act as a missionary in Frisia was sanctioned, blessed and granted by papal mandate. He went to Rome twice, first in 690 to be consecrated as bishop and later in 696 when he was made an archbishop, 'as Pippin had requested'.[111] But his ability to function in such a role – and to succeed in the longer term – depended (as Bede implied) on the logistical local support which he gained from Pippin II and his clan, especially Pippin's wife, Plectrude. Bede describes something of the use which Pippin II made of Willibrord and his followers. He refers to the generous reception offered by the *dux Francorum* to the 12 missionaries when they had arrived *altra mare in francea*.[112] Pippin, Bede says, sent Willibrord *ad citeriorem Fresiam,* having just expelled Radbod from that region. While there, Pippin gave the missionaries the benefit of his *imperiali auctoritate*, guarding them from molestation and supporting them with gifts to bestow on any person who would convert to the Christian faith. The importance of Pippin's patronage – or, rather, the lack of such support – can be seen in the premature attempts to take the mission to regions which were, at this time, far beyond the reach of Frankish influence. In the same chapter of the *Ecclesiastical History*, Bede describes the lynching, mutilation and subsequent murder of two Anglo-Saxon missionaries, both named Hewald, by a Saxon mob. Pippin, now the *gloriosissimus dux Francorum*, though unable to protect the missionaries in life, honoured the two martyrs in death by having their bodies buried *cum multa gloria* in the church of the city of Cologne which was one of the foremost centres of Pippinid power.[113] Likewise, Suidbert's attempts to convert the *Broctuarii* in southern Westphalia, although initially successful, failed when the Saxons invaded the lands of that tribe. Willibrord's own mission to Denmark, as described by his biographer, was bound to fail not least because the lines of support from western Frisia, and Francia beyond, were stretched too thinly to sustain such an enterprise.[114] Beyond the marchlands of the Frankish kingdom, Christianity and those who brought it were mistrusted as agents of Frankish

---

[111] Bede, *HE*, V.11; Alcuin, *Vita Willibrordi*, c. 6–7. K.-F. Werner, 'Le rôle d'aristocratie dans la christianisation du nord-est de la Gaule', *Revue de l'histoire de l'église de France*, 62 (1976), 45–74; Fouracre, *Charles Martel*, 42–47.

[112] Bede, *HE* V.10.

[113] *Ibid*. Their death is commemorated on 4 October on fo. 39 recto of Willibrord's Calendar, although the Fulda martyrology and the OE martyrology follow Bede's date of 3 October

[114] Alcuin, *Vita Willibrordi*, c. 9. Alcuin's biography of his kinsman Willibrord was written between 785 and 797 and may have been cast, in part, as a contemporary commentary on Charlemagne's anti-pagan campaigns; see Wood, *The Merovingian Kingdoms*, 319–20.

dominion; the spread of Frankish authority and Christianization were inseparable.

Pippin's patronage of the Anglo-Saxon missionaries, dead and alive, was continued over time and was supported by generous grants of land. He was instrumental in the consecration of Willibrord as Archbishop of the Frisians by Pope Sergius in Rome in 696 and gave the new archbishop a site for his metropolitan see at Traiectum (Utrecht) *in castello suo inlustri*.[115] This was a momentous move not just for the status of the mission in western Frisia but also because it effectively sealed and formalized Frankish control there – as well as giving the papacy an unprecedented role in the election of bishops within the Frankish Church. Pippin's wife Plectrude also provided a refuge for the dispossessed Bishop Suidbert at Kaiserswerth after the collapse of his mission to the *Broctuarii*, just as her mother had earlier given Willibrord the land for the monastery of Echternach.[116] This strong bond between Willibrord, the Anglo-Saxon mission, and the Carolingian family was maintained into the following generations. His support proved critical in Charles Martel's bid for power in the crisis years after the death of Pippin II in 714 as support within the Carolingian dynasty ebbed away from Charles's cause to the faction led by his stepmother Plectrude. These divisions and the dynastic instability among the Austrasian nobility prompted a counteralliance between the Neustrians and Frisians, thereby exacerbating the crisis within Francia.[117] A consequence of this realignment of Frankish factions after Pippin's death was to jeopardize the lifetime achievements of Willibrord in Frisia. In this light, Willibrord's decision to abandon the faction of Plectrude (whose family owned the territory around his beloved monastery at Echternach) in favour of her stepson Charles Martel (whose powerbase was closer to Willibrord's Frisian dependencies) is understandable. It was a gamble which proved to be a turning point for the success of Charles, of the Anglo-Saxon mission, and for the future relationships between the two.

Willibrord's new alliance was publicly demonstrated when he baptized Martel's son, the future Pippin III, probably shortly after Charles's first victory against the Neustrian army at Amblève in late spring of 716.[118] Martel's decisive victory occurred about a year later at Vinchy on 21 March 717. But in the months between Martel's victories at Amblève and Vinchy, two more highly influential Anglo-Saxon clergymen arrived in Francia, one at the end of his career and the other whose greatness still lay ahead. The first of these was Ceolfrid, Bede's own abbot from Wearmouth and Jarrow. Ceolfrid left his North-

---

[115] Bede, *HE* V.11; J. M. Wallace-Hadrill, *The Frankish Church* (Oxford, 1983), 145, 154.

[116] For Irmina's gift to Willibrord see Gerberding, *The Rise of the Carolingians*, 102. For Plectrude's gift to Suidbert see, Bede, *HE* V.11.

[117] Gerberding, '716: A Crucial Year', 205–7.

[118] For a discussion of the dating of Pippin's baptism see ibid., 210–11 and Alcuin, *Vita Willibrordi*, c. 23.

umbrian monastery for the last time on Thursday 4 June 716.[119] Accompanied by about 80 companions (as well as the *Codex Amiatinus*), he arrived in Frankish territory some two months later on 12 August. Ceolfrid and his party avoided the troubled areas to the east and travelled instead through Neustrian lands. There his anonymous biographer says that he was warmly received and honoured by King Chilperic II (the Neustrian king and rival to Charles Martel) who perhaps saw in the presence of this Northumbrian party at his court a useful and high-profile antidote to the influence of their compatriot Willibrord with Charles. With suitable royal largesse, the king gave Ceolfrid many gifts and letters of commendation and protection for the remainder of his journey through Frankish and Lombard territory.[120] Chilperic's actions towards Ceolfrid were remembered by the Northumbrians, who recorded the king's generosity for posterity not just in the anonymous *Vita* but also, it seems, in the Northumbrian *Liber Vitae,* where his name, *Helpric*, is recorded in the list of *reges* and *duces* for whom prayers were to be said at the monastery to which the book belonged.[121]

The other Englishman to arrive on continental shores was Boniface, perhaps the most famous of the eighth-century Anglo-Saxon missionaries to *Germania* and one of the driving forces behind the reform of the Frankish and Anglo-Saxon churches in the first half of that century.[122] According to his biographer, Boniface sailed on a Frisian merchant ship from London to the Frisian emporium of Dorestad early in 716 only to find that, 'a fierce quarrel had broken out' between Charles and Radbod which 'caused a great disturbance among the population of both sides' and 'the dispersion of priests', as well as 'the restoration of pagan shrines and (what is worse) the worship of idols'.[123] His biographer notes that – hardly surprisingly – the conditions were not right for missionary work. Nevertheless, Boniface obtained an audience with King Radbod who had regained the fortress at Utrecht, and spent the summer and autumn of that year touring the country, to discover (so the author of the *Life* states), 'what possibility there might be of preaching the Gospel there in the

---

[119] The dates of Ceolfrid's final voyage are given by his anonymous biographer in the *Vita Ceolfridi*, c. 31–32.

[120] Anon. *Vita Ceolfridi*, c. 32.

[121] Figure 4.1, on the manuscript and its provenance see further, below Chapter 4, 102–4. The orthography of Chilperic's name in the Northumbrian *Liber Vitae* is the same as given by the anonymous author of the *Vita Ceolfridi*; c. 32; C. Plummer (ed.), *Venerabilis Bedae Opera Historica*, 2 vols (Oxford, 1896), Vol. 1, 400; Wood, *The Merovingian Kingdoms*, 268.

[122] Levison, *England and the Continent*, 70–93; T. Schieffer, *Winfrid-Bonifatius und die christliche Grundlegung Europas* (Freiburg, 1954); C. Raabe, H. Büttner and S. Hilpisch (eds), *Sankt-Bonifatius. Gedenkgabe zum zwölfhundertsten Todestag* (Fulda, 1954); T. Reuter (ed.), *The Greatest Englishman: Essays on St. Boniface and the Church at Crediton* (Exeter, 1980); Wallace-Hadrill, *The Frankish Church*, 150–61; R. McKitterick, 'Anglo-Saxon Missionaries in Germany: Personal Connections and Local Influences', Vaughan Papers 36 (Leicester, 1990) reprinted as Chapter I in R. McKitterick, *The Frankish Kings and Culture in the Early Middle Ages* (Aldershot, 1995).

[123] Willibald, *Vita Bonifatii*, ed. W. Levison, MGH SS rer. Germ. LVII (Hanover and Leipzig, 1905), c. 4; *The Anglo-Saxon Missionaries in Germany*, trans. C. H. Talbot (London, 1954), 25–64.

future'. As a result, Boniface aborted his mission and returned to his own monastery in Wessex for, 'two winters and a summer' to await a better time to begin his mission. On his return in 718, he mimicked Willibrord's actions 20 years earlier and set off almost immediately to Rome to obtain the papal mandate that was to make him *legatus Germanicus catholicae et apostolicae Romanae ecclesiae*.[124]

One of the reasons for Boniface's enduring fame is the quantity and quality of historical data about him, surviving from his lifetime or shortly afterwards. Some of it is by his own hand; the surviving corpus of letters – though partial – is one of the largest from the period. His *Life*, written by the priest Willibald, was composed before 767, within 13 years of his death. The veracity and internal balance of the *Life* has been called into question, and much recent scholarship has been devoted to resurrecting and emphasizing the depth of the Merovingian contribution to Boniface's missionary work to the east of the Rhine, as well as his reforms within the Frankish Church.[125] Boniface comes across in the sources (and particularly in his own letters) very much as a kind of St Paul of the Anglo-Saxon mission, as a self-styled apostle to the pagans, labouring among the gentiles as St Paul himself had done.[126] Similarly, he was an outspoken conscience of the early medieval church, and his caustic criticism of the public and private morality of secular leaders and of the men chosen to lead the Church of the day, show him to have been a hard task-master and thus an easy man to dislike. His famous letter to King Æthelbald of Mercia written in 747 denounced the morals not just of the powerful Mercian king but also condemned the lifestyles of his predecessor King Ceolred and also King Osred, Ceolred's contemporary in Northumbria.[127] William of Malmesbury (writing at the turn of the twelfth century) preserved a copy of this letter to Æthelbald in his *Gesta Anglorum*. William's copy, which may preserve the original version sent to England rather than that copied into the Fulda collection, includes Charles Martel in this array of damnable monarchs, accused of despoiling Church property and abusing ecclesiastical privilege.[128]

---

[124] 'Legate for Germany of the catholic and apostolic church of Rome'; *Bonifatius und Lullus*, ed. Tangl, no. 78 to Cuthbert, the archbishop of Canterbury (747) and no. 91 to Archbishop Ecgberht of York (747–754); *The Letters of Saint Boniface*, trans. Emerton, nos 62 and 75.

[125] Wallace-Hadrill, 'A Background to St. Boniface's Mission', 35–48; *idem, The Frankish Church*, 143–61; R. Fletcher, *The Conversion of Europe: From Paganism to Christianity 371–1368 AD* (London, 1997), 203–4; Fouracre, *Charles Martel*, 127–29 .

[126] E. Ewig, 'Milo et eiusmodi similes', in *Sankt Bonifatius,* 412–40, reprinted in H. Atsma (ed.), *Spätantikes und Fränkisches Gallien*, Beihefte der Francia, 3 (Zurich and Munich, 1976); Wallace-Hadrill, 'A background to St. Boniface's Mission', 45; *Bonifatius und Lullus*, ed. Tangl, at 316–17.

[127] *Bonifatius und Lullus*, ed. Tangl, no. 73; *Letters*, trans. Emerton, no. 49 and *EHD* 1, trans. Whitelock, no. 177. This letter contains nine quotations from writings of St Paul.

[128] Levison, *England and the Continent*, 280–81; Thomson, *William of Malmesbury*, 44; Fouracre, *Charles Martel*, 123–25, 134–36. For the argument that the addition of Martel's name to

But, despite his criticisms of Martel's moral authority, Boniface – like Willibrord before him – needed the practical support of the ruling Carolingian aristocracy to fulfil his papal vocation. Writing to Bishop Daniel of Winchester, Boniface noted his dependence on Pippin: 'without the patronage of the Frankish prince I am unable to govern the members of the Church, nor defend the priests, clerics, monks or nuns of God, nor can I prohibit pagan rites and sacriligious idolators in Germany without his orders and the fear inspired by him'.[129] His mission first to Hesse, and then beyond to Thuringia and Bavaria extended the remit of the Anglo-Saxon mission to those Germanic tribes which held a similar place in the cultural memory of the Franks as the Old Saxons did for the English.[130] In these regions Boniface was able to draw on the achievements of earlier insular missionary pioneers such as St Pirmin and St Corbinian, and his letters show him to be more concerned with the restoration and establishment of churches, chapels and monasteries than with primary evangelization.[131] Indeed, it was Boniface's skills as a church reformer for which the Frankish Church was perhaps most indebted. It was largely through his lobbying that the important series of church councils and reforming synods were held under Charles's sons Carloman and Pippin in the 740s – synods which were also to influence reforms in the English Church, especially the provisions of the Council of Clofesho in 747.[132] And, despite the evident irritation which Boniface caused to Charles and subsequently to his two sons, the Carolingians were not slow to appreciate the value of this energetic and vocal Englishman. After his brutal death at the hands of pagan Frisians in 754 there was something of an unholy struggle to take control of the body of the martyr and of the site of his martyrdom (which Willibald reports but does little to clarify).[133] Pippin wanted

---

the rogues' gallery was made by Boniface himself, see T. Reuter, '"Kirchenreform" und "kirchenpolitik" im zeitalter Karl Martells: begriffe und wirklichkeit', in J. Jarnut et al. (eds), *Karls Martell in seiner Zeit* (Sigmaringen, 1994), 51–58. Cf. Wallace-Hadrill, 'A background to St. Boniface's Mission', 46, where he notes that the first detailed charges against Martel were levied by Hincmar of Rheims. See also Wood, *The Merovingian Kingdoms*, 279–80, for the discussion on the attribution of the interpolation concerning Martel to Ecgberht, Archbishop of York who also received a letter from Boniface at this time (*Bonifatius und Lullus*, ed. Tangl, no. 75; *Letters*, trans. Emerton, no. 59). Wood downplays the extent of Charles Martel's anti-Church policies, arguing that they were sensible and pragmatic actions against his secular enemies, depriving them of powerbases and putting monasteries and bishoprics into the hands of his own supporters.

129 Boniface, *Epistola ad Daniel*, 742–44; *Bonifatius und Lullus*, ed. Tangl, no. 63; Haddan and Stubbs (eds), *Councils* III, 343–46; *Letters*, trans. Emerton, no. 51 and *EHD* 1, trans. Whitelock, no. 175; McKitterick, 'Anglo-Saxon Missionaries in Germany', 7.

130 Wallace-Hadrill, 'A background to St. Boniface's Mission', 35.

131 Ibid., 42; McKitterick, 'Anglo-Saxon Missionaries in Germany', 7.

132 C. Cubitt, *Anglo-Saxon Church Councils, c. 650–850* (London, 1995), 99–124; Wallace-Hadrill, *The Frankish Church*.

133 Willibald, *Vita Bonifatii*, c. 8, with reference to the site of the martyrdom at Dokkum. Eigil in his *Life* of Abbot Sturm of Fulda emphasized Boniface's wishes to be buried at Fulda; Eigil, *Vita Sturmi*, c. 5. On the site at Dokkum and the archaeological evidence for the presence of ecclesiastical buildings on the site dating from c. 900, see H. Halbertsma, 'Dokkum', *Bulletin van de*

the body to remain in Utrecht; it took a miracle, according to Willibald, for him to allow it to be removed and taken up the Rhine to Mainz. The bishop of that city, the Anglo-Saxon, Lul, wanted to keep the body of his venerable compatriot and predecessor in the church there but Boniface was eventually buried, in accordance with his wishes, at Fulda. The last chapter of his *Vita* shows Pippin's men taking charge of the site of Boniface's martyrdom (in compensation, per-haps, for losing direct control of the martyr's body) and describes the decision taken, 'on the advice of the ecclesiastical authorities and the majority of the Frisian people', to raise a large mound of earth over the spot where he and his companions had been killed and to build a cult church dedicated to Boniface and his apostolic mentor, St Paul.[134]

This period of Christianization and restructuring of the Frankish Church is notable in general for the proliferation and establishment of a structured ecclesi-astical hierarchy based around the principle of a metropolitan province supported by dependent bishoprics. This was just the type of structure that Gregory the Great had planned for the new Church in Anglo-Saxon England and which he had sent Augustine to implement at the turn of the seventh century. It is no coincidence that it was Anglo-Saxons – Willibrord and Boniface in particular – who headed attempts to introduce such a structure to the Church in Francia and its new dominions in *Germania* in the early decades of the eighth century.[135] Nor, perhaps, is it a coincidence that it was this same period that witnessed a revival in Northumbria of the campaign to re-establish an archbishopric in York with an extended circle of bishops more widely distributed throughout the kingdom than had previously existed. It is Bede's well known letter to Ecgberht, who was then only bishop of York, written in November 734 which best encap-sulates this idea.[136] Bede's motives in writing to Ecgberht were undoubtedly many, and there is no direct evidence that he knew of the campaigns in Francia to establish such networks of bishoprics. Indeed, in contrast to his extensive knowledge of Willibrord's activities, nowhere, even in the *Ecclesiastical History*, does he mention Boniface or his continental achievements.[137] Bede's primary concerns were the establishment of effective pastoral organization and a desire to bring to fruition the plan of Gregory the Great which had lain unfulfilled for a

---

Koninklijke Nederlandse Ouheidkundige Bond, 69 (1970), 33–52; W. A. van Es, H. Sarfatij and P. J. Woltering (eds), *Archeologie in Nederland. Die rijkdom van het bodemarchief* (Amsterdam, 1988), 184–86.

134 Willibald, *Vita Bonifatii*, c. 8; Fulda, and the relics of Boniface, were belatedly brought under Pippin's control a few years later after a revolt against the abbot; see R. McKitterick, *The Frankish Kingdoms under the Carolingians* (London, 1983), 57.

135 Wallace-Hadrill, *The Frankish Church*, 157, Levison, *England and the Continent*, 86–89. For the letter of Pope Zacharias concerning the *pallia* for new Frankish metropolitans, see *Bonifatius und Lullus*, ed. Tangl, no. 57; *Letters*, trans. Emerton, no. 45.

136 *Venerabilis Baedae Opera Historica*, ed. C. Plummer (Oxford, 1896), 405–23.

137 Ibid., 346. In her Jarrow lecture, Whitelock suggests that the ignorance was mutual and that Boniface learned about the *Ecclesiastical History* only after Bede's death; Whitelock, *After Bede*, 6.

century. One hundred years had passed between the granting of the pallium to Paulinus and the date of Bede's letter to renew that office in York, and Bede may have been prompted to action by that centenary anniversary.

Was the renewal of the York pallium and equivalent developments in Francia a simple coincidence? The missions of Willibrord and Boniface can be seen as the ecclesiastical sword in an essentially political and military campaign by proto-royal Carolingian princes; so too the elevation of the brother of the Northumbrian king to archiepiscopal status had profound political ramifications in that kingdom. Indeed, the collaboration between the brothers Ecgberht and Eadberht posed a concentration of secular and ecclesiastical power in the hands of one family such as had not previously been seen in any Anglo-Saxon kingdom. But the *amicitia* which Symeon tells us had existed between the courts of Eadberht and Pippin III suggests that ideas of metropolitan grandeur and its temporal value could also have passed between the two regions.[138] In the same chapter of his *Libellus* Symeon, also uniquely, claims that Ecgberht had spent time earlier in his life in Rome with another brother, named Ecgred. If this information is correct, Ecgberht may have been more closely aware of Frankish episcopal restructuring and reform than we might otherwise have supposed.[139] It is thus arguable that the re-establishment of York to metropolitan status should be seen within the broader context of developments in the Frankish Church. That these Frankish developments were initiated by the Northumbrian Willibrord suggests that the Northumbrian events should by no means be seen as an evolution of the Frankish ones, but rather as a mutual development in which the general goal of a metropolitan network was established in both places through the impetus of the political motives of local magnates.

Patronage and politics: Carolingian continuity

The contacts between England and Francia prior to 750 were both longstanding and diverse. The English owed much to Franks in the period of their conversion, and the Franks (particularly the Carolingian family) had a reciprocal debt to several Anglo-Saxon missionaries from the 670s onwards. The nature of the sources emphasizes the role of a few prominent players in these processes but a theme that emerges consistently in the later seventh and early eighth century is one of cooperation between Anglo-Saxon churchmen and the Pippinid nobility. Perhaps the most explicit example of this bond is the part played by some

---

[138] Letters exist dating to 746–54 from Boniface to Ecgberht of York and to Hwaetberht of Wearmouth Jarrow verifying the existence of such channels of communication in the period after York had acquired metropolitan status; *Bonifatius und Lullus*, ed. Tangl, nos 75–76, 91, 156–9, 206–8; *Letters*, trans. Emerton, no. 59–60, 75.

[139] Symeon, *Libellus*; Symeon of Durham, ed. and trans. Rollason, II.3.

Anglo-Saxons established within the Frankish ecclesiastical hierarchy in the process that elevated the Carolingian family to royal rank between 749 and 751. The Anglo-Saxon bishop, Burchard of Würzburg, accompanied Fulrad, the Abbot of St Denis, to Rome to ask Pope Zacharias who had the right to be king in Francia – he who held power or he who wore the crown? The answer to this question legitimized the Carolingian *coup d'état* and, although the sources are problematic on this point, it may have been Boniface who performed the *coup de grace* over the Merovingian dynasty by anointing Pippin and his queen in the ceremony at Soission in 751, which secured Pippin as king of the Franks.[140]

With hindsight, it is easy to overemphasize the symbiotic relationships that were built up between men such as Willibrord and Pippin II. Alcuin himself, when writing the *Life* of his relative, Willibrord, between 785 and 797 anachronistically accentuated the cooperation between Pippin II and the papacy in the plan to make Willibrord a bishop, and even referred to Pippin II and Charles Martel as kings when plainly he knew that they had never acquired that rank.[141] Indeed, the spin which he put on his narrative account of Willibrord's mission may have had as much to do with his disapproval of Charlemagne's harsh anti-pagan polices against the Saxons and Avars as with earlier attitudes towards the Frisians.[142] But the links created between Anglo-Saxon and Frankish courts by the opening of the missionfield, and the role of the English churchmen and churchwomen within it, were contemporary and real. English kings continued to sponsor missionary activity abroad and, in doing so, kept open direct links to the Carolingians. It is this situation which provides a context for the type of contacts which existed between Eadberht and Pippin III after the Carolingians had become a royal dynasty.

This sort of relationship can be traced further. An otherwise unknown English abbot by the name of Eanwulf wrote two letters on consecutive days, 24 and 25 May 773, one to Lul, Boniface's successor in Mainz, and another to Charlemagne himself.[143] The letter to Lul responds to one received and requests reciprocal confraternal prayers. It is preserved in the same manuscript

---

[140] See *Annales regni Francorum* 750 with reference to Boniface's participation in the event although he is not named in the more closely contemporary *Continuation to the Chronicle of Fredegar*, ch. 33; see J. M. Wallace-Hadrill (ed. and trans.), *The Fourth Book of the Chronicle of Fredegar and its Continuations* (London, 1960), 102. Nor is Boniface mentioned in the controversial *Clausula de unctione Pippini* accepted by some as a contemporary account; MGH *SS rer. Merov.* I, 465–66. McKitterick argues that Chrodegang of Metz, rather than Boniface, was likely to have been the churchman involved in the anointing of Pippin; see McKitterick, *The Frankish Kingdoms*, 56 and *idem*, 'The illusion of royal power in the Carolingian Annals', *EHR*, 115 (2000), 1–20 at 9, 15–16.

[141] Wood, *The Merovingian Kingdoms*, 318.

[142] Ibid., 319–20

[143] Tangl, *Bonifatius und Lullus*, nos 119–20; MGH Epp. III, no. 119 and 120. The letter of Eanwulf to Charlemagne is translated by Whitelock, *EHD* 1, no. 186. It may be significant that an abbot Eanwulf is named on fo. 20v of the Northumbrian *Liber Vitae*, on which see, further, Chapter 4 below, 102–4; J. Gerchow, *Die Gedenküberlieferung ser Angelsachsen* (Berlin and New York, 1988), 306.

as Eanwulf's letter to Charlemagne who is addressed by the abbot as *Domino gloriosissimo atque praecellentissimo regi Francorum*.[144] This letter quotes extensively from one (cited by Bede) which Pope Gregory the Great had written to King Æthelberht of Kent in the earliest years of the mission of Augustine to England, exhorting him to greater efforts to spread the faith of Christ and to destroy idols and temples thereby rendering 'the fame of your glory even more glorious to posterity'.[145] But at the point in the original version where Gregory provided Æthelberht with an analogy of the Emperor Constantine's campaign against paganism, Eanwulf abandoned his source and petitioned Charlemagne directly for patronage and protection with the promise of perpetual prayers for him and his people:

> ... beseeching your majesty to deign to be mindful of us and to receive us as friends, that we, who urgently commend you to the Lord in frequent prayers, may have you as our protector and patron.[146]

The plea for a Frankish *patronus* recalls Charles Martel's letter of protection granted to Boniface in 723 as well as what we know of Pippin II's patronage of Willibrord and his companions.[147] The context for Eanwulf's letter to Charlemagne was, most likely, the ongoing campaign being waged by Charlemagne against the pagans in Saxony, accounts of which were incorporated into contemporary Northumbrian annals. In 772 Charlemagne's army had destroyed the sacred pagan grove known as the Irminsul but in doing so had suffered considerable losses from Frankish ranks (as a Northumbrian annalist had noted).[148] That Eanwulf chose the words of the greatest missionary pope to exhort Charlemagne not to lose heart but to redouble his efforts was undoubtedly deliberate. The letter indicates continued interest by sections of the Anglo-Saxon Church in the Frankish campaigns among the pagan tribes of *Germania* as well as close and personal links with the Carolingian king.

---

[144] Vienna, Nationalbibliothek MS Lat. 751, Eanwulf's letter to Charlemagne is copied on fos 53v–54r and that to Lul is on fo. 59 r–v; F. Unterkircher (ed.), *Sancti Bonifatii Epistolae*, Codices Selecti phototypice impressi, 24 (Graz, 1971). The Vienna codex is the most important of the surviving manuscripts of Boniface's letters. It is mid-ninth century in date and is copied in a Carolingian minuscule which retains some insular features and is close to Boniface's originals; see Levison, *England and the Continent*, 280–81 and P. Chaplais, 'The Letter from Bishop Waldhere of London to Archbishop Brihtwold of Canterbury: The Earliest Original "Letter Close"', in M. B. Parkes and A. G. Watson (eds), *Medieval Scribes* (London, 1978), 3–24 at 9–10, reprinted in his *Essays in Medieval Diplomacy and Administration* (London, 1981), 3–13.

[145] Bede, *HE* I.32. This implies that Abbot Eanwulf had access either to a copy of the *Historia Ecclesiastica* or to the copies of Gregory's letters which Nothhelm had made in the papal *scrinium* at Rome, brought back to London and then supplied to Bede.

[146] *Ipsi te protectorem habere valeamus et patronum*; Eanwulf, *Epistola ad Carolum*; MGH *Epp.* III, no. 120; *EHD* 1, trans. Whitelock, no. 186.

[147] *Bonifatius und Lullus*, ed. Tangl, no. 22, 36–38; *Letters*, trans. Emerton, no. 14; Bede, *HE* V.10. Gerberding, '716: a crucial year', 208; Wallace-Hadrill, 'A background to Saint Boniface's Mission', 45.

[148] *Historia regum* (*York Annals*), 772.

This interest is also reflected in another letter copied between the two from Eanwulf in the same Vienna manuscript that contains the only extant copies of all three. This third letter, also addressed to Lul, should be dated sometime between late 771 and Easter 774, and almost certainly dates to the earlier months of 773.[149] This letter is written in the name of King Alhred of Northumbria (765–74) and his wife Osgifu.[150] They thanked Lul for letters and gifts, and for his concerns about the social unrest in Northumbria, they sent him gifts (12 cloaks and a gold ring) and begged him to include their names, 'and those of friends and relations' in the confraternity book of his church, just as they had done with the list of names that Lul had earlier sent to them.[151] In an echo of the bond of friendship which Symeon later tells us had existed between Charlemagne's father, Pippin III, and Alhred's predecessor, Eadberht, Alhred also asked Lul to help and care for his legates who he was sending on to Charlemagne, in order that *pax et amicitia* might be 'firmly strengthened' between the two kings. Alhred is known to have been active in support of the Northumbrian mission to the Continent, sponsoring the activities of Willehad, who subsequently became the first bishop of Bremen,[152] and it was during his reign that Aluberht came to York to be consecrated bishop of the Old Saxons by Archbishop Ælberht, and when the Frisian convert Liudger came to Northumbria to be schooled by Alcuin.[153] Indeed, Alhred's letter to Lul may well be associated with Liudger's return to the Continent in the early months of 773; the *Vita Liudgeri* says that he was accompanied by a deacon from York named Pyttel who was sent as an escort by Alcuin with instructions to continue Rome.[154]

---

149 Vienna, Nationalbibliothek MS Lat. 751, fo. 57v–58r. The chronological parameters of the letter are established by the date of Charlemagne's accession to all Francia after his brother's death in December 771 and Alhred's deposition in 774. On the dating of this letter see D. A. Bullough, '*Albuinus deliciosus Karoli regis*. Alcuin of York and the Shaping of the Early Carolingian Court', in L. Fenske, W. Rösener and T. Zotz (eds), *Institutionen, Kultur und Gesellschaft im Mittelalter* (Sigmaringen, 1984), 73–92, at 82–83, where he argues that the letter from Alhred was not necessarily sent with those from Abbot Eanwulf.

150 MGH Epp. III, no. 121; *EHD* 1, trans. Whitelock, no. 187.

151 On confraternal commemoration see (for example) S. Keynes, *The Liber Vitae of the New Minster and Hyde Abbey, Winchester*, EEMF 26 (Copenhagen, 1996), 49–58, and R. McKitterick, 'Social Memory, Commemoration and the Book', in S. Ridyard (ed.), *Reading and the Book in the Middle Ages*, Sewanee Medieval Studies 11 (Sewanee, TN, 2001), pp. 5–26. For the continental scholarship on *libri vitae* see, most recently, A. Angendent, D. Geuenich and U. Ludwig (eds), *Der Memorial- und Liturgicodex von San Salvatore / Santa Guilia in Brescia*, MGH Libri Memoriales et necrologia, NS 4 (Hanover, 2000), and see, further, Chapter 8 below, 220.

152 His *Life* was written by his successor at Bremen, Anskar; MGH *SS* II, 378–90.

153 *Historia regum* (*York Annals*), 767; Altfrid, *Vita Liudgeri*, c. 10–12; Rollason, *Sources for York*, 131–32. A close parallel to Liudger's consecration at York occurred in 692–93 when Suidbert was sent to Wilfrid, at that time resident in Mercia, to be consecrated bishop for Frisia and for the tribe of the Broctuarii; Bede, *HE* V.11. Bullough, '*Albuinus deliciosus Karoli regis*', 78.

154 Altfrid, *Vita Liudgeri*, ed. G. H. Pertz, MGH SS11 (Berlin, 1829), c. 12.

Alhred's actions reaffirmed the type of connections made and sustained by the Anglo-Saxon mission to the Continent in earlier decades, the difference being that he now sent his legates to the royal court of the Carolingians. We do not know for certain the purpose of the Northumbrian legates' mission to Charlemagne as mentioned in Alhred's letter to Lul but it is possible that their journey was connected with the collection of the pallium for Archbishop Ælberht which, the annals embedded in the *Historia regum* tell us, arrived in York sometime in 773. The *Royal Frankish Annals* for that year record that the Lombards had closed all the roads to Rome thereby forcing papal envoys to Charlemagne's court to travel there by sea.[155] The message which these emissaries brought to Charlemagne presaged the invasion of the *Regnum Langobardorum* by two Frankish armies in the late summer of 773; the emissaries alleged that the Lombard king, Desiderius, had failed to comply with territorial demands stipulated by the pope, and Charlemagne (as *legitimus tutor et defensor* of the Roman Church) was bound to act. The war between the Lombards and the Franks culminated the following year with the annexation of the Lombard kingdom to Frankish dominion. Any Northumbrian legate intending to travel to Rome in the spring of 773 may, under these circumstances, have been forced to divert to Charlemagne's court in order to obtain up-to-date information about the onward route to take to Rome. The mission of Alhred's legates to Charlemagne may also have had another dimension that was connected to the 'disturbances in our churches and people' to which Alhred had alluded in his letter to Lul.[156]

Alhred's reign came to an abrupt end not long after his letter to Lul was composed. The civil disturbances to which he alluded in his letter swelled sufficiently to force him into exile at Easter 774, 'with the consent of all his household'.[157] We hear no more of Alhred except that he fled initially to Bamburgh and thence to the protection of Cynoth, king of the Picts. His pleas to Lul to secure a strong bond of 'peace and friendship' with the Frankish king had probably gone unheard in the storm brewing over Lombard Italy, but this letter demonstrates the continuing interest of the Northumbrian Church in the Frankish missionfield and also shows that a Northumbrian king, in trouble at home, was at pains to secure both the moral and spiritual support of a foreign bishop as well as the *pax et amicitia* of the Carolingian king. Alhred's letter should certainly be seen in the light of the continued interest of Northumbrians in the Frankish mission, but it also points to potentially more significant political links with the Carolingians.

---

[155] *Annales regni Francorum* 773; the annals name one of the envoys as *Petrus*. The *Liber Pontificalis* makes it clear that Charlemagne sent another mission to Italy to check the veracity of the information coming from the court of Desiderius and the Pope; see Bullough, '*Albuinus deliciosus Karoli regis*', 73–76.

[156] *Historia regum* (*York Annals*), 773. The next pallium for an archbishop of York was collected from Rome by Alcuin who returned via Charlemagne's court in 781, to historic effect.

[157] *Historia regum* (*York Annals*), 774.

Chapter 3

Bishop George and the Legates' Mission to England

Bishop George of Ostia and Amiens

The messengers who carried King Alhred's and Abbot Eanwulf's letters to Bishop Lul and to Charlemagne in the spring of 773, and those who travelled on to Rome to collect the pallium on behalf of Archbishop Ælberht of York, would have witnessed a high degree of diplomatic activity as embassies hurried back and forth between the courts of Charlemagne, Pope Hadrian and Desiderius in attempts to persuade the Lombard king to abandon territory to which the papacy laid claim.[1] When diplomatic persuasion and repeated offers of financial compensation failed to make Desiderius comply with the demands of Pope Hadrian, Charlemagne resorted to force and took a Frankish army across the Alps to subdue the Lombards, in fulfilment of his father's pledges and his own duties as *patricius Romanorum*. The victories of his armies at the sieges of Pavia and Verona, and the capture of Desiderius with 'the whole kingdom of Italy', were hailed as triumphs by contemporary chroniclers – Anglo-Saxons among them. The Northumbrian chronicler whose work is preserved in the *Historia regum* recorded with evident approval the victory at Pavia, 'the most noble city of the Lombards', and the capture there of King Desiderius.[2] The Anglo-Saxon scholar Cathwulf who was writing from within Francia, probably from the Abbey of St Denis, interpreted Charlemagne's victory in Italy as proof that God had marked him out for special glory.[3]

One of the key figures in the diplomatic manoeuvres which had preceded the Frankish conquest of Lombard Italy was George, bishop of the Roman see of Ostia and, after 767, of the Neustrian see at Amiens as well. George is a rather shadowy figure in the extant sources, but his longevity and recorded activity on behalf of his papal and Carolingian patrons over a period of more than 40 years makes him one of the lynchpins of the Franco-papal relationship in the second half of the eighth century.[4] As holder of two important dioceses, one close to Rome

---

[1] D. A. Bullough, '*Albuinus deliciosus Karoli regis*. Alcuin of York and the Shaping of the Early Carolingian Court', in L. Fenske, W. Rösener and T. Zotz (eds), *Institutionen, Kultur und Gesellschaft im Mittelalter* (Sigmaringen, 1984), 73–92.

[2] *Historia regum* (*York Annals*), 774.

[3] Cathwulf, *Epistola ad Carolum*, ed. E. Dümmler, MGH Epp. IV, no. 7 at 501–4; J. E. Story, 'Cathwulf, Kingship, and the Royal Abbey of Saint-Denis', *Speculum*, 74 (1999), 1–20.

[4] George is first recorded as bishop of Ostia in 753 and is last heard of officiating the

and the other to the north of Paris, George was well placed to act as *missus* between the papal court and that of Charlemagne. By the time of the Lombard crisis in the early 770s, he was already an experienced and well-travelled diplomat. Letters in the *Codex Carolinus*, from Popes Stephen II and Paul I, testify to his employment as an official legate between the papal and Frankish courts in the 750s and 760s, often at times when the papacy was under severe pressure from militant Lombard aggression.[5] He and another papal *missus* were sent by Stephen II to Pippin early in 756 with letters begging the Frankish king and his people to intervene decisively against Aistulf, king of the Lombards. The *Liber Pontificalis* and the correspondence from a subsequent pope, Hadrian I, make it clear that George remained an important element in the diplomacy which preceded Charlemagne's advance into Lombard territory. He was sent by Charlemagne with Abbot Wulfhard of Tours and the layman Albuinus from the court at Thionville to Rome in the spring of 773 to examine the conflicting news from Italy; their report supported the pope's claims of Lombard non-compliance with demands to return territory in central Italy to papal control, and so laid the way for the mobilization of the Frankish armies.[6] George continued to be used as an envoy after the Frankish annexation of the *Regnum Langobardorum*, and, in a letter to Charlemagne dated *c.* 782, Hadrian described George as 'your bishop and ours', confirming the plurality of his office and his bipartisan allegiances.[7]

The legates' mission to England: sources and context

A decade or so after the conquest of Lombard Italy, when other men with 30 years' service might have contemplated a peaceful retirement, George was sent by Pope Hadrian on another high-level mission, accompanied by Theophylact of Todi, a fellow Italian bishop, but this time *trans mare in gentem Anglorum*. The same Northumbrian chronicle that had recorded Charlemagne's victories in Italy noted the arrival of George's mission in England.

> At that time legates were sent to Britain from the apostolic see by the Lord Pope Hadrian, and the venerable Bishop George held primacy among them; they renewed the ancient friendship between us and the

consecration of churches belonging to Saint-Riquier in 798; see W. Levison, *England and the Continent in the Eighth Century* (Oxford, 1946), 127–29; *Liber Pontificalis. Texte, introduction et commentaire*, 3 vols (rev. edn), ed L. Duchesne (Paris, 1955), Vol. 1, 457 n. 25, 482 nos 29–30, 515; *The Lives of the Eighth-Century Popes*, trans. R. Davis (Liverpool, 1992), 61, 96, 134; L. Duchesne, *Fastes épiscopaux de l'ancienne Gaul*, 3 vols (Paris, 1907–15), Vol. 3, 128–29.

[5] *Codex Carolinus*, ed. F. W. Gundlach, MGH *Epp.* III, Epistolae karolini Aevi (Berlin, 1892), 476–653 at 494–507, nos 8, 9, 11, 16–18, 21, 37; T. F. X. Noble, *The Republic of St. Peter: The Birth of the Papal State 680–825* (Philadelphia, 1984), 91–92.

[6] Levison, *England and the Continent*, 154 n. 3; *Liber Pontificalis*, 494; Davis, *Lives of the Eighth-Century Popes*, 134–35.; Bullough, '*Albuinus deliciosus Karoli regis*, 75–77.

[7] *Codex Carolinus*, no. 73 at 604 [lines 20–21]; *Liber Pontificalis*, ed. Duchesne, 494; Levison, *England and the Continent*, 128.

catholic faith which St Gregory taught through the blessed Augustine, and they were honourably received by kings and bishops, and by
princes and nobles of this country, and they returned home in peace
bearing great gifts, as was proper.[8]

The legates were received by the leading men of the kingdom with the pomp and
ceremony that was due to the official representatives of the pope. Given his
previous experiences as *missus* both to the papacy and the Carolingian kings, the
choice of Bishop George to lead the legation in 786 marks out the mission as an
event of major significance for the secular and ecclesiastical elites in later eighth-
century England. Not since 679 when Pope Agatho commissioned John, the
archcantor of St Peter's and the abbot of the monastery of St Martin in Rome, had
an emissary been sent from Rome to inquire into the beliefs of the English
Church. John had accompanied Benedict Biscop to Northumbria to teach the
monks the latest and most correct form of the Roman chant necessary for the
proper performance of the liturgy; he had also been instructed by the pope to
ensure that the Church in Britain was free from the 'heretical contagion' of
monothelitism which had been condemned by a papal council in 649. Accompanied by helpers from the Abbey of St Martin's at Tours, John and Archbishop
Theodore (himself sent from Rome in 669) had duly secured the adherence of the
English Church to the precepts of that Council at the synod held at Hatfield.[9]
Bede's comments about these helpers from St Martin's suggest that they had been
sent to assist John with his papal commission to examine the English Church for
signs of heresy rather than in connection with his instruction to teach Roman
chant to the Northumbrian monks. In choosing George and Theophylact as his
emissaries (both of whom had Greek names), Pope Hadrian may well have been
hoping to emulate the successes of two earlier Greek-speaking clerics sent to
England from Rome – namely, Archbishop Theodore and Abbot Hadrian of Canterbury.[10] But as the Northumbrian chronicler noted, and as George himself was
later to record, the perceived precedent for this mission was that of St Augustine
who Pope Gregory the Great had sent in the late 590s to convert the Anglo-Saxons
from paganism. The prime objective of George's mission, the Northumbrian chronicler said, was to reaffirm the bond between the Christians in England and the
Church of Rome. George's instructions from the Pope were as follows:

---

8 *Historia regum* (*York Annals*), 786; T. Arnold (ed.), *Symeonis Monachis Opera Omnia*, RS,
75.ii (London, 1885), 51; , *EHD* 1, trans. Whitelock, no. 3 at 271.

9 Bede, *HE* IV.17–18. On John the archcantor see also, Bede, *HAB*, c. 6 and *HAA*, c. 10. On
the Council of Hatfield see, C. Cubitt, *Anglo-Saxon Church Councils, c. 650–c.850* (London,
1995), 252–58, and *idem*, 'Finding the Forger: An Alleged Decree of the 679 Council of Hatfield',
EHR, 114 (1999), 1217–48.

10 Bede, *HE* IV.1–2. On the influence of Greek learning on the School at Canterbury set up
by Archbishop Theodore and Abbot Hadrian, see M. Lapidge, 'The School of Theodore and
Hadrian', *ASE*, 15 (1986), 45–72; *idem*, 'The Study of Greek at the School of Canterbury in the
Seventh Century', in M. Herren (ed.), *The Sacred Nectar of the Greeks: The Study of Greek in the
West in the Early Middle Ages* (London, 1992), 169–94; *idem*, 'The Career of Archbishop Theodore',
Settimane di studio del Centro italiano di Studi sull'alto medioevo, 39 (Spoleto, 1992), 137–91.

... trans mare in gentem Anglorum peragrare ... ut si qua zizania messem optimo semine satam, quam beatus Gregorius papa per os sancti Agustini seminavit, inritasset, funditus eradicare quod noxium et fructum saluberrimum stabilire summo conamine studuissemus.[11]	... to travel across the sea to the people of the English ... so that if any tares had spoilt the crop which blessed Pope Gregory had sown through the mouth of St Augustine, we might uproot anything noxious and ensure the propagation of only the healthiest fruit.

Significantly for our understanding of the mission, Bishop George's own account of its progress is preserved in a Frankish collection of canon law, copied *c.* 1000 and now kept in the ducal library at Wolfenbüttel.[12] His account, written in the first person and composed in the form of a letter of report to Pope Hadrian, provides a detailed description of the progress of the mission through Britain and of the social and ecclesiastical reforms which George and his companion, Bishop Theophylact, recommended to the assembled councils of the English kingdoms. His letter tells of the legates' journey across the Channel to Kent and their reception at Canterbury by Archbishop Jaenberht. Having 'rested there awhile', the legates travelled northwards to the court of King Offa of the Mercians who, George says, received them and the letters from Pope Hadrian, 'with immense joy and great honour on account of his reverence for St. Peter and your apostolic office'. A council was called and attended by King Offa and the bishops and elders of Mercia, and by Cynewulf, ruler of the West Saxons. The mission divided after this first Mercian council, with Theophylact going 'to visit the King of the Mercians and the parts of Britain' – presumably that is, to Wales – while George and his companions travelled to Northumbria where a further council was held in the presence of King Ælfwald, Archbishop Eanbald, and all the leading men of that kingdom. It is this Northumbrian council and its proceedings that are described and scrutinized most closely by George in his

---

[11] George of Ostia, *Epistola ad Hadrianum*, ed. E. Dümmler, MGH Epp. IV, no. 3, 20–29, at 20 (lines 12–14). The pastoral motif is also used by Alcuin in his *York Poem* and is derived from Christ's call to evangelism, Matt. 9:37 and Luke 10:2; *Alcuin: The Bishops, Kings, and Saints of York*, ed. and trans. P. Godman (Oxford, 1982), 10–11. See also Bede, *HE* I.29.

[12] Wolfenbüttel, Herzog-August-Bibliothek, MS Helmstadt 454, fos 113v-127v; O. von Heinemann (ed.), *Die Handschriften der Herzoglichen Bibliothek zu Wolfenbüttel. Vol. 1: Die Helmstedter Handschriften* (Wolfenbüttel, 1884), 356–57. The manuscript is now incomplete, a quire of eight folios (fo. 118r-125v) having been lost since the codex was paginated and since the text was transcribed in the late sixteenth century by the Magdeburg Centuriators; see *Ecclesiastica historia, integram eccleisae Christi ideam ... congesta per aliquot studiosos et pios viros in urbe Magdeburgica*, 13 vols (Basle, 1561–74), cent. 8, cap. ix, cols 574–87. That transcription forms the basis of subsequent editions, the best of which is by Dümmler, MGH Epp. IV. no. 3, at 20–29. An incomplete edition which (like the Centuriators) omits the dating clause and opening sentence is in Haddan and Stubbs, *Councils*, III, 447–61. The remainder of the manuscript consists of a collection of canon law associated with Rotger, Archbishop of Trier in the early tenth century, on which see P. Fournier and G. Le Bras, *Histoire des collections canoniques en Occident depuis les Fausses Décretals jusqu'au Décret de Gratien*, 2 vols (Paris, 1931), Vol. 1, 300–5.

letter to Hadrian. After business had been concluded in Northumbria, George and his companions travelled back south where a second Mercian council was convened by King Offa and the reforms proposed by George in Northumbria were read out to the assembled Mercian company which readily agreed to implement the recommendations. At this point, the only manuscript copy of the letter comes to an abrupt end without the formal closure that we would ordinarily expect in an important communication with the pope. This implies that either the scribe of the Wolfenbüttel manuscript omitted to copy out fully the exemplar before him, or that the exemplar was itself incomplete.

The core of George's letter to Pope Hadrian as it survives thus concerns the Northumbrian council which he attended and the reforms which were proposed to the assembled Northumbrian elite.[13] This northern bias of the letter corresponds with the provenance of other contemporary accounts of the legates' mission. As noted above, notice of the mission is recorded in the contemporary *York Annals*, now embedded within the twelfth-century historical compilation known as the *Historia regum*.[14] The northern recension of the *Anglo-Saxon Chronicle* contains the same information, *s.a.* 785. The OE annal reads like an epitome of the Latin version as preserved in the *Historia regum*, and as such provides important evidence for the textual relationship between these two early Northumbrian chronicles. The common emphasis on the parallel between George's mission and that of St Augustine suggests that these northern chronicles were ultimately drawn from a tradition very like the introduction to George's own letter to Hadrian, which held that the papal legates had indeed been sent to Britain to reinforce the message of Gregory, the Apostle of the English.

Tempore illo legati ab apostolica sede a domino Adriano papa ad Britanniam directi sunt, in quibus venerabilis episcopus Georgius primatum tenuit; **qui antiquam inter nos amicitiam et fidem catholicam quam sanctus Gregorius papa per beatum Augustinum docuit innovantes, honorifice suscepti sunt** a regibus et a præsulibus sive a

And in þas tid wæron ærendracan gesend of Rome fram Adrianum papan to Englalande to niwanne þone geleafan and þa sibbe þe sanctus Gregorius us sende þurh þone biscop Augustinum and hi man wið weorðscype underfeng and mid sibbe ongæn sænde.[15]

---

[13] The Northumbrian aspect of the legates' report is stressed by Cubitt in her detailed and important analysis of the mission; Cubitt, *Anglo-Saxon Church Councils*, 153–90. On the Mercian aspects of the Report see P. Wormald, 'In search of King Offa's "Law Code"', in I. Wood and N. Lund (eds), *People and Places in Northern Europe, 500–1600. Essays in Honour of Peter Sawyer* (Woodbridge, 1991), 25–45; H. Vollrath, *Die Synoden Englands bis 1066* (Paderborn, 1985), 162–81.

[14] On the *Historia regum* (*York Annals*) see, further, Chapter 4, below, 95–113.

[15] *ASChron.* DEF, 785. Only manuscript D contains the last clause, 'and mid sibbe ongæn sænde' which corresponds to the phrase in the *York Annals*, 'in pace domum reversi sunt'; *The Anglo-Saxon Chronicle. A Collaborative Edition. MS D*, ed. G. P. Cubbin, Vol. 6 (Cambridge, 1996), 16.

principibus hujus patriae, **et in
pace domum reversi sunt** cum
magnis donis, ut justum erat.[16]

It is notable that no contemporary records of the mission survive from
Southumbria, although a version of George's report does seem to have been
preserved in the south; a version of the proceedings of the legates' council seems
to have been known in England in the tenth century as several of its canons
clearly lie behind the *Constitutiones* of Archbishop Oda (941–58) and may also
have been known to King Alfred.[17] Important details concerning the legates'
mission are corroborated by another, continental source. In 798 Pope Leo III
wrote to Coenwulf of Mercia in response to a letter concerning the archbishopric
of Lichfield, and in it he referred to a promise made by Offa of an annual gift
which was to be sent to Rome. Leo claimed that a vow was made in front of a
synodal meeting of all the bishops and noblemen of the island of Britain as well
as the two papal legates.

... Offa rex ... coram synodo tam omnibus episcopis seu principibus atque optimatibus cunctoque populo insulæ Bryttanniæ morantibus quamque et nostri fidelissimi missi Georgii et Theophilacti, sanctissimis episcopis ... ut per unumquemque annum scilicet quantos dies annus habuerit, tantos mancusas eidem Dei Apostolo ecclesiæ nimirum CCCLXV pro alimoniis pauperum et luminariorum concinnationes emittere ... .[18]	... King Offa ... made a vow before a synod of all bishops and princes and nobles and all the people dwelling in the island of Britain and before our most loyal envoys George and Theophylact, most holy bishops ... that each and every year he would send as many mancuses as the year has days, that is, 365, to the same Apostle of the Church of God for the support of the poor and the provision of lights ... .

Leo's reference to *nostri fidelissimi missi*, George and Theophylact, and to the
synod held in the presence of King Offa and his bishops, princes and leading
men of the kingdom, makes it certain that this letter refers to one of the two
Mercian councils held during the legates' mission in 786. Theophylact is named

---

[16] *Historia regum* (*York Annals*), 786. The words *et primatibus* are interlineated in the
manuscript, Cambridge, Corpus Christi College, MS 139.

[17] G. Schoebe, 'The Chapters of Archbishop Oda (942/6) and the Canons of the Legatine
Council of 786', *Bulletin of the Institute of Historical Research*, 35 (1962), 75–83; D. Whitelock et
al. (eds), *Councils and Synods with other Documents Relating to the English Church, I, AD 871–
1204*, 2 vols (Oxford, 1981), Vol. 1, no. 20, at 67–74; P. Wormald, 'Offa's Law Code' and *idem, The
Making of English Law: King Alfred to the Twelfth Century* (Oxford, 1999), Vol. 1, 106–7, 306, 310.

[18] Leo, *Epistola ad Coenwulf*; ed. K. Hampe, MGH Epp. IV, no. 127 at 187–89; trans.
Whitelock, *EHD* 1, no. 205; Haddan and Stubbs (eds), *Councils* III, 445; Levison, *England and the
Continent*, 31; *Alfred the Great: Asser's Life of King Alfred and Other Contemporary Sources*, trans.
S. Keynes and M. Lapidge (Harmondsworth, 1983), 268.

by George in the preamble of his letter to Hadrian, and both of their names are recorded in the dating clause which precedes the letter.

Charlemagne, Alcuin and the legates' mission

All these sources – that is, George's letter to Hadrian, Leo's letter to Coenwulf, and the accounts given in the *York Annals* and the northern recension of the *Chronicle* – state that the legates were commissioned to go to England by the pope. The sources imply that the mission's primary concern was to ensure ecclesiastical conformity and to enforce reform where appropriate. However, a close examination of the context of the mission in 786, and of the content and structure of the letter to Hadrian, reveals an important Frankish component to the mission and to the recommendations which were proposed to the English. George's long experience as a *missus* for the Frankish king and his longstanding possession of the see at Amiens near the Channel coast are but two clues which point to a significant element of Carolingian influence within the legates' mission to England. George's letter to Hadrian reveals features that demonstrate a Carolingian contribution to the mission at a variety of levels. The letter is dated in the introductory address (among other methods) by the regnal years of Charlemagne. More explicitly, George tells us that the Frankish king also sent his own envoy, an abbot named Wigbod, who was sent by Charlemagne to act as an 'assistant' (*adiutor*) for the legates.[19] Wigbod travelled with George's delegation to Northumbria after the first Mercian council, and was considered by George to be a man *probatae fidei,* a term used elsewhere to compliment a particularly trustworthy and loyal Carolingian official.[20] Wigbod was a respected scholar at Charlemagne's court and may have been abbot of St Maximin's at Trier. He was the author of a *Commentary on Genesis* which he dedicated to Charlemagne and, indeed, it was to him that Levison attributed the survival of George's letter in Frankish scholarly circles.[21] Levison argued that the Wolfenbüttel manuscript

---

[19] George, *Epistola ad Hadrianum*, ed. E. Dümmler, MGH, Epp. IV, no. 3, at 20 [lines 30–32]. Charlemagne described himself as a *humilis adiutor* in the preface to the reform capitulary written in 789, the *Admonitio Generalis*; MGH Capit. no 22.

[20] A similar expression is used by Alcuin to describe the loyalty of Torctmund, who avenged the assassination of King Æthelred, 'virum in fide probatum, strenuum in armis'; Alcuin, *Ep.* no. 231, MGH Epp. IV; *Alcuin of York, c.A.D. 732 to 804: His Life and Letters*, trans. S. Allott (1974) no. 52 and *EHD* 1, trans. Whitelock, no. 206. He uses it again in his letter to Archbishop Æthelheard in exile, 'just as tested loyalty (*veritas probata*) always shines clear in a perfect man'; Alcuin, *Ep.* no. 128, MGH Epp. IV; *Alcuin of York*, trans. Allott, no. 49, and *EHD* 1, trans. Whitelock, no. 203.

[21] For comments on Wigbod's work and the access which he had to the Lorsch library see D. A. Bullough, *Carolingian Renewal* (Manchester, 1991), 14, 30, 140; Levison, *England and the Continent*, 128 n. 9; M. Gorman, 'The Encyclopedic Commentary on Genesis prepared for Charlemagne by Wigbod', *Recherches Augustiniennes*, 17 (1982), 173–201; *idem*, 'Wigbod and Biblical Studies under Charlemagne', *Revue Benedictine*, 107 (1997), 40–76; Cubitt, *Anglo-Saxon Church Councils*, 257–58, n. 18.

which contains the letter alongside other canonical material had been compiled there for Archbishop Rotger, and noted that the Trier library also contained an early manuscript of Wigbod's biblical commentary.[22] Although the attribution of the Wolfenbüttel manuscript to Trier is no longer widely accepted, the evidence remains that Wigbod was a learned man who knew Charlemagne personally and who had access to the king at court. His opening verses to the *Commentary* praise Charlemagne for his care in collecting books: 'who can count the great series of books which your decree has brought together from many lands, reviving the writings of earlier holy fathers'.[23] Alcuin's concern for supplementing book collections in Francia is well known, and Wigbod seems to have been the sort of man with whom Alcuin would have had considerable affinity.

It is no surprise to find that Alcuin was also part of the missionary party that met at the Northumbrian court. George told the pope that Alcuin and his companion, Pyttel, had acted as *legati* for the Northumbrian king and archbishop, and that they had travelled south with the legates' party to the second Mercian council.[24] The decision to include Alcuin in the mission was an obvious one given his acquaintance with the Carolingian court and his intimate knowledge both of York and of the archbishop's household, having spent nearly 40 years there as deacon, teacher, and custodian of the archbishop's famous library. In later years he wrote numerous letters to the noble men and women of the Mercian court, and the legates' mission would have provided an ideal forum for an entry into the network of the Mercian elite.[25] The contacts made and the status acquired through involvement in the mission would have stood him in good stead in later years. By 786 Alcuin had been associated with Charlemagne and his court for perhaps as long as five years, so his participation in the legates' mission to England should be considered in the light of his recent experiences with Frankish ways.[26] Pyttel also had experience of life abroad; he had escorted the Frisian scholar Liudger back to Frisia in early 773 and, with Alcuin's blessing and instruction, had continued on to Rome. He may have been in the Northumbrian party that brought back the *pallium* for Archbishop Ælberht in late 773 and, indeed, could have crossed paths with George's embassy to Pope Hadrian earlier in the same year.[27]

---

[22] Levison, *England and the Continent*, 128, n. 9; M. Wasserschleben, *Beiträge zur Geschichte der vorgratianischen Kirchenrechtsquellen* (Leipzig, 1837), 162–64. It has been claimed more recently that the Wolfenbüttel manuscript should be dated *c.* 1000 and that it originated at Hildesheim; Bullough, 'Albuinus deliciosus Karoli regis', 80, n. 24; Cubitt, *Anglo-Saxon Church Councils*, 270–71; Wormald, *The Making of English Law*, 107 n. 371.

[23] Bullough argues that this decree was sent *c.* 780; see Bullough, 'Albuinus deliciosus Karoli regis', 140. See also B. Bischoff, 'The Court Library of Charlemagne', in his *Manuscripts and Libraries in the Age of Charlemagne*, trans. M. Gorman, Cambridge Studies in Palaeography and Codicology, 1 (Cambridge, 1994), 56–76, at 63.

[24] George, *Epistola ad Hadrianum*, 28 [line 11].

[25] See, further, Chapter 6, below, 181–84.

[26] D. A. Bullough, 'Alcuin before Frankfort', in R. Berndt (ed.), *Das Frankforter Konzil von 794* (Mainz, 1997), 571–85 at 581.

[27] Bullough, 'Albuinus deliciosus Karoli regis', 78–82. Ælberht would not (at this date) have

Overall, Alcuin has a low profile in the account sent to Hadrian; George mentions him only once when describing the return journey of the Northumbrian expedition to Mercia. Alcuin has, however, been credited with a major role in the composition of key sections of a document interpolated by George into his report to Hadrian. George wrote to the pope saying that, on his arrival in Northumbria, it had been drawn to his attention that, in addition to the Mercian errors which he had already dealt with, 'additional, no-less serious vices needing correction were related to us in our hearing'. Consequently, he laid out a programme of reform which he deemed necessary to deal with these matters. This programme of reform, composed in response to reported Northumbrian vices, is interpolated wholesale into George's letter to Hadrian, and it is this programme – or at least part of it – which Cubitt and others attribute to the hand and intellectual concerns of Alcuin.[28] On the basis of comparisons between this interpolated document, some of Alcuin's later letters and the seminal Carolingian reform capitulary of 789 known as the *Admonitio Generalis*, Cubitt has argued that Alcuin was probably responsible for drafting the part of George's letter which deals with the reform of vices encountered by the team after their arrival in Northumbria, and particularly with those sections which deal with the temporal relationship between a king, his bishops and his people.[29] Cubitt has observed that the political thought displayed in this part of George's report is paralleled by the concepts and terminology used by Alcuin in his later letters, especially those addressed to Northumbrian kings, and has argued that the parallels are sufficiently close to claim that the leading mind in the formation of that part of the report was Alcuin's. It is not difficult to imagine Alcuin taking the opportunity to draw to the eminent bishop's attention some of the ills which he perceived in his own *patria,* using the occasion of a papal legation to promote an appropriate programme of reform.

The degree of Alcuin's influence on the reform programme embedded in George's letter to Hadrian is, though, a matter for continued debate, since it is possible that George and his mission provided a formative context for the development of Alcuin's later opinions.[30] Bishop George was a man of considerable authority and worldly experience, and a man who Alcuin held in great respect as a spiritual superior. In a letter written to Abbot Adalhard of Corbie in 790 when he found himself once again in Northumbria at the start of Æthelred's second reign, Alcuin asked Adalhard, 'to send greeting to my father George, and

---

collected the pallium himself; see Levison, *England and the Continent*, 241–48; contra M. Lapidge in *The Blackwell Encyclopaedia of Anglo-Saxon England* (Oxford, 1998), 6, 352.

[28] That is, *capitula* 11–14 of the Legates' Capitulary as discussed below. See Cubitt, *Anglo-Saxon Church Councils*, 166–90.

[29] Ibid., 165, 181–82; F.-C. Scheiber, 'Alcuin und die Admonitio Generalis', *DA*, 14 (1958), 221–29 and *idem*, 'Alcuin und die Briefe Karls des Grossen, *DA*, 15 (1959), 181–93. For an analysis which places a greater emphasis on the influence of Bishop George, see Wormald, 'Offa's Law Code'.

[30] Wormald, 'Offa's Law Code'; Cubitt, *Anglo-Saxon Church Councils*, 168.

ask him not to forget Alcuin, his spiritual son'.[31] Corbie was close to George's
see at Amiens and Alcuin, stuck against his will in Northumbria, may well have
recalled an earlier, happier, sojourn in Northumbria in the company of George's
entourage. It is also significant that Alcuin does not refer to many of his other
ecclesiastical superiors in this tone; the best parallel is his devotion for Ælberht,
the archbishop of York under whom Alcuin had spent his most formative years
and who had recognized and promoted his talent. In some ways, George seems
to have replaced the mentor which Alcuin lost when Ælberht died in 778. In his
York Poem, Alcuin describes the occasion when Ælberht, *praesul perfectus*,
handed over control of his precious library to Alcuin.

Tradidit ast alio caras super omnia gazas	Father-like he entrusted his books, treasures he valued above
librorum gnato, patri qui semper adhaesit,	all, to his other son [Alcuin], who was constantly at his side
doctrinae sitiens haurire fluenta suetus. ...	and whose thirst for learning Ælberht would satisfy....
pontificis summi, nostri patris atque magistri.[32]	that archbishop, our father and teacher.

Bishop George's report to Pope Hadrian: date, form and function

George's report on the mission is divided into four distinct sections: the formulaic dating address; a narrative introductory passage; the canons agreed upon at
the councils; and the attestations of those who agreed to them. The formulaic
address which precedes the narrative introduction contains a fourfold dating
system which enables the timing of the legates' mission to Britain to be established more precisely than the *anno domini* date provided by the northern
chronicle evidence. The combined dating formulae indicates that the synod was
held in the autumn of 786, a common season for Church gatherings.[33] The year
is fixed by an *anno domini* date and the season is ascertained through a combination of Charlemagne's regnal years and by reference to the indiction.

Synodus que facta est in anglorum saxnia **temporibus ter beatissimi et coangelici domini Hadriani** summi pontificis et universalis pape	The synod which was held in English Saxony **in the days of thrice-blessed and co-angelical Lord Hadrian**, supreme pontifex and univer-

---

[31] Alcuin, *Ep.* no. 9, MGH Epp. IV; *Alcuin of York*, trans. Allott, no. 10.

[32] Alcuin, *York Poem*. The translation here is taken from *Alcuin: On The Bishops, Kings and
Saints of York*, ed. and trans. P. Godman (Oxford, 1982), 120–21, lines 1525–28, 1575. On this
poem and on Alcuin's role in the production of the texts of 786 and 789 see also Bullough's
forthcoming 1980 Ford Lectures, *Alcuin: Achievement and Reputation*.

[33] Cubitt, *Anglo-Saxon Church Councils*, 270.

regnante gloriosissimo Karolo excellentissimo rege Francorum et Langobardorum seu patricio Romanorum, **anno regni ipsius XVIII** missis a sede apostolica Georio [*sic*] Ostiensi episcopo et Theophylacto venerabili episcopo sancte Tudertine ecclesie regnante domino nostro iesu christo in perpetuum **anno incarnationis eiusdem domini nostri DCCLXXXVI, indictionis X**.[34]

sal pope, **in the reign of the most glorious Charles**, most excellent king of the Franks and Lombards and patrician of the Romans, **in the eighteenth year of his reign**, when George bishop of Ostia and Theophylact, venerable bishop of the Church of Todi, had been sent by the apostolic see, our Lord Jesus Christ reigning for ever, **in the year of the incarnation of the same Lord 786, the tenth indiction.**

The *Royal Frankish Annals* state that Charlemagne had been made king in 768 at Noyon on 9 October (the feast day of St Denis) after Pippin's death on 24 September.[35] Charlemagne's eighteenth year as king, thus, stretched from 9 October 786 to the eighth day of that month the following year. The indiction (the tenth in the 15-year cycle) also tallies with a date in the latter part of the year, as the tenth indiction lasted from 1 September 786 to 31 August 787.[36] The 'Synod held in English Saxony' seems, therefore, to have been held sometime between 9 October 786 AD and Christmas, which marked the end of that year. The only ambiguity concerns which of the three councils convened by George is being referred to here as 'the synod'. However, since George's letter concentrates on the Northumbrian council we might assume that the dating formulae refer to that meeting.

There are other references within the letter which confirm this date. Some of the people who attended the Northumbrian and Mercian councils could only have done so if those councils had been held in the latter part of 786. The *York Annals* for 786 describe the episcopal consecration of Alduulf and the choice of Aldberht as abbot of Ripon. Alduulf and Aldberht, using their new titles, subsequently signed as witnesses to the proceedings of the Northumbrian council which was copied into George's letter (see Figure 3.4, lines 4 and 12). Since Alduulf had been consecrated to the bishopric of Mayo in Ireland, it is likely that the northern council was held relatively soon after his consecration *æt Corabrige*

---

[34] George, *Epistola ad Hadrianum*, MGH, Epp. IV, no. 3, at 20 [lines 1–7].

[35] *Annales regni Francorum*, 768.

[36] Indiction dates are generally calculated in 15-year cycles starting from the year 312 when the system was first introduced by the Emperor Constantine I. This calculation is based on the Greek Indiction which started on 1 September. The other possible starting date of the Indiction, 24 September, as used by Bede, would not alter the timing of the Northumbrian council, since the starting date of both calculations fall before 9 October, the day of Charlemagne's accession. See K. Harrison, *The Framework of Anglo-Saxon History to A.D. 900* (Cambridge, 1976), 38–42; R. Cheney (ed.), *Handbook of Dates for Students of English History*, Royal Historical Society Guides and Handbooks, No. 4, revised by M. Jones (Cambridge, 2000), 2–3.

before he returned to his diocese across the sea. The same source describes how Abbot Aldberht of Ripon died barely a year later during a synod held at *Wincanheale* on 2 September 787. In addition, George's letter records the presence of Cynewulf, King of the West Saxons, at the first Mercian council but his name was not included among the list of witnesses who attended the second Mercian meeting. It seems likely, therefore, that this second Mercian council, called to ratify the canons of the Northumbrian council, was held after the infamous assassination of Cynewulf outside his mistress' bedchamber at *Meretun*.[37] Also indicative of a pre-787 date is the fact that Hygeberht is titled the Bishop of Lichfield. It was not until the following year at the Synod of Chelsea that he was controversially promoted to archiepiscopal rank.[38]

The timing of the legates' councils to the last three months of 786 is significant in relation to Charlemagne's actions in that year. The corpus of Frankish annals states that, following the Easter celebrations, he sent his army into Brittany.[39] The Breton campaign was concluded 'with astonishing speed' and Charlemagne's seneschal, Auduulf, was able to bring the Breton leaders as hostages to the August assembly at Worms. With the defeat of the Bretons in a single campaigning season, Charlemagne found that, unusually, 'he had peace throughout his realms' and so decided to go to Rome to give thanks 'at the threshold of the blessed apostles' and to subdue the Lombards of Benevento.[40] He set out for Rome in the autumn, reaching Florence in time to celebrate Christmas 786 there, a date confirmed by the revised version of the *Royal Frankish Annals* which says that he entered Italy with his troops, 'in the cold of winter'.[41] The first episode in the annal for the subsequent year 787, describes how he entered Rome and was received, 'with great honours by the Lord Pope Hadrian'.

Thus, in the same year in which Hadrian commissioned Theophylact and George to go to Britain, Charlemagne decided to make his third visit to Rome. The chronology of Charlemagne's itinerary and the dating of George's synod to the autumn of 786 raises the possibility that Theophylact's arrival in Francia to collect George en route to Britain had spurred Charlemagne's decision to visit Rome. The location of Theophylact's bishopric at Todi, in central Italy near Spoleto, means that he cannot have avoided contact with the vagaries of Lombard politics and his opinions would doubtless have been of interest to Charlemagne. George, being resident at that time in Francia, would probably also have needed Charlemagne's

---

[37] *Historia regum* (*York Annals*), 786; *ASChron.* 755 (for 757) and 784 (for 786); *Continuatio Bedae*, 757. On the implications of the reference to the assassination of Cynewulf to the dating of the *Continuatio*, see *Bede's Ecclesiastical History of the English People*, ed. and trans. B. Colgrave and R. A. B. Mynors (Oxford, 1968), lxix and 575, n. 9.

[38] *ASChron.* 787. C. J. Godfrey, 'The Archbishopric of Lichfield', *SCH*, 1 (1964), 145–53; N. P. Brooks, *The Early History of the Church of Canterbury* (Leicester, 1984), 118–20.

[39] *Annales regni Francorum*, 786. See also J. M. H. Smith, *Province and Empire: Brittany and the Carolingians* (Oxford, 1992), 58.

[40] *Annales Laureshamenses*, 786; *Annales regni Francorum*, 786.

[41] *Annales regni Francorum*, 786.

permission before he could leave for England. An assembly such as that held at Worms in August was the usual place for foreign dignitaries to pay their respects to the king and it is more than likely that an important papal emissary such as Theophylact would have visited Charlemagne.[42] Furthermore, given that George's letter to Hadrian cannot have been written until the last weeks of 786, after the second Mercian meeting, and allowing for the time a letter would take to get to Rome from Britain in winter, it is possible that George's report concerning the English mission may have reached Rome during Charlemagne's sojourn in Italy between Christmas and Easter 787. The outcome of the legates' mission to Britain may have been one of the items discussed by Charlemagne and Hadrian in the 'several days' which they spent together early in 787 or during their shared Easter celebrations in the city.[43] The chronology suggested by the *Royal Frankish Annals* and by George's letter is sufficiently flexible that George and Theophylact may have known before they left for Britain that Charlemagne intended to travel to Rome for the winter; if so, the entire report to Hadrian could have been written with the foreknowledge that Charlemagne would be in Italy when George's letter arrived. This could account for the eulogistic reference to Charlemagne in the address, which corresponds exactly with the formula that the papal chancery used when writing to the Frankish king at this date.[44]

One of the letters contained in the *Codex Carolinus* provides a further piece of evidence relating to Franco-papal collaboration in 786. A letter from Hadrian to Charlemagne, written in the early months of the year, discusses the days of prayer and thanksgiving which Charlemagne had requested as spiritual support for his ongoing campaign against the Saxons.[45] Hadrian announced that three days be set aside for this purpose – namely, the vigils of St John the Baptist, SS John and Paul, and St Peter, all of which fall in late June.[46] To this effect Hadrian, 'decreed and sent forth orders into all our lands' and recommended that Charlemagne should send word, 'throughout all your territories, and to those regions beyond the sea where Christian people are to be found, for the performance of three days of litanies in this fashion'.[47] A mission such as

---

[42] R. McKitterick, *The Frankish Kingdoms under the Carolingians, 751–987* (London, 1983), 97–98.

[43] *Annales regni Francorum*, 786.

[44] *Codex Carolinus*, no. 73 and 74.

[45] *Codex Carolinus*, no. 76; *Charlemagne: Translated Sources* trans. P. D. King (Kendal, 1987), no. 30, at 293–94. On the importance of these days of prayer in support of the Carolingian regime see M. McCormick, 'The Liturgy of War in the Early Middle Ages: Crisis, Litanies, and the Carolingian Monarchy', *Viator*, 15 (1984), 1–23.

[46] That is, 24, 26, and 29 June respectively. The feast day of St Peter, as the chief of the apostles, was a favoured feast day for prayer and the celebration of military campaigns. Cathwulf, writing to Charlemagne in 775, suggests that public masses be said on behalf of the 'Christian army' on the feast days of SS Michael and Peter; Cathwulf, *Epistola ad Carolum*, 504 [line 28].

[47] *Codex Carolinus*, no. 76 at 608 [lines 11–18]. See also Alcuin's letter to the bishops of Britain, accompanying gifts with requests for requiem masses to be said for Pope Hadrian; Alcuin, *Ep.* 104, MGH Epp. IV; *Alcuin of York*, trans. Allott, no. 25.

that led by George would have been an ideal mechanism in which to declare this message throughout the Christian kingdoms of Anglo-Saxon England. George and Theophylact read out messages from the pope, which could conceivably have included instructions of this type, before the first Mercian and Northumbrian assemblies. However, given that the days of thanksgiving were to be held in June of that year and the English synod was held sometime after 9 October, a time lapse of several months would need to have occurred between the arrival of the papal messengers and the holding of the synod. George's description of the progress of the mission through Kent, Mercia and Northumbria gives the impression of a fairly speedy journey, and a delay of this order seems unlikely. If, as Hadrian's letter implies, the Christian peoples of Anglo-Saxon England are to be included in the reckoning of a Christian, 'region beyond the sea', this letter suggests that the papal decree for the three days of prayer in June were transmitted, possibly via a Carolingian agent as the letter recommends, prior to the mission of George and Theophylact. It seems possible, therefore, that two sets of Franco-papal envoys were sent to Britain in 786, the first perhaps acting as a precursor to the second, bigger mission.

After the initial dating address, a lengthy narrative introduction describes the progress of the mission through Britain. Having described the journey from Kent, through Mercia to the Northumbrian court, George continues his report with a list of the 20 canons of reform which were read out to and ratified by the assembled companies, first in Northumbria and afterwards at the second council in Mercia. The letter continues with a witness list of the 'signatures' or attestations of those Northumbrians and Mercians who pledged to obey the legates' reforms. The process by which the noblemen affirmed their consent is important and was obviously considered so at the time since the method by which it was done is described by George with particular attention to detail. The witnesses vowed, 'with all devotion of mind' to respect and obey the pronouncements – a vow which they confirmed as George made the sign of a cross, 'on your [Hadrian's] behalf, in our hand'.[48] In a second and quite distinct action, the signatories themselves made the sign of the cross as a symbol of their commitment to its precepts, 'with a careful pen on the page of this charter'.[49] It is important to note here that autograph crosses were a regular feature of papal bulls but are not normally found in Anglo-Saxon diplomatic. The unique manuscript copy of the letter at this point gives an example (*ita*) of the type of cross used to mark the approval of the various Northumbrian witnesses (Figure 3.3, line 17). In the manuscript, the first three names, those of Archbishop Eanbald, King Ælfwald, and Bishop Tilberht of Hexham, are indeed followed by crosses of this type.[50]

---

[48] *in vice vestra in manu nostra*. This is the manuscript reading. Dümmler erroneously has *in vice nostra in manu nostra*; MGH Epp. IV, no. 3 at 27 [line 32].

[49] *stilo diligenti in charta huius pagine;* MGH Epp. IV, no. 3 at 27 [lines 33–34].

[50] Cf. Wormald, 'Offa's Law Code', 31. The attestation of Archbishop Eanbald in the Wolfenbüttel manuscript is written at the foot of fo. 126r (Figure 3.3) after the attestation of

None of the other Northumbrian or Mercian attestations on following folios are accompanied by crosses but some of the Northumbrian 'signatures' have a space left after the word *crucis* which may indicate the presence of a cross in the exemplar omitted by the copyist, who perhaps intended to fill them in at a later stage.[51]

The placing of the name of Tilberht, Bishop of Hexham, immediately after that of the king reflects the special bond between King Ælfwald and Hexham (see Figure 3.3, lines 18–21). This link was maintained after the king's assassination in 788 with the development of a cult at Hexham dedicated to Ælfwald's memory.[52] Similarly, the name of Hygeberht, the bishop (soon-to-be archbishop) of Lichfield follows Offa's 'signature' in the Mercian list (Figure 3.5, lines 12–14). The other Northumbrian episcopal witnesses to the document were Higbald, Æthelberht, and Alduulf who were the bishops of Lindisfarne, Whithorn, and Mayo[53] respectively, along with an otherwise unknown bishop named Æthelwine. The report records the consent of this otherwise unknown bishop in a way which is noticeably different from the others – *Ætheluuinus episcopus per legatos subscripsi* – a style which seems to suggest that, whereas the other delegates of the Northumbrian council had witnessed the original document themselves, Æthelwine was not actually present at the meeting and his consent was ascribed on his behalf, 'through the legates' (Figure 3.4, line 5).[54] This may account for the fact that Æthelwine's name and see are not recorded in any other context.[55] Abbots Aldberht and Eghard also

---

Tilberht of Hexham. It was copied in a lighter ink after the page was finished but evidently by the same scribe. The omission and proper place for Eanbald's attestation is signalled through use of characteristically insular abbreviation symbols (similar to those used to abbreviate the words *dominus* and *iesus*) and which are used elsewhere in the manuscript (for example, fo. 117v, line 4); see R. McKitterick, 'The Diffusion of Insular Culture in England and on the Continent: The Manuscript Evidence, c. 650–c. 850', in H. Altsma and K.-F. Werner (eds), *La Neustrie: Le pays au nord de la Loire de 650 à 850*, Beihefte der Francia 16/11 (Sigmaringen, 1989), 395–431 at 399.

[51] Such a space is left for example in the 'signatures' of Siguulf, Aldberht and Eghard, fo. 126v [11–13], Figure 3.4 [lines 11–13].

[52] *Historia regum* (*York Annals*), 788.

[53] Alduulf was in Northumbria in 786 for his consecration which took place 'in monasterio quod dicitur Et-Corabridge'; *Historia regum* (*York Annals*), 786. The legates' council must have taken place after this event but before he returned to Ireland. Dümmler suggested that the council may have been held at the same monastery in which Alduulf was consecrated; MGH Epp. IV, at 28, n. 1.

[54] George, *Epistola ad Hadrianum*, MGH Epp. IV, no. 3, at 28 [line 2].

[55] There is no other known northern bishopric which he may have represented. Three alternative explanations suggest themselves; firstly that Æthelwine may have been a continental bishop who was being consecrated in York (for which there is a precedent in the *Historia regum* (*York Annals*) for 767) or that the scribe who copied the report into the Wolfenbüttel manuscript wrote *episcopus* after the name of Æthelwine in error of another title. His name is the last in the list of bishops. Another suggestion is that Æthelwine was Bishop Elfod of Bangor; see M. Deansley, *The Pre-Conquest Church in England* (London, 1963), 228.

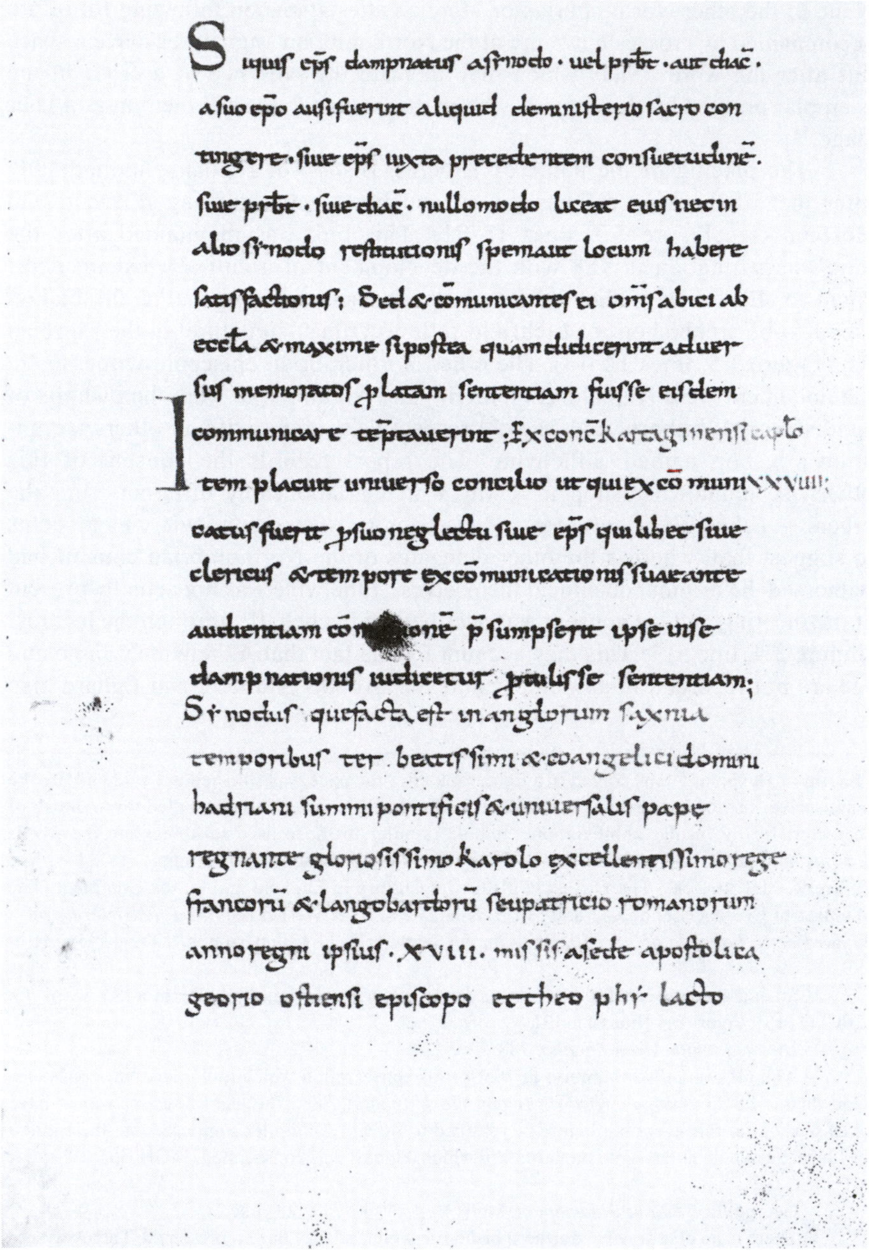

Siquis eps dampnatus a synodo · uel prbtr · aut diac ·
a suo epo ausi fuerint aliquid de ministerio sacro con
tingere · siue eps iuxta precedentem consuetudine͂ ·
siue prbtr · siue diac · nullomodo liceat eius nec in
alio synodo restitutionis spem aut locum habere
satisfactionis; Sed & comunicantes ei omis abici ab
eccta & maxime si postea quam didicerint aduer
sus memoratos plaiam sententiam fuisse eisdem
communicare teptauerint ; Ex conc Kartaginensi capto
tem placuit uniuerso concilio ut qui ex comuni XXVIII ·
catus fuerit p suo neg lectu siue eps qui libet siue
clericus & tempore excomunicationis suae ante
audientiam communione p sumpserit ipse in se
dampnationis uidetur pulisse sententiam;
Si nodus que facta est in anglorum Saxnia
temporibus ter beatissim & euangelici domni
hadriani summi pontificis & uniuersalis pape
regnante gloriosissimo Karolo excellentissimo rege
francoru & langobardoru seu patricio romanorum
anno regni ipsius · XVIII · missis a sede apostolica
georio ostiensi episcopo et theo phr lacto

Fig. 3.1   Wolfenbüttel, Herzog-August-Bibliothek, Cod. Guelf. 454 Helmst.,
fo. 113v

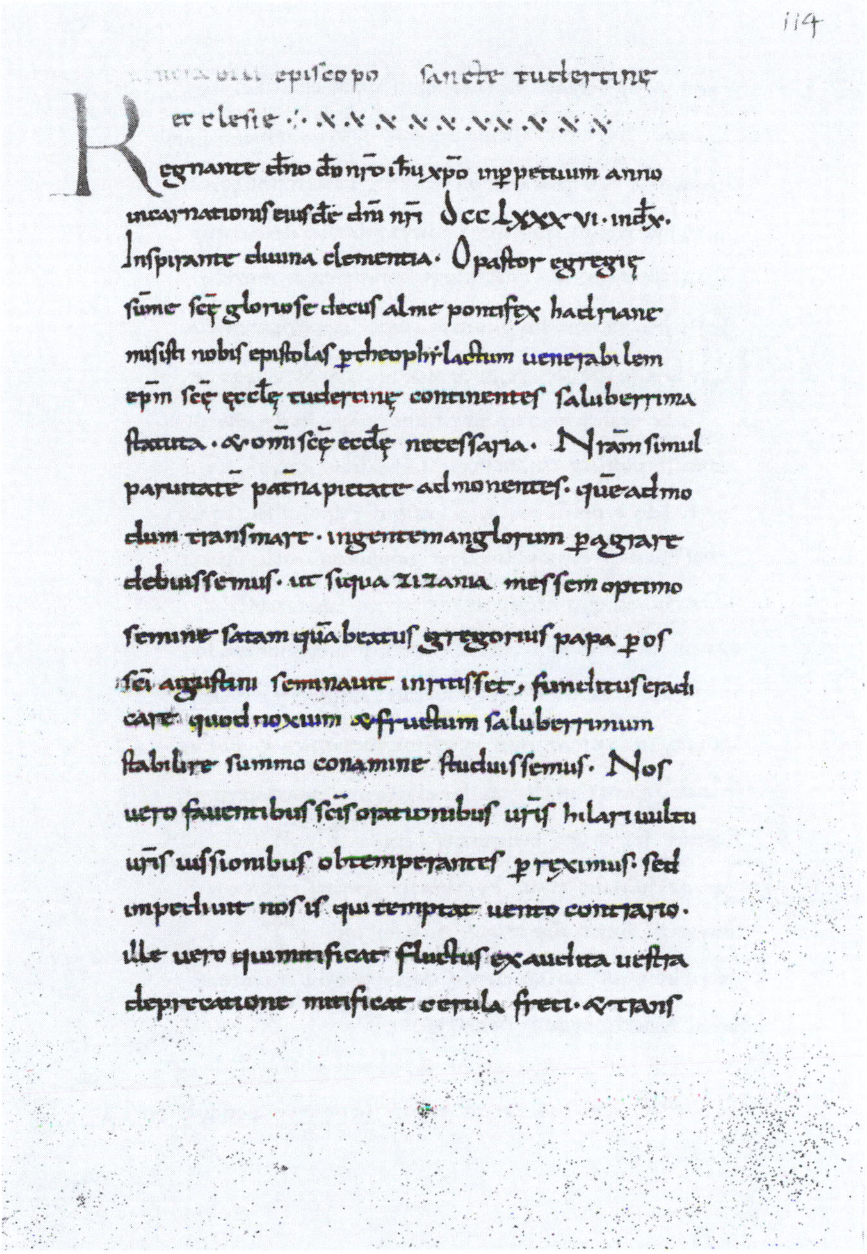

114

episcopo sanctæ tudertinæ
ecclesie ·:· x x x x x x x x x x x
Regnante æterno dno nro ihu xpo inpperium anno
incarnationis eiusdæ dni nri dcc lxxx vi indx.
Inspirante diuina clementia · O pastor egregius
sume sce gloriose decus alme pontifex hadriane
misisti nobis epistolas p theophylactum uenerabilem
epm sce ecce tudertinæ continentes saluberrima
statuta · & omni sce ecce necessaria · Nram simul
paruitate patna pietate admonentes· que admo
dum transmare · ingentem angloum paggiare
debuissemus· ut siqua zizania messem optimo
semine satam qua beatus gregorius papa p os
sci augustini semnauit inruisset·s sanelttus eradi
care quod noxium & fructum saluberrimum
stabilire summo conamine studuissemus· Nos
uero fauentibus scis oratoonibus uris hilari uultu
uris uissionibus obtemperantes proximus· sed
impediuit nos is qui temptat uento contrario·
ille uero qui mitificat fluctus exaudita uestra
deprecatione mitificat cerula freti· & trans

Fig. 3.2 Wolfenbüttel, Herzog-August-Bibliothek, Cod. Guelf. 454 Helmst.,
fo. 114r

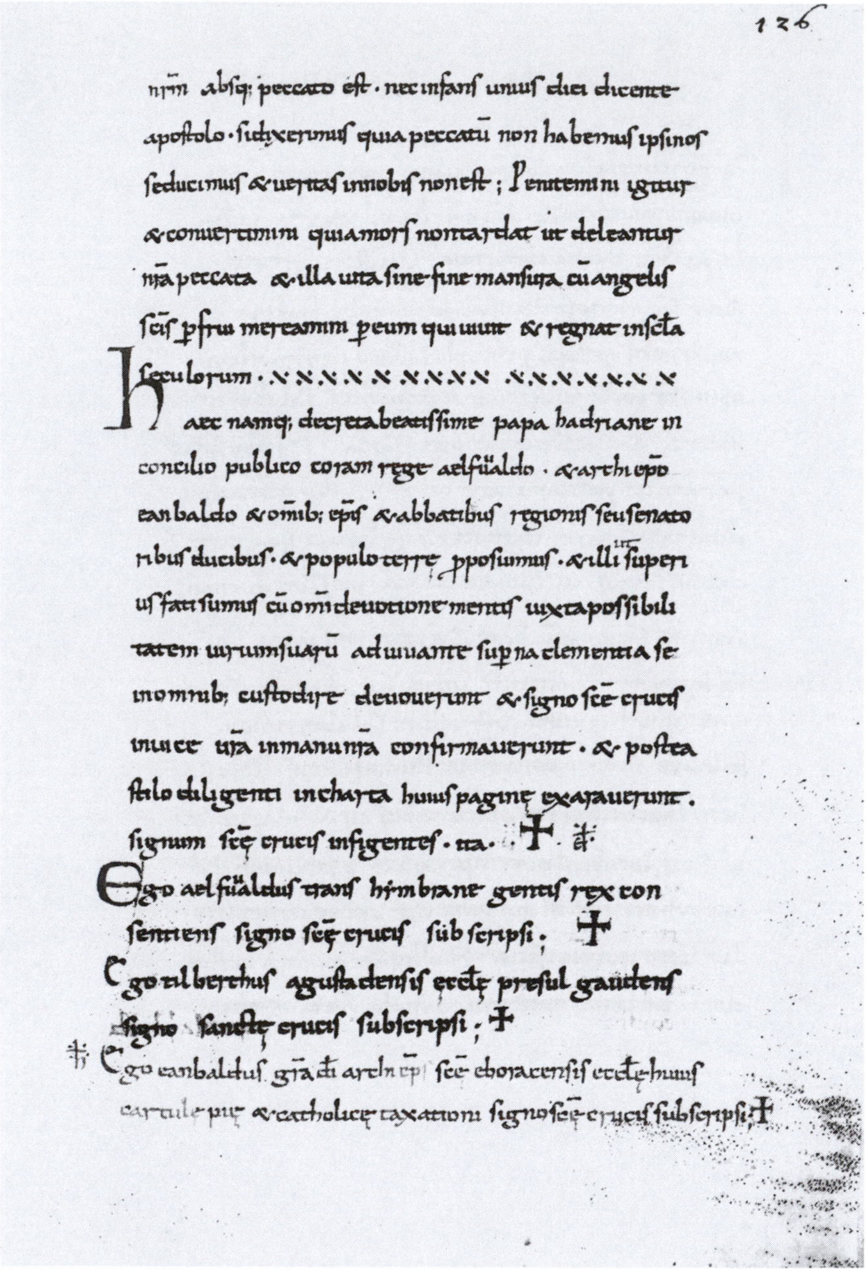

126

nम्रn absq; peccato est . nec infans unus diei dicente
apostolo . sidixerimus quia peccatu non habemus ipsinos
seducimus & uertas innobis noñest ; Penitemini igitur
& conuertemini quia mors nomtardat ut deleantur
nřa peccata & illa uita sine fine mansura cu angelis
scīs pfrm mereamur peum qui uiuit & regnat inscla
sēculorum . x x x x x x x x x x x x x x x x x
aec namq; decreta beatissime papa hadriane in
concilio publico coram rege aelfuualdo . & archi epo
eanbaldo & omibः epis & abbatibus regionis seu senato
ribus ducibus . & populo terre pposuimus . & illi superi
us fati sumus cu omi deuotione mentis iuxta possibili
tatem uirumsuaru adiuuante supna clementia se
mo mnibः custodire deuouerunt & signo scē crucis
inuicem uia inmanunřa confirmauerunt . & postea
stilo diligenti incharta huius paginę exarauerunt.
signum scē crucis infigentes . ita . ✠ ✠
Ego aelfuualdus trans hymbrane gentis rex con
sentiens signo scē crucis subscripsi ; ✠
Ego tilberthus agustadensis ęcclę presul gaudens
signo sanctę crucis subscripsi ; ✠
✠ Ego eanbaldus gratia di arch eps scē eboracensis ęcclę huius
cartule pur & catholicę taxationi signo scē crucis subscripsi ✠

Fig. 3.3 Wolfenbüttel, Herzog-August-Bibliothek, Cod. Guelf. 454 Helmst.,
fo. 126r

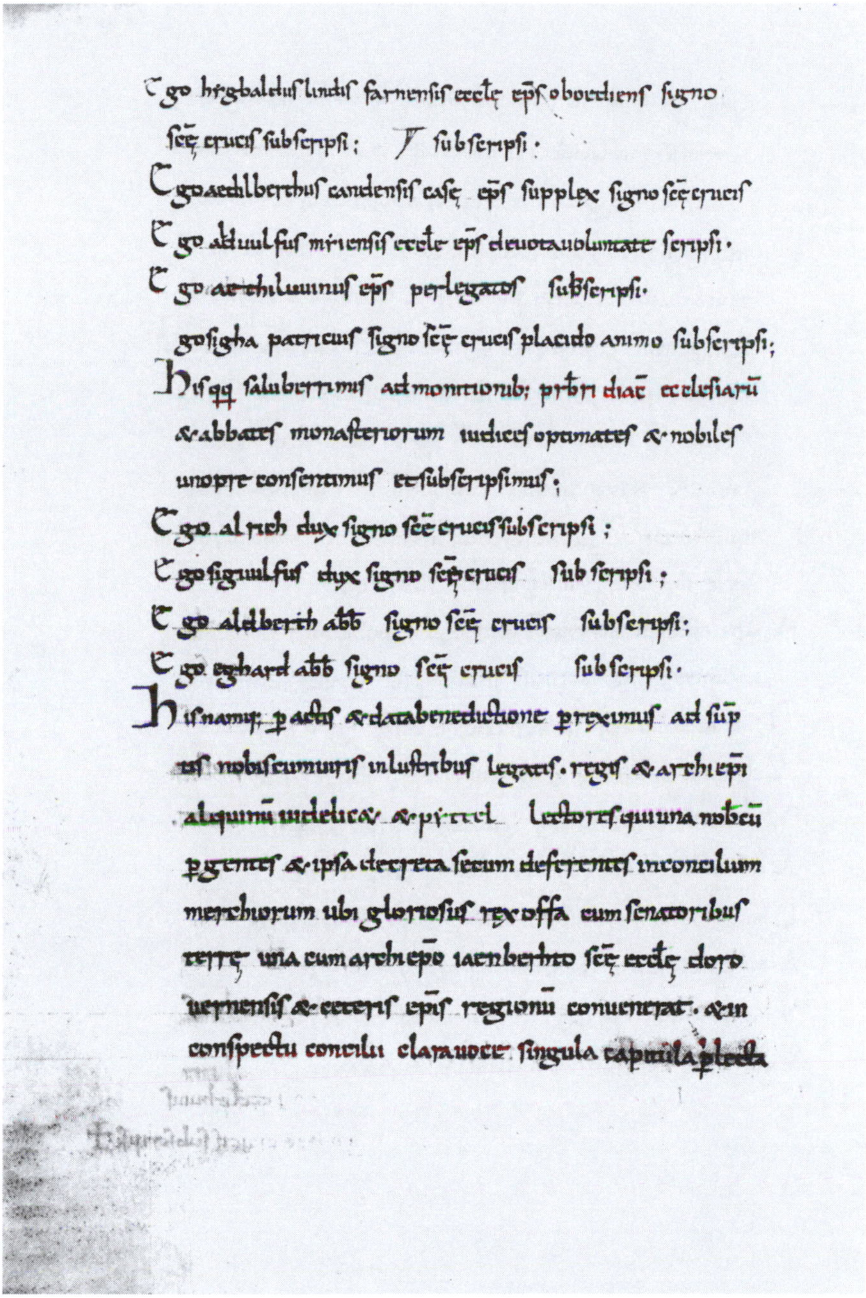

Ego hygbaldus lindis farnensis eccle eps oboediens signo
sce crucis subscripsi; ☩ subscripsi.
Ego aethilberhtus candensis casæ eps supplex signo sce crucis
Ego alduulfus mirensis eccle eps deuota uolumtate scripsi.
Ego aethiluuinus eps per legatos subscripsi.
gosigha patricus signo sce crucis placido animo subscripsi;
Hisqq saluberrimis admonitionib; prbri diac ecclesiarū
& abbates monasteriorum iudices optimates & nobiles
unopere consentimus et subscripsimus;
Ego alrich dux signo sce crucis subscripsi;
Ego siguulfus dux signo sce crucis subscripsi;
Ego aldberht abb signo sce crucis subscripsi;
Ego eghard abb signo sce crucis subscripsi.
His namq; pactis & data benedictione proximus ad sup
os nobiscum mittis inlustribus legatis. regis & archiepi
alquinū uidelica; & pyttel lectores qui una nobcū
pgentes & ipsa decreta secum deferentes inconcilium
merchiorum ubi gloriosus rex offa cum senatoribus
terre una cum archiepo iaenberhto sce eccle doro
uernensis & ceteris epis regionū conuenerat. & in
conspectu concilii clarauoce singula capitula plecta

Fig. 3.4   Wolfenbüttel, Herzog-August-Bibliothek, Cod. Guelf. 454 Helmst.,
fo. 126v

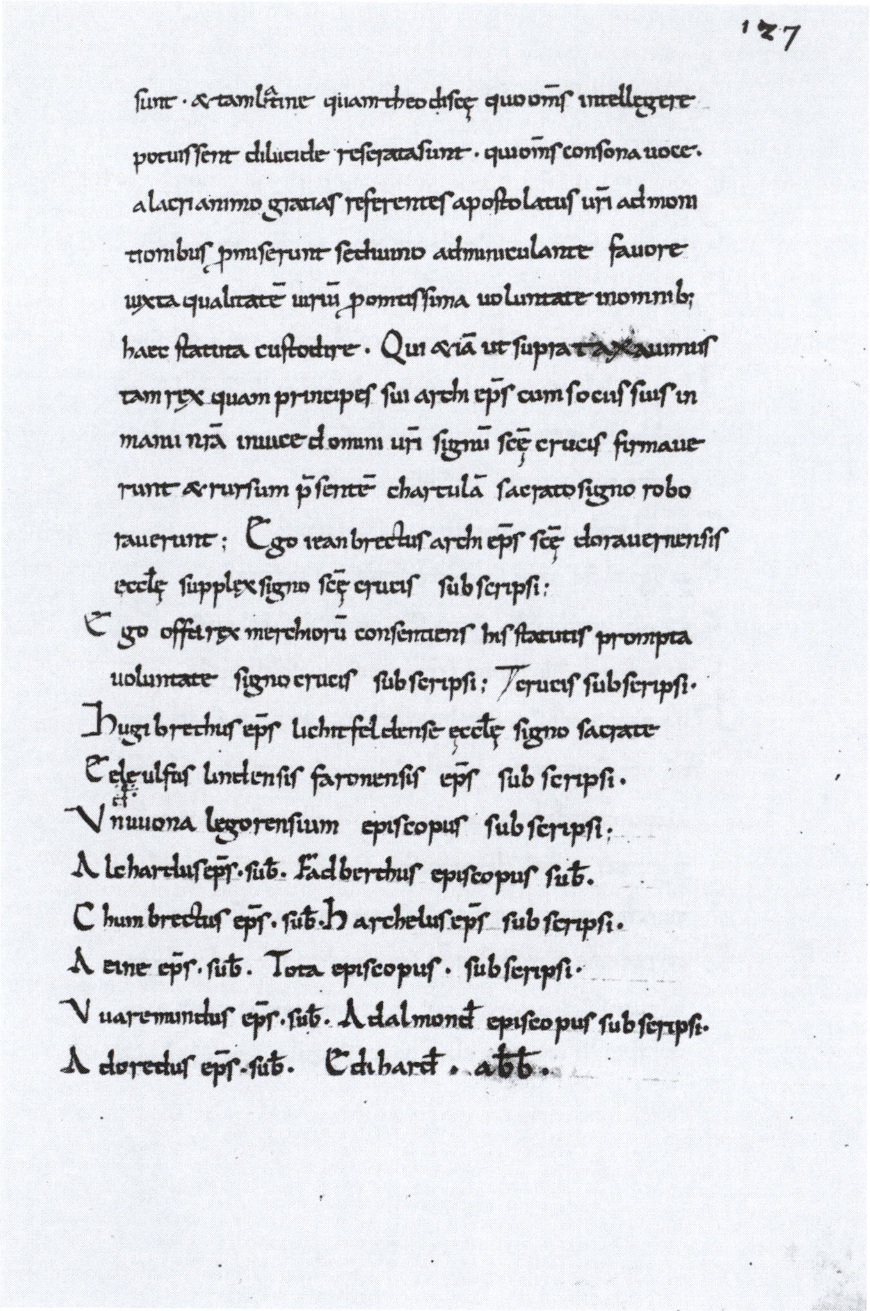

127

sunt · & tam latine quam theodisce quo omnes intellegere
potuissent dilucide reserata sunt · quo omnes consona uoce ·
alacri animo gratias referentes apostolatus uri admoni
tionibus pmiserunt se diuino adminiculante fauore
iuxta qualitate uiriu promtissima uoluntate in omnib;
haec statuta custodire · Qui etiā ut supra taxauimus
tam rex quam principes sui archi eps cum sociis suis in
manu nrā in uice domini uri signū scē crucis firmaue
runt & rursum psente chartulā sacrato signo robo
rauerunt ; Ego ieanbrectus archi eps scē dorauernensis
ecclē supplex signo scē crucis subscripsi ;
Ego offa rex merciorū consentiens his statutis prompta
uoluntate signo crucis subscripsi ; ✝ crucis subscripsi ·
Hugibrechus eps lichitfeldense ecclē signo sacratae
Ceoleulfus lindensis faronensis eps subscripsi ·
Unuuona legorensium episcopus subscripsi ;
Alchardus eps · sub · Eadberchus episcopus sub ·
Chumbrectus eps · sub · Harchelus eps subscripsi ·
Aeine eps · sub · Tota episcopus · subscripsi ·
Uuaremundus eps · sub · Adalmond episcopus subscripsi ·
Aldredus eps · sub · Echhard · abb ·

Fig. 3.5 Wolfenbüttel, Herzog-August-Bibliothek, Cod. Guelf. 454 Helmst., fo. 127r attested their support of the canons as did Sigha, Ælfwald's *patricius*, and two Northumbrian *duces*, Alrich and Siguulf.[56]

After the Northumbrian 'signatures', George describes, in a short narrative passage, the journey from the north to Mercia and notes that, on this occasion, they were accompanied by the *lectores*, Alcuin and Pyttel.[57] At the second Mercian council a similar procedure to approve the canons was followed; the decrees were propounded out aloud again but on this occasion, 'in Latin and in the vernacular [*theodisc*]', an oral pledge was made by the assembled council, and their pledge was blessed by George on behalf of the pope *in manu nostra in vice domini vestri* with a cross, and the written document (*chartula*) which listed the decrees was signed by the Mercian witnesses, including the 12 bishops of the southern metropolitan province.[58] After the Mercian attestations, the letter terminates abruptly and the scribe of the extant manuscript continues without a break to the next item, which suggests that scribe's exemplar was probably incomplete.

The 20 canons promulgated by George at the Northumbrian council and the attestations which follow them form a discrete document interpolated wholesale into George's narrative account of the mission. The format of this document and its diplomatic affiliations are important. The double process of attestation, with the sign of the cross made first by the hand of George, deputizing for Pope Hadrian, and subsequently by each of the signatories (except Æthelwine, the unidentified bishop whose consent was affirmed *per legatos*) is reminiscent of the format of contemporary charters. The first sign of the cross, made by George when blessing the oral consent of the council to the decrees, is similar in function to the written chrismon which is found in the top left-hand corner of contemporary charters and which acts as a stamp of sanctity and inviolability over the whole document. The rulings of the Synod of Chelsea in 816 describe the ceremonial importance of the signing of the cross and the imposition of hands over a legal document, emphasizing the ritual significance and symbolic gravitas of the act.[59] In 786 George used the words *charta* and *chartula* to describe the documents affirmed by the Northumbrian and Mercian nobility

---

[56] The *Historia regum* (*York Annals*) for 786 also describes how Aldberht was elected and consecrated as abbot of Ripon after the death of Botwine. The same chronicle records in the following year that Aldberht died, probably during a synod which was held at *Winchala* on 2 September. The subsequent fate of Sigha is also recorded in the *Historia regum* (*York Annals*), 788 and 793, on which see below, 92.

[57] See Figure 3.4 (line 16). The plate indicates that the Pyttel's name was added in a lighter ink with a different pen but probably by the same scribe. It was written into a space too large for his name, possibly over an erasure. Bullough notes that the spelling of Pyttel's name is the correct OE version whereas the name of Alcuin on the same line is spelt in the late tenth-century continental style – *Alquinum;* Bullough, '*Albuinus deliciosus Karoli regis*', 80, n. 24.

[58] On the use of orality and law in Anglo-Saxon England and Francia see J. L. Nelson, 'Literacy in Carolingian Government', in R. McKitterick (ed.), *The Uses of Literacy in the Early Middle Ages* (Cambridge, 1990), 265–67.

[59] Cubitt, *Anglo-Saxon Church Councils*, 95. On the Synod of Chelsea see *ibid.*, 191–203.

respectively; the diminutive *chartula* signed by the Mercians could be understood literally, that a summarized version or appendix to the longer Northumbrian document was signed at the second Mercian council.[60] Another feature of the document produced by the legates (as preserved in the Wolfenbüttel manuscript) which is reminiscent of Anglo-Saxon legal diplomatic is the observation that the lesser names (*Alchardus episcopus* to *Edihard* (*sic*) *abbas*) in the list of Mercian attestations were copied into the manuscript two to a line, suggesting that they were copied from a list written in two columns (Figure 3.5, lines 17–21). Again this structure is commonplace in Anglo-Saxon charters. The presence of the attestations accompanied by pledge crosses suggests that the document compiled by George was presented to the Anglo-Saxon nobility in the familiar guise of a legal document, an idea which is complemented by other structural features of the letter as preserved in the manuscript.

In the extant manuscript, the formulaic dating clause which precedes George's letter merges into the narrative introduction to the report. The scribe copied the initial part of the address in a lighter (red) ink, starting on line 15 of fo. 113v (Figure 3.1), and the address was continued in the same lighter ink for two lines on the top of fo. 114r as far as the words *episcopo sancte Tudertine ecclesie* (Figure 3.2, lines 1–2). The remainder of the second line is taken up with *x*-shaped line fillers. The first letter of the next word, *regnante*, is written as a large capital letter in the same lighter coloured ink at the head of line 3. But the rest of the introductory dating clause – [R]*egnante domino ... Ind[ictionis] X* – is written in the blacker ink of the main body of the text, thereby making the second part of the dating clause appear indistinguishable in presentational terms from the start of the text of the letter. This division of the dating clause could be dismissed as a copying quirk of the scribe who transcribed the letter into our manuscript *c.* 1000, although it does at least confirm that the dating clause was an intrinsic part of the exemplar he copied and was not his own invention. Yet this arrangement, which merges the second part of the dating clause into the start of the text of the letter proper, provokes other observations. Presented like this, the report commences in black ink at the head of fo. 114r (Figure 3.2) with a striking formulaic invocation to Christ; *Regnante domino nostro Ihesu Christo in perpetuum... .* This was the usual sentence by which records of Anglo-Saxon synodal proceedings commenced and was also used as the invocation in some of Offa's surviving charters.[61] While often employed in eighth-century insular

---

[60] A possible parallel is the scribal memorandum of attestations sewn to a Kentish charter of 843 (BL Stowe Charter 17) *BCS* 442 / *S* 293.

[61] See, for example, the introduction to the Council of Clofesho, 747, Haddan and Stubbs, *Councils* III, 362. The issue of synodal diplomatic custom is discussed by Cubitt, *Anglo-Saxon Church Councils*, 78–83. See, for example, BM Cotton Aug. II.4, Hartleford 779 (BCS 201/S 106, *ChLA* 184) and BM Cotton Aug. II 26.27, Chelsea 767 (BCS 230/S 114, *ChLA* 186). Intriguingly, the *Regnante* invocation is also used in a 'provincial' South-Saxon charter that was subsequently confirmed by Offa. The Mercian confirmation is written in a rather more sophisticated script than the text of the charter; Chichester, West Sussex Record Office Cap. 1/17/2, Selsey 780; S. E. Kelly,

documents, this opening invocation was less used on the Continent, although when it is found, the context is significant. It is, for example, the formula which opens the *Admonitio Generalis* of 789, Charlemagne's first major reform capitulary which, on close inspection, has many parallels with the content of the legates' report – parallels which scholars have attributed to Alcuin's involvement in the composition of both.[62] Furthermore, the earliest copy of the *Admonitio* is found in a late eighth- or early ninth-century manuscript written in Anglo-Saxon minuscule on parchment prepared in insular fashion at an Anglo-Saxon centre in Germany, probably Fulda.[63] It is also the highly unusual opening to the proceedings of the Roman Council of 769 at which we find Bishop George playing a prominent role. This council condemned the papal usurper Constantine and, by use of 'this singular expression' instead of imperial regnal years, openly flaunted papal freedom from Byzantium in favour of the new relationship with the Franks.[64]

The combined evidence of the ritual process of confirmation (the signing of crosses, the oral pronouncement of the decrees, the oral agreement of the assembled counsellors to uphold the decrees, the *Regnante* invocation, and the list of attestations at the end of the letter) all support the suggestion that the Mercian and Northumbrian noblemen would have identified the written document which they were being asked to attest with a charter-style legal document. Despite the late date of the unique manuscript copy of George's letter, the physical impression of Anglo-Saxon charter diplomatic within the letter is striking and is an important observation, not least because no charters have survived from Northumbria in this period. The legates' report is not a charter in the sense of a record of land transfer or a grant of privilege, and its charter-like affinities are closest to Mercian charters of Offa's reign, yet this was a document initially produced in Northumbria and, as it stands, it is the closest surviving thing to a formal, secular legal document from pre-Viking Northumbria.[65]

Charters of Selsey, Anglo-Saxon Charters IV (Oxford, 1997), no. 11; BCS 1334/S 1184, *ChLA* no. 236. Charters of Offa with a *Regnante* invocation in non-contemporary manuscripts are BCS 195/S 105, BCS 229/S 115 (of dubious authenticity), and BCS 188/S 143. See also Cubitt, *Anglo-Saxon Church Councils*, 257 and n. 34; and *idem*, 'Finding the Forger', 1232.

[62] See footnote 29 *supra*.

[63] Wolfenbüttel, Herzog-August-Bibliothek MS Guelf. 496a Helmstadt; *CLA* IX, no. 1381 where Lowe attributes the manuscript 'presumably' to Fulda, an attribution supported by Bischoff, *Manuscripts and Libraries in the Age of Charlemagne*, 43, n. 113 and H. Mordek, *Bibliotheca capitularium regum Francorum manuscripta*, MGH *Hifsmittel* 15 (Munich, 1995), no. 22 at 949–52, 1082.

[64] MGH *Conc.* II.1, 79; P. Classen, 'Karl der Große, das Papsttum und Byzanz', in *idem*, *Karl der Große: Lebenswerk und Nachleben*, 1 (Düsseldorf, 1965), 537–608 at 545; Noble, *The Republic of St. Peter*, 118; W. Hartmann, *Die Synoden der Karolingerzeit im Frankenreich und in Italien* (Paderborn, 1989), 84–86. On the Council of Rome see below, 89.

[65] There is one forged charter ascribed to Northumbria in this period (*S* 66) although it is known from references in the *Vita Wilfridi* and in Bede's *Epistola ad Ecgberti* that the Northumbrians did produce such documents; S. Kelly, 'Anglo-Saxon Lay Society and the Written Word', in R. McKitterick (ed.), *The Uses of Literacy* (Cambridge, 1990), 36–62 at 38, n. 10.

It was common practice for grants of land and privilege to be confirmed and witnessed at synods where the secular and ecclesiastical elite had gathered.[66] Nor was it uncommon for synodal proceedings concerning ecclesiastical matters (which may, of course, have had secular implications) to be witnessed in this manner, but normally only by clergymen, even when the king was present.[67] It was *not* normal practice for the secular members of an Anglo-Saxon synodal council during this period to ratify a document that was even partially ecclesiastical in content. The legates' mission seems to have provoked an innovative amalgamation of ecclesiastical synodal conventions with secular charter-type practice in a single document concerned with both Church and lay matters. An alternative explanation for the unusual form of the document as we have it, is that the document signed by the Anglo-Saxon elite was based on a different, non-native model, so that its ratification required a new attestation procedure. The obvious places to look for such a model are the *patriae* of the author of the report, Carolingian Francia and papal Italy.

Carolingian affinities in the Legates' 'Capitulary'

The clearest affinity of the document which lists the decisions of the Northumbrian council, and which was interpolated into George's letter, lies with Frankish legislative documents, as Wormald and Cubitt have emphasized.[68] This is true not just of the structure of the legates' report but also of its contents. One of the most striking aspects of the legates' mission to Britain, as it was reported by George to Hadrian, is the parallel between the Northumbrian council and a Carolingian assembly. The comparison is valid for the form of the council and of the document which it produced. Four common features stand out: the meeting was summoned by the king and was held in the presence of the gathered secular and ecclesiastical elite of the kingdom; a document called a 'capitulary' was produced with the proceedings of the council summarized in numbered paragraphs; this capitulary dealt with a combination of ecclesiastical and secular issues, practical procedures and moral reforms; the document was proclaimed orally to the gathered assembly thereby giving it a degree of legal authority. Thus, when King Ælfwald heard of George's arrival in Northumbria he, 'straight way with great joy ordered a day for a council, at which gathered all the principle men of the region both ecclesiastical and secular'.[69] Of the document produced and its oral transmission to the assembled company, George recorded that:

---

[66] See, for example, the land grants and privileges enacted at the Synod of Clofesho in 798; Haddan and Stubbs (eds), *Councils* III, 512–14.

[67] For example, the Councils of Hatfield (*HE* IV.5) and Clofesho 803; Haddan and Stubbs (eds), *Councils* III, 542–47.

[68] Wormald, 'Offa's Law Code', 34; Cubitt, *Anglo-Saxon Church Councils,* 160; Wormald, *The Making of English Law*, 50, 106–7.

[69] George, *Epistola ad Hadrianum*; MGH Epp. IV, no. 3, at 20 [lines 35–36] to 21 [line 1].

Scripsimus namque **capitulare** de singulis rebus et per ordinem cuncta disserentes auribus illorum protulimus. ... **Haec namque decreta**, beatissime papa Hadriane, **in concilio publico coram rege Ælfuualdo et archiepiscopo Eanbaldo et omnibus episcopis et abbatibus regionis seu senatoribus, ducibus et populo** terre proposuimus et illi ... cum omni devotione mentis ... confirmaverunt.[70]

We wrote a **capitulary** concerning each matter and we produced them each in order in their hearing ... **These decrees**, most blessed pope Hadrian, we propounded **in the public council before King Ælfwald and Archbishop Eanbald and all the bishops and abbots of the region, and the counsellors, leaders and people of that land** and they with all devotion of mind ... confirmed them.

George refers to the document which he produced for the Northumbrian council as a 'capitulary', and the canons within it are termed *decreta, statuta* or *capitula*.[71] It was presented to the most important men of the kingdom, lay and clerical, who readily affirmed it, 'with all devotion'. This description can be compared usefully with the introduction to Charlemagne's first major decree, promulgated at the palace of Herstal in March 779.

Anno feliciter undecimo regni domni nostri Karoli gloriosissimi regis in mense Martio factum **capitulare** qualiter congregatis **in unum sinodali concilio episcopis abbatibus virisque inlustribus comitibus, una cum piissimo domno nostro** secundum Dei voluntatem pro causis oportunis consenserunt **decretum**.[72]

In the eleventh year of the reign of our most glorious king Charles, in the month of March, a **capitulary** having been made as to the content of a decree to deal with pertinent matters **which was agreed together by our most pious lord and by bishops abbots and illustrious counts, gathered together in one synodal council**, in accordance with the will of God.

The Herstal Capitulary, like George's report to Hadrian is dated by Charlemagne's regnal years and was presented to an assembled group of important laymen and their ecclesiastical counterparts, who willingly affirmed the *decreta* concerned with 'relevant matters'. It continues with 23 short *capitula*, the first few concerning ecclesiastical matters and the rest detailing matters of secular concern. This is also the recipe of the document produced for the Northumbrian

---

[70] Ibid., at 21 [lines 3–5], 27 [lines 28–33].

[71] Ibid., at 21 [lines 4–8], 27 [line 28], 28 [lines 15, 19, 24].

[72] MGH Capit. I, no. 20, at 47; trans. King, *Charlemagne,* no 2, at 203–5; F. L. Ganshof, *Recherches sur les Capitulaires* (Paris, 1958), 4; *idem*, 'The Use of the Written Word in Charlemagne's Administration', in *The Carolingians and the Frankish Monarchy*, trans. J. Sondheimer (London, 1971), 125–42 at 128; Hartmann, *Die Synoden*, 99; Mordeck, *BCRFM*, no. 20 at 1081–82. The capitulary is dated to the month of March in the eleventh year of Charlemagne's reign – that is, 779 – and the *Annales regni Francorum* (revised version) 779 says that Charlemagne spent Easter at Herstal before moving on to Compiègne.

council; the first ten *capitula* relate to ecclesiastical concerns and the next ten to secular issues. Thus, at both Herstal in 779 and in Northumbria in 786, a document which is labelled a capitulary was promulgated at a council where the ecclesiastical and secular elite of the kingdom had gathered. To the *decreta* of the Herstal Capitulary, also, the assembled company enthusiastically agreed. *Capitula* 13 of the Herstal Capitulary says that the *precariae* or 'orders' were issued *de verbo nostro*, implying that the royal decisions were pronounced orally.[73] Once again, this is reminiscent of the proclamation of the Legates' Capitulary to the Northumbrian and Mercian councils; the personnel of the assembly which ratified the Herstal Capitulary mirrors the structure of the council which agreed to the Capitulary composed by George in Northumbria in 786.[74]

The terminology which George used to describe the document of reform recommendations which he presented to the Northumbrian council is significant; this is the first occasion that a 'capitulary', in the technical sense of treatise arranged in chapters concerning secular as well as ecclesiastical issues, is found in an Anglo-Saxon context.[75] Furthermore, the word is found in the context of a document, the external trappings of which were recognizably legal to an Anglo-Saxon audience. The use of the term is important because the capitulary is a form of document which is synonymous with Carolingian government; it is not an indigenous Anglo-Saxon form of document. In Francia the capitulary was used as a vehicle for disseminating the instructions of the king that had been issued at central assemblies. There is much debate as to how these documents worked in practice, whether they were simple *aides mémoires* for local counts or if they carried legal force as pronouncements of the royal will; it is at least clear that, as a genre, the function, format and use of capitularies evolved rapidly during Charlemagne's reign.[76] The use of the term in the legates' report of 786 indicates a mind familiar with emerging Carolingian legal practices at work on the composition of the document which is dovetailed into George's letter. It is, of

---

[73] In his seminal study of Carolingian capitularies, Ganshof argued that it was the verbal pronouncement of the Frankish capitulary which gave them legal force; Ganshof, *Recherches*, 18–21. He cites the introduction to the capitulary of Mantua (MGH Capit. I no. 90); the capitulary of Herstal (MGH Capit. I, no. 20); the so-called *Capitulare de Villis*, (MGH Capit. I, no. 32), and the Capitulary of the Saxon (MGH Capit. I, no. 32). On this point see also P. Wormald, '*Lex Scripta* and *Verbum Regis*: Legislation and Germanic Kingship from Euric to Cnut', in P. H. Sawyer and I. N. Wood (eds), *Early Medieval Kingship* (Leeds, 1977), 105–38 at 118; Nelson, 'Literacy in Carolingian Government', 265–67, 280; R. McKitterick, *The Carolingians and the Written Word* (Cambridge, 1989), 28.

[74] For example, the Synod of Frankfurt and the *Capitulare Saxonicum*, ratified at Aachen in 797; MGH Capit. I, nos 27 and 28.

[75] *Dictionary of Medieval Latin from British Sources*, Fasc. 2, ed. R. E. Latham et al. (London, 1981), 271, col. 3.

[76] The key discussion here remains that of Ganshof, *Recherches*, but see also H. Mordek, 'Karolingische Kapitularien', in H. Mordek (ed.), *Überlieferung und Geltung normativer Texte des frühen und hohen Mittelalters* (Sigmaringen, 1986), 25–50. See also Nelson, 'Literacy in Carolingian Government' and Wormald, *The Making of English Law*, 49–53.

course, possible that this person was George himself, and that he was drawing on his years of experience in the Frankish and papal courts when constructing a document for Northumbrian ecclesiastical and social reform.

The use of the word *capitulare* in the legates' report is in fact one of the earliest uses of the word outside a papal context. The word *capitulum* had been employed in earlier papal documents, where it referred to a chapter heading or a summary of a complex series of points, rather than a generic label for a type of legislative document.[77] In this sense, the word had long been in use in strictly ecclesiastical contexts, even in seventh-century England where it was used in the canons of the Synod of Hertford, according to the text preserved by Bede.[78] By contrast, the word *capitulare* (plural *capitularia*) as applied to a legal-style treatise proposed by a secular ruler and broken down into individual *capitula*, is a word which has become associated specifically with the legislative documentation of Carolingian government, although there has been a tendency to apply the term anachronistically, using it to describe a variety of Merovingian and early Carolingian documents. A survey of the word *capitulare* in Frankish material indicates that, although the genre has clear precursors in earlier legislative methods, the term was seldom used before 800 and very rarely before 786.[79] The *Capitulare* of Herstal in 779, discussed above, is the earliest unequivocal example in Charlemagne's reign. The noun *capitula* occurs in only a few documents belonging to the reign of Charlemagne's father, Pippin III. The Council of Ver which was held in July 755 produced a document concerning mostly ecclesiastical issues which were divided into 21 sections and referred to in the introductory preamble as *capitula,* meaning, simply, 'head(ing)s'.[80] Twelve items in another document promulgated by Pippin, which Ganshof considered to be innovative in form and function, concerned ecclesiastical and secular problems in Aquitaine and are referred to in a preliminary title as *capitula*.[81] However, the title of this latter document was attached later and refers to Charlemagne's reaffirmation of his father's Aquitanian decrees. Charlemagne produced his own 'Capitulary on Aquitanian Issues' in 789, which was closely based on his father's decrees, suggesting that the reference to Pippin's decrees as *capitula* may well date closer to 789.[82]

---

[77] *Gregorii I Papae Registrum Epistolarum*, ed. P. Ewald and L. M. Hartman, MGH Epp. I (Berlin, 1891–99) I, no. i.39a, at 53 [line 9], no. i.40 at 55 [line 9] and *Gregorii I Papae Registrum Epistolarum*, Vol. 2, MGH Epp. II, no. viii.7 at 9 [line 28] , no. ix.186 at 178 [line 14], no. xiii.19 at 386 [line 6], xiii.47 at 410 [line 11]. C. DuCange, *Glossarium mediae et infirmae Latinis*, 10 vols (Niort, 1883–87), Vol. 2, 140, col. 2.

[78] Bede, *HE* IV.5.

[79] Ganshof, 'The Use of the Written Word', 125–26.

[80] MGH Capit. I, no. 14, at 33 [line 34]; Hartmann, *Die Synoden*, 68–72.

[81] Ganshof, 'The Use of the Written Word', 125–27; Mordek, *BCRFM*, no. 18 at 1081.

[82] MGH Capit. I, no. 18, at 42 [line 31]. The title is as follows: *Incipiunt capitula quas bone memorie genitor Pipinus sinodaliter [instituit] et nos ab hominibus conservare volumus.* Charlemagne's own capitulary on Aquitanian issues is MGH *Capit.* I, no. 24 at 65–66; Mordek, *BCRFM*, no. 24 at 1083.

Apart from the Herstal Capitulary, the only other true Carolingian capitularies which pre-date the one produced by the legates in Northumbria come from the Frankish territories of Lombard Italy.[83] This may reflect a level of experimentation with capitularies as a mechanism for imposing Carolingian government over a newly annexed territory, rather than differential preservation of evidence. The relatively high proportion of early Carolingian capitularies relating to Italy encouraged Ganshof to see Lombard practice as an important influence in the development of the capitulary as a documentary genre in Carolingian Francia.[84] There are three documents issued by Charlemagne or his son, Pippin, concerning Lombard Italy which are dated before 786, and one other which is dated *c.* 780–90.[85] The so-called Capitulary of Mantua is particularly interesting in the context of the typological precursors to the Legates' Capitulary.[86] It lists 'each *capitula*' which was presented 'to the general assembly' (*ad placitum generale*) and, as with the Legates' and Herstal Capitularies, the Mantuan document is a mixture of episcopal and secular issues, of moral, fiscal and military matters all designed to reinforce Carolingian institutions and methods of government in Frankish territories in Italy. It would be an exaggeration to equate the Legates' Capitulary with an equivalent attempt to introduce Carolingian-style governance into Anglo-Saxon England but it is notable that the recipe of *capitula* is similar for both regions. An obvious feature of the Mantuan Capitulary (which recurs in Frankish capitularies concerning the control of the newly conquered Saxons) is the way in which the Church, its needs and institutions, were an intrinsic part of the implementation of Carolingian government.[87] Unlike the Lombards or the pagan Saxons, the Anglo-Saxons posed no challenge to Frankish authority. Nevertheless, the Legates' Capitulary proposed a programme of reform more subtle than that imposed upon the annexed territories of Carolingian Francia, but one that demonstrates similar concerns and broadly analogous methods of implementing them. The Legates'

---

[83] On the 'Italian' capitularies see Ganshof, *Recherches*, 16–18. Ganshof redated the *Capitulare episcoporum* (for which Boretius had '780?') to 792–3; Ganshof, *Recherches*, 109; MGH Capit. I, no. 21, at 52–53.

[84] Ganshof, *Recherches*, 5–6, quoting the edict of Aistulf of March 750 which appears to use the word *capitulare* in the introduction to a group of decrees.

[85] MGH Capit. I, nos 88–91, at 187–93. Boretius dated the first of these 776 or 781, Ganshof supported the earlier date; Ganshof, *Recherches*, 17, n. 56.

[86] MGH Capit. I, no. 90; Mordek, *BCRFM*, no. 90 at 1089. The dating of the Mantuan Capitulary which is particularly important for understanding the chronology of the introduction of Carolingian-style monetary reforms into Lombard Italy, is not certain. Boretius, Ganshof, Grierson, and Mordek have dated it to 781 or thereabouts. Other scholars have suggested that it may be slightly later, at 803–13. Ganshof preferred the earlier date because of the close parallels of the Mantuan Capitulary to the Herstal Capitulary (*capitula* 5, 7, 8). See Ganshof, *Recherches*, 19, n. 63, P. Grierson, 'Chronologia delle riforme monetari di Carolo Magne', *Riuista Italiana di Numismatica*, 5th Ser., 56 (1954), 65–79, 66–72 and reprinted as Chapter 17 in P. Grierson, *Dark Age Numismatics, Selected Studies* (Aldershot, 1979); and M. A. S. Blackburn, 'Money and Coinage', in *NCMH* 2, 538–59 at 549. Wormald accepts the later date; see his 'Offa's Law Code', 34, n. 20.

[87] MGH Capit. I, no. 26 and 97, at 68–70, 203–4.

Capitulary resembles its Carolingian equivalents both in its idealism and as a response to local needs.

The context for the Mantuan Capitulary seems likely to have been Charlemagne's journey to Rome in 781 when his sons Pippin and Louis were baptized and consecrated by Hadrian as sub-kings of the Lombards and Aquitanians respectively. A letter of introduction survives, written by Pope Hadrian to Charlemagne, concerning an embassy led by George between the Frankish and papal courts, and dated sometime between April 781 and April 783.[88] There is no evidence to link George with the creation of the Mantuan Capitulary but we should be mindful that, in the early 780s, Lombard issues were the special concern of this man who was sent a short while later to Northumbria. The close interest in Lombard affairs in the early Carolingian capitularies, and Ganshof's suggestion that the methods of the Lombard kings may have influenced the development of Carolingian capitularies, should make us look hard at the Italian context. George, in his capacity as the Franco-papal *missus* with a special interest in Lombard Italy, is likely to have come into contact with early capitulary-style documents. That George used this particular form of document in Northumbria arguably ties him even closer to the development of the capitulary tradition within Carolingian Francia itself.[89]

The capitulary became a commonplace legislative document in Francia only in the 790s after the production of the seminal reform capitulary of 789, the *Admonitio Generalis*. It is after this date that the label becomes used in the Carolingian sense by papal writers.[90] The format of the legates' document was, therefore, innovatory and sophisticated in that it seems to combine something of the ritual of Anglo-Saxon charter diplomatic with the new type of legislative document emerging in Francia – the capitulary. The document produced by the papal legates in England in 786 is thus an early example of the type of document which was developed by the Carolingians as a mechanism for governing their vast realms. As such, the appearance of a capitulary in England – in Northumbria initially – is remarkable; it is apparently the first time that such a document was seen or used in Anglo-Saxon England. An innovation of this type begs the question as to whether the content of this legislative document was as foreign as its format. The form, of both the legates' document and of the council at which it was presented, is entirely consistent with emerging Carolingian methods of legislation. Although the mission was nominally papal in origin, the document produced by the legates to fulfil their missionary objectives was Carolingian in typology; yet the Legates' Capitulary, which was created in England and ratified by Anglo-Saxon assemblies, was of a type that, in 786, was still relatively unusual in Francia.

---

[88] *Codex Carolinus*, no. 73 at 604.

[89] See the decrees of the Synod of Compiègne, *s.a.* 757; MGH Capit. I, no. 15 at 38 [lines 38, 45] and 39 [line 16]; Mordek, *BCRFM*, no. 15 at 1081.

[90] See the letters of Popes Hadrian and Leo III to Charlemagne; MGH Epp. V, no. 2, at 7, [line 13], at 31, [line 30] and at 40, [line 34]; no. 10, at 102 [lines 15, 16, 18].

Northumbrian problems: Carolingian solutions

The author of the legates' report to Hadrian was clear about the immediate inspiration for the contents of the Capitulary contained within it. George says that, after the Northumbrian elite had been summoned to the council, 'it was related in our hearing ... that there were many no less serious vices requiring correction'. It was because of these vices that he wrote the Capitulary, 'concerning each single thing in order' which was subsequently read out and ratified by the assembly.[91] This statement implies that, however Frankish in its mode of presentation, the content of the Legates' Capitulary was prompted by the need to correct domestic Northumbrian problems. Since, as George tells us, the Capitulary was presented to the Northumbrian assembly before the pronouncement of the papal letters brought by the legates, it is apparent that the *capitula* were something other than the issues which had provoked the mission to England.

It is not easy to cross-check how many of the *capitula* do indeed relate specifically to Northumbrian ills since the Capitulary provides an almost unique insight into Northumbrian society in the 780s. A few of the *capitula* have references which seem to relate directly to observation of Anglo-Saxon practices. *Capitulum* 12 ends with the comment, all too pertinent in the 780s, that 'killing of lords occurs often among you'. In Northumbrian terms, this reference to the sin of regicide had uncomfortable echoes with the murder of King Ælfwald's own father, Oswulf, in 758 as well as Æthelbald's assassination in Mercia the previous year.[92] Unfortunately for Ælfwald, the strictures of the legates went unheeded and he was himself murdered two years later. It seems that regicide was indeed a Northumbrian vice, although the killing of Cynewulf of Wessex in the very year of the legates' mission shows that it was a social ill not restricted to the Northumbrians. In a letter to King Æthelred written in 793, Alcuin bemoans a collapse in Northumbrian morals, and of indulgence in incest, adultery and fornication. These vices, he said, had inundated the land 'since the days of Ælfwald' implying a decline in social mores in the years since the legates' mission.[93] Several of the Capitulary canons find close parallels in Alcuin's letters but, without exception, these letters were written several years after the council and are, therefore, likely to have received inspiration from the Capitulary rather than vice versa.

The reference in *capitulum* 10 to the prohibition on bishops judging secular cases seems also to be based on first-hand observation of Northumbrian practice, since it is introduced by a verb in the first person.[94] The reference in the same chapter to chalices and patens made of horn also reads like an

---

[91] George, *Epistola ad Hadrianum*, MGH Epp. IV, no. 3, at 21 [lines 1–4].

[92] *Historia regum* (*York Annals*) 758; *ASChron.* 755 (for 757).

[93] Alcuin, *Ep.* no. 16; MGH Epp. IV, at 43; *Alcuin of York*, trans. Allott, no. 12; Cubitt, *Anglo-Saxon Church Councils*, 182.

[94] George, *Epistola ad Hadrianum*; MGH Epp. IV, no. 3, at 23 [lines 10–11].

observation of local practice. The comment in *capitulum* 19 concerning pagan behaviour is similar in tone, and is mirrored by another of Alcuin's subsequent letters to Æthelred in which he berated the king and his nobles for having their hair and beards cut in the manner of pagans. Alcuin admonishes them for their luxurious clothing which he says is beyond their needs and divergent from the traditions of their forefathers. The pagans with whom Alcuin equates these fashions are those 'whose terror threatens us' – that is, presumably, the Viking pirates whose raid on Lindisfarne prompted his letter to Æthelred – suggesting that the Northumbrians were familiar with Scandinavian ways before the hostile raids began.[95] However, the pagans and gentiles who are mentioned in *capitulum* 19 of the Legates' Capitulary are those whom, George says, 'your fathers expelled by force of arms', a comment which has led to one suggestion that these people (though nominally Christian by this date) might have been Picts.[96] The writer of the Capitulary marvels that 'it is a remarkable thing and no less stupifying, that those whose life you always hate, you desire to imitate'.[97] The implication is that the Northumbrians were particularly partial to the fashions of their northern neighbours which, to a continental eye, seemed to be pagan. Equally, the reference to the eating of horsemeat which 'no Christian does in the East' is evidently the opinion of an outsider, used to a Mediterranean lifestyle.[98]

There are other details in the Legates' Capitulary which imply that its compilation was overseen by someone who was not native to Anglo-Saxon England. The suggestion in *capitulum* 4 that monks, nuns and canons conduct themselves with suitable sobriety in the manner of Eastern monks and canons is a further example of familiarity with Eastern customs. In addition, this reference to canons and their lifestyle as being distinct from that of regular monks is the earliest of its kind in any Anglo-Saxon source, again suggesting external influence.[99] Another feature suggestive of Frankish concerns is the request for the

---

[95] Alcuin, *Ep.* no. 16; MGH Epp. IV, no. 16, at 43 [lines 23–24]; *Alcuin of York*, trans. Allott, no. 12.

[96] George, *Epistola ad Hadrianum*, MGH Epp. IV, no. 3, at 27 [lines 5–6]. Wormald rightly points out that the Picts were Christian by this date, but that their appearance would have been bizarre to a man who had spent much of his long life in Italy and Francia; Wormald, 'Offa's Law Code', 33. On the Pictish contact with the Frankish world see G. Henderson, *From Durrow to Kells: The Insular Gospel-books, 650–800* (London, 1987), 93–97; R. G. Lamb, 'Carolingian Orkney and its Transformation', in C. E. Batey, J. Jesch and C. D. Morris (eds), *The Viking Age in Caithness, Orkney and the North Atlantic* (Edinburgh, 1993), 260–71; E. James, 'The Continental Context', in S. Foster (ed.), *The St. Andrew's Sarcophagus: a Pictish Masterpiece and its International Connections* (Dublin, 1998), 240–50.

[97] George, *Epistola ad Hadrianum*, MGH Epp. IV, no. 3, at 27 [lines 6–7].

[98] There are several papal letters which forbid the consumption of horses as a pagan attribute. Pope Gregory II, writing to Boniface, forbade the custom in the newly Christianized regions of Germany and, in a reply to Pope Zacharias, Boniface remarked that the custom of eating horseflesh was a barrier to conversion; F. J. Simoons, *Eat not this Flesh: Food Avoidances from Prehistory to the Present* (2nd edn) (Madison, WI, 1994), 187–88.

[99] Wormald, 'Offa's Law Code', 34.

proper payment of tithe and the use of fair weights and measures as found in *capitulum* 17 of the Legates' Capitulary. Economic regularity is a common concern of Frankish legislation but is an issue not found in Anglo-Saxon sources prior to this reference.[100]

The Legates' Capitulary is the earliest English document to demand the payment of tithe and, as Levison noted, this 'may have been a reflection of the continental situation'.[101] One of Boniface's letters notes that Pippin had made it a universal duty to pay tithe.[102] Tithe was employed by Charlemagne as a method of ensuring lasting control over the newly conquered tribes of the Saxons and Avars; Alcuin wrote to various Frankish potentates voicing his concerns that excessive tithe payments would harm the nascent faith of these newly Christianized tribes.[103] Cathwulf in his letter to Charlemagne incorporated those who did not pay tithes amongst his list of evildoers which included pagans, sorcerers, slave-traders and adulterers.[104] In legislative terms, tithe was insisted upon in *capitulum* 17 of Charlemagne's first Saxon Capitulary where, 'in accordance with God's demands', a tenth part of acquired wealth was to be given to the Church and its priests.[105] Tithe was also the subject of the seventh and thirteenth items in the Herstal Capitulary of 779, which like the Legates' Capitulary also mentions the payment of ninths as well as tenth-part tithes. The use of fair weights and measures had been advocated by Pippin back in 744 at the Council of Soissons (*capitulum* 6) and in the council held in 751–55 (*capitulum* 5).[106] The reference to ecclesiastical tribute in *capitulum* 14 of the Legates' Capitulary in which the tribute levied on churches is to be no more than in 'Roman law and the ancient custom of aforegone emperors, kings and princes' is paralleled by *capitulum* 15 of Charlemagne's Herstal Capitulary where the king commanded that the longstanding arrangements for the levy of tithe were to be honoured.[107]

Another recurring theme in the Legates' Capitulary which is also commonly found in Frankish capitulary legislation are the references to canonical marriage. The Legates' Capitulary contains several references to the proper ordering of marriage in *capitula* 3 and 15, and the subject is implicit in the chapters on illegitimacy and the inheritance rights of the offspring of illegal

---

[100] See, for example, the Capitulary of Mantua, c. 9; MGH Capit. I, no. 90; Grierson, 'Chronologia delle riforme monetari', 66.

[101] Levison, *England and the Continent*, 106–7.

[102] *Die Briefe des heiligen Bonifatius und Lullus*, ed. M. Tangl, MGH, Epp. Sel., 1 (Berlin, 1916), no. 118, at 254.

[103] Alcuin, *Ep.* no. 110, MGH Epp. IV, (to Charlemagne); 111 (to Magenfrith); no. 107 (to Arn); no. 174 (to Charlemagne); *Alcuin of York*, trans. Allott, nos 56–57, 59 and 103 respectively.

[104] Cathwulf, *Epistola ad Carolum*, MGH Epp. IV, 504 [line 15].

[105] MGH Capit. I, no. 26, 68–70 [lines 26–28]. The first Saxon Capitulary is dated 785 by Ganshof and 782 (?) by King, *Charlemagne*, 205–8 and Mordeck, *BCRFM*, no. 26 at 1083.

[106] MGH Capit. I, no. 12, at 30 [lines 1–3] and no. 13, at 32 [lines 12–14]; Mordeck, *BCRFM*, nos. 12–13, at 1080.

[107] MGH Capit. I, no. 20, at 50 [lines 37–39].

marriages (*capitula* 12 and 16).[108] Again the Herstal Capitulary (*capitulum* 5) gives the bishop the right to punish those guilty of incest, just as the Legates' Capitulary ordered bishops in *capitulum* 3 to separate incestuous relationships. Illicit marriages are also condemned in *capitulum* 20 of the first Saxon Capitulary. Sanction against improper carnal union is also found in the legislation of Pippin's rule; the decrees produced at the Council of Soissons in 744 refers to illicit sexual union with nuns, and the first major decree of Pippin's reign as king starts *De incestis*. This council, which met at Compiègne in 757, produced a set of 21 decrees that were concerned almost entirely with the complexities of canonical marriage. Given the quantity of references in the Legates' Capitulary to the ramifications of illegitimacy, it is significant that the presence of George of Ostia was specifically recorded at the Council of Compiègne, some 30 years prior to the mission to Northumbria. His consent is recorded against three of the decrees promulgated there.[109]

The proceedings of a synod held at Ver in 755 shows perhaps the closest overall parallels in Pippin's legislation with the Legates' Capitulary.[110] Apart from the fact that it is one of the earliest Frankish conciliar documents to use the word *capitula* to divide its findings, it also refers to the need by bishops to correct the regular and secular clergy of his diocese (as *capitula* 3 and 4 in the Legates' Capitulary). *Capitulum* 4 of the Ver proceedings orders that two synods be held annually – one on the Kalends of March and another on the Kalends of October. This is another precept which is also included in the Legates' Capitulary and which stands out as being 'contrary to English usage'.[111]

Bishop George and kingship

The final aspect of the contents of the Legates' Capitulary which displays the author's familiarity with contemporary political thought and practice is perhaps the most significant. References to the anointing of kings appear twice in *capitulum* 12, once in a passage which likens the sin of regicide to the sin of Judas, and once with reference to the need to choose a king from legitimate stock, 'because, just as in our times following the canons it is not possible for a bastard to be a priest, nor is it possible for a man who is not born of a legitimate

---

108 On this subject see Wormald, 'Offa's Law Code', 38–39. On Frankish family ties and views on marriage more generally see E. James, *The Origins of France, from Clovis to the Capetians, 500–1000* (London, 1982), 78–81.

109 *Capitula* 14, 16 and 20. MGH Capit. I, no. 15, at 38 [lines 38, 45] and 39 [line 16]; Hartmann, *Die Synoden*, 76–79; Mordek, *BCRFM*, no. 15 at 1081.

110 Wormald, 'Offa's Law Code', 34 n. 21.

111 Wormald, 'Offa's Law Code', 33. The holding of two annual synods was, however, a condition of chapter 7 of the Canons of the Council of Hertford held in 672, although the same meeting decided *quia diversae causae impediunt*, to meet only once a year at Clofesho on 1 August; Bede, *HE* IV.5.

marriage to be the Lord's anointed (*christus Domini*) and king of the whole kingdom and heir to the fatherland'.[112] A Frankish context for the references to royal anointing in the Legates' Capitulary is uncontroversial but it can be shown that they are particularly appropriate to the circumstances of George's career. The innovative use of anointing in the ceremony which made Pippin king of the Franks in 751 symbolized divine approval and ecclesiastical sanction of the Carolingian coup over the Merovingian dynasty.[113] The dynastic prerogative of his two sons to rule after him was affirmed three years later when Pope Stephen II made an unprecedented journey to Francia seeking protection for Rome from the Lombard threat.[114] In a ceremony held at St Denis, probably on 24 July 754, Stephen anointed the young princes, Charlemagne and Carloman, and reaffirmed with his own hand the earlier anointing of Pippin and his wife by members of the Frankish episcopacy.[115] The *Liber Pontificalis* describes Stephen's journey to Francia and lists the people who accompanied the pontiff from Rome. George of Ostia is the first in the list. Thus the man who wrote the Legates' Capitulary was in Francia at this most critical moment in Carolingian history – the moment which not only cemented the right of Pippin's dynasty to rule Francia but also forged the symbiotic link between the Carolingians and the papacy on which so much of that right was founded. Indeed, it was this papal ceremony in 754, rather than the bloodless coup in 751, by which Einhard marked the demise of the Merovingians.[116] The presence of George at St Denis in 754 seems to have had a lasting effect on his career; he quickly became an important and respected figure in Frankish circles as demonstrated by his presence and prominent participation in the Council of Compiègne held three years later in 757.

It is clear that George formed a close working relationship with the man who he had helped to make king of the Franks. Five letters survive in the *Codex Carolinus* from Stephen II or his successor, Paul I, testifying to the several missions which George undertook as an official legate between the papal and

---

[112] George, *Epistola ad Hadrianum*; MGH *Epp.* IV, no. 3, at 24 [lines 1–3].

[113] J. L. Nelson, 'The Lord's Anointed and the People's Choice: Carolingian Royal Ritual', in D. Cannadine and S. Price (eds), *Rituals of Royalty: Power and Ceremonial in Traditional Societies* (Cambridge, 1987), 137–80, reprinted in her *The Frankish World* (London and Rio Grande, OH, 1996), 99–132.

[114] On this event see chapters 23–27 of the *Vita Stephani*; *Liber Pontificalis*, ed. Duchesne, 476–78; trans. Davis, *Lives of the Eighth-Century Popes,* 61–64. See also *Annales regni Francorum,* 754.

[115] The Frankish annalistic sources do not provide a date for the ceremony in which Pippin and his family were anointed. The *Liber Pontificalis* says that it occurred 'some days after' the Pope had travelled to St Denis when 'the season of winter was pressing'. This is contradicted by the account of the ceremony given in the text known as the *Clausula de unctione Pippini regis*, which is generally (but not uncontroversially) assumed to be a near-contemporary account written by a monk of St Denis. The date given by the *Clausula* is 28 July 754. The *Clausula* is edited in MGH SS XV.1, at 1; P. E. Dutton trans., *Carolingian Civilization: A Reader* (Peterborough, Ontario, 1993), 12. On the debate over the authenticity of this text see Noble, *The Republic of St. Peter,* 87; *Lives of the Eighth-Century Popes,* trans. Davis, 64, n. 64; Nelson, 'The Lord's Anointed', 151 n. 37; R. McKitterick, 'The Illusion of Royal Power in the Carolingian Annals', *EHR,* 115 (2000), 1–20.

[116] Einhard, *VK*, c. 1.

Frankish courts between 756 and 759.[117] To these pontiffs George was 'our most reverend and most holy brother and co-bishop'. By 761 George's affection for Francia led Pope Paul to give him permission to remain there,[118] although, after Paul's death in 767, this permission was temporarily withdrawn by Pope Constantine II, whose uncanonical election to papal office was nullified in August the following year.[119] As bishop of Ostia and primary among the suburbicarian bishops of Rome, George played an important role in the confirmation of a new pope.[120] The bishop of Ostia was traditionally the first of the consecrators of a new pontiff, and it seems that Constantine needed George in Rome in order to legitimize his election to papal office and to minimize the negative publicity surrounding his uncanonical promotion. George refused to obey Constantine's demands, a decision which seems to have prompted Pippin to grant him the bishopric of Amiens which thereafter he held concurrently with the benefice of Ostia.[121] This duality of office is reflected in the proceedings of a synod held in Rome in 769 at the start of the pontificate of Stephen III and which sanctioned the dismissal of Constantine (who had already been blinded) and reversed the decisions made by him and the ordinations authorized under his leadership. The *Liber Pontificalis* records how 12 Frankish bishops were sent to Rome – men who were 'learned in the divine scriptures and in the holy canons'.[122] George was one of those present at this council; he was recorded in the *Liber Pontificalis* as Bishop of Amiens but in the proceedings of the council as the Bishop of Ostia.[123] The precepts of this Roman council may lie behind the

---

117 *Codex Carolinus*, no. 8, at 494–98; no. 11, at 504–7; no. 16, at 513–14; no. 17, at 514–17; no. 18, at 518–19.

118 *Codex Carolinus*, no. 21, at 522–4 and 73, at 547–50.

119 J. N. D. Kelly, *The Oxford Dictionary of Popes* (Oxford, 1986), 93–94. There is no Life of Constantine in the *Liber Pontificalis* although his misdeeds are recorded in the Lives of Popes Paul I and Stephen III. A letter survives from him to Pippin III written in 767, after 31 August, in which he demands that George and the priests Peter and Marinus return to Rome; *Codex Carolinus*, no. 99 at 649–53. On this Peter see Bullough, '*Albuinus deliciosus Karoli regis*', 73, n. 3.

120 Noble, *The Republic of St. Peter*, 215.

121 Levison, *England and the Continent*, 128 and Bullough, '*Albuinus deliciosus Karoli regis*', 75, n. 9. An interesting new angle on the importance of the bishopric of Ostia has been revealed by the recent discovery of the Constantinian basilica to the south of the city. The fourth-century basilica, which, including the atrium, is some 80 metres in length, appears to have been continuously used until the late eighth/early ninth century. Preliminary archaeological evaluation of the site points to the gradual abandonment of the basilica in the later eighth century and its systematic spoliation in the early ninth, which the excavators have linked to the building of the new *burgos* by Pope Gregory IV (827–42), although we might wonder what effect the extended absence of Bishop George in Francia had on the status and use of the site in the later eighth century. See F. A. Bauer and M. Heinzelmann, 'The Constantinian Bishop's Church at Ostia: Preliminary Report on the 1998 Season', *Journal of Roman Archaeology*, 12 (1999), 342–53.

122 *Liber Pontificalis*, ed. Duchesne, 473.

123 Ibid. and MGH *Conc.* II.1, no. 14, at 74–92. This contradiction has led to some speculation that George did not attend the Roman synod at all or that he was the thirteenth bishop at the synod, especially since 13 bishops' names are recorded in the list interpolated into the French *Liber Pontificalis* manuscript. See *Liber Pontificalis*, ed. Duchesne, 482, n. 30; trans. Davis, *Lives of the*

'contradictory and puzzling' reference in *capitulum* 8 of the Legates' Capitulary, in which all the ancient privileges granted by the Roman see were to be respected except those which had been written *contra canonica instituta* with 'the assent of evil men'.[124] The identical expression is used in the *Liber Pontificalis'* account of the proceedings of the 769 Roman Council which condemned Constantine, a synopsis of which is included in the same manuscript which preserves George's letter to Hadrian.[125]

George was, therefore, a prominent and influential person in the Franco-papal diplomatic axis of Pippin's reign, and he maintained this role during Charlemagne's reign, although his career became increasingly weighted towards Francia. The *Liber Pontificalis* refers to George's status as an envoy of Charlemagne in a mission to Hadrian in 773, ostensibly to enquire whether the Lombard king, Desiderius, had 'restored the stolen cities and all St. Peter's rights'.[126] This mission was of the highest diplomatic importance, since the lack of cooperation by the Lombard king as reported by George and his fellow ambassadors to Charlemagne was a catalytic factor prompting the invasion of Lombard Italy the following year, which resulted in its annexation to the Frankish crown.[127] Lombard issues were the recurrent and persistent theme of George's missions between Rome and the Frankish kings; the Lombard threat to papal security had been the issue which had brought Stephen II to Francia in 754 which culminated in the ceremonial anointing of Pippin's family. It is a reflection of George's high status and obvious ability that the continued monitoring of the Lombard problem was largely entrusted to him.[128]

The Legates' Capitulary represents a Franco-papal response to the problems of later eighth-century Northumbria. George's Franco-papal career provides an entirely plausible context for introduction of such a sophisticated document into Northumbria in 786. The text is not simply an advanced reform programme, its format as a capitulary is also precocious. Ganshof's suggestion that the capitulary format owes much to Lombard practice fits neatly with George's 30-year career as a Franco-papal legate with a special interest in the affairs of Lombard Italy. That it was he who subsequently produced what is essentially an

---

Eighth-Century Popes, 96, n. 42–45. However, the proceedings of the council intermix the names of the Frankish and Italian delegates and do not specify how many bishops travelled from Francia.

[124] Cubitt, *Anglo-Saxon Church Councils*, 158. An alternative suggestion is provided by Brooks, *The Early History*, 178–79.

[125] Wormald, 'Offa's Law Code', 40; MGH *Conc.* II.1, no. 14, at 78 [lines 19–20].

[126] *Liber Pontificalis*, ed. Duchesne, 494. George was accompanied on this mission by Wulfhard, abbot of St Martin's at Tours and by a man named Albuinus. On the controversy surrounding the identification of the latter of these envoys see Bullough, '*Albuinus deliciosus Karoli regnis*', 73.

[127] *Annales regni Francorum*, 773–74.

[128] Ganshof noted that it was traditional practice for the *missi* of the pope and Frankish kings to concentrate their diplomatic activity within a tight sphere of influence; F. L. Ganshof, 'The Frankish Monarchy and its External Relations, from Pippin III to Louis the Pious', in his *The Carolingians and the Frankish Monarchy. Studies in Carolingian History*, trans. J. Sondheimer (London, 1971), 161–204 at 168.

early example of a Carolingian reform capitulary on his mission to Northumbria in 786 corroborates the notion that he was a key figure in the development of this characteristically Carolingian form of government.

The influence of the legates' mission

Our information about the Northumbrian and Mercian meetings is of unequal quality. Much of the Mercian aspect is assumed by inference from later events. Offa's decision to create a third metropolitan see and to have his son anointed the following year must also be seen in the context of Carolingian precedents and, given its Frankish components, of the legates' mission as well.[129] The Northumbrian aspect of the mission was undoubtedly influenced by Alcuin's years of experience at the archiepiscopal and royal courts in York, and it may be that we should attribute to the influence of the legates' mission the elaborate ecclesiastical ceremony which made Eardwulf king in York a decade later, in 796.[130] George's mission seems also to have had a major influence on Alcuin, and on his attitudes to the political network of his *patria* and to its ruling elite, both secular and ecclesiastical.

In procedural terms George effectively merged Carolingian, papal and Anglo-Saxon methods of producing a document which he hoped the Northumbrian and Mercian elite would honour. The Carolingian-style capitulary with its tradition of oral pronouncement was combined with the ritualized Anglo-Saxon procedures of synodal and charter records. The decrees were written down as a capitulary but were attested like a charter and presented in synodal diplomatic form. The result of this combined methodology was a defined ritual of confirmation, oral proclamation of the decrees followed by oral agreement, followed by a blessing of the decrees (a sign of the cross made with the hands over the parchment and perhaps at the head of the folio), followed by the attestation by signature with a cross. This procedure was used at the Northumbrian meeting and repeated at the Mercian one. The motive for combining both Carolingian and Anglo-Saxon methodology may have arisen for one of several reasons – out of habit of the author of the Capitulary, out of a need to make the document comprehensible to the secular portion of the Northumbrian and Mercian assembly, or perhaps for ensuring maximum authority in order to ensure that the decrees were upheld.

But how effective was this injection of Frankish ideology and practice into Anglo-Saxon political life? The references to the protected status of an anointed king have been regarded as a prelude to Offa's decision to force through the ritual hallowing of his son Ecgfrith at the Synod of Chelsea the following year. The concept also rubbed off in Northumbria; a decade later Eardwulf was

---

[129] See, further, Chapter 6, below, 177–80, 197.
[130] See Chapter 5, below, 157–60.

consecrated king in a ceremony at York which has all the hallmarks of a Carolingian-style inauguration ritual.[131] But, in Northumbria, the intervening decade between the legates' mission and Eardwulf's elevation to the throne witnessed the assassination of two kings, the exile of two more – one of whom was later murdered – and the slaughter of the ætheling sons of Ælfwald. Most telling, though, was the murder of Ælfwald himself in 788 at *Scythlesceaster* near the Roman wall at the hands of his own *patricius*, Sigha, who had witnessed the Legates' Capitulary beneath the name of his king. Sigha's own death five years later on 22 February 793 was also carefully recorded by the Northumbrian chroniclers, to which the author of the *York Annals* adds the unusual observation that he had died by his own hand.[132] Records of death by suicide are very rare in pre-Conquest sources.[133] Quite astonishing is the York annalist's subsequent note that some two months later, on 23 April, Sigha's body was taken to Lindisfarne and, it seems, accepted for burial. As a suicide and regicide, Sigha died a sinner twice over and, furthermore, died in full knowledge of the severity of his sin, having signed the Legates' Capitulary which contained pronoucements on the sanctity and inviolability of kingship, and which had been read out to him and to his assembled companions in the vernacular to ensure total comprehension. Sigha's suicide and the transportation of his body to Lindisfarne in that portentous year implies that the community of St Cuthbert was deeply involved in the secular political intrigues of the day – an involvement which was to merit divine punishment in the form of the infamous Viking attack barely six weeks later on 8 June. In Alcuin's telling words to Bishop Higbald, the Viking raid, 'has not happened by chance, but is the sign of some great sin'.[134]

---

[131] See Chapter 5, below, 157–60.

[132] *Historia regum* (*York Annals*), 793; *ASChron*. DE, 793.

[133] A. Murray, *Suicide in the Middle Ages*, Vol. 1: *The Violent Against Themselves* (Oxford, 1998), 363, 431.

[134] Alcuin, *Ep.* no. 29, MGH, Epp. IV; *Alcuin of York*, trans. Allott, no. 26.

Chapter 4

Chronicled Connections: Frankish Annals and the *Historia regum*

Letters and chronicles: sharing news

Alcuin and his collected writings are a rich source of evidence about contacts between England and Francia at the end of the eighth century. His presence at the Frankish court before 796 and at Tours until his death in 804, facilitated the transit of people and information between England and the Continent, and his contemporary reputation as one of the foremost scholars of the Carolingian *renovatio* provided a motive for the preservation of that information during his lifetime and after his death.[1] Alcuin's scholarly letters of advice and friendship (though often preserved as monuments to epistolary style) told his correspondents about, or enquired after, events in countries far from his own place of residence. As such, his letters often reveal important information about the transmission of newsworthy events in later eighth-century Europe – events which were current affairs to Alcuin and his correspondents but were potentially the stuff of historical record to other readers. His correspondence is full of such historical details, and the flow of information was certainly two-way. In a letter to Colcu, an Irish scholar from Clonmacnoise and visitor to Northumbria, Alcuin tells 'of recent doings in the world' and brings his friend up-to-date on news of the conversion of the Frisians and Saxons, of a Byzantine campaign and the Avar raids against the Franks' allies in Italy, and of Charlemagne's military campaigns in Spain against the Saracens and against the Slavic tribe of the Wends.[2] Details of the Viking raid on Lindisfarne in June 793 quickly reached Alcuin in Francia; in shocked response, his letters to the Northumbrian monastic communities urged spiritual stoicism and self-reflection as well as the practical reassurance that Alcuin would ask Charlemagne to help recover the brothers taken into captivity by the Norsemen.[3] His letters concerning the raid mention a visit to Francia from the Anglo-Saxon, Hwita (Candidus), who told Alcuin of the dreadful events in Northumbria and, in return, carried his letters and his news from Francia back across the Channel.[4] The raid on Lindisfarne is a particularly

---

[1] W. Levison, *England and the Continent in the Eighth Century* (Oxford, 1946), 169.

[2] Alcuin, *Ep.* no. 7; *Alcuin of York c. A.D. 732 to 804: His Life and Letters*, trans. S. Allott (York, 1974), no. 31 and *EHD* 1, trans. Whitelock, no. 192. Colcu's death is recorded in the *Historia regum* (*York Annals*), 794.

[3] Alcuin, *Ep.* no. 20; *Alcuin of York*, trans. Allott, no. 26.

[4] Alcuin, *Ep.* nos 20, 22, 24; *Alcuin of York*, trans. Allott, nos 26, 28, 30.

prominent example of a newsworthy event of Europe-wide significance, details of which can be shown to have travelled far and quickly.

It was through just such epistolary mechanisms, and in the memories of the travellers themselves, that raw data concerning distant lands was exchanged and made available for insertion into contemporary chronicles. Through the very fact of recording events in a far-off land, these self-consciously historicizing records of annual events captured evidence of indirect contact with those distant places. The blunt reference in the *Anglo-Saxon Chronicle s.a.* 779 to a battle between the Franks and the 'Old' Saxons is a lone eighth-century example of a note about Frankish events in that particular Old English source.[5] Its placement there might reasonably be regarded as further evidence of interest by an Anglo-Saxon audience in the fate of the Continental Saxons; the prefix *Eald* is a comparative term employed by the Saxon inhabitants of Britain (rather than the Franks) to distinguish themselves from their Continental cousins. It is a term (taken ultimately from Bede) which is found elsewhere in Alcuin's letters and in other early chronicles, notably in the *Historia regum* (*York Annals*) for 767 when Aluberht was sent to York for consecration as bishop of the *Ealdsaxones*.[6] By contrast, from the other side of the Channel, Einhard classified Alcuin as a man 'from Britain, of Saxon stock' (*de Britannia Saxonici generis*).[7]

Frankish material is sparse in the *Anglo-Saxon Chronicle* before the mid-ninth century when Viking raids in the Channel and marriage links between the West Saxon and West Frankish dynasties provided a local political imperative for recording Frankish events.[8] But the low density of recorded information concerning eighth-century Frankish affairs in the *Anglo-Saxon Chronicle* contrasts with the contents of Latin chronicles which originated north of the Humber. One of the most important, though least understood, is the *Continuatio Bedae* which (as its name suggests) continues the chronological recapitulation concluding Bede's *Historia Ecclesiastica* as far as the year 766.[9] Although relatively

---

[5] *ASChron.* 779 (for 782); see also the revised version of the *Annales regni Francorum*, 782. The next vernacular reference to Francia in the *Chronicle* is to the death of Charlemagne; *ASChron.* 812 (for 814). For the later interpolation of Latin annals relating to Francia in manuscripts of the *Anglo-Saxon Chronicle*, see note 21 below.

[6] *Historia regum* (*York Annals*), 767; Bede, *HE* V.9–11, using the Latin equivalent, *Antiqui Saxones*, for the pagans who were targeted by the Anglo-Saxon missionaries; *Venerabilis Baedae Opera Historica*, ed. C. Plummer (Oxford, 1896), 286; Levison, *England and the Continent*, 92. See also Asser's *Vita Alfredi*, c. 94 with reference to John, abbot of Athelney, *Eald-Saxonum genere*; *Asser's Life of King Alfred, with the Annals of St. Neots Erroneously Attributed to Asser* ed. W. H. Stevenson (Oxford, 1904), 81; *Alfred the Great: Asser's Life of King Alfred and other Contemporary Sources*, trans. S. Keynes and M. Lapidge (Harmondsworth, 1983), 103–5, 260, n. 169.

[7] Einhard, *VK*, c. 25; M. Springer, 'Geschichtsbilder Urteile und Vorurteile', in C. Stiegemann and M. Wemhoff (eds), *799 Kunst und Kultur der Karolingerzeit. Karl der Große und Papst Leo III in Paderborn*, 3 vols (Mainz, 1999), Vol. 3, 224–32.

[8] See Chapter 7, below, 224–43.

[9] *Venerabilis Baedae Opera Historica*, ed. Plummer, 361; *Bede's Ecclesiastical History of the English People*, ed. and trans. B. Colgrave and R. A. B. Plummer (Oxford, 1969), lxvii–lxix, 573–77.

little is known about the compilation and transmission of this chronicle – it is found only in a group of late manuscripts with a north Rhenish provenance – it has at its core the same stock of information as the so-called *York Annals* which are preserved in the *Historia regum* and, like them, includes some Frankish data. Though complicated by the late, continental origin of the manuscripts, it is possible that the Frankish elements in the *Continuatio* are of contemporary Anglo-Saxon compilation rather than wholesale interpolations inserted after its prototype arrived on the Continent. The *Continuatio* contains an entry recording the martyrdom of St Boniface in Frisia in 754, adding a local clause to the effect that 'Hrethgar was consecrated archbishop in his place by Pope Stephen'.[10] News of Boniface's murder certainly reached England quickly; a letter survives addressed to Boniface's successor at Mainz, from Archbishop Cuthbert of Canterbury in which he congratulated Lul on the blessed nature of Boniface's death at the hands of pagans and tells him of a recent synodal decision to institute an annual commemoration of the holy martyrdom.[11] The *Continuatio Bedae* also records the death of Charles Martel in 741 and the accession of his sons Carloman and Pippin. Erroneously though, the *Continuatio* refers to Martel as *rex Francorum*, a title he never attained. This could be an error due to the late dates of the surviving manuscripts, when confusion with royal successors of the same name would have been an easy error to make. It is notable that Alcuin also conflated notions of kingship with Charles' correct status as *dux*; in his *Life of Willibrord* Alcuin says that Charles 'received the sceptre of the kingdom' on his father's death, and refers to Charles' father, Pippin II, as 'king of the Franks'.[12]

The York Annals

Related to the *Continuatio Bedae* are the *York Annals*, so named by Hunter-Blair by virtue of their focus on that city and its environs.[13] This set of annals covers

---

[10] *Continuatio Bedae*, 754; *Historia regum* (*York Annals*), 754. Hrethgar is known more commonly as Chrodegang (of Metz); see R. McKitterick, *The Frankish Kingdoms under the Carolingians, 751–987* (London, 1983), 56–57.

[11] Cuthbert, *Epistola ad Lullum*; Haddan and Stubbs (eds), *Councils* III, 390–94; *Die Briefe des helligen S. Bonifatius und Lulius*, ed. M. Tangl, MGH Epp. Sel. I (Berlin, 1916), no. 111; C. Cubitt, *Anglo-Saxon Church Councils, c. 650–c. 850* (London, 1995), 267–68.

[12] Cf. Pauli who argued that this error meant that the *Continuatio* cannot have been compiled earlier than the tenth century; R. Pauli, 'Karl de Große in northumbrischen Annalen', *Forschungen zur deutschen Geschichte*, 12 (1872), 137–66, at 157. Alcuin, *Vita Willibrordi*, ed. W. Levison, MGH Ser. rer Merov. VII, no. 5, c. 13, at 115 and 127; I. N. Wood, *The Merovingian Kingdoms, 450–751* (London, 1994), 319–20. See also the *Annales Cambriae*, 714 recording the death of Pippin II; *Annales Cambriae*, ed. J. Williams, RS, 20 (London, 1860), 9.

[13] The nomenclature of this set of annals varies confusingly between commentators. The term *York Annals* will be used here to refer to the annals as they currently exist within the *Historia regum*, and not as a label for the hypothetical eighth-century chronicle which lies as the root of our extant text and which is, indeed, presumed to be behind several other northern sources for the eighth century; D. W. Rollason, *Sources for York History to AD 1100* (York, 1998), 17–18. P. Hunter-Blair, 'Some Observations on the "Historia regum" attributed to Symeon of Durham', in

the years 732–802 and is now embedded within the twelfth-century historical compilation known as the *Historia regum* and commonly attributed to Symeon of Durham, a text which provides the framework for the history of Northumbria from the 730s up to the Norman period.[14] Significantly for our purposes, these *York Annals* also contain 14 entries which relate directly to contemporary affairs on the Continent.[15] Viewed collectively, these entries constitute an important, largely independent set of annals for Frankish history, and shed further light on the contacts which existed between Northumbria and Francia in the eighth century.[16]

Some of these annals form the only element in the entry for a particular year, whereas in other years the Frankish information is incorporated within a longer annal relating to Anglo-Saxon issues. These eighth-century Frankish entries in the *York Annals* fall into two basic types – those which are concerned with continental events (Frankish or papal) and those which are of mutual relevance for the history of Anglo-Saxon and Frankish history. The martyrdom in 754 of St Boniface and 53 companions at the hands of Frisian pagans is recorded here, as is the ordination in York in 767 of Aluberht as bishop of the Old Saxons. Notice of the Franco-papal mission to England is recorded under the entry for the year 786, and the annal for 792 records a not dissimilar gathering in Northumbria to discuss Alcuin's response to a book sent by Charlemagne concerning the controversy in the Eastern Church over iconoclasm.[17] News of purely Frankish events is recorded in a further six annals, five of which fall within an eight-year span from 768 to 775. The death of Pippin III is noted in 768 as is the death of his son Carloman in 771 and the consequent accession

---

N. K. Chadwick (ed.), *Celt and Saxon: Studies in the Early British Border* (Cambridge, 1963), 63–118, 98–99; M. Lapidge, 'Byrhtferth of Ramsey and the Early Sections of the *Historia regum* attributed to Symeon of Durham', *ASE*, 10 (1982), 97–122, at 115–16, reprinted in Lapidge, *Anglo-Latin Literature. Vol. 2: 900–1066* (London, 1993), 317–42; *idem*, 'Latin Learning in Ninth-century England', in *Anglo-Latin Literature. Vol.1: 600–899* (London, 1996), 409–54, at 429–30; D. N. Dumville, 'Textual Archaeology and Northumbrian History Subsequent to Bede', in D. M. Metcalf (ed.), *Coinage in Ninth-century Northumbria*, BAR Bri. Ser. 180 (Oxford, 1987), 43–55 at 49. The *York Annals* are translated by Whitelock, *EHD* 1, 113.

[14] *Symeonis Dunelmensis Opera et Collectanea*, ed. H. Hinde, Surtees Society 51 (London, 1868), 1–131; *Symeonis Monachis Opera Omnia*, ed. T. Arnold, RS 75.ii (London, 1885), 3–283, at 30–66; Hunter-Blair, 'Some Observations'. Lapidge classifies the *York Annals* as Part III.1–29 of the version of the *Historia regum* which was known to Byrhtferth of Ramsey in the late tenth century; a new edition of the work as known to Byrhtferth is in preparation by M. Lapidge.

[15] *Annales Northumbranei*, MGH SS XIII, 154–56; Hunter-Blair, 'Some Observations', 92–94, 98–99; Lapidge, 'Byrhtferth of Ramsey', 115; Rollason, *Sources for York History*, 17–18 (S.37), 27 (S.59).

[16] Pauli, 'Karl de Große', 137–66; H. Löwe, 'Eine Kölner Notiz zur Kaisertum Karl der Große', *Rheinische Vierteljahrsblätter*, 14 (1949), 7–34; P. E. Schramm, *Kaiser, Könige und Papst*, 4 vols (Stuttgart, 1968), Vol. 1, 257–59, 263; Hunter-Blair, 'Some Observations', 92–94.

[17] The 786 annal was not regarded as part of the series of Frankish annals by Hunter-Blair although it has a clear Frankish context (see Chapter 3, 55–92); *Symeonis Monachis Opera Omnia*, ed. Arnold, 2, 51, 53–54.

of Charlemagne 'to the whole kingdom of the Franks'. There are annals concerning Charlemagne's military campaigns: against the Saxons in 772 and 775; against the Lombards in Italy in 774; and a further annal under the year 795 recording Charlemagne's destruction of the Avars and the capture of their fabulous treasure hoard. The *York Annals* also tell in great detail of Charlemagne's imperial coronation in 800. Of papal events, we hear of the death of Pope Hadrian in 794 (for 795) and of Charlemagne's commission of a marble epitaph to the memory of his friend, as well as details of the attempted assassination of Pope Leo III in 799. But this last story is of a different style from those which had preceded it and, like the story recorded in the annal for 802 concerning the flight of Eadburh, the West Saxon queen, to Francia, it seems (as we shall see) to have been a rather later addition to the corpus of Frankish-related material in the *York Annals*.[18]

All the Frankish events recorded in the *York Annals* are known about and corroborated by other sources produced in Francia and in Rome.[19] However, the *York Annals* often add colour and detail which is unparalleled elsewhere, and they are remarkable for the persistence of their interest in the Carolingian dynasty and its successes under Charlemagne. The level of detail and accuracy in these annals means that (excluding the entries for 799, 802 and possibly 800, discussed below) they are unlikely to be derivatives of a Frankish chronicle and can be considered primary sources of information about eighth-century Francia.[20] What is more, these Frankish annals seem to have been incorporated into this Latin chronicle at a very early stage in its production in the late eighth or early ninth century, relatively soon after the dates of the events recorded. This near-contemporaneous inclusion of Frankish material sets the *York Annals* apart from other Anglo-Saxon historical sources such as the *Annals of St. Neots* or Version E of the *Anglo-Saxon Chronicle* both of which contain retrospective interpolations of Latin entries from the Rouen recension of the so-called *Norman Annals*.[21] As such, the Frankish entries in the *York Annals* are a major addition to the corpus of evidence concerning the nature and extent of Frankish contacts with

---

[18] Hunter-Blair, 'Some Observations', 100.

[19] Pauli, 'Karl der Große', 160 where he expresses the opinion that the closest Frankish source to the *Historia regum* here is the *Annales regni Francorum*; see also Schramm, *Kaiser, König und Papst*, 257.

[20] Hunter-Blair, 'Some Observations', 93; Pauli, 'Karl der Große', 160; C. R. Hart, 'Byrhtferth's Northumbrian Chronicle', *EHR*, 97 (1982), 558–82, at 562. A similar claim is made for the preservation within this section of the *Historia regum* of a fragmentary Pictish chronicle by K. Forsyth, 'Evidence for a Lost Pictish Source in the *Historia regum Anglorum* of Symeon of Durham', in S. Taylor (ed.), *Kings, Clerics and Chronicles in Scotland, 500–1297* (Dublin, 2000), 19–34.

[21] Stevenson, *Asser*, 101, 103 n.1, 112 n. 5; *The Annals of St. Neots with Vita Prima Sancti Neoti*, ed. D. Dumville and M. Lapidge, The Anglo-Saxon Chronicle, a collaborative edition, 17 (Cambridge, 1985), xliii–xlvii; *Two of the Saxon Chronicles Parallel*, 2 vols, ed. J. Earle and C. Plummer (Oxford, 1889–92), xl, xlv–xlvii; D. N. Dumville, 'Annalistic Writing at Canterbury', *Peritia*, 2 (1983), 23–57, at 32–34, 55–57.

Anglo-Saxon England during the reign of Charlemagne, since their presence there argues for the existence of contemporaneous channels of communication.

The record of the death, in 771, of Charlemagne's brother, Carloman, is a case in point. He had ruled half of the kingdom alongside his brother since their father's death three years earlier. Although the scribe of the *Historia regum* manuscript glosses his name with the epithet *famosissimus*, Carloman's name and memory was quickly eclipsed by his brother's achievements on the battle-field in Italy and against the Saxons.[22] Notice of Carloman's death is, thus, scarce outside the central corpus of Frankish annals and, when found in a late manuscript, is a sign that the scribe had before him a text which had made use of a good, near contemporary source. Even the *Royal Frankish Annals* are cursory in their account of Carloman in the period of joint rule, choosing always to emphasize deeds of 'the lord king Charles' over those of Carloman who is accorded the title of king only in the entry for his death. Contemporary Frankish sources strongly imply that there was no love lost between the two brothers; to one commentator Carloman's demise was 'not the least sign of blessedness' in Charlemagne's career.[23] At Carloman's sudden and premature death, Charle-magne moved fast to claim his brother's half of the kingdom and to exclude his nephews from the succession. The 'York annalist' correctly notes the suddenness (*subita*) of Carloman's death and, closely echoing the words of the *Earlier Metz Annals*, says that Charlemagne 'obtained sole-rule over all the kingdom'.[24] The death of Carloman is recorded in one other contemporary Anglo-Saxon source, in a letter written early in 775 from within Francia by the Anglo-Saxon scholar Cathwulf to Charlemagne in the immediate aftermath of the Lombard cam-paign.[25] Charlemagne's actions on Carloman's death, and the swift switch of

---

[22] *Famosissimus* is an interlinear gloss added by the hand of the main scribe of Cambridge, CCC MS 139; see Hunter-Blair, 'Some Observations', 97. On glosses in CCCC MS 139 see D. N. Dumville, 'The Corpus Christi "Nennius"', *Bulletin of the Board of Celtic Studies*, 25 (1972–74), 369–79; and Hart, 'Byrhtferth's Northumbrian Chronicle', 579–82.

[23] Cathwulf, *Epistola ad Carolum*, ed. E. Dümmler, MGH Epp. IV, *Epistolae Variorum*, no. 7, 502–5, at 502.

[24] '... et unxerunt super se dominum suum Carolum gloriosissimum regem et obtinuit feliciter monarchiam totius regni Francorum'; *Annales Mettenses Priores*, 771, MGH Ser. rer. Germ. VII.10, 57–58; *Charlemagne, Translated Texts*, trans. King (Kendal, 1987), 150. The early twelfth-century copy of this text, Durham, DCL MS C.IV.15, was certainly in Durham by the second half of the twelfth century (although its place of origin is obscure); A. J. Piper, 'The Historical Interests of the Monks of Durham', in D. Rollason (ed.), *Symeon of Durham, Historian of Durham and the North* (Stamford, 1998), 301–32, 311–12, 328.

[25] On Cathwulf, see H. H. Anton, *Fürstenspiegel und Herrscherethos in der Karolingerzeit*, Bonner historische Forschungen, 32 (Bonn, 1968), 75–79; M. Garrison, 'Letters to a King and Biblical Exempla: The examples of Cathwulf and Clemens Peregrinus', *EME*, 7 (1998), 305–28; J. E. Story, 'Cathwulf, Kingship, and the Royal Abbey of St-Denis', *Speculum*, 74 (1999), 1–20. His death is also recorded in a set of chronicle-style notes compiled in *c.* 1125 by Symeon of Durham. It is just possible that the *Annales Mettenses Priores* (Durham, DCL C.IV.15) were the source here since this chronicle focuses elsewhere on the early history of the Carolingian dynasty; see *idem*, 'Symeon as Annalist', in Rollason, *Symeon of Durham*, 202–13.

allegiance by his brother's aides, had forced Carloman's wife and sons to flee for protection to the court of the Lombard king Desiderius. This move provided Charlemagne with a further pretext to invade northern Italy and, ultimately, to annex the Lombard kingdom entirely. Cathwulf saw a direct causal link between Carloman's death and the aggrandizement of Charlemagne's status in his brother's territory and in Italy; as a result Charlemagne had been 'exalted in honour to the glory of the kingdom of Europe'. The 'York annalist' likewise recorded the conquest of Italy by Charlemagne, *Francorum rex invictissimus*.[26] To the annalist, the Lombard capital was 'the most noble city' (*nobilissimam urbem*); to Cathwulf it was 'most opulent' (*opulentissimam civitatem*). The fall of Pavia after a long siege is recorded by the annalist as is the capture of its king, Desiderius, and with him the whole kingdom of Italy. Though brief, the note in the *York Annals* is accurate and accords with Frankish records of the event; its closest equivalent is the revised version of the *Royal Frankish Annals* which, like the *York Annals*, gives Pavia its Roman name, *Ticinia*. News of this most glorious of Charlemagne's military achievements to date had evidently reached Cathwulf and, it seems, other Anglo-Saxon ears as well.

The *York Annals* diverge from Cathwulf's discreet political agenda with its knowledge of, and interest in, the Saxon war waged by Charlemagne's armies alongside his Lombard campaign. Once more, the *York Annals* are detailed and have the air of authority. However, in its two references to the opening campaigns of the Saxon war (*s.a.* 772, 775) no mention is made of Frankish objectives to convert the Saxons to Christianity, a sequel to Frankish lordship. This is surprising given Anglo-Saxon interest in the Christianization of the Saxons, exemplified in Northumbria by Alhred's and Osgifu's closely contemporary letter to Lul, dated May 773, as well as their sponsorship of Willehad's mission and Aluberht's consecration earlier in Alhred's reign.[27] This observation is the more pronounced when the Frankish sources which describe the prolonged Saxon campaign are consulted. The various Frankish annals for 772 all stress the destruction of the important pagan sanctuary known as the Irminsul.[28] By contrast, the *York Annals* give a rather negative account of the campaign for that year stating that, 'having collected together a strong force and the warlike men of his realm', Charlemagne had to 'return to his own lands, having lost many of his leaders and noblemen'.[29] The only Carolingian references to the loss of any

---

[26] For the use of superlatives in the *Historia regum* see Lapidge, 'Byrhtferth of Ramsey', 102. But see also Nelson's comments about contemporary use of superlatives to describe Carolingians; J. L. Nelson, 'Fulk's Letter to Alfred Revisited', in J. Roberts, J. Nelson, M. Godden (eds), *Alfred the Wise* (Rochester, NY, 1997), 137, n. 8.

[27] *Bonifatius und Lullus*, ed. Tangl, no. 121; *EHD* 1, trans. Whitelock, no. 187.

[28] *Annales regni Francorum*, 772; *Annales Mosellanni*, 772; *Annales Laureshamenses*, 772. On the campaign against the Saxons see Stiegemann and Wemhoff (eds), *799 Kunst und Kultur*, Vol. 1, 264–311.

[29] '... multisque ex principibus ac nobilibus viris suis', *Historia regum* (*York Annals*), 772; J. L. Nelson, *The Frankish World* (London and Rio Grande, 1996), xxix.

Frankish noblemen while fighting the Saxons are to be found in Einhard's *Vita Karoli* as a general comment on the whole Saxon war, and in the revised version of the *Royal Frankish Annals* for 782.[30] The latter account tells of a premature attack on the Saxon camp by a headstrong and undisciplined unit of the Frankish cavalry who were unprepared for the marshalled ranks of the Saxons. The ensuing slaughter of two Frankish legates, four counts, as well as 20 other 'men of distinction' and their bodyguards, culminated in the judicial execution at Verden of 4500 Saxons at Charlemagne's command when their leaders refused (or were unable) to hand over the ringleader of the initial rebellion.

It is possible that that the compiler of the Frankish material in the *York Annals* retrospectively conflated news of several seasons' campaigning against the Saxons or, alternatively, may have dated the 782 setback a decade too soon. But this scenario is unlikely for several reasons, not least since the chronology of the *Royal Frankish Annals* makes it quite clear that Charlemagne marched immediately into Saxony on receiving the news of the death of his warriors in order to exercise the fearsome revenge of a warlord whose authority had been so seriously challenged. The *York Annals*, on the other hand, tell us of Charlemagne in retreat to his own lands (*in sua se recepit*). The correctly dated detail offered in accompanying *York Annals* concerned with the Saxon war also makes conflation improbable. The annal for 775 tells of the capture by the Franks of two cities (*urbes*), Syburg and Eresburg, as well as the reconquest of the whole *provincia Bohweri* which had previously been under Frankish control. The capture and refortification of these Saxon strongholds is well attested in the major sets of Frankish annals in which Syburg and Eresburg are referred to as *castra*. The *Bohweri* of the Anglo-Saxon annal are the *Bucki* of the Frankish annals whose powerbase was centred on the *oppidum* at Bückeburg some 50 miles to the north of Eresburg on the River Weser.[31] In the Frankish corpus of annals Charlemagne is here described as 'most gentle' (*mitissimus*), 'pious and illustrious' (*pius et praeclarus*); the *York Annals* label him *bellicosissimus rex Francorum*, 'the most war-like king of the Franks'. The entry for 775 is a dramatic, bloodthirsty account of the campaign which describes the Carolingian king in classicizing prose, 'raging with fire and sword, because he was furious in spirit'.[32] This description of Charlemagne's uncontrolled fury is unlike any Frankish version of the event although the formulaic 'fire and sword' element does appear in the 772 description in the revised version of the *Royal Frankish Annals*.[33] Nevertheless, the description of Charlemagne's hot temper is corroborated by

---

[30] *Annales regni Francorum* (revised version), 782; *Charlemagne*, trans. King, 116–17; Einhard, *VK*, c. 8.

[31] *Annales regni Francorum* (revised version), 775; *Annales Mosellanii*, 775.

[32] *igne ferroque debacchans, quia erat consternatus animo*; *Historia regum* (*York Annals*), 775.

[33] A. Lampen, 'Sachsenkriege, sächsischer Widerstand und Kooperation', in Stiegemann and Wemhoff (eds), *779 Kunst und Kultur*, Vol. 1, 264–72; W. Best, R. Gensen, P. R. Hömberg, 'Burgenbau in einer Grenzregion', in ibid., Vol. 3, 328–45.

other contemporary Frankish accounts and so is entirely plausible in this context.[34]

The description of the outcome of the war against the Avars in the *York Annals s.a.* 795 is one of only two entries dedicated entirely to a single continental event, the other being the martyrdom of St Boniface in 754. The annal tells in unusual detail of the extraordinary treasure taken by the Carolingian army, 'after having driven away the chief of the Avars and overcoming their army':

... sublatis inde xv plaustris auro argentoque paliisque olosericis preciosis repletis, quorum quodque quatuor trahebant boves. ...[35]	... [he] carried away from there fifteen wagons laden with gold and silver and precious robes of silk, each one drawn by four oxen. ...

No equivalent Frankish source defines so precisely the quantity of treasure taken from the Avar Ring, although many refer to its quality. The account rings true with the sources which describe the campaign and the subsequent distribution of the treasure.[36] The closest contemporary source is the *Lorsch Annals* which tell of 'a great abundance of treasure' but it is only Einhard, writing in the 820s, who used the words *auri et argenti* to describe the contents of the hoard, although its great wealth is implicit in other accounts of its subsequent distribution among Charlemagne's *fideles*.[37] News of the victory and of the wealth of plunder certainly reached Anglo-Saxon England; the 'York annalist' also noted that Charlemagne distributed treasure from the 'God-given victory' among the poor and the 'churches of Christ'.[38] In a close echo of this account, a famous letter from Charlemagne to Offa refers to the Avar sword, baldric, and two silken robes (*duo pallia serica*) which he was sending to him in Mercia, and of equivalent gifts to Æthelred in Northumbria, as well as to the metropolitan sees of England (Canterbury, York and presumably Lichfield too). Alcuin's subsequent letter to Offa, written a few months later in early summer 796, tells of Charlemagne's rage at hearing of the recent assassination of Æthelred and of his threat to withdraw his 'generous gifts' from the Avar treasure which he had sent to Northumbria.[39] Given these references in letters recording the distribution of

---

[34] *Annales regni Francorum*, 783, 795, 796.

[35] *Historia regum* (*York Annals*), 795.

[36] J. Déer, 'Das Untergang des Awarenreiches', in W. Braunfels (ed.), *Karl der Große. Lebenswerk und Nachleben* (Düsseldorf, 1965–68), Vol. 1, 719–91; T. Reuter, 'Plunder and Tribute in the Carolingian Empire', *TRHS*, 5th ser. 35 (1985), 75–94.

[37] Einhard, *VK*, c. 13; *Annales Laureshamenses*, 795; *Charlemagne*, trans. King, 141–42. On the Avar campaign see also Charlemagne's letter to Fastrada, MGH Epp. IV, *Epistolae Variorum*, no. 20, 528–29; H. R. Loyn and J. Percival (trans.), *The Reign of Charlemagne: Documents of Carolingian Government and Administration* (London, 1975), no. 40, 134–35.

[38] *Historia regum* (*York Annals*), 795.

[39] Alcuin, *Ep.* no. 101; *Alcuin of York*, trans. Allott, no. 41 and *EHD* 1, trans. Whitelock, no. 197. Alcuin's letter must have been written between the death of Æthelred of Northumbria on 18 April and Offa's death on 29 July; *Historia regum* (*York Annals*), 796.

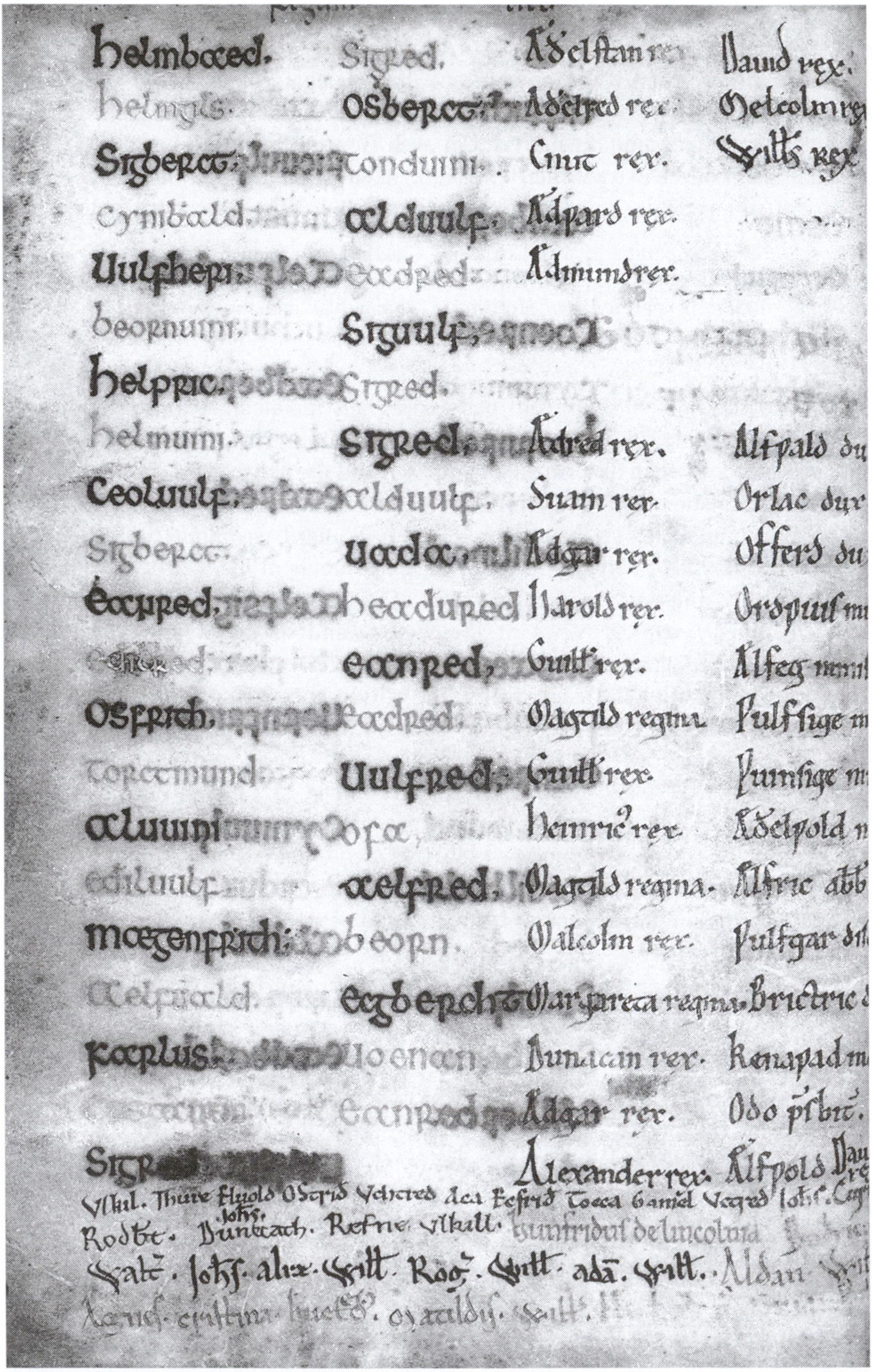

Fig. 4.1　London, British Library, Cotton MS Domitian A. vii, fo. 15v

items from the Avar treasure hoard to the kingdoms of England it is perhaps not surprising that such a detailed account of the collection of the treasure should have found its way for inclusion into an eighth-century Northumbrian chronicle. And in a society obeying the etiquette of gift exchange, the context of these gifts and their implicit political significance as a symbol of Charlemagne's largesse and growing authority would not have been missed by the recipients.

An echo of these exotic gifts lies behind the entries in another important source, the Northumbrian *Liber Vitae*. This manuscript, long associated with St Cuthbert's community at Durham, records lists of benefactors to a major but as yet unidentified ninth-century Northumbrian church.[40] The first column on fo. 15v includes two Frankish names, *Mægenfrith* and *Karlus* within the list of *Reges et Duces* for whom prayers were to be said by the community (see Figure 4.1). The roughly chronological listing of names makes it highly probable that *Karlus* refers to Charlemagne himself. This being so, the first name is very likely to refer to Alcuin's *carissimus amicus*, Mægenfrith, who was one of Charlemagne's military commanders and, significantly in this context, his treasurer.[41] Mægenfrith was certainly active in the war against the Avars, being on campaign along the Danube with Charlemagne in 791 when the revised version of the *Royal Frankish Annals* refers to him as Charlemagne's *camerarius*, or chamberlain. Given this military experience against the Avars, and his role as Charlemagne's treasurer, he is likely to have been the official responsible for the distribution of the treasure hoard gathered from the Avars after their defeat in 795. Alcuin wrote to him in 796 reminding him, as the *regalis palatii arcarius*, to be lenient in demanding tithe from newly conquered converts.[42] The *De ordine palatii* written in 882 by Hincmar of Rheims, though based on a treatise by Charlemagne's courtier Adalhard of Corbie, lists the distribution of gifts to foreign legations as one of the duties of the *camerarius*.[43] Thus, the distribution

---

[40] London, BL MS Cotton Domitian A.vii. See Chapter 8 below, 220. These names are numbers 79 and 77 respectively according to the numeration in the most recent edition; J. Gerchow, *Die Gedenküberlieferung der Angelsachsen* (Berlin and New York, 1988), 304–20. The book is normally ascribed either to Lindisfarne or to Wearmouth-Jarrow. The latest datable names written by the original scribe date the manuscript to *c.* 840. On this important manuscript (and the debate over its provenance) see also *Liber Vitae Ecclesiae Dunelmensis*, ed. J. Stevenson, Surtees Soc. 13 (London, 1841) and the facsimile of the text by A. H. Thompson, Surtees Soc. 136 (London, 1923); A. G. Watson, *Catalogue of Dated and Datable Manuscripts c.700–1600 in the Department of Manuscripts in the British Library* (London, 1979), Vol. 1, 101, no. 527; L. Webster and J. Backhouse, *The Making of England: Anglo-Saxon Art and Culture, AD 600–900* (1991), no. 97. On the importance of the spelling of the Pictish names in this manuscript and in the *York Annals*, see Forsyth, 'Evidence for a Lost Pictish Source', 25–28.

[41] For Alcuin's grief on hearing of Mægenfrith's death in Benevento in 801 see Alcuin, *Ep.* no. 211; *Alcuin of York*, trans. Allott, 64. On Mægenfrith, see S. Abel and B. Simson, *Jahrbücher des fränkischen Reiches unter Karl dem Großen. Vol. 2: 789–814* (Berlin, 1883), 548.

[42] Alcuin, *Ep.* no. 111; *Alcuin of York*, trans. Allott, no. 57 and *Charlemagne*, trans. King, 316–17.

[43] *Hinkmar von Rheims, De Ordine palatii*, ed. and trans. T. Gross and R. Schieffer, MGH Fontes *NS* IV (Hanover, 1980), 72–75; trans. P. E. Dutton, *Carolingian Civilization: A Reader*

of a portion of the Avar treasure to the royal and ecclesiastical courts of Anglo-Saxon England provides a reasonable context for the inclusion of the names of Charlemagne and his treasurer into the Northumbrian *Liber Vitae*, recording them in perpetuity in this memorial book of confraternal prayer. And such a context could thus point to metropolitan York as the origin of this sumptuous volume with the names of its benefactors written in burnished gold and silver leaf.[44]

The death of Pope Hadrian

Hunter-Blair and Pauli noted in their analyses that of all the continental entries in the *York Annals* only one contained a demonstrable factual error.[45] The entry for 794 records the death of Pope Hadrian on *.vii. Kalends Januarii* – that is, on the day after Christmas. The day of his death is correct but is placed a year too soon; the 'official' papal biography in the *Liber Pontificalis* records that Hadrian died on 26 December 795. The error can be explained as a confusion over the starting date of the year,[46] and a similar error occurs in the *Royal Frankish Annals* which tended to start the new year with the Christmas feast.[47] Christmas 794 was therefore considered Christmas 795 by the Franks and, knowing that Hadrian had died on the day after Christmas, various Frankish sources thus noted his death *sub anno* 796 (a year too late by our reckoning which begins the year on 1 January). Yet the *York Annals* entry concerning Hadrian gives more detail than either the *Royal Frankish Annals* or its revised version, attempting to give a calculation of the years, months and days of Hadrian's rule: according to the *York Annals*, Hadrian reigned *annos xxvi* (26 years), *menses decem* (10 months), *et dies xii* (12 days). The correct calculation is provided in the *Liber Pontificalis* which, however, states that he ruled 23 years, 10 months, and 17

(Peterborough, Ontario, 1993), no. 72. In this, the duties of the Carolingian *camerarius* were not dissimilar to those of the late antique *comes sacrae largitionum*, listed in the *Notitia Dignitatium*; P. C. Berger, *The Insignia of the Notitia Dignitatum* (London and New York, 1981), 67–75.

44 See also Alcuin's letter to Abbot Æthelbald requesting that his name be included in the confraternity book of Wearmouth-Jarrow; Alcuin, *Ep.* no. 67; *Alcuin of York*, trans. Allott, no. 24. Alcuin's name is recorded in the Northumbrian *Liber Vitae* (fo. 19v, no. 7), correctly within the list of priests holding the rank of deacon. We should be mindful here, too, of Bishop Wilfrid of York's gift to Ripon of a copy of the Gospels, 'written out in letters of purest gold on purpled parchment'; *The Life of Bishop Wilfrid by Eddius Stephanus*, ed. and trans. B. Colgrave (Cambridge, 1927), 36–37, c. 17. Gerchow prefers to associate the inclusion of these Frankish names with the letter which Alcuin wrote to Bishop Higbald of Lindisfarne after the Viking raid in 793, thereby tying the manuscript to that monastery; Gerchow, *Die Gedenküberlieferung*, 139.

45 Hunter-Blair, 'Some Observations', 93; Pauli, 'Karl der Große', 162.

46 R. L. Poole, *Studies in Chronology and History* (Oxford, 1934), 8–11; Levison, *England and the Continent*, 265–79. On this debate see Alcuin's letter to Charlemagne in which he expressed a preference for beginning the new year with the coming of light (that is, Christ's birth in December) rather than with the coming of winter darkness (that is, September / Michaelmas); Alcuin, *Ep.* no. 145; *Alcuin of York*, trans. Allott, no. 78.

47 *Annales regni Francorum*, 796.

days, his accession having occurred on 9 February 772. While the error in the *York Annals* seems substantial – being inaccurate by four years and five days – they do correctly cite the number of months of Hadrian's rule in words and not in numerals. Moreover, the Roman numerals for the years and days of Hadrian's rule could very easily have been miscopied by a scribe writing *xxvi* for *xxiii*, and *xii* for *xvii*, suggesting an error caused in manuscript transmission rather than in original fact. Only the so-called *Lorsch Annals* among the Frankish corpus of chronicles gives the correct year and date for Hadrian's death, but they do not provide a calculation for the length of his reign.

More striking than this, though, is the evidence which the *York Annals* provide concerning the epitaph which Charlemagne commissioned for Pope Hadrian. The *York Annals* describe the marble memorial which was to rest over the pope's tomb, recording his 'good deeds written in verse and in golden lettering'.[48] The annal states that 'Charlemagne himself ordered this marble slab to be made out of loving memory for the Pope'. Once again, it is only the *Lorsch Annals* from the Frankish chronicle corpus which comes close to the level of detail provided in the Northumbrian source. The *Lorsch Annals* for 795 state that:

> Hadrian the supreme pontiff died; and the lord king, once he had ceased his mourning asked that prayers be said for him throughout the whole Christian people within his lands and sent an abundance of alms for him and ordered an epitaph, written in gold letters on marble, to be made in Francia so that he might send it to Rome to adorn the sepulchre of the supreme pontiff Hadrian.[49]

The reference to the golden lettering, which is common to both descriptions of the marble epitaph, is also noted in another contemporary source – the poem to Hadrian written by Theodulf of Orléans which commences with the words:

Aurea funereum complectit littera carmen	Golden lettering embraces the funereal song
Verba tonat fulvus et lacrimosa color.[50]	The gilded colour intones tearful words.

---

[48] *Historia regum* (*York Annals*), 794; J. Ramackers, 'Die Werkstattheimat der Grabplatte Papst Hadrians I', *Römische Quartalschrift*, 59 (1964), 36–78; J. B. De Rossi, 'L'Inscription du tombeau d'Hadrien I composée et gravée en France par ordre de Charlemagne', *École Française de Rome. Mélanges d'archéologie et d'histoire*, 8 (1888), 478–501; H. LeClercq, 'Hadrien I, (épitaph de)', in *Dictionnaire d'Archéologie Chrétienne et de liturgie*, ed. H. LeClercq, 15 vols (Paris, 1924–53), 6.ii, cols. 1964–67; N. Gray, 'The Palaeography of Latin Inscriptions in the Eighth, Ninth and Tenth Centuries in Italy', *Papers of the British School at Rome*, 16, ns III (1948), 38–162, at 97–100; S. Morison, *Politics and Script* (Oxford, 1972), 170–73, pl. 172; R. Favreau, *Épigraphie Médiévale*, L'Atelier du Médiéviste, Vol. 5 (Turnhout, 1997), 63–68.

[49] *et ebitaffium aureis litteris in marmore conscriptum iussit in Francia fieri, ut eum partibus Roamae transmiitteret ad sepultura summi pontificis Adriani ornandum*; *Annales Laureshamenses*, 795; Ramackers, 'Die Werkstattheimat', 37.

[50] Theodulf, *Carmen ad Hadriani*, ed. E. Dümmler, MGH PLAC I (Berlin, 1881), no. 26, 489–90.

The concurrence of the reference to golden lettering by Theodulf and by the authors of the *Lorsch* and *York Annals* is striking, and supports the suggestion that the Northumbrian description was based on a contemporary source. Significantly, Hadrian's Carolingian epitaph is preserved in the portico of St Peter's in Rome and is the most outstanding piece of early medieval epigraphy to have survived in the city; it is a masterpiece of Carolingian craftsmanship (see Figure 4.2).[51] Although there now exists no visible sign of the golden lettering mentioned in the *York Annals* and parallel sources, it is possible that the incised letters had originally been gilded, inlaid with burnished gold leaf, to enhance the aesthetic and intrinsic value of the piece. The slim, elegant form of the letters makes it unlikely that burnished bronze letters had been used (although this technique is known from other surviving examples of Carolingian epigraphy) since the lead surround required to fix them in place demands a deeper, more substantial incision into the surface of the marble than is used here.[52] The references to golden letters rather than the more commonplace (but still valuable) polished bronze is surely a contemporary emphasis to highlight the exceptional adornment of this inscription which was to be sent as a final gift from Charlemagne to his dear friend in Rome.

The very high value of this gift is implicit in another feature of the epitaph. The marble used is black – suitably sombre for a sepulchral inscription but of a material so scarce that, prior to the creation of Hadrian's epitaph, very little evidence exists that black stone had ever been used for this purpose.[53] The choice of black marble for Hadrian's epitaph was innovative and artistically bold; the uniformly black surface provided a striking background for the golden lettering of the classicizing inscription and vine-scroll border.

The bold design and unusual choice of stone for this epitaph also had a political dimension. In the Roman world black marble was exceedingly unusual, so much so that the black form of porphyry (extracted from a corner of the

[51] *Epitaphia Hadriani papae*, MGH PLAC I, 101, 113–14. The letter-forms imitate second-century *capitalis quadrata*; D. A. Bullough, *The Age of Charlemagne* (London, 1973), 66, pl. 19; R. Krautheimer, *Rome: Profile of a City 312–1309* (Princeton, NJ, 1980), 140, fig. 115; Gray, 'The Palaeography of Latin Inscriptions', 97.

[52] U. Lobbey, J. Mitchell and P. Peduto, 'Inschriften', in Stiegemann and Wemhoff (eds), *799 Kunst und Kultur*, 2, 570–74; J. Mitchell, 'Literacy Displayed: The Use of Inscriptions at the Monastery of San Vincenzo al Volturno in the Early Ninth Century', in R. McKitterick (ed.), *The Uses of Literacy in Early Medieval Europe* (Cambridge, 1990), 186–225, at 205–15; De Rossi, 'L'Inscription du tombeau d'Hadrien', 488; LeClercq, 'Hadrien I', 1966.

[53] A fragment of a tombstone made of black limestone from Namur, Belgium with a late fifth- or early sixth-century inscription was recovered from the fabric of the church of Saint-Servaas in Maastricht; T. Panhuysen, 'Maastricht, centre de production de sculptures gallo-romaines et d'inscriptions paléo-chrétiennes', in H.-J. Häßler and C. Lorren (eds), *Studien zur Sachsenforschung* 8 (Hildesheim, 1993), 83–96, at 95 (frag. no. 4); W. Boppert, 'Die frühchristlichen Grabinschriften aus der Servatiuskirche in Maastricht', in C. G. De Dijn (ed.), *Sint-Servatius, bisschop van Tongren-Maastricht. Actes du Colloque à Alden Biesen* (Tongres and Maastricht, 1984), 64–96, at 80–83 (my thanks to Wim Dijkman for these references).

Fig. 4.2   The epitaph of Pope Hadrian I (772–95), portico, St Peter's, Vatican City

imperial quarries at Mons Porphyrites in Egypt) was prized by emperors over
and above red porphyry, itself highly valued for its imperial colour: indeed,
black porphyry may have had 'a value almost beyond comprehension'.[54] With
Pope Hadrian's permission, Charlemagne imported black porphyry columns
from imperial Ravenna for his new chapel at Aachen, and it seems very likely
that he understood the imperial connotations of this most rare stone.[55] The artist
of the evangelist page of the early ninth-century Fleury Gospels depicted the
attributes of the evangelists enclosed within two arches constructed by an outer
pair of red porphyry columns and a central one which is black; the hand of God
is shown emerging from the top of the central black column, graphically sym-
bolizing the rarity and value of that stone.[56] The marble used to make Hadrian's
epitaph was not black porphyry but, significantly, a stone quarried (it seems)
from within Charlemagne's own realm.[57] As the *Lorsch* annalist noted, Charlemagne had ordered the epitaph to be made *in Francia*. Black stone famed for its
homogenous colour and fine grain was certainly quarried from the Tournai
region of Belgium from the twelfth century onwards, and it is possible that this
was also the source of the material used for Hadrian's large epitaph, although
such an interpretation would imply that the quarries were worked very much
earlier than is normally thought to have been the case. Another possible location
was the region around Namur and Dinant. An alternative explanation is that the
slab, like the columns, was Roman *spolia*.[58] The use of black stone must have
been a deliberate choice in order to make an unambiguous statement about
Charlemagne's access to scarce, quasi-imperial resources – a message that would

---

[54] D. P. S. Peacock, 'Charlemagne's Black Stones: The Re-use of Roman Columns in Early
Medieval Europe', *Antiquity*, 71 (1997), 709–15, at 712; M. Greenhalgh, *The Survival of Roman
Antiquities in the Middle Ages* (London, 1989), 120–22. For black marbles from Africa see G.
Borghini (ed.), *Marmi Antichi* (Rome, 1998), no. 73, 88, 101, 114, 115, with a note about the
exploitation of Namur *'nero del Belgio'* as no. 102; R. Gnoli, *Marmora Romana* (Rome, 1971,
reprinted 1988), 192–95.

[55] *Codex Carolinus*, no. 81, ed. F. W. Gundlach, MGH *Epp*. III. Alcuin discussed the Aachen
columns with one of the women at court and in a letter to Charlemagne; Alcuin, *Ep*. 149; *Alcuin of
York*, trans. Allott, no. 80. Peacock argues that Offa of Mercia also desired status-enhancing black
stones of this type; Peacock, 'Charlemagne's Black Stones'; 709; Alcuin, *Ep*. 100; *Alcuin of York*,
trans. Allott, no. 40 and *EHD* 1, trans. Whitelock, no. 197. See also R. Hodges, *Towns and Trade in
the Age of Charlemagne* (2000), 64–67 and below, 196.

[56] Berne, Burgerbibliothek, MS 348, fo. 8v; F. Mütherich and J. E. Gaede, *Carolingian
Painting* (1977), pl. 11.

[57] See Ramackers, 'Die Werkstattheimat', 46–53 where it is argued that the slab was quarried
near Dinant, Belgium. Contrast De Rossi's argument that the marble came from nearer Tours, a
comment based on his belief that the epigraphy of the monument was most like the palaeography of
manuscripts produced in contemporary Tours; De Rossi, 'L'Inscription', 485. My thanks to Professor Eric Robinson for his help with this material.

[58] Peacock, 'Charlemagne's Black Stones', 709. On the use of Tournai stone for grave slabs
in the twelfth century, see J.-C. Ghislain, 'La production funéraire en pierre de Tournai à l'époque
romaine. Des dalles funéraires sans décor aux œuvres magistrales du 12e siècle', *Les Grands-
Siècles de Tournai*, Tournai Art et Histoire, 7 (Louvain-la-Neuve, 1993), 115–208.

not have been lost on the Roman recipients and viewers of the epitaph. Hadrian's 'Frankish' epitaph certainly had a 'startling and dramatic' impact on Roman epigraphers; for a long while afterwards the epigraphic style of inscriptions produced in Rome conforms to the new Carolingian standards visible in Charlemagne's remarkable epitaph for his friend.[59]

There is, furthermore, a good context for the contemporary transmission of details about the pope's death and his marble memorial to Northumbria. The verse epitaph that was ordered to be carved on the stone slab was composed by Alcuin himself, having won the commission from Charlemagne after a poetic duel with his rival, Theodulf, bishop of Orléans.[60] After Hadrian's death, Alcuin wrote to the bishops of Britain informing them of Charlemagne's decree that prayers be said for the soul of the deceased pope, and that the king had sent monks and priests 'with little gifts' to ensure that this was done.[61] It is thus entirely plausible that news of Alcuin's success in the competition for the composition of the official papal epitaph reached England simultaneously with details of the physical appearance of the commissioned memorial. The corrupted note in the *York Annals* regarding the length of Hadrian's rule could have been derived indirectly from Alcuin's poem which concludes with the correct calculation. Even the use of the unusual word *platoma* (*sic* for *platonia*) in the *York Annals* as a synonym for *marmor*, has a relevant and contemporary papal parallel which, given the contact outlined above, could account for its use in this Northumbrian context. The use of the word in the *York Annals* (in an entry which is so rich and accurate in other respects) need not therefore necessarily be condemned as a pretentious graecism used as a gloss by a later editor of the text.[62]

The *Lorsch Annals* entry for 795 bears further scrutiny since, as noted above, it is also the closest in the Frankish annalistic corpus to the description of the Avar treasure hoard as found in the *York Annals*. Can it be coincidence that the information concerning the Avars and Hadrian's death which is found in such exceptional detail in the Northumbrian source is most closely paralleled by a single entry in the *Lorsch Annals*? The information about the two incidents in both these sources is not sufficiently close to suggest direct verbal borrowing from one to the other, but might be taken to suggest that the two sets of annals shared a common source. What is more, the *Lorsch Annals* are considered at this point to be a contemporary account and survive (uniquely among the corpus of Frankish annals) in what appears to be an autograph manuscript, compiled year

---

[59] Gray, 'The Palaeography of Latin inscriptions', 97.

[60] L. Wallach, *Alcuin and Charlemagne: Studies in Carolingian History and Literature* (Ithaca, 1959), 178–97; *Poetry of the Carolingian Renaissance*, trans. P. Godman (London, 1985), 11, 17.

[61] Alcuin, *Ep.* no. 104; *Alcuin of York*, trans. Allott, no. 25.

[62] *platonias* posuit diversisque pictoris mirae magnitudinis opus decoravit; *Liber Pontificalis, Vita Leonis III*, c. 97; *The Lives of the Eighth-Century Popes*, trans. R. Davis (London, 1992), 225 and n. 187; Du Cange, *Glossarium mediae et infirmae latiniatis*, 7 vols (Paris, 1845), Vol. 5, 296; Pauli, 'Karl der Große', 162; Lapidge, 'Byrhtferth of Ramsey', 100.

on year by different scribes. This observation enhances considerably the value of the parallel information recorded in the *York Annals* since the contemporaneity of the *Lorsch Annals* is also mirrored in the details of the Northumbrian source.[63]

Leo, Eadburh and the imperial coronation

All the Frankish entries in the *York Annals* up to and including the year 795 fit easily into the linguistic style of the great majority of neighbouring annals about events in eighth-century England; the Frankish annals merge seamlessly into the Anglo-Saxon, and the language displays no jarring stylistic changes, suggesting either the hand of a skilful editor or of contemporary compilation. The remaining three continental entries for the years 799, 800 and 802 differ in this respect. That for 799 which describes the assassination attempt on Pope Leo III is written in a verbose, flowery Latin with a distinct partisan flavour which is stylistically at odds with the other Frankish entries in the *York Annals*.[64] Similarly, the last entry in this section, that for 802, can be dismissed immediately as a later interpolation into the text. It too reads very differently from most of the other annals in this section and, in fact, is an extract from part of Asser's *Life of King Alfred*.[65] It is a jeering account of the humiliation and downfall of Eadburh, a daughter of Offa and the estranged widow of Beorhtric, king of Wessex. Standing accused of the accidental poisoning of her husband, Eadburh fled to Charlemagne's protection in Francia but made the error of preferring his eldest son to the king himself. She was consequently confined to a Frankish nunnery from which she soon lapsed in honour again, ending her days begging with just a slave-boy for company on the street of the Lombard capital, Pavia. This moral tale has obvious apocryphal elements, although it may echo a residual memory

---

63 Vienna, Nationalbibliothek, Cod. 515; *CLA* X, no. 1482; W. Wattenbach, W. Levison and H. Löwe, *Deutschlands Geschichtsquellen im Mittelalter. Vorzeit und Karolinger*. 2: *Die Karolinger vom Anfang des 8. Jahrhunderts bis zum Tode Karls des Großen* (Weimar, 1953), 187–88; S. Käuper, 'Annales Laureshamenses (Lorscher Annalen)', in Stiegemann and Wemhoff (eds), *799 Kunst und Kultur*, 1, 38–40; L. Halphen, *Études critiques sur l'Histoire de Charlemagne* (Paris, 1921), 26–31; F. Unterkircher, *Das Wiener Fragment der Lorscher Annalen*, Codices selecti 15 (Graz, 1967); H. Fichtenau, *Karl der Große und das Kaisertum*, Mittelungen des Instituts für Österreichische Geschichtsforschung, 16.iii (Darmstadt, 1971), 257–334, at 287–309; P. Classen, *Karl de Große, das Papsttum und Byzanz, die Begründung des Karolingischen Kaisertums*, Beiträge sur Geschichte und Quellenkunde des Mittelalters 9, 2 vols (Sigmaringen, 1985–88), Vol. 2, 58, pl. 2; *Charlemagne*, trans. King, 19–20.

64 See below, 123–25.

65 Asser, *Vita Alfredi* c. 14–15. The exact relationship of the *Historia regum* to the (destroyed) Cotton manuscript of Asser's *Vita* is not yet clear; Hunter-Blair, 'Some Observations' 99–102; Lapidge, 'Byrhtferth of Ramsey', 121–22; *Alfred the Great*, trans. Keynes and Lapidge, 71–72, 254; D. Whitelock, *The Genuine Asser*, Stenton Lecture 1967 (Reading, 1968); A. P. Smyth, *Alfred the Great* (Oxford, 1995), 157–60. The same story was interpolated directly from Asser by Gerald of Wales, writing at Asser's see of St David's in the twelfth century, which implies that he had access there to a copy of the *Vita Alfredi*.

of aborted marriage negotiations between the Frankish and Mercian courts in the 780s.[66]

The inclusion of the story within the annal for 802 is interesting and deserves comment since its placement shows a certain subtlety; the figure of Charlemagne resonates with earlier Frankish annals, and the reference to the miserable, impecunious death of Eadburh in Pavia harks back to the annal for 774 which records Charlemagne's siege and capture of the city as a triumphant conqueror. Eadburh's story is inserted into the *York Annals* after what appears to be a genuine entry recording both the death of her husband Beorhtric, who had ruled Wessex 'most nobly' for 17 years, and the accession there of Ecgberht who was 'from the royal stock of that people'.[67] This affirmation of Ecgberht's ancient regal lineage is not found in the *Anglo-Saxon Chronicle* until 855–58 when the death of his son Æthelwulf is recorded after notice of his marriage to the Frankish princess, Judith.[68] This later ninth-century context was also that which Asser used to tell Eadburh's unfortunate story, to explain 'the perverse and detestable practice' of the West Saxon kings who were accustomed to deny their wives their rightful title of queen.[69] Asser's use of Eadburh is politically charged. On the one hand, she stands as a parallel to Judith (queen both of Æthelwulf and, after his death, of his son Æthelbald), a woman whom Asser (and Alfred) saw as a cause of dynastic unease within Wessex. On the other hand, she acts as a foil to Alfred's own pious Mercian wife, Ealhswith, who was never accorded the title of queen.[70] That the interpolator of this story from Asser into the *York Annals* clearly understood its significance to the 'foundation myth' of Alfred's brand of dynastic politics is demonstrated by the fact that he linked it directly with Ecgberht's succession. Implicit too, perhaps, is the interpolator's knowledge of Ecgberht's own exile to Francia which was forced by the marriage of Eadburh to Beorhtric in 789.[71] Technically, therefore, the Eadburh story belongs to the subsequent section of the *Historia regum*, which

---

[66] It was probably not Eadburh who was the intended bride for Charlemagne's son; see F. M. Stenton, *Anglo-Saxon England* (Oxford, 1971), 220, n. 4. See also, Smyth, *Alfred the Great*, 175–80 and Chapter 6, below, 188.

[67] *ASChron.* 800 (for 802); *Historia regum* (*York Annals*), 802. The annalistic reference to the succession is repeated after the Eadburh story with the addition of a (Byrhtferthian) reference to his 'coronation' and the beginnings of a king-list to Alfred; Lapidge 'Byrhtferth of Ramsey', 108; Hunter-Blair, 'Some Observations', 99–104.

[68] *ASChron.* 855–58; P. Stafford, 'The King's Wife in Wessex 800–1066', *Past and Present*, 91 (1981), 3–27; A. Scharer, 'The Writing of History at King Alfred's Court', *EME*, 5.2 (1996), 177–206; and see, further, Chapter 7, below, 240–43.

[69] The story was told to Asser by King Alfred himself; Asser, *Vita Alfredi*, c. 13; *Alfred the Great*, trans. Keynes and Lapidge, 235–36, n. 28.

[70] Eadburh's demise in Pavia can also be read as a sideswipe at Alfred's own sister Æthelswith who had followed her husband Burgred into exile at Pavia in 874. See S. Keynes, 'Anglo-Saxon Entries in the "Liber Vitae" of Brescia', in Roberts et al., *Alfred the Wise*, 99–120. That Ealhswith's mother was also named Eadburh adds an extra dimension to the story which is unlikely to have been lost on Alfred's contemporaries.

[71] *ASChron.* 787 (for 789) and 839 after recording Ecgberht's death; *Alfred the Great*, trans. Keynes and Lapidge, 236, n. 30. See also Chapter 5, below, 144–45.

contains a Wessex-centred chronicle for the years 849–87 and which is also closely dependent on Asser's *Vita Alfredi*; it sets up the marked shift in focus from Northumbria to Wessex in the ninth-century section of that text.[72] In practice, though, the Eadburh story also has relevance for the eighth-century *York Annals*, not least through its Frankish connections.

The *York Annals* entry for 800 is rather more difficult to evaluate, since (as we shall see) features of the text suggest that it has been tampered with and adapted at more than one stage in its evolution. It discusses the events surrounding the coronation of Charlemagne as Emperor in Rome on Christmas Day 800 in unusual depth and, with the exception of the interpolated entry for 802, is by far the longest entry on Frankish affairs. Like the other Frankish entries up to 795, the information contained therein is of high quality and detail. The annal for 800 tells of Charlemagne's adornment of the churches of St Peter and St Paul in Rome with 'gold, silver, and precious gems', of the trial and fate of Pope Leo's accusers, of the imperial coronation ceremony itself, and of the arrival of legates bearing marvellous gifts from Constantinople and Jerusalem. Much of the detail here can be paralleled by relevant entries in the *Liber Pontificalis* and the *Royal Frankish Annals*. For example, the only comparable reference to Charlemagne's generous gifts to the churches of St Peter and St Paul is found in the *Liber Pontificalis* which records precisely the Frankish donations after its account of the imperial coronation.[73] Nowhere, though, in the Franco-papal corpus of descriptions of this event do we find a direct source from which all the material in the Northumbrian annal for 800 can have been derived. And there are further problems: the section which records the request by the legates from Jerusalem that Charlemagne should act as their 'helper and defender' of the holy city to 'preserve the holy *coenobia* of the Christian religion … against insurgent peoples' sounds, as Pauli noted, rather more akin to crusading ideals expressed in the twelfth century than to the Frankish world of the ninth.[74] Indeed, the closest parallels to the sentiments expressed in the *York Annals* entry for 800 concerning Charlemagne's relationship with the East are found in the popular early twelfth-century text known variously as the *Iter Hierosolymitanum Caroli Magni*, the *Relatio*, or the *Descriptio*. This text tells the legend of Charlemagne's journey to Constantinople in response to the Byzantine emperor's request for help, and how he continued from there to Jerusalem to save the holy places from the infidel, returning victorious with gifts of precious relics.[75]

---

[72] This seems to be the function of the story when copied into the *Historia post Bedam* in the mid-twelfth century, *Chronica Magistri Rogeri de Houedene,* ed. W. Stubbs, RS 51 (London, 1868–71), Vol. 1, 18–19; Hunter Blair, 'Some Observations', 99–104.

[73] *Liber Pontificalis. Texte, introduction et commentaire*, ed. L. Duchesne 2 vols (Paris, 1886–92), Vol. 2, no. 98, c. 24–25; *Lives of the Eighth-Century Popes*, trans. Davis, 191–92. Einhard talks generally of Charlemagne's love of St Peter's as a prelude to his account of the coronation; Einhard, *Vita Karoli*, c. 27.

[74] Pauli, 'Karl de Große', 163–65.

[75] 'A wearisome recitation of palpable falsehoods': the main purpose of this text was to

Immediately following this, and similarly incongruous with the style of preceding entries, is the topos that worldly rulers must be students of wisdom. The phrase, as it stands in the *York Annals*, is a quotation from the prose version of Boethius's *Consolation of Philosophy*, a text which became popular in England from the time of Alfred and which is quoted elsewhere in the *Historia regum*, especially in its metres.[76] The context for the inclusion of this Boethian quotation may thus relate to a later age, but it is worth noting that Alcuin also used the same idea (citing Plato) in a letter written to Charlemagne in 801 in the immediate aftermath of his imperial coronation.[77] Also reminiscent of Alcuin's ideas is the annalist's 'curious note' that Charlemagne deserved coronation, 'so that he might be called emperor of the whole world (*imperator totius orbis appellaretur*)'.[78] Another of Alcuin's well-known letters to the king, written in May 799, talks of three world powers and implies that, of these, it was only Charlemagne who could protect the churches of Christ, with 'greater powers, clearer insight and more exalted royalty', than either the pope or the emperor in Constantinople.[79] A similar notion of pan-Christian duty lies behind the *Lorsch* annalist's important account of the ceremony where it is noted that 'it seemed to the *apostolicus* Leo, to all the holy fathers present at the council, as well as the rest of the Christian people, that they ought to bestow the name of emperor upon Charles … since it seemed to them to be right that, with the help of God and of the entire Christian people, he should have that name'.[80]

---

validate the relics of the crown and keys held at Saint-Denis; *A Thirteenth-Century Life of Charlemagne*, trans. R. Levine, Garland Library of Medieval Literature, Series B, Vol. 80 (New York, 1991). See also R. N. Walpole, 'Charlemagne's Journey to the East: The French Translation of the Legend by Pierre of Beauvais', *University of California Publications on Semitic Philology*, 11 (1951), 433–52, at 435–37; F. Castets, 'Iter Hierosolymitanum ou voyage de Charlemagne à Jérusalem et à Constantinople. Texte latin d'après le MS de Montpellier', *Revue des langues romanes*, 36 (1892), 417–74. See also S. Runciman, 'Charlemagne and Palestine', *EHR*, 50 (1935), 606–19; R. Morrisey, *L'empereur à la barbe fleurie: Charlemagne dans la mythologie et l'histoire de France* (Mesnil-sur-l'Estrée, 1997), 91–93.

[76] Lapidge, 'Byrhtferth of Ramsey', 114, n. 45.

[77] 'Happy is the people ruled by a good and wise prince, as we read in Plato's dictum that kingdoms are happy if philosophers, that is lovers of wisdom, are their kings, or if kings devote themselves to philosophy. For nothing in the world can be compared to wisdom'; Alcuin, *Ep.* no. 229; *Alcuin of York*, trans. Allott, no. 67; Anton, *Fürstenspeigel und Herrscherethos*, 98.

[78] Wallace-Hadrill, 'Charlemagne and England', 169.

[79] Alcuin, *Ep.* no. 174; *Alcuin of York*, trans. Allott, no. 103. This letter was written after the attack on Leo in Rome in 25 April. Charlemagne was himself in Tours in late May (the *Annales regni Francorum* note the death and burial there of Queen Liutgard on 4 June) and undoubtedly sought Alcuin's advice on the turmoil in Rome on which he had been kept closely informed by Bishop Arno (Alcuin, *Ep.* no. 184; *Alcuin of York*, trans. Allott, no. 65). A later letter indicated that Charlemagne had asked Alcuin to travel with him to Rome, though Alcuin refused on grounds of ill-health; Alcuin, *Ep.* no.177; *Alcuin of York*, trans. Allott, no. 104.

[80] *Annales Laureshamenses*, 800; *Charlemagne*, trans. King, 144. Here the Lorsch annalist explicitly cites the existence of the Byzantine empress, Irene, as fair cause for the elevation of Charlemagne to imperial rank; Classen, *Karl der Große*, 60–61.

Aspects of the vocabulary in the *York Annals* for 800 are paralleled by the entry for 801 in the *Royal Frankish Annals*, although the convergence may reflect the wording of a pontifical *ordo*, commonly known to the authors/editors of both these extracts.

Ipsa die sacratissima natalis Domini, cum rex ad missam ante confessionem beati Petri apostoli ab oratione surgeret, <u>Leo Papa coronam capiti eius imposuit</u> ... .[81]	On that same most holy day of the Lord's birth, when the king, at mass, arose from prayer before the confessional of the blessed apostle St. Peter, Pope Leo placed a crown on his head.
... in qua a domino <u>Leone papa</u> purpura regaliter induitur; <u>cui corona</u> aurea <u>capiti inponitur,</u> et regale sceptrum in manibus datur.[82]	... in which place he was robed regally in purple by Pope Leo, who placed a crown of gold on his head and a royal sceptre in his hand.

Lapidge has interpreted this extract from the *York Annals* as evidence of editorial interference in that text by a late tenth-century scholar, and it is possible that the contemporary description of ceremony has been amplified here with reference to a 'royal sceptre' and the king 'being robed regally in purple'.[83] But the verbal parallel with the coronation phraseology in the *Royal Frankish Annals* shows that, at its core, the vocabulary of the *York Annals* used here is contemporary. The same entry from the *Royal Frankish Annals* provides the information that Charlemagne travelled back to Aachen via Ravenna after the ceremony, a detail which is also noted in the *York Annals*. Both also give notice of the ambassadors sent by the patriarch of Jerusalem who came to see Charlemagne and note especially the gifts which they brought. The *Royal Frankish Annals* record it thus:

... qui benedictionis causa <u>claves sepulchri Dominici ac loci calvariae,</u> claves etiam civitatis et montis <u>cum vexillo</u> detulerunt.[84]	... in token of [his] blessing they brought the keys of the Lord's Tomb and of Calvary, and even the keys to the city and Mount [Sion] together with the standard.

Although it is less specific about the exact nature of the gifts, the vocabulary of the *York Annals* echoes this Frankish version:

... <u>vexillum</u> argenteum inter alia munera regi ferentes, <u>clavesque locorum sanctorum Dominicae resurrectionis aliorumque ei optulerunt</u> ... .[85]	... carrying to the king a silver standard among other gifts, they brought him the keys of the holy sites of Christ's resurrection and of other places ... .

---

[81] *Annales regni Francorum*, 801.

[82] *Historia regum* (*York Annals*), 800.

[83] Lapidge, 'Byrhtferth of Ramsey', 108.

[84] *Annales regni Francorum*, 800.

[85] *Historia regum* (*York Annals*), 800.

The *York Annals* entry for 800 also provides some details about the fate of the conspirators against Leo, saying that some were executed for their involvement but that others were exiled. This differs from both the Frankish and papal versions of the trial which say that Leo had magnanimously intervened on behalf of his accusers in order to save their lives. The *York Annals* also depart from the Franco-papal narrative by placing the trial of Leo's accusers before the coronation ceremony, whereas the Franco-papal sources stress that judgement was only passed on them after Charlemagne had received imperial coronation. The implication of the latter account is that Charlemagne had lacked the judicial authority to condemn the conspirators when he was simply *patricius romanorum* but that he was able to act as judge in Rome once he had been made emperor. The *York Annals*, if misplaced in the timing of the trial of the conspirators, is correct in the sense that much debate had taken place in the early weeks of December about who could adjudicate the serious charges levelled against the pope himself.[86] The solution devised was to make Leo swear his innocence on a copy of the Gospels in the pulpit of St Peter's, with God as his judge.[87] Also apparently out of chronological sequence is the reference in the *York Annals* to the arrival of Byzantine envoys, 'bringing great gifts'. There is no reference to their arrival in the Frankish annals for 800–801 or in the *Liber Pontificalis*, although Greek delegates had been at Charlemagne's court in 798 and returned 'in order to conclude peace' between the Franks and the Empress Irene in 802.[88] And, although it is possible that Greek envoys may have been present in Rome a year or so previously, it is most improbable that they would have begged Charlemagne, as the *York Annals* claim they did, 'to receive their kingdom and empire'.[89] This phrase, too, reads like a later interpolation, probably derived from the same source as the allusion to Charlemagne's legendary crusade to the East.

The Northumbrian annal and the *Iter Hierosolymitanum* similarly conflate the arrival of envoys from Jerusalem and Constantinople. In its account of Charlemagne's journey, the *Iter Hierosolymitanum* displays the unshakeable confidence of the First Crusade in the superiority of the West over the East – a belief inherent also in the fictitious plea put into the mouths of the Greek envoys in the *York Annals*, which is unrecorded in contemporary accounts.[90]

---

[86] *Liber Pontificalis*, ed. Duchesne, no. 98, c. 26; *Lives of the Popes*, trans. Davis, 192; *Annales regni Francorum*, 801.

[87] *Liber Pontificalis*, ed. Duchesne, no. 98, c. 22; *Lives of the Eighth-Century Popes*, trans. Davis, 190; *Annales regni Francorum*, 800; Alcuin had already advised Charlemagne of the lack of canonical precedents for the trial of a pope; Alcuin, *Ep.* no. 179; *Alcuin of York*, trans. Allott, no. 102.

[88] *Annales regni Francorum*, 798 and 802.

[89] See Einhard's comments on the irritation of the authorities in Constantinople caused by Charlemagne's coronation; Einhard, *Vita Karoli*, c. 28.

[90] Walpole, 'Charlemagne's Journey to the East', 437. The mid-twelfth-century catalogue of books of the library at Durham includes a reference to *De Itinere Jerusalem libri duo* which may provide a clue to the incorporation of this material into the *Historia regum* (*York Annals*) entry for 800; Piper, 'The Historical Interests of the Monks of Durham', 301–32, at 312.

The *Historia Regum* and the *York Annals*: structure and transmission

The assumption hitherto has been that the Frankish entries in the *York Annals* are, with the exceptions outlined above, primary sources for Frankish history. It is also assumed that the information they contain was circulating in Anglo-Saxon England in the later eighth century or shortly afterwards when the archetype of the *York Annals* (now embedded in the *Historia regum*) was being compiled.[91] Despite the quality of the information and our understanding of the widespread links between England and the Continent in this period, this is not a claim that can be made lightly and without further investigation. The transmission of chronicles over time, as any student of the *Anglo-Saxon Chronicle* knows, is inherently complex. The open-ended structure of chronicle-style texts and the usual anonymity of their authors meant that such texts were freely copied, corrected and adapted; they tended to be subject to interpolation, addition and removal of information at each and every stage in their development, with the result that every copy can a claim to be regarded as a free-standing text in its own right.[92] Identifying the extant sources to sections of early chronicles is difficult; searching for a lost archetype is akin to looking for the proverbial needle in a haystack which has long since been blown to the four winds.

However, given the central significance of the *Historia regum* for our understanding of post-Bedan England (and its links to Francia), it is essential that, as far as possible, we have a clear understanding of the evolution of this text. The *Historia regum* in its present form is a complex, composite text which survives as Item 7 in a single manuscript of late twelfth-century date; Cambridge, Corpus Christi College, MS 139 (fo. 51v-129v).[93] A rubric at the head of the *Historia regum* gives a date of 1164, corresponding with the palaeographic analysis of the major text hands in the volume which have been dated to the third quarter of the twelfth century.[94] The manuscript is a composite volume containing 26 historical texts, many of which relate to the Anglo-Saxon and early Norman history of northern England and several of which, the *Historia regum* included, are unique copies not found elsewhere. The *Historia regum* itself is a loose amalgam of nine distinct sections, some of which are chronological, some

---

91 Rollason, *Sources for York History*, 17, 27.

92 A. Gransden, *Historical Writing in England, c. 550 to c. 1307* (London, 1974), 29; and A. Gransden, 'The Chronicles of Medieval England and Scotland, Part 1', *JMH*, 16 (1990), 129–50.

93 M. R. James, *A Descriptive Catalogue of the Manuscripts of Corpus Christi College, Cambridge* (Cambridge, 1909–12), Vol. 1, 317–23; D. Baker, 'Scissors and Paste: Corpus Christi, Cambridge MS 139 again', *SCH*, 11 (1975), 83–124; B. Meehan, 'A Reconsideration of the Historical Works Associated with Symeon of Durham; Manuscripts, Texts and Influences', unpublished PhD thesis, University of Edinburgh (1979), 183–221. The *Historia regum* is translated by W. H. Stevenson, *The Church Historians of England, III, part ii: containing the Historical Works of Symeon of Durham* (Lampeter, 1885, reprinted 1987).

94 Hunter-Blair, 'Some Observations', 78; Dumville, 'The Corpus Christi "Nennius"', 370–71.

narrative in structure.[95] The *York Annals* (732–802) constitute the fourth of these nine sections, lying between material derived from Bede and an Asser-based chronicle for the years 849–87. It is quite apparent that the whole text, as preserved in this manuscript, has undergone several phases of editing and has acquired many textual accretions and modifications over time; but it is equally clear that at its core, there is a group of high-quality texts composed before *c.* 950 (see Figure 4.3).[96]

Because of the importance of its contents and the complexity of its structure, the manuscript has provoked contentious debate concerning its place of origin.[97] It can certainly be placed a century or so after it was written to the small Cistercian foundation at Sawley in north Yorkshire, which was a daughter cell of Newminster (itself a dependent foundation Fountains Abbey), as is indicated by an extant *ex libris*. However, its place of origin is still in doubt, since a good case can be made for linking its production to the monastic scriptorium and library at Durham – an association implied by close textual connections with extant volumes from Durham which have a secure link to that scriptorium.[98] Items 2 and 4 in the manuscript, for example, can be shown to have been copied directly from two extant (and indisputable) Durham manuscripts.[99] Furthermore, the copies of the *Historia Brittonum* and the *Life of Gildas* in the *Historia regum* manuscript were used to update the copies of those same texts in another important Durham manuscript, Durham, DCL MS B.II.35.[100]

Symeon of Durham

Significant, too, is the traditional attribution of the *Historia regum* itself to Symeon, who was cantor at Durham in the first quarter of the twelfth century. Symeon's authorship of the *Historia regum*, first claimed in the rubrics to the

---

[95] Hunter-Blair, 'Some Observations', 76–77.

[96] Ibid., 87, 116; Rollason, *Sources for York History*, 27. Particularly significant is the set of annals for 888–957 (section 6 of the *Historia regum*) which appear to be a contemporary compilation.

[97] On this debate (and that concerning the companion volume to CCCC MS 139 now split between Cambridge, UL MS Ff 1.27 and CCCC MS 66) see C. Norton, 'History, Wisdom and Illumination', in D.W. Rollason (ed.), *Symeon of Durham, Historian of Durham and the North* (Stamford, 1998), 61–105 and Dumville, 'The Corpus Christi "Nennius"'.

[98] D. W. Rollason, 'Symeon's Contribution to Historical Writing in Northern England' in *idem*, *Symeon of Durham*, 5–6; Norton, 'History, Wisdom and Illumination', ibid., 71–89; B. Meehan, 'Durham twelfth-century manuscripts in Cistercian houses', in D. W. Rollason, M. Harvey, and M. C. Prestwich (eds), *Anglo-Norman Durham, 1093–1193* (Woodbridge, 1994), 439–49.

[99] Item 2 (fos 19r-37v) which is a copy of part of the *Chronicon* of Regino of Prüm seems to have been copied from a Durham exemplar (Durham, DCL MS C.IV.15) in which identical passages have been marked up; Meehan, 'Durham Twelfth-century Manuscripts' 442. Item 4 (fos 48r-50v) is a short chronicle based on the Six Ages of the World, on which see Story, 'Symeon as Annalist', 202–3.

[100] Dumville, 'The Corpus Christi "Nennius"'.

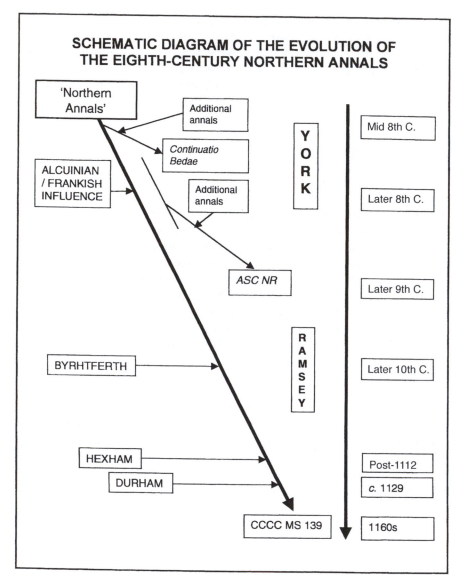

Fig. 4.3   Schematic diagram of the evolution of the eighth-century 'Northern Annals'

copy in CCCC 139 (fo. 51v), is now discounted for all bar the annals from 1119 to 1129.[101] However, he clearly knew and used the text because he incorporated

---

[101] Symeon may also have been responsible for additions to the previous section which is an amplified version of the *Chronicle* of John of Worcester; Rollason, *Sources for York History*, 27.

extracts from it into his own *Tract on the Origins and the Progress of this Church of Durham* and into other minor chronicle compilations.[102] A convincing case has been made for the identification of Symeon's own handwriting based on the observation of the hand which added notations to the Cantor's Book (Durham, DCL MS B.IV.24) at a time when Symeon is known to have held that office.[103] The hand which added these notes (mainly obits) can be shown to have worked on many other products from the Durham scriptorium, all of which are datable to the period during which Symeon was known to be active. Particularly interesting, given his reputation as an historian and his alleged involvement with the *Historia regum*, are the autograph copies of two chronicle-style texts both of which show an interest in the history of Anglo-Saxon England and Francia. One of these, known as the *Annals of Lindisfarne and Durham*, is interesting chiefly because it is a rare English example of a chronicle copied in the margin of an Easter table; its contents (in all except one entry) are derivative but show Symeon to have been an avid collector of historical material from a wide variety of sources and an able scholar who was well able to use and rework that material to his own ends.[104] The other text, which now forms the flyleaves to a later twelfth-century copy of Bernard of Clairvaux's commentary on the *Song of Songs*, is a short chronicle compilation, based on Bede's concept of the Six Ages of the World, running from Adam until the death of the Emperor Henry V in 1125.[105] As such, it is unremarkable except for the fact that Symeon incorporated some Frankish history in it and attempted to cross-reference this material with contemporaneous events in Anglo-Saxon England. His attempt was only partially successful but, again, this short piece demonstrates Symeon's intellectual capability as an historian and illustrates that he had access to a rich library of information about the Anglo-Saxon past, which seems also to have included some Frankish history.[106]

Both of these short chronicle texts, as well as his *Tract on the Origins and the Progress of this Church of Durham*, reveal Symeon's passing interest in the history of Francia in so far as it illuminated or enhanced his understanding of the

---

[102] *Symeon of Durham: Libellus de exordio atque procursu istius, hoc est Dunelmensis, ecclesiae. Tract on the Origins and Progress of this Church of Durham* ed. and trans. D. W. Rollason (Oxford, 2000), xlvi–l; Rollason, *Sources for York History*, 25–26 (S.55); see Chapter 2, above, 20.

[103] A. J. Piper, 'The Durham Cantor's Book (Durham, Dean and Chapter Library, MS B.IV.24)', in Rollason et al., *Anglo-Norman Durham*, 79–92 and M. Gullick, 'The Scribes of the Durham Cantor's Book (Durham, Dean and Chapter Library, MS B.IV.24) and the Durham Martyrology Scribe', ibid., 93–110.

[104] W. Levison, 'Die "Annales Lindisfarnenses et Dunelmenses" kritisch Untersucht und neu Herausgegeben', *Deutsches Archiv für Erforschung des Mittelalters*, 17 (1961), 447–506; Story, 'Symeon as Annalist', 205–9.

[105] Durham, DCL MS B.IV.22, fos 3–5v; *Symeon of Durham*, ed. Rollason, pl. 32–37.

[106] This short chronicle text was the immediate exemplar to Item 4 in CCCC MS 139, the scribe of which misread and miscopied the peculiar layout of the chronicle as devised by Symeon in Durham, DCL MS B.IV.22; Story, 'Symeon as Annalist', 203–4.

Anglo-Saxon past; his intellectual interest in Frankish history may have been an attempt to place his own Anglo-Norman present in some kind of longer historical perspective. And these chronicles certainly demonstrate that Symeon had access at Durham to good-quality sources of Frankish history. However, it is unlikely that Symeon (or any of his colleagues) had been responsible for the insertion of the Frankish entries into *York Annals*, as there is no evidence from extant manuscripts or from the medieval library catalogues of the Durham library that he had had access to sufficient Frankish data to have provided him with all of the Frankish annals in the *York Annals*, even though the library of Symeon's day probably contained a copy of the *Annales Mettenses Priores* and Regino's *Chronica* (Durham, DCL C.IV.15).[107] Had Symeon been responsible for the insertion of the Frankish material into the *Historia regum* one would expect to see a greater sharing of information between the texts on which he is known (through textual or palaeographic analysis) to have worked. Where there is any correlation in content between the Frankish entries in *York Annals* and other Symeon texts, the borrowing is much more likely to have been from the former to the latter rather than vice versa. More decisively, aspects of the *York Annals*, including the Frankish entries, show clear evidence of having been affected by the editorial tampering of an earlier, late tenth-century editor, which argues that the Frankish material must have been present in the text when it arrived on Symeon's desk at Durham in the early twelfth century.

Byrhtferth of Ramsey

The analysis of these annals also needs to address the late tenth-century phase of the *Historia regum* – a phase which is characterized by the editorial intervention of Byrhtferth, a monk of the abbey of Ramsey near Peterborough.[108] Byrhtferth's influence over the text is now well established; Lapidge has argued that he was the scholar responsible for amalgamating the early sections of the *Historia regum* into a loosely structured unit of four parts with each part subdivided into numbered chapters, some of which are identified by rubrics.[109] The eighth-century *York Annals*, including our Frankish ones, constitute Part III:1–29 of Byrhtferth's version of the text as re-edited by Lapidge. Byrhtferth's editorial contribution to the *Historia regum* can be observed through distinctive linguistic and literary parallels between these first four sections of the *Historia regum* and

---

[107] This is probably the manuscript which is referred to as the *Gesta Francorum* in the book catalogue contained in DCL B.IV.24 and is certainly that later called the *Cronica Pippini* in the catalogue for 1391; B. Botfield (ed.), *Catalogi Veteres Librorum Ecclesiae Cathedralis*, Surtees Soc. 7 (London, 1838), 3, 30; Piper, 'The Historical Interests of the Monks of Durham', 311–12; Meehan, 'Durham Twelfth-century manuscripts', 442.

[108] Lapidge, 'Byrhtferth of Ramsey'; C. Hart, 'Byrhtferth's Northumbrian Chronicle', *EHR*, 97 (1982), 558–82.

[109] Hunter-Blair's sections 1–5 in 'Some Observations', 77–78; *Symeonis Monachis Opera Omnia*, ed. Arnold, 2, 30–68.

other texts written by him, such as the *Vita S. Ecgwini,* the *Vita S. Oswaldi,* his preface or *Epilogus* to his *Computus,* and especially his *Enchiridion,* the last of which is also divided into four parts.[110] It is these linguistic characteristics and literary predilections which define Byrhtferth's editorial touch. There is no suggestion that Byrhtferth composed any of the *Historia regum* from scratch; rather that his contribution was as editor, compiler, and occasional glossator of the text, adding phrases and rubrics in his own distinctive style.

Commentators have not been kind to Byrhtferth and his interventions; Thomas Arnold was of the opinion that the Latin style of this tenth-century editor was 'pretentious and bombastical on the one hand, obscure and ineffectual on the other', and Hunter-Blair noted the interference of 'an editor who delighted in conceits of syntax, the use of uncommon words and the most bombastic language which his ingenuity could devise'.[111] Byrhtferth's literary choices included a tendency to use complex words when simple ones would have sufficed, to use elaborate constructions to record the deaths of great men, an interest in coronations and the works of Boethius, and the frequent use of superlatives, threefold participles, polysyllabic adverbs, agentive nouns and the like. Regardless of our opinions of Byrhtferth's literary style, the identification of his contribution to the text is important since it proves a definite pre-Conquest stage in the text-history of the *Historia regum.* Furthermore, the linguistic elements identified by Lapidge as characteristic of Byrhtferth's work can also be identified in the Frankish entries in the *York Annals,* which is lexical proof that they were present in that text by the tenth century and cannot have been a later, Norman interpolation dating from Symeon's day. The question then becomes one of whether Byrhtferth himself could have interpolated some or all of the Frankish annals when he was working on the text. He may have had access to information about Frankish history through Abbo, the computistical master of Fleury, who had arrived in England in 985 at the invitation of Oswald of Worcester and had taught for two years at Byrhtferth's own monastery at Ramsey. It is likely to have been through Abbo and his network of contacts that information reached Ramsey about the Viking attack on Fleury in 881 and the emergency removal of the relics of St Benedict, an event which is recorded in Part IV:13 of Byrhtferth's version of the *Historia regum.*[112]

The Historia post Bedam

One of the most important (and least understood) texts relating to the *Historia regum* and which may be able to cast light on this question of Byrhtferth's

---

110 P. S. Baker and M. Lapidge (eds), *Byrhtferth's Enchiridion,* EETS SS 15 (Oxford, 1995); Sharpe, *Handlist,* 174.

111 *Symeonis Monachis Opera Omnia,* ed. Arnold, 2, xxv; Hunter-Blair, 'Some Observations', 81, 114.

112 *Symeonis Monachis Opera Omnia,* ed. Arnold, 2, 85.

contribution to the Frankish entries in the *York Annals* is a work known as the *Historia Saxonum vel Anglorum post Bede obitum* (*HpB*), as yet unprinted and unedited.[113] This historical compilation, which seems to have been written in Durham perhaps in the 1120s, opens with two components of the *Historia regum* – namely, the genealogy of Northumbrian kings followed by the *York Annals* to 802 including some, but not quite all, of their Frankish elements.[114] The *HpB* then continues with extracts from Henry of Huntingdon (covering the years 732–866), further excerpts from the *Historia regum* to 1121 (with extra details added from Asser, Eadmer and John of Worcester), finally completing the text with verbatim extracts from Henry of Huntingdon down to the year 1148. The compiler of this rather sophisticated history added little of his own work but did include extra excerpts concerning St Cuthbert and Durham, thereby displaying knowledge of Symeon's *Tract of the Origin and Progress of this the Church of Durham* and betraying his own community's interests.[115]

The *HpB* seems to have had a relatively limited circulation (it survives complete in two manuscripts) but was then taken up by Roger of Howden in the late twelfth century who copied it almost verbatim as the opening section of his *Chronica*.[116] The significance of the *HpB* for our purposes lies in the fact that its compiler seems to have used a copy of the *Historia regum* before it was altered and adapted by Symeon. The *HpB* therefore seems to preserve an earlier version of the *York Annals* than that which survives under Symeon's name in CCCC MS 139. Consequently, the debate rests on the date at which the version of the *York Annals* in the *HpB* was produced. In his work on Howden's *Chronica*, Stubbs recognized the presence of a 'poetical editor' at work in the *York Annals* (which he called the 'Northumbrian Chronicle') and argued that the compiler of the *HpB* had 'pruned the somewhat ambitious language' of this editor.[117] Knowing, as we now do, that this 'poetical editor' was Byrhtferth of Ramsey, Stubbs' argument implies that the 'pruned' version of the *York Annals* in the *HpB* was produced at some point after Byrhtferth's intervention in the late tenth century but before Symeon's in the 1120s.

This interpretation contrasts with recent analysis of the *HpB* which regards the text as representing not a cut-down version of Byrhtferth's compilation but as his 'first draft'. Thus, Hart refers to the *HpB* as 'representing what

---

[113] The *Historia post Bedam* is found in two manuscripts; London, BL MS Royal 13.A.vi (*s.* xii[med.]) and Oxford, St. John's College MS 97 (Durham, *s.* xiii[in]). It is discussed and printed as the first part of Roger of Howden's *Chronica Magistri Rogeri de Houedene*, ed. W. Stubbs, RS 51 (London, 1868–71), Vol. 1, xxvi–vii, xxxi–xl; Rollason, *Sources for York History*, 17.

[114] Hunter-Blair's sections 2 and 4 respectively; *Symeonis Monachis Opera Omnia*, ed. Arnold, 2, 13–15 and 27–69, without the extracts from Bede's *Historia Ecclesiastica* at 28–29; Hunter-Blair, 'Some Observations', 76–99; Piper, 'The Historical Interests of the Monks of Durham', 302 and n. 8.

[115] *Chronica*, ed. Stubbs, Vol. 1, xxxi–iii; one of the *HpB* manuscripts London, BL MS Royal 13.A.vi has many marginal annotations by the rubricator explaining obscure Durham place names.

[116] Sharpe, *Handlist*, no. 1571.

[117] *Chronica*, ed. Stubbs, Vol. 1, xxxiii.

survives from the text of Byrhtferth's first recension of his Northumbrian Chronicle', thereby dating it slightly earlier in the tenth century than the version which has ended up in the *Historia regum* attributed to Symeon of Durham in CCCC MS 139.[118] Were Hart's interpretation to be correct, an analysis of the *HpB* would reveal whether all the Frankish references were included in Byrhtferth's first draft, or if some were added or altered for inclusion in the second draft which was ultimately incorporated into the *Historia regum* as we have it today. Such an analysis could also strengthen the case that the Frankish entries were part of the *York Annals* as available to Byrhtferth at Ramsey.

This process of comparison between the *HpB* and the *Historia regum* reveals some interesting points, since the eighth-century Frankish entries in the *HpB* are all but identical to those in the *York Annals*, in all bar two occasions (799 and 800). The account of the attempted assassination of Pope Leo III is entirely absent from the *HpB*, whereas in the *Historia regum* it forms one of the longest of the *York Annals*. The compiler of the *HpB* may, of course, simply have omitted the account precisely because of its length, although he did choose to include the long entry for 802 concerning Eadburh. Analysis of the substance and style of the 799 annal as it is found in the *Historia regum* today shows how different it is from earlier Frankish entries (and in this respect it serves to emphasize the quality and stylistic cohesion of the preceding Frankish annals in the *Historia regum*). The *Historia regum* version of the assassination attempt on Pope Leo is interesting in that it follows the papal version of events rather than the Frankish. Two versions of this event circulated shortly after the controversy was resolved – one put out by the papal curia in the *Liber pontificalis*, the other found in Frankish sources.[119] The papal version naturally emphasized the heretical injustice of the attack and the miraculous recovery of the pope; the reader is left in no doubt that the pope was left for dead in a Roman gutter, with his eyes gouged out and his tongue cut off. This version of the story regards his recovery from these injuries as proof of his innocence and worthiness to be restored to power. Almost as an afterthought, the *Liber pontificalis* refers to the arrival in Rome of the Duke of Spoleto who, on witnessing Leo's miraculous recovery, escorted him out of the city. From thence, the *Liber pontificalis* says, the pope made his way to Charlemagne who was resident at Paderborn although the reason for Leo's journey is not explained.

Frankish accounts are markedly different. The revised version of the *Royal Frankish Annals* is openly sceptical about the veracity of the pope's serious injuries and the miraculous nature of his recovery, adding phrases to the narrative such as *ut aliquibus visum est* ('as some saw it').[120] Central to the

---

[118] Hart, 'Byrhtferth's Northumbrian Chronicle', 578.

[119] M. Becher, 'Karl der Große und Papst Leo III', in Stiegemann and Wemhoff (eds) *799 Kunst und Kultur*, 1, 22–36.

[120] *Annales regni Francorum* (revised version) 799; *Charlemagne*, trans. King, 129. Einhard is rather more credulous of the papal account; Einhard, *VK*, c. 28.

Frankish version is the role of Charlemagne in the pope's rescue and political restitution. According to the Frankish sources, the pope had to be smuggled by night from his prison, spirited to Spoleto by the duke and taken from thence by him to Paderborn where Charlemagne was campaigning against the Saxons.[121] Alcuin's letters show that inflammatory allegations against the pope had been circulating in Francia during the summer of 799. He answered a worrying letter from Arno (who was acting as Charlemagne's special envoy in Italy) which contained 'some complaints about the behaviour of the Pope', adding that, as he 'did not want [Arno's] letter to get into other hands, so Candidus was the only one to read it with me, and then it was put into the fire, lest any scandal should arise though the carelessness of the man who keeps my correspondence'.[122] A subsequent letter from Arno tells of the pope's safety, but adds that there still existed in Rome 'many rivals of the Pope who wished to depose him by scheming accusations, seeking charges of adultery or perjury against him'.[123] Charlemagne was evidently in close correspondence with Alcuin about affairs in Rome, and turned to him for advice about how to act; he was certainly in Tours for 'some time' in early summer 800 before the Mainz assembly at which he announced his intention to lead an expedition into Italy.[124]

Contrary to what might be expected, given the depth of Frankish detail and interest in Charlemagne's military campaigns, the annal for 799 in the *Historia regum* follows the papal version of events and fails to mention Charlemagne at all. The author of this annal goes into florid detail about the murder attempt, using examples of the words and phrases ascribed to Byrhtferth's latinity.[125] That it is not included at all in the *HpB* might be taken as evidence that all the information for this annal was imported into the *Historia regum* by Byrhtferth in a second draft (following Hart) or simply omitted as overlong or irrelevant by a later editor of that text (following Stubbs). At any rate, the 799 annal may be taken as evidence of the interpolation of some continental material into the *York Annals* some considerable time after the event itself had occurred and on a separate occasion from the incorporation of the rest of the Frankish material into those annals.

This pro-papal version of Leo's story is that which is found in all other English chronicles including the late ninth-century copy of the *Anglo-Saxon Chronicle* MS A, although there it is found in a more concise form. It is this concise version which is found in another chronicle text produced at Byrhtferth's monastery. These so-called *Ramsey Annals* are incorporated into a computistical

---

[121] Symeon's short chronicle in Durham, DCL B.IV.22 (fo. 5r) says that he was at Herstal, not Paderborn, but the source of this statement is obscure; Rollason, *Symeon of Durham*, pl. 36.

[122] Alcuin, *Ep.* no. 41; *Alcuin of York*, trans. Allott, no. 65.

[123] Alcuin, *Ep.* no. 179; *Alcuin of York*, trans. Allott, no. 102.

[124] Alcuin, *Ep.* 178; *Alcuin of York*, trans. Allott, no. 71; *Annales regni Francorum*, 800 notes that Queen Liutgard died at Tours and was buried there on 4 June.

[125] Lapidge, 'Byrhtferth of Ramsey', 103, 114–15.

manuscript closely associated with Byrhtferth's work.[126] Entirely contrary to the *HpB*, the *Ramsey Annals* do not incorporate any of the continental material found in the *Historia regum*, with the sole exception of the *Chronicle*'s version of the papal annal for 799.[127] This might be taken as further evidence for the inclusion of the credulous account of Leo's recovery into the *Historia regum* by Byrhtferth at Ramsey, but implies that the compiler of the *Ramsey Annals* deliberately chose to omit the other Frankish annals as irrelevant to his purpose.

As noted previously, the entry for the year 800 in the *York Annals* is also of a different character to the earlier Frankish entries therein. Whereas the other Frankish annals up to 799 are incorporated verbatim into the *HpB*, the basic facts of the 800 annal are included but in a much more concise format and under the year 801:

Hoc anno potentissimus rex Francorum Karolus Rome summus imperator declaratur ab omni senatu, imposito capiti eius diademate imperiali a domino papa.[128]	In this year, Charles the most powerful king of the Franks was declared highest emperor by all the senate, an imperial diadem having been placed on his head by the lord pope.

The word *potentissimus* is a typical Byrhtferthian superlative and the last clause is close to the *York Annals* version (which, like the account in the *Royal Frankish Annals*, uses *corona* rather than *diadema*). Following Hart's interpretation of the *HpB* this entry could be a feasible first draft. But, if Hart's interpretation is correct, the second version of the account of the imperial coronation, as found in the *Historia regum s.a.* 800, must be regarded entirely as a late tenth-century composition by Byrhtferth. Because it is concerned with a coronation ceremony, Lapidge has argued that it betrays the editorial preoccupations of Byrhtferth.[129] As noted above, the *York Annals* entry for 800 certainly contrasts with the other Frankish entries in that text in terms of its length, but it mirrors annals such as the 795 description of the Avar treasure hoard in that it contains details which are not readily found in native Frankish sources. Whereas the annal for Leo in 799 was based on a non-Frankish source and was, it seems, not part of the original set of Frankish annals incorporated into the *York Annals*, the same

---

[126] Oxford, St John's College MS 17, fos 139r–143v and London, BL Cotton MS Nero C vii, fos 80r–84v which contains the section of the Ramsey Annals for 961–1421AD; C. R. Hart, 'The Anglo-Saxon Chronicle at Ramsey', in Roberts et al., *Alfred the Wise*, 65–88. On the relationship between the *York Annals* and the *Ramsey Annals* see Lapidge, 'Latin Learning', 430.

[127] Hart has argued that the *Ramsey Annals* preserve the original Latin form of the annal (ie: without the chronological dislocation of *ASChron.* 'A' which places these events in 797) which had been translated into OE for *ASChron.* 'A' in the ninth century; Hart, 'The Anglo-Saxon Chronicle at Ramsey', 83 at n. 70; see also Lapidge, 'Byrhtferth of Ramsey', 121; and *The Anglo-Saxon Chronicle MS* A. *A Collaborative Edition* 3, ed. J. Bately (Cambridge, 1986), xcvii, 40.

[128] *Historia post Bedam*, 801; *Chronica*, ed. Stubbs, Vol. 1, 18.

[129] Lapidge, 'Byrhtferth of Ramsey', 108.

argument cannot be advanced for the account of Charlemagne's imperial coronation.

In summary, it is evident that the *York Annals* entry for 800 is broadly
based on a Frankish description of the event but the immediate source of that
description is obscure, and in this respect it resembles the *York Annals* for 774–
95. It certainly contains some of the stylistic devices attributed to Byrhtferth but
these come across as editorial additions to a pre-existing text rather than as a
wholesale composition by this author. On balance, it seems that the annal for
800 should be regarded alongside the earlier Frankish annals in the *York Annals*,
and that it was abbreviated for inclusion in the *HpB*, but whether it was included
in the *York Annals* at the same stage as the other Frankish entries is debatable.

Byrhtferth and Alcuin: the vocabulary of kingship

Lapidge and Hart's work on the œuvre of Byrhtferth of Ramsey has identified
the literary fingerprint of the tenth-century editor whose involvement with the
text of the *Historia regum* has long been suspected.[130] It is an identity built up
from the recognition of numerous, often commonplace, literary and linguistic
devices which, in combination, clarify the predilections and choices of a particular writer. But problems of detail arise since many of the component parts of this
literary fingerprint were devices often also favoured by other writers. An example is Byrhtferth's preoccupation with coronations: the ceremonies of Coenwulf
of Mercia in 798, Charlemagne in 800, and Ecgberht of Wessex in 802 are
manifestations in the *Historia regum* of Byrhtferth's interest in the subject. And,
as Lapidge notes, these examples may be compared profitably with his description of Edgar's coronation in the *Vita S. Oswaldi*,[131] and coronations are a
recurring theme linking the several sections of the *Historia regum* worked on by
Byrhtferth with other texts composed by that author. But the implication of this
argument is that the kingship vocabulary used to describe these ceremonies was
anachronistically applied by Byrhtferth to the eighth-century *York Annals* in the
Historia regum. However, as we have seen with the example of Charlemagne's
imperial coronation cited above, this type of vocabulary has unambiguous contemporary parallels. Thus, the emphasis on coronations, which is such a defining
feature of Byrhtferth's hand, may in fact mask vocabulary which was current in
an earlier age. The distinction is subtle since, by Byrhtferth's day, the rituals of
kingmaking such as the coronation and the ecclesiastical sanction of new monarchs were commonplace whereas in the later eighth century these rituals were
only just beginning to be deployed in Anglo-Saxon England. These observations

---

130 *Symeonis Monachis Opera Omnia*, ed. Arnold, 2, xvii; *Chronica*, ed. Stubbs, Vol. 1, xxix;
The Chronicle of John of Worcester, ed. and trans. R. R. Darlington and P. McGurk (Oxford, 1995),
Vol. 1, lxxx.

131 Lapidge, 'Byrhtferth of Ramsey', 108; Hart, 'Byrhtferth's Northumbrian Chronicle', 569–
70; J. Raine (ed.), *The Historians of the Church of York*, RS 71, 3 vols (London, 1879), Vol. 1, 438.

have important historical implications for our understanding of the development of kingship in Anglo-Saxon England in the eighth century, since, beneath the embellishments of Byrhtferth, a complex contemporary political vocabulary is visible in the *York Annals*.

There are several authors to whose writings Byrhtferth evidently had access and from whom he drew inspiration in both content and style.[132] That Byrhtferth was something of a literary magpie is to be expected from a man of his intellect and education – his quotations from Boethius, Asser and even Alcuin were a self-conscious parade of his range of learning. But, in the particular context of the *Historia regum*, it is important to recall that Byrhtferth's deliberate use and emulation of earlier sources blurs the contributions of others to earlier versions of that text. This is especially true of the *York Annals* which make up Part III of Byrhtferth's 'historical miscellany' in which Hart cites the work of Alcuin as an important source.[133] It becomes, therefore, a matter of debate whether the reader regards the Alcuinian phraseology in the *Historia regum* as further evidence of Byrhtferth's use of Alcuin's writings, anachronistically introduced during his revisions of the text in the later tenth century, or as contributions to that text incorporated by scholars who were directly and contemporaneously connected with Alcuin and his school at York. This is true of the content and vocabulary of the Frankish entries incorporated into the *York Annals* as well as those which tell of eighth-century events in the kingdoms of England.

That there is an eighth-century core to Byrhtferth's Part III is self-evident. The very close parallels of many of the annals concerning Northumbria with other contemporary chronological material such as that which was incorporated into the northern recension of the *Anglo-Saxon Chronicle*, the annalistic continuation to the Moore manuscript, and the *Continuatio Bedae* demand the recognition of a strong, independent chronicle-keeping tradition in Northumbria in the decades which followed Bede's death.[134] The case for York as one such centre is longstanding and well made and, given what is known of Alcuin's career at York and in Francia, it is natural to look to his work and to those of his contemporaries for evidence of an earlier pre-Byrhtferthian stratum of editorial activity and intellectual influence. In his *York Poem*, Alcuin uses much of the kingship vocabulary of the type found in the *York Annals*:

line 115	qui mox **accipiens sceptri regalis** honorem
line 154	qui mihi concessit vitam **regnique coronam**
line 506	Osui germano terrestria **sceptra** reliquens

---

[132] Lapidge, 'Byrhtferth of Ramsey', 112–18.

[133] Hart, 'Byrhtferth's Northumbrian Chronicle', 562.

[134] Rollason, *Sources for York History*, 17–18. On the annalistic continuation to the Moore Manuscript (Cambridge, UL MS Kk.5.16) see *Bede's Ecclesiastical History*, ed. and trans. Colgrave and Mynors, 572–73; P. Hunter-Blair, 'The Moore Memoranda on Northumbrian History', in C. Fox and B. Dickins (eds), *The Early Cultures of North West Europe* (Cambridge, 1950), 245–57; and *idem*, *The Moore Bede, Cambridge University Library* MS Kk.5.16, EEMF, 9 (Copenhagen 1959).

lines 575–76   Ecgfrido tradens proprio **diademata** gnato,
                Ecgfrido moriens **regalia sceptra** reliquens.
lines 1274–75   Cuius frater item Tyrio nutritus in ostro
                sumpserat Eadberctus gentis **regalia sceptra**.
line 1281   ille **levat capiti veterum diademata** patrum
line 1286   ille annis tenuit ter septem **sceptra** parentum.

Although it is arguable that Alcuin may have used words such as *corona, sceptra,* and *diademata* as generic labels of kingly rank rather than as words to describe specific items of royal regalia, it remains true that these words were current in an eighth-century vocabulary of kingship.[135] And Alcuin was not the only eighth-century insular writer to use these terms in this way; Cathwulf proclaimed Charlemagne's superiority saying that God 'has blessed you over your ancestors with a crown of glory (*corona gloriae*)' and Boniface praised Æthelbald of Mercia for 'guiding the renowned sceptre of imperial rule over the English'.[136] Coenwulf of Mercia used similar terminology in a letter to Pope Leo III in 801 when he refers euphemistically to 'this sceptre of the Mercians'.[137] In a charter of 799 (the second year of his reign – *secundo [anno] imperii nostri*) he is styled *rector et imperator Merciorum regni* and in another charter of 811 his kingdom is termed as *imperii piissimi regis Merciorum*.[138] These contemporary references correspond closely to the 'Byrhtferthian' terminology used in the *York annal* for 798 describing his accession to the Mercian throne after crushing the Kentish rebels, and for which evidence of the contemporary use of the word *imperium* as a synonym for *regnum* is particularly significant.[139]

Alcuinian influence on Byrhtferth's work stretches beyond Part III; several distinctive phrases are found both in Alcuin's *York Poem* and in Part IV of the *Historia regum* (the Asser-based chronicle which lies outside the eighth-century element of interest to us here) and implies that Byrhtferth did indeed have direct or indirect access to some of Alcuin's writings.[140] But the links to Alcuin's own works are strong: the reference in the *York Annals s.a.* 800 to Rome as *Romulea urbs* is mirrored in the *York Poem* as is the formulation of 'gold, silver, and gems' in the same annal.[141] Alcuin, like Byrhtferth, frequently used superlatives

---

[135] See above, 95 for Alcuin's use of the word *sceptra* in Chapter 13 of his *Vita Willibrordi.*

[136] Cathwulf, *Epistola ad Carolum*, MGH *Epp.* IV, *Epistolae Variorum*, no. 7, 502; *Die Briefe des heiligen Bonifatius und Lullus*, ed. Tangl, no. 73; *EHD* 1, trans. Whitelock, no. 177; J. Nelson, 'The Earliest Royal Ordo: Some Liturgical and Historical Aspects', in *idem, Politics and Ritual in Early Medieval Europe* (London and Rio Grande, 1986), 341–60, at 356.

[137] Haddan and Stubbs (eds), *Councils* III, 521–23; *EHD* 1, trans. Whitelock, no. 204.

[138] BCS 289, 335 / S153, S168.

[139] Lapidge, 'Byrhtferth of Ramsey', 108; Levison, *England and the Continent*, 121–25; F. M. Stenton, 'The Supremacy of the Mercian kings', in D. M. Stenton (ed.), *Preparatory to Anglo-Saxon England* (Oxford, 1970), 48–66; Wallace-Hadrill, 'Charlemagne and England', 169.

[140] Alcuin, *The Bishops, Kings and Saints of York*, ed. and trans. P. Godman (Oxford, 1986); *armipotens*, line 125 (and *Historia regum, s.a.* 868); *bellator*, line 659 (and *Historia regum, s.a.* 887).

[141] Alcuin, *The Bishops, Kings and Saints of York*, ed. and trans. Godman, lines 1455, 277, 389; see also Einhard, *Vita Karoli*, c. 27.

and agentive nouns as well as threefold participles for emphasis.[142] He also refers to the presence of copies of Boethius's writings in the library of the school at York (although he was not prone to such extensive quotation from that author as Byrhtferth undoubtedly was).[143] Alcuin's letters and other poems offer further examples of literary constructions also familiar to readers of Byrhtferth; Charlemagne and other kings are often addressed in superlative terms and referred to using allusions such as *rector, defensor, amator, adjutor et protector* and *gubernator*, for example.[144] That some of these constructions are also found in a letter which survives from Alcuin's pupil Eanbald to the incumbent archbishop of York indicated that he, and probably others too, were able to write in a style akin to that employed by their master Alcuin.[145] Certainly Abbot Eanwulf and Cathwulf, writing to Charlemagne in 773 and 775 respectively, addressed the king in superlative terms as *praecellentissimus, gloriosissmus, piissimus* and *carissimus rex Francorum.*[146]

One phrase used in the *York Annals* has an even more venerable Frankish pedigree. With reference to the accession of Eardwulf to the Northumbrian throne in 796, the annalist used the phrase *regni infulis est sublimatus*, meaning 'raised to the regalia of kingship'. This technical expression is first recorded in the late seventh-century *Passion of St. Leudgarius, s.a.* 673 in the context of a solemn customary ritual – *solemniter, ut mos est.*[147] This phrase, in combination with the element of consecration, is next used in the *Continuation to the Fourth Book of the Chronicle of Fredegar* describing the ceremony which elevated Pippin III to the throne of the Franks:

Pippinus electione totius Francorum in sedem regni <u>cum consecratione episcoporum</u> et subiectione principum una cum regina Bertradne, ut antiquitus ordo deposcit, <u>sublimatur in regno.</u>[148]	Pippin, having been elected by all the Franks to the throne of the kingdom, <u>with the consecration of the bishops</u> and subjection of the leading men with his queen Bertrada, was <u>raised to the kingship,</u> as an ordo of former times stipulates.

---

[142] Alcuin, *The Bishops, Kings and Saints of York*, ed. and trans. Godman, lines 99, 131, 232, 365, 267, 291, 569, 773, 1237, 1450.

[143] Ibid., line 1548; Lapidge, 'Byrhtferth of Ramsey', 114–15.

[144] Alcuin, *Alcuini Carmina*, ed. E. Dümmler, MGH *PLAC* 1.i, 245; J. Celini, *Le vocabulaire politique et Social dans la Correspondance d'Alcuin*, Travaux et Mémoires, 12 (Aix-en-Provence, 1959), lxxii; *The Bishops, Kings and Saints*, ed. Godman, civ–vi; Nelson, 'Fulk's Letter to Alfred Revisited', 137, n. 8.

[145] Alcuin, *Ep.*, no. 46, *ammonitionis, benedictionis et promissionis ... remunerator.*

[146] Eanwulf, *Epistola ad Carolum; Bonifatius und Lullus*, ed. Tangl, no. 120; *EHD* 1, trans. Whitelock, no. 186; Cathwulf, *Epistola ad Carolum*, MGH Epp. IV, *Epistolae Variorum*, no. 7.

[147] *Passiones Leudgarii* I, c. 5; MGH Ser. rer. Merov. V, 287; J. Nelson, 'Inauguration Rituals', in *idem, Politics and Ritual in Early Medieval Europe* (London, 1986), 283–308, at 286.

[148] *The Fourth Book of the Chronicle of Fredegar and its Continuations* ed. and trans. J. M. Wallace-Hadrill (London, 1960), 102.

The whole description of Eardwulf's kingmaking ceremony in the *York Annals* resonates with analogies to similar Frankish ceremonies – analogies that are emphasized by other evidence of close ties between this king and the Frankish court. The elaborate description of the consecration and elevation of this Northumbrian *dux* to the throne of his kingdom at the altar of St Paul in the church of St Peter in York where the first Northumbrian Christians had been baptized seems an entirely plausible description of an attempt to legitimize the claims of a new dynasty to royal power in Northumbria. That the ceremony is described in almost identical terms in the vernacular Northern Recension of the *Anglo-Saxon Chronicle* only serves to underline the significance of the ceremony and of the contemporaneity of the phraseology used to describe it.[149] It seems that the weight and significance of this technical Frankish phrase was understood by the chronicler of the 796 Northumbrian event, and that its use in this context was deliberate and measured.

Much of the evidence which links Alcuin to the *York Annals* is circumstantial – his composition of Hadrian's epitaph, for example – but, as Stubbs suggested in 1868, Alcuin may have been 'instrumental in a remote way' in the original collection of the annals, both Frankish and Anglo-Saxon, which form the basis of (Byrhtferth's) Part III of the *Historia regum*. Stubbs argued that, 'the references to events of European rather than domestic interest and especially the history of the great Emperor seem to imply it. It ends too about the time of Alcuin's death, as if the writer had not thought it worthwhile to continue it.'[150] This last point about the cessation of the *York Annals* in 802 needs to be set alongside the similar hiatus in the ninth-century portion of the Northern Recension of the *Anglo-Saxon Chronicle* which ends in 806 – a cessation which underlines the interdependence of these two key witnesses to the history of Alcuin's homeland. Stubbs' scenario is one of distant influence with Alcuin as the transmitter of the Frankish information rather than having a more direct editorial input into the text. Given Alcuin's continual presence in Francia for at least the last 12 years of his life from late 792, this must certainly be the case for the annals included after that date. However, contrary to Stubbs' claim that there are 'few allusions and no direct references' in the *Historia regum* to the contents of his letters, a close inspection of Alcuin's poetic and epistolary output does reveal parallels in both content and vocabulary. Several of Alcuin's letters to Anglo-Saxon and Frankish correspondents are directly concerned with events recorded in the *York Annals*. His letters to Charlemagne, the treasurer Mægenfrith, Archbishop Arno of Salzburg, Paulinus the patriarch of Aquileia, as well as the Irish *magister* Colcu, concerning the conquest and conversion of the Avars and Saxons, are important sources illustrating the Carolingian insistence on the conversion to the Christian faith as a means of enforcing Frankish lordship.[151]

---

[149] See Chapter 5, below, 157.

[150] *Chronica*, ed. Stubbs, Vol. 1, xi n. 2.

[151] Alcuin, *Ep.* nos 99, 110–11, 113; *Alcuin of York*, trans. Allott, nos 58, 56, 57, 137.

The ordination of Aluberht as bishop of the Old Saxons as described in the annal for 767 has a more direct connection with Alcuin, as the *Life of St. Liudger* notes. Chapter 10 tells of the arrival in Utrecht of Aluberht, *de terra Anglorum*, who had arrived hoping to assist with the missionary work started by Willibrord among the Frisians.[152] Unable to consecrate Aluberht himself, Abbot Gregory instructed him to return 'to the land from which [he had] come' to acquire canonical ordination from its bishop with whose 'permission and advice' he had embarked for Frisia. Aluberht returned to York accompanied by two members of the Utrecht community, Liudger and Sigibod, who, when Aluberht was ordained bishop, were ordained deacon and priest respectively. 'And in that place', the author of the *Life* continues, 'Alcuin was master, who afterwards in the time of Charles was in charge of the teaching at Tours and in the Frankish kingdom'. The three men remained in York for a year; Liudger became Alcuin's pupil and, having returned to Frisia, chose to return to York to continue his studies there for a further three and a half years. The *Life* of this Frisian saint, therefore, confirms Alcuin's presence and position of authority in York at the time of Aluberht's episcopal consecration, as recorded in the *York Annals* under the year 767. The connection between Alcuin and the text in the *York Annals* is again tangential and may in fact reflect the connection of the early chronicle with York rather than with Alcuin *per se*, but the *Life* reminds us that Alcuin was at this time a venerated *magister* and was just the sort of figure who may have inspired the keeping of accurate records about his *patria* and its contacts. Furthermore, the *Life of St. Liudger* indicates that Alcuin was attracting students from abroad – students who would have brought with them information about events in Francia and beyond. Alcuin's subsequent fame and influence at the Frankish court (as the author of Liudger's *Life* notes) would, if anything, have enhanced the keeping of records about distant events in the years after he left for service at the Frankish court.

That Alcuin may have been the catalyst for the collection of Frankish information into an essentially Northumbrian chronicle is further suggested by the *York Annals* for 792. This entry tells how Charlemagne sent a synodal book from Constantinople to Alcuin in Britain. This book was full of 'many inconveniences and arguments against the true faith', reporting the outcome of the second Council of Nicaea held in 787 concerning image worship.[153] Alcuin's presence in Northumbria at this time is confirmed by several letters that he wrote back to his friends in Francia, complaining to Joseph that 'the new reign

---

[152] Altfrid, *Vita Liudgeri;* MGH SS II, 403–19; *EHD* 1, trans. Whitelock, no. 160. On this incident see D. A. Bullough, '*Albuinus deliciosus Karoli regis*. Alcuin of York and the Shaping of the Early Carolingian Court', in L. Fenske, W. Rösener, and T. Zotz (eds), *Institutionen, Kultur und Gesellschaft im Mittelalter* (Sigmaringen, 1984), 73–92, at 78–83.

[153] On the wider context of the controversy over image-worship and the authorship of the *Libri Carolini*, see A. Freeman, 'Carolingian Orthodoxy and the Fate of the Libri Carolini', *Viator*, 16 (1985), 65–108.

[of Æthelred] keeps me here against my will so that I cannot come to you'.[154]
The Byzantine book and Alcuin's letter 'supported marvellously by the authority
of the divine scriptures' seems to have provided Alcuin with sufficient excuse to
return to Francia where he was in residence by June 793, as confirmed in his
letters to Bishop Higbald and the Northumbrian monastic communities concerning the Viking raid on Lindisfarne. The 792 annal is significant not least because
it states that Alcuin's tract against image worship was affirmed 'by all the
bishops and nobility of our people', an event which must have echoed in the
minds of the Northumbrian people with memories of the assemblies which met
to affirm the Legates' Capitulary in 786, at which Alcuin was present. In 792 the
Northumbrian ecclesiastical and lay elite met once again to add their assent to a
Frankish demand for religious conformity to a document drawn up by Alcuin
and sent to their attention by Charlemagne.

That Alcuin was involved at some point in the evolution of the *York
Annals* is widely accepted. Hunter-Blair's seminal article on the text emphasized the York focus of this section of the annals, but he was sceptical of
Stubbs' desire to link their production too closely to Alcuin saying that, 'there
are likely to have been many others in a position to secure and transmit to
Northumbria information of the kind recorded in these entries'. This is self-
evident; someone must have brought the synodal book to Alcuin in 792.
Alcuin's stylistic influence over the *York Annals* is detectable although it is
debatable whether this is a consequence of direct editorial influence or a
secondary borrowing from his own compositions by a contemporary or later
editor of those annals. If (as is argued here) much of the kingship vocabulary
can be attributed to an eighth-century editor of the *York Annals*, then it provides significant implications for the development of royal authority and ritual
in Anglo-Saxon England at that date.

With regard to the Frankish entries incorporated into the *York Annals* it is
noteworthy not so much that the section on English affairs terminates just before
Alcuin's death in 804, but that contemporary Frankish annals cease to be included after Alcuin had retired to Tours in 796. Only a few letters in the extant
collections from Alcuin to Northumbrian noblemen can be dated after 796 and,
other than the slightly difficult description of Charlemagne's imperial coronation in 800, after 795 no further Frankish annals are found in the *York Annals*.
Alcuin's retirement to Tours coincided with (and may have been partially prompted
by) a dramatic year in Anglo-Saxon England; Offa of Mercia died on 26 July
and Ecgfrith, his anointed son and heir, followed him to the grave before the end
of the year.[155] In Northumbria Æthelred was assassinated on 18 April and his

---

154 Alcuin, *Ep.* nos 8, 9; *Alcuin of York*, trans. Allott, nos 9, 10; D. A. Bullough, 'Alcuin and
the Kingdom of Heaven: Liturgy, Theology and the Carolingian Age', in U.-R. Blumenthal (ed.),
Carolingian Essays (Washington, 1983), 1–69, at 35–38; *idem*, 'Alcuin before Frankfort', in R.
Berndt (ed.), *Das Frankforter Konzil von 794* (Mainz, 1997), 571–85, at 581–82.

155 *Historia regum* (*York Annals*), 796.

successor Osbald survived only 27 days before being expelled and exiled to Pictland. Alcuin's lifelong friend Eanbald I, the archbishop of York, died on 10 August and was replaced four days later by Alcuin's pupil, also named Eanbald. Alcuin's letters to Eanbald II show his increasing apprehension about Northumbrian stability, berating the new archbishop about his luxurious lifestyle, questioning him about the need for armed retainers, and warning him against antagonizing the new king Eardwulf by sheltering his enemies.[156] And, although he wrote to Eardwulf expressing hope of a new beginning, he was soon expressing doubts about the king's political prospects having offended God by setting aside his wife in favour of a concubine.[157] By the end of 796 Alcuin's carefully constructed network of diplomacy centred on the families of Offa and Æthelred had collapsed, and different noble families were controlling both Northumbria and Mercia. His own health failing, Alcuin retired exhausted to Tours, and the flow of information to Northumbria from the Carolingian court simply slowed.

---

[156] Alcuin, *Ep.* nos 232–33, see also 114, 116, 125, 226; *Alcuin of York*, trans. Allott, nos 20–21, 6–7 and 18–19.

[157] Letters to Eardwulf and a Mercian nobleman; Alcuin, *Ep.* nos 108, 122; *Alcuin of York*, trans. Allott, nos 16, 46.

Chapter 5

Exiles and the Emperor

The accumulated evidence demonstrates that aspects of Carolingian political thought were current in intellectual circles in Anglo-Saxon England in the later eighth century. The evidence of the chronicles, the *York Annals* in particular, shows that both the events in Francia and the language of Carolingian kingship were known, at least in Northumbria, by this stage. But did this information have any impact on the practice of politics and kingship in Anglo-Saxon England? What was the impact of this theorizing and moralizing by Carolingian thinkers on the reality of temporal power in Anglo-Saxon England?

The most immediate fall-out from the legates' mission in 786 was witnessed, of course, in Mercia. Reason and chronology suggests a close connection between George's statements within his capitulary on the sanctity of kingship and respect owed to bishops by kings and princes, with the events of the contentious Synod of Chelsea a few months later when the new metropolitan see of Lichfield was carved out of Canterbury's, and when Offa's son, Ecgfrith, was 'hallowed' to kingship. After all, it can only have been with papal approval that Offa was permitted to deviate from the episcopal plan for England as devised by Pope Gregory the Great.[1] Alcuin's presence in Bishop George's legation supplied the element of continuity between that mission and the Frankish contribution to Anglo-Saxon political life which Alcuin and his network of contacts were able to sustain in the following decades. It was after 786 that he composed his 65 or so surviving letters addressed to Anglo-Saxon men and women – letters which are imbued with Carolingian thinking on the nature of temporal power which he himself was doing so much to shape and define. Although many of his surviving letters to Anglo-Saxons often seem to have been written as a reaction to a political event or crisis, on close reading many of them show that he was striving to change the behaviour of his correspondents through advice and admonition – behaviour which he believed was undermining their political authority as well as their spiritual health.

It is important to remember that Alcuin was also present in England for an extended period between 790 and mid-792 during which time he encountered several significant issues which impinged on aspects of the relationship between the English kingdoms and Francia. It seems that he had arrived in England in the wake of the row which had broken out between King Offa and Charlemagne concerning the break-up of marriage negotiations between their children. Alcuin's impartiality was evidently called into question since he was at pains to affirm

---

[1] N. P. Brooks, *The Early History of the Church of Canterbury* (Leicester, 1984), 123.

his loyalty to Offa and to the English in a letter to the priest Beornwine.[2] The dispute between the Mercian and Frankish kings was settled eventually through the diplomatic ministrations of Abbot Gervold of St Wandrille, but Alcuin's contacts may have been behind the subsequent marriage of Offa's daughter to Æthelred of Northumbria at Catterick on 29 September 792.[3] If this was the girl whom Charlemagne had accepted and then rejected as a suitable bride for his eldest son Charles, then it is possible that Alcuin had been instructed to find a match for the girl which would redeem the bruised pride of King Offa as well as being an acceptable compromise to Charlemagne in Francia.[4] What we know of Æthelred's subsequent cross-Channel contacts certainly points to his status as the legitimate king of Northumbria and that he had been accepted and was even cultivated by the Franks. Alcuin was certainly present in Northumbria in 792 and had been there since the beginning of Æthelred's reign in 790 when he was able to offer advice to the new king, and claims to have been working 'against injustice … with certain men of power'.[5] As we have seen, Alcuin was in direct contact with Charlemagne in 792 when the Frankish king sent to Britain a copy of the decrees of the second Council of Nicaea concerning image worship. Prior to its account of Æthelred's marriage, the *York Annals* record Alcuin's composition of a letter condemning this tract, which he subsequently took to back Charlemagne with the approval of all the bishops and secular leaders of Northumbria.[6]

The extent and depth of Carolingian involvement in Anglo-Saxon politics in the 790s reveals itself in another way: through Charlemagne's treatment of and hospitality towards a number of political exiles from England. The epistolary and chronicle sources reveal the names of at least five powerful Anglo-Saxons who came to Charlemagne to plead their cases, and the same sources imply that many more accompanied these exiled men in their retinues. By this date Charlemagne's status was such that his court often received the disgruntled or dispossessed nobility of neighbouring kingdoms, from as far afield as Asturias and Denmark, from the Slavic peoples, and even from the caliphate of Cordoba.[7]

---

[2] Alcuin, *Ep.* no. 82; *Alcuin of York c. A.D. 732 to 804: His Life and Letters*, trans. M. Allott (York, 1974), no. 39.

[3] *Historia regum* (*York Annals*), 792. The marriage took place at Catterick where Æthelred's parents had been married thirty years previously; ibid., 762. On Abbot Gervold's actions see the *Gesta Sanctorum Patrum Fontanellensis coenobii*, ed. F. Lohier and R. P. J. Laporte (Rouen and Paris, 1936), c. 12.2, 86–87; *EHD* 1, trans. Whitelock, no. 20. On the marriage dispute with Charlemagne see Chapter 6, below, 184–88.

[4] F. M. Stenton, *Anglo-Saxon England* (Oxford, 1971), 218. Offa's other daughter, Eadburh, had been married to Beorhtric of Wessex in 789, *ASChron.* A, 787.

[5] Alcuin, *Ep.*, no. 9; *Alcuin of York*, trans. Allott, no. 10.

[6] C. Cubitt, *Anglo-Saxon Church Councils c. 650–c. 850* (London, 1995), 64 and n. 15; H. Vollrath, *Die Synoden Englands bis 1066*, Konziliengeschichte Reihe A Darstellungen (Paderborn, 1985), 179–81; D. A. Bullough, 'Alcuin before Frankfort', in R. Berndt (ed.), *Das Frankforter Konzil von 794* (Mainz, 1997), 571–85, at 581ff.

[7] F. L. Ganshof, 'The Frankish Monarchy and its external relations, from Pippin III to Louis

These men hoped for financial or military support, or even just the moral backing of the Frankish king in their struggles to avoid assassination at home and regain status and power in their *patriae*. The presence of Anglo-Saxon political exiles at the Frankish court around the turn of the ninth century is, therefore, perhaps not as surprising as it might first seem. But their presence there, and Charlemagne's interest in, and assistance with, their causes, should undoubtedly be seen in the light of his (and Alcuin's) longstanding and deep interest in the affairs of Anglo-Saxon England, and more particularly, in the growing power of Mercia and its king.

The followers of Hringstan

The first recorded example of such an Anglo-Saxon exile at Charlemagne's court is revealed in a letter written in Charlemagne's name and addressed to Æthelheard, Offa's Mercian archbishop of Canterbury, and to Ceolwulf the bishop of Lindsey, sometime between 793 and mid-796.[8] The letter requested their intervention with King Offa, Charlemagne's 'dearest brother', on behalf of the followers of a man named Hringstan who, it seems, had died while in exile in Francia and went on to say that Charlemagne was sending Hringstan's men back to England under the protection of this letter of introduction. Charlemagne reminded Æthelheard and Ceolwulf of the bonds of friendship which they had pledged, 'in loyal words, when once we were together', and instructed the bishops to intercede with Offa to allow the men to return and live peacefully in their own land, 'without unjust oppression of any kind'. But if Offa was unforgiving in their case, Charlemagne continued, Æthelheard and Ceolwulf were charged to return the men uninjured to Francia for, he said, 'it is better to live in exile than to perish, to serve in a foreign land than to die in one's own'. According to the letter, Hringstan and his retinue had fled to Francia 'in danger of death'. He had come to Charlemagne to whom he had protested his innocence and was, 'ever ready to purge himself with an oath from all disloyalty'. Charlemagne clearly thought that Hringstan would have maintained faith with Offa had he been able to remain in his homeland but, as he had fled, he had kept Hringstan and his party with him at court 'for some little time' out of the desire for reconciliation rather than emnity – or so he said.

However, Charlemagne evidently realized that Offa might mistrust his display of Christian altruism and might yet demand the men's continued exile, or something even worse. Charlemagne therefore makes much of the notion of

---

the Pious', in his *The Carolingians and the Frankish Monarchy: Studies in Carolingian History*, trans. J. Sondheimer (London, 1971), 162–204.

[8] Alcuin, *Ep.*, no. 85; Haddan and Stubbs (eds), *Councils* 3, 487–88; *EHD* 1, trans. Whitelock, no. 196. The letter must postdate Æthelheard's consecration in 792–93 and Offa's death in July 796. See F. C. Scheiber, 'Alcuin und die Briefe Karls des Großen', *DA* 15 (1959), 181–93. According to Einhard, Charlemagne also referred to the Byzantine emperors as 'brothers'; Einhard, *VK*, c. 28.

fidelity: the fidelity of Hringstan's followers to their lord; of Hringstan to Offa; and of the English bishops to Charlemagne himself through their 'special bond of Christian friendship' which they had pledged in his presence. By playing on this notion of fidelity Charlemagne was able to pressurize the bishops into action on behalf of the exiles and to cast real doubt on Offa's willingness to trust the loyalty of a band of men who (rather admirably in the eyes of the Frankish king) had held faith with their lord, and had followed him even into exile abroad. To Offa these men were guilty by association with Hringstan; to Charlemagne their guilt was only that they had stayed true to their lord, a bond which was now absolved by his death. The letter tells us much about Offa's reputation for ruthlessness towards his opponents but perhaps rather more about Charlemagne's notions of friendship, fidelity and the abilities of a distant king to intervene in the internal disputes of another's kingdom.

The reference to face-to-face contact between Charlemagne, Æthelheard, and Ceolwulf is important. The power of Charlemagne's argument in the letter is amplified by reference to this personal contact. We have no independent note of the date of this meeting but it is tempting to recall Charlemagne's own assertion that British representatives had been present at the important reforming Synod of Frankfurt held in the early summer of 794.[9] One wonders if Æthelheard and Ceolwulf were, with Alcuin, the 'learned men from Britain' referred to by Charlemagne in a letter written in his name to Elipand, the Bishop of Toledo.[10] Although the main focus of the synod was the rebuttal of the heresy of adoptionism, other important issues were discussed which were likely to have been of interest to Offa, not least the actions which Charlemagne took against a rebellious magnate. In the same year that Offa brutally repressed an apparent rebellion against Mercian supremacy in East Anglia and subsequently ordered King Æthelberht to be beheaded, Charlemagne used the synod as a stage for the final denunciation and ritualized humiliation of Tassilo, the *dux Baiuwariorum*, who had broken his oaths of vassalage to the king and had challenged Carolingian authority in Bavaria.[11] The parallel with Tassilo was a pertinent one; Charlemagne had used the sanction of the synod rather than the sword to suppress the

---

[9] *Annales regni Francorum, s.a.* 794; MGH Capit. I, no. 28; MGH Conc. II, 110–71; Haddan and Stubbs (eds), *Councils*, 3, 481–82; Stenton, *Anglo-Saxon England*, 219; W. Levison, *England and the Continent in the Eighth Century* (Oxford, 1946), 122, 156, 316; D. Berndt (ed.), *Das Frankfurter konzil von 794*, 2 vols (Mainz, 1997).

[10] MGH, Conc. II, 157–64; Wallach argued that Alcuin was the author of the letter sent in Charlemagne's name and that he was the only Englishman at the synod, acting only in his capacity as adviser to the Frankish king; L. Wallach, *Alcuin and Charlemagne: Studies in Carolingian History and Literature* (Ithaca, 1959), 165–68. This opinion on the authorship of the letter is supported by Bullough, 'Alcuin before Frankfort', 582, but for alternative views see the articles cited by Bullough, ibid., 583, n. 48 and J. M. Wallace-Hadrill, 'Charlemagne and England' in W. Braunfels (ed.), *Karl der Große: Lebenswerke und Nachleben* (Dusseldorf, 1965), vol. 1, 164.

[11] R. McKitterick, *The Frankish Kingdoms under the Carolingians, 751–987* (London, 1983), 65–67; C. E. Odegaard, *Vassi and Fideles in the Carolingian Empire* (Cambridge, MA, 1945), 24–32; S. Reynolds, *Fiefs and Vassals: The Medieval Evidence Reinterpreted* (Oxford, 1994), 86.

challenge to his authority in a once-independent region which lay beyond his familial powerbase. Also of interest to Offa, given recent developments in Mercia, were the references at Frankfurt to the standardization of weights and measures, the acceptance of the new Carolingian pennies (which Offa's moneyers were imitating), the enforcement of monastic discipline and the definition of the jurisdiction of metropolitans and bishops.[12]

As his name is not recorded in any other source, Hringstan's zone of activity prior to his exile remains unknown, but the kingdoms of East Anglia or Kent are obvious candidates. Offa had ordered the decapitation of Æthelberht in 794 presumably as a reaction to the emergence of opposition to Mercian overlordship in East Anglia.[13] Kent, though quiet after the death of Archbishop Jaenberht in 792, maintained a latent and festering mistrust of its Mercian overlords, both secular and ecclesiastical – a mistrust which resurfaced in open rebellion shortly after Offa's death in July 796. However, the quality of the charter evidence for Kent during this period is such that we might expect Hringstan to have left some trace in that material had he, in fact, been active in that region. Another possibility is that Hringstan had come from the kingdom of Lindsey which had been subsumed by Mercia *c*. 770. Although we have no direct evidence of resistance to Mercia in that kingdom it may be significant that both the recipients of Charlemagne's letter were Lindsey men: Archbishop Æthelheard had been abbot of the monastery at Louth before being elevated to Canterbury in 792.[14] It may also be relevant that the other recipient of Charlemagne's letter, Bishop Ceolwulf of Lindsey, left England a couple of years later in 796, but where he went, or whether he went voluntarily, is unknown.[15]

Odberht / Eadberht Præn and the Kentish rebellion, 796–98

The case of Hringstan's followers is, in some respects, unusual; it is not often that we hear of such high-level and explicit interventions on behalf of a group of men such as this. But their situation as Anglo-Saxon exiles at the Frankish court was by no means unique. Another group of English exiles were with Charlemagne by the early months of 796, 'having taken refuge under the wings of our protection'. This second group of men, who had 'bound themselves together with a vow', had fled England, once more *timore mortis*. Their leader was a priest, named Odberht in the Frankish sources. On this occasion Charlemagne

---

[12] MGH Capit. I, no. 28; *Charlemagne. Translated Texts*, trans. P. D. King (Kendal, 1987), 224–30; MGH, Conc. II.1, no. 19; and see, further, Chapter 6, 194.

[13] *ASChron*. A, 792 (for 794).

[14] *ASChron*. F, 790 (for 792). On Lindsey in the Anglo-Saxon period see P. H. Sawyer, *Anglo-Saxon Lincolnshire*, A History of Lincolnshire, Vol. 3 (Lincoln, 1998).

[15] *ASChron*. A, 794 (for 796) and *ASChron*. D, 796 on his death in the same year. Ceolwulf left with Ealdbald, the bishop of London, an event which Brooks sees as symptomatic of the unravelling of Mercian control after Offa's death; Brooks, *The Early History*, 122.

wrote directly to King Offa, rather than through episcopal intermediaries, in response to letters from the Mercian king concerning this group of exiles.[16] Acknowledging a difference of opinion, Charlemagne informed Offa that he had sent Odberht and his companions to Rome to plead their case before Pope Leo, since 'what could be safer for us than that the opinion of the apostolic authority should determine a case in which the views of others disagree'. This time Offa had sent Archbishop Æthelheard directly to Rome to present the Mercian argument and to force a papal judgement over the exiles who had fled beyond his writ into Francia. It may have been that Odberht's status as a priest was doubtful, and this had forced the issue into the jurisdictional domain of the papacy; it is also possible, given Charlemagne's proven willingness and ability to intervene on behalf of Offa's opponents (as the case of Hringstan and his followers had recently shown), that Offa hoped to circumvent and curtail any potential action by Charlemagne by sending his archbishop to Rome and appealing to the pope for judgement, thereby pressurizing the Frankish king into compliance with a papal ruling on the case.

Charlemagne was certainly at some pains to placate Offa over this affair. With the same letter he sent Offa precious gifts from the Avar treasure hoard and granted legal protection to English merchants travelling in Francia.[17] Alcuin reinforced Charlemagne's affection for 'his dearest brother' by adding in another, contemporaneous letter that, 'the lord king Charles has often spoken to me of you in a most loving and loyal way, and in him you certainly have a most loyal friend'.[18] But despite Charlemagne's protestations to Offa that Odberht intended to 'live abroad for the love of God' on his return from Rome, Offa's fears about the continued challenge posed by Odberht and his companions-in-exile were entirely justified. Soon after Offa's death in July 796 the anti-Mercian sentiments of the Kentishmen were reasserted, with Odberht – given his Anglo-Saxon name, Eadberht Præn ('the Priest') – at their head. The rebellion in Kent was successful enough for Archbishop Æthelheard, who had stood against Eadberht in Rome, to be forced into exile in Mercia, and to allow Eadberht to mint coins at Canterbury using moneyers who had previously worked for King Offa.[19] For two years, until 798, Kent remained free of Mercian dominion.

Is there a connection here between Charlemagne's explicit support for Eadberht in exile and the successful rebellion in Kent a few months later? There is no direct evidence of Carolingian involvement in the return of Eadberht to Kent in 796, but it is hard to believe that Charlemagne would not have

[16] Alcuin, *Ep.*, no. 100; *Alcuin of York*, trans. Allott, no. 40. K. P. Witney, *The Kingdom of Kent* (London, 1982), 198–214; Brooks, *The Early History*, 114, 121–25.

[17] Wallace-Hadrill, 'Charlemagne and England', 164–67. On the Avar treasure and Charlemagne's letter to Offa, see also Chapter 4, above, 101–4 and, Chapter 6, below, 195–96.

[18] Alcuin, *Ep.*, no. 101; *Alcuin of York*, trans. Allott, no. 41.

[19] C. E. Blunt, 'The Coinage of Offa' in R. H. M. Dolley (ed.), *Anglo-Saxon Coins* (London, 1958), 39–62. Æthelheard went in exile to the court of Ecgfrith and was given the monastery of *Pectanege*; BCS 291; Brooks, *The Early History*, 121.

known about, if not actively supported, Eadberht's return to England. Charlemagne's correspondence about the case dates to the first few months of 796
and the Kentish rebellion was certainly underway before the end of the year,
making it likely that it commenced before the premature death of Offa's son,
Ecgfrith, in mid-December.[20] Given Eadberht's period of exile in Francia
immediately prior to these events, and Charlemagne's sponsorship of his cause
in Francia and in Rome, it seems improbable that his successful return after a
period of exile abroad could have been achieved without external patronage of
some sort.[21] If this is the case, and Eadberht enjoyed at least tacit Frankish
support, it moves Charlemagne's interventions in English politics on to a new
level.

The events of Eadberht's revolt are murky; Alcuin disapproved of
Æthelheard's decision to desert his diocese, and wrote to both the archbishop
and to the men of Kent begging them all to reconsider since, 'disobeying the
priests and driving away the preachers of salvation always means the ruin of a
people'.[22] Alcuin must also have found it hard to reconcile the coup in Kent with
Eadberht's apparent profession as a priest. Forced tonsuring or expulsion into
internal exile in a monastic prison were techniques used by both Franks and
Anglo-Saxons who wished to dispose of troublesome opponents.[23] Receiving
the crown of Christ (even reluctantly) debarred men from accepting royal office
on Earth, and Offa may well have tried this technique on his Kentish opponent.[24]
Eadberht evidently considered himself an exception to this rule, but Pope Leo
did not. In a response to a letter from Ecgfrith's successor, Coenwulf, and
another from Æthelheard, Leo compared Eadberht with Julian the Apostate and
demanded that:

> ... [concerning] the apostate cleric who has mounted the throne ...
> we excommunicate and reject him, having regard for the safety of his
> soul. For if he still should persist in that wicked behaviour, be sure to
> inform us quickly, that we may send the apostolic reminder to all in
> general, both to princes and to all people dwelling in the island of
> Britain, exhorting them to expel him from his most wicked rule and
> to procure the safety of his soul.[25]

---

[20] *ASChron.* D, 796 and *ASChron.* A, 755 (for 757).

[21] D. P. Kirby, *The Earliest English Kings* (London, 1991), 185.

[22] Alcuin, *Ep.*, nos 128 and 129; *Alcuin of York*, trans. Allott, nos 49 and 50.

[23] Most notable in Francia was the deposition of the last Merovingian monarch, Childeric III;
Einhard, *VK.* ch.1; For the same practices in Northumbria see Æthelwulf's *Carmen de abbatibus*,
ed. and trans. A. Campbell (Oxford, 1967), ch. 7, as well as the fate of Bede's king, Ceolwulf;
Bede's Ecclesiastical History of the English People, ed. and trans. B. Colgrave and R. A. B. Mynors
(Oxford, 1968), 572–73. For the context to this phenomenon see C. Stancliffe, 'Kings who Opted
Out', in P. Wormald (ed.), *Ideal and Reality in Frankish and Anglo-Saxon Society: Studies Pre-
sented to J. M. Wallace-Hadrille*, (Oxford, 1983), 155, 158.

[24] The exception was Ceolwulf, Bede's king who was deposed and tonsured in 732, but was
restored to his throne shortly afterwards; *Continuatio Bedae*, 732.

[25] MGH, Epp. 4, no. 127; *EHD* 1, trans. Whitelock, no. 205.

Coenwulf's response was brutal. In 798 he broke the Kentish resistance, captured Eadberht and installed his own brother as king in his stead.[26] Eadberht was
mutilated in punishment; his hands were amputated and his eyes poked out, but
his life was preserved – perhaps in recognition of his priestly rank or perhaps as
a reminder to others that the new king of Mercia could be as ruthless with
opponents as Offa had been. Later tradition has it that Eadberht was consigned
to the monastery at Winchcombe which Coenwulf had newly founded. The
incarceration of political dissenters in a family monastery also has Carolingian
precedents – consider Desiderius imprisoned at St Denis (according to later
tradition) or Tassilo of Bavaria who was similarly said to have been incarcerated
at Jumièges, or Charlemagne's own son, Pippin the Hunchback, who was condemned to the monastery of Prüm after the collapse of his uprising in 792.[27]

Pope Leo had not foreseen this outcome to the Kentish crisis – he had
demanded Eadberht's immediate return to exile – and the mutilation and viola-
tion of even a reluctant priest was more than he could have sanctioned. It is
rather ironic, then, that Pope Leo himself suffered a similar indignity barely a
year later, in 799, when political opponents ambushed him outside the church of
St Silvestro in Rome. According to papal sources, several attempts were made to
gouge out Leo's eyes and chop off his tongue. He was then imprisoned in a
monastery from where he was rescued and fled, an exile himself, to Charlemagne's protection.[28] The Frankish and papal sources differ on the detail of
these events, but whichever version of the story we follow, two things are clear:
Leo was undoubtedly the most important exile to have arrived at Charlemagne's
court to date, and Charlemagne's actions in support of the pope produced the
most significant repercussions, since the restoration of Leo to his papal throne
culminated in Charlemagne's imperial coronation in Rome on Christmas day in
800.

---

[26] *ASChron.* A, 796 (for 798). The surviving charter evidence suggests that Canterbury may
have been sacked in 798 since no original documents from the monastery survive prior to 798 but
authentic, original documents survive in great numbers after that date. See Brooks, *The Early
History*, 120–25; S. Keynes, 'The Control of Kent in the Ninth Century', *EME*, 2.2 (1993), 111–31,
at 113.

[27] On Desiderius and Tassilo see *Francorum monasterii Sancti Dionysii*, ed. G. H. Pertz,
MGH *SS* IX (Hanover, 1851), 395–406 at 400; D. A. Bullough, *The Age of Charlemagne* (London,
1973), 96; McKitterick, *The Frankish Kingdoms*, 58. On the revolt of Pippin see the *Annales regni
Francorum*, 792.

[28] The papal sources suggest that Leo went voluntarily to Charlemagne after he had re-
established some authority in Rome; see *The Lives of the Eighth-Century Popes*, trans. R. Davis
(Liverpool, 1992), 185–87. Compare the Frankish sources which say that he was spirited out of
Rome under the guard of the Duke of Spoleto; *Annales regni Francorum* (revised version), 799. M.
Becher, 'Karl der Große und Papst Leo III', in C. Stiegemann and M. Wemhoff (eds), *799 Kunst
und Kultur in der Karolingerzeit. Karl der Große und Papst Leo III in Paderborn* (Mainz, 1999),
Vol. 1, 22–36.

Torctmund

The next group of Anglo-Saxons to arrive at Charlemagne's court were not exiles, but they had brought with them a man who had good reason to flee his homeland in the expectation that he would find a sympathetic audience at the Frankish court. This man was a Northumbrian nobleman named Torctmund, who joined the company of Archbishop Æthelheard and the Mercian ealdorman Ceolmund on their journey to Rome in 801 in order to obtain papal permission to dissolve the metropolitan see of Lichfield. Alcuin wrote three letters on this occasion, one to the Archbishop informing him of the provisions he had made to ease their journey through Francia and how his party ought to behave in Charlemagne's presence, and another to Archbishop Eanbald of York.[29] The third was a letter of introduction to Charlemagne announcing the imminent arrival of the Anglo-Saxon party at the Frankish court.[30] In this letter to Charlemagne Alcuin describes Torctmund as a *fidelis* of King Æthelred of Northumbria who had been murdered by members of his household in 796. So faithful was Torctmund to his lord that, in 799, he perjured his own soul by killing the *dux* Ealdred who had assassinated Æthelred three years previously.[31] Alcuin clearly approved of Torctmund's actions and thought the Frankish king would too: he describes him to Charlemagne as, 'a man of proven loyalty (*in fide probatum*) and valiant in arms who has bravely avenged the blood of his lord'. Given the references in the Legates' Capitulary to the sanctity of kingship and Alcuin's own comments on Charlemagne's fury at the news of Æthelred's murder, Torctmund was assured a warm welcome in Francia.[32] The politics surrounding this situation in Northumbria were complex; Torctmund had taken advantage of the new Northumbrian king's campaign against the anti-Æthelred faction in order to kill Ealdred. But the new king, Eardwulf, was himself an implacable enemy of the murdered king, having narrowly survived an execution ordered by Æthelred in 790.[33] Under these circumstances, Torctmund evidently considered it safer to leave Northumbria in self-imposed exile and to travel abroad in the company of the archbishop, in order to secure his secular reputation and spiritual redemption. Tortcmund's journey must have fulfilled its function since he suffered no *damnatio memoriae* in his own country; his name is recorded in the mid-ninth-century Northumbrian *Liber Vitae* in the list of *reges et duces* on the same folio as that of Charlemagne and the Frankish treasurer Mægenfrith.[34]

---

[29] Alcuin, *Ep.*, nos 230 and 232; *Alcuin of York*, trans. Allott, nos. 51 and 20.

[30] Alcuin, *Ep.*, no. 231; *Alcuin of York*, trans. Allott, no. 52.

[31] *Historia regum* (*York Annals*), 799.

[32] Alcuin, *Ep.*, no. 101; *Alcuin of York*, trans. Allott, no. 41.

[33] *Historia regum* (*York Annals*), 790.

[34] See above, Figure 4.1, line 14.

Ecgberht of Wessex

The Kentishman Eadberht Præn was not the only Anglo-Saxon ætheling who had spent time in Francia before returning to claim the throne of his homeland. The *Anglo-Saxon Chronicle* for 839 recorded the death of King Ecgberht of Wessex, and noted that, sometime prior to his accession, he too had been forced to flee in exile to Francia. The reason for his flight, suggests the *Chronicle*, was that Offa and the West Saxon king Beorhtric had allied against him in a pact which was sealed by the marriage of the Mercian princess, Eadburh, to Beorhtric in 789.[35] The *Chronicle* says that Ecgberht had spent three years in Francia during Beorhtric's 13-year reign, although the precise dates of his exile are ambiguous. If, as seems likely, Ecgberht had fled abroad for three years shortly after the establishment of the coalition against him – that is in 789–90 – we have no notion of where he had spent the remaining ten years of Beorhtric's reign (although if the chronicler had mistakenly omitted a single numeral, it may have been that he had spent the entire 13 years of Beorhtric's reign in Francia).[36] After Beorhtric's death in 802, Ecgberht was able to mount a successful bid for power in Wessex. Unlike the cases of Hringstan and Eadberht Præn, we have no surviving letters to amplify our understanding of Carolingian involvement in Ecgberht's case, although we should note that Ecgberht's exile in Francia was concurrent with the serious breakdown in communication between Offa and Charlemagne over the marriages of their children. As with Eadberht's coup in Kent in 796, there is no explicit proof linking Charlemagne with Ecgberht's rather more successful coup in Wessex in 802. But the parallels are pressing; an Anglo-Saxon nobleman, having spent a period of exile in Francia, was able to return to his *patria* having retained sufficient status and resources to claim the throne. As Stenton argued, 'it cannot have been without Charlemagne's approval that Egbert, the rival of Offa's protégé Byrhtric [*sic*] of Wessex, lived in Frankish territory after Byrhtric and Offa had driven him from England'.[37] Kirby would have us push the evidence further, arguing that Ecgberht's return from Francia, 'was also probably a consequence of Carolingian and possibly even papal influence'.[38] It was certainly to his period of Frankish exile that William of Malmesbury retrospectively attributed Ecgberht's skills in 'the arts of good government'.[39]

There is another twist to Ecgberht's story; Scharer has argued that the West Saxon chronicler, who was responsible for compiling the *Anglo-Saxon Chronicle*

[35] *ASChron.* A, 839 and 789. See also the *Historia regum* (*York Annals*) 802 and Asser's *Life of King Alfred*, ed. W. H. Stevenson (Oxford, 1959), ch. 14–15 for Eadburh's fate; also *Alfred the Great, Asser's Life of King Alfred and other Contemporary Sources*, trans. S. Keynes and M. Lapidge (Harmondsworth, 1983), 71–73, 236; Wallace-Hadrill, 'Charlemagne and England', 162.

[36] See Chapter 7, below, 214–18.

[37] Stenton, *Anglo-Saxon England*, 220.

[38] Kirby, *The Earliest English Kings*, 186.

[39] William of Malmesbury, *Gesta Regum Anglorum: The History of the English Kings*, ed. and trans. R. A. B. Mynors, R. M. Thompson and M. Winterbottom (Oxford, 1998), vol. I, 152–3.

during the reign of Ecgberht's grandson, Alfred, had assimilated a Kentish spin on the history of Ecgberht's dynasty, in order to accommodate and conceal the fact that Alfred's family was ultimately descended from the dynasty which had ruled Kent in the mid-eighth-century before it had succumbed to Mercian rule.[40] Although there are some difficulties with this idea it is certainly the case that the West Saxon genealogy given in the *Anglo-Saxon Chronicle* for 855–58 names one Ealhmund as Ecgberht's father, a name belonging to a king of Kent who ruled there in the early 780s before Offa's annexation of that kingdom. The early twelfth-century bilingual Canterbury version of the *Chronicle*, represented by manuscript F, makes an explicit link between Ecgberht's father and the Kentish king of the same name.[41] If this blood-link between the non-Mercian kings of Kent and the ninth-century West-Saxon dynasty is genuine, it adds an interesting gloss to the notion of Carolingian support for Ecgberht in exile. A link with Kent would add consistency to Charlemagne's attitude towards Anglo-Saxon exiles, giving protection, and perhaps active support, to men who valued a Kent free from Mercian control. It is this broader context, surely, which supplies the kernel of truth behind the rumour peddled by Matthew Paris in the thirteenth century that Archbishop Jaenberht had been prepared to allow Charlemagne's army access to England via Canterbury should he have chosen to challenge Offa by force.[42] Condoning Ecgberht's actions in Wessex would have complemented Charlemagne's concerns for Kent, which by 802 had reverted to Mercian control, as well as extending his interests and influence within Wessex.

Eardwulf of Northumbria

The evidence of Carolingian support for Ecgberht is tantalizing but sparse, but we are on rather firmer ground with our next example of an Anglo-Saxon exile at the Carolingian court. Perhaps the most remarkable of the Anglo-Saxon exiles to Charlemagne came from Alcuin's own homeland in Northumbria. In the last entry that is unique to its Northern Recension, the *Anglo-Saxon Chronicle* states in the annal for the year 806 that Eardwulf, king of Northumbria, was expelled from his kingdom.[43] The event is stated simply, between accounts of a lunar

---

[40] Kirby, *The Earliest English Kings*, 166–67; A. Scharer, 'The Writing of History at King Alfred's Court', *EME*, 5.2 (1996), 177–206. See also Alcuin's comment to the Kentishmen that, 'scarcely anyone is found now of the old stock of kings'; Alcuin, *Ep.*, no. 129, *Alcuin of York*, trans. Allott, no. 50.

[41] *ASChron.* F, 784.

[42] *Vitae duorum Offae, Matthæi Paris Historia Major*, ed. W. Watts (1684), 978–9. Brooks argues that, although this 'may simply be a typical fabrication by Matthew Paris ... it is possible that a genuine tradition had been preserved at St. Alban's, the house that Offa founded, and therefore that Carolingian interest in Kentish politics was real'; Brooks, *The Early History*, 115–16. See also Wallace-Hadrill, 'Charlemagne and England', 162.

[43] *ASChron.* DE, 806.

eclipse and the death of Eanberht, the bishop of Hexham. The dating of the eclipse is accurate; it was witnessed also in Francia and recorded in a set of annals compiled at the Carolingian court.[44] The bald narration of these events in the *Anglo-Saxon Chronicle* reveals nothing which might suggest that the expulsion of Eardwulf from Northumbria was anything other than the common fate which befell so many of his predecessors in the politically volatile eighth century. The northern annals which supplied the *Anglo-Saxon Chronicle* with information about the affairs of Northumbria cease after this entry and, thus, no more is heard of Eardwulf in any near-contemporary Anglo-Saxon source.

But Eardwulf's political career was not yet finished. The *Royal Frankish Annals*, having noted the lunar eclipse, also recorded in some detail the subsequent movements of the exiled Northumbrian king. This set of annals, compiled at the Frankish court, relates several surprising events within its entry for the year 808, and as such preserves a record of events which cannot be found in any Anglo-Saxon source.

Interea rex Nordanhumbrorum de Brittania insula, nomine Eardulf, regno et patria pulsus ad imperatorem, dum adhuc Noviomagi moraretur, venit et patefacto adventus sui negotio Romam proficiscitur; Romaque rediens per legatos Romani pontificis et domni imperatoris in regnum suum reducitur. Praeerat tunc temporis ecclesiae Romanae Leo tertius, cuius legatus ad Brittaniam directus est Aldulfus diaconus de ipsa Brittania, natione Saxo, et cum eo ab imperatore missi abbates duo, Hruotfridus notarius et Nantharius de sancto Otmaro.[45]

Meanwhile the king of the Northumbrians from the island of Britain by the name of Eardwulf, having been expelled from his kingdom and his native land, came to the Emperor while he was still residing at Nijmegen, and having made known the reasons for his coming, he went on to Rome; and returning from Rome he was escorted back into his own kingdom by legates of the Roman pontiff and the Lord Emperor. This happened when Leo III ruled of the Roman church, his legate Aldulf the deacon was sent to Britain – being himself from Britain from the Saxon race, and with him were two abbots Hruotfrid, the notary, and Nantharius of St Omer sent by the Emperor.

According to the *Royal Frankish Annals*, after his expulsion Eardwulf had crossed the sea into lands which constituted part of the territory of the Empire of Charlemagne. He travelled to the imperial palace at Nijmegen on the Rhine

---

[44] The dating of the lunar eclipse by the *ASChron.* DE to 1 September 806 is accurate. The *Annales regni Francorum* record the same eclipse (*iv Non. Sept.*, that is, 2 September) in the annal for 807 but as a reference to the preceding year. The eclipse occurred around midnight on 1–2 September 806; D. J. Schove and A. Fletcher, *Chronology of Eclipses and Comets, AD 1–1000* (Woodbridge, 1984), 174.

[45] *Annales regni Francorum*, 808.

where Charlemagne's court was in residence for the season of Lent. There he pleaded his case to the emperor; immediately after this, Eardwulf proceeded to Rome for an audience with Pope Leo III. The Frankish annals state explicitly that, on his return from Rome, Eardwulf was, 'escorted back to his own kingdom by legates of the Roman Pontiff and the Lord Emperor'. Three men who accompanied him are named. The papal legate, Aldulf, a Saxon from Britain, is named in several papal letters of the period.[46] Charlemagne was represented on the mission to Northumbria by two abbots, Nantharius from the monastery of St Omer[47] and Hruotfrid, who was probably abbot of the monastery of St Amand further to the east near the River Scheldt.[48] The geographical situation of both of these monasteries means that they are likely to have been familiar to Anglo-Saxons travelling to the Continent, and thus their abbots may well have been familiar in the English kingdoms.[49] The presence of a notary in the escort which returned Eardwulf to Northumbria also suggests that the process was to be formalized by written record; indeed, Hruotfrid's name is recorded in the list of abbots in the Northumbrian *Liber Vitae*.[50]

The international dimension of Eardwulf's journey to Charlemagne and the pope is reinforced by another continental source. A single manuscript, the precise original provenance of which is unknown but which is certainly of

---

[46] MGH, Epp. V. no. 2, 3, and 4.

[47] Nantharius is also listed as abbot of St Omer in other sources such as the *Lamberti Audomarensis series abbatum St Bertini*, MGH, SS XIII, 390–1 and in the *Gesta Abbatum S. Bertini Sithiensium* written by Folcuin in the third quarter of the tenth century; ibid., 613. Nantharius (the second abbot of that name at St Omer) died in 820 and was succeeded as abbot by Fredegisius, Alcuin's pupil and friend, on whom see Levison, *England and the Continent*, 165.

[48] The St Amand Rotfrid was first identified as the notary in the *Annales regni Francorum* annal by Pertz; MGH, SS I, 195 n. 66, but the attribution is not certain. There was an abbot by the name of Rotfrid at St Amand who died in 827 according to the *Annales Elnonenses Maiores*; MGH, SS V, 1, although the entry giving the obituary of Rotfrid is in a twelfth-century hand. However, the same list appears to show that a certain Adalricus was abbot of the community between 787 and 819. Adalricus may have taken over as abbot when Arno (Alcuin's great friend) was promoted to the metropolitan see of Salzburg in 785. A man named Hruotfrid is recorded as a royal *missus* acting in the Chalons–Rheims region in 825; see R. Hennebicque-le Jan, 'Prosopographica Neustrica, les agents du roi en Neustrie de 639 à 840', in H. Atsma (ed.), *La Neustrie, le pays au nord de la Loire de 650 à 850*, Beihefte der Francia 16/1 (Sigmaringen, 1989), 231–70, 245, no. 168.

[49] The reality of the contacts with Anglo-Saxon England is revealed by the insular elements in the books produced at both these monasteries. Both were important centres of the Franco-Saxon style of book production in the ninth century, on which see R. McKitterick, 'The Diffusion of Insular Culture in Neustria between 650 and 850: The Implications of the Manuscript Evidence', in Atsma and Werner, *La Neustrie*, 395–432, and reprinted as Chapter 3 in R. McKitterick, *Books, Scribes and Learning in the Frankish Kingdoms, 6th–9th Centuries* (Aldershot, 1994).

[50] London, BL MS Cotton Domitian A.vii, fol. 20r. J. Gerchow, *Die Gedenküberlieferung der Angelsachsen*, Arbeiten sur Frümittelalterforschung, 20 (Berlin and New York, 1988), 306, no. 24 in the 'Abbots List'; *Liber Vitae Ecclesiae Dunelmensis*, ed. J. Stevenson, Surtees Society, 13 (London, 1841), 9 and *Liber Vitae Ecclesiae Dunelmensis. A collotype facsimile of the original manuscript with introductory essays and notes*, ed. A. H. Thompson, Surtees Society, 136 (London, 1923).

Frankish origin and which dates palaeographically to the second quarter of the ninth century, contains the only surviving copies of ten letters written by Pope Leo III to Charlemagne.[51] Of these ten letters, three refer directly to Eardwulf and to the mission to return him to Northumbria.[52] The remainder are concerned with places and issues of considerable international significance such as relations with the Saracens, Pippin and Italy, Ravenna and the Byzantine succession.[53] The inclusion of papal letters in this Frankish manuscript makes it a successor to the *Codex Carolinus* in which letters written by popes to Carolingian kings of previous decades were transcribed as an official record.[54] Leo's letters cast light not only on the pope's perception of his role in the affair but also reveal important information about the embroilment of Archbishop Eanbald II of York, Coenwulf of Mercia, and the Northumbrian nobleman Wada, all of whom are known to have been actively hostile towards Eardwulf and all of whom, Leo records, had sent messengers and letters to Rome on the subject of the Northumbrian king.[55]

Leo's letters to Charlemagne describe a frenetic coming-and-going of messages and envoys about the trouble in Northumbria and imply a considerable degree of activity between Northumbria, Mercia, Francia and Rome in the months preceding Eardwulf's departure from his kingdom. His subsequent expulsion and journey to Rome via Charlemagne's court was evidently only one aspect of a long-running dialogue concerning his kingship – a dialogue which had involved the kings and bishops of Northumbria and Mercia, as well as the Frankish emperor and the pope. As a consequence of these letters the intrigue surrounding the internal politics of Northumbria around the year 808 and, more significantly, the international ramifications of these events are illuminated from a variety of angles and in unusual detail. In Eardwulf's case we can see quite clearly, from the evidence of the *Royal Frankish Annals* and Leo's letters, that

---

[51] The manuscript which is now preserved as Wolfenbüttel, Herzog-August-Bibliothek, Helmstadt MS 254 also includes the only surviving copy of the important Carolingian capitulary known as the *Capitulare de Villis;* O. von Heinemann (ed.), *Katalogue der Herzog-August-Bibliothek, Wolfenbüttel. Vol. 1: die Helmstedter Handschriften* (Frankfurt, 1884, repr. 1963), 214; Stiegemann and Wemhoff (eds), *799 Kunst und Kultur*, 1, 93–96. The ten letters by Leo from this manuscript were edited in MGH, Epp. V, 85–104, and those concerning Eardwulf were also printed in part by Haddan and Stubbs (eds), *Councils*, 3, 562–67. On the capitulary collection in this manuscript see R. McKitterick, 'Some Carolingian Law Books and their Function', in P. Linehan and B. Tierney (eds), *Authority and Power: Studies on Medieval Law and Government* (Cambridge, 1980), 13–27 and reprinted as Chapter II in McKitterick, *Books, Scribes, and Learning*.

[52] The letters which refer to Eardwulf are numbers 2, 3, and 4; MGH, Epp. V and 5, 8, and 7 in the manuscript, fos 4r–5r, 7 and 6 respectively. The quire in which these letters are found is now bound at the front of the manuscript, although there is a quire number (which appears to be contemporary with the script of the text) on fo. 8v, which indicates that it had originally been the thirteenth quire in a codex.

[53] MGH, Epp. V, no. 1, 5–10.

[54] MGH Epp. III, 476–653 and *Monumenta Carolina*, ed. P. Jaffe (Berlin, 1867), 1–334.

[55] MGH, Epp. V, no. 3, 91–92, where Leo had to excuse Aldulf for bypassing the Carolingian court and refer to Charlemagne copies of all the letters which had been sent to him on the case.

the emperor and the pope went to considerable efforts on behalf of this Anglo-Saxon king, and also that their collaborative diplomatic efforts were sufficient to ensure that, late in 808, Eardwulf could return to his own kingdom, thereby (presumably) overturning the wishes of the native faction which had deposed him.

No historical analysis has yet provided a completely satisfactory context for this 'extraordinary incident'.[56] Levison simply incorporated the facts of the case as part of his broader commentary on Northumbrian contact with Francia as background to his central analysis of the Anglo-Saxon mission to the Continent.[57] The only really detailed examination of the evidence tried primarily to resolve the issue of temporal authority.[58] Karl Hampe, writing in 1894, argued that the only way in which Charlemagne could have effected a change in Northumbria was to use papal pressure to enforce his wishes on the Archbishop of York, whom Hampe perceived to have been the major instigator of Eardwulf's demise. Hampe's main aim, however, was to use the evidence of this incident to disprove the 'accepted opinion' that Leo's participation reflected the true power of the papal throne over and above that of Charlemagne. If Hampe's thesis is acceptable, its implication must be that the emperor rather than the pope provided the impetus behind the restoration of Eardwulf in 808. Underpinning Hampe's analysis is the basic assumption that Charlemagne was prepared to become actively involved in the domestic politics of Northumbria. By turning up as a political exile at Charlemagne's court Eardwulf had brought this domestic incident firmly on to the international diplomatic stage. Charlemagne, and Leo too, could have ignored the Northumbrian plaintiff, but instead chose not to do so, and plainly put a considerable effort into returning Eardwulf to Northumbria. Evidently, sufficient pressure had been brought to bear on Charlemagne and subsequently on the pope to do something about Eardwulf's problems. In essence, the incident reveals both a remarkable willingness by Charlemagne to become involved in the affairs of a distant kingdom, as well as an ability to achieve that goal.

Wallace-Hadrill has questioned how this was achieved in practice, while admitting that the whole incident was, 'an awkward piece of evidence'.[59] It is awkward precisely because it demonstrates the reality of Carolingian interest and practical involvement in the secular political issues of a kingdom which lay outside the territorial boundaries of Charlemagne's empire. The fundamental question, therefore, must be not so much how the restoration of Eardwulf was achieved but why it was even attempted. Was Charlemagne's motive just a question of 'moral importance' (as Wallace-Hadrill has supposed) or was

---

56 Wallace-Hadrill, 'Charlemagne and England', 170. A full description of the events is given by S. Abel and B. Simson, *Jahrbücher des Fränkischen Reiches unter Karl dem Großen, 789–814*, 2 vols (Berlin, 1883, reprinted 1969), 2, 380–3, 398–9.

57 Levison, *England and the Continent*, 114.

58 K. Hampe, 'Die Wiedereinsetzung des Königs Eardulf von Northumbrien durch Karl den Großen und Papst Leo III', *Deutsche Zeitschriften für Geschichtswissenschaft*, 9 (1894), 352–59.

59 Wallace-Hadrill, 'Charlemagne and England', 170.

Charlemagne in any way obliged to respond to Eardwulf's plea for help? What was the nature of the relationship between Eardwulf and the Carolingian emperor? Was it unique to Eardwulf or can a similar type of contact be distinguished in the historical accounts of the reigns of other Northumbrian kings? Or is this incident just an unusually tangible example of Charlemagne's ability to monitor and influence events in independent kingdoms which lay beyond the militarily defined borders of his empire?

The significance of Charlemagne's intervention on Eardwulf's behalf becomes more dramatic in light of the long-held historiographical assumption that Eardwulf was actually reinstated to royal office on his return to his native kingdom in 808 and that he enjoyed a second reign as king. This assumption is implicit in the title of Hampe's analysis and has been followed by subsequent scholars. Contemporary proof of a reinstatement is, however, lacking; the *Royal Frankish Annals* simply state that Eardwulf was returned *in regnum suum* (the emphasis being on the possessive pronoun). But the possibility that a reinstatement to the Northumbrian kingship did occur is circumstantially implicit in the claims made by the authors of two later medieval chronicles that kings Eanred and Æthelred II were, respectively, the son and grandson of Eardwulf – a relationship which implies that Eardwulf was able to create and maintain an hereditary dynasty in Northumbria in the early decades of the ninth century. Although this does not in itself constitute proof of a second reign for Eardwulf, these later sources do imply that his family overcame the faction which had usurped him and were able to maintain a dynastic supremacy in Northumbria which lasted until the mid-ninth century. If genuine, such a domination of the Northumbrian kingship by a single family had been unknown since the days of Oswald, Oswiu and Ecgfrith in the seventh century, and under these circumstances the intervention by Charlemagne and the pope, as described by the *Royal Frankish Annals*, would seem to have been of longlasting significance for Northumbrian kingship.[60]

The issue of Eardwulf's fate after his return 'to his own kingdom' in 808 has aroused debate, primarily because the question of a second reign naturally has a knock-on effect for the basic regnal chronology of the Northumbrian kings of the pre-Viking ninth century. It also reflects the degree of influence wielded by Eardwulf's Frankish *patronus*. It is, therefore, a problem which demands closer attention not least because the nature of the evidence has a direct bearing on the quality of information deriving from it. The historian of ninth-century Northumbria is faced with a virtual hiatus in the chronicle sources for the majority of the first half of the century, with the consequence that only the thinnest scatter of events are recorded in the historical sources which discuss the period. The source(s) which supplied the Northern Recension of the *Anglo-Saxon Chronicle* and its related text, the *York Annals*, comes to an end in the

---

[60] A similar situation occurred in Wessex after Ecgberht's return. His reign was followed by that of his son Æthelwulf in the first direct father-to-son succession in Wessex since 641.

early ninth century.[61] Thereafter, the regnal chronology of the Northumbrian kings of the first half of the ninth century is insecure; what is known of the regnal chronology must be deduced partly from later medieval texts and partly from extensive, but complex, numismatic evidence.[62] The essence of the argument is this: the written sources which provide most information about Eardwulf's successors are all creations of a later age, predominantly the twelfth and thirteenth centuries,[63] and these later sources do not provide entirely consistent evidence for the dates of the reigns of the early ninth-century Northumbrian kings. The inconsistencies are such that a period of three to four years remains unaccounted for between the demise of Ælfwald II (who usurped Eardwulf) and the death of King Aelle in 867, a gap which provides sufficient time for a second reign by Eardwulf.[64] Thus, it has been argued that the failure of any contemporary Anglo-Saxon sources to record Eardwulf's restoration to power and, therefore, to incorporate the correct number of years for his second reign into the narrative sources, resulted in incongruities in the Northumbrian regnal chronology as recorded by later tradition.

The problem can perhaps be solved by analysing the date at which Eardwulf was initially expelled from Northumbria. The Northern Recension of the *Anglo-Saxon Chronicle* states that Eardwulf was expelled in 806.[65] This is the last entry in the *Chronicle* before the Northern Recension is temporarily lost. Its record of the lunar eclipse on 1 September 806 is accurate, strongly suggesting

---

[61] This section of the *Historia regum* (*York Annals*) ends in the year 802 and the *ASChron.* DEF in 806.

[62] H. E. Pagan, 'Northumbrian Numismatic Chronology in the Ninth Century', *BNJ*, 38 (1969), 1–15; D. N. Dumville, 'Textual archaeology and Northumbrian History Subsequent to Bede', in D. M. Metcalf (ed.), *Coinage in Ninth-century Northumbria*, BAR British Series 80 (Oxford, 1987), 43–56; E. J. Pirie, 'Earduulf: A Significant Addition to the Coinage of Northumbria', *BNJ*, 65 (1996), 20–31. Only two coins of Eardwulf are known; *EMC* 1995.6001 and *EMC* 1997.6002.

[63] The twelfth-century sources are the *Libellus de exordio* by Symeon of Durham; T. Arnold, ed. *Symeonis Monachis Opera Omnia*, ed. T. Arnold, RS 75, 2 vols (London, 1882–85) 1, 3–135; the *De primo Saxonum adventu*, ibid., 2, 365–84, 377; the *Series regum Northymbrensium*, ibid., 389–93; *The Chronicle of Melrose AD 735–1270, a facsimile of Cotton MS Faustina B ix*, ed. A. O. Anderson and M. O. Anderson (London, 1936); the *Annales Lindisfarnenses*, W. Levison, 'Die "Annales Lindisfarnenses et Dunelmenses" kritisch untersucht und neu herausgegeben', *DA*, 17 (1961), 447–506. See also the early thirteenth-century *Flores Historiarum*; *Rogeri de Wendover, Chronica sive Flores Historiarum*, ed. H. O. Coxe (London, 1841), Vol. 1, 270–71.

[64] Kirby, *The Earliest English Kings*, 156, 196. The argument rests on the fact that an eleventh-century text, known as the *Historia de Sancto Cuthberto* (and which has a tenth-century core), implies that Osberht lost his life within a year of being challenged by Aelle in 866 rather than in 861–62. As Kirby says, this readjustment of the Northumbrian regnal chronology leaves a gap of three to four years which may correspond to the second reign of Eardwulf. On the *Historia de Sancto Cuthberto* see L. Simpson, 'The King Alfred/St Cuthbert episode in the *Historia de Sancto Cuthberto*: Its Significance for Mid-tenth-century English History', in G. Bonner, C. Stancliffe and D. Rollason (eds), *St Cuthbert, his Cult and Community to A.D. 1200* (Woodbridge, 1989), 397–412 and P. H. Sawyer, 'Some Sources for the History of Viking Northumbria', in R. A. Hall (ed.), *Viking Age York and the North*, CBA Research Report, 27 (London, 1978), 3–7.

[65] *ASChron.* DEF, 806.

that the other two events in the same annal also occurred in that year. Given the precision of the date of Eardwulf's accession in both the *Anglo-Saxon Chronicle* and the *York Annals*,[66] it is reasonable, on the basis of this evidence, to assume that he had an initial reign which lasted ten years. Indeed, this was the assumption made by the scholars of twelfth-century Durham priory. The *Libellus de exordio*, the *De primo Saxonum adventu*, the *Annales Lindisfarnenses et Dunelmenses*, and the *Series regum*, all Durham texts dating from the first decades of the twelfth century, concur on this point.[67] Therefore, according to the *Anglo-Saxon Chronicle*, King Eardwulf was expelled in the same year that Bishop Eanberht of Hexham died – that is, 806. However, Richard of Hexham, writing a history of his church sometime after the translation of the Hexham saints in 1155 (*De statu et episcopis ecclesiae Hagustaldensis*), placed Bishop Eanberht's death in 813, seven years after the *Anglo-Saxon Chronicle*'s date.[68] Offler has explained this anomaly as an error in the *De statu* probably deriving from Richard's confused conflation of a variety of late sources,[69] concluding that Eanberht most probably died in the same year as Eardwulf's expulsion – that is, either 806 or 808. Offler offers the second option because, although he prefers the authority of the *Anglo-Saxon Chronicle*, he noted two problems. First, the section of the *Chronicle* in which this annal occurs is subject to a fairly systematic chronological dislocation, which has resulted in events being consistently placed a couple of years too early, so that the 806 entry might therefore really refer to events which occurred in 808. Second, the continental chronicles which discuss Eardwulf's demise, as well as some post-Conquest English sources, place Eardwulf's expulsion in 808.[70] For Offler, these two observations combined to make the date of Eardwulf's expulsion (and Bishop Eanberht's death) uncertain – that is, 806 or 808.

A solution can be proposed for the first of Offler's problems. It is true that the annals of the *Anglo-Saxon Chronicle* suffer a chronological dislocation between the years 756 and 845 whereby those annals which are common to all versions of the *Chronicle* (manuscripts A–F) are dated two, or sometimes three, years too early. As Whitelock notes, this error is found in all versions of the *Chronicle*, including Æthelweard's Latin translation, and so must have been present in their common archetype.[71] However, those elements of the *Chronicle* which are found only in manuscripts D, E and F (that is, the Northern Recension)

---

[66] His accession is dated by the *ASChron*. DE, 795 (for 796) and the *Historia regum* (*York Annals*), 796 to 26 May. Both sources also record an eclipse on 28 March (the date is given as a marginal note in the *Historia regum* manuscript, CCCC MS 139).

[67] See footnote 63 *supra*.

[68] *The Priory of Hexham: The History and Annals of the House*, ed. J. Raine, Surtees Society, 44 (London, 1864).

[69] H. S. Offler, 'A Note on the Last Medieval Bishops of Hexham', *Archaeologia Aeliana*, 4th series, 40 (1962), 163–69.

[70] Ibid., 166.

[71] *EHD* 1, trans. Whitelock, no. 124, 175 n. 5.

do not suffer from this systematic chronological error between those years.[72] Therefore, those annals from the Northern Recension of the *Chronicle* which tell of events in Northumbria between the years 756 and 845 are deemed to be correctly dated and, thus, can be cross-checked with the annals found in the *York Annals* which are similarly unaffected by any chronological slippage. It is unfortunate that the *York Annals* which corroborate the *Chronicle* annals in this way come to an end in the year 802, so that there is no comparative annal for the *Anglo-Saxon Chronicle* entry for 806 which describes Eardwulf's expulsion and Bishop Eanberht's death. However, given that this annal is found only in the Northern Recension of the *Chronicle* and is not included in its main West Saxon Recension (manuscripts A, B and C), the dates which it provides are likely to be correct.

There might also be a way of resolving Offler's second problem of the difference between the *Anglo-Saxon Chronicle* dates and those provided by the continental sources for Eardwulf's expulsion. The *Royal Frankish Annals* describe Eardwulf's arrival in Francia in 808 but makes no direct statement concerning the date of Eardwulf's expulsion from Northumbria.[73] They refer to the expulsion only in an explanatory subclause which acts as an introduction for the major subject of the sentence which was the audience granted by Charlemagne to this exiled Anglo-Saxon king. The *Royal Frankish Annals* state that Eardwulf visited Charlemagne at the imperial palace of Nijmegen. The same annal also says that Charlemagne was resident at Nijmegen only between the beginning of spring and Easter of that year – that is, the 40 days of Lent. After this, the Frankish annals say, the emperor returned to Aachen. Easter fell on 16 April in 808, meaning that Charlemagne was at Nijmegen for certain only between the beginning of March and mid-April of that year. Thus, the Frankish annals do not say that Eardwulf was expelled from Northumbria in 808, only that he arrived in Francia in the early months of that year. The Frankish account goes on to describe Eardwulf's return journey to Northumbria in the company of the papal legate and Frankish abbots. That Eardwulf's return to Northumbria occurred later in the same year as his initial audience with Charlemagne is confirmed by the entry in the *Royal Frankish Annals* for the following year, 809, which describes the safe return of the Frankish abbots and the capture of the papal legate by pirates, 'after Eardwulf, king of Northumbria, had been returned to his kingdom' (*reductus est in regnuum suum*).[74] Eardwulf's safe return is also implicit in a letter from Pope Leo to Charlemagne dated 31 December. Unfortunately, this letter is dated only by day and month, not by its year of composition;

---

[72] This point is (unsurprisingly) often misunderstood; see J. Booth, 'Coinage and Northumbrian History: *c.* 790–810', in Metcalf, *Coinage in Ninth-century Northumbria*, 57–90, 63.

[73] *Annales regni Francorum*, 808.

[74] Ibid., 809 and MGH, Epp. V. no. 4, 93–93. Aldulf was captured on the crossing back to Francia and was returned to Britain where his ransom was paid by one of Coenwulf's *homines*. Charlemagne's abbots made the return journey safely.

its editor dates it to 808 by comparison with the *Royal Frankish Annals*.[75] One other factor suggests that that the Frankish legates were back in their homeland by 809; if the abbot named Hruotfrid in the *Royal Frankish Annals* for 808 was indeed the leader of the community of St Amand, as is customarily assumed, then it is likely that, as abbot of his community, he would have been present when the body of their patron saint was transported to a new resting place on 20 September 809.[76]

Another source which provides an *anno domini* date for Eardwulf's expulsion, and to which great weight has been attached, is the *Flores Historiarum* written by Roger of Wendover in the early thirteenth century.[77] Although writing from St Albans, he evidently had access to a source concerning northern England which contained information about ninth-century events lost to all other sources.[78] It is likely that he obtained this information via the monastery at Tynemouth which, by the mid-twelfth century, was a dependent cell of St Albans, ceded to that monastery by Durham.[79] Roger ascribes the usurpation and expulsion of Eardwulf by a man named Ælfwald II to the year 808. Ælfwald, he says, ruled for two years – that is, 808–10. However, were Roger's chronology to be correct, it would imply that Eardwulf was returned *in regnum suum*, during the 'occupation' of Ælfwald. Also, it suggests that, under these conditions, Eardwulf did not challenge Ælfwald and that Ælfwald tolerated Eardwulf's presence in the kingdom. Both these suggestions seem unlikely given Eardwulf's bellicose reputation, his influence with Charlemagne and Leo, as well as the suggestion that it was Eardwulf's son, not Ælfwald's, who eventually succeeded to the throne.

Had Eardwulf really been expelled from Northumbria in 808 (as Roger's chronology implies) the crisis which had brought about his political demise, his expulsion and the journey from Northumbria to Francia must have taken place during the earliest months of the year when the seas would have been least hospitable to travellers between England and the Continent. Of course, it is not impossible that Eardwulf's journey from Northumbria was made at this time especially since the Frankish annals state that the winter that year was 'unheathily mild' (*hiemps mollisima*),[80] but, given the strong likelihood that the date provided by the *Anglo-Saxon Chronicle* for Eardwulf's expulsion is correct, it is

---

[75] MGH, Epp. V, no. 3, 91–92.

[76] See, for example, the entries recorded under the year 809 in the *Annales sancti Amandi, pars secunda*, MGH, SS I, 14; the *Annales S. Amandi breves*, MGH, SS II, 184; the *Annales Elenonenses Maiores*, MGH, SS V, 11.

[77] *Rogeri de Wendover*, ed. Coxe, 1, 270–71. For the significance attached to Roger's account see Booth, 'Coinage and Northumbrian History', 60, 63–64.

[78] Roger includes a unique reference to King Redwulf whom, he says, ruled in Northumbria for a short while in 844; *Rogeri de Wendover*, ed. Coxe, 1, 270–71. Roger's reference is corroborated by coins minted in this king's name; see P. Grierson and D. M. Metcalf, *Medieval European Coinage: The Early Middle Ages, 5th to 10th Centuries* (Cambridge, 1986), 299–302.

[79] D. Knowles et al., *Heads of Religious Houses, England and Wales 940–1216* (London, 1972), 96–97.

[80] *Annales regni Francorum*, 808.

necessary to reconcile it with the Frankish account. An alternative pattern for this series of events can be proposed by following the chronology hinted at in the *Anglo-Saxon Chronicle* and the regnal lists of post-Conquest sources. The *Chronicle* states that Eardwulf was expelled in 806. The regnal list embedded within twelfth-century Durham texts agrees with this by according Eardwulf a reign of ten years and his successor Ælfwald II a reign of two years. There is no controversy as to the date of Eardwulf's accession; both the *Anglo-Saxon Chronicle* and the *York Annals* describe in detail Eardwulf's accession ceremony and its date, 26 May 796. A ten-year reign would have made Eardwulf king until May 806. It is probable, therefore, that the political crisis which brought about Eardwulf's expulsion occurred *c.* May 806. This would then have given Eardwulf some 18 months to amass the evidence and money to pursue his case with Charlemagne and subsequently in Rome. In combination with the evidence that Eardwulf was returned to Northumbria late in the year 808, the hypothesized time lapse between his expulsion and return provides the necessary space for a two-year reign for the usurper Ælfwald – that is, mid–late 806 until mid–late 808.

This revised chronology disagrees with that given by Roger of Wendover who was writing some 400 years after the event. However, the chronological accuracy of many of Roger's other early chronicle entries is suspect. In several places he ascribes an event to a year two or three years after the event is known from other sources to have occurred.[81] Thus his annal for 783 which describes the mission to Rome to collect the pallium for Archbishop Eanbald I should more correctly be dated to 780–81. The entry for 828 is also incorrectly dated, and the annal for 844 is dated to 843. It may be that Roger's annals for 808 and 810 are simply two years too late.

In the last resort, whether or not Eardwulf was restored to the Northumbrian throne cannot be precisely ascertained on the basis of the available evidence. What can be said with certainty is that both the numismatic and textual evidence is sufficiently flexible to allow the possibility that Eardwulf enjoyed a second period of power in Northumbria. Nevertheless, the debate over Eardwulf's possible second reign does not in fact alter the observation that he was returned to Northumbria under escort by Carolingian and papal envoys. Since it is inherently unlikely that the usurper Ælfwald would have been able to tolerate the presence of his rival in the kingdom, the burden of probability argues that Eardwulf's return to his homeland prompted the demise of Ælfwald and, therefore, that the rule of the latter extended from 806 to 808. This interpretation, albeit hypothetical in the absence of contemporary historical or explicit numismatic sources, is supported by the twelfth-century claim that the next two kings of Northumbria were direct descendents of Eardwulf. Thus, a real possibility remains that not only was Eardwulf returned to Northumbria from exile with the assistance of imperial and papal legates, but that he may also have regained

---

[81] *EHD* 1, trans. Whitelock, no. 4.

power in his kingdom. Indeed, it could be argued that Charlemagne would have been unlikely to have expended energy on the plan for Eardwulf to be *in regnum suum reducitur* without his protégé regaining some political status, and one might wonder whether the letters concerning his reinstatement would have been preserved had the intervention been ineffective.

Northumbrian kings and Francia before 808

The idea that this incident was not an isolated event, but that it formed part of a longer-term relationship between Northumbrian and Carolingian kings has found favour. Kirby has pointed out that 'the contacts and connections which secured for Eardwulf Carolingian and papal support in 808 are unlikely to have been suddenly extinguished and may well have helped to create the stable conditions of Eanred's reign'.[82] He also surmises that Eardwulf must have been the 'recipient of Carolingian favours' earlier in his reign in order to warrant the intervention in 808.[83] In contrast to the lack of sources after his exile, a fair amount of background information exists concerning Eardwulf's major period of rule from 796 to 806, which can be scrutinized for evidence of Carolingian contacts with that king. The most explicit statement in this respect is found in the minor Durham chronicle known as the *Annales Lindisfarnenses et Dunelmenses* for 797.[84] This annal claims that Eardwulf married a daughter of Charlemagne, *duxit uxorem filiam regis Karoli*. This is the only unique piece of evidence found in these annals, the remainder being derived from a variety of other sources. The *Annales Lindisfarnenses* are a compilation of the early twelfth century, probably made (and certainly copied) by Symeon of Durham. But, although they are clearly based on earlier material, the reference to Eardwulf's possible dynastic union with the Carolingians is usually considered spurious.[85] Levison thought

---

[82] Kirby, *The Earliest English Kings*, 197.

[83] *Ibid.*, 157.

[84] See Chapter 4, above, 119. The *Annales Lindisfarneses* are one of the few true paschal chronicles surviving in an English manuscript, the entries being written in the margins of a Dionysiac Easter cycle. On this text and its authorship see W. Levison, 'Die *Annales Lindisfarnenses et Dunelmenses* Kritisch Untersucht und neu Herausgegeben', *DA* 17, 447–506; M. Gullick, 'The Scribes of the Durham Cantor's Book (Durham, Dean and Chapter Library, MS B.IV.24) and the Durham Martyrology Scribe', in D. W. Rollason, M. Harvey and M. Prestwich (eds), *Anglo-Norman Durham* (Woodbridge, 1994), 93–110; J. E. Story, 'Symeon as Annalist', in D. W. Rollason (ed.), *Symeon of Durham: Historian of Durham and the North* (Stamford, 1998), 202–13. The reference to Eardwulf is found on the last line of the table on fo. 21r of the manuscript, Glasgow University Library, MS Hunter 85; see J. Young and P. H. Aitken, *A Catalogue of the Manuscripts in the Hunterian Library of the University of Glasgow* (Glasgow, 1908), 91–94; N. Thorpe, *The Glory of the Page: Medieval and Renaissance Illuminated Manuscripts from Glasgow University Library* (London, 1987), 57; R. A. B. Mynors, *Durham Cathedral Manuscripts to the End of the Twelfth Century* (Durham, 1939), 55–56, no. 71.

[85] Levison, *England and the Continent*, 114; *Two Saxon Chronicles Parallel*, ed. C. Plummer

the reference was a twelfth-century confusion with Æthelwulf's marriage to Judith, the daughter of Charles the Bald in 856.[86] This is a possible explanation, but a surprising one given the dissimilarity in the names of kings concerned. Indeed, given Eardwulf's other connections with Charlemagne and Francia, the allegation that Eardwulf had dynastic connections with the emperor's family perhaps ought to be taken more seriously. Even if mistaken in detail, the *Annales Lindisfarneses* reference echoes a tradition that, during his time as king of Northumbria, Eardwulf had been closely associated with Charlemagne.[87]

This is especially interesting given that further evidence survives which suggests that Charlemagne might have had a longer-standing interest in Eardwulf's career. This is illustrated by the two surviving accounts of Eardwulf's accession ceremony in 796 and recorded in the *York Annals* and the *Anglo-Saxon Chronicle*.

Her wæs se mona aþystrod betwux hancræde 7 dagunge on .v. kalendas Aprilis. 7 Eardwulf feng to Norðanhimbran cynedome on .ii. idus Mai, 7 and he wæs syððan gebletsod 7 his cynestole ahafen on .vii. kalendas Iunii on Eoforwic fram Eanbalde arcebiscop 7 Æþelberhte 7 Higbalde 7 Badwulfe.[88]	In this year there was an eclipse of the moon between cockcrow and dawn on 28 March and Eardwulf succeeded to the Northumbrian kingdom on 14 May; and he was afterwards blessed and raised to the throne on 26 May in York by Archbishop Eanbald and Æthelberht and Higbald and Badwulf.
Eardulf enim, de quo supra diximus, filius Eardulfi de exilio vocatus, regni infulis est sublimatus, et in Eboraca in ecclesia sancti Petri ad altare beati apostoli Pauli, ubi illa gens primum perceperat gratiam baptismi, consecratus est .vii. Kalendas Junii.[89]	However, Eardwulf, the son of Eardwulf, about whom we spoke above, was called from exile and was raised to the crown of the kingdom and was consecrated in York on 26 May in the church of St Peter at the altar of the apostle Paul, where the people first received the grace of baptism.

The accession of Eardwulf to the throne of Northumbria in 796 is described in the Anglo-Saxon sources in vocabulary which would not have seemed out of

---

and J. Earle, 2 vols (Oxford, 1889–92) 2, 68. Levison's argument rests partly on Einhard's statement in chapter 19 of his *Vita Karoli* that Charlemagne did not allow any of his daughters to marry during his lifetime; see *Charlemagne's Courtier: The Complete Einhard*, trans. P. E. Dutton (Peterborough, Ontario, 1998), 28–29.

86 See, further, Chapter 7, below, 240–43.

87 Wallace-Hadrill, 'Charlemagne and England', 696.

88 *ASChron.* D, 795 (for 796); *The Anglo-Saxon Chronicle, MS D. A Collaborative Edition*, 17, ed. G. P. Cubbin (Cambridge, 1996), 6, 18.

89 *Historia regum* (*York Annals*), 796.

place in a contemporary Carolingian chronicle.[90] In both the Anglo-Saxon and
the Latin descriptions of the event, significant terms were employed to describe
the ceremony. This is the first time in a Northumbrian context that we hear of an
elaborate kingmaking ceremony held in the presence of the four highest-ranking
clergymen of the kingdom, and it is complete with ideological overtones of the
divine confirmation of kingship which are implicit in the references to the
'enthronement' and 'consecration' of the new king.[91] It is also significant that
the kingmaking rituals took place at the ecclesiastical heart of the kingdom in
the church of St Peter at the altar of St Paul 'where the nation first received the
grace of baptism' (*ubi illa gens primum perceperat gratium baptismi*); a dedica-
tion which recalls both Canterbury and Rome.[92] This type of kingmaking
ceremony seems to have been innovative not just in a Northumbrian context, but
also within a broader Anglo-Saxon perspective. Eardwulf's accession was a
high-profile event, imbued with ritual significance and contemporary, continental connotation. The only previous allusion to a similar type of event is the
famous reference in the *Anglo-Saxon Chronicle* for 787, referring to the 'hallowing' of Offa's son, Ecgfrith, after the contentious Synod of Chelsea – a ceremony
which echoed the anointing of Charlemagne's sons by the pope in 781.[93] What
was so different about the accession of Eardwulf that it necessitated such a
departure from tradition? Why did such a strong, ritualized statement need to be
made in Northumbria at this date?

The ceremony described in the *York Annals* and the Northern Recension of
the *Anglo-Saxon Chronicle* is reminiscent, in terms of content and vocabulary, of
the description of the consecration, elevation and anointing of Pippin in 751.[94]
This was the event that legitimized the claim of the Carolingian dynasty to usurp

[90] R. Pauli, 'Karl der Große in Northumbrischen annalen', *Forschungen zur deutschen
Geschichte*, 12 (1872), 139–66; J. L. Nelson, 'National Synods, Kingship as Office, and Royal
Anointing: An Early Medieval Syndrome', *Studies in Church History*, 7 (1971), 41–59; M. Lapidge,
'Byrhtferth of Ramsey and the Early Sections of the *Historia regum* (*York Annals*) Attributed to
Symeon of Durham', *ASE*, 10 (1982), 97–112.

[91] The *Historia regum* (*York Annals*), 774 and 790 uses similar vocabulary when describing
certain aspects of the reign of Æthelred; he is said to have been *tanto honore coronatus* and *iterum
per gratiam Christi regni solio est subtronizatus*. However, for neither of Æthelred's reigns is there
any mention of an accession ceremony of the type enjoyed by Eardwulf in 796 and the 'Carolingian'
terminology used in the Æthelred contexts seems to be the choice of the chronicler; see above
Chapter 4.

[92] The whereabouts of St Peter's is not known for certain; see R. K. Morris, 'Alcuin, York and
the *alma sophia*', in L. A. S. Butler and R. K. Morris (eds), *The Anglo-Saxon Church: Papers on
History, Architecture and Archaeology in Honour of Dr H. M. Taylor*, CBA Research Report, 60
(London, 1986), 80–89; E. James, 'Introduction Part 2: The Post Roman Period to AD 1069', in D.
Phillips and B. Hayward (eds), *Excavations at York Minster: From Roman Fortress to Norman
Cathedral*, (London, 1995), 1, 9–15.

[93] *ASChron.* A, 787; *Annales regni Francorum*, 781. For a discussion of the problems concerning the 787 incident see J. L. Nelson, 'Inauguration Rituals' in P. H. Sawyer and I. N. Wood
(eds), *Early Medieval Kingship* (Leeds, 1977), 50–71; Brooks, *The Early History*, 118–19.

[94] See Chapter 4 above, 129–30.

the Merovingians and to rule Francia in their stead.[95] Eardwulf, like Pippin, had been born into a noble, but non-royal, family. His father, also called Eardwulf, may have been one of the two men, both holding the title *dux* indicating high secular rank, named *Eaduulf* in the *York Annals* whose deaths were recorded *s.a.* 774 and 775.[96] The latter of these seems to have been murdered (*per insidias*), and was one of the several high-ranking Northumbrians who lost their lives during Æthelred's turbulent first reign (774–78).[97] It is thus probably no coincidence that the first target of Æthelred's second reign (790–96) was Eardwulf himself who survived an execution ordered by the king to take place outside the walls of the monastery at Ripon in 791.[98] Well before his creation as king in 796, Eardwulf had been a man of considerable political significance within Northumbria and possibly posed a second-generation threat to Æthelred's authority. Both Pippin in 751 and Eardwulf in 796 were, therefore, in the business of transforming a high-ranking noble family into a royal dynasty, and both used the highest clerical authority available in their kingdoms to accomplish this goal.

The parallel between the 751 and the 796 ceremonies extends to the vocabulary used to describe both events. The text known as the *Continuation to the Fourth book of the Chronicle of Fredegar*, like the *York Annals*, also uses the phrases *sublimatur in regno* and *cum consecratione episcoporum* in its description of the 751 kingmaking ceremony.[99] Admittedly, there is no specific reference to anointing in the accounts of Eardwulf's accession ceremony; the Old English word used in this context is *gebletsod* ('blessed') whereas the verb *gehalgian* ('to hallow') is used to describe the Mercian events in 787.[100] The latter of these words has overtones of ordination and, in an episcopal context at this date, such a ceremony may well have involved the process of anointing. The verb used in the 796 account has more of a sense of blessing which nevertheless has overtones of ecclesiastical sanction. The author of the *York Annals* entry used the word *infulis* (*infula, ae* f.) which, in a classical context, specifically referred to

---

[95] J. L. Nelson, 'The Lord's Anointed and the People's Choice: Carolingian Royal Ritual', in D. Cannadine and S. Price (eds), *Rituals of Royalty: Power and Ceremonial in Traditional Societies* (Cambridge, 1987), 137–80.

[96] *Historia regum* (*York Annals*), 774 and 775. The man killed in 775 was murdered *per insidias* during Æthelred's first reign.

[97] See also the account of the murders of the *duces* Ealdwulf, Cynewulf, and Ecga *ASChron.* DE, 778 and *Historia regum* (*York Annals*), 778.

[98] *Historia regum* (*York Annals*), 791. This incident may be the origin of the association between Eardwulf and St Hardulf to whom the church at Breedon-on-the-Hill in Leicestershire is dedicated. The Peterborough chronicler, Hugh Candidus, refers to the dedicatee at Breedon as *Sanctus Hardulfus rex*; *The Peterborough Chronicle of Hugh Candidus*, trans. C. and W. T. Mellows (Peterborough, reprinted 1997), 28; D. W. Rollason, 'Lists of Saints' Resting Places in Anglo-Saxon England', *ASE*, 7 (1978), 61–93.

[99] *The Fourth Book of the Chronicle of Fredegar and Continuations*, ed. J. M. Wallace-Hadrill (London, 1960), 102, and see, further, Chapter 4, above, 129.

[100] For an analysis of the Old English *gehalgian*, see P. Hunter-Blair, *An Introduction to Anglo-Saxon England* (Cambridge, 1959), 205 and comments by Cubitt, *Church Councils*, 185–86.

the headband worn by a priest. It could be argued that a tangible noun of this type was implied in the 796 context, with the word meaning something akin to a crown. Indeed, it was in the context of ritual headgear in which Isidore of Seville, writing in the seventh century, discussed the meaning of the word.[101] However, the noun is plural, thereby mitigating against this impression, and the alternative sense of the word as a sign of religious consecration and inviolability is perhaps implied. This sense of inviolability is very much the scriptural reasoning behind anointing: 'Touch not mine anointed.'[102] Although it is stretching the evidence too far to assert that Eardwulf must have been anointed in 796, the evidence from the two chronicles implies that he was created king in a ceremony brimming with religious connotations and ecclesiastical ritual. The Carolingian affinities of Eardwulf's accession ceremony go beyond the allusions in the vocabulary used by the authors of the accounts found in the *York Annals* and the *Anglo-Saxon Chronicle* (or indeed, by the author of the archetype which supplied the information for these two chronicles). The ceremony in which Eardwulf was made king seems to have been different to anything which had been recorded in Northumbria before. Apart from the 787 'hallowing' of Ecgfrith referred to above, this is the first definite occasion that such a kingmaking ceremony is described in an Anglo-Saxon context. Indeed, the *Chronicle*'s account of the Northumbrian ceremony is much fuller than the single-line statement describing the better-known Mercian event. Is it too much to suppose that something akin to the legitimization of a new regime was intended in York in 796 just as it had been at Soissons in 751? The organizers of the later event must have been aware both of the force and of the enduring success of the earlier Frankish ceremony.

Another source pointing to other longstanding connections between Eardwulf and Charlemagne is Leo's letter to the emperor, referred to earlier, which discussed the plight of the king and the circumstances of his expulsion.[103] In it, Leo describes his reaction to the news that Charlemagne had taken steps to intervene in the Northumbrian crisis, saying that 'much joy and great happiness' had arisen in his heart, because Charlemagne, in his great piety, had sent Eardwulf's own messengers to Northumbria, to lead Eardwulf 'alive all the way to you [Charlemagne]'. The pope then goes on to describe Eardwulf as *vester semper fidelis*. This phrase is remarkable since, taken literally, it implies that

---

[101] *Isidore Hispalensis Episcopi, Etymologiarum sive originum, Libri XX*, ed. W. M. Lindsay, 2 vols (Oxford, 1911), 2, xix.30.4. In later medieval Latin, *c.* 1300, the word becomes interchangeable with 'chasuble', maintaining the ritual context but for a garment worn on the body as opposed to the head. However, it is still used to describe the bands on a bishop's mitre, reviving the connotation with religious headgear. See for example the Salzburg *infulae* as discussed by H. Granger-Taylor, 'The Weft-patterned Silks and their Braid: The Remains of an Anglo-Saxon Dalmatic of *c.* 800?', in G. Bonner et al. (eds), *St Cuthbert, his Cult and Community to A.D. 1200* (Woodbridge, 1989), 303–27.

[102] Ps. 105:15; see also I Sam. 26:9, 'for who can stretch forth his hand against the Lord's anointed, and be guiltless?'.

[103] MGH, Epp. V. no. 127.

Eardwulf owed some sort of loyalty or fidelity to Charlemagne. Was this 'fidelity' merely a turn of phrase used by the pope or did it really imply that some sort of alliance, either informal or formal, existed between the two rulers? Some understanding of Leo's usage of the word *fidelis* is important when trying to evaluate Eardwulf's relationship to Charlemagne. In Frankish sources the word often implied a quasi-formal degree of mutual obligation between the emperor and his *fidelis* – a *fidelis* being a 'royal servitor' under oath to a Carolingian overlord.[104] Wallace-Hadrill has interpreted Leo's words as a reference to the loyalty which Eardwulf owed to Charlemagne after he had been reinstated. He argued that 'Eardwulf, doubtless heartened with a share of Carolingian *munificentia*, returned to his throne as the *fidelis* of an emperor who had exercised the power of *imperialis defensio*'.[105] However, this passage explicitly states that Eardwulf had been Charlemagne's 'faithful man' *semper* – that is, 'always'. This corroborates the hints in other sources that Eardwulf had strong links with the continental powers earlier in his career, and certainly before his expulsion from Northumbria in 806, since the pope says in the same breath that Eardwulf had been 'accustomed to send his messengers to us' (that is, to Rome) presumably whilst still acting in his capacity as king.[106] Significantly perhaps, the same word is used earlier in the letter to describe the loyalties of a certain Count Helmengaud, *vester nosterque fidelis*. Helmengaud had been present at Charlemagne's imperial coronation in Rome in 800[107] and had acted as his envoy to the Byzantine court in 802.[108] He was obviously, therefore, one of Charlemagne's highest-ranking followers and was entrusted with important missions.[109] The evidence from this letter (and indeed, all of Leo's surviving letters) is difficult to deal with, since his diplomatic epistolary style frequently seems intentionally ambiguous.[110] What the phrase meant in this context, as opposed to Frankish usage of the term, is unclear: it is possible that the pope was recognizing that Eardwulf had been a longstanding ally of the emperor simply in the sense that he was not actively hostile to him. But the literal implication of this passage from Leo's letter is that Eardwulf, as a *fidelis* of the emperor, had been rescued from England by *missi* sent by Charlemagne and was escorted by them to Charlemagne's presence.

The last sentence of this part of Leo's letter is particularly intriguing: 'because of this thing [Eardwulf's escape], everywhere repeatedly echoes with your defence of the empire'. The phrase *vestra imperialis defensio* seems to

---

[104] Odegaard, *Vassi and Fideles*, 51–68.

[105] Wallace-Hadrill, 'Charlemagne and England', 170–71.

[106] The imperfect tense of the verb *dirigere* suggests that Eardwulf sent messengers to the papal court occurred more than once.

[107] *Liber Pontificalis. Texte, introduction et commentaire*, ed. L. Duchesne, 2 vols (Paris, 1886–92), 2, 1–34, ch. 23; *Lives of the Eighth-Century Popes*, trans. Davis, 191.

[108] *Annales regni Francorum*, 802.

[109] Ganshof, 'The Frankish Monarchy and its External Relations', 169.

[110] G. F. Browne, *Alcuin of York* (London, 1908), 112.

imply that by 'defending' his *fidelis* in this way, Charlemagne's *imperium* extended even to Northumbria. Whether this comment was meant literally or was yet another example of Leo's obsequious flattery towards the emperor is a moot point; it may simply reflect his ignorance of Anglo-Saxon geography. Nevertheless, Leo's language carries significant implications: that Charlemagne's broad *imperium* correlated with the territory of the emperor's *fideles* and that whatever land was under the control of one of Charlemagne's *fideles* was considered by the pope to have been part of the wider Carolingian *imperium*. Furthermore, inclusion in that *imperium* came about as a result of the pro-Carolingian affiliation of the ruler of the kingdom, the implication being that Charlemagne's *imperium* could expand though political and diplomatic alliances as well as by military conquest. In Leo's eyes, Charlemagne's *imperium* was not restricted by geopolitical frontiers.[111]

Æthelred and the Avar treasure

Eardwulf was not the only Northumbrian king to be paid particular attention by Charlemagne: Æthelred, his opponent, who had reigned twice from 774–78 and 790–96, was the recipient or subject of many letters from Alcuin.[112] Undoubtedly, the quantity of Alcuin's letters to and about Æthelred is due largely to the coincidence of his second reign with Alcuin's most prolific and prominent period of influence at the Carolingian court and, as such, Æthelred was a particular target of Alcuin's proselytizing about the duties and responsibilities of kings. These letters provide an insight into Alcuin's opinions on another Northumbrian monarch, and through him to Charlemagne's attitudes. Writing to King Offa in 796, Alcuin described the Frankish king's dramatic reaction to the news of Æthelred's assassination in April 796.[113] Even allowing Alcuin some leeway for dramatic effect, his description of Charlemagne's reaction is extraordinary. After hearing the news of Æthelred's assassination from his legates who had travelled home via *Scotia* (a point of note in itself), Charlemagne recalled his gifts to the Northumbrians, threatening direct action and revenge against such people who could murder their lord and whom he considered to be 'worse than pagans'. In light of other evidence for Charlemagne's temper this description of his ire is entirely plausible, even if slightly melodramatic.[114] But why should Charlemagne have reacted to the assassination of a Northumbrian king, as Wallace-Hadrill has said, 'with a display of anger that looks disproportionate in

---

111 On Carolingian land frontiers see J. M. H. Smith, '*Fines imperii*: The Marches', in *NMCH2*, 169–89; T. Reuter, 'The End of Carolingian Military Expansion', in P. Godman and R. Collins (eds), *Charlemagne's Heir* (Oxford, 1990), 391–405; T. F. X. Noble, 'Louis the Pious and the Frontiers of the Frankish Realm', in Godman and Collins, *Charlemagne's Heir*, 333–47.

112 Alcuin, *Ep.*, nos 8–10, 16, 18, 30, 79, 101–2, 105, 122, 231.

113 Ibid., no. 101; *Alcuin of York*, trans. Allott, no. 41.

114 See *Annales regni Francorum* (revised version), 795 for Charlemagne's extreme fury at the news of the murder of Witzan, his Abodrite ally.

a foreign king'? Indeed, Alcuin specifically says that Charlemagne was prepared 'to remove all good things from them' (*eis boni abstrahere*), and 'to make mischief' (*mali machinare*) as vengeance for this deed. This is fairly drastic action for the Frankish king to consider. Luckily for the Northumbrians, Alcuin graciously interceded on their behalf thereby sparing them the wrath of his Frankish lord. But, again, why should Charlemagne have reacted in this way?

One reason is perhaps to be found behind the 'generous gifts' which Charlemagne retracted 'in such great anger against that people'. It appears that Charlemagne had sent gifts to both the king of Northumbria *et ad suas episcopales sedes*. These 'generous gifts' are mentioned elsewhere, most notably in the letter concerning Eadberht Præn written by Charlemagne to Offa in early spring 796.[115] The 'worldly treasure' referred to in this letter was part of the spoils of the war fought against the Avars which had culminated in a resounding victory for the Frankish forces in the previous year. Charlemagne had promised Offa an Avar sword, a baldric and two precious robes from the treasure. The redistribution of parts of this treasure to English kings and the bishops of the *metropolitanas civitates* (York, Lichfield, and Canterbury) may be the context for the inclusion of Charlemagne's name and that of his treasurer, Mægenfrith, in the Northumbrian *Liber Vitae* (see Figure 4.1).

The dissemination of the treasure abroad raises significant questions when the Frankish sources are consulted. The *Royal Frankish Annals* for 796 tell how Charlemagne (a *vir prudentissimus atque largissimus*), sent a large part of the treasure from Aachen to Rome, 'but the remainder he bestowed upon his *optimates*, both clergy and laymen, and upon his other *fideles*'.[116] The so-called *Lorsch Annals* – which are based on the *Royal Frankish Annals* but which in this section incorporate extra information – also say that *fideles* were among the recipients of the treasure.[117] Taken literally, this seems to imply that, in the eyes of the Frankish chroniclers who recorded these events at the royal court, the Anglo-Saxon recipients of Charlemagne's largesse were also considered his *fideles*. This is unlikely with a king of Offa's rank and power, yet given the papal usage of the word with regard to Eardwulf and his subsequent restoration by the emperor, as well as Alcuin's prolonged contact with Æthelred and Charlemagne's

---

[115] Alcuin, *Ep.*, no. 100; *Alcuin of York*, trans. Allott, no. 40. On Charlemagne's campaign against the Avars see *Annales regni Francorum*, 795 and Charlemagne's letter to his queen, Fastrada: MGH, Epp. IV, *Epistolae Variorum*, ed. E. Dümmler, no. 20; *The Reign of Charlemagne*, trans. H. R. Loyn and J. Percival, Documents of Medieval History, 2 (London, 1975), no. 40, 134–35; W. Pohl, *Die Awaren: Ein Steppenvolk in Mitteleuropa, 567–822* (Munich, 1988), 312–32; J. Déer, 'Das Untergang des Awarenreiches', in W. Braunfels (ed.), *Karl der Große, Lebenswerk und Nachleben* (Düsseldorf, 1965), 1, 719–91.

[116] *Annales regni Francorum*, 796.

[117] *Annales Lareshamenses*, 795; MGH SS 1, 36. On the authorship of these annals and their place in the Frankish annalistic literature see S. Käuper, 'Annales Lareshamenses (Lorsch Annalen)', in Stiegemann and Wemhoff (eds), *799 Kunst und Kultur*, 1, 38–40; L. Halphen, *Études critiques sur l'histoire de Charlemagne* (Paris, 1921), 26–36, and D. A. Bullough, 'Europae Pater: Charlemagne and his Achievement in the Light of Recent Scholarship', *EHR*, 85 (1970), 59–105, at 65.

violent reaction to the news of his murder, it is at least possible that both Æthelred and Eardwulf maintained a relationship with Charlemagne which the Frankish chroniclers understood as a form of *fidelitas*. The parallel of Æthelred's successful restoration in 790 with that of Eardwulf's in 808, further points in this direction, although, without direct proof, such suggestions must necessarily remain speculation. Nevertheless, the donation of gifts, especially robes, should certainly be regarded as part of the complex etiquette which oiled the wheels of long-distance diplomacy in the political world of the eighth century.[118] By accepting gifts from the Carolingian king, these Anglo-Saxon kings were acknowledging a relationship which involved concepts of obligation and debt to the giver. The perception of that relationship may have differed in the Anglo-Saxon and Frankish courts but, as the accumulated evidence cited above indicates, these links were real and had a significant impact on the political life of each kingdom.

To this one could add the evidence of the *Scotti*, who – if we are to believe Einhard – were so impressed by Charlemagne's generosity and goodwill that they, 'publicly declared that he was certainly their lord and that they were his subjects and servants'.[119] Letters survived, said Einhard, which proved their affection towards the Frankish king. These letters have since been lost and so Einhard's claim is impossible to verify, but it is undoubtedly significant that the Frankish envoys who took the Avar treasure to the English are said by Alcuin to have returned home by way of *Scotia*.[120] Though not mentioned in other lists of beneficiaries, Alcuin's comment suggests that the leaders of the *Scotti* were also in receipt of war-gear from the Carolingian victory and were similarly considered by the Frankish audience to have acknowledged the might and superiority of their benefactor.[121]

---

[118] On the role of treasure and tribute see J. Campbell, *Essays in Anglo-Saxon History* (London, 1986), 92–95 and T. Reuter, 'Plunder and Tribute in the Carolingian Empire', *TRHS*, 5th series, 53 (1985), 75–94. On the diplomatic relationship which developed between the Carolingian court and the Abbasid caliphate and the importance of the robe of honour in that link, see F. W. Buckler, *Harunu'l-Rashid and Charles the Great* (Cambridge, MA., 1931) and M. Borgolte, *Der Gesandtenaustausch der Karolinger mit den Abbasiden und mit den Patriarchen von Jerusalem* (Munich, 1976).

[119] Einhard, *Vita Karoli*, ch. 16.

[120] Alcuin, *Ep.*, 101; *Alcuin of York*, trans. Allott, no. 41.

[121] Bullough has suggested that Einhard may have confused the claims of the *Scotti* with those of the Northumbrian kings; see Bullough, *The Age of Charlemagne*, 161. It is not entirely clear exactly to whom Einhard was referring in this case, and whether the kings of the Irish or those resident in Scotland were implied by the term. For the suggestion that even the Welsh kings may have been included under the label see Wallace-Hadrill, 'Charlemagne and England', 172 and Kirby, *The Earliest English Kings*, 176. On the debt of Pictish sculptors to continental art forms see, S. Foster (ed.), *The St Andrew's Sarcophagus: A Pictish Masterpiece and its International Connections* (Dublin, 1998), 118–40, 240–49. On the Irish mission to Francia in 848 see Chapter 7, below, 230–31.

Fidelitas

After its description of the distribution of the Avar treasure, the *Lorsch Annals* for 795 add a further note which is relevant in this context. This annal also records the death of the Roman pontiff Hadrian and states that Charlemagne had ordered prayers to be said in memory of his friend throughout the whole Christian people 'within his own boundaries' (*infra terminos suos*).[122] Ordinarily, this latter phrase might reasonably be taken to refer to Frankish territory under direct Frankish command and administration. However, a letter survives addressed by Alcuin, 'son of the holy church of York', to the bishops of Britain, which he evidently wrote shortly after Hadrian's death.[123] In it, Alcuin repeats the statement of the *Lorsch Annals*, that Charlemagne 'greatly desires your prayers for the soul of the most blessed Pope Hadrian', and adds a request that prayers be said for, 'the king himself, for the stability of his kingdom, and for the spread of Christianity'.[124] This demand from Alcuin for public prayer to support Charlemagne and to buttress the spiritual security of his kingdom is pointed; such demands were made by Frankish kings in times of military or spiritual crisis and were used by them as a liturgical tool to bind the service and loyalty of their subjects to the Carolingian cause. As McCormick has noted, towards the end of the eighth century the proper performances of these litanies or special prayers were considered as 'acts of loyalty towards the monarch' and that 'failure to perform them was ground for an accusation of *infidelitas*'.[125]

Such liturgical instructions from the centre harnessed the power of prayer for the ruling elite and bound distant regions to the political, spiritual or military projects of the court. That Alcuin was extending this royal command to the bishops of Britain supports the accumulated evidence that, towards the end of the eighth century, some sections of the Frankish political elite regarded Anglo-Saxon England as an outlying cog of the Frankish machine. Charlemagne, Alcuin adds, had sent monks and priests *cum benedictionis munusculis* in order to ensure that his instruction regarding the performance of the prayers was fulfilled. These gift-bearing messengers may have been those who not only broke the news of Hadrian's death (with Charlemagne's orders for prayers to be said in his memory) but who also carried Charlemagne's letter and the Avar treasure to Offa, to Æthelred in Northumbria and to the metropolitan bishops. If this were not the case, we have evidence of the presence of another formal Frankish legation touring England early in 796. More significantly, Alcuin's letter reflects his perspective that Anglo-Saxon England was considered to be

---

122 *Annales Laureshamenses*, 795.

123 Alcuin, *Ep.*, no. 104; *Alcuin of York*, trans. Allott, no. 25.

124 Alcuin, *Ep.* no. 104, lines 25–26; Wallace-Hadrill, 'Charlemagne and England', 164–65. The request for prayers for the *populus christianus* is echoed in Charlemagne's letter to Offa which accompanied the gifts; Alcuin, *Ep.*, no. 100; *Alcuin of York*, trans. Allott, no. 40.

125 M. McCormick, 'The Liturgy of War in the Early Middle Ages: Crisis, Litanies, and the Carolingian Monarchy', *Viator*, 15 (1984), 1–23.

within the *termini* of Charlemagne's authority as defined by the author of the *Lorsch Annals*. Alcuin closed his letter to the bishops with his seal (*sigillum*) so that they could be sure of its authenticity.[126] It is possible that the *munusculis* brought by Charlemagne's envoys were similarly intended to authenticate the Frankish king's instructions. In later medieval contexts the word could refer to 'signet rings'; such a use in this context would make the connotations of *fidelitas* between Frankish monarch and the Anglo-Saxon kingdoms even stronger.[127]

Eardwulf's case has obvious and explicit echoes with the experiences of other high-ranking Anglo-Saxons who were exiled from their kingdoms towards the end of the eighth century: like Eadberht Præn, Eardwulf travelled to Francia and Rome to plead his case; like Eadberht Præn and Ecgberht too, Eardwulf later returned to his own kingdom. With Eardwulf, though, the sources are quite explicit about Carolingian involvement in the plan to return him to his kingdom; and this evidence increases the likelihood of Carolingian involvement in the successful installation of kings who had been exiled across the Channel into Kent and Wessex in 796 and 802 respectively, especially since all three men had had a history of hostility towards Mercia. But Eardwulf's story is all the more remarkable because the kingdom involved was Northumbria. Unlike Mercian-controlled Kent, or even Wessex, Northumbria posed no kind of political or economic challenge to Francia, and its fractured politics ensured that no Northumbrian king could rival the status of Offa in Mercia, let alone Charlemagne in Francia. This means that the motives for Carolingian involvement in the return of Eardwulf to Northumbria transcended the demands of security, mercantile flexibility or even the niceties of 'fraternal' diplomatic rivalry with the Mercian king, all of which could be proposed as motives for tacit intervention in the affairs of the southern kingdoms.

It seems that Charlemagne's motive for involvement in Eardwulf's problems had a different trajectory and one which is epitomized by the events in Rome on Christmas Day in 800. As the eighth century drew to a close, Charlemagne's self-image evolved towards the concept of himself as emperor of the *populus christianus*, as did the attitude of the Anglo-Saxon rulers towards him. Alcuin clearly thought that Charlemagne had responsibilities to the whole

---

[126] *Hec ut nostra credatis, nostro sigillo subter sigillavimus*; Alcuin, *Ep.*, no. 104, at 151 [line 9]; *Alcuin of York*, trans. Allott, no. 25.

[127] R. E. Latham, *Revised Medieval Latin Word-List from British and Irish Sources* (London, 1965), 308. Wallace-Hadrill argued that Carolingian seals may have provided the inspiration for Offa's portrait coinage; 'Charlemagne and England', 160. On the pre-eleventh-century circulation of the impressions of seal matrixes as means of authentication independent of written instructions see P. Chaplais, 'The Anglo-Saxon Chancery: From the Diploma to the Writ', *Journal of the Society of Archivists*, 3 (1966), 160–76, repr. in F. Ranger (ed.), *Prisca Munimenta* (London, 1973), 43–62, at 50–52 and P. D. A. Harvey and A. McGuinness, *A Guide to British Medieval Seals* (London, 1996), 3–4, with particular reference to the double-sided leaden seal of Coenwulf of Mercia (796–821) and the mid-ninth-century seal matrix of a Bishop Æthelwold, probably bishop of East Anglia. On the latter see also, A. B. Tonnochy, *Catalogue of British Seal-Dies in the British Museum* (London, 1952), 1.

Christian people;[128] as this sense of duty grew so Anglo-Saxon England was drawn more closely into the political, cultural and religious hegemony that was Carolingian Francia. Here, we see Charlemagne acting as a fulcrum and magnet for the exiled and dispossessed nobility of Anglo-Saxon England who turned to him for restitution and rehabilitation. Significantly, by the beginning of the ninth century, Charlemagne had both the inclination and the ability to intervene decisively on their behalf.

---

[128] See Alcuin's letter on the subject of the three world powers; Alcuin, *Ep.*, no. 174; *Alcuin of York*, trans. Allott, no. 103.

Chapter 6

Francia and the Mercian Supremacy

The political and cultural dominance of Mercia within Anglo-Saxon England in the eighth and earlier ninth centuries has led to the characterization of the period as one of 'Mercian supremacy'; when the kings of Mercia dominated the lands south of the Humber which lay outside the traditional powerbase of Mercian royalty in the middle Trent valley.[1] This Mercian hegemony – which had its roots in Penda's battlefields – was consolidated during the long reign of King Æthelbald (716–57) whom Bede recognized in 731 as the *de facto* overlord of Southumbria.[2] It reached its apogee in the second half of the eighth century under King Offa (757–96) who forged a new type of polity by systematically degrading the status of neighbouring kingdoms and attempting, with varying degrees of success, to make them Mercian provinces under his direct rule. Succeeded only briefly by his son, Offa's legacy was taken up by a distant relative named Coenwulf (796–821) who maintained Mercian military and political seniority. After Coenwulf's death in 821, succession to the Mercian throne was contested between several noble families and, in a manner not unlike the Northumbrian experience of the later eighth century, dynastic rivalry served to undermine Mercian authority over the rest of Anglo-Saxon England. It is, then, a simple matter of chronological fact that the heyday of Mercian power in England was matched in Francia by the rise to prominence of the Carolingian family, and that it was a 'Mercian century' in England, *c.* 720–*c.* 820, which paralleled the *floruit* of Carolingian power across the Channel. This simple observation demands that Mercia be at the forefront of any analysis of Carolingian relations with the kingdoms of England. Although the ruling elite of other Anglo-Saxon kingdoms (particularly Northumbria, Kent and Wessex) clearly had independent connections with the Carolingians, much of the Frankish response to them was conditioned by the state of diplomacy with Mercia. As we have seen, much of the evidence discussed in previous chapters concerning Charlemagne's dealings with political exiles, and the cross-Channel exchange of ideas, advice and news, is to be found in the wake of Franco-Mercian contacts particularly with the court of King Offa.

---

[1] F. M. Stenton, 'The supremacy of the Mercian kings', *EHR*, 33 (1918), 433–52, reprinted in his *Preparatory to Anglo-Saxon England: Collected Papers* (Oxford, 1970), 48–66; *idem*, *Anglo-Saxon England* (3rd edn) (1971), 205–24. S. Keynes, 'England, 700–900', in *NCMH*, 2, ed. R. McKitterick (Cambridge, 1995), 18–42, at 27–37.

[2] Bede, *HE* V.23. Æthelbald's status is affirmed by the Ismere diploma which styles him *rex Britanniae* and 'king not only of the Mercians but also of all the provinces which are called by the general name "South English"'; *BCS*, 154, S 89; *EHD* 1, trans. Whitelock, no. 67.

The contemporaneous emergence of the Mercian and Carolingian polities was, to all intents and purposes, an unconnected historical coincidence – although around the turn of the eighth century communities on both sides of the Channel undoubtedly benefited from the expansion and profitability of the Frisian North Sea trade network.[3] Cross-Channel contacts with Francia were not directly significant (so far as we can tell) to the consolidation of Mercian power in England in the early decades of the eighth century. In Francia, though, the Carolingians maximized the opportunities for self-aggrandizement offered by the activities of the Anglo-Saxon missionaries in Frisia and the Rhineland, and men and women from Mercia were prominent among Boniface's circle of colleagues and correspondents.[4] This personal connection provided the context for Boniface's vociferous and condemnatory letter to King Æthelbald in 746 which, along with a letter to Archbishop Cuthbert, set the agenda for the reforming council called by the Mercian king at *Clofesho* the following year.[5] As is well known, some of the canons of that council closely mirrored provisions already enacted by Boniface at Frankish councils.[6] This letter from Boniface was received when Æthelbald was at the peak of his authority and in a position of sufficient influence to convene and preside over a council of all the bishops of England, and is thus a reflection of the reality of Mercian hegemony in southern England. Once Mercian and Carolingian dominance was firmly established, for the rulers of both kingdoms cross-Channel contacts became a sure sign of their exalted status at home. Thus, for the Mercian kings, the arrival of gifts, embassies and letters from continental courts (even overtly critical ones) was not only a potent symbol of their own importance within England but was also emblematic of the breadth of their fame and success. The same held true, though to a differing degree, for Carolingians who gave audience to messengers from Mercia.

The fact that the Mercian supremacy in Anglo-Saxon England was contemporary with that of the Carolingians in Francia has inevitably encouraged historians to search for evidence that cross-Channel contact was a factor in the sustained success of both regimes. This is particularly tempting for the latter part of the eighth century when, under Offa and Charlemagne, there is a quantitative and qualitative increase in evidence for political and economic contacts between the Anglo-Saxons and the Franks. The question is whether this increased visibility is a result of real change or a product of broader cultural developments

---

[3] S. Lebecq, 'Routes of Change: Production and Distribution in the West (5th–8th centuries)', in L. Webster and M. Brown (eds), *The Transformation of the Roman World AD 400–900* (London, 1997), 67–78; *idem, Marchands et navigateurs frisons du haut moyen âge*, 2 vols (Lille, 1983), vol. I, 49–97; D. Jellema, 'Frisian Trade in the Dark Ages', *Speculum*, 30 (1955), 294–99; M. A. S. Blackburn, 'Money and Coinage', in *NCMH* 2 (Cambridge, 1995), 538–59, at 545–48.

[4] R. McKitterick, 'Anglo-Saxon Missionaries in Germany: Personal Connections and Local Influences', Eighth Brixworth Lecture (Leicester, 1990).

[5] Boniface, *Epistolae*, nos 73 and 78; *The Letters of Saint Boniface*, trans. E. Emerton (New York, 1940), nos 57 and 62.

[6] C. Cubitt, *Anglo-Saxon Church Councils, c. 650–c. 850* (London, 1995), 102–10. Cf. H. Vollrath, *Die Synoden Englands bis 1066* (Paderborn, 1985), 150–56.

that enabled the preservation of more primary sources.[7] Wallace-Hadrill coun-
selled against assuming direct exchange of influence in historical situations
where similar problems may have been resolved by similar solutions, independently attained.[8] Certainly, pressures of governance in the later eighth century
were as acute for Offa as they were for Charlemagne; both were faced with
immediate military challenges on their accession and both were concerned to
ensure the succession of their own offspring in preference to rival relatives. It is
similarities such as these in the circumstances of their reigns, as well as the
various mechanisms of government which they devised and employed to maintain their dynastic rule, which attract attention and raise the question of whether
the mechanisms and solutions of rulership owed anything to the practices of
governance across the Channel. And, aided by the eyes of Alcuin in particular,
sufficient evidence of direct contact survives to suggest that interaction between
Carolingians and Mercians was both personal and institutional, and that their
kings were mutually cognizant of events occurring across the Channel.

One feature common to both Carolingian and Mercian hegemonies was the
longevity of their kings. Calculating longevity is a blunt tool with which to
examine the impact and achievements of rulers, but a long reign was thought
noteworthy by contemporary chroniclers and does, at the very least, suggest that a
ruler was doing something right.[9] In a world of warrior societies where conquest,
plunder and tribute-taking were yardsticks of a king's prowess and the means by
which he satisfied noble ambition, a long reign was a direct reflection of a king's
abilities on the battlefield as well as in the chamber of politics. The fundamental
achievements of Mercian and Carolingian kings are amplified in this respect by
comparison with the less salubrious record of kingship in neighbouring kingdoms
– most obviously in Northumbria where, in the period corresponding to Offa's
rule, eight different kings claimed the throne – one of them twice. In contrast,
apart from the brief reigns of Beornred (757) and Ecgfrith (796), neither of which
lasted more than a few weeks, no Mercian king of the eighth or earlier ninth
centuries ruled for less than a full quarter-century; Æthelbald (716–57), Offa
(757–96) and Coenwulf (796–821). These figures compare favourably with
Carolingian rulers: Pippin III was in power for 27 years, 17 as king; Charlemagne
reigned 46 years and Louis for 36. More practically though, the contemporaneous
presence of long-lived rulers in Mercia and in Francia provided the context for the
development of a more complex political relationship than would ordinarily have
been feasible. Political longevity permits continuity of contact and evolution of

---

[7] On the context of the preservation of Alcuin's letters see, M. Lapidge, 'Latin Learning in
Ninth-century England', in *idem, Anglo-Latin Literature. Vol. 1: 600–899* (London and Rio Grande,
1996), 409–54, at 429.

[8] J. M. Wallace-Hadrill, 'Charlemagne and Offa', in *idem, Early Germanic Kingship in
England and on the Continent* (Oxford, 1971), 109; *idem*, 'The Franks and the English in the Ninth
Century: Some Common Historical Interests', *History*, 35 (1950), 202–18, at 211, reprinted in his
Early Medieval History (Oxford, 1975), 201–16.

[9] See, for example, *ASChron. DE*, 757 recording the accession of Offa.

diplomacy between individuals, and creates the conditions for a different sort of impact than is possible with one-off embassies. If fortunate with source survival, historians have the opportunity to examine the development of long-distance links between individuals – links which had time to evolve and change. In this respect, the second half of the eighth century provides an unusual opportunity to trace the development of connections between England and Francia through the contacts that linked the royal and ecclesiastical courts of Offa and Charlemagne.

Sources for the Mercian supremacy, 720–820

A paradox of this period of 'Mercian supremacy' is that its chronological param-
eters were defined not by Mercian observers but by outsiders; Bede recorded the authority of Æthelbald over all the kingdoms south of the Humber in the closing chapters of his *Ecclesiastical History* and, in doing so, he implicitly recognized the passing of power within England away from his own Northumbrian *patria*.[10] Similarly, the decline of Mercian dominance was marked by the West-Saxon compiler of the *Anglo-Saxon Chronicle* who ignored a century or more of Mercian domination when he acclaimed Ecgberht of Wessex in 829 as the eighth *Bretwalda* in direct succession to Bede's seventh-century Northumbrian kings.[11] The chronicler's claim for the West-Saxon ascendant was based on an account of the defeat of the Mercian army in that year and the submission of the Northumbrians to Ecgberht in a string of military victories which Kirby has attributed, in part, to Carolingian support for the West-Saxon cause.[12] The extent of Frankish support for Ecgberht in the 820s remains a matter for discussion; nevertheless, the *Chronicle's* record symbolizes the eclipse of Mercian hegemony in England and marks a further southerly shift in the balance of power in favour of Wessex. What is more, the perception of change is enhanced considerably by the *Chronicle's* subsequent records of the Carolingian connections between the courts of Ecgberht's son, Æthelwulf, and that of Charles the Bald in the 850s.[13]

---

[10] Bede, *HE* V.23–24; *Bede's Ecclesiastical History of the English People*, ed. and trans. B. Colgrave and R. A. B. Mynors (Oxford, 1969), 558–59, 566–67. See also N. P. Brooks, 'The Formation of the Mercian Kingdom', in S. R. Bassett (ed.), *The Origins of Anglo-Saxon Kingdoms* (London, 1989), 159–70, reprinted in his *Anglo-Saxon Myths: State and Church, 400–1066* (London, 2000), 61–78.

[11] *ASChron.* A 827 (for 829). P. Wormald, 'Bede, the Bretwaldas, and the Origins of the *Gens Anglorum*', in P. Wormald et al. (eds), *Ideal and Reality in Frankish and Anglo-Saxon Society* (Oxford, 1983), 99–129.

[12] D. P. Kirby, *The Earliest English Kings* (London, 1991), 192–93.

[13] Wallace-Hadrill, 'The Franks and the English in the Ninth Century'; J. L. Nelson, 'The Franks and the English in the Ninth Century Reconsidered', in P. E. Szarmach and J. T. Rosenthal (eds), *The Preservation and Transmission of Anglo-Saxon Culture* (Kalamazoo, 1997), 141–58 reprinted, as Chapter VI, in her *Rulers and Ruling Families in Early Medieval Europe: Alfred Charles the Bald and Others* (Aldershot, 1999); P. Stafford, 'The King's Wife in Wessex, 800–1066', *Past and Present*, 91 (1981), 3–27. See also Chapter 7, below, 224–43.

It is one of the anomalies of the eighth century that no native Mercian historian or chronicler emerged to document the power of his own kingdom within England. We have no 'Life of King Offa' to set alongside Einhard's *Life of Charlemagne* or Asser's *Life of King Alfred*, and it is the outsider's view of Mercia which prevails in the contemporary record.[14] Bede tells us about the importance of Mercian monasteries, and of the appointment in 731 to the archbishopric of Canterbury of a Mercian scholar called Tatwine, who came from the monastery of *Briudun*, probably Breedon-on-the-Hill near Repton. Bede says that Tatwine was a man 'renowned for his devotion and wisdom and excellently instructed in the Scriptures'.[15] Two of his works survive to corroborate Bede's opinion – a collection of 40 riddles or *enigmata* and a Latin grammar. There is, however, no surviving sign that Tatwine or any of his contemporary compatriots produced an account of Mercia to set alongside Bede's own retrospective history of Northumbria or the West-Saxon-focused *Anglo-Saxon Chronicle*. Historical material in the form of regnal genealogies and episcopal lists were available in Mercia to a scribe who copied a Northumbrian list *c.* 812,[16] but narrative accounts of eighth-century Mercia were written by outsiders, often at some remove from Mercia itself and often for non-Mercian readers. Felix wrote his *Life* of the Mercian saint, Guthlac, for an East-Anglian patron. Although Felix knew the scholarship of Bede and Aldhelm, there are hints in his work which suggest that he may not have been of English birth.[17] Bishop George of Ostia and Amiens wrote his account of the Mercian and Northumbrian assemblies in 786 for the eyes of Pope Hadrian and Charlemagne, and Boniface (a West Saxon) and Alcuin (a Northumbrian) wrote their surviving letters to the Mercian elite while resident in Francia. We know of Offa's legislative achievements only from hints in Bishop George's letter, from a letter from Charlemagne to Offa, and from the *Preface* of King Alfred's Law Code which was penned a century after Offa's death.[18] It is not until the early years of the

---

[14] P. Wormald, 'The Age of Offa and Alcuin', in J. Campbell (ed.), *The Anglo-Saxons* (Oxford, 1982), 110–11; Keynes, 'England 700–900', 29–30.

[15] Bede, *HE* V.23; R. Sharpe, *A Handlist of the Latin Writers of Great Britain and Ireland before 1540* (Turnhout, 1997), no. 1681; F. H. Whitman, 'Aenigmata Tatwini', *Neuphilologische Mitteilungen*, 88 (1987), 8–17; N. P. Brooks, *The Early History of the Church of Canterbury* (Leicester, 1984), 98–99.

[16] London, BL MS Vespasian B.VI (fos 104–9); R. I. Page, 'Anglo-Saxon Episcopal Lists, Parts I and II', *Nottingham Medieval Studies*, 9 (1965), 71–95, at 74–77; *idem*, 'Anglo-Saxon Episcopal Lists, Part III', *Nottingham Medieval Studies*, 10 (1966), 2–24, at 3–7; D. N. Dumville, 'The Anglian Collection of Royal Genealogies and Regnal Lists', *ASE*, 5 (1976), 23–50; J. Morrish, 'Dated and Datable Manuscripts Copied in England During the Ninth Century: A Preliminary List', *Medieval Studies*, 50 (1988), 512–38, at 517; M. P. Brown, *The Book of Cerne: Prayer, Patronage and Power in Ninth-century England* (London and Toronto, 1996), 168–72.

[17] Sharpe, *A Handlist*, no. 296 *Felix's Life of St. Guthlac*, ed. and trans. B. Colgrave (1956).

[18] P. Wormald, 'In Search of King Offa's "Law Code"', in I. N. Wood and N. Lund (eds), *People and Places in Northern Europe, 500–1600* (Woodbridge, 1991), 25–45. Charlemagne's letter to Offa, concerning the rights of merchants, presupposes the existence in Mercia of recognized judicial authority in the hands of the king.

tenth century that we get a chronicle which is identifiably Mercian in origin, although even this so-called 'Mercian Register' survives only as an interpolation into two copies of the West-Saxon recension of the *Anglo-Saxon Chronicle*.[19]

The enigmatic *Tribal Hidage* most probably belongs to the period of Mercian hegemony, although the context for its creation and function remains contentious.[20] Of the surviving administrative documents from the period, charters provide the greatest insight into the mechanisms and chronology of the extension of Mercian power, and the royal styles accorded to Mercian kings in these charters are the closest thing historians possess to a Mercian expression of regal ideology.[21] But even documents such as these, as witnessed by the kings of the Mercian supremacy, relate mostly to the regions outside the heartlands of the middle Trent valley, recording grants of lands in non-Mercian territory to pro-Mercian allies. The Mercian kings of the later seventh and eighth centuries became adept at using charters – bookland – to insert their own men within, and to assert their own authority over, the kingdoms that bordered of their own. As such, it is the regions on the periphery of the Mercian powerbase which are illuminated by charters rather than the core of the Mercian kingdom itself.[22] The kingdom of the Hwicce around the river Severn is a good example; annexed by the Mercians at the end of the seventh century, its charters (preserved via the bishopric at Worcester) show how the Mercian kings gradually dispersed the landholdings of the native rulers of the Hwicce to the point where Offa was able to refer to the Hwiccan king, Ealdred, as a *subregulus* as a prelude to the total absorption of the kingdom into 'greater' Mercia.[23] A similar pattern of absorption and demotion of a native dynasty can be observed through the charters of other kingdoms such as that of the South Saxons and Kent.[24]

Similarly placed outside the areas of traditional Mercian power were the mints of Canterbury and London (and Rochester after 810) which produced coinage for their Mercian lords. With the possible exception of an unlocated

---

[19] *ASChron*. B and C, 903–924; Whitelock, *EHD* 1, 112–13, 208–18.

[20] Keynes, 'England 700–900', 21–25; D. N. Dumville, 'The Tribal Hidage: An Introduction to its Texts and their History', in S. Bassett (ed.), *The Origins of the Anglo-Saxon Kingdoms*, (London, 1989), 225–30; N. J. Higham, *An English Empire: Bede and the Early Anglo-Saxon Kings* (Manchester, 1995), 74–111.

[21] Stenton, 'The Supremacy of the Mercian Kings', 53ff; Wallace-Hadrill, 'Charlemagne and Offa', 110–12 and 'Charlemagne and England', 684; S. Keynes, 'Changing Faces: Offa, King of Mercia', *History Today*, 40 (1990), 14–19; *idem*, 'England, 700–900', 29.

[22] E. John, *Reassessing Anglo-Saxon England* (Manchester, 1996), 50–54.

[23] S. Bassett, 'In Search of the Origins of Anglo-Saxon Kingdoms', in S. Bassett (ed.), *The Origins of the Anglo-Saxon Kingdoms* (London, 1989), 3–27; D. Hooke, *The Anglo-Saxon Landscape: The Kingdom of the Hwicce* (Manchester, 1985); H. P. R. Finberg, 'Princes of the Hwicce', in his *Early Charters of the West Midlands* (Leicester, 1964), 167–80; P. Sims-Williams, *Religion and Literature in Western England, 600–800* (Cambridge, 1990), 16–53.

[24] Brooks, *Early History*, 112–13; S. E. Kelly, *Charters of Selsey*, Anglo-Saxon Charters 6 (Oxford, 1998); P. Brandon, *The South Saxons* (London, 1978); M. Welch, 'The Kingdom of the South Saxons: The Origins', in S. Bassett (ed.), *Origins*, 75–96.

mint in the upper Thames Valley, Mercia itself had no mints of its own, a factor which undoubtedly lies behind the ongoing concern of the Mercian kings to control London and the south-east.[25] Even the great linear earthwork between the kingdom of Powys and Mercia, which is Offa's best known legacy, marks his attempts to control the most westerly march of his kingdom.[26] Indeed, it is only in terms of extant architecture, sculpture and manuscripts that we can see the skills of Mercian artisans and understand the cultural vibrancy of the Mercian supremacy at work in the core of the kingdom itself. The grandeur of Mercian ambition is self-evident at Brixworth – thought by some to be the lost site of *Clofesho* – a church which proclaims, in equal measure, its stylistic debt to continental building techniques as to Anglo-Saxon traditions.[27] The mausoleum, which now forms the lower part of the east end of the church at Repton and which was constructed by mid-ninth century, contains four monolithic twisted columns recalling the antique columns around the apostle's tomb in the old basilica of St Peter in Rome.[28] Similarly exotic inspiration lies behind the astonishing set of architectural sculpture which survives in the twelfth-century rebuilding of Tatwine's church nearby at Breedon-on-the-Hill, the closest parallels for which are antique and Byzantine, possibly filtered through the Carolingian world.[29] Other examples of monumental sculpture in Mercia, such as the crosses from Sandbach in Cheshire, have iconographic traits which may also be linked

---

[25] P. Grierson and M. A. S. Blackburn, *Medieval European Coinage with a Catalogue of the Coins in the Fitzwilliam Museum, Cambridge. Vol. 1: The Early Middle Ages* (Cambridge, 1986), 272–82. On the possible existence of a mint in the upper Thames valley see D. M. Metcalf, 'Monetary Expansion and Recession: Interpreting the Distribution-Patterns of Seventh and Eighth-Century Coins', in P. J. Casey and R. Reece (eds), *Coins and the Archaeologist* (2nd edn) (London, 1988), 230–53, at 230.

[26] C. Fox, *Offa's Dyke: A Field Survey of the Western Frontier Works of Mercia in the Seventh and Eighth Centuries AD* (Oxford, 1955); D. Hill, 'Offa's Dyke: Pattern and Purpose', *Antiquaries Journal*, 80 (2000), 195–206.

[27] R. H. C. Davis, 'Brixworth and Clofesho', *JBAA*, 25 (1962), 71; H. M. Taylor and J. Taylor, *Anglo-Saxon Architecture* (Cambridge, 1965), Vol. 1, 108–14; D. Parsons, 'Brixworth and its Monastery Church', in A. Dornier (ed.), *Mercian Studies* (Leicester, 1977), 173–90; E. Fernie, *The Architecture of the Anglo-Saxons* (London, 1983), 65–69; S. Keynes, *The Councils of Clofesho*, University of Leicester, Vaughan Paper, 38 (Leicester, 1994).

[28] H. M. Taylor, 'St. Wystan's Church, Repton, Derbyshire. A Reconstruction Essay', *Archaeological Journal*, 144 (1987), 205–45. Cf. Fernie, *The Architecture of the Anglo-Saxons*, 116–21 where the author argues for a tenth/eleventh-century date for the insertion of the spiral columns. The date which provides a watershed for the construction of the crypt is 873–74 when, according to the *ASChron.*, the Great Viking Army overwintered in Repton; see M. Biddle and B. Kjølbye-Biddle, 'Repton and the Vikings', *Antiquity*, 66 (1992), 36–51.

[29] R. J. Cramp, 'Schools of Mercian Sculpture', in Dornier, *Mercian Studies*, 191–231; R. Jewell, 'The Anglo-Saxon Friezes at Breedon-on-the-Hill', *Archæologia*, 108 (1986), 95–115; S. J. Plunkett, 'The Mercian Perspective', in S. M. Foster (ed.), *The St Andrews Sarcophagus: A Pictish Masterpiece and its International Connections* (Dublin, 1998), 202–26, at 215–20; A. Dornier, 'The Breedon Lion and its Associates: A Comparative Study of Anglo-Saxon and Frankish Architectural Animal Panels', in J. Bourne (ed.), *Anglo-Saxon Landscapes in the East Midlands* (Leicester, 1996), 37–52; D. Parsons, 'Before the Parish: The Church in Anglo-Saxon Leicestershire', in ibid., 11–36, at 15–16.

to Carolingian theological developments.[30] Relatively few surviving manuscripts can be linked to Mercia in this period, but those which can are testimony to the calligraphic and artistic achievements of Mercian scholarship. A number of the books thought to have been produced in Mercian scriptoria (Lichfield or Worcester being likely centres of production) are intimate prayerbooks for personal devotion, and the content and decoration of at least two such books was influenced by Carolingian developments.[31] Apart from this important, but relatively restricted, body of material evidence produced in Mercia itself, the reality of the Mercian supremacy is visible primarily through the written output and artefacts of those neighbouring kingdoms which were the targets of Mercian aggression; by contrast, the heart of the aggressor remains shrouded.

Alcuin and the Mercian court

Another complicating factor for historians of the Mercian supremacy is the imbalance in the chronological distribution of sources. The decade of the 790s is among the best documented in the entire Anglo-Saxon period, thanks largely to Alcuin's concern for his compatriots while resident at the Frankish court. The sources which tell of Carolingian contacts with Mercia in the last decade or so of the eighth century are very much superior to those which survive from adjacent decades. Is this haziness on either side of the 790s real or apparent – a genuine reflection of the significance of Alcuin's role at the Frankish court or a function of the preferential preservation of his writing over time? Despite the continued presence of Anglo-Saxon and Irish scholars at centres close to the Frankish court,[32] after Alcuin's death in 804 no ninth-century scholar takes up the role of commentator on the Franco-Mercian relationship in the last decade of Charlemagne's reign or during that of his son.

Alcuin was one of the most prolific writers of his day and, as a political theorist and scholar of the Bible, he was one of the most influential. His letters to members of the Mercian court are a particularly interesting element of his epistolary output, revealing something of the dynamics of Mercian politics and

---

[30] J. Hawkes, 'A Question of Judgement: The Iconographic Programme of Sandbach, Cheshire', in C. Bourke (ed.), *From the Isles of the North* (Belfast, 1995), 213–20; *idem*, 'Constructing Iconographies: Questions of Identity in Mercian Sculpture', in M. P. Brown and C. A. Farr (eds), *Mercia: An Anglo-Saxon Kingdom in Europe* (2001), 230–45.

[31] BL Harley 7653; BL Royal 2.A.XX, BL Harley 2965; CUL MS Ll.I.10 (The Book of Cerne); Oxford Bodleian Library MS Hatton 93. The latter manuscript contains the Carolingian explication of the mass, 'Primum in ordine'. On this text and these manuscripts see, Morrish, 'Dated and Datable Manuscripts'; Brown, *The Book of Cerne*, esp. 164–72; L. Webster and J. Backhouse (eds), *The Making of England: Anglo-Saxon Art and Culture, AD 600–900* (London, 1991), 195–96 and no. 162–66.

[32] M. Garrison, 'The English and the Irish at the Court of Charlemagne', in P. L. Butzer, M. Kerner and W. Oberschelp (eds), *Karl der Grosse und sein Nachwirken. 1200 Jahre Kultur und Wissenschaft in Europa*. Vol. 1: *Wissen und Weltbild* (Turnhout, 1997), 97–124.

also Alcuin's aspirations for better governance of the Mercian polity under Offa's control. Alcuin's hopes for Anglo-Saxon kingship were shaped both by his education in Northumbria as well as by his experience of kingship under the Carolingians. In his view, the adherence of kings to the will of God brought health and wealth to a people; defeat, hunger or moral decline were signs of poor governance and divine displeasure. Whereas he despaired for the spiritual and political stability of his own Northumbrian people, he saw in Offa of Mercia a man with ruthless ambition and the ability to succeed. His letters to Offa, and to the men and women of the Mercian court, were often written in reaction to news of events in England. But Alcuin also wrote to influence attitudes and to encourage suitable behaviour becoming of a king, although it is debatable whether he wrote to harness Offa's own enthusiasm for Carolingian-style reforms or rather to channel Offa's raw energy to prevent it from spilling over into a very un-Carolingian tyranny.

The earliest firm evidence for contact between Alcuin and the Mercian court dates to 786 when he joined Bishop George, the Franco-papal legate, on his journey back south into Mercia after the Northumbrian council. George's report to Hadrian names Alcuin and his companion Pyttel as the representatives of King Ælfwald and Archbishop Eanbald to the Mercian court (Figure 3.4, fo. 126v, line 16, p. 73). As noted above, it is likely that Alcuin's role in the legates' mission was more substantial than the brief reference in George's letter implies, and he may have helped George to draft the tenets of the capitulary reported to Hadrian. If, as is commonly supposed, Alcuin already had some experience of Charlemagne's court prior to the mission, his presence at the Northumbrian and Mercian councils is an important element in the Frankish dimension to the proceedings.[33] Certainly, his inside knowledge of Anglo-Saxon political geography and social mores would have been invaluable when Bishop George was planning the mission. It is likely also, although we cannot prove it, that Alcuin was a key informant concerning Offa's political and ecclesiastical ambitions in the late 780s. George's mission preceded the 'contentious synod at Chelsea' by a matter of months.[34] It is difficult not to conclude that the key issues at Chelsea must also have been raised in the conciliar meetings held by the Franco-papal legates in 786, since both the principal outcomes from the Chelsea synod had continental dimensions on which the legates would have had a view. Thus, Offa's decision to divide the metropolitan see of Canterbury and to create a new archbishopric at Lichfield needed papal consent since the policy strayed from the episcopal structure of the English Church laid down by Gregory the Great. And having secured a compliant archbishop for Mercia, the subsequent consecration of Offa's son, Ecgfrith, at Chelsea as king alongside his father must be

---

[33] Cf. D. A. Bullough, 'Alcuin before Frankfort', in R. Berndt (ed.), *Das Frankfurter Konzil von 794. Kristallisationspunkt karolingischer Kultur. Vol. 2: Kultur and Theologie* (Mainz, 1997), 571–85, at 578.

[34] *ASChron.* 785 (for 787).

assessed (as has long been recognized) in the light of the recent Carolingian experiment with 'the magic of unction'.[35]

The 'anointing' of Ecgfrith

A Carolingian language of sacral kingship permeates George's report to Hadrian. The capitulary signed by the worthies of both the Mercian and Northumbrian courts laid down two relevant principles on royal inheritance and regicide: that only men born to a legitimate marriage may be *christus domini ... et rex totius regni*, 'the Lord's anointed and king of the whole kingdom'; and the instruction 'Let no-one dare to conspire to kill a king, for he is the Lord's anointed'.[36] The Legates' Capitulary was pronounced to the assembled companies both in the vernacular and in Latin to ensure total comprehension among the secular, as well as ecclesiastical, nobility. Although Wallace-Hadrill has been sceptical about attaching a technical meaning to these phrases used by George, it should be noted that the language of sacral kingship in the Legates' Capitulary is not forced – it reads like a natural aspect of the vocabulary of its author.[37] And in that normalizing environment it is easy to envisage how the presence of George and his companions at the Mercian court could have nurtured an idea in Offa's mind to use ecclesiastical ceremony to underpin his son's birthright.

The immediate precedent for Ecgfrith's consecration seems likely to have been the ceremony which had taken place in Rome at Easter 781 when Charlemagne fulfilled a promise to Hadrian and brought his son Pippin to Rome for baptism. Pippin was also anointed king of Italy alongside his brother, Louis, who was anointed king of Aquitaine in the same ceremony.[38] The revised version of the *Royal Frankish Annals* says that Hadrian also crowned the young boys as an outward display of their new status. This event mirrored Charlemagne's own consecration alongside his brother Carloman, at the hands of Pope Stephen III at St Denis in 754.[39] On both these occasions young Carolingian

---

[35] Wallace-Hadrill, 'Charlemagne and Offa', 117; *idem*, 'Charlemagne and England', in W. Braunfels (ed.), *Karl der Grosse: Lebenswerke und Nachleben* (Düsseldorf, 1965), Vol. 1, 683–98, reprinted in his *Early Medieval History*, 155–80, at 159; W. Levison, *England and the Continent in the Eighth Century* (Oxford, 1946), 116–19; P. E. Schramm, *A History of the English Coronation* (Oxford, 1937), 15.

[36] Haddan and Stubbs (eds), *Councils* III, 453.

[37] Wallace-Hadrill, 'Charlemagne and Offa', 115.

[38] *The Lives of the Eighth-Century Popes*, trans. R. Davis (Liverpool, 1992), 113–14. E. John, *Orbis Britanniae* (Leicester, 1966), 28–35. For arguments for an insular background to the Mercian ceremony and for a slight modification to this stance see *idem*, *Reassessing Anglo-Saxon England*, 59–61, and J. L. Nelson, 'Inauguration Rituals', in her *Politics and Ritual in Early Medieval Europe* (London and Rio Grande, 1986), 283–307, at 285.

[39] *Annales regni Francorum*, 754; *Clausula de unctione Pippini*, ed. B. Krusch, MGH SS rer. Merov. (Hanover, 1885), 465–56; *Carolingian Civilization: A Reader*, trans. P. E. Dutton (Peterborough, Ontario, 1993), 12. On the veracity of the latter text see A. Stoclet, '"La Clausula de

princes were anointed as kings while their father was still alive. The pre-mortem recognition of a son's rights to rule clearly did not affect the father's authority, but it did transfer his elevated status on to his legitimate offspring thereby marking out the next generation for rulership and simultaneously creating a further hurdle for the ambitions of non-anointed rivals. However, it is important to remember that, by 781, the Carolingian theory and practice of royal anointing was still evolving. The initial experiment at Soissons in 751 had shown its worth but, since we lack evidence that all of Charlemagne's legitimate sons were anointed, it seems that the ceremony cannot yet have been considered a prerequisite for kingship, even in Francia.[40] It is particularly notable that Charlemagne's oldest legitimate son and namesake does not appear to have been anointed at the ceremony in which he was made subking of Neustria in 790, and probably had to wait until his father's trip to Rome in 800–1 to receive an equivalent ceremonial inauguration.[41] Charlemagne's motive for the anointing ceremony in Rome in 781 seems, therefore, to have been pragmatic rather than dynastic; he used the ritual to cement an alliance with the pope and as a means of demonstrating Carolingian lordship over two traditionally independent and potentially troublesome areas of his realm. In this way he could satisfy the nobility of Italy and Aquitaine with a local ruler, while still maintaining the Carolingian dynastic agenda.[42]

Nevertheless, to Offa, the practice of anointing or consecrating an heir had much to commend it. He had come to power in the aftermath of a coup in which Æthelbald, a king of more than 40 years' standing, had been assassinated through the treachery of his personal bodyguard.[43] Carolingian-style royal anointing, and the legates' wise words about the divine protection conferred on an anointed monarch, must have seemed an interesting notion to him. Why not add the armour of Christ to the measures he could take himself against mortal enemies of his regime; if it was working for the Carolingians, why not the Offingas? We know from other evidence that Offa was concerned to establish the long-term legitimacy of his regime; the use of a genealogy, inserted in the *Anglo-Saxon Chronicle* under the date of his accession, displayed Offa's impeccable descent from Eowa, a brother of Penda, and from

---

unctione Pippini regis": mises au point et nouvelle hypothèses', *Francia*, 8.1 (1980), 1–42 and R. McKitterick, 'The Illusion of Royal Power in the Carolingian Annals', *EHR*, 115 (2000), 1–20.

[40] R. McKitterick, *The Frankish Kingdoms under the Carolingians, 751–987* (London, 1983), 193; Nelson, 'Inauguration Rituals', 291–93.

[41] On the younger Charles and Neustria see the *Annales Sancti Amandi*, 790, MGH SS 1, 12 and the *Annales Mettenses Priores*, 789, MGH SRG 10, 77; *Charlemagne: Translated Texts*, trans. P. D. King (Kendal, 1985), 157. See also Nelson, 'Inauguration Rituals', 292. On his involvement in the events in Rome in 800–81 see the *Liber Pontificalis, Vita Leonis III*, c. 24 (*Lives of the Ninth-Century Popes*, trans. Davis, 191) and R. Collins, *Charlemagne* (Basingstoke, 1998), 156–57.

[42] Coins were briefly issued for Louis in Aquitaine; Grierson and Metcalf, *MEC* 1, 207 and 213; S. Coupland, 'Money and Coinage under Louis the Pious', *Francia*, 17.1 (1990), 23–54 at 24–25.

[43] *Historia regum (York Annals)*, 757.

him back to Woden.[44] These 'Woden genealogies' were used by Christian Anglo-Saxon kings at moments of dynastic uncertainty to bolster the royal credentials of the ruling family. Eric John has shown that Woden-descent was restricted to royal families and, as such, was 'an important validating concept'.[45] In a similar fashion to the practice of anointing, these genealogies limited access to the royal title – in this case, to those who could demonstrate their blood-right by proving descent from historical and mythical ancestors of their kingdom.

There was another reason why the idea of royal anointing may have been raised in England in the 780s. By coincidence, Alcuin had also been in Rome in 780–81, having been sent there to collect the pallium from Hadrian for his friend Eanbald who was to succeed their mentor Ælberht as archbishop in York.[46] Eanbald had been selected on Ælberht's retirement two years previously but it seems that a request for the pallium had been delayed until after Ælberht's death on 8 November 780. According to the author of the ninth-century *Vita Alcuini*, it was on his return journey north that Alcuin met Charlemagne at Parma and, famously, received an invitation from the king to join the Frankish court.[47] Charlemagne, having spent Christmas at Pavia, travelled south via Parma to Rome in time for the Easter celebrations on 15 April.[48] If this interpretation of the evidence is correct, Alcuin did not witness any of the ceremonies of baptism, anointing and coronation performed by Hadrian on the Carolingian princes, but he cannot have failed to appreciate the buzz of anticipation around the papal court in the build-up to Charlemagne's arrival. At the very least, he would have learned the purpose of Charlemagne's journey to Rome during his encounter with the Carolingian court at Parma. Alcuin would thus have returned to England with the pallium for Eanbald, with stories of Franco-papal *amicitia*, an invitation from Charlemagne to return to Francia, and with news also of a Carolingian anointing ceremony.

---

[44] *ASChron.* 757. On the contemporary, 'Anglian Collection' of genealogies, compiled probably during the reign of the Northumbrian king, Alhred (765–74), see D. N. Dumville, 'The Anglian Collection', 23–50; and K. Sisam, 'Anglo-Saxon Royal Genealogies', *Proceedings of the British Academy*, 39 (1953), 287–348; H. Moisl, 'Anglo-Saxon Royal Genealogies and Germanic Oral Tradition', *JMH*, 7 (1981), 215–48; C. R. Davis, 'Cultural Assimilation in the Anglo-Saxon Royal Genealogies', *ASE*, 21 (1992), 23–36.

[45] E. John, 'The Point of Woden', *ASSAH*, 5 (1992), 128–34 and also his *Reassessing Anglo-Saxon England*, 55–56. See also Wallace-Hadrill, 'Charlemagne and England', 168.

[46] *ASChron.* DEF, 780; *Historia regum* (*York Annals*), 780. Bullough, 'Alcuin before Frankfort', 577.

[47] *Vita Alcuini* c. 5–6, ed. W. Arndt, MGH SS XV.1, 190; Charlemagne signed a privilege at Parma on 15 March 781; MGH Dipl. I, no. 132 at 182–83. See also, Levison, *England and the Continent*, 154, 243 and *Alcuin. On the Bishops, Kings and Saints of York*, ed. and trans. P. Godman, (Oxford, 1982), xxxvi–viii, and lines 1522–24 and 1562–64.

[48] *Annales regni Francorum*, 781; Revised *Annales regni Francorum*, 781.

Letters to ladies

Among the most interesting of Alcuin's letters to his English correspondents are those which he wrote to the women of the Mercian court, and which are matched by a selection which he wrote to the ladies of Charlemagne's entourage. In total, 26 letters survive addressed to the noblewomen of Anglo-Saxon England and Francia, which is about 9 per cent of the surviving collection.[49] The letters to these ladies are different in tone to those written to their male relatives; they are more intimate and personal, and they often refer to the exchange of gifts – they are letters between friends. They do, however, often discuss or allude to affairs of state, and Alcuin quite clearly realized that these women had influence at court and that their friendship was worth cultivating.

It seems very likely that Alcuin knew Offa's wife and daughters personally, and quite probably that he had met them when he accompanied Bishop George to the Mercian court in 786. He may have had other, unrecorded opportunities to meet them prior to that date, but on the occasion of the legates' mission he was present as a formal envoy of the Northumbrian king and archbishop, and possibly as a representative of Carolingian interests too. The ladies' presence is not mentioned in George's report to Hadrian; however, Offa's queen, Cynethryth, was clearly used to accompanying her husband to meetings of Mercian councils as proven by her habit of countersigning his charters.[50] On such a grand occasion as the arrival of legates from Rome it is unthinkable that Cynethryth and her children would not have been involved with hospitality to their distinguished guests.

There are no surviving letters from Alcuin to the queen, although there are indications that letters may have passed between them. Writing to a nun named Hunðryð, who clearly had good access to the Mercian court, Alcuin asks if she would speak to Cynethryth on his behalf to assure her that he was eager to communicate with her and that he would have written a letter 'if the King's business had permitted her to read it'.[51] This rather cryptic comment suggests that Cynethryth had already contacted Alcuin for advice but that Alcuin felt that Offa would not have taken too kindly to a reply. 'Let her rest assured', Alcuin continues, 'that I am as faithful to her ladyship as I can be' – the clear implication being that he would continue to work on her behalf. What it was that concerned Cynethryth is not known for sure, although Alcuin's command that Hunðryð, 'be sure to greet my son Ecgfrith' may provide a clue. Writing separately to Ecgfrith, Alcuin advised him to be worthy of his noble parents and to learn the virtue of *pietas* from Cynethryth.[52]

---

49 Alcuin, *Ep.* 15, 32, 36, 50, 62, 68, 69, 72, 79, 84, 102, 103, 105, 106, 154, 195, 204, 213, 214, 216, 228, 241, 279, 297, 300, 309, MGH Epp. IV.

50 See BCS 207 / S 140; BCS 216 / S 104; BCS 236 / S116; BCS 234 / S117; BCS 247 / S 123; BCS 245 / S124; BCS 248 / S125; BCS 251 / S 127; BCS 253 / S 129; BCS 259 / S 133; and BCS 203 / S59; BCS 237 / S 1184; trans. Whitelock, *EHD* I, no. 74, 76.

51 Alcuin, *Ep.* 62; MGH Epp. IV; *Alcuin of York*, trans. Allott, no. 36.

52 Alcuin, *Ep.* 61, MGH Epp. IV; *Alcuin of York*, trans. Allott, no. 35.

Cynethryth was clearly a woman of considerable stature and determination. Alcuin refers to her in his letters as *dispensatrix domus*, the 'controller of the household'.[53] In this respect, Alcuin plainly recognized Cynethryth's role to resemble that of a Carolingian queen; the *De ordine palatii* (compiled by Hincmar in 882 but based on material from Charlemagne's day) assigns the management and provisioning of the palace to the queen and her chamberlain.[54] Hincmar envisaged the royal palace as a microcosm of the empire; the smooth running of the palace was thus a pre-requisite for a stable and prosperous kingdom, and in this the queen played an essential role. A Carolingian queen's attention was required especially for the 'trappings of royalty' (*ornamento regali*). But unlike any Carolingian or other Anglo-Saxon queen, coins were minted in Cynethryth's name bearing her portrait and rank, *regina M[erciorum]*. With this overt expression of her status, the royal moneyers may have been reflecting an awareness of the coinage of the Empress Irene, Cynethryth's contemporary in Constantinople who controlled the eastern empire between 780–802.[55] Cynethryth's prominence at the Mercian court is further demonstrated by the inclusion of her name alongside that of her husband in a privilege granted by Pope Hadrian to the royal monasteries in which they had a familial interest.[56]

Cynethryth's high profile did not diminish after her husband's death in 796. As was usual for a royal widow, she retired into a monastery becoming abbess of the community at Cookham in Berkshire, close to Offa's burial place in Bedford, both houses having been bequeathed into her personal control by her husband.[57] Another letter from Alcuin may refer to this moment of transition from queen to abbess. He commends the carrier of the letter to the recipient, an unnamed nun, and asks her to 'greet that dear lady in my name', and to send the messenger to 'my lady' in order that he might be returned through her good office to his own country.[58] Echoing his earlier letter to Hunðryð, he adds, 'we

---

[53] Alcuin, *Ep.* 101, MGH Epp. IV; *Alcuin of York*, trans. Allott, no. 41.

[54] *Hincmarus, De ordine palatii*, ed. T. Gross and R. Schieffer, MGH *Fontes ius* III (Hanover, 1980), c. 22, at 72–75; Dutton, *Carolingian Civilization*, 458–99, at 493. See also the *Capitulare de villis* (*c.* 800), especially chs 16, 27, 47 and 58; MGH Capit. I, no. 32; *The Reign of Charlemagne*, trans. H. R. Loyn and J. Percival (London, 1975), 64–73.

[55] During her period of sole rule 797–802 (that is *after* Offa's death), Irene issued coins with her image on both obverse and reverse sides. Prior to that she appears alongside her son, Constantine VI. See P. Grierson, *Catalogue of the Byzantine Coins in the Dumbarton Oaks Collection* (Washington, 1966–73), Vol. 3, 336–51; Grierson and Blackburn, *MEC* 1, 279–80. Cf. S. Zipperer, 'Coins and Currency: Offa of Mercia and his Frankish Neighbours', in U. von Freeden, W. Koch and A. Wieczorek (eds), *Völker an Nord- und Ostsee und die Franken. Akten des 48. Sachsensymposiums in Mannheim vom 7 bis 11 September 1997* (Bonn, 1999), 121–28, where the case for a Roman prototype is pressed. On Irene see S. Runciman, 'The Empress Irene the Athenian', in D. Baker (ed.), *Medieval Women: Essays Presented to Rosalind Hill*, SCH Subsidia 1 (1978), 101–18.

[56] Her name is preserved in one of the formulaic privileges (no. 93) in the *Liber Diurnus*; Levison, *England and the Continent*, 29–31.

[57] Ibid., 251; Brooks, *The Early History*, 116; Haddan and Stubbs (eds), *Councils* III, 512; *EHD* 1, trans. Whitelock, no. 79.

[58] Alcuin, *Ep.* 103, MGH Epp. IV; *Alcuin of York*, trans. Allott, no. 43.

have always been loyal to her'. With reference to recent widowhood, he continues that he has 'always desired her progress towards the salvation of her soul, for which she has always had to strive, but now most of all since she has survived the death of her most excellent lord the King. I wish her to live in happiness and to serve God faithfully.' The precise context of this letter is ambiguous and it may be that it should be associated with Cynethryth's daughters, Abbess Æthelburh and Ælfflæd, queen of Æthelred of Northumbria who (much to Alcuin's chagrin) had died a few weeks before Offa on 18 April 796 at the hands of an assassin. The letter does, however, fit equally well with Alcuin's contacts with Cynethryth in the preceding decade and of her retirement to Cookham.

Alcuin was on particularly friendly terms with Offa's daughter, Abbess Æthelburh.[59] He wrote her at least three letters, possibly four if that to the unnamed nun was also for her.[60] Picking up on the meaning of her Old English name ('noble city'), he addresses her as 'Eugenia' – meaning 'nobly born'. Nicknames, as he says in a letter to the Frankish noblewoman Gundrada, 'arise from familiarity'.[61] This friendship was reinforced with the exchange of gifts which bound the giver and receiver more closely, and prompted the recipient for prayers and action on behalf of the donor. Alcuin sent Æthelburh a chalice and paten with which she might make daily offerings at the altar, and so remember Alcuin in her prayers. He also forwarded to her the gift of a dress from Charlemagne's fifth wife, Liutgard, and asked her to include the queen's name 'with those of your sisters in the records of the church'. One is reminded of the Northumbrian *Liber Vitae* (*c.* 840) and the inclusion therein of Charlemagne's name (Figure 4.1). This letter shows Alcuin, through the exchange of gifts and the promise of prayer, actively building a female friendship-network between the most prominent women of the Frankish and Mercian courts. Although these networks are difficult to access in the surviving records, the significance of their ties should not be underestimated; as Alcuin reminded Æthelburh, the friendship of Charlemagne's wife Luitgard, 'is honourable and useful to you'.[62]

Alcuin's letters to Æthelburh touched on matters of high politics too. He wrote to her at least twice in 796 offering solace and advice in that most difficult

---

[59] Levison thought that she was the abbess of the same name at Fladbury; Levison, *England and the Continent*, 251, n. 2. Others disagree, arguing that Abbess Æthelburh of Fladbury was in fact a member of the Hwiccan royal dynasty; Sims-Williams, *Religion and Literature*, 38–39, 132, and Kirby, *The Earliest English Kings*, 163.

[60] Alcuin, *Ep.*, nos 102, 36, 300, and possibly also no. 103; *Alcuin of York*, trans. Allott, nos 42, 44, 45.

[61] M. Garrison, 'The Social World of Alcuin: Nicknames at York and at the Carolingian Court', in L. A. J. R. Houwen and A. A. MacDonald (eds), *Alcuin of York. Scholar at the Carolingian Court,* Germania Latina, 3 (Groningen, 1998), 59–80.

[62] On Alcuin's use of these friendship and confraternity networks see, J. Gerchow, *Die Gedenküberlieferung der Angelsachsen* (Berlin and New York, 1988) and Bullough, 'Alcuin before Frankfort', 571–73.

of years.[63] The assassination of King Æthelred in Northumbria had made a widow of Ælfflæd, causing 'hot tears for your beloved sister'. Alcuin urged Æthelburh to bring Ælfflæd into a cloister, so that 'her temporal grief may lead to eternal joy'. It may have been this new sense of responsibility for her sister that prevented Æthelburh from departing on a long journey, probably a pilgrimage to Rome, which she had previously discussed with Alcuin. Two charters from Lucca in Italy show that Æthelred's sister, Adaltruda, had already made the journey to Italy; in 782 she bought a church in the town for 70 gold coins.[64] But Æthelburh's fate in England was sealed after the death of her own father in July later the same year. Alcuin wrote to her again after Offa's death, talking to her of new tyrant kings in England and offering consolation for her inability to commence her voyage.[65] 'God was planning something better for you,' he says. 'Spend on the comfort of the poor what you prepared as travelling money for your long journey.' The two sisters, Æthelburh and Ælfflæd, are subsequently found as witnesses to a confirmation of a papal privilege from Pope Leo III granted in 798 to the monastery at Glastonbury, as 'relatives' (*cognatae*) of Abbess Cynethryth.[66] Clearly Offa's wife and daughters did not sink into obscure retirement under the new reign.

Gervold and the marriage dispute

Alcuin's acquaintance with the ladies of the Mercian court may have been connected with his involvement in the diplomacy surrounding marriage negotiations between the offspring of Charlemagne and Offa in 789–90. Several letters survive from him, referring to the serious arguments which resulted when the negotiations were halted by Charlemagne.[67] Things had soured badly after Offa, apparently having agreed to the marriage of one of his daughters to Charlemagne's eldest son Charles, insisted that a reverse match should also be made and that Charlemagne's daughter, Bertha, should marry his son Ecgfrith.[68] The marriage negotiations demonstrate the very real esteem in which Offa was held at the Frankish court; the only other foreign court with which Charlemagne

---

[63] Alcuin, *Ep.*, nos 102, 300, and possibly 103, MGH Epp. IV; *Alcuin of York*, trans. Allott, nos 42, 45, and 43 respectively.

[64] Æthelred's sister (Æthelburh's sister-in-law) Adaltruda is described in a contemporary charter dated August 782 as 'Saxa Dei ancilla filia Adeluualdi qui fuit rex Saxonorum ultramarino', a reference to her (and Æthelred's) father, Æthelwald Moll, who had been king in Northumbria from 758/59 to 765; D. Barsocchini, *Memorie e documenti per servire all'istoria del ducato di Lucca*, Vol. V.ii (Lucca, 1837), nos 186 and 187, at 107–9; *ChLa* XXXVII, no. 1082, at 47–51.

[65] Alcuin, *Ep.*, no. 300, MGH Epp. IV; *Alcuin of York*, trans. Allott, no. 45. Alcuin honours her education by quoting Isidore of Seville's definition of kingship in explication of her troubles.

[66] Levison, *England and the Continent*, 251.

[67] Alcuin, *Ep.* nos 7, 9, and 82, MGH Epp. IV; *Alcuin of York*, trans. Allott, nos 31,10, and 39.

[68] *Acts of the Abbots of St Wandrille*, c. 12.ii, at 86–87.

entered into marriage negotiations for his children was that of the Byzantines.[69] Charlemagne's own chequered marital career demonstrates how politically sensitive such matters were.[70] Offa's insistence on a return match shows just how far his self-confidence had developed by the late 780s. Not content with the highly prestigious union of his daughter with the eldest son of the most powerful ruler in the west, Offa required a Carolingian at his own court, bringing Charlemagne's bloodline into his own. By now, Ecgfrith was a consecrated king, but there is no evidence that the same was true for the younger Charles. However, unlike Charles, Ecgfrith's father had had to fight a bloody coup to win his crown, and had been only a distant relative of previous kings. Offa's ambitions for his son's security included a Carolingian bride, and he wished to augment Ecgfrith's authority through union with the most powerful family in western Europe. Offa did not, however, bargain on Charlemagne's volatile temper and his slightly curious relationship with his daughters. Charlemagne's biographer, Einhard, says that he refused to allow any of his daughters to marry during his lifetime, preferring to keep them close beside him at court at all times.[71] Yet he did not, apparently, object to their love affairs; Ecgfrith's intended bride, Bertha, eventually had two illegitimate sons by Angilbert, a friend of Alcuin and one of Charlemagne's favourite court poets to whom he gave the lay-abbacy of St Riquier in Picardy.[72]

Wallace-Hadrill attributed the collapse of the marriage negotiations not so much to Charlemagne's damaged sense of his own superiority, but rather to the suggestion that Offa may have wanted Bertha as a hostage for her father's good behaviour in case the presence of the Mercian princess in Francia gave Charlemagne cause to intervene against his enemies in England.[73] This seems a convoluted explanation for Offa's plan to secure a Carolingian bride for his son. Much more plausible, if indeed Bertha was the intended bride, is that the match complemented Offa's other schemes to secure his son's inheritance. To carry the

---

[69] His eldest daughter Rotrude was betrothed (but not married to) the Emperor Constantine VI; Einhard, *VK*, ch. 19 and the *Annals of Lorsch*, 781, MGH SS 1, 32. P. Classen, 'Karl der Große, der Papsttum und Byzanz, in W. Braunfels (ed.), *Karl der Große: Lebenswerk und Nachleben* (Düsseldorf, 1965–67), Vol. 1, 537–608, at 558–63.

[70] J. L. Nelson, 'Women at the Court of Charlemagne: A Case of Monstrous Regiment?', in J. C. Parsons (ed.), *Medieval Queenship* (New York, 1993), 43–61, reprinted in her *The Frankish World*, 223–42; *idem*, 'Making a Difference in Eighth-century Politics: The Daughters of Desiderius', in A. C. Murray (ed.), *After Rome's Fall. Studies in Honour of Walter Goffart* (Toronto, 1998), 171–90.

[71] Einhard, *VK*, c. 19.

[72] Alcuin, *Ep.* no. 9, MGH Epp. IV; *Alcuin of York*, trans. Allott, no. 10. Their son, Nithard, was author of the important account of the civil wars between the sons of Louis the Pious in the mid-ninth century; *Nithard: Histoire des fils de Louis le Pieux*, ed. P. Lauer, Les classiques de l'histoire de France au moyen âge, 7 (Paris, 1926); *Carolingian Chronicles*, trans. B. W. Scholz (Michigan, 1972); Levison, *England and the Continent*, 112. For comments on degrees of illegitimacy (according to a mother's social rank) see, John, *Reassessing Anglo-Saxon England*, 60.

[73] Wallace-Hadrill, 'Charlemagne and Offa', 115; 'Charlemagne and England', 162.

Carolingian analogy of Ecgfrith's consecration at Chelsea in 787 to its logical conclusion, Offa would have required a subkingdom for his son. Where more obvious than the kingdom of Kent which, by 785, Offa had secured for Mercia, having removed its native dynasty? And what more appropriate for a Kentish king than a Frankish bride named Bertha? There was a powerful resonance here for an Anglo-Saxon audience of the successful union between the Merovingian princess, also named Bertha, and the Kentish 'Bretwalda' Æthelberht, which had presaged the arrival of St Augustine's mission to convert the English. Offa's dynastic aspirations cannot have been more explicit; in marrying his son to a Frankish princess named Bertha, he was laying claim to the memory and inheritance of Æthelberht, the first Christian king of the English and 'Bretwalda'. That Offa intended Kent for Ecgfrith could account for the strength of Archbishop Jaenberht's opposition to the consecration of the young prince at Chelsea in 787. The negotiations surrounding Ecgfrith's marriage must have followed on quickly from that event since it was barely three years later, by early 790, that the negotiations with Charlemagne had collapsed and trade sanctions had been imposed by the Frankish king.[74] Offa's desire to make Kent into a formal subkingdom of Mercia is rendered all the more plausible by the actions of Offa's successor, Coenwulf, who, in 798 after brutally suppressing the rebellion led by Eadberht Præn, installed his own brother, Cuthred, as subking of Kent.[75]

Most of the facts of this episode are known from the records of the monastery of St Wandrille, sited near the mouth of the Seine, a few miles downstream from Rouen. The abbot of St Wandrille's, named Gervold, was another of Charlemagne's regular envoys to England. The mid-ninth-century author of the *Acts of Saint-Wandrille* says that Gervold was 'closely connected in friendship to Offa, the most mighty king of the English or Mercians' and that he 'many times discharged diplomatic missions to King Offa by order of the most invincible Charles'.[76] At the time of writing, the author says, the monastery's archives still contained letters sent from Offa to the abbot. Despite this partisan commentary from Gervold's own community, it is clear that the abbot was an important cross-Channel envoy. His ability to fulfil this role was enhanced by his appointment as Charlemagne's *procurator*, or toll-collector, for the trading ports and towns on the Frankish side of the Channel. As such, he was well placed to defuse the row which ensued when Charlemagne punished Offa for his impudence by ordering that, 'no-one from the island of Britain and the English race was to land on the sea-coast of Gaul for the sake of commerce'.[77] Alcuin too, talks of the severity of the situation in a letter to his Irish friend Colcu

---

[74] Alcuin, *Ep.*, no. 7, MGH Epp. IV; *Alcuin of York*, trans. Allott, no. 31.

[75] *ASChron.* 796 (for 798).

[76] 'Unde Offae regi Anglorum siue Merciorum potentissimo, in amicitiis ualde cognoscitur adiunctus ... nam multis uicibus ipse per se iussione inuictissimi regis Karoli ad praefatum regem Offam legationibus functus est'; *Gesta sanctorum*, ed. Lohier and Laporte, 86–87.

[77] 'ut nemo de Brittania insula ac gente Anglorum mercimonii causa littus Oceani maris attingeret in Gallia'; ibid.

saying that Offa had retaliated so that 'on both sides the passage of ships has been forbidden to merchants and is ceasing'.[78] The author of the *Acts* credits Gervold with defusing the row, but Alcuin had also been under pressure from some in Francia to go to Mercia 'in the interests of peace'.[79] Another letter to the priest Beornwine (probably datable to 790) also concerns this dispute. Reading between the lines, it seems that an earlier attempt to intercede had backfired, with the result that Alcuin was accused of split loyalties, with his good intentions misunderstood by Beornwine, and possibly Offa too:

> I have received your tender letter of explanation, full of sweet thoughts, and I trust its sincerity more than the lying version of others. For trust should be placed in a friendly heart, not a fickle tongue. I wish I were worthy to preach peace instead of sowing discord, to carry the banner of Christ, not the arms of the devil. I would never have written to you if I had not wanted to be at peace with you and to go on as we began in Christ. Truly, I have never been disloyal to King Offa or the English people (*gens Anglorum*). I shall be as loyal as I can to the friends here whom God has given me but no less to those I have left behind in my own country. ... let no suspicion of any disagreement between us remain in your mind.[80]

Alcuin did return to England some time in 790, before the dispute was settled. Late in that year he wrote from Northumbria to Adalhard at Corbie asking for news about affairs in Francia and for Adalhard's opinion on the cause of the dispute 'between old friends'. 'It seems', he says, 'that I and our poor company are to go to try to make peace. If you have any knowledge of the reason for this quarrel ... do let me know, we must be peace-makers between Christian peoples.'[81] His presence in Northumbria in 790 coincided with the banishment of Osred and the reinstatement of Æthelred, 'again enthroned by the Grace of Christ'.[82] Alcuin wrote a housekeeping letter to Colcu's protégé, Joseph, who he had left in charge of his affairs in Francia, saying that the new reign obliged him to remain awhile in Northumbria.[83] To Adalhard he added that Æthelred's behaviour was less than he had hoped for and that he was 'working against injustice ... with certain men of power'. The cause of this injustice may have been the series of events focused on York and spoken of by the annalist whose work is preserved in the *Historia regum*. This annalist says that the deposed king, Osred, was forcibly tonsured at York having been deprived of his kingdom, 'by the guile of his nobles'.[84] This (rather Frankish) form of enforcing secular impotence was followed by banishment from the kingdom rather than enforced enclosure in a

---

[78] Alcuin, *Ep.* no. 7, MGH Epp. IV; *Alcuin of York*, trans. Allott, no. 31.

[79] Alcuin, *Ep.* nos 7 and 9, MGH Epp. IV; *Alcuin of York*, trans. Allott, nos 31 and 10.

[80] Alcuin, *Ep.* no. 82, MGH Epp. IV; *Alcuin of York*, trans. Allott, no. 39.

[81] Alcuin, *Ep.* no. 9, MGH Epp. IV; *Alcuin of York*, trans. Allott, no. 10.

[82] *Historia regum* (*York Annals*), 792.

[83] Alcuin, *Ep.* no. 8, MGH Epp. IV; *Alcuin of York*, trans. Allott, no. 9.

[84] *Historia regum* (*York Annals*), 790.

monastery.[85] Alcuin returned to Francia sometime before June in 793, by which time Æthelred (like Offa in Mercia) had begun systematically to eliminate his opponents. The king attempted to execute Eardwulf at Ripon, then the æthlings Œlf and Œlfwine were seduced from sanctuary in York and lured to their deaths at *Wonwaldremere*. And on 14 September 792 the ex-king, Osred, having ill-advisedly returned from exile, was executed at *Aynburg* and buried at Tynemouth.[86] Barely two weeks later at Michaelmas, Æthelred married Offa's daughter, Ælfflæd, at Catterick where his own parents had been married 30 years before.[87] This was the girl who, a year or two before, had been the object of the failed marriage negotiations with the Carolingians. Alcuin's involvement in the fall-out from those negotiations and his presence in Northumbria throughout the early period of Æthelred's second reign would have left him well placed to advise on Ælfflæd's eventual match with the Northumbrian king, perhaps as an attempt to curb the excesses of Æthelred's blood-lust.

Coinage and commerce

The method by which Charlemagne chose to signal his irritation with Offa is illuminating. His decision to close the Frankish ports to English merchants signals the importance of cross-Channel trade, and his ability to enforce the stoppage – and Offa's tit-for-tat retaliation – demonstrates the control which late eighth-century kings had over merchants and their trade routes. It also shows that those links between England and Francia which were essentially economic could be politicized. Royal interest in economic matters is demonstrable in eighth-century historical and archaeological records in a way that is not easily paralleled in earlier periods in Anglo-Saxon England or Francia.[88] This interest is signalled particu-larly in Anglo-Saxon charters which record toll exemptions granted to particular monasteries, and Carolingian capitulary legislation, as well as by the minting of coinage under royal prerogative on both sides of the Channel.[89] The importance of

[85] He was exiled to the Isle of Man according to a later Durham source; *Symeon of Durham, On the Origins and Progress of this Church of Durham*, ed. and trans. D. W. Rollason (Oxford, 2000), 86–87, Book II.4.

[86] Alcuin's excuse to return to Francia was Charlemagne's request for his analysis of the proceedings of the Council of Nicaea (787), a translation of which had been sent to him in Northumbria; *Historia regum* (*York Annals*), 790–92. D. W. Rollason, 'The Cults of Murdered Royal Saints in Anglo-Saxon England', *ASE*, 11 (1983), 1–22.

[87] *Historia regum* (*York Annals*), 762 and 792; *ASChron.* DE, 792.

[88] Grierson and Blackburn, *MEC* 1, 128–30; P. H. Sawyer, 'Kings and Merchants', in P. Sawyer and I. N. Wood (eds), *Early Medieval Kingship* (Leeds, 1977), 139–58. For a Danish example of royal interest in the profits of trade – as interpreted by a Frankish annalist – see *Annales regni Francorum*, 808.

[89] S. E. Kelly, 'Trading Privileges from Eighth-century England', *EME*, 1 (1992), 3–28. For the continuity of tight monetary control in the first half of the ninth century see Coupland, 'Money and Coinage'.

coining as an expression of royal authority partly depends on our interpretation of the function of coinage and the scale of the monetary economy in this period. This debate, though difficult to resolve, is central to our understanding of the political, as well as economic, importance of coinage, and informs our understanding of the motives for kings' involvement in coin production in the later eighth century. The maximal interpretation – which assumes that only a small fraction of minted coin has been recovered in hoards or as single finds – argues for a widespread use of coinage in everyday transactions.[90] The minimalist view is that coin use was not widespread and that it was restricted to the elite economy, providing primarily a medium of exchange for luxury goods traded over long distances. Under such circumstances, coinage was of high prestige and the design was a highly political statement intended for observation by an elite audience.[91]

Intensification of royal control over trade and exchange has also been proposed as a reason for the development and sustained success of a particular type of coastal and riverine settlement in this period. These so-called *wic* sites, which emerged in the seventh century, were at first seasonally occupied but seem to have rapidly become permanent settlements.[92] They are discernible around the North Sea and Channel coasts and – because of their location and archaeology – are interpreted primarily as trading settlements. The coastal accessibility of such sites, and the high proportions of foreign and luxury artefacts uncovered by excavation, has encouraged their interpretation as nodal points for long-distance, international trade with an emphasis on outward zones of interaction rather than with the domestic hinterland. Recent work has shown this to be a partial picture; the *wics* also had a role in local and interregional trade which was complemented by other types of permanent settlement and seasonal fairs.[93] The establishment of *wics* during the seventh century has tradi-

---

[90] D. M. Metcalf, 'The Monetary Economy of Ninth-century England South of the Humber: A Topographical Analysis', in M. A. S. Blackburn and D. N. Dumville (eds), *Kings, Currency and Alliances, History and Coinage of Southern England in the Ninth Century* (Woodbridge, 1998), 167–98, at 170–71; *idem*, 'Monetary Expansion and Recession: Interpreting the Distribution-pattern of Seventh-and Eighth-century coins', in P. J. Casey and R. Reece (eds), *Coins and the Archaeologist* (2nd edn) (London, 1988), 231–53, esp. n. 1; *idem*, 'Monetary Circulation in Southern England in the First Half of the Eighth Century', in D. H. Hill and D. M. Metcalf (eds), *Sceattas in England and on the Continent*, BAR Bri. Ser. 128 (Oxford, 1984), 159–64; *idem*, 'The Prosperity of Western Europe in the Eighth and Ninth Centuries', *EcHR*, 2nd ser. 20 (1967), 344–57.

[91] P. Grierson, 'Commerce in the Dark Ages: A Critique of the Evidence', *TRHS*, 5th ser. 9 (1959), 123–40, reprinted as ch. XV in his *Dark Age Numismatics* (Aldershot, 1979).

[92] R. Hodges, *Dark Age Economics: The Origins of Towns and Trade A.D. 600–1000* (London, 1982); *idem*, 'Trade and Market Origins in the Ninth Century: Relations between England and the Continent', in M. T. Gibson and J. L. Nelson (eds), *Charles the Bald: Court and Kingdom* (2nd rev. edn) (Aldershot, 1990), 203–23, at 205–9; *idem*, *Towns and Trade in the Age of Charlemagne* (London, 2000).

[93] On these so-called 'productive sites' see K. Ulmschneider, 'Settlement, Economy and the "Productive" Site: Middle Anglo-Saxon Lincolnshire AD 65–780', *Medieval Archaeology*, 44 (2000), 53–80. M. Bonser, 'Fifteen Years of Coin Finds from Productive Sites', *The Yorkshire Numismatist*, 3 (1997), 15–38; and J. D. Richards et al. 'Cottam: An Anglian and Anglo-Scandinavian Settlement

tionally been interpreted as an element in the process of state consolidation and kingdom-building in north-western Europe. The extent to which they were *de novo* creations set up under royal authority is debatable, but it seems irrefutable that, once established, these trading sites attracted the attention of kings who were keen to control the wealth resources of their kingdom. Sometimes, though not invariably, the *wics* also acted as sites for mints, as well as locations where incoming merchants and travellers could be taxed and tolls exacted. It is particularly noticeable that there are, as yet, no *wic* sites associated with central Mercia – apart, perhaps, from the inland salt-producing settlement at Droitwich – and this may have been one reason behind Æthelbald's and Offa's desire to expand Mercian hegemony into Kent, East Anglia and Essex.[94] Moreover, during Offa's reign, the major mints operating south of the Humber were located in these kingdoms, at Canterbury and London, and at an unidentified site in East Anglia, probably Ipswich, all of which produced coinage in the name of their Mercian lord.[95]

The enforcement of a centralized royal monopoly on minting in Francia in the second half of the eighth century is one of the most striking features of the production of coin in the early medieval period. Under the Merovingians, coin production seems to have been largely unregulated, with a great many mints operating outside centralized control. This situation changed with the accession of the Carolingian dynasty; in 754–55 Pippin ordered a reform of the coinage that was clearly designed to drive out the old Merovingian issues. Pippin's coins were to be produced to a new, heavier standard (1.24g rather than 1.1g) and on an appreciably broader and thinner flan (14–16mm rather than 10–12mm). They also carried his name and rank, *rex Pippinus* or *rex Francorum*.[96] Charlemagne continued this process, enforcing uniformity of weight and a coin design incorporating the king's name or monogram as a standard feature. He also began to reduce the number of mints permitted to issue this coinage, undoubtedly as a matter of policy.[97] Several of these changes

---

on the Yorkshire Wolds', *Archaeological Journal*, 156 (1999), 1–110. See also P. H. Sawyer, 'Fairs and Markets in Early Medieval England', in N. Skyum-Nielsen and N. Lund (eds), *Danish Medieval History: New Currents* (Copenhagen, 1981), 153–68.

[94] P. H. Sawyer, 'Early Fairs and Markets in England and Scandinavia', in B. L. Anderson and A. J. H. Latham (eds), *The Market in History* (London, 1986), 59–78, at 62; D. Hooke, 'The Droitwich Salt Industry: An Examination of the West Midlands Charter Evidence', in *ASSAH*, 2, BAR Bri. Ser. 92 (1981), 123–69. The site at Meols in Wirral is also significant, on which see, D. Griffiths, 'Trade and Production Centers in the Post-Roman North: The Irish Sea Perspective', in *The Archaeology of Gudme and Lundeborg. Papers Presented at Svendborg, October* 1991, Archaeologiske Studier 10 (Copenhagen, 1994), 184–88; J. D. Bu'Lock, 'The Celtic, Saxon and Scandinavian Settlement at Meols in Wirral', *Transactions of the Historical Society of Lancashire and Cheshire*, 112 (1961), 1–28.

[95] The mint at Rochester, which was certainly operating in the early ninth century, may also have been active earlier, and there is evidence of intermittent minting during the eighth century in Wessex, probably at Hamwic (rather than Winchester as was later to be the case); Grierson and Blackburn, *MEC* 1, 274 and 281.

[96] MGH Capit. I, no. 13 at 31–32; Grierson and Blackburn, *MEC* 1, 108, 203–4.

[97] Grierson and Blackburn, *MEC* 1, 196.

were mirrored in England during Offa's reign, although there are hints that increasing regulation may have begun rather earlier in the eighth century.[98] Before the reforms of Offa's reign, small, chunky silver pennies, known to numismatists as 'sceattas', were minted in a wide variety of types from *c.* 675 to *c.* 760. In its early phases, a certain degree of regulation of this sceatta currency is evidenced by a reasonable consistency of weight and metal fineness. It is, however, far from clear that this regularity was imposed by royal authority and, in any case, the rapid debasement of the sceatta coinage of southern England in the second quarter of the eighth century is so marked that some numismatists have argued for a major collapse of the currency during the 740s and 750s.[99] It is only in Northumbria that we have explicit evidence of royal involvement in coin production prior to the reforms of Offa's day, when King Aldfrith (d. 704) issued coins bearing his own name. This remarkably early innovation was revived after a break in production by Eadberht (738–58), who restored the silver content of his Northumbrian coin to the levels of the early sceattas, in marked contrast to the falling standards of contemporary southern issues. Eadberht's explicitly royal issues (which in all probability pre-date Pippin's) seem to have provided the inspiration for another attempt to restore the silver content of the debased southern sceatta coinage, this time in East Anglia by Beonna, *c.* 760.[100] But both the East Anglian and Northumbrian reforms retained the small, thick shape of the old-style sceattas rather than employing the new, thinner Frankish module as devised for Pippin.

The Carolingian reforms did, however, affect coin production in England during Offa's reign, particularly at the mints of Canterbury and London.[101] The first reform (which effectively initiated the familiar penny coinage of medieval England) came after a period when large-scale coin production had almost ceased in southern England. Metcalf has argued that Carolingian coin may have circulated in England to fill this vacuum and, while there are reasons to modify aspects of his argument, the choice of early Carolingian coins as a model (rather than the reformed sceatta coinage of East Anglia and Northumbria) should be

---

[98] Ibid., 158–59.

[99] D. M. Metcalf, *Thrysmas and Sceattas in the Ashmolean Museum, Oxford* (London, 1993–94), Vol. 1, 10; Grierson and Blackburn, *MEC* 1, 184–86. For the notion of a serious monetary decline in the middle decades of the eighth century see J. P. C. Kent, 'From Roman Britain to Saxon England', in R. H. M. Dolley ed., *Anglo-Saxon Coins. Studies presented to F. M. Stenton on the occasion of his 80th Birthday* (London, 1961), 1–22 at 12, and Metcalf, 'Monetary Expansion and Recession', 234–36.

[100] See Chapter 2, above, 23–26; also M. M. Archibald, 'The Coinage of Beonna in the Light of the Middle Harling Hoard', *BNJ*, 55 (1985), 10–54; Blackburn, 'Money and Coinage', 546.

[101] C. E. Blunt, 'The Coinage of Offa', in Dolley, *Anglo-Saxon Coins*, 39–62, at 40–42; I. Stewart, 'The London Mint and the Coinage of Offa', in M. A. S. Blackburn (ed.), *Anglo-Saxon Monetary History. Essays in Memory of Michael Dolley* (Leicester, 1986), 27–44. Cf. Zipperer, 'Coins and Currency', 125–26. For a refinement of aspects of Blunt's chronology see D. Chick, 'Towards a Chronology for Offa's Coinage: An Interim Study', *The Yorkshire Numismatist*, 3 (1997), 47–64, and G. Williams, 'Mercian Coinage and Authority', in Brown and Farr (eds), *Mercia: An Anglo-Saxon Kingdom in Europe*, 210–28.

seen in the light of this hiatus.[102] There were, undoubtedly, pragmatic motives for choosing the Carolingian model for the new-style Anglo-Saxon penny. After the downturn in the production of coinage in the middle decades of the century, Carolingian coinage provided a source of good silver and, certainly for the mint at Canterbury, reinforced longstanding links with Carolingian Frisia and the Rhineland (both the known examples of Pippin's reformed deniers found in Kent are from the mint at Dorestad).[103] Analysis of the metal alloy used in Offa's earliest issues demonstrates that his source of silver was the same as that used by Carolingian moneyers, derived, it seems, from recoining imported deniers rather than the old-style, home-produced sceattas.[104] But the introduction of the new Carolingian fabric also had a political resonance, the implications of which would not have been lost on contemporary users and patrons of the reformed coins.

In this respect, it is significant that very early in the reform process, new-style coinage was minted in the names of two minor Kentish kings, Heahberht (king in East Kent acc. c. 764) and Ecgberht II (king in West Kent c. 765–c. 779) both of whom posed a challenge to Offa's ambitions in Kent. The adoption at Canterbury of a new-style coinage, which corresponded to Carolingian denarial reforms rather than that of the East Anglian or Northumbrian sceattas, clearly had a political dimension as well as fulfilling the demands of economic pragmatism. Given the complexities of interpreting the evidence, numismatists have long debated the possibility that credit for introducing the new Carolingian-style pennies to Anglo-Saxon England may in fact belong to these Kentish kings rather than to Offa.[105] Kentish charters illustrate the fluctuating fortunes of Heahberht and Ecgberht II; the witness lists indicate that, by 764–65, both kings were obliged to acknowledge Offa's authority over bookland in Kent, and suggest that, by the early 770s, the native dynasties were being suppressed.[106]

---

[102] Metcalf, 'Monetary Expansion and Recession', 237 and, with a similar argument proposed for the presence of Carolingian coins in England in the ninth century, in 'The Monetary Economy of Ninth-Century England', 175–77.

[103] The Kentish coins of Pippin were found at Richborough and West Hythe and published, respectively, in Grierson and Metcalf, *MEC* 1, no. 719 (also *EMC* 1986.8719) and 'Coin Register', *BNJ*, 68 (1998), no. 109 (also *EMC* 1998.0028). See also Hodges, 'Trade and Market Origins', 209–12. On the Dorestad mint in the Carolingian period see S. Coupland, 'Dorestad in the Ninth Century: the numismatic evidence', *JMP*, 75 (1988), 5–26, and on the (East Anglian) coin of Offa from Dorestad, see C. E. Blunt and G. Van der Meer, 'A New Type for Offa', *BNJ*, 38 (1969), 182–83.

[104] D. M. Metcalf and J. P. Northover, 'Coinage Alloys from the Time of Offa and Charlemagne to c. 864', *Numismatic Chronicle*, 159 (1989), 101–20, at 105.

[105] See Chick, 'Towards a Chronology', which resolves much of the complexity of the chronology. Important too is C. C. S. Lyon, 'Historical Problems of Anglo-Saxon Coinage – (1)', *BNJ*, 36 (1967), 215–21, and Blunt, 'The Coinage of Offa', 39–62 for the view that the Kentish reforms preceded those of Offa; also Metcalf, 'Monetary Expansion and Recession', 240. Stewart puts the case for the involvement of London moneyers, noting that almost double the number were minting Offa's 'light' coinage in London than were working in Canterbury; Stewart, 'The London Mint'.

[106] Brooks, *The Early History*, 112–13.

Conversely, Ecgberht's charters of the later 770s imply a resurgence of Kentish independence, since he was able to grant land with no reference to consent from Offa. This period of resistance was followed by a Mercian crackdown; certainly by 785 Offa was granting away Kentish land in his own right as *Rex Merciorum*, and no more is heard of the native dynasties.

New-style pennies exist for both Heahberht and Ecgberht II, in imitation of the broader and heavier Carolingian style. They also display the name of the king around a central monogram of the word *Rex*, in which the diagonal descender of the capital letter 'R' is crossed to form the letter 'x'. The use of this abbreviation for *Rex* is also found on Pippin's coins, and the monogram used here is a feature of some of Charlemagne's earlier issues.[107] The issue of such a novel and explicitly royal coinage by these Kentish kings, whose independence was under direct threat from Mercia, clearly had political dimensions. Furthermore, that these coins were issued at Canterbury implies the cognizance of Archbishop Jaenberht. It is probably significant that the single surviving example of Heahberht's coinage was recovered in Rome, and it may be (as Brooks has argued) that Jaenberht and Ecgberht II hoped to secure support from powers abroad in their struggle to secure Kentish independence from Mercia.[108]

The numismatic chronology suggests that the new-style Kentish coins preceded the great majority of Offa's own Canterbury issues, and that the coins of Ecgberht II seem to represent a resurgence of Kentish autonomy after the defeat of Offa's forces at the Battle of Otford in 776.[109] However, recent finds suggest that one of Offa's East Anglian moneyers, Wilred, was minting the new-style coinage in the 760s – that is, in advance of the issues of the Kentish kings.[110] In addition, the coinage produced for Offa by another moneyer, named Mang, is also typologically early. Mang seems to have worked in London, and

---

[107] Grierson and Blackburn, *MEC* 1, nos 730–33. Some of Offa's moneyers also used this monogram, as did some of the later eighth-century Northumbrian issues; ibid., 279, 298. See also ibid., 208, for the suggestion that these Kentish coins could have provided a model for the design of Charlemagne's Class 3 issue. It has been argued that one of Charlemagne's early Strasbourg coins, minted 768–70, was based on the design of a coin of Ecgberht II which, if correct, would place the adoption of the new-style pennies in England securely in the 760s; D. M. Metcalf, 'Fiufar or Arfiuf = Strasbourg', *Hamburger Beiträge sur Numismatik*, 20 (1966), 380–84. But for another possible source from Beonna's reformed sceatta coinage, see M. Archibald, 'The Coinage of Beonna in the Light of the Middle Harling Hoard', *BNJ*, 55 (1985), 10–54.

[108] C. E. Blunt, 'Anglo-Saxon Coins Found in Italy', in M. A. S. Blackburn (ed.), *Anglo-Saxon Monetary History* (Leicester, 1986), 159–69 at 163–64; Brooks, *The Early History*, 115–16.

[109] Chick, 'Towards a Chronology', 49–50, 53, 59. Only the 'B10' coins of the Canterbury moneyer Eoba issued for Offa may predate the battle of Otford, although, as Eoba also minted for Ecgberht II, his coins for Offa could follow, rather than precede, his coins for the Kentish king. The reference to the outcome of the Battle of Otford in the *Anglo-Saxon Chronicle* is ambiguous; *ASChron.* A, 773 (*recte* 776). Key to the interpretation of the battle are the charters which show that Ecgberht II was able to issue land grants in Kent in 778 and 779 with no reference to Offa; F. M. Stenton, 'Anglo-Saxon Coinage and the Historian', in D. M. Stenton (ed.), *Preparatory to Anglo-Saxon England* (Oxford, 1970), 371–82; Brooks, *The Early History*, 113.

[110] Chick, 'Towards a Chronology', 49.

Chick has suggested that he may have been striking coins for Offa from the London mint simultaneously with the production of coins at Canterbury for the independent Kentish kings.[111] In conclusion, it seems that Offa was able to produce coinage in the London and East Anglian mints sporadically during the 760s and 770s but, with the exception of some coins of the moneyer Eoba, was not able to exploit the mint at Canterbury until after the removal of Ecgberht II. It is only in the 780s that Canterbury became a major Mercian mint.

Rather less contentious is the chronology for Offa's introduction of the second major coin reform in the last years of his reign. Again, the precedent was Carolingian; Charlemagne had ordered a new reform of weights and measures in the *Admonitio generalis* of 789, and his *novi denarii*, bearing 'the monogram of our name', were discussed at the Council of Frankfurt in May 794, implying that the new coinage was in existence by that date.[112] These 'new deniers' were issued to a heavier standard of 1.7g on a wider flan of 19–20mm, with a uniform design on both sides which, with its large letters surrounding an encircled cross or monogram, may have been modelled on the earlier Kentish 'Rx' coins. Anglo-Saxon moneyers correspondingly adopted a heavier and broader style for their coin (weight 1.45g, diameter 18–19mm). The adoption of this new standard in England can be dated 792–93 since all the coins minted in the name of Archbishop Æthelheard (consecrated on 21 July 793) conform to the new type, whereas those of his predecessor Jaenberht (who died on 12 August 792) were all of the lighter variety.[113] The adoption of the heavy coin therefore dates to the period when Gervold and Alcuin were dealing with the fall-out from the breakdown of the marriage negotiations between Charlemagne and Offa, which suggests either that the blockades were ineffective or that Charlemagne's decision to block the ports was specifically aimed at hurting the southern Anglo-Saxon economy which had, in monetary terms at least, become closely aligned with that of Francia.

In any event, it is clear that the design and form of southern Anglo-Saxon coinage produced during Offa's reign owed much to monetary reforms enacted by the Carolingians. But the borrowing was not all one-way, nor was the debt slavishly pursued.[114] For a start, Anglo-Saxon moneyers continued their practice of putting their own names on the reverse of their coins instead of following the Carolingian practice of using the mint name. Also it is widely acknowledged that the artistic creativity of Offa's moneyers was far superior to anything which Charlemagne's die-cutter's could yet produce. Nowhere is this more apparent

---

[111] Ibid., 56–59.

[112] MGH Capit. I, no. 28, c. 5. Grierson and Blackburn, *MEC* 1, 208–9; P. Grierson, 'Money and Coinage under Charlemagne', in Braünfels, *Karl der Große, Lebenswerk und Nachleben*, 501–36, at 507–11, 528–30; See also Chapter 5, above, 138 on the possibility of the presence of bishops from Britain at the 794 synod.

[113] Blunt 'The Coinage of Offa', 47–49; *MEC* 1, 280.

[114] D. M. Metcalf, 'Artistic Borrowing, Imitation and Forgery in the Eighth Century', *Hamburger Beitrage sur Numismatik*, 20 (1966), 379–92.

than in the remarkable series of portrait-coins which were struck for Offa before
the 792–93 reform and which pre-date the portrait coins of Charlemagne's
magnificent imperial issue by at least 20 years. Offa's portrait coins are so fine
and so original that it is easy to suppose that the die-cutter(s) responsible had
made a genuine attempt at achieving a likeness of their king. Uncomfortable
with this evidence of Mercian artistic innovation, Wallace-Hadrill has argued
that Offa's portrait coins were a response to the royal images on seals, stamped
on the base of Carolingian documents.[115] There is little corroborative basis for
this view and it seems likely that the models for these coins, such as they are,
were Roman, perhaps filtered through the medium of papal issues. Some have
preferred to see the majority of Offa's coins of this type dated to the period after
the legates' mission in 786 on the grounds that Offa's status and self-confidence
had been boosted by the favourable outcome of the mission. But Offa had good
grounds for such self-confidence earlier, especially after he had retaken Kent in
785. And if, as seems likely, we can date to 784–85 a letter from Hadrian to
Charlemagne which discussed issues concerning the Mercian king, we have
further evidence that Offa was of sufficient importance by that date to have sent
envoys to Charlemagne and to Rome where they were received 'with willing
heart' by the pope.[116]

Charlemagne's letter to Offa

The sophistication of the relationship which developed between the two kings is
encapsulated in the well-known letter written by Charlemagne in the early months
of 796. The letter refers to the death of Pope Hadrian on 26 December 795 but
pre-dates the assassination of King Æthelred of Northumbria on 18 April 796.[117]
In this letter, which Stenton rather grandiosely termed the first English trade
treaty, Charlemagne covered a wide range of topics which were of mutual
interest.[118] He discussed the rights and legal obligations of pilgrims and merchants travelling through England and Francia, the trade of luxury goods, the
donation of gifts in memory of the late pope and in celebration of his own
victories against the Avars. He refers also to the fate of the Kentish exiles at his
court and his desire to see the controversy resolved by the new pope. Charlemagne's letter makes it clear that this was only one of several letters which had
passed between the two men. None of Offa's letters survive, and we must

---

115 Wallace-Hadrill, 'Charlemagne and England', 160. On forged Mercian seals see H. Atsma
and J. Vezin, 'Le dossier suspect des possessions de Saint-Denis en Angleterre revisité (VIIIe–IXe
siècles)', in MGH *Schriften* 33.4, *Falschungen im Mittelalter* 4, *Diplomatische Fälschungen* 2
(Hanover, 1988), Vol. 4, 211–36, at 215–16 and pl. 3.

116 See below, 198–99.

117 Alcuin, *Ep.* no. 100, MGH, Epp. IV; Haddan and Stubbs, *Councils* III, 496–98; *Alcuin of
York*, trans. Allott, no. 40 and *EHD* 1, trans. Whitelock, no. 197.

118 Stenton, *Anglo-Saxon England*, 221.

surmise his wishes from Charlemagne's responses. The letter is remarkable for its tone; it presumes a like-minded audience. Charlemagne here speaks directly to Offa, perhaps not quite as an equal, but as a fellow monarch who understands the dignity of kingship as well as its daily responsibilities. He expects equitable judgement and protection for Frankish merchants under English law, and pre-supposes that the Mercian king is able to control the export of English cloth in the same way as he himself is able to control the scarce supplies of the 'black stones' which Offa wished to import. If Peacock and Greenhalgh are correct in deducing that this is a request for Roman *spolia*, the letter reveals that the Mercian king had a sophisticated sense of the contemporary relevance of the trappings of Roman imperialism.[119]

This letter represents the pinnacle of the long relationship between the two rulers who, by this date, had ruled alongside each other – not always harmoni-ously – for nearly three decades. It is direct and businesslike, it is respectful and diplomatic but not affectionate: 'if we are ordered by our Lord's command to untie the knots of enmity, how much more care ought we to take to tie the links of love?' Charlemagne pointedly refers to Offa as his 'dear brother', a term he only used elsewhere in correspondence with the Emperor of Byzantium. The epithet was surely a compliment but we would do well to remember that Charle-magne's relationship with his own brother, Carloman, had been strained to breaking point; in Francia a brother was always a potential challenger.[120] With no sense of irony, Charlemagne prefaced his letter with comments on the need for brotherhood between kings and on his pleasure at Offa's defence of the Church. But he also subtly reinforces his own superiority; he is king of the Franks and Lombards, and Patrician of the Romans where Offa is merely king of the Mercians. It is Charlemagne who is orchestrating the official intercession for the soul of the dead pope, although Offa clearly had his own reasons to be grateful to Hadrian. It is only through Charlemagne that Offa will get the black stones he requires and he must send another envoy before Charlemagne will part with any. Furthermore, Offa's exiled enemies will receive protection at the Frankish court. Through the donation of precious gifts, Charlemagne is a patron of Offa's churches, and the name of the Frankish king is to be remembered in the prayers of English Christians.

---

[119] D. P. S. Peacock, 'Charlemagne's Black Stones: The Re-use of Roman Columns in Early Medieval Europe', *Antiquity*, 71 (1997), 709–15; M. Greenhalgh, *The Survival of Roman Antiqui-ties in the Middle Ages* (London, 1989), 120–22.

[120] For the animosity between Carloman and Charlemagne see Einhard, *Vita Karoli*, c. 3, and also the request by Pope Stephen II for peace between the brothers; *Codex Carolinus*, MGH Epp. 3, 558–60. J. Story, 'Cathwulf, Kingship and the Royal Abbey of Saint-Denis', *Speculum*, 74 (1999), 1–20, at 5–7.

Mercia and the papacy: Offa and Hadrian

The interaction between Offa and Charlemagne's court was unparalleled for a Mercian king but it represented only one aspect of his reputation abroad. The third point in the diplomatic triangle was Rome, and here too it is clear that Offa maintained a high profile, particularly with Pope Hadrian I. The dynamics of the relationship between Hadrian and Offa are important not least because, in a very real sense, the success of Offa's dynastic project depended on papal approval of his plans for a second metropolitan see south of the Humber. The laconic reference in the *Anglo-Saxon Chronicle* to the 'contentious synod at Chelsea' in 787 implicitly links the elevation of Hygeberht to the archbishopric of Lichfield with Ecgfrith's consecration. Clearly, Offa needed a compliant archbishop to perform the religious ceremony which would secure his son's royal credentials. It is a measure of the stubborn persistence of Archbishop Jaenberht and of Kentish resistance to Mercian authority that Offa was unable to force Canterbury to comply with his wishes. In this sense, as Brooks has argued, the establishment of an archbishopric at Lichfield was a 'second-best' solution, since undoubtedly Offa would have preferred to have had his son consecrated by Augustine's heir with the support of all the bishops of the southern province. On the other hand, the implementation of the Lichfield scheme represents a considerable diplomatic achievement by Offa and his agents in that they were able to persuade Hadrian to sanction a departure from the episcopal structure which Pope Gregory had devised for the English Church. In a later letter, Leo III claimed that Hadrian's consent was only given because Offa had lied. Leo told Coenwulf that consent had been granted because:

> … your excellent king Offa, testified in his letter that it was the united wish and unanimous petition of you all, both on account of the vast size of your lands and the extension of your kingdom, and also for many more reasons and advantages. For these reasons chiefly did the lord apostolic Hadrian send the dignity of the *pallium* to the bishop of the Mercians.[121]

By 801 when this letter was written, it was politically convenient for Leo and Coenwulf to accuse Offa of pulling the wool over Hadrian's eyes, and to blame him for the unsatisfactory division of the southern province. The accusation of deception was repeated in the formal decree produced at *Clofesho* in 803 which demoted the status of Lichfield back to a bishopric subject to Canterbury.[122] Nevertheless, there is other evidence which demonstrates that Offa was on good terms with Hadrian. A privilege survives in the eighth-century papal formulary known as the *Liber Diurnus*, from Hadrian to an unnamed ruler (*excellentia vestra*) and his wife, *Cynedrida regina*, which can only refer

---

[121] Alcuin, *Ep.* no. 127, MGH Epp. IV; *EHD* 1, trans. Whitelock, no. 205.
[122] *BCS* 310; Haddan and Stubbs, *Councils* III, 542–44; *EHD* 1, trans. Whitelock, no. 210.

to Offa and his queen Cynethryth.[123] This privilege grants the king exclusive control over all the monasteries which he had acquired or built and which he had dedicated to St Peter, along with all the property associated with them. It demonstrates that Offa was prepared to go to the highest ecclesiastical authority to gain full proprietorial rights over what he considered to be his monastic property, and that Hadrian considered it appropriate that Offa had this privilege.

A rather more extraordinary story is preserved in the *Codex Carolinus* in a letter which Hadrian wrote to Charlemagne, concerning a dastardly rumour which alleged that Offa and Charlemagne were conspiring to replace Hadrian with a pope of Frankish birth.[124] Hadrian had been unaware of this story until Charlemagne had alerted him by letter, having been prompted into action by messengers from Mercia. According to Hadrian's letter, Offa's envoys had gone to Charlemagne with information that 'some enemies of himself and yourself had brought to our apostolic notice that the same King Offa was suggesting to you that, with his advice and encouragement, you should remove us from the holy seat of our office and place another upon it from your own people'. Charlemagne quickly sent his own envoys to Rome, accompanied by Offa's messengers, to denounce the rumour and to reassure Hadrian of the loyalty and affection of both kings. He assured Hadrian that the allegations were 'most certainly false', and the pope magnanimously dismissed the 'foul assertions recounted by Offa', adding that not even a pagan would countenance such a sin. The letter is illustrative of the very close bond which had developed between Charlemagne and Hadrian; the remainder of the text deals with Hadrian's sincere concern for the well-being of Charlemagne and his family. It also demonstrates the respect which Offa's messengers could expect at Charlemagne's court and in Rome. Charlemagne had acted immediately on hearing the allegations brought by Offa's messengers, and they were received in Rome by the Pope 'with a joyful countenance out of respect for [Charlemagne's] distinguished excellence'.

The precise context for this intriguing letter is unclear. It is not possible from internal evidence to date the letter more closely than 784–91, nor is it certain which 'enemies' were responsible for spreading the rumour in the first place. Unless we hypothesize a cunning double-bluff by Offa, a plausible case can be made against the Kentish rebels from Jaenberht's circle, who may have wished to discredit Offa in the eyes of the pope as the debate concerning the elevation of Lichfield escalated. If so, we could date Hadrian's letter and the journey of Offa's messengers to Francia and Rome, to the years 784–85 when Offa had regained control of Kent. It may then have been this incident which prompted Hadrian to send his legates to England in 786 with a brief to 'uproot

---

[123] H. Foester (ed.), *Liber Diurnus romanorum pontificum* (Bern, 1958), 172–73; Brooks, *The Early History*, 184–85; Levison, *England and the Continent*, 29–30, 35.

[124] *Codex Carolinus*, no. 92; *The Reign of Charlemagne*, trans. Loyn and Percival, no. 39.

completely anything harmful' and, 'to renew the faith and friendship which St. Gregory sent'.[125]

Coenwulf, Canterbury, and the Continent

Offa's Mercian archbishopric did not long outlast him, and by 803 the primacy of Canterbury had been upheld and the metropolitan see at Lichfield was declared invalid by papal mandate and by a full council of the southern English Church.[126] Jaenberht had died in August 792, and was succeeded in Canterbury by Æthelheard, the abbot of the monastery at Louth in Lindsey. It is likely that Offa was instrumental in the appointment of this pro-Mercian, non-Kentish archbishop to a post which, under Jaenberht, had become closely identified with Kentish resistance to Mercia. On Alcuin's advice, it seems likely that Æthelheard was consecrated by the other archbishop in the southern province, namely Hygeberht of Lichfield, in a ceremony which would have underlined the seniority of the new Mercian archbishopric.[127] But, ironically, from this moment onwards, the political imperative for a separate Mercian metropolitan declined as Offa now had a sympathetic archbishop installed at Canterbury. The rapidity with which the new metropolitan see was dismantled after Offa's death is perhaps indicative of its short-term political purpose – that of providing Offa with a cooperative archbishop. But, as the new metropolitan had required papal approval to be established, so it needed permission from the new pope to be dismantled.

This was not a straightforward process. A mechanism had to be found which, on the one hand, restored the canonical balance of the southern province and, on the other, satisfied the political demands of Coenwulf who needed to consolidate his authority in Mercia after the unexpected death of Offa's son, Ecgfrith. It also had to preserve the dignity of Hygeberht who had, after all, received a 'charter sent from the Roman see by Pope Hadrian about the *pallium* and the archiepiscopal see in the church of Lichfield'.[128] It was imperative, too, that the papacy should not be seen to lose face by reversing a solemn decision made so recently without very good cause. These diplomatic considerations were compounded by the disruption of violent rebellion, first in Kent with the uprising of Eadberht Præn which forced Æthelheard to flee from Canterbury, and then in Rome in April 799 when Pope Leo was himself deposed and imprisoned. Between 797 and 801 Coenwulf had to send three

---

[125] *ASChron*. D, E, 786; Alcuin, *Ep.* no. 3, MGH Epp. IV.

[126] Haddan and Stubbs (eds), *Councils* III, 542–44; *EHD* 1, trans. Whitelock, no. 210.

[127] Alcuin's letter to Offa on this subject, in which he refers to the two metropolitans in Offa's kingdom, is one of the very few which survives outside the manuscript standard collections; Levison, *England and the Continent*, 245–46. See also his subsequent letter to Æthelheard; Alcuin, *Ep.* no. 128, MGH Epp. IV; *Alcuin of York*, trans. Allott, no. 49.

[128] Haddan and Stubbs (eds), *Councils* III, 542–44; *EHD* 1, trans. Whitelock, no. 210.

separate delegations to Rome in pursuit of his claim against Lichfield. The
first envoy, Abbot Wada, was sent in 797 when Kent was still in rebellion and
Æthelheard remained in exile. But Abbot Wada's intervention was incompetent and failed to resolve the matter to Coenwulf's satisfaction, so the following
year he sent three more messengers, Byrne the priest, and two thegns, Cildas
and Ceolberht, with a gift of 120 mancuses to ease the negotiations. This
second group also took with them letters composed by Æthelheard in the
presence of 'all our provincial bishops', concerning 'his own affairs and needs,
and those of all Britain'.[129] On this occasion, Coenwulf presented a novel
solution to the pope and suggested that, as a means of repairing the 'rent in
Christ's coat'[130] and resolving the problem of Æthelheard's continued exile
from Canterbury, the seat of the southern archbishop should be moved to
London. London had been a Mercian city for many years, and Coenwulf
argued that Pope Gregory the Great had initially intended that it, not Canterbury, should be the home of the southern metropolitan. Leo refused to
countenance this suggestion arguing, not unreasonably, that it would not do to
rectify one mistake with another decision which had no precedent in the
canons or in the privileges granted by his predecessors. He also condemned
the Kentish rebel, Eadberht, as an apostate cleric and recommended his immediate excommunication and exile. He finished not by thanking Coenwulf for
his gift of 120 mancuses, but by reminding the king that Offa had in fact
pledged, 'for himself and for his successors in that kingdom, for ever and in
perpetuity', to send 365 mancuses every year to Rome. 'And if your excellency wishes to have ampler victories and honours in that same kingdom', Leo
continued, 'paying the same contribution, let it remain likewise confirmed
more amply by your excellency in perpetuity.'[131]

Coenwulf's response to Leo's letter has already been noted. The rebellion in Kent was brutally crushed, Æthelheard was restored to Canterbury, and
Coenwulf installed his own brother, Cuthred, as sub-king of Kent. The final
resolution of the Lichfield problem, though, had to wait until 801 by which
time Leo had been restored to the papal throne by Charlemagne and had
absolved himself of the charges of corruption which the rebels had laid against
him. This third mission to Rome was led by Archbishop Æthelheard himself,
joined by three high-ranking companions: Cyneberht, the bishop of Winchester; Ceolmund who had been a thegn of King Offa; and the Northumbrian

---

[129] Haddan and Stubbs (eds), *Councils* III, 521–23; *EHD* 1, trans. Whitelock, no. 204; Cubitt,
Church Councils, 277–78.

[130] This metaphor of the Church as the seamless cloak of Christ is used three times in relation
to the resolution of the Lichfield dispute: by Coenwulf in his letter to Leo of 798 (Haddan and
Stubbs (eds), *Councils* III, 521–23; *EHD* 1, trans. Whitelock, no. 204); by Alcuin in his letter to
Æthelheard written in 802 (Alcuin, *Ep.* no. 255, MGH Epp. IV; *Alcuin of York*, trans. Allott, no. 53);
and in the proceedings of the Council of *Clofesho* in 803 (Haddan and Stubbs (eds), *Councils* III,
542–44; *EHD* 1, trans. Whitelock, no. 210).

[131] Alcuin, *Ep.* no. 127, MGH Epp. IV; *EHD* 1, trans. Whitelock, no. 205.

nobleman, Torctmund.[132] Æthelheard and his companions were received at St Judoc's near Quentovic, and Alcuin sent letters of introduction to Charlemagne on their behalf.[133] The archbishop returned to England the following year with a charter of privilege from Leo confirming his rights and that of the church at Canterbury to pre-eminence in England. Leo's judgement was confirmed by a full council of the southern English province at *Clofesho* on 12 October 803.[134] Although the detail of Leo's charter, as it survives in an eleventh-century copy, may have been manipulated slightly by later copyists (for instance, it ignores the rights of York), it is unambiguous in its support for Æthelheard himself and for the traditional rights of the see of Canterbury.[135] Personal support from the pope for Æthelheard may have been significant, since his own consecration had probably been performed by Hygeberht of Lichfield whose authority to act in this capacity, though legitimate at the time, had been gained (as everyone now agreed) by deceit.[136] In untangling the Lichfield problem, Æthelheard had to be very careful not to undermine his own already tenuous authority.

In a period of a little more than five years between the arrival of Eadberht Præn and his detractors in late spring of 796 and the journey of the archbishop and his companions in 801, four formal Mercian missions had been dispatched to Rome. It is possible – and unprecedented, if true – that Archbishop Æthelheard himself made the journey twice, once to argue the case against Eadberht and again to put the case for the abolition of Lichfield and the supremacy of Canterbury within the English Church. The high profile which Coenwulf and Æthelheard held at the papal court was maintained during the episcopacy of Æthelheard's successor, Wulfred, although – to Pope Leo's distaste – the relationship between king and archbishop reverted to one of opposition and antagonism rather than the cooperation which had been necessary to resolve the crisis over Lichfield. Wulfred, like Æthelheard, was not a Kentishman; his family allegiances seem to have been in Middlesex rather than in Kent. There are indications, however, that he was, in his own right, a wealthy and therefore powerful individual who was able to endow his church at Canterbury with considerable landed estates and

---

132 *ASChron.* 799 (recte 801); Alcuin, *Ep.* nos 231–32, MGH Epp. IV; *EHD* 1, trans. Whitelock, no. 206–7 and *Alcuin of York,* trans. Allott, no. 52 and 20. In the second of these letters Alcuin says that two bishops accompanied Æthelheard to the Continent. On Torctmund see above, Chapter 5, 143.

133 Alcuin, *Ep.* no. 230 and 231, MGH Epp. IV; *Alcuin of York,* trans. Allott, no. 51 and 52.

134 Editions of the proceedings of the council are in *BCS* 310 and Haddan and Stubbs (eds), *Councils* III, 542–44; *EHD* 1, trans. Whitelock, 210. See also *BCS* 312, Haddan and Stubbs (eds), *Councils* III, 545–47, promulgated at the same council, prohibiting lay lordship of monasteries on which see Cubitt, *Church Councils,* 279–80 and Brooks, *The Early History,* 179.

135 William of Malmesbury, *De Gestis Pontificum,* I.37; *BCS* 305, Haddan and Stubbs (eds), *Councils* III, 536–37; *EHD* 1, trans. Whitelock, no. 209.

136 Even Alcuin realized that Offa's motive had been 'a desire for power' and recommended the reassertion of the primacy of Canterbury, Alcuin, *Ep.* no. 128, MGH Epp. IV; *Alcuin of York,* trans. Allott, no. 49.

material wealth from his own resources.[137] He was also, as the charters and council reports from his period of office imply, strongly Francophone in his theological tastes and ambitions for the reform of the English Church – all of which brought him into conflict with his Mercian master.

A rich vein of Canterbury charters survive, often in contemporary form, for the first quarter of the ninth century, and these charters – in combination with a few papal letters preserved in Frankish manuscripts – demonstrate that both the Mercian king and the archbishop of Canterbury continued to send messengers and letters to Rome and the Carolingian court.[138] A significant continental dimension therefore continued to influence the major domestic issues confronting early ninth-century rulers in Anglo-Saxon England. In one of the letters which Leo wrote to Charlemagne concerning problems in England in 808, the pope noted that Coenwulf 'does not yet have peace with his archbishop'.[139] The precise disagreement here is unknown, but it seems (at least in Pope Leo's analysis) to have been related to the problems of the Northumbrian king, Eardwulf, whose banishment was the primary topic of the letter. It is apparent that Charlemagne had received numerous letters from interested parties in England which he had sent on to Leo for information and advice. Leo's postbag included correspondence from Coenwulf, Archbishop Eanbald II of York, and a man named Wada (who was probably the *dux* who had led an army against Eardwulf in 798 rather than the inept abbot of the same name whom Coenwulf had sent to Rome in 797).[140] Both Coenwulf and Eanbald had been accused of harbouring Eardwulf's enemies including (presumably) *dux* Wada and his followers who had fled in defeat after the battle at Billington Moor in 798.[141] Coenwulf's support for Eardwulf's enemies escalated into full-scale war between Mercian and Northumbrian forces. This conflict was resolved in 801 only 'after a long campaign' by the intercession of the English bishops, when the two kings pledged firm peace and everlasting friendship over a copy of the Gospels.[142] Leo's letter to Charlemagne implies that this pact had unravelled by 806 when Eardwulf's position in Northumbria became untenable; one explanation for the dispute between Coenwulf and Wulfred to which Leo alludes in his letter to the emperor is that the archbishop of Canterbury had provided refuge for Eardwulf en route to Francia and Rome.

---

[137] Brooks, *The Early History*, 132.

[138] On the Canterbury charters see ibid., 167–74. On the letters of Pope Leo in Wolfenbüttel, Herzog-August-Bibliothek, MS Guelf. 254 Helmstadt see above, 148.

[139] Haddan and Stubbs (eds), *Councils* III, 562–64.

[140] *Historia regum* (*York Annals*), 798.

[141] Eanbald had been reprimanded by Alcuin for his involvement and immoderate behaviour which, Alcuin suspected, had antagonized Eardwulf. In a strongly worded letter Alcuin had persuaded Eanbald not to flee York in the face of the armed conflict (as Æthelheard had done in 796); *Historia regum* (*York Annals*), 801 and Alcuin, *Ep*. no. 232, MGH Epp. IV, *Alcuin of York*, trans. Allott, no. 20.

[142] *Historia regum* (*York Annals*), 801.

Whatever the cause of their quarrel in 808, a number of Canterbury charters, datable to the years immediately following, record mutually agreeable land transactions between archbishop and king, suggesting that an understanding between them had been reached – and it is possible that the Carolingian and papal envoys who returned with Eardwulf to England in 809 played a part in the conciliation between them. The papal legate, Aldulf, certainly had cause to be grateful to Coenwulf. On the return journey, according to the account in the *Royal Frankish Annals*, he was captured by pirates and taken by them 'to Britain' where he was freed after being ransomed by one of Coenwulf's *homines*.[143] It was in this period at the end of the first decade of the ninth century that Wulfred embarked on a far-reaching reform of the clergy who served the archbishop's church at Canterbury, a process which can be traced through the charters which span the remainder of his period of office and which was to have major implications for the organization of the Anglo-Saxon Church in future decades.[144] A solemn diploma, datable to 808–813 and witnessed by all the leading men of the community, declared that Wulfred had 'revived the holy monastery of the church of Canterbury by renewing, restoring, and rebuilding it with the aid of his priests, deacons, and all the clergy of the same church'.[145] The charter demanded the regular attendance of the cathedral clergy in church at the proper canonical hours, that they make use of a communal dormitory and refectory, and that they observed a common rule of life. Wulfred's reforms restructured the clergy serving his archiepiscopal church; they were headed now by a priest-abbot rather than a provost and archdeacon as before.[146] Subsequent charters record the archbishop making provision for a sick-bay within the monastery, and ordering the proper regulation of alms-giving and psalm-singing. Wulfred also maintained and extended the Canterbury practice of ensuring endowments of land specifically for the benefit of the community's table and their clothing needs.[147] The objective of Wulfred's reforms was the restoration of the archbishop's household at Canterbury to a *communis congregatio,* a 'common community', which would live according to a structured 'rule of life of monastic discipline'.[148] Significantly, aspects of these reforms at Canterbury are comparable to the principles and practices of Carolingian *ordines* which governed the life-

---

[143] *Annales regni Francorum*, 809.

[144] Brooks, *The Early History*, 133, 155–64.

[145] *BCS* 342 / S 1265. Also, Haddan and Stubbs (eds), *Councils* III, 575–76. The dating formulae are inconsistent but the original charter is now lost and is known only from an antiquarian transcript; Brooks, *The Early History*, 155–57.

[146] Brooks, *The Early History*, 160–64.

[147] Brooks has shown that this practice of the so-called 'division of the *mensa*' between requirements of the bishop and the community was practiced at Canterbury at least since the 780s and so predates the early ninth century Carolingian evidence for this practice; ibid., 157–59.

[148] On the phase of rebuilding which may belong to this period of reform see K. Blockley, *Canterbury Cathedral Nave: Archaeology, History, and Architecture*, The Archaeology of Canterbury, NS Vol. 1 (Canterbury, 1997), and R. Gem, 'Architecture of the Anglo-Saxon Church, 735 to 870: From Archbishop Ecgberht to Archbishop Ceolnoth', *JBAA*, 146 (1993), 29–66, at 35–38.

style of secular canons who lived a structured, communal life but without monastic vows.

Comprehensive reform of the archbishop's community had been urged by Alcuin – in typical fashion – back in the dark days of Æthelheard's exile from Canterbury. A letter to Æthelheard included advice on encouraging learning and reading, and the proper training of a choir to sing the holy offices. This he said should be done in order to restore the bruised dignity of the archiepiscopal church and to ensure that talent was nurtured at Canterbury so that future archbishops could be chosen from within the community.[149] A subsequent letter reminds the archbishop more generally of the widespread corruption and secularization of clergy throughout England, to the extent that 'their only distinction [from the laity] seems to be the tonsure'.[150] Æthelheard's successor was indeed chosen from the Christ Church *familia*; Wulfred had been Æthelheard's archdeacon and seems to have been groomed for succession.[151] While Alcuin's advice may have contributed to a mood for reform at Canterbury, in his enthusiasm for high educational and liturgical standards and the regularization of clerical life, he was part of a much broader reform movement within the Frankish church, and his advice to Canterbury (and indeed to other ecclesiastical establishments in England) should be seen in that light.

An awareness in Canterbury of Frankish ecclesiastical practice is suggested by the timing and content of Wulfred's policies which were contemporaneous with reforms of cathedral communities in Francia. Parallels with Wulfred's reforms can be found in the proceedings of the Reform Councils of 813, held in five provincial centres around Francia and culminating in a great assembly in Aachen, and which were the pinnacle of Charlemagne's ecclesiastical reforms.[152] The progress made at the 813 meetings was consolidated and extended at the major series of councils convened by Louis the Pious at Aachen from 816–19, the decisions of which were ordered by imperial capitulary to be propagated *in toto regno suo*.[153] It is unlikely to be a coincidence that Wulfred's charter, which signals the start of the reform process at Canterbury, also bears the incarnation date of 813, and that at Chelsea in 816 he too convened an assembly of the southern province of the English Church.

---

[149] Alcuin, *Ep.* no. 128, MGH Epp. IV; *Alcuin of York*, trans. Allott, no. 49.

[150] Alcuin, *Ep.* no. 230, MGH Epp. IV; *Alcuin of York*, trans. Allott, no. 51.

[151] Brooks, *The Early History*, 132.

[152] The individual agreements from Councils at Arles, Rheims, Mainz, Chalons and Tours were collected together and brought for discussion to Aachen; MGH Conc. II.i, nos 34–38, 248–97. MGH Capit. 1, no. 77, pp. 170–72. On the 813 Reform Councils see R. McKitterick, *The Frankish Church and the Carolingian Reforms, 789–895* (London, 1977), 12–15, 217; J. M. Wallace-Hadrill, *The Frankish Church* (Oxford, 1983), 229–31, 262–64; and W. Hartmann, *Die Synoden der Karolingerzeit im Frankenreich und in Italien* (Paderborn, 1989), 128–40.

[153] *Capitula Notitiarum*, MGH Epp. V, *Epistolae Variorum*, no. 4 at 302–4. The decisions affecting monastic communities (as opposed to secular canons and canonesses) are edited by J. Semmler, 'Legislation Aquisgranensis', in K. Hallinger (ed.), *Corpus Consuetudinum Monasticorum*, 1 (Sieburg, 1963), 423–582. See also Hartmann, *Die Synoden*, 156–64.

Langefeld has argued that Wulfred's reforms were intended to return the Canterbury community to the purist ideals of a monastic rule, rather than to enforce its transformation into a Frankish-style community of canons.[154] Although the Canterbury texts do not use the term *canonici* to describe the members of the reformed community, the timing of Wulfred's reforms links them to the contemporary reform movement in Francia and demonstrates a desire for reform of episcopal communities in Kent and in Francia. And, given what we know of Wulfred's contact with the Continent, it would be perverse to disassociate the two reform processes entirely; at least in timing, if not in precise detail, the two movements were comparable. Significantly, the only occasion prior to this that the notion of the canonical lifestyle had been raised was in chapter 4 of the capitulary produced by George of Ostia during the legates' mission of 786.[155] The two texts of particular importance in defining Frankish practice were the *Regula canonicorum* devised by Chrodegang of Metz in the mid-eighth century, and the revised and expanded version of Chrodegang's *Regula*, known as the *Institutio canonicorum*, which was compiled at the first synod of Aachen in August 816.[156] Chrodegang's *Regula*, instituted at the Synod of Ver in 755,[157] had provided, for the first time in Francia, a distinction between the rules which guided the lifestyles of communities of monks or nuns, and canons or canonesses. It required its adherents to live a structured, communal life in the manner of strict monastic rules such as that of St Benedict of Nursia but permitted, among other differences, the possession of private property. It was partly for this reason that Chrodegang's *Regula* was widely adopted and taken up by some of the most powerful and wealthy ecclesiastical communities in Francia such as St Denis in Paris, as well as Chrodegang's own archiepiscopal community at Metz.[158] The reforms of the Frankish clergy which had begun in Pippin's reign took on a new lease of energy in the years following Charlemagne's imperial coronation, and were pursued energetically in the south-west of the kingdom where the reforming zeal of Benedict of Aniane was harnessed and sponsored by Charlemagne's son Louis, when sub-king of Aquitaine.[159]

---

[154] B. Langefeld, '*Regula canonicorum* or *Regula monasterialis vitae*? The Rule of Chrodegang and Archbishop Wulfred's Reforms at Canterbury', *ASE*, 25 (1996), 21–36.

[155] George of Ostia, *Epistola ad Hadrianum*, ed. E. Dümmler, MGH Epp. IV (Berlin, 1895), no. 3, 20–29, at 22; Brooks, 'The Cathedral Community' at Canterbury, 597–1070', in P. Collinson and N. Ramsey (eds), *The History of Canterbury Cathedral* (Oxford, 1995), reprinted in his *Anglo-Saxon Myths: State and Church 400–1066* (London, 2000), 101–54, at 115–116; Wormald, 'In Search of King Offa's "Law Code"', 25–45; B. Langefeld, '*Regula canonicorum* or *Regula monasterialis vitae*?: 'The Rule of Chrodegang and Archbishop Wulfred's Reforms at Canterbury', *ASE*, 25 (1996), 26–27.

[156] Chrodegang's *Regula Canonicorum* is edited in J. P. Migne, *PL* Vol. 139, cols 1097–1120; the text of the 816 *Institutio canonicorum* is in MGH Conc. II.i, no. 39, 309–421. The 816 *Institutio sanctimonialium* for canonesses is MGH Conc. II.i, no. 39, 421–56.

[157] Mordek, *BCRFM*, no.14 at 1081.

[158] McKitterick, *The Frankish Kingdoms*, 58–59, 110.

[159] McKitterick, *The Frankish Church*, 12–15 and *idem*, *The Frankish Kingdoms*, 109–24; Wallace-Hadrill, *The Frankish Church*, 229–30

After Louis's accession to the imperial throne, the pressure for the reform of monastic communities and the clergy which served the episcopal churches spread to other parts of Francia under the personal patronage and enthusiasm of the new emperor. Councils were held in Aachen in August 816 and July 817 at which Louis and Benedict of Aniane sought to impose reforms, revising and extending the *Regula canonicorum* for canons and demanding the primacy of the rule of St Benedict for monks. The synod of 816 produced three major documents: the *Institutio canonicorum* for canons; the *Institutio sanctimonialium* for canonesses; and a set of *ordines* for monks based on a more pure version of the rule of St Benedict than had been available in Chrodegang's day.[160] The new rules for canons and canonesses were based on Chrodegang's *Regula,* but were rigorously revised by detailed reference to instructions from patristic texts and decrees of councils of the early Church. Like Chrodegang's *Regula,* these new rules expected canons to be closely connected to a bishop and his cathedral. The decisions of the 816 synods were submitted to the emperor for his approval, who then wrote a letter to all the bishops of his kingdom instructing that the new rule for canons was to be copied and disseminated throughout Francia.[161] Louis also announced that he would be sending inspectors out to check that his orders had been followed. The large number of extant manuscripts of the *Institutio canonicorum* from a wide variety of centres suggests that Louis's instruction was indeed carried through.[162]

There is no indisputable manuscript evidence that copies of either the 813 Reform Councils or the decrees of the Aachen synods of 816 and 817 were available in Canterbury in Wulfred's day, although the rule for monks which Benedict of Aniane drafted in 818–19, known as the *Codex Regularum,* became very important for the Benedictine revival in England in the tenth century.[163]

---

160 The monastic ordines of 816 were edited in MGH Capit. I, 343–49 and again by J. Semmler, *Corpus Consuetudinum* 1, 457–68. Benedict of Aniane's revised Benedictine rule for monks, the *Codex Regularum* produced in 818–19, is in ibid., 515–36.

161 MGH *Leges* I, 219–23.

162 Werminghoff lists 73 manuscripts of the *Institutio Canonicorum;* MGH Conc. II.i, 310–11.

163 *Corpus consuetudinum,* ed. J. Semmler, 1, 506–7, 515–36. Eleventh-century manuscripts of Benedict of Aniane's *Regula* with an English provenance include BM Harley MS 5431, fos 107r–114r; Cambridge, Corpus Christi College MS 57, fos 37v–40v; BM Cotton MS Tiberius A.iii, fos 169r–173r; BM Cotton MS Titus A.iv fos 107r–111r; Cambridge, University Library MS Ll.I.14 fos 105v–108v. On these manuscripts and the importance of Benedict of Aniane's work to the tenth-century reform movement in England see M. Gretsch, 'Æthelwold's Translation of the Rule of St. Benedict and its Latin Exemplar', *ASE,* 3 (1974), 125–51; V. Ortenberg, *The English Church and the Continent in the Tenth and Eleventh Centuries* (Oxford, 1992) 245; P. Wormald, 'Æthelwold and his Continental Counterparts: Contacts, Comparison, Contrast', in B. A. E. Yorke (ed.), *Bishop Æthelwold: His Career and Influence* (Woodbridge, 1988), 13–42, at 31; J. Barrow, 'English Cathedral Communities in the Late Tenth and Eleventh Centuries', in D. Rollason et al. (eds), *Anglo-Norman Durham* (Woodbridge, 1994), 25–39. The earliest surviving Anglo-Saxon copy of Chrodegang's *Regula* is a Worcester manuscript of the earlier tenth century; Brussels, Bibliothèque Royale, MS 8558–8562 (2496). See also B. Langefeld, '*Regula canonicorum* or *Regula monasterialis vitae?'*, 26.

There is some evidence that, in the first quarter of the ninth century, some Canterbury scribes were using parchment prepared in Frankish fashion rather than the traditional insular style.[164] This observation may reveal no more than the passing presence of Frankish-trained manuscript craftsmen but it does reinforce the sense that, at quite a fundamental and practical level, the intellectual culture at Canterbury was informed by Frankish practices. Nevertheless, close parallels between specific aspects of Wulfred's reforms and decrees from contemporary Frankish synods make a link between the two movements a conclusion which is hard to avoid. Most explicit is the sanction against Irish priests whose proper canonical consecration could not be guaranteed; this canon is found in the proceedings of the Synod of Chelsea and in the proceedings of the 813 Council of Chalons.[165] Wulfred's insistence in his charter of 808–13 on a communal dormitory and refectory is paralleled in the provisions of four of the Reform Councils of 813.[166] His insistence at Chelsea on the proper observance of canons' lifestyle, on maintenance of peace and concord, and on the Catholic faith are all mirrored in 813 Reform Councils' proceedings. Wulfred's provision of a sick-house for the community's use likewise mirrors provisions in Chrodegang's *Regula* and the *Institutio canonicorum*;[167] similar also is Wulfred's insistence on the keeping of the office at proper canonical hours and the use of the dormitory according to 'monastic discipline' while permitting the continued ownership of private houses and cells – as long as the clergy never used them for feasting or sleeping, or as an attempt to alienate them from the community.[168] Comparable, too, is the use which Wulfred made in the proceedings at Chelsea of the decrees of councils of the early Church, particularly the Council of Chalcedon. This text was widely quoted by the authors of the *Institutio canonicorum*.

Wulfred's links with the Continent are implicit in the reforms embedded in his charters and in the proceedings of the Synod of Chelsea in 816; they are explicit in his actions during the years leading to this synod. The *Anglo-Saxon Chronicle* records that, in 814, Wulfred went to Rome accompanied by Bishop Wigberht of Sherborne. He had returned by March the following year 'with Pope Leo's blessing'. The chronicler says nothing of direct contact with the Franks but Wulfred must have journeyed through Francia, and it seems unthinkable that he would not have paid his respects to the new emperor since, despite the precedent set by Æthelheard, the journey of an archbishop to Rome was still

---

[164] M. P. Brown, 'Continental Symptoms in Insular Codicology: Historical Perspective', in P. Rück (ed.), *Pergament: Geschichte, Struktur, Restaurierung, Herstellung* (Sigmaringen, 1991), 57–62. On the paradox between the highly skilled calligraphy and the poor quality of Latin written in Canterbury by the second and third quarters of the ninth century see Brooks, *The Early History*, 164–74.

[165] Co. of Chelsea, c. 5; Co. of Chalons, c. 43.

[166] Co. of Rheims, c. 23; Co. of Arles, c. 6; Mainz c. 9; Tours c. 23; MGH Conc. II.i, 248–96.

[167] *Reg.* c. 28; *Inst.* c. 142.

[168] Brooks, *The Early History*, 156.

extremely unusual. It is not impossible, then, that Wulfred himself picked up at least the sense of the drive for reform which Louis and Benedict of Aniane were so keen to establish throughout Francia, and which inspired him to continue with his own programme of change at Canterbury. Indeed, whichever route he took to and from Rome, he would probably have passed through one of the provincial capitals which had hosted one of the Reform Councils in 813. It may, then, have been at Chalons-sur-Saone or one of its dependent bishoprics that he heard of the provision against Irish priests and noted it as being particularly applicable to his own Church.

That Wulfred was indeed known to the emperor is perhaps implied by a comment reported to have been made by Coenwulf in 821 when the king threatened the archbishop with impoverishment and exile from his see, which 'neither the mediation of the pope nor of the emperor, nor any other ruler would regain for him'.[169] The same Canterbury charter reveals that the archbishop had already suffered a diminution of his authority caused by the 'enmity, violence and avarice of King Coenwulf, both by his actions in this our own nation, but also overseas by his embassies and instructions at the Apostolic See'. The text of this charter presents a one-sided, pro-Canterbury view of the dispute; the issue under contention boiled down to the thorny question of lay-lordship over ecclesiastical property, which had been brought to a head by a dispute over the Kentish monasteries of Reculver and Minster-in-Thanet. This issue also lay at the heart of the 816 Synod of Chelsea and, it seems, probably lay behind Wulfred's journey to Rome in 814–15. Its importance is further underlined by Coenwulf's decision (as reported in the Canterbury charter) also to send embassies to Rome to discredit Wulfred's position. It is perhaps to these messengers that we should attribute the two papal privileges granted to the king by Leo III sometime before 815 and again by Paschal I in December 817, both of which reinforced and supported the rights of lay patronage that had been granted earlier by Hadrian to Offa and Cynethryth.[170]

At the Synod of Chelsea, Wulfred sought to stem the cumulative loss of ecclesiastical property and episcopal privileges brought about by many decades of the creeping extension of lay-lordship over monastic lands and appointments. The acts of the synod indicate that Wulfred tried to extend episcopal control over monastic appointments, subordinating the rights of both the *familia* and the king or other lay-lords to nominate the abbots of family monasteries. This went against established English practice and, it seems, contradicted the spirit and word of the papal privileges granted to Coenwulf. Leo's privilege to Coenwulf had granted him the exclusive right to deal with 'all the monasteries (*omnia monasteria*) and various places in the *insula Saxonia*, that he had inherited from his kinsfolk or had justly acquired and reasonably'.[171] Paschal's privilege re-

---

[169] S 1436 / *BCS* 384; Brooks, *The Early History*, 180–83, 322–23.

[170] *BCS* 337 (Leo III) and 363 (Paschal I), on which see Levison, *England and the Continent*, 255–57; and Brooks, *The Early History*, 186–87.

[171] Levison, *England and the Continent*, 29–32, 255; Brooks, *The Early History*, 185–86.

used the formula of Hadrian's privilege to Offa and reaffirmed the king's hereditary rights. Its date is significant; dated late December 817, it seems that Coenwulf had sought the charter of privilege from the new pope as explicit papal reaffirmation for his case against Wulfred after the Synod of Chelsea and the onset of the dispute over the two Kentish monasteries.

Although focused on the fate of these two houses, this conflict between Coenwulf and Wulfred was of profound significance for wider Anglo-Saxon society since, in essence, it concerned the control of landed estates, with all their human wealth and natural resources. Wulfred's attempts to secure episcopal prerogatives over monasteries went against the grain of a century or more of tradition which had evolved through donations of land by laymen for the sake of their souls, and cumulative papal privileges which sought to secure monastic rights against interference from greedy or interfering bishops. The severity of the implications of the dispute concerning the Kentish monasteries can be gauged by Coenwulf's response; although we only have the Canterbury version of the dispute settlement, it seems that the archbishop was out of favour for at least six years, that he was deprived of his authority, and that his rehabilitation was secured only after he had agreed to pay the sum of £120 – literally a king's ransom – and yield to the king an estate of 300 hides in compensation for the monasteries at Reculver and Minster-in-Thanet.[172] In return, Coenwulf agreed to clear the archbishop's stained reputation at Rome. The value of the principles at stake in this dispute had been sufficient to take Wulfred to Rome and for Coenwulf to send envoys to secure further privileges from the Apostolic See to reaffirm his traditional hereditary rights. Paradoxically, it seems that both Coenwulf and Wulfred had expected and secured a measure of papal support for their respective cases. The new emperor's attitude was equally ambiguous; Louis was certainly sympathetic to Coenwulf's position since, at the Aachen synod of 818–19 he also acted to ensure royal prerogative in the filling of abbatial vacancies.[173] On the other hand, Louis would also have approved of Wulfred's drive to reform the Anglo-Saxon clergy in a manner similar to the Frankish reforms which he had ordered to be enforced *in toto regno suo*.

Ninth-century continuity

Despite the change in the nature and scale of the written evidence after Alcuin's death, it is clear that, in the first quarter of the ninth century, Mercian politics retained a high profile on the Continent in a manner similar to, but less well

---

[172] The Council of London (821) reported in the proceeding for the Council of 825; Haddan and Stubbs (eds), *Councils* III, 587–88. On the price of a Mercian king's *wergild* see F. Liebermann (ed.), *Die Gesetze der Angelsachsen*. Vol. I: *Text und Übersetzung* (Halle, 1903), 462; and Brooks, *The Early History*, 182–83, 364.

[173] Wallace-Hadrill, *The Frankish Church*, 264; Brooks, *The Early History*, 182.

documented than, the period of Offa's reign. The number of Mercian missions to Rome in the years around the turn of the ninth century is remarkable. It is notable, too, that contact with the Frankish court was sustained beyond the death of Charlemagne. Although the sources for contacts with Frankish Europe in the early years of Louis's reign are derived overwhelmingly from Canterbury-centred sources, and are much more limited than from Alcuin's years, there is every reason to see the contacts with Louis's court as an extension of the type of interest which Charlemagne had developed in Anglo-Saxon affairs. The difference that we see in emphasis, from Charlemagne's sponsorship of political exiles to Louis's encouragement of ecclesiastical reform, could be a result of differential source survival as well as a reflection of personal preferences. We only have the evidence of Coenwulf's warning at the Council of London in 821 against the possibility of direct papal or imperial action on behalf of the archbishop to indicate that, in the opinion of the Mercian king, active intervention in English politics remained as much an option for Louis as it had been for his father. Kirby regarded this as evidence that Coenwulf was 'increasingly estranged from the political community of Frankish Europe',[174] but it is also scarce evidence that Mercian politics in the early ninth century retained a continental dimension which impinged on the king's decisions.

More tangible is the evidence which links the timing of Wulfred's reforms to contemporaneous developments in the Frankish Church. Whether deliberately (as part of Louis's instructions to disseminate the Aachen decisions) or fortuitously (as a result of passing contact) it is no surprise that news of developments in Frankish ecclesiastical policy reached Canterbury. We should not forget that Charlemagne had sent a synodal book to Northumbria in 792 for comment, nor that English bishops were said to have attended the Council of Frankfurt in 794, or that Charlemagne's instructions for the commemoration of Pope Hadrian had also been sent to England in 796. The opportunities for information about developments in Francia to have reached Canterbury during Coenwulf's reign were many. Apart from the formal legations to Rome, the chronicles reveal the existence of many other journeys: the messenger who took the news of Æthelheard's death to Rome and returned with a pallium for Wulfred in 806; the journey of the East Saxon king Sigeric in 798; of the arrival of Abbots Hruotfrid and Nantharius and the papal envoy Aldulf with Eardwulf in 808–9; let alone the carriers of the news about the death of Charlemagne and the deaths and elections of three popes which were recorded in the *Anglo-Saxon Chronicle* for the years 814, 815, 816 and 817. At some point between 817 and 821, one of Coenwulf's moneyers issued a silver penny for Coenwulf which closely mimicked the new gold solidus of Emperor Louis.[175] In an echo of the events surrounding Eardwulf's restoration, a charter from a synod held at *Clofesho* in

---

[174] Kirby, *The Earliest English Kings*, 187.

[175] C. F. Keary, *A Catalogue of English Coins in the British Museum. Vol. 1: The Anglo-Saxon Series*, 1 (London, 1887), no. 64, at 34 and Plate VIII.5. See also Chapter 7, below, 245–46.

824 notes the otherwise unrecorded presence of a papal legate by the name of Nothhelm indicating that papal concern for the Mercian Church continued after Coenwulf's death in 821.[176] In 848 the Mercian king, Berhtwulf, granted privileges to the Mercian monastery at Breedon-on-the-Hill, close to the royal centre at Repton. His charter of privilege released the community from a variety of obligations to the king, but not from the requirement to provide hospitality to envoys from the West Saxons or Northumbrians, nor to the ambassadors who came to visit the Mercian king from overseas.[177]

---

[176] BCS 379 / S 1433; Haddan and Stubbs (eds), *Councils* III, 592–94; Cubitt, *Anglo-Saxon Church Councils*, 220–21.

[177] BCS 454 / S 197; D.A. Bullough, 'What has Ingeld to do with Lindisfarne', *ASE*, 22 (1993), 93–125, at 121–22; S. Keynes, 'King Alfred and the Mercians', in M. A. S. Blackburn and D. N. Dumville (eds), *Kings, Currency and Alliances* (Woodbridge, 1998), 1–46, at 6; C. R. Hart, *The Early Charters of Northern England* (Leicester, 1975), no. 34.

Chapter 7

Francia and the Rise of Wessex

The first quarter of the ninth century shows a continuity of contact between Mercia and Francia of a type familiar from the reign of Offa. The Canterbury evidence highlights the ripple effect of the Frankish monastic reform movement of these years and shows that Archbishop Wulfred was actively implementing a parallel reform of his own. Wulfred's contacts with Rome and his travels through Francia are indicative of his wide vision and breadth of experience, and serve to underline the similarities between his ecclesiastical reforms and those being implemented throughout the Carolingian *regna*. The spotlight on the Canterbury evidence accentuates the scarcity of comparable material from the heartlands of the Mercian kingdom; lacking a commentator like Alcuin, Coenwulf's attitudes are filtered through the less-than-sympathetic Canterbury sources. A similar problem confronts analysis of the kingdom of Wessex in these years – a problem which is particularly frustrating given the pinpricks of light which illuminate the rising importance of Wessex under the command of Ecgberht. In 825 a Mercian army was defeated by the West Saxons at *Ellendun*, and Ecgberht sent his son Æthelwulf, with Bishop Ealhstan of Sherborne and Ealdorman Wulfheard in the vanguard of a large armed force into Kent; thereafter West Saxon affairs impinged directly on the interests of the church at Canterbury and consequently the West Saxon kings and their methods of governance become visible in the Canterbury sources.[1]

Prior to 825 the task is much more difficult, and written sources for this crucial period in the formation of the West Saxon polity are very limited. In this context, the references in the *Anglo-Saxon Chronicle* to the visits of two West Saxon bishops to Rome assume more than usual significance.[2] On both occasions the West Saxon bishop was accompanying the Archbishop of Canterbury; Cyneberht of Winchester with Archbishop Æthelheard in 801, Wigberht of Sherborne with Archbishop Wulfred in 814. We are told by Alcuin that the earlier of the two missions travelled via Charlemagne's court and it is likely that, as a distinguished cleric who shared a personal interest in monastic reform with the new emperor, Wulfred would also have visited the Carolingian court in 814–15. The *Chronicle* does not reveal whether either of the West Saxon bishops returned to their sees but the chronology of their successors' careers does not exclude the possibility.[3] The silence concerning their return journey is

---

[1] S. Keynes, 'The Control of Kent in the Ninth Century', *EME*, 2.ii (1993), 111–32; N. P. Brooks, *The Early History of the Church of Canterbury* (Leicester, 1984), 143–49, 197–203.

[2] *ASChron.* 799 (for 801) and 812–13 (for 814–15).

[3] E. B. Fryde et al., *Handbook of British Chronology* (3rd edn), Royal Historical Society

not necessarily a problem; it is, after all, only Alcuin who tells us that a second (unnamed) bishop travelled with Cyneberht and Æthelheard to Rome in 801.[4] It is possible that both Cyneberht and Wigberht may simply have been taking advantage of high-profile missions to Rome to make their own personal pilgrimages and that they were unconnected with the important matters of state which drove the archbishops to Rome. However, if this seems unlikely, at the very least, their presence would have added considerable gravitas to the archbishops' deputations and provided a semblance of episcopal solidarity within the southern English province for continental audiences. Their presence may also point to the involvement of West Saxon bishoprics in the Canterbury reform movement and of the desire of the archbishops to reassure the pope and the curia in Rome of West Saxon attitudes to these and other issues.

It is also important to note that both these missions by high-ranking Anglo-Saxon churchmen followed key transitional moments in Carolingian dynastic history; it would not be beyond the bounds of historical probability to suppose that the English delegations would have wished to capitalize on the fortuitous timing of their journeys to assess for themselves the changed political circumstances in Francia. If both bishops returned to Wessex – and it seems likely that Wigberht at least came back to Sherborne – both would have returned with experience of the Frankish court and of Rome and, in their experience of foreign lands, they had something in common with their new king, Ecgberht.

Ecgberht and Louis the Pious

Alfred's grandfather, Ecgberht, fled into exile in Francia in 789 when the West Saxon king Beorhtric became Offa's son-in-law. The *Anglo-Saxon Chronicle* states that his flight abroad was a direct consequence of the marriage alliance between the Mercian princess Eadburh and Beorhtric and, furthermore, that the West Saxon king had acted against Ecgberht on Offa's orders.[5] This is important as it implies that (in the mind of the chronicler) Ecgberht's safety had been

---

Handbooks 2 (London, 1986), 222–23. Cyneberht's successor at Winchester, Ealhmund, attests the proceedings of the Council of Chelsea in 803, the year after the archbishop returned from Rome; Haddan and Stubbs (eds), *Councils* III, 541–47. Wigberht's successor, Ealhstan, died in 867, having been bishop for 50 years (*ASChron*. 867; Asser, *Vita Alfredi*, c. 28), implying that he became bishop in 817, two years after Wulfred returned from Rome. It is possible, then, that Wigberht did return and lived until 816–17. See M. A. O'Donovan, 'An Interim Revision of Episcopal Dates for the Province of Canterbury, 850–950, Part I', *ASE*, 1 (1972), 23–44, *idem*, 'Part II', *Anglo-Saxon England*, 2 (1973), 91–114.

    [4] Alcuin, *Ep*. no. 232; *Alcuin of York, c. A.D. 732 to 804: His Life and Letters*, trans. S. Allott (York, 1974), no. 20.

    [5] *ASChron*. 836 (for 839). William of Malmesbury envisaged a different scenario, arguing that the marriage was a consequence of Ecgberht's flight to Offa's court; *William of Malmesbury: Gesta Regum Anglorum: The History of the English Kings*, ed. and trans. R. A. B. Mynors et al. (Oxford, 1998–99), c. 106.

jeopardized by the new alliance with Mercia rather than by Beorhtric's kingship *per se*. Despite the fact that, as a descendant of Ine's brother, Ecgberht was (as he proved to be) a potential dynastic challenger for the West Saxon throne, he does not seem to have been involved in the blood-feud which brought Beorhtric to power.[6] It is possible that he was just too young in 786 to be a serious challenger in the confused aftermath of the assassination of Cynewulf. The year of Ecgberht's birth is unknown but he died, according to the *Chronicle,* in 839, 50 years after fleeing England for Francia. If (for the sake of argument) he had been the same age as his contemporary, Louis the Pious (778–840), Ecgberht would have been about eight years old when Beorhtric came to power in Wessex, 11 when he went to Francia, 47 when he won victory at *Ellendun* in 825, and in his early sixties when he died. Give or take a few years, this age range is unlikely to be too far out, so it is possible that Ecgberht reached the age of majority when in exile in Francia. Ecgberht's non-appearance in the feud which brought Beorhtric to power is an argument in favour of him having been quite young in 786 – too young to have fronted a feasible armed challenge.[7] However, by the time of Beorhtric's marriage three years later in 789 Ecgberht was clearly old enough for the new strategic alignment between Wessex and Mercia to have made his continued presence in England politically untenable, since he would now pose a threat to the offspring which Offa must have hoped would result from the marriage of his daughter to Beorhtric. Offa's desire to see Ecgberht removed thus corresponds with the kin-killing which he practised in Mercia on his own son's behalf.[8] All this implies that the young Ecgberht's political affiliations were necessarily anti-Mercian and that, by marrying into the Mercian ruling family, Beorhtric had aligned himself with Ecgberht's political enemies. Ecgberht's youth makes it improbable that his own actions had been the cause of Offa's enmity and rather more likely that he had been born into a political inheritance; this adds credence to the statement (made in one late copy of the *Chronicle*) that Ecgberht's father, Ealhmund, had for a period during the early 780s been one of several independent kings ruling in Kent, challenging Offa's authority there.[9]

---

[6] *ASChron.* 755 (for 757) and 784 (for 786); Asser, *Vita Alfredi,* c. 1. Beorhtric seems to have been unrelated to preceding West Saxon kings, a point underlined by his choice of marital alliance; B.A.E. Yorke, *Wessex in the Early Middle Ages* (London and New York, 1995), 81, 94.

[7] By comparison, 14-year-old Charles the Bald was granted a portion of his father's realm in 837, supplemented with oaths of loyalty from leading men. He was only 'invested with arms' as a symbol of his adulthood and consequent ability 'to wield the indispensable instruments of power' in September 838 after he had reached his fifteenth birthday, the age of majority among the Franks; J. L. Nelson, 'Ninth-century Knighthood: The Evidence of Nithard', in C. Harper-Bill et al. (eds), *Studies in Medieval History presented to R. Allen Brown* (Woodbridge, 1989), 255–66, reprinted in her *The Frankish World, 750–900* (London and Rio Grande, 1996), 75–88, at 84 (subsequent references are to this reprint).

[8] Alcuin, *Ep.* no. 122; *Alcuin of York,* trans. Allott, no. 46.

[9] *ASChron.* F 784 states that a King Ealhmund ruled in Kent and that this Ealhmund was the father of Ecgberht, father of Æthelwulf. *ASChron.* F (Lat.) has a relationship, as yet not fully worked out, with the Christ Church Cartulary which notes the gift of Sheldwich by Ealhmund to Reculver

The *Chronicle* for 825 explains the submission of the kingdoms of the south-east to Ecgberht's army with the statement that 'they had been wrongfully forced away from his kinsmen'.[10]

Ecgberht's presence in Francia with his anti-Mercian stance and possible Kentish background could have been a factor in the disintegration of the relationship between Offa and Charlemagne *c.* 790 caused by the disagreement over the betrothal of their children.[11] As shown by the West Saxon alliance, Offa had very recently used the marriage of one daughter to strengthen an ally and to dispose of a potential enemy; the betrothal of another daughter into the Carolingian family would have been a further obstacle to Ecgberht's future rehabilitation in Wessex (or in Kent) as well as a formidable buttress for his own son's authority in Mercia. The severity of the breach between the Frankish and Mercian kings was perhaps as much an indication of Charlemagne's sympathy for Ecgberht's cause as a reflection of his distaste for Offa's methods of dynastic aggrandizement.

According to the *Chronicle*, Ecgberht remained in Francia for three years. Where he resided for the remainder of Beorhtric's reign is unknown, although a simple scribal error in the archetype of the *Chronicle* may have disguised the fact that he remained in Francia for 13 years – that is, for the duration of Beorhtric's marriage in 789 until his death in 802.[12] This was a problem which vexed twelfth-century historians; William of Malmesbury assumed that Ecgberht must have stayed in Francia for 13 years whereas John of Worcester thought that he returned after three and lived quietly in England until 802.[13] Had Ecgberht remained in Francia till 802, Alfred's story of Eadburh's humiliation at Charlemagne's court, could have come directly from his grandfather's entourage – 'from men' as Asser says 'who remembered the event in all its particulars'.[14] In either case, Ecgberht spent a substantial proportion of his formative years in

---

(*BCS* 243/*S*38). It is possible that the compiler of the cartulary was the author of *ASChron*. F. (Lat.). On Ecgberht's Kentish pedigree see A. Scharer, 'The Writing of History at King Alfred's Court', *EME*, 5.2 (1996), 177–206, at 184–85; *Alfred the Great: Asser's Life of Alfred and Other Contemporary Sources*, trans. S. Keynes and M. Lapidge (Harmondsworth, 1983), 236, n. 30.

[10] *ASChron.* 823 (for 825).

[11] See Chapter 6, above, 184–88. See also, *Asser's Life of King Alfred together with the annals of St. Neots erroneously ascribed to Asser*, ed. W. H. Stevenson (Oxford, rev. edn, 1959), 206–8 and F. M. Stenton, *Anglo-Saxon England* (3rd edn) (Oxford, 1971), 220.

[12] Stenton (ibid.) objected to this idea on the grounds that the figure *.iii.* was common to all manuscripts of the *Chronicle* and that, if *.xiii.* had been meant, the error must have been made in the archetype, which in itself is quite possible. On this point see *Two Saxon Chronicles Parallel*, ed. C. Plummer and J. Earle (Oxford, 1892–99), Vol. 2, 75.

[13] *William of Malmesbury: Gesta Regum Anglorum*, ed. and trans. Mynors et al., Vol. 1, 152–55, Vol. 2, 75–77; *The Chronicle of John of Worcester. Vol. 2: 450 to 1066*, ed. and trans. R. R. Darlington et al. (Oxford, 1995), 230 n.1, 252–55. Note that William assumes that Ecgberht was of marriageable age in 789.

[14] Asser, *Vita Alfredi*, c. 13–15; *Alfred the Great*, trans. Keynes and Lapidge, 70–72, 236. On the inclusion of the name of an Abbess Eadburh in the Reichenau *Liber Vitae* see H. Becher, 'Das königliche Frauenkloster San Salvatore/Santa Giulia in Brescia im Spiegel seiner Memorialüberlieferung', *Frühmittelalterlich Studien*, 17 (1983), 299–392, at 380–81.

Francia and, unless we suppose that Ecgberht and his companions sat in Quentovic meekly waiting for the political tide to turn, we can safely assume that observing Charlemagne's Francia prepare for war against the Avars in the early 790s would have been a useful apprenticeship for a career as king of Wessex.[15] Clearly, the author of the *Chronicle* entry for 839 retrospectively regarded the period of Ecgberht's Frankish exile as an important factor behind Ecgberht's subsequent achievements as king. The same entry records the smooth transition of the succession to Æthelwulf, the first occasion since 641 that a son had directly succeeded his father to the kingdom of the West Saxons. The chronicler's inclusion of the record of Ecgberht's exile in Francia at this seminal moment in the creation of a dynasty is surely meaningful.

The contemporary sources are almost silent about Ecgberht's succession and the early years of his rule. The *Chronicle* describes a battle on the day of his accession between the men of Wiltshire and the Hwicce which seems to have realigned the frontier between Wessex and Mercia in favour of the West Saxons, and records a campaign by Ecgberht in Cornwall in 815.[16] Ten years later he was fighting again in the southwest; the *Chronicle* records a battle between the Britons and the men of Devon in 825, and a pair of Winchester charters show that, in August of that year, Ecgberht and his army were with them.[17] The silence of these early years (like the period of his exile) is undoubtedly deceptive; the first half of Ecgberht's reign must have been characterized by a cumulative acquisition of military and political authority to the point where his consolidated strength dominated the south-west and, by 825, the Mercian king was roused to attack him. Kirby has speculated that a continuation of Carolingian support may have been a factor behind not just Ecgberht's coup in 802 but also the spectacular successes of his armies which the *Chronicle* records in the later 820s.[18] West Saxon forces defeated the Mercian army at *Ellendun* in 825 in a victory which precipitated the collapse of Mercian authority in Kent and East Anglia, and which was a prelude to the conquest of Mercia in 829 and the submission of the Northumbrians at Dore. The historic significance of the events of 829 was not lost on the chronicler writing later in the ninth century who famously proclaimed Ecgberht as the eighth *bretwalda* south of the Humber.[19] Kirby has drawn attention to the parallel dynamics of West Saxon and Carolingian fortunes

---

[15] K. Leyser, 'Early Medieval Warfare', in J. Cooper (ed.), *The Battle of Maldon* (London, 1993), 87–108 reprinted in T. Reuter (ed.), *Communications and Power in Medieval Europe: The Carolingian and Ottonian Centuries* (London, 1994), 29–50, at 30.

[16] *ASChron.* 800 (for 802); Yorke, *Wessex*, 64, 94.

[17] *BCS* 389/*S* 273 and *BCS* 390/*S* 272; *EHD* 1, trans. Whitelock, 185, n. 4.

[18] D. P. Kirby, *The Earliest English Kings* (London, 1991), 192–93. For the suggestion that, like Offa, Ecgberht spent the early years of his reign (on which the *Chronicle* is silent) 'reducing his cousinage' to secure his son's accession, see A. Woolf, 'Pictish Matriliny Reconsidered', *Innes Review*, 49.2 (1998), 147–67.

[19] *ASChron.* AG, 827 (for 829). On this passage see S. Keynes, 'England, 700–900', in *NCMH* 2, 17–42, at 38–41.

in these years, noting the coincidence of Ecgberht's retrenchment after the high point of 829 and the re-emergence of Mercian independence under Wiglaf with the beginning of the serious rebellion in Francia against Louis the Pious. Postulating a continuity of imperial patronage from the days of Ecgberht's exile in his youth, Kirby has argued that the downturn in West Saxon fortunes is best explained by 'a relatively sudden withdrawal of Frankish support' in the aftermath of the revolt against Louis the Pious in February 830 and the ónset of the domestic conflict between the emperor and his sons culminating in his ritual penance and temporary deposition at Soissons in 833.[20]

It is difficult to see how the Carolingian regime could have influenced West Saxon military fortunes so directly; moral sponsorship would have been valued and may have contributed to a sense of self-confidence among the West Saxon ruling elite but it is doubtful that even the withdrawal of any direct Carolingian material aid that had been given could account for the retrenchment of the West Saxon advances in the early 830s.[21] It is quite possible, though, that Ecgberht's strategies for success in the 820s did owe something to his years of exile in Francia. We may note in passing, for example, that it is in Ecgberht's reign that the bishops of Wessex became deeply involved in military campaigning (like their Carolingian counterparts) and that it is in the early decades of the ninth century that obligations for bridge-building and repair began to be reserved in West Saxon charters as had customarily been demanded in Francia and latterly in Mercia.[22]

One Frankish source does, however, point to direct contacts with Louis's court right at the end of Ecgberht's reign which may presuppose existing diplomatic contacts. The *Annals of St Bertin* record the arrival of a legation from 'a king of the Angles' in 839, the year of Ecgberht's death.[23] The envoys of the English

---

[20] Astronomer, *Vita Hludovici Imperatoris*, ed. E. Tremp, MGH SS rer. Germ. LXIV (Hanover, 1995), c. 3, 288–93; *Son of Charlemagne. A Contemporary Life of Louis the Pious*, trans. A. Cabaniss (Syracuse, 1965), 33–34; *AB* 840.

[21] For evidence of Louis's strength in the period after 833 see J. L. Nelson, 'The Last Years of Louis the Pious', in P. Godman and R. Collins (eds), *Charlemagne's Heir* (Oxford, 1990), 147–60 reprinted in *idem, The Frankish World* (London and Rio Grande, 1997), 37–50. For an alternative view of the Mercian–West Saxon relationship during these years see S. Keynes, 'King Alfred and the Mercians', in M. A. S. Blackburn and D. N. Dumville (eds), *Kings, Currency, and Alliances: History and Coinage of Southern England in the Ninth Century* (Woodbridge, 1998), 1–46, at 2–11.

[22] Ealhstan of Sherborne and his successor Heahmund are the only ninth-century Anglo-Saxon bishops recorded in military service. See *ASChron*. 823 (for 825), 845 (for 848) and 871; also J. L. Nelson, 'The Church's Military Service in the Ninth Century: A Comparative View?', *SCH*, 20 (1983), 15–30 reprinted in *idem, Politics and Ritual in Early Medieval Europe* (London, 1986), 117–32, at 120–21. On bridgework see N. P. Brooks, 'The Development of Military Obligations in Eighth- and Ninth-century England', in P. Clemoes and K. Hughes (eds), *England Before the Conquest* (London, 1971), 69–84, reprinted in N. P. Brooks, *Communities and Warfare 700–1400* (London, 2000), 32–47 (references hereafter are to this reprint). See also J. L. Nelson, 'England and the Franks in the Ninth Century Reconsidered', in P. E. Szarmach and J. T. Rosenthal (eds), *The Preservation and Transmission of Anglo-Saxon Culture* (Kalamazoo, MI, 1997), 141–58 at 146–48.

[23] *AB* 839; *The Annals of St. Bertin*, trans. J. L. Nelson, Ninth Century Histories, 1 (Manchester,

king came to Louis after Easter as he was making his way back from Alemannia into Francia. Prudentius of Troyes, who was the continuator of the *Annals of St Bertin* from 835 (at least) to 861 and who was at this stage writing at Louis's court, does not specify which English king had sponsored the mission but notes that the purpose of the envoys' mission was to secure permission for their king to travel through Francia on pilgrimage to Rome. The envoys also brought Louis a letter from the English king which contained a detailed account of a portentous dream which had recently been revealed to a local priest.[24] This vision had troubled the English king and his advisers so greatly that he was anxious Louis should hear it too, and heed its message. In the dream the priest was led by a guide into a fantastic land filled with marvellous buildings. One of the buildings was a church in which the priest saw a group of boys reading from books written out in alternate lines of black ink and blood. When he asked the meaning of this strange sight, the priest was told that the bloody lines represented the errors of the Christian people and the boys were the saints who prayed continuously for them to be forgiven. 'You will remember', the guide added, 'that this very year fruit came forth in abundance on the land and on the trees and on the vines, but because of the sins of men most of this fruit withered and was never used by anyone.' Christians every-where, the guide explained, needed urgently to reform in order to avoid being engulfed by a dense fog and scourged for their sins by pagan warriors. The scriptural allusion is both apocalyptic and evangelical, recalling both the Revela-tion of St John and Christ's call for evangelism among those who had yet to hear his message 'Truly the harvest is great but the labourers are few'.[25] The sins of these ninth-century Christians are thus compounded; they have turned their back on Christ's harvest of souls and are complacently disregarding the manifold gifts of God, to the peril of their present lives and future salvation.

The metaphors used to convey this message repay investigation. The im-age of a land of plenty is a commonplace of insular political thought which equated good harvests and clement weather with the rule of a righteous king; conversely, famine and hard winters were associated with an unjust ruler or one who harboured sin.[26] As Alcuin said in an open letter to the Northumbrian court of King Æthelred, 'We read that a good king means a prosperous nation, victori-ous in war, temperate in climate, rich in soil, blessed with sons and a healthy people'.[27] The picture of a crop unharvested thus represents a just, hard-working

---

1991), 7–9, 42–43. On the authorship of the *AB* see J. L. Nelson, 'The Annals of St. Bertin', in M. T. Gibson and J. L. Nelson (eds), *Charles the Bald* (2nd edn) (Aldershot, 1990), 23–40.

[24] P. E. Dutton, *The Politics of Dreaming in the Carolingian Empire* (Lincoln, NB 1994), 107–9.

[25] Matt, 9:37; Luke 10:2; Rev. 20:12. See also Bede, *HE* I.29.

[26] H. H. Anton, *Fürstenspiegel und Herrscherethos in der Karolingerzeit* (Bonn, 1968), 66–79.

[27] Alcuin, *Ep.* no. 18, *Alcuin*, trans. Allott, no. 13. See also the comments of the Astronomer on the clement weather which coincided with the rehabilitation of Louis at St Denis in March 834; Astronomer, *Vita Hludovici Imperatoris*, c. 51; MGH *SRG ius* LXIV, 488–91; *Son of Charlemagne*, trans. Cabaniss, 101–2.

king whose people squandered the rewards of his equitable government – an inversion of the familiar explanation for the fluctuation of the abundance and disasters of nature and, crucially, one for which the king was not solely to blame. Equally, the books of blood are a grotesque distortion of the familiar concept of a 'Book of Life', well-known to both Anglo-Saxon and Carolingian audiences.[28] For example, the Northumbrian *Liber Vitae* – copied *c*. 840, contemporaneously with the account of this vision – was also written in lines of alternate colours, in gold and silver.[29] The names in that book were those of long-dead benefactors to the community who used the book to pray for their souls – the souls of the saved. Paradoxically, the boys with the books of blood prayed for the unsaved – for living sinners. The boys were the saints themselves who 'grieve every day over the sins and crimes of Christians and intercede for them so that they may finally be turned to repentance some day'.[30]

The detailed inclusion of this story in the *Annals of St Bertin* is intriguing and significant. Until 843 Prudentius was a palace clerk compiling his annals at court and, up to 840, his focus was the activity of Louis the Pious and the promotion of imperial stability.[31] His reference to the arrival of the English envoys and the dream of the priest sits amid news of other events of 'international' significance: the fearful story of the conversion to Judaism of an Alemanian deacon named Bodo and his public entry into the Spanish town of Zaragoza; devastating floods in Frisia; and a detailed account of the arrival, at the palace of Ingelheim, of Greek envoys accompanied by men from the Swedish people known as the *Rus*.[32] The remainder of the annal is devoted to the *rapprochement* between the ageing emperor and his son Lothar, with an account of the subsequent division of the kingdom. Prudentius's motive for including the verbatim

---

[28] Rev. 20:12: 'And I saw the dead, small and great, stand before God; and the books were opened: and another book was opened, which is the book of life: and the dead were judged out of those things which were written in the books, according to their words ... '. On the shared development of the genre of remembrance represented by the *Libri Vitae* among the Franks and Anglo-Saxons see S. Keynes (ed.), *The Liber Vitae of the Newminster and Hyde Abbey, Winchester*, EEMF 26 (Copenhagen, 1996), 49–58; R. McKitterick, 'Social Memory, Commemoration and the Book', in S. J. Ridyard (ed.), *Reading and the Book in the Middle Ages*, Sewanee Medieval Studies II (Sewanee, TN, 2001), 5–26.

[29] On the dating of the Northumbrian *Liber Vitae* see A. G. Watson, *Catalogue of the Dated and Dateable Manuscripts c. 700–1600 in the Department of Manuscripts, the British Library* (London, 1979), no. 527; Keynes, *The Liber Vitae* 56–58; J. Gerchow, *Die Gedenküberlieferung der Angelsachsen* (Berlin and New York, 1988), 109–49; J. Morrish, 'Dated and Datable Manuscripts Copied in England during the Ninth Century: A Preliminary List', *Mediaeval Studies*, 50 (1988), 512–38, at 523–24; L. Webster and J. Backhouse (eds), *The Making of England: Anglo-Saxon Art and Culture, AD 600–900* (London, 1991), no. 97; *Liber vitae ecclesiae Dunelmensis*, ed. A. H. Thompson, Sur. Soc. 136 (1923).

[30] *AB* 839.

[31] Nelson, 'The Annals of St. Bertin', 177–78

[32] On Bodo see A. Cabaniss, 'Bodo-Eleazar: A Famous Jewish Convert', *Jewish Quarterly Review*, n.s. 43 (1952–53), 313–28 and R. Collins, *Early Medieval Spain* (London, 1983), 191–92; J. Shepard, 'The Rhos Guests of Louis the Pious: Whence and Wherefore?', *EME*, 4.1 (1995), 41–60.

account of the English priest's vision probably had as much to do with his own fears about the future governance of the empire under the quarrelsome sons of Louis the Pious as about the threat of pagan raiders, which had undoubtedly been the scourge envisaged by the English king. It is clear, though, that Prudentius understood the complex nuances of the English priest's vision; the care with which he recorded it suggests that Louis – at whose court the *Annals* were then being compiled – had heard and understood it too.[33] The image of the unpicked harvest was a particularly sympathetic metaphor for the troubled later years of Louis's reign since it implied that Louis's subjects bore a considerable burden of culpability for the unrest of the 830s. At this stage, the *Annals* were still a product of the palace and intended for a courtly audience; by copying the account into the *Annals*, Prudentius thought to preserve the Englishman's vision for future readers and rulers.[34] The vision is also a reminder of the commonality of the Anglo-Saxon and Frankish experience; the English king having heard and understood this vision, knew that the Carolingian king should hear and would understand it too. It reflects an understanding in Anglo-Saxon England that the English and the Franks were part of the confraternity of Christ, against whom God threatened to unleash a pagan plague because of complacency and lack of piety among Christians.

Louis's sensitivity to interpretations of collective responsibility within such portents is borne out by another contemporary story. At Easter the previous year, Louis's anonymous biographer, known to historians as the Astronomer, was summoned by the emperor to judge the meaning of a comet which had recently appeared.[35] The Astronomer records his nervous conversation with the emperor, evidently fearful that Louis had heard the rumour circulating around the court that the comet foretold upheaval in the kingdom and the death of a prince. But the emperor shrugged off this populist scaremongering, arguing that, if the comet was indeed a celestial portent, 'it affects both me and everyone jointly' – *communiter*.[36] In response, Louis took steps to remind his courtiers of their mutual responsibility before God by summoning them the next day to witness his alms-giving, to say mass with him, and to join him on the hunt which, the Astronomer notes approvingly, was more than usually successful.

---

[33] Dutton, *The Politics of Dreaming*, 109.

[34] On the transition *c.* 843 of the *AB* from a court product to a private project see Nelson, 'The Annals of St. Bertin', 178–85; *The Annals of St. Bertin*, trans. J. L. Nelson, Ninth Century Histories I (Manchester, 1991) 7–9.

[35] Astronomer, *Vita Hludovici Imperatoris*, c. 58; MGH *SRG ius*, LXIV, 518–25; *Son of Charlemagne*, trans. Cabaniss, 113–14. See also Nelson, 'The Last Years of Louis the Pious', 39. The sighting was of Halley's comet or of a comet in its aftermath; D. J. Schove and A. Fletcher, *Chronology of Eclipses and Comets AD 1–1000* (Woodbridge, 1984), 295.

[36] On Louis and the politics of consensus see J. Hannig, *Consensus Fidelium: Frühfeudale Interpretation des Verhältnisses von Königtum und Adel* (Stuttgart, 1983) and J. L. Nelson, 'Legislation and Consensus in the Reign of Charles the Bald', in P. Wormald et al. (ed.), *Ideal and Reality in Frankish and Anglo-Saxon Society* (Oxford, 1983), 202–27, reprinted in Nelson, *Politics and Ritual in Early Medieval Europe* (London, 1986), 91–116, at 108.

The identity of the English king who sent this confraternal message to Louis is not known for sure; potential candidates include Wiglaf of Mercia or Eanred of Northumbria, both of whom seem to have died around 840 and who, conceivably, may have wished to end their days in Rome.[37] However, it is widely assumed – given the origin of the remaining Anglo-Saxon information in Prudentius's section of the *Annals of St Bertin* – that the king was West Saxon.[38] The call for repentance and reform in the priest's dream could account for the desire of the unnamed English king to visit Rome, as atonement for the sins of his people, although the annalist does not link the two aspects of the mission explicitly. If so, the king in question was most probably Ecgberht.[39] In 838 Ecgberht had secured at a council held at Kingston effective recognition of Æthelwulf's succession, together with a promise of perpetual support for himself and his heirs from the archbishop of Canterbury 'and all his successors'. This pledge was made in exchange for the restoration of extensive estates at 'Malling' and a compromise over the old dispute concerning the lordship of Kentish *monasteria*.[40] The protracted negotiations were witnessed by the archbishop of Canterbury and 'many other bishops', and the decisions were ratified a few months later by the secular nobility of Wessex at an assembly at Wilton and confirmed by a full synod of the province of Canterbury *æt Æstran* in 839.[41] The importance of the Kingston council is highlighted by the preservation of three contemporary copies of the discussion; the palaeography of these charters and of the contemporary endorsements from Kingston, Wilton and *Æstran* demonstrates the care with which widespread consensus was achieved among the political elites in both Kent and Wessex.[42] The agreement was a

---

[37] Roger of Wendover, *Flores Historiarum,* 840; ed. *Rogeri de Wendover Chronica, sive Flores historiarum,* ed. H. O. Coxe (London, 1841–42), I, 271, 281; Whitelock, *EHD* 1, no. 4. But the numismatic chronology may push Eanred's date of death forwards into the 850s; see H. E. Pagan, 'Northumbrian Numismatic Chronology in the Ninth Century', *BNJ*, 38 (1969), 1–15; *Sources for York History to AD 1100*, ed. D. W. Rollason, The Archaeology of York, 1 (York, 1998), 55. Wiglaf's dates are inferred by the dates of adjacent kings; Kirby, *Earliest English Kings,* 194.

[38] Prudentius's reference to the king as a *Rex Anglorum* is not a barrier to his identity as a West Saxon. Prudentius's terminology is fluid; later entries label Æthelwulf variously as *rex occidentalium Anglorum* (*AB* 856), *rex Anglorumsaxonum* (*AB* 855), *rex occidentalium Saxonum* (*AB* 858). The Brescia *Liber Vitae* provides *Ædeluulf rex anglorum* which is the same formulation used in the address of a fragmentary papal letter, on which see footnote 97 below.

[39] Kirby, *The Earliest English Kings*, 192, 210; S. Keynes, 'Anglo-Saxon Entries in the "Liber Vitae" of Brescia', in J. L. Nelson and M. Godden (eds), *Alfred the Wise* (Woodbridge, 1997), 99–119, at 113 n. 57. Most other commentators have attributed the mission to Æthelwulf, an error which originates in the dislocation of the chronology of the main West Saxon recension of the *Anglo-Saxon Chronicle* which places events two or three years too early, and hence appears to place Ecgberht's death in 836; *EHD* 1, trans. Whitelock, nos 124 and 187. The West Saxon regnal lists, however, note the length of his reign as 37 years and 7 months (*ASChron.* 836 recte 839) and, as he became king in 802, he is unlikely to have died before July 839; D. N. Dumville, 'The West Saxon Genealogical Regnal list: Manuscripts and Texts', *Anglia*, 104 (1986), 1–32, at 24; and *idem*, 'The West Saxon Genealogical Regnal List and the Chronology of Early Wessex', *Peritia*, 4 (1985), 21–66, at 23, 46, 49.

[40] Brooks, *The Early History*, 137, 145–46; Keynes, 'The Control of Kent', 121.

[41] Brooks, *The Early History*, 146–47, 197–203.

political landmark since it secured the commitment of the southern province of Canterbury to the nascent dynasty in Wessex, and the alliance also provided the Kentish churches with a protector who was closer to hand than the Mercian kings had ever been.[43] Given the implications of these decisions, it is not impossible that the Kingston meeting culminated in some type of ceremony which solemnized the approval of Ecgberht's lineage and recognized Æthelwulf's succession; certainly by the tenth century Kingston (which marked the place where the River Thames ceased to be tidal) had become the favoured site for West Saxon kingmaking rituals.[44] Thus, the assembly there in 838 marked the ecclesiastical sanction of Ecgberht's dynasty and symbolized, in a very real sense, the shift in power from Mercian hegemony in the south to a West Saxon one. An English king's *ordo* is thought to have provided the underlying structure for the service of coronation and anointing devised by Hincmar of Rheims for the marriage of Judith to Æthelwulf in 856; it would have been singularly appropriate if Hincmar's exemplar had been used previously to affirm Æthelwulf's regality at Kingston in 838.[45]

Æthelwulf, whom Ecgberht had made king in Kent shortly after the victory at *Ellendun* in 825,[46] is another candidate for the sponsor of the dream text and the mission to Louis in 839 – the more so since he eventually went on pilgrimage to Rome in 855 – but it is improbable that he would have wished to leave his kingdom at such a sensitive time in the transition of power to his own generation. It is much more likely that it was Ecgberht who, having secured widespread support from the secular and ecclesiastical nobility of the southern English for his son's succession, planned to end his days at the threshold of the Apostles. Following in the footsteps of his illustrious forbears Cadwalla and Ine – the latter of whom, like Ecgberht, had ruled Wessex for 37 years – this journey would have been an appropriate royal 'sacrifice' for the sake of his people, and an action which balanced the Frankish exile of his youth.[47] However, these well-laid plans came to naught. Ecgberht died in the summer of 839, a couple of

---

[42] *BCS* 421/*S* 1438 (BL Cotton Aug. II. 21, 20, and 37); an account of the palaeography is given by Brooks, *The Early History*, 323–35.

[43] Keynes, 'The Control of Kent', 124.

[44] P. Wormald, 'The Ninth Century', in J. Campbell (ed.), *The Anglo-Saxons* (Oxford, 1982), 132–57, at 140; J. Blair, *Early Medieval Surrey: Landholding, Church and Settlement before 1300* (Stroud, 1991), 99–101; S. Keynes, *The Diplomas of King Æthelred the Unready, 978–1016* (Cambridge, 1980), 270–71.

[45] Hincmar's exemplar does not survive, but for the argument that it was indeed English (and probably West Saxon) see C. Holher, 'Some Service Books of the Later Saxon Church', in D. Parsons (ed.), *Tenth-Century Studies* (London, 1975), 60–83 and J. L. Nelson, 'The Earliest Surviving Royal Ordo: Some Liturgical and Historical Aspects', in B. Tierney and P. Lineham (eds), *Authority and Power: Studies in Medieval Law and Government Presented to W. Ullmann* (Cambridge, 1980), 29–48 reprinted in her *Politics and Ritual in Early Medieval Europe* (London, 1986), 341–60, at 350–53 (subsequent references are to this reprint).

[46] *ASChron.* 823 (for 825) and *BCS* 395 / *S*271; Keynes, 'The Control of Kent', 121.

[47] *HE* V.7. On royal pilgrimages to Rome see C. Stancliffe, 'Kings who Opted Out', in Wormald et al., *Ideal and Reality in Frankish and Anglo-Saxon Society*, 154–76.

months after his envoys had spoken to Louis, and Æthelwulf inherited the kingdom of Wessex as well as Kent: consequently, the plan for a pilgrimage to Rome by a West Saxon king had to wait.[48]

Æthelwulf, Vikings, and Charles the Bald

When Æthelwulf succeeded his father to the kingdom of Wessex in the late summer of 839 he had already acquired at least a decade's experience of leadership, having been sent by his father with a large armed force into Kent at *Ellendun* in 825. Although the precise process by which West Saxon lordship was recognized in the kingdoms of the south-east is obscure (the chronology was certainly more protracted than the slick narrative of the *Chronicle* implies), it is clear from the surviving charters that the new West Saxon kings of Kent operated a system of lordship which was much more local and direct than Mercian government of the region had ever been.[49] Whereas the Mercian kings operated their interests in Kent from afar and dealt with Kentish affairs from councils and assemblies held in Mercia, Æthelwulf, as sub-king under his father and then as king in his own right, often came to Kent himself and was careful to involve the local elite in the prosecution of his objectives. After Ecgberht's death Æthelwulf continued his father's policy and gave Kent as a subkingdom first to his eldest son Æthelstan and then, after Æthelstan's death in 851x855, to his third son, Æthelberht.[50] Unlike his father, however, Æthelwulf retained for himself minting rights and the sole authority to issue charters, thereby restricting his sons' ability to establish their own patronage networks – a similar policy to that which was pursued by Charles the Bald with regard to his sons' *regna* of Neustria and Aquitaine.[51] As a matter of routine, Æthelwulf seems to have dealt with the demands of each kingdom separately.[52] For this reason, his rulership of southern England has been called schizophrenic but, in recognizing and respecting the traditional differences between the two regions of Wessex and Kent, Æthelwulf's achievements were considerable. Despite increased pressure from Viking warbands, he sustained and strengthened his father's legacy of West Saxon lordship over the kingdoms in the south-east which had no previous history of submission to Wessex and, although he never reached the heights of

---

[48] For another aborted, but well-planned, trip to Rome at about this time (837) see Astronomer, *Vita Hludovici*, c. 55.2; *Son of Charlemagne*, trans. Cabaniss, 109.

[49] Keynes, 'The Control of Kent', 124–28; *idem*, 'England 700–900', 18–42, at 40–41.

[50] *ASChron.* 836 (for 839). The date of Æthelstan's death is not known; the last record of him is in the *ASChron.* 851. His younger brother, Æthelberht, attests the most reliable of the so-called 'Decimation Charters' (S 315; *BCS* 486; *EHD* 1, trans. Whitelock, no. 89) as *rex* in 855, on which see *Alfred the Great*, trans. Keynes and Lapidge, 15, 232–34.

[51] J. L. Nelson, *Charles the Bald* (London and New York, 1992), 163–64; *idem*, 'The Frankish Kingdoms, 814–898: The West', in *NCMH* 2, 110–41, at 125.

[52] Keynes, 'The Control of Kent', 127.

'Britain-ruler' which the chronicler claimed for his father (however temporary the achievements of 829 were in reality), Æthelwulf acquired and cultivated a reputation both in Francia and in Rome that is unparalleled in the sources since the height of Offa and Coenwulf's power at the turn of the ninth century.

Æthelwulf's contacts with Francia and Rome were memorable. The contemporary evidence records the development of frequent, high-status connections between the courts of Æthelwulf and Charles the Bald in the 850s. These contacts culminated with the remarkable marriage of Æthelwulf to Charles's 12- or 13-year-old daughter, Judith, at the palace of Verberie sur L'Oise on 1 October 856. That ceremony was preceded by Æthelwulf's 'state visit' to Rome in 855 and by a preliminary mission two years previously when the young prince Alfred was the object of a solemn papal ceremony, the precedents for which are undeniably Carolingian. This earlier journey is the less well attested of the two West Saxon missions to Rome; it was recorded by the West Saxon chronicler and by Asser, and in a fragment of a letter from Pope Leo IV preserved only in a late eleventh-century collection.[53] By contrast, Æthelwulf's expedition in 855–56 is recorded in a number of contemporary sources from England, Francia and Italy: his journey is noted in the preamble of a charter granting land in Kent, and is recorded in the *Chronicle* and discussed at length by Asser; Prudentius noted both his outward and return journeys in the *Annals of St Bertin*; and his stay in Rome was recorded in some detail by the author of Benedict III's biography in the *Liber Pontificalis*.[54] In addition, the passage of Æthelwulf's party through northern Italy is recorded in the *Liber Vitae* from the church of S. Salvatore in Brescia, and the same source may also preserve a record of the earlier mission in 853.[55]

Æthelwulf's contemporary fame in Francia probably also accounts for the forged charter issued in his name on behalf of the Abbey of St Denis, near Paris.[56] The charter claims that Æthelwulf confirmed the rights of the Frankish abbey to property in Sussex and in London, supported to this effect by a forged diploma from Pope Benedict III.[57] The earliest copy of this charter was made at the turn of the thirteenth century but the claims it makes for St Denis to English property are made in other forged charters issued in the names of King Offa

---

[53] *ASChron.* 853; Asser, *Vita Alfredi*, c. 8, 11. See also Kirby, *The Earliest English Kings*, 198–204 and footnote 97 below.

[54] S 315; *EHD* 1, trans. Whitelock, no. 89; *ASChron.* 855–58; Asser, *Vita Alfredi*, c. 11–17; *AB* 855–56; *Liber Pontificalis*, no. 106, c. 34.

[55] S. Keynes, 'Anglo-Saxon Entries', 99–120. The *Liber Vitae* is now Brescia, Biblioteca Queriniana, MS G.VI.7, on which see A. Angenendt et al. (eds), *Der Memorial- und Liturgiecodex von San Salvatore/Santa Giulia in Brescia*, MGH *Libri memoriales et necrologia*, n.s. 4 (Hanover, 2000).

[56] H. Atsma and J. Vezin, 'Le dossier suspect des possessions de St. Denis en Angleterre revisité (VIIIe–IXe siècles)', in MGH *Schriften* 33.4, *Falschungen im Mittelalter* 4, *Diplomatische Fälschungen* 2 (Hanover, 1988), Vol. 4, 211–36, at 218–19.

[57] S214; E. E. Barker, 'Sussex Anglo-Saxon Charters, Part 2', *Sussex Archaeological Collections*, 87 (1948), 112–63, no. 23. Atsma and Vezin, 'Le dossier suspect', 217; *PL* 115, col. 701–2.

(757–96) and King Edgar (959–77).[58] These other charters are copied on insular-style parchment in hands which mimic pre-Conquest insular minuscule, thus implying that the forgers had access to genuine Anglo-Saxon charter material. The claims made in these documents on behalf of St Denis are a blatant exercise in late eleventh-century opportunism, but it is a sign of Æthelwulf's reputation at that time (alongside those of Offa and Edgar) that a later medieval forger thought that his reign provided a plausible context for a lucrative grant to a Frankish monastery.

The reasons behind this intensification of activity between the West Saxon, West Frankish and papal courts in the 850s have been much discussed, with particular importance being attached to the escalation of Viking attacks on western Europe in the same period.[59] Sources from Ireland and Francia, as well as Anglo-Saxon England, demonstrate independently that, from the mid-830s, attacks by seaborne pirates were increasing in scale and frequency across western Europe. In Francia the damage was exacerbated by the civil conflict between Louis the Pious and his sons; not only did the unstable political situation provide openings for opportunistic raids but Carolingian princes encouraged attacks by Northmen on rivals' resources.[60] Particularly vulnerable were the coastal trading emporia; Dorestad was attacked annually from 834–37 in raids which (the annalists claimed) were encouraged by Lothar as a means of damaging his father's reputation and resources.[61] Encouraged by the profitability of such ventures, greater numbers of Northmen began to plunder communities on both sides of the Channel and along the coast of Aquitaine. The Frankish and Anglo-Saxon sources make two things clear: first, the highly mobile raiding groups could move across the Channel unhindered and at will; and, second, chroniclers in Francia and Anglo-Saxon England heard about and recorded attacks on both sides of the Channel. This implies that, despite the danger, messages and news were still able to be exchanged. For example, in its entry for 842 the *Chronicle* recorded an attack on Quentovic as well as raids closer to home in London and Rochester. In Francia, the soldier–historian Nithard noted attacks on Hamwic and Northannwic in England, in addition to the attack on Quentovic, during the same year.[62]

---

[58] S133, S686; Atsma and Vezin, 'Le dossier suspect', 215–19, 225–27; Barker, 'Sussex Anglo-Saxon Charters', 118–26 nos 18–19.

[59] Nelson, 'England and the Franks '; M. J. Enright, 'Charles the Bald and Aethelwulf of Wessex: The Alliance of 856 and Strategies of Royal Succession', *JMH*, 5 (1979), 291–302; P. Stafford, 'Charles the Bald, Judith and England', in M. T. Gibson and J. L. Nelson (eds), *Charles the Bald: Court and Kingdom*, (2nd edn) (Aldershot, 1990), 139–53; Stenton, *Anglo-Saxon England*, 245; E. John, *Reassessing Anglo-Saxon England* (Manchester, 1996), 71–72.

[60] S. Coupland, 'The Vikings in Francia and Anglo-Saxon England to 911', in *NCMH*, 2, 190–201, at 192.

[61] AB 841; Nithard, *Historiarum Libri IV,* IV.2, *Carolingian Chronicles*, trans. B. W. Scholtz (Ann Arbor, MI, 1970), 166–7.

[62] *ASChron.* 839 (recte 842); Nithard, *Historiarum Libri IV*, IV.3; *Carolingian Chronicles*, trans. Scholz, 167.

The success of these attacks, and the lack of organized resistance to them, encouraged a further change in Viking tactics, with warbands choosing to remain through the winter in the west rather than returning to their Danish (or Irish) bases as they had done previously.[63] In 851 Vikings from Aquitaine overwintered for the first time on the Seine. The 850–51 campaigning season also saw an escalation in the scale of the Viking assault on Anglo-Saxon England, and comparable developments in military tactics and in the size and number of hostile warbands. The *Anglo-Saxon Chronicle* for 851 records five separate strikes in Æthelwulf's realms in southern England, a tenfold increase in the size of the fleet which sailed into the Thames, and its first record of Vikings overwintering on Anglo-Saxon territory on the Isle of Thanet.[64] The Frankish annalists interpreted these attacks, and those on northern Frankish coasts, as an indirect result of feuding and warfare in Denmark itself.[65] Whatever the cause, this escalation in Viking aggression in the 840s and early 850s had serious implications for the immediate security and longer-term stability of the Frankish and Anglo-Saxon kingdoms that were the targets of the Viking warmongers. This increasingly hostile environment provides one important context for Æthelwulf's interest in Rome and Francia. It is a key question for historians of Wessex and Francia alike whether the intensification of Viking hostility in these years drove domestic policy or was incidental to it; a secondary issue is whether the Viking threat was sufficiently grave that an alliance against a mutual enemy was the catalyst for a closer alliance between Æthelwulf and Charles.

Æthelwulf's actions in the 850s have not always been viewed in a positive light; rather like the Emperor Louis, his legacy has been clouded by accusations of excessive piety which (to modern sensibilities at least) has seemed at odds with the demands of early medieval kingship.[66] This impression is founded partly on early medieval accounts, particularly from Asser, which emphasized Æthelwulf's religiosity and preference for consensus politics. Similar traits of governmental style have often been regarded negatively by historians of ninth-century Francia as evidence of the rise of aristocratic power at the expense of king and empire.[67] Describing the king's last will and testament, Asser empha-

---

[63] '*Insulam quandam ingressi, convectis a continentibus domibus, hiemare velut perpetuis sedibus statuerunt*'; *AB* 843; *AB*, trans. Nelson, 55–56, nn. 1, 3; Coupland 'The Vikings in Francia and Anglo-Saxon England', 193–96.

[64] *ASChron.* 851. The annalist records a fleet of 350 ships, ten times bigger than the fleets of 836, 840 and 843. This relative increase is surely what is implied, rather than a literal count of enemy ships; P. H. Sawyer, *The Age of the Vikings* (London, 1971), 125–26; N. P. Brooks, 'England in the Ninth Century: The Crucible of Defeat', *TRHS*, 5th ser. 29 (1979), 1–20. *Alfred the Great*, trans. Keynes and Lapidge, 13, 210–11. Asser has the Isle of Sheppey not Thanet; ibid., 68, 231.

[65] *AF* 850, 854; *AB* 850, 854; Nelson, *Charles the Bald*, 181.

[66] On Louis's piety and epithets see B. Simson, *Jahrbücher des fränkischen Reichs unter Ludwig dem Frommen* (Leipzig, 1876), 1, 33–46 and T. F. X. Noble, 'Louis the Pious and his Piety Re-reconsidered', *Revue belge de philologie et d'historie*, 58 (1980), 297–316.

[67] For references and discussion on this point see Nelson, 'Legislation and Consensus', 92 and 108.

sized Æthelwulf's dispositions for the sake of his soul, 'which from the first flower of his youth he was keen to care for in all respects'. The king's deep devotion was further asserted when he booked (by charter) a tenth of his land to the churches of his kingdom 'for the sake of his soul and those of his predecessors' before leaving for Rome in 855.[68] On his return in 856, it is not with any great sense of enthusiasm that Asser describes the concessions made by Æthelwulf to his rebellious elder son to avoid the threat of civil war; with 'indescribable forbearance' Æthelwulf partitioned the kingdom in a manner which Asser evidently considered was demeaning to the status of the senior ruler and to the dignity of the kingdom as a whole.[69] Stenton has referred to Æthelwulf as 'a religious and unambitious man, for whom engagement in war and politics was an unwelcome consequence of rank'; to others, he 'appears to have been an impractical religious enthusiast' and a king of 'more than conventional piety'.[70] His reputation for 'dramatic piety' has been artificially enhanced by the traditional, but misplaced, association of the 839 dream story in the *Annals of St Bertin* with Æthelwulf rather than his father, alongside the better attested evidence of Æthelwulf's sponsorship of two formal West Saxon missions to Rome in 853 and 855, one of which he made himself. Lurking unsaid is the distasteful suspicion that the king was in some way irresponsible in electing to go to Rome himself just at the point when Viking warbands had started to overwinter on the Anglo-Saxon mainland and thus began (with the benefit of hindsight) to threaten the fundamental structure of Anglo-Saxon society. Æthelwulf's engagement in continental politics can thus be presented in the light of a personal piety pursued at the expense of the needs of his kingdom, combined with a need to acquire Frankish support against pagan hostilities with which he was increasingly unable to cope.[71] In this light, his decision to marry Charles's daughter has been described as 'the folly of a man senile before his time' and, in a more measured way, as an early example of a series of cross-Channel matrimonial alliances brokered in response to increasingly serious Viking aggression.[72]

A more optimistic view sees rather more reason for confidence in Æthelwulf's Wessex. Key to this is the evidence, as presented by the partisan voices of the *Chronicle*, that in the 840s and early 850s West Saxon armies were in fact gaining the upper hand in campaigns against the Vikings, despite the unambiguous evi-

---

[68] Asser, *Vita Alfredi*, c. 11 and 16. On Æthelwulf's so-called decimation charters (all bar one of which are suspect in their current form) see *Alfred the Great*, trans. Keynes and Lapidge, 232–34, and *EHD* 1, trans. Whitelock, no 89.

[69] Asser, *Vita Alfredi*, c. 12–13.

[70] Stenton, *Anglo-Saxon England*, 245. See also Enright, 'Charles the Bald and Aethelwulf of Wessex', 291; Wormald, 'The Ninth Century', 140.

[71] J. M. Wallace-Hadrill, 'The Franks and the English in the Ninth Century: Some Common Historical Interests', *History* (1950), 202–18, at 212; Stenton, *Anglo-Saxon England*, 245.

[72] R. H. Hodgkin, *A History of the Anglo-Saxons* (Oxford, 1935), 514, cited by Enright, 'Charles the Bald and Aethelwulf of Wessex', 291; Stafford, 'Charles the Bald, Judith and England', 143.

dence from both sides of the Channel that, in the same period, Viking warbands were growing larger and becoming more persistent in their attacks. During Æthelwulf's reign the *Chronicle* records only one definitive defeat of a West Saxon army led by the king – at Carhampton in 843. The language of the *Chronicle* is equivocal concerning battles at Portland in 840 and Thanet in 853 in which experienced ealdormen were killed and which must have been serious setbacks for the West Saxons; but on both those occasions the *Chronicle* mitigates the negative impact by claiming initial successes for the West Saxon and/or Kentish forces. Of four other clashes during Æthelwulf's reign where a 'great slaughter' is recorded and the Anglo-Saxons seem to have come off worse, none explicitly involved a West Saxon army – though the death of the Kentish ealdorman Hereberht 'and many men with him' at Romney Marsh in 841 was undoubtedly a blow to the West Saxon hegemonic reputation in the south-east.[73]

However, this patchwork of Viking victories is outweighed in the chronicler's account (and entirely eclipsed in Asser's) by records of West Saxon successes against Vikings; of particular significance was Æthelwulf's triumph, with Æthelbald's assistance, at *Aclea* in 851. This followed a victory by a contingent of Devon soldiers under the command of Ealdorman Ceorl and was consolidated by yet another victory the same year, this time at Sandwich in Kent, with an army led by Æthelstan and Ealdorman Ealhhere. The *Chronicle* does not disguise or minimize the reality of the threat caused by the Vikings in Æthelwulf's reign, but it does emphasize victories of armies led by Æthelwulf or his sons. Although the *Chronicle* is not, strictly speaking, a contemporary source for the mid-ninth century and is partial in its coverage of the Viking raids for the earlier part of the century,[74] its account does make it clear that the achievements of the West Saxon armies against the Vikings in 851 were immensely important. The late ninth-century chronicler lays bare the long-term psychological significance of Æthelwulf's victory at *Aclea* against the large Viking army which had already attacked London and Canterbury and had routed the army of the Mercian king; it was 'the greatest slaughter of a heathen army that we have ever heard of until this present day'.[75]

These West Saxon triumphs in 851 provided a stark contrast to the rout of Mercian forces and King Berhtwulf's flight from London in the same year. Æthelwulf's military reputation was boosted further in 853 when the new Mercian king, Burgred, in consultation with his council, requested Æthelwulf's help with a campaign against the Welsh. Soon afterwards, this new military alliance with Mercia was ritually sealed by the marriage of Æthelwulf's daughter, Æthelswith, to Burgred. The ceremony was held at Chippenham on West Saxon territory and, in line with Mercian practice and in an important precedent for the events of

---

[73] *ASChron.* 841 recording conflict in Kent, Lindsey and East Anglia; *ASChron.* 842 recording a great slaughter in London, Quentavic, and Rochester; *ASChron.* 851 against the Mercians.

[74] Brooks, 'The Development of Military Obligations', 42–43.

[75] *ASChron.* ABC 851; Asser, *Vita Alfredi*, c. 3–5.

856, Æthelswith was probably made Burgred's queen as well as his wife – she certainly attests later with the title *regina*.[76] This background of considerable military successes and renewed alliance with Mercia provides a second essential context for Æthelwulf's flirtation with continental politics – his elder sons had proved themselves winners in battle against Vikings and his daughter was joined in a prestigious marriage to a military ally. In 853 Æthelwulf's outlook was good.

Æthelwulf in the Frankish sources: Prudentius, Lupus and Felix

Information about Æthelwulf's Wessex continued to reach Prudentius who, 'still scribbling away at many things', continued to include information from Britain in the years after Ecgberht's death, although after 843 the character of his annals changed as he was no longer writing from the court, having been promoted to the bishopric of Troyes.[77] After that date, his annals reflect his rather more provincial perspective and, following the division of the empire at the Treaty of Verdun, are more narrowly focused on the West Frankish kingdom of Charles the Bald.[78] Although he occasionally recorded information which came his way concerning events in Lothar's Middle Kingdom or from the East Frankish kingdom of Louis the German, Prudentius's remaining annals overwhelmingly focus on events in West Francia and on the activities of Charles the Bald. Consequently, after 843 the entries in the *Annals of St Bertin* lack the close focus on events at the palace and cease to have the same role as an 'official' record. Distant from court, Prudentius could be more critical of the king, more partial in his narrative, and more political in his omissions. He remained in touch, though, with wider events and maintained (in so far as he was able) a running commentary on the progress of hostile Viking armies around the coasts and rivers of Francia, Frisia and the British Isles. Reminiscent of his record of the arrivals of envoys from the English king in 839 is that for 848 in which he recorded a major victory by the Irish against a group of Vikings to whom they had been forced to make regular tribute payments. As a consequence of this victory, Irish envoys brought gifts to Charles seeking permission for their king to travel through Francia on pilgrimage to Rome and, moreover, to forge a treaty of 'peace and friendship'.[79] In a vivid echo of Einhard's eulogy on the relationship between

---

[76] She is named *regina* in the Brescia *Liber Vitae* (fo. 31v); footnote 55 *supra*. The inscription on the gold ring from Aberford also calls her "Queen Æthelswith'; Webster and Backhouse, *The Making of England*, no. 244.

[77] Nelson, 'The Annals of St. Bertin', 179–85. In *AB* 861 Hincmar of Reims (who had his own agenda) noted that Prudentius died 'still scribbling away at many things that were mutually contradictory and contrary to Faith'.

[78] *AB* 843; *AF* 843.

[79] *AB* 847 and 848: ... *rex Scottorum ad Karolum pacis et amicitiae gratia legatos cum muneribus mittit* ... ; Nelson, *Charles the Bald*, 155–56 and *idem*, 'The Annals of St. Bertin', 179.

the kings of the *Scotti* and Charlemagne, Prudentius's entry for 848 is a reminder that Irish rulers also regarded the Frankish king as an important benefactor
and ally in times of need, and that Charles (like his grandfather) was happy to
encourage such an expression of indebtedness by distant rulers.[80]

Prudentius's information about Viking attacks on the English is noticeably
restricted to conflict with Wessex. He records in 844 the defeat of the English
forces after a three-day battle but then has no further information until the
entries for 850 and 860 in which he makes passing reference to Anglo-Saxon
victories in the context of Viking attacks on Francia. In none of these cases does
he record the location of the battle or the names of the combatants, although his
comments are sufficient to link the incidents he mentions with battles fought by
Æthelwulf at Carhampton in 843 and in the campaign of 850–51, and the victory
for the men of Hampshire and Berkshire over 'a great ship-army' that had
attacked Winchester in 860 after campaigning in the Somme valley.[81] From
Prudentius's perspective in Troyes, the Viking impact on England was significant in so far as it provided the Vikings with an alternative target to the Frankish
kingdom. Yet the fact that he was able to record these sparse but accurate details
about West Saxon and Irish conflicts with the Vikings demonstrates that in the
mid-ninth century the Channel was by no means an impassable domain of
Viking pirates.

Frankish knowledge of Æthelwulf's victory against the pagans in 851 and
his status within Anglo-Saxon England is demonstrated further in a series of
letters written by Lupus, abbot of the monastery at Ferrières and its dependent
cell at St Judoc's. Lupus was not only a close friend of Einhard and a bibliophile
and voracious scholar of classical literature, but was also one of the most
prolific letter writers of his day.[82] Four letters survive to correspondents in
England (including Æthelwulf) which seem to have been written in 852 shortly
after Lupus had reclaimed the ownership of St Judoc's which had been granted
to Ferrières by Louis the Pious but disputed between his quarrelling sons.[83] St
Judoc's was located close to Quentovic and had customarily provided hospitality
for Anglo-Saxon travellers and pilgrims, having been given to Alcuin by Charle-

---

See also Chapter 2, above, 53–54 for the use of the same expression by other, Anglo-Saxon, kings.
Doyle has suggested that Sedulius Scottus may have left Ireland in 848 and travelled to Francia
with this group; *Sedulius Scottus: On Christian Rulers and The Poems*, trans. E. G. Doyle
(Binghampton, 1983), 12.

[80] Einhard, *VK*, Ch. 16; *Charlemagne's Courtier: The Complete Einhard*, trans. P. E. Dutton
(Peterborough, Ontario, 1998), 25–26.

[81] *AB* 844, 850, 860; *ASChron.* 840 (for 843), 851, 860.

[82] *Loup de Ferrières: Correspondence*, ed. L. Levillain Les Classiques de l'Histoire de
France au Moyen Age, 2 vols (Paris, 1927–35); *The Letters of Lupus of Ferrières*, trans. G. W.
Regenos (The Hague, 1966).

[83] Lupus, *Ep.* nos 84–87 and see, below, 243–44; R. McKitterick, *The Frankish Kingdoms
under the Carolingians 751–987* (London, 1983), 181–82; Stafford, 'Charles the Bald, Judith and
England', 140–42. For Lupus's 19 letters on the subject of the loss of St Judoc's see Lupus, *Ep.* nos
19, 32, 36, 42–43, 45, 47–50, 60, 62, 65, 82, 84, 86–87.

magne for that purpose.[84] With the monastery restored to him, Lupus was able to tap into the collective memory of its members and to the network of news from England of which it was invariably a part. While at St Judoc's Lupus learned – or at least had it confirmed – that the most powerful king among the Anglo-Saxons was Æthelwulf of Wessex, who had recently defeated the 'foes of Christ', a reference probably to the West Saxons' victory over the Vikings at *Aclea* in 851, news of which had also reached Prudentius at Troyes. 'Lowliest' Lupus is effusive in his praise of the king's piety, the strength of his rule and the fervour of his faith; he prays that Æthelwulf 'may be invincible against the enemies of the Christian name'.[85] This much (and probably more) Lupus had heard from contact with Æthelwulf's notary, a Frank named Felix who was responsible for the king's official letters.[86] Felix also received a letter from Lupus, reminding him of the occasion when they had met at the monastery of Faremoûtiers-en-Brie and asking him to intercede with his master on Lupus's behalf.[87] These letters provide the only direct information about Felix and his duties at the West Saxon court; they offer a tantalizing glimpse of the presence of a Frank close to Æthelwulf in the early 850s, on whose influence on the literate culture of the West Saxon court we can but speculate.[88]

The object of Lupus's letters was a petition to Æthelwulf for a gift of lead with which to repair the roof of the church at Ferrières. In the accompanying letter, he asked Felix to press the king to this act of Christian charity and to oversee the transport of the metal across the Channel to the village of Étaples, near Quentovic. The request implies that Æthelwulf had access to scarce lead resources, probably from the Mendip hills in Somerset where quantities of lead had certainly been extracted in the Roman period.[89] In exchange, Lupus offered

---

[84] On Alcuin's use of St Judoc's see Alcuin, *Ep.* no. 230; *Alcuin of York*, trans. Allott, no. 51 and Lupus, *Ep.* no. 18.

[85] ... *omnium servorum Dei ultimus Lupus*, like Cathwulf's address to Charlemagne; Lupus, *Ep.* no. 84; *EHD* 1, trans. Whitelock, no. 217.

[86] ... *qui epistolarum vestrarum officio fungebatur*. This comment has raised much debate over Frankish influence on the production of charters in Æthelwulf's 'chancery'; *Asser's Life of King Alfred*, ed. Stevenson, 203, 225–26 modified by P. Chaplais, 'The Origin and Authenticity of the Royal Anglo-Saxon Diploma', *Journal of the Society of Archivists*, 3.2 (1965), 48–61, reprinted in *Prisca Munimenta*, ed. F. Ranger (London, 1973), 28–42 at 37–38. See also M. P. Parsons, 'Some Scribal Memoranda for Anglo-Saxon Charters of the Eighth and Ninth Centuries', *Mitteilungen des Österreichischen Instituts für Geschichtsforschung*, 14 (1939), 13–32. If Felix was responsible for drafting Æthelwulf's letters to Frankish and papal recipients what impact would such letters have had on their recipients? Would the form and script of the letters have made Æthelwulf seem more familiar to Frankish eyes, and what would the pope have made of a letter from an Anglo-Saxon king written, perhaps, in Caroline minuscule?

[87] Lupus, *Ep.* no. 85; *EHD* 1, trans. Whitelock, no. 218.

[88] On the use, in southern England, of parchment prepared in continental style see M. P. Brown, 'Continental Symptoms in Insular Codicology: Historical Perspective', in P. Rück ed., *Pergament: Geschichte, Struktur, Restaurierung, Herstellung* (Sigmaringen, 1991), 57–62.

[89] A lead 'pig' produced in Britain during the reign of Nero (54–68) was recovered near the mouth of the Somme just south of Étaples. Similar lead pigs of Vespasianic date (69–79) have been

the king the prayers of his brethren and any other service which would be of assistance to the king. Lupus's request for lead from an English king recalls similar correspondence from the likes of Alcuin and Einhard. In 834 Einhard had written to Abbot Fulco of the monastery of St Wandrille about a delivery of lead to cover the roof of his new church at Seligenstadt.[90] It is possible, given the location of St Wandrille's on the Channel coast and the traditional role of the abbey in the management of cross-Channel trade and diplomacy, that Einhard's lead was also an English export.[91] But, unlike Lupus, Einhard had to pay hard cash to secure his supplies of the metal. Some years earlier Alcuin had sent a gift of tin weighing a hundred pounds to cover the bell-tower of the church at York.[92] Pope Hadrian I had also managed to extract a gift of lead from Charlemagne and, like Lupus, tried to persuade the donor to deal with the transport of the material, asking Charlemagne to send his gift in small parcels in the diplomatic baggage of the emissaries whom he would, in any case, have been sending to Rome so as to circumvent the involvement of merchants.[93]

Whether Æthelwulf conceded to Lupus's request is not known but the abbot and his monasteries at St Judoc's and Ferrières were well placed to assist with Æthelwulf's own ambitious plans to travel to Rome. The timing of Lupus's request neatly precedes the reference in the *Anglo-Saxon Chronicle* to a West Saxon mission to Rome in 853. The precedent of missions from Wessex in 839 and Ireland in 848 as recorded in the *Annals of St Bertin* suggest that, in the mid-ninth century, it was 'normal practice' to send an advance party to consult with the authorities in Francia in order to obtain the necessary permissions and to ensure an appropriate reception for a king who wished to follow on pilgrimage to Rome.[94] On this pattern, if a mission was sent from Wessex some time before 855 in order to lay the ground for the grand pilgrimage planned for Æthelwulf, it is likely that the *Chronicle* entry for 853 encapsulates a record of such a journey. The 853

---

found at the Roman fort of *Clausentum*, on Southampton Water, indicating the probable place of export of West Country lead across the Channel; see B. Cunliffe, *Wessex to AD 1000* (London, 1993), 229–30, 259, 323.

[90] Einhard, *Ep.* no. 36, ed. K. Hampe, MGH Epp. V; *Charlemagne's Courtier*, trans. Dutton, 154–55. A charter of 835 records the annual payment of 300 shillings of lead by a Mercian ealdorman named Hunberht to the Archbishop of Canterbury in lieu of land at Wirksworth, Derbyshire; S1624, *BCS* 414; Keynes, 'The Control of Kent', 124; Wormald, 'The Ninth Century', 143.

[91] On Abbot Gervold's dual role as tax collector at Quentovic and royal envoy to England see Ch. XII.2 of the *Acts of the Abbots of Fontanelle* and above 184–88; *Gesta sanctorum patrum Fontanellensis coenobii*, ed. F. Lohier and J. Laporte (Rouen and Paris, 1936), 86–87; *EHD* 1, trans. Whitelock, no. 20. On the mission of the *praefectus* of Quentovic, Grippo, to Britain and the miraculous intercession of St Wandrille on his behalf, see Stafford, 'Charles the Bald, Judith, and England', 142.

[92] Alcuin, *Ep.* no. 226.

[93] P. Grierson, 'Commerce in the Dark Ages: A Critique of the Evidence', *TRHS*, 5th ser. 9 (1959), 123–40, at 128–29.

[94] For another example – but going in the other direction – see the account of the journey of Stephen IV to Francia; *Annales regni Francorum*, 816.

mission looks rather like a preliminary, fact-finding journey of that type. Lupus's offer to 'be ready in anything possible that you may ask of us', and his acquaintance with Felix would have provided Æthelwulf with a ready-made network of contacts to facilitate the logistical organization of such an ambitious enterprise. Lupus had himself been to Rome in 849–50 as an agent of Charles the Bald and thus had had recent experience of the logistics of such a journey. Keynes's suggestion that Marcward, once a monk at Ferrières and then abbot of the royal monastery at Prüm until his retirement in 853, may have accompanied Æthelwulf over the Alps into Italy in 855 points additionally to the involvement of Lupus's circle of contacts in the planning and execution of the West Saxon missions of the 850s.[95] Marcward was a frequent recipient of letters from Lupus and his name is found immediately after Æthelwulf's in the Brescia *Liber Vitae*.[96]

The mission of 853 was not noted by Prudentius in his annals despite the fact that he had attended the king's councils at Soissons and Quierzy in April and May of that year and may be expected to have heard about a West Saxon mission had it passed through northern Francia in the spring. But two other sources (one of which is in a contemporary manuscript) allude to the journey; the *Liber Vitae* of S. Salvatore in Brescia and part of a letter from Pope Leo IV to King Æthelwulf. The fragmentary papal letter survives in a single canon-law collection of *c.* 1100,[97] but the Brescia *Liber Vitae* is contemporary and, rather like a ninth-century visitors' book, includes two groups of Anglo-Saxon names.[98] Keynes has argued that the first group of names (on fol. 27v) relates to the two West Saxon missions of 853 and 855, whereas a second, distinct group of names at the top of fol. 31v are more obviously linked to a pilgrimage made in 874 by King Burgred of Mercia, his West Saxon queen, Æthelswith, and their companions.[99] Both these sources support the *Chronicle* entry for 853 which claims that Æthelwulf's youngest son, Alfred, was included in the West Saxon party which travelled to Rome in that year. Alfred is the subject of the fragment of Leo's letter and his name is placed second in the primary group of Anglo-Saxon names

[95] Keynes, 'Anglo-Saxon Entries', 108, 114. On the suggestion that Marcward may have retired to Ferrières in 853 (rather than staying at Prüm) see Becher, 'Das königliche Frauenkloster', 379.

[96] Lupus, *Ep.* nos 18, 28, 30, 33, 35, 58, 60, 65, 68, 70, 77, 83, 88, and also nos 5, 11, 110.

[97] The so-called *Collectio Britannica* (now BL MS Add. 8873, a central Italian manuscript of the late eleventh century), on which see W. Ullmann, '"Nos si aliquid incompetenter … " Some Observations on the Register of Fragments of Leo IV in the Collectio Britannica', *Ephemerides Iuris Canonici*, 9 (1953), 3–11, reprinted as c. 7 in his *The Church and the Law in the Earlier Middle Ages* (London, 1975); Nelson, 'The Problem of King Alfred's Royal Anointing', 311; A. P. Smyth, *King Alfred the Great* (1995), 13. R. Somerville and S. Kuttner, *Pope Urban II, the Collectio Britannica, and the Council of Melfi (1089)* (Oxford, 1996). The extract of Leo's letter is edited in MGH *Epistolae Karolini Aevi* III, *Epistolae* 5 (Berlin, 1899), no. 31; *EHD* 1, trans. Whitelock, no. 219. The letter is not found in Leo IV's register.

[98] Keynes, 'Anglo-Saxon Entries', 107–10.

[99] Ibid., Angenendt, *Der Memorial- und Liturgiecodex*, 92–93, Pl. 27v (A2–B2) and Pl. 31v (B1,2–C1,2). On the circumstances for the later mission see *ASChron.* 874.

in the Brescia manuscript. Alfred's name in the *Liber Vitae* is preceded by that of his elder brother, Æthelred, which implies by analogy that he too was part of the expedition. However, Æthelred's name is not included in any other account; either he did not complete the journey to Rome or, more probably, given their Alfredian date of compilation, sources such as the *Chronicle* and Asser's *Life* focused on the participation of Alfred at the expense of his less distinguished elder brother.[100] Likewise, the surviving extract from Pope Leo's letter is so short that, as it stands, it can prove nothing about the actions of other participants in the 853 mission.

The fragment of Pope Leo's letter to Æthelwulf briefly describes a ceremony performed by the pope on the young West Saxon prince. If we can accept that Leo's letter is genuine and that the fragment is unadulterated in its current form – its late and fragmentary preservation engender reasonable caution on this point – careful account must be taken of the extract, which is precise in its terminology and specific in the ceremony it describes, the emphasis of which was secular and military. Because he 'gave himself into our hands', Leo decorated Alfred 'as a spiritual son, with the dignity of the belt and the vestments of the consulate, as is customary with Roman consuls'.[101] The allusion to Roman imperial custom is important; military and civic status was defined and displayed by regalia that was strictly controlled and classified according to rank. Buckled sword-belts (known from the third century as *cinguli*) and cloak brooches (*fibuli*) were particularly significant as 'badges of office'.[102] The sophisticated system of display used in the late Roman Empire in the West was certainly known in Carolingian circles through the illustrated text known as the *Notitia Dignitatum*, at least one copy of which was available in Francia at this time.[103] In early medieval contexts the *cingulum militare* retained its symbolic, as well as practical, significance as a sign of a masculinity, social rank, free status and military service; gifts of such gear reflected the donor's endorsement of a recipient's status as well as reinforcing the bonds and expectations between them.[104]

---

[100] Keynes argues that Æthelred did not reach Rome and that Alfred travelled on alone; Keynes 'Anglo-Saxon Entries', 112–13.

[101] ' ... *quasi spiritalem filium consulatus cinguli honore vestimentisque, ut mos est Romanis consulibus, decoravimus* ... '; *Epistolae selectae Leonis IV*, MGH Epp. V, no. 31.

[102] M. C. Bishop and J. C. N. Coulston, *Roman Military Equipment from the Punic Wars to the Fall of Rome* (London, 1993), 96–98, 173–79.

[103] J. J. G. Alexander, 'The Illustrated Manuscripts of the *Notitia Dignitatum*', in R. Goodman and P. Bartholomew (eds), *Aspects of the Notitia Dignitatum*, BAR Suppl. Ser. 15 (Oxford, 1976), 11–25, at 19–20. On the interpretation of the images showing the regalia of rank see P. C. Berger, *The Insignia of the Notitia Dignitatum* (London and New York, 1981).

[104] This has a particular bearing on Charlemagne's gift to Offa of a baldric (*baletus*), sword and silken cloaks from the Avar hoard. See K. Leyser, 'Early Medieval Canon Law and the Beginnings of Knighthood', in L. Fenske et al. (eds), *Institutionen, Kultur und Gesselschaft im Mittelalter* (Sigmaringen, 1984), 549–66, reprinted in T. Reuter (ed.), *Communications and Power in Medieval Europe: The Carolingian and Ottonian Centuries* (London, 1994), 51–73, at 55–64. See also Alcuin's use of the work; Alcuin, *Ep.* no. 240 and 257; *Alcuin of York*, trans. Allott, no. 69 and 70.

Ninth-century canon law demanded that penitents or those accused of serious crimes were ritually 'unmanned' – required to relinquish their sword-belt and to refrain from sexual activity with their wives.[105] Equally, the girding of a sword-belt marked a right of passage into manhood and adult responsibility. In royal contexts donning a sword-belt also symbolized 'kingworthiness' in a prince who was destined for a secular rather than an ecclesiastical career.

Carolingian examples are plentiful: the Astronomer describes how, having reached the age of majority (14), Louis was summoned to Regensburg in 791 and girded with a sword. A similar ceremony was performed by Louis on Charles (the Bald) during the public assembly at Quierzy in 838 as a prelude to crowning and the receipt of a kingdom.[106] There are examples of papal involvement too; the best parallel to Alfred's experience in 853 is given in the *Annals of St Bertin* for 844 when Lothar's son Louis II, accompanied by his great-uncle Bishop Drogo of Metz, was sent to Rome and was 'received with due honour by the pope [Sergius II] who, when negotiations had been concluded, consecrated Louis king by anointing him and invested him with a sword-belt (*cingulo decoravit*)'.[107] The political context of that particular ceremony was as much a show of strength by Lothar in the aftermath of an unauthorized papal election as a move to establish the credentials of his son, but it was undoubtedly Carolingian precedents of this sort that the pope and his advisers had in mind when the West Saxon party turned up in Rome.

The ceremony performed by Leo on Alfred in 853, though, had two differences: first, there is no equivalent reference to papal anointing in Leo IV's letter; and, second, Alfred was only four years old at the time, very much younger than the age of majority. For this reason alone, the 853 ceremony should be regarded as more-than-usually aspirational in tone – of status desired rather than status attained. In that sense, Alfred's experience recollects the occasion in November 753 when Charlemagne, aged only five, was sent by his father at the head of a procession to meet Pope Stephen II who had made an unprecedented crossing of the Alps to seek out the Franks as protectors of the papacy, and who ritualized the new relationship through the ceremonial anointing of Pippin and his family at St Denis the following year. Similar also to Alfred's experiences are the accounts of ceremonies in 781 when Charlemagne brought two of his infant sons to Rome to be baptized and anointed as kings of Aquitaine and Italy by Pope Hadrian I, although that event (more than 70 years earlier) is

---

[105] Leyser, 'Early Medieval Canon Law', 59–61. For the use of the term in mid-ninth-century canon law formulated at the councils of Mainz (October 847 and October 852) and Pavia (850) see, MGH Conc. III, no. 14, c. 20 and c. 24; no. 23, c. 12; no. 26, c. 11. For a contemporary example see the west Frankish annalist's account of the 'lunacy' of Charles the Fat; *AB* 873.

[106] Nithard, *Libri Historiarum IV*, 1.6; *AB*, 838, Astronomer, *Vita Hludovici imperatoris*, c. 59. On this passage see J. L. Nelson, 'Ninth-century Knighthood', 75–87, at 84.

[107] *AB* 844: *honorifice suscepti sunt, peractoque negotio, Hludowicum pontifex Romanus unctionem in regem consecratum cingulo decoravit.* See also *AB* 850 for the imperial anointing of Louis II in Rome that year; and *The Annals of St. Bertin*, trans. Nelson, 57 n. 3, 69.

unlikely to have been the primary inspiration for the actors in the 853 events. But if Alfred had indeed been accompanied by his elder brother Æthelred, the parallel with the events of 781 is even closer. Enriched and enrobed (like Benjamin at Pharaoh's court) Alfred could return home bringing glory on his father's house.[108]

The claim made in the *Chronicle* (elaborated by Asser) that Alfred was also consecrated (*gehalgod*) or anointed (*unxit*) to kingship by Pope Leo IV in the manner of a Carolingian king has naturally generated copious debate.[109] Many have suspected that this entry was either entirely false or had been embellished by a later contributor to the *Chronicle*, who wrote during Alfred's reign when the king's reputation was assured and who wilfully misinterpreted papal ceremonies of confirmation and ritual investiture with arms to include kingmaking rituals.[110] The entry certainly has a hagiographical ring to it, predicting greatness in a young child. Others have suggested that Æthelwulf may have used the mission to mark out Alfred, as the youngest of his five sons, for a career in the Church, and that the ceremonies in Rome in 853 were in fact preparing him for life in the clergy. Some have doubted whether Alfred went to Rome at all in 853, arguing that Asser's claim that the young boy went for a second time with his father in 855 was projected back by the chronicler to the genuine preliminary mission 853 in order to engineer a meeting between Alfred and a pope with the auspicious name of Leo.[111] By the time Æthelwulf reached Rome in 855 Pope Leo IV had been succeeded by Pope Benedict III whose name had none of the resonance of the epoch-making events of 800.[112]

However, the inclusion of Alfred's name in the Brescia *Liber Vitae* makes it hard to contradict the statements made variously in the *Chronicle*, by Asser and in the letter from Leo, that Alfred did indeed go to Rome as a young boy; that his name is included twice in the first group of English names in the *Liber Vitae* supports Asser's suggestion that Alfred also joined his father's expedition in 855. Surprising as this may sound to modern ears (and the tight turnaround didn't leave much time for little Alfred to learn a book of vernacular poetry for his mother),[113] it is not impossible that the little boy did go to

---

[108] Gen. 46: 22–28.

[109] *ASChron.* 853 and Asser, *Vita Alfredi*, c. 8; *Alfred the Great*, trans. Keynes and Lapidge, 232.

[110] *EHD* 1, trans. Whitelock, 123; *Alfred the Great*, trans. Keynes and Lapidge, 232 n.19. Cf. John, *Reassessing Anglo-Saxon England*, 72–74 and Smyth, *King Alfred the Great*, 12–17.

[111] Asser, *Vita Alfredi*, c. 11; *Alfred the Great*, trans. Keynes and Lapidge, 234.

[112] Nelson, 'The Problem of King Alfred's Royal Anointing', 309–27. Nelson has since amended her view on this point and now concedes the probability of Alfred's journey in 853; see her 'England and the Franks in the Ninth Century', 145.

[113] Asser, *Vita Alfredi* c. 23; *Alfred the Great*, trans. Keynes and Lapidge, 75, 239. On this point and the possibility that Alfred's mother may have been repudiated by Æthelwulf rather than having died before his marriage to Judith in 856 see J. L. Nelson, 'Reconstructing a Royal Family: Reflections on Alfred from Asser', Chapter 2, in I. Wood and N. Lund (eds), *People and Places in Northern Europe, 500–1000* (Woodbridge, 1991), 47–66, at 54–55 and references therein.

Rome, not so much because he was the favourite son destined for greatness and kingship (as Asser and the chronicler would have us believe) but because he was the most expendable representative of Æthelwulf's family under the circumstances. Alfred's (and Æthelred's) presence would have added prestige to the preliminary 'fact-finding' mission, and publicly demonstrated the value and importance that Æthelwulf attached to his own planned pilgrimage. Unlike his older brothers, Alfred the toddler was much too young to be of any material assistance to his father's military campaigns against the Vikings but by his quiet presence on the mission to Rome he could act as herald for Æthelwulf's forthcoming stage-managed visit to Rome and the court of Charles the Bald.

Prudentius incorporated into his annals a brief account of Æthelwulf's arrival in Charles's kingdom in 855: 'Charles gave an honourable reception to King Æthelwulf of the Anglo-Saxons who was hastening on his way to Rome. Charles gave him all the supplies a king might need and had him escorted right to the boundary of his realm with all the courtesies due to a king'.[114] We know little more of Æthelwulf's journey before he reached Italy, although Keynes has suggested that he may have turned east into Lothar's kingdom and travelled with Abbot Marcward of Prüm through Lotharingia via the central Alpine Septimer Pass to Lake Como and Brescia, rather than following the more usual westerly route through the Great St Bernard Pass to Vercelli and Pavia. This hinges on the interpretation of the context for the inclusion of the names in the Brescia *Liber Vitae*: whether they were placed there directly or came to be copied into that manuscript through contact with the dependent monastery of S. Maria Britonum in Pavia which, as its name suggests, was a well-established destination for Anglo-Saxon pilgrims.[115]

Prudentius's comments give a clue to the grandeur and stateliness of Æthelwulf's company; his rank was clearly recognized by Charles who seems to have met the West Saxon party on its southbound journey. The image of regal splendour is reinforced by the account given in the *Liber Pontificalis*. Though problematic in some details – the account is out of chronological order in the text and may conflate events of 855 with an account of the legacy left to the pope by the king in 858 – the author of the *Vita* of Benedict III enumerates the precious artefacts which Æthelwulf brought as gifts for St Peter.[116] These gifts are notable for the quantity of gold and for the regalia of kingship: a gold crown

---

[114] *AB* 855.

[115] Keynes, 'Anglo-Saxon Entries',103–5, 116 n. 72; Angenendt, *Der Memorial- und Liturgiecodex*, 92–93. Had Æthelwulf travelled through Lotharingia, he would have learned of the grave illness of the Emperor Lothar who died in September that year having spent his last weeks as a monk at Prüm; *AB* 855, *AF* 855.

[116] *Texte, introduction et commentaire*, ed. L. Duchesne (Paris, 1955), *Liber Pontificalis*. no. 106, c. 34; *The Lives of the Ninth-Century Popes*, trans. R. Davis (Liverpool, 1995), 164, 186–87 and the glossary of terms at 309–18. On the legacy which Æthelwulf left to Rome in his will see Asser, *Vita Alfredi*, c. 16; *Alfred the Great*, trans. Keynes and Lapidge, 73, 237.

(*corona*) weighing four pounds; two gold goblets (*baucae*)[117]; a sword (*spatha*) bound with gold; two small images (*imagines minores*) 'in fine gold'; four silver-gilt Saxon bowls (*gabathe saxisce de argento exaurato*); a silk tunic with gold-studding (*cum chrisoclavo*); and another silk tunic – this one with roundels and gold studding, and two large gold-interwoven veils. Benedict's biographer, whose job it was to list the treasures lavished on St Peter during the pontificate and who was used to such generosity, was impressed with the largesse of this Saxon king. He continues, that when pressed by the pope for further donations, the king of the Saxons gave gold to the clergy and leading men of Rome and a smaller gift of silver to the people of the city.[118] Æthelwulf's gifts easily rivalled those of Carolingian donors, or those sent to Benedict by the Byzantine emperor as described in the preceding chapter of the *Vita*, and were clearly chosen to reflect the personal generosity and spiritual wealth of the West Saxon king; here was no Germanic 'hillbilly' from the backwoods of the Christian world but, rather, a sophisticated, wealthy and utterly contemporary monarch.[119] Such an image must have been equally apparent to Charles the Bald on Æthelwulf's journey south.

The novelty of Æthelwulf's journey, however, was not that he visited Rome or was received by a Frankish king – the same had happened to Eardwulf, after all – but that he made the journey while retaining full royal authority and seems from the outset to have intended returning as king to his own realm. Prior to 855 every Anglo-Saxon king who had travelled through Francia to Rome did so as an exile – either on a voluntary basis in order to die at the threshold of the apostles or as an involuntary, political exile, forcibly ejected from his homeland and hoping for adjudication abroad.[120] Benedict's biographer similarly assumed that Æthelwulf was both pilgrim and political exile when he arrived in Rome: he 'came for the sake of prayer; he left all that he had, having lost [*amisit*] his own kingdom, and made his way to the homes of Peter and Paul, the apostles in Rome, with a multitude of people'. This may well represent a confusion on the part of the Benedict's biographer concerning the arrangements which Æthelwulf had made for the governance of his kingdom prior to leaving Wessex.[121] Just as his father had done before him in 838, Æthelwulf prepared for his journey by sorting out the succession of his kingdom – he made Æthelbald ruler in Wessex and Æthelberht king in Kent and the south-east – and by making substantial provisions from his own possessions for the sake of his soul. The biographer's comments underline

[117] *Lives of the Ninth-century Popes*, trans. Davis, 309. Nelson translates *baucae* as 'armrings'; Nelson, 'England and the Franks', 146.

[118] Davis has suggested that this part of the gift may have been conflated by the biographer with the details of the legacy left by Æthelwulf to St Peter after his death in 858; *Lives of the Ninth-century Popes*, trans. Davis, 186 n. 84.

[119] *Liber Pontificalis,* 106 c. 33; *Lives of the Ninth-century Popes*, trans. Davis, 164

[120] Stancliffe, 'Kings who Opted Out'.

[121] *Lives of the Ninth-Century Popes*, trans. Davis, 186, n. 84; *Alfred the Great*, trans. Keynes and Lapidge, 235.

just how unusual Æthelwulf's intentions were in relation to past practice. To all intents and purposes, and in the light of all precedents, Æthelwulf must have given the impression that he was retiring to Rome, leaving the way open for his sons to succeed. It is perhaps then not a surprise that (as Asser has it) 'when King Æthelwulf was returning from Rome, his son Æthelbald, with all his councillors attempted to perpetrate a terrible crime, expelling the king from his own kingdom'.[122]

Æthelwulf and Judith

The blot on Æthelwulf's copybook, in the eyes of many historians, is his marriage to Charles's 13-year-old daughter Judith at Verberie on 1 October 856. It was an event not easily explained; even those analysts who look upon his actions in the early 850s as deriving from a position of strength interpret the marriage as a display of the subordination of West Saxon status to West Frankish interests and a tacit acknowledgement by Æthelwulf that his original plans for dynastic continuity and stability had gone awry.[123] Those who prefer to see the marriage as the ritual cement in a Franco-West Saxon alliance against the Vikings cannot easily account for the apparent naïvety of a union which would so obviously threaten the rights of Æthelwulf's four surviving sons by his first marriage and thereby augment the Viking threat with that of filial civil war. Furthermore, the implications of the marriage in terms of future offspring would seem to negate entirely the extra special effort which Æthelwulf had taken in 853 to have the royal rights of his youngest son recognized by the pope in a manner familiar to Carolingian politics. The parallel of Æthelwulf's second marriage with Louis the Pious's profoundly destabilizing marriage to Judith's grandmother and namesake in 819 is so obvious that it is impossible to suppose that neither Æthelwulf nor Charles the Bald (who was the product of that union) could have entered into the marriage alliance in 856 without an awareness of the consequential ramifications of filial rebellion in Wessex. Æthelbald, like Louis's eldest son Lothar, was an experienced warrior and ruler in his own right at the time of his father's second marriage, so the dangers of rebellion against Æthelwulf in Wessex in 856 were thus present and considerable. The potential threat of filial (rather than fraternal) rebellion was high on Charles's agenda too; in 853 he had taken precautions to eliminate the possibility of recent history repeating itself among the next generation by taking the unprecedented step of having a legitimate but 'superfluous' son, Carloman, tonsured and dedicated to God – a striking contrast to Æthelwulf's treatment of Alfred the same year.[124] Historians who favour the

---

122 Asser. *Vita Alfredi*, c.12; *Alfred the Great*, trans. Keynes and Lapidge, 235. For a different interpretation of the division of the kingdom see, Kirby, *The Earliest English Kings*, 201. The rebellion is not mentioned in the *ASChron*.

123 Nelson, 'England and the Franks', 146.

124 This policy (probably prompted by a lack of subkingdoms – Charles only had two,

explanation of an alliance against the Vikings as a motive for the marriage need therefore to explain why Æthelwulf would have added the threat of civil war to the burdens on his kingdom. Two explanations present themselves; either, as Enright proposed, Æthelbald's rebellion prompted the marriage (rather than vice versa) or that the potential benefit of marriage into the Carolingian bloodline outweighed, in Æthelwulf's opinion, any short-term discomfort to his existing sons.[125]

The marriage was also considered extraordinary by contemporary observers since it represented a departure from Carolingian and West Saxon traditions alike. In Francia the marriage of a Carolingian princess was highly unusual and marriage to a foreigner virtually unheard of, let alone to a foreigner from 'beyond the sea'. Charlemagne, famously, did not permit any of his daughters to marry during his lifetime, and the normal fate of a Carolingian princess was to enter a monastery where her name and position would still command influence but where there would be no chance of the birth of legitimate offspring with a maternal claim to Carolingian rank.[126] The liturgical innovations behind the queenmaking rituals in 856 also confirm the unusual nature of that aspect of the proceedings in Francia; that Hincmar of Rheims had perforce to adapt a king's *ordo* as the basis for the queenmaking ceremony implies that no queen's *ordo* was available to him.[127] While Judith's elevation provided an enduring boost to the formal status of queenship among the Carolingians, the same cannot be said for the West Saxons for whom Judith's anointing remained politically anomalous. As the St Bertin annalist noted, this was something 'not previously customary to [Æthelwulf] or to his people'.[128] This comment by the Frankish annalist must have been picked up from contemporary Anglo-Saxon observers and, crucially, it agrees with Asser's testimony that traditionally, 'the West Saxons did not allow the queen to sit beside the king, nor indeed did they allow her to be called "queen" (*regina*) but rather "king's wife" (*regis coniugam*)'.[129] Asser amplified

---

Neustria and Aquitaine) ultimately backfired as Carloman rebelled in 870 against his father and the monastic profession. Carloman's three younger brothers likewise seem to have been tonsured; J. L. Nelson, 'Charles the Bald and the Church in Town and Countryside', *SCH*, 16 (1979), 103–18, reprinted in her *Politics and Ritual* (London, 1986), 75–90, at 81–82.

[125] Enright, 'Charles the Bald and Æthelwulf'; see also Nelson, *Charles the Bald*, 182.

[126] J. L. Nelson, 'Women at the Court of Charlemagne: A Case of Monstrous Regiment?', in J. C. Parsons (eds), *Medieval Queenship* (New York, 1993), 43–61, reprinted in her *The Frankish World, 750–900* (1996), 223–42.

[127] J. L. Nelson, 'Early Medieval Rites of Queen-Making', in A. Duggan (ed.), *Queens and Queenship in Medieval Europe* (Woodbridge, 1997), 301–15, at 303–6.

[128] *AB* 856. The sentence on the marriage gives Hincmar a leading role in the ceremonies which may indicate that it is a self-congratulatory interpolation incorporated by Hincmar into Prudentius's narrative after he took over the compilation of the *AB*; *The Annals of St. Bertin*, trans. Nelson, 15.

[129] Asser, *Vita Alfredi*, c. 14–15 This is one of the few passages in which Asser is supported by a totally independent witness and which therefore argues in favour of a ninth-century core to his work; cf. Smyth, *King Alfred the Great*, 149–367.

the point with one of Alfred's favourite stories illustrating the foolishness of queens, suggesting that, even in Alfred's day, it was the ritual elevation of Judith's status (rather than her Frankishness) which was remembered and considered to be different.[130] As Stafford has shown, with reference to evidence drawn from across the ninth century, this West Saxon practice to refuse the king's wife any regal status in her own right was probably a mechanism to prevent the dilution of the royal bloodline, and which consequently encouraged 'horizontal' succession between brothers rather than 'vertical' succession to sons and nephews.[131] It seems furthermore to have been a policy pursued most vigorously by Æthelwulf's own dynasty.[132] Later ninth-century evidence indicates that the precedent set by Judith's elevation was insufficient to change the practice within Wessex; Asser's pointed reference to it as a 'perverse and detestable custom' suggests that, as an outsider, he too found West Saxon attitudes strange. But the political implications of Judith's enhanced value as an anointed queen is evident both by her rapid remarriage after Æthelwulf's death in 858 to her son-in-law, Æthelbald, and by her father's furious reaction when, after Æthelbald's death in 860, she promptly eloped with Count Baldwin of Flanders.[133]

Our revised impression of Æthelwulf as a wealthy king, victorious against the Vikings and self-consciously able to emulate the Carolingian practice of dynastic enhancement through papal ceremonial sits awkwardly alongside the negative aspects of the marriage to Judith with its consequential implications of subordination to a Frankish father-in-law, denigration of legitimate sons (including Alfred) and provocation of filial rebellion. Nelson has argued that the marriage alliance was an opportunistic piece of power-politics brokered after Æthelbald's uprising forced Æthelwulf to abandon his own well-laid 'quasi-imperial' strategies of succession and to throw in his lot with the self-confident Frankish king who had ambitious plans of his own for an extended 'family of kings'.[134] One wonders, however, if Æthelwulf's dynastic aspirations were quite so easily thrown off-course; we should not forget that, among the gifts he gave to the pope, was a crown (a definitive Carolingian symbol of royalty by this date) and that someone in his company seems to have carried (or had memorized) an Anglo-Saxon *ordo* for the consecration of a king.[135] Although there is no evidence to suppose that

---

[130] Asser, *Vita Alfredi*, c. 13–15.

[131] P. Stafford, 'The King's Wife in Wessex, 800–1066', *Past and Present*, 91 (1981), 3–27.

[132] Nelson, 'Reconstructing a Royal Family', 55.

[133] *AB* 858, 862. Note the different treatment in these annals of Judith's actions; the earlier annal blandly notes her marriage to her son-in-law without judgement (cf. Asser c. 17 who is scathing, saying it was contrary to canon law) whereas her third marriage precipitated charges of uncanonical behaviour and adultery in Francia. Prudentius was the author of the 858 annal, Hincmar the author of the second. See *The Annals of St. Bertin*, trans. Nelson, 7–13.

[134] Nelson, 'England and the Franks', 143–46; *idem*, *Charles the Bald*, 182.

[135] This is the implication of Nelson's argument that Hincmar used an English king's ordo as the basis of the one he devised for Judith's queenmaking; Nelson, 'The Earliest Surviving Royal *Ordo*', 351–53.

Æthelwulf hoped for formal papal recognition of his own regality in 855, it is less difficult to suppose that he would not have welcomed the opportunity to bring his style of kingship more in line with Mercian and Carolingian practices. The surprise, perhaps, is not that he sought a Carolingian bride but that he married her himself rather than seeking her hand for his son, as Offa had done.

Wessex and beyond: Carolingian coinage in Anglo-Saxon England

Lupus of Ferrières also sent letters to Northumbria, seeking to renew bonds of confraternity with Wigmund, archbishop of York and Ealdsige, abbot of the monastery in the same city. His correspondence with leading churchmen in York recalls the connections that Alcuin had fostered and demonstrates that, in the early 850s, York was still renowned as a storehouse of scholarship. Fifty years after Alcuin's death, Frankish scholars were still writing to York for copies of texts that were difficult to obtain in Francia. Lupus petitioned Ealdsige for copies of four books, the *Libri Institutionum Oratorium* by the first-century author Quintilian, the commentaries by St Jerome on Jeremiah with his *Quaestiones* on the Testaments, and Bede's work on the same subject. He asked whether copies of these works could be sent to St Judoc's where they might be handed over for copying to a scribe named Lantramn. This scribe, Lupus says, 'is well known to you' suggesting that, directly or otherwise, Lantramn had already been in touch with the scholarly community at York. Lupus subsequently wrote to Pope Benedict III asking if the papal libraries contained copies of Jerome on Jeremiah and Quintilian's work on training orators.[136] We have other evidence that Lupus requested multiple copies of works from different libraries in order to collate and correct texts, and his request to Rome for the same books as he sought from York is likely to reflect the thoroughness of his scholarship rather than deficiencies at the York library.[137]

The contacts revealed by Lupus's letters to clerics in Northumbria in the 850s are scarce but not surprising evidence for the continued cultural importance of York to the Frankish scholars who were the heirs of Alcuin. Lupus says that the 'pestilential discord which cruelly vexed all Gaul and Germany' had slowed the exchange of letters and gifts but could not diminish the prayers and memories of alliance between York and the Frankish monasteries which had been bestowed on Alcuin.[138] The disorder to which he refers resulted from the

---

[136] Lupus, *Ep.* no. 100; *Lives of the Ninth-century Popes*, trans. Davis, 166; McKitterick, *The Frankish Kingdoms*, 212.

[137] Cf., M. Lapidge, 'Latin Learning in Ninth-century England', in his *Anglo-Latin Literature. Vol. I: 600–899* (London and Rio Grande, 1996), 409–54, at 427. See also Stafford, 'Charles the Bald, Judith and England', 141. On the survival of Quintilian's work see L. D. Reynolds (ed.), *Texts and Transmission: A Survey of Latin Classics* (Oxford, 1983), 332–34.

[138] Lupus, *Ep.* no. 86–87; *EHD* 1, trans. Whitelock, nos. 215–16.

civil conflict between the sons of Louis rather than the increasingly persistent incursions of the Vikings, which points to a date of composition for these letters shortly after Charles and his brothers had signed a capitulary of peace and concord at Meersen in May 851.[139]

The evidence of the coinage supports Lupus's assertion that communication between Northumbria and Francia was not broken during the difficult decades of the 830s and 840s. An eloquent example is the unique gold solidus struck in the name of one of Lupus's correspondents, Archbishop Wigmund of York (837(?)– 854) (see Figure 7.1(c)).[140] The prototype of the reverse die of Wigmund's coin was a gold solidus issued by Louis the Pious, which showed on its reverse a cross encircled by a wreath surrounded by the declamatory inscription – *Munus divinum*, 'the divine gift' (see Figure 7.1 (a)).[141] The obverse of Louis's coin shows a bust of the emperor in profile wearing a Roman-style laurel wreath with his name and title, D[OMINUS] N[OSTER] HLVDOVVICVS IMP[ERATOR] AUG[USTUS]. The motif of the wreath thus cradles both the cross and the head of the emperor, signifying the sacred duty of the emperor as secular guardian of the message of salvation through Christ's sacrifice on the Cross – a powerful evocation of the centrality of faith to Louis's notion of the role of temporal government. These scarce gold coins were probably struck as a commemorative issue to celebrate the 'divine gift' of Louis's imperial office after his coronation by Pope Stephen V at Rheims on 5 October 816.[142] An alternative (but less likely) date for their production is 825 when the Synod of Paris condemned any dishonour shown to the image of the Cross.[143] The reverse design of Louis's gold issue, as copied by Wigmund's moneyer, is so good and true to the Frankish original that we must suppose that he had a genuine coin (or very high-class copy) at his disposal. In contrast, the obverse design of Wigmund's coin shows a frontal portrait of the archbishop wearing his pallium which was inspired by papal coins rather than Carolingian designs, perhaps filtered indirectly through coins issued for contemporary arch-

---

[139] *The Annals of St Bertin*, trans. Nelson, 70–73.

[140] The weight of the coin is less than its Carolingian prototype and it may therefore have been intended as a mancus rather than a solidus; see Grierson and Blackburn, *MEC* 1, 330; Webster and Backhouse, *The Making of England*, no. 120; C. E. Blunt, 'Ecclesiastical Coinage in England (Part 1 to the Norman Conquest)', *Numismatic Chronicle*, 20 (1960), i–xvii, at iv–vii; I. Stewart, 'Anglo-Saxon Gold Coins', in R. A. G. Carson and C. M. Kraay (eds), *Scripta Nummaria Romana: Essays Presented to Humphrey Sutherland* (London, 1978), A.123, 143–72, at 166; P. Grierson, 'The Gold Solidus of Louis the Pious and its Imitations', *Jaarboek voor Munt- en Penningkunde*, 38 (1951), 1– 41 at 16–17, reprinted with corrections as Ch. XXII in his *Dark Age Numismatics* (Aldershot, 1979).

[141] Grierson, 'The Gold Solidus'; Grierson and Blackburn, *MEC* 1, 329; S. Coupland, 'Money and Coinage under Louis the Pious', *Francia*, 17.i (1990), 23–54, at 27.

[142] Grierson, 'The Gold Solidus', 3; *idem* 'La date des monnaies d'or de Louis le Pieux', *Le Moyen Age*, 69 (1963), 67–74, at 72–73, reprinted as Ch. VIII in his *Dark Age Numismatics*; M. Prou, *Catalogue des monnaies française à la Bibliotheque Nationale. Les monnaies carolingiennes* (Paris, 1896), xxxii–iii.

[143] K. F. Morrison, 'The Gold Medallions of Louis the Pious and Lothaire I and the Synod of Paris (825)', *Speculum*, 36 (1961), 592–99.

bishops of Canterbury.[144] It should be noted, though, that Wigmund's portrait is modelled in relief in the manner of the Carolingian imperial portraits and is not engraved as was the practice of contemporary papal die-cutters.[145] The archbishop's tonsure is a prominent feature of the portrait on Wigmund's coin and so retains something of the emphasis and meaning of the laurel wreath worn by the Carolingian emperor. Wigmund's portrait is thus closer to the Carolingian prototype than is apparent on first sight. Perhaps Wigmund wished to commemorate the 'divine gift' of his own elevation to archiepiscopal office (or his receipt of the pallium), and used appropriate continental models to demonstrate the significance of the event.[146]

This heavy, large gold coin would have been in total contrast to the small format, brass 'stycas' that were the normal product of the York mint at the time. This could suggest that Wigmund's gold coin was in fact minted south of the Humber, possibly at London where the portrait on the obverse of a silver penny of Coenwulf may also have been inspired by the *Munus divinum* solidus of the Frankish emperor, although the prototype could equally have been a silver imperial denier bearing a portrait of Louis or of his father, Charlemagne (see Figure 7.1(e)).[147] Coenwulf's portrait on this coin is unlike any other produced by the London moneyer, Ceolbeald, although the reverse can be paralleled elsewhere. The same die-cutter is likely to have been responsible for a second silver penny, minted, again in London for Coenwulf, by the moneyer Aelhun (see Figure 7.1(g)).[148] Like the gold solidi, the laureate bust, with diadem and robes, fills most of the field on the obverse of the Coenwulf coins and is not ringed by an inner circle, in a manner which suggests that the die-cutter had a good specimen of a genuine Frankish solidus (or denier) before him. However, as Grierson noted and as the letters of Lupus demonstrate, York in the 850s was still an important cultural centre and it is possible that Archbishop Wigmund hoped to initiate a serious commercial coinage with his Carolingian-style coin, and that it was not simply a commemorative issue.[149] There is some corrobora-

---

[144] The ultimate model for the frontal portraits is Byzantine; see P. D. Whitting, 'The Byzantine Empire and the Coinage of the Anglo-Saxons', in Dolley, *Anglo-Saxon Coins*, 23–38, at 34, although Grierson argued for a Beneventan model; Grierson, 'The Gold Solidus', 16.

[145] Stewart, 'Anglo-Saxon Gold Coins', 155 and n. 80.

[146] Nelson has suggested that the grant of Wigmund's pallium may be linked to the *AB* 839 reference to the arrival of English envoys at Louis court; Nelson, 'England and the Franks', 153, n. 15.

[147] Assuming that the prototype for the coin was indeed a solidus, 817 is the earliest possible date for this London coin, allowing time for Louis's solidus to reach England after the coronation in October 816 and for Coenwulf's die-cutters to copy the style. See Grierson, 'La date des monnaies', 74 n. 14; C. F. Keary, *A Catalogue of English Coins in the British Museum. Vol. I: The Anglo-Saxon Series* (London, 1887), 34, no. 64, plate VIII.5; C. E. Blunt, C. S. S. Lyon, B. H. I. H. Stewart, 'The Coinage of Southern England, 796–840', *BNJ*, 32 (1964), 1–74, at 33 and plate VII, *Cn* 95. Ceolbeald also minted coins for Coenwulf's successor, Ceolwulf I.

[148] EMC 1985.0048.

[149] Grierson, 'The Gold Solidus', 17.

(a)   Louis the Pious, gold solidus; Grierson Loan no. 12, 578

(b)   Louis the Pious gold solidus, cut quarter; found Louth, Lincolnshire; *EMC* 1997. c.101

(c)   Gold solidus of Archbishop Wigmund of York (*c.* 837–54); BM, *BMC* 718

(d)   Louis the Pious, gold solidus; BM, *BMC* 77

(e)   Silver penny of Coenwulf of Mercia (796–821) by London moneyer Ceolbeald; BM, *BMC*, p. 34, no. 64

(f)   Imitation gold solidus, found River Cam, Cambridgeshire; *MEC* 1, 753; *EMC* 1986.8753

(g)   Silver penny of Coenwulf of Mercia by London moneyer Aelhun, found Methwold, Norfolk; *EMC* 1985.0048

(h)   Gilt bronze-plated forgery of a Louis the Pious gold solidus; found between Gainsborough and Lincoln; *BNJ CR* 1995, no. 127; *EMC* 1995.0127

Fig. 7.1   Carolingian and Anglo-Saxon coins

tive evidence to support the notion that demand for gold coins existed in England, including Northumbria, in the second quarter of the ninth century. The issue of Louis's gold coinage was small-scale – Grierson estimates that the entire output was made with four pairs of dies – yet it seems clear that this gold coinage was known, and used as coin, in Anglo-Saxon England. A cut quarter of an original Louis solidus has been found near Louth in Lincolnshire (see Map 3, no. 1; Figure 7.1(b)); its precise division into a quarter of the weight of the original coin suggests that this fragment had a commercial, monetary function and was not simply regarded as bullion.[150]

Also, there is good evidence that unofficial, imitative copies of Louis's solidi circulated concurrently with the official Frankish issue, and continued to be made and to circulate up to the end of the century. The concentrated distribution of these imitative solidi to the north of the empire and beyond its borders, suggests that they were being minted in Frisia and possibly also in Anglo-Saxon England. To date, at least 11 of these imitations have been found in Britain – three of which are contemporary forgeries, gilt on a bronze core (see Map 3, nos 2–4; Figure 7.1(h)).[151] Grierson's intriguing suggestion that some of these imitative solidi may have been minted in Anglo-Saxon England has been underpinned recently by the discovery of a lead trial-piece from an (as yet) unlocated 'productive site' 'near Torksey' in Lincolnshire which bears impressions of dies for striking imitations of Louis's solidi.[152] The dies shown on the trial-piece cannot be tied to any of the known imitative solidi or plated forgeries yet discovered in the British Isles but the possibility that a local atelier was responsible for the trial-piece is rendered all the more plausible by the proximity of the findspot of the genuine cut-quarter as well as a plated

---

[150] The Louth fragment weighs 1.16g – marginally more than a quarter of the full weight of a solidus; 'Coin Register', *BNJ*, 67 (1997), no. 101. See also the *Early Medieval Coin* corpus held online at the Fitzwilliam Museum Cambridge, (hereafter *EMC*); *EMC* 1997.0101 and M.A.S. Blackburn, 'Finds from the Anglo-Scandinavian Site of Torksey, Lincolnshire', in B. Paszkiewicz (ed.), *Moneta Mediaevalis: studia numizmatyczne i historyczne ofiarowane Profesorowi Stanisławowi Suchodolskiemu w 65. rocznicę vrodzin* (Warsaw, 2002) 89–101, pl. 51. Another genuine gold solidus which may have had a British provenance is no 147a in Webster and Backhouse, *The Making of England*. On the use of gold see M. A. S. Blackburn, 'Gold in England during the Ninth and Tenth Centuries', in J. Graham-Campbell and G. Williams (eds), *Silver Economy in the Viking Age* (forthcoming).

[151] Imitative solidi are known from Cambridge (Cambridgeshire), *EMC* 1986.8753, Figure 7.1(f); Southampton (Hampshire), *EMC* 1992.9424; Stamford Bridge (North Yorkshire), *EMC* 1986.5037; Kirk Maughold (Isle of Man), *EMC* 1999.0154; Elgin (Morayshire); Lewes (Sussex); Porchester (Hampshire); Therfield (Hertfordshire). Gilt bronze forgeries were found at near Gainsborough (Lincolnshire), *EMC* 1995.0127; Exeter (Devon); Hindringham (Norfolk). Up to seven more are known from nineteenth-century records, several of which may have had a British provenance. See H. E. Pagan, 'The Imitative Louis the Pious Solidus from Southampton and Finds of Other Related Coins in the British Isles', in P. Andrews (ed.), *The Coins and Pottery from Hamwic*, Southampton Finds, Vol. 1 (1988), 71–72. See also the cast bronze brooch apparently modelled on a solidus; Wormald, 'The Ninth Century', 142 fig. 133. Also recent finds from London; G. Egan, 'Material from a Millennium: Detritus from a Developing City', *Transactions of the London and Middlesex Archaeological Society*, 50 (1999), 29–37, at 30.

[152] Grierson 'The Gold Solidus', 11, 25–26, 34; The trial-piece from Torksey is illustrated and described in Blackburn, 'Finds from the Anglo-Scandinavian Site of Torksey'. On 'productive sites' in Lincolnshire see K. Ulmschneider, 'Settlement, Economy and the "Productive" site: Middle Anglo-Saxon Lincolnshire AD 65–780', *Medieval Archaeology*, 44 (2000), 53–80, and *idem, Markets, Minsters and Metal-Detectors: The Archaeology of Middle Saxon Lincolnshire and Hampshire Compared*, BAR Bri. Ser. 307 (Oxford, 2000).

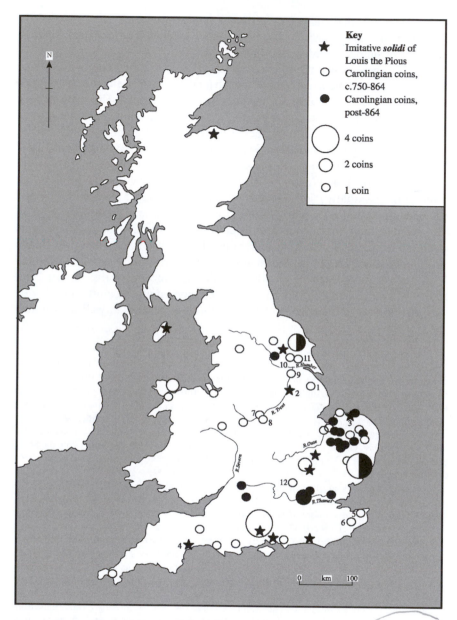

Map 3 Distribution of single finds of Carolingian coins minted *c.* 750–*c.* 900 in the UK

forgery found near Gainsborough, barely seven miles from Torksey (Map 3, no. 2).[153]

The presence of these imitative Carolingian coins in Anglo-Saxon England demands attention, since there would have been little point forging or importing such coins had there been no demand for the genuine item. The Louth cut-quarter, with the Coenwulf and Wigmund derivatives, demonstrates that genuine Louis the Pious solidi were known in England. If the design of the Coenwulf penny is indeed derived from the portrait of Louis on the solidus, then we can be sure that genuine Frankish gold coins were available – at least in London – between 816 and 821. Wigmund's dates of office place their use in northern England at the very latest by 854. This range accords with the dates suggested by Grierson for the earlier of the imitative issues based on the limited evidence of the hoards which contain relevant examples.[154] The issue of gold coinage during this period in England or Francia was unusual, so it is likely that Louis's gold coins remained in circulation comparatively longer than was normal for contemporary silver coinage which was much more susceptible to recall and recoining.[155] The scarcity of gold coinage is likely to have been a factor behind the demand for, and evident popularity of, the unofficial issues outside imperial control. However, the quantity of gold in Æthelwulf's gifts to Pope Benedict III in 855 acts as a reminder that gold wealth was stored in forms other than coinage.

The concentration of the unofficial imitations of Louis's solidi to the north of the empire has encouraged interpretation of their production and distribution as a reflection of Viking activity in Frisia and Anglo-Saxon England, rather than as products of direct Frisian or Frankish trade routes across the Channel and around the North Sea. It is likely that Viking activity was behind the loss of imitative solidi recovered from Elgin in Grampian and on the Isle of Man – areas which were beyond Anglo-Saxon political control.[156] But the reasons for the location of similar coins within Anglo-Saxon kingdoms is not as clear-cut. The discovery of the lead trial-piece 'near Torksey' lends support to the idea of Viking involvement in the distribution of such coins, since it was at Torksey on the River Trent that the great Viking army established one of its major camps in the winter months of 872–73, staying there possibly for as long as a year with tribute taken from defeated Anglo-Saxons in London and York.[157] However, the

---

153 'Coin Register', *BNJ*, 65 (1995), no. 127.

154 Grierson, 'The Gold Solidus', 9–10.

155 On the debate over the extent of gold coinage in western Europe in this period see, Grierson and Blackburn, *MEC* 1, 326–31. See also M. A. S. Blackburn and M. Bonser, 'A Carolingian Gold Coin Struck from a Die of Chartres and Found at Congham, Norfolk', *Numismatic Circular*, 92 (1990), 304–6.

156 See footnote 150 *supra*. The Elgin coin is part of Grierson's Type 1, which he thinks 'may have originated in Britain', *c*. 850. Other representatives of this type were found in the Hon hoard in Norway; Grierson, 'The Gold Solidus', 9–11, 25–27.

157 *ASChron.* 873. P. H. Sawyer, *Anglo-Saxon Lincolnshire*, History of Lincolnshire 3 (Lincoln, 1998), 196–97; Ulmschneider, "Settlement, Economy, and the "Productive" Site', 65–67.

character of the total assemblage from the 'near Torksey' site (which includes coin weights, contemporary Northumbrian stycas and a large number of Islamic dirhems), in so far as it can currently be assessed, suggests commercial activity rather than the distribution of ill-gotten booty.[158] It is important, though, to note that, without further knowledge of the underlying archaeology, it is impossible to be sure of the function of sites known only through metal detector scatters and, in the absence of positive proof to the contrary, the possibility that these finds do in fact come from a hoard cannot be discounted. In particular, the finds from 'near Torksey' are reminiscent of the content of the Croydon hoard, which Brooks and Graham-Campbell have argued belonged to a member of the Danish army in London in 871–72.[159]

The activities of Vikings, broadly defined, were undoubtedly one route through which continental (and Arabic) coinage came to be gathered, used and lost in England in the second half of the ninth century. Uncertainty caused by the threat of Viking warfare may account for the deposition of hoards but the activity of traders (including Vikings), and peaceful means of exchange at temporary fairs or on permanent settlements, is more likely to account for the loss of individual coins. Grierson favoured the notion of trade rather than piracy as the primary mechanism for the distribution of the derivative solidi around Anglo-Saxon England. In this respect, it is significant that the distribution of those coins closely mirrors the pattern of single finds of genuine Carolingian coins minted before 864. Map 3 shows the location of single finds of Carolingian silver coins, classified into those which were certainly minted before 864 (open circles) and those issued after Charles the Bald's major reform of the Frankish coinage in 864 up to c. 900 (filled circles).[160] This distribution pattern, which will change as more finds are recovered and reported by metal detectorists and in archaeological excavations, could be criticized as a reflection of modern differences in reporting rather than a genuine reflection of regional coin use in the second half of the eighth and ninth centuries. Nevertheless, notwithstanding the vagaries of differen-

---

[158] Blackburn, 'Finds from the Anglo-Scandinavian Site of Torksey'. A similar range of material has been recovered from the settlement site at Flixborough, Lincolnshire; Ulmschneider, 'Settlement, Economy, and the "Productive" Site', and C. Loveluck, 'A High-status Anglo-Saxon Settlement at Flixborough, Lincolnshire', *Antiquity*, 72 (1998), 146–61.

[159] N. P. Brooks with J. Graham-Campbell, 'Reflections on the Viking-Age Silver Hoard from Croydon, Surrey', in M. A. S. Blackburn (ed.) *Anglo-Saxon Monetary History* (Leicester, 1986), 91–101.

[160] On The Edict of Pîtres and Charles the Bald's monetary reform of 864 see MGH Capit. II, no. 273; Grierson and Blackburn, *MEC* 1, 232–33; P. Grierson, 'The *Gratia Dei Rex* coinage of Charles the Bald', in M. Gibson and J. L. Nelson (eds), *Charles the Bald: Court and Kingdom* (2nd edn) (Aldershot, 1990), 52–64; S. Coupland, 'The Early Coinage of Charles the Bald, 840–864', *Numismatic Chronicle*, 151 (1991), 121–58; Nelson, *Charles the Bald*, 207–9. The 864 reform is used because, at present, it is extremely difficult to distinguish between the coins issued at the mint of Melle by Charlemagne and by his grandson and namesake Charles the Bald; both rulers minted coins bearing the mint name +METVLLO and the *Karolus* monogram. After 864 Charles the Bald's coins bear the legend 'GDR' (*Gratia Dei Rex*).

tial retrieval and recording, we can follow widely held numismatic assumptions that singly recovered coins are likely to represent losses from the everyday use of coins and that such coins were likely to have been lost within a decade or so of minting, to argue that distribution patterns of single finds broadly reflect the contemporary geographical and chronological range of coin use.[161]

In 1963 Morrison and Dolley (who knew of only a handful of single finds) argued forcefully that, 'from the time of Offa onwards ... continental pieces were excluded from currency in Wessex, Mercia, and Kent and perhaps East Anglia as well'.[162] Since then about 70 single finds of Carolingian coins have been reported in Britain, forcing a reassessment of Morrison's and Dolley's conclusion. This number, though not high in absolute terms, could represent as much as 4 per cent of the die output of Anglo-Saxon moneyers in the ninth century.[163] Furthermore, the concentration of single finds of Carolingian coins dating from the mid-eighth century in relatively discrete geographical zones points to the existence of long-lived routes of exchange established well before the Vikings became a seriously destabilizing factor in north-western Europe, and – more controversially still – to the notion that Carolingian coinage played a bigger part in Anglo-Saxon monetary economies of the later eighth and ninth centuries than has previously been assumed.

The current British distribution pattern of Carolingian coins minted between *c*. 750 and *c*. 900 is remarkably consistent. With the exception of the outlying finds from Elgin and the Isle of Man, the locations of the imitative and forged solidi of Louis the Pious correspond closely with the distribution pattern of official silver deniers, suggesting that both types of coin functioned within the same monetary network, despite the fact that the 'gold' solidi would not have been used as commonly for everyday transactions.[164] Single finds of Carolingian coins recovered to date in Britain cluster in three distinct areas; (1) along the south coast, (2) in East Anglia, and (3) around the Humber

---

161 D. M. Metcalf, 'The Monetary Economy of Ninth-century England South of the Humber: A Topographical Analysis', in M. A. S. Blackburn and D. N. Dumville (eds), *Kings, Currency, and Alliances: History and Coinage of Southern England in the Ninth Century* (Woodbridge, 1998), 167–98, at 171–73, and M. Bonser, 'Single Finds of Ninth-century Coins from Southern England: A listing', in ibid., 199–240, at 226–28 and fig. 7. Metcalf's argument is summarized by R. Hodges, *Towns and Trade in the Age of Charlemagne* (London, 2000), 107–11. On the interpretation of and problems raised by single finds, see especially D. M. Metcalf, *An Atlas of Anglo-Saxon and Norman Coin Finds, c. 973–1086* (London and Oxford, 1998).

162 See R. H. M. Dolley and K. F. Morrison, 'Finds of Carolingian Coins from Great Britain and Ireland', *BNJ*, 32 (1963), 75–87, at 86. Cf. the important discussion by Metcalf, 'The Monetary Economy', 175–77.

163 Metcalf, 'The Monetary Economy', 175–77. Metcalf's calculations are based on the number of ninth-century Carolingian coins that were known in 1991. A more recent audit of reported finds from the period 750–900 lists more than 70 items, on which see M. A. S. Blackburn and S. Miller, *Corpus of Early Medieval Coins*, Fitzwilliam Museum, Cambridge at http://www.fitzmuseum.cam. ac.uk/Coins/emc.html.

164 Metcalf, 'The Monetary Economy', 177.

estuary with its tributaries, the Trent and Yorkshire Ouse. The gaps are equally apparent, with no Carolingian finds as yet from Bernicia, or the central Midlands between the Trent, Severn and Cambridgeshire Ouse. Only isolated finds, which are either very early or very late in the series, are found in Kent, London and the Thames valley. With the exception of two rare denarii of Pippin III from Richborough (Map 3, no. 5) and West Hythe (Map 3, no. 6) in Kent, there are no Carolingian coins minted before Charles the Bald's major reform in 864 from the south-east. This 'gap' is likely to represent the success of the major mints at London and Canterbury in intercepting imported Carolingian coins, which (as has already been noted) provided the raw material for the output of those mints during the reign of Offa and in the early decades of the ninth century.[165]

Particularly notable is the northern distribution pattern around the Humber and its tributary rivers. This 'Humbrian zone' mirrors the distribution patterns of other types of imported artefact and provides some corroborative evidence for a long-lasting network of exchange centred on the Humber and its links to the North Sea.[166] The Carolingian coins (Map 3, nos 7 and 8) retrieved close to the royal site at Repton in the Mercian heartlands have previously been considered very peripheral to a distribution pattern orientated on the south and east; but they are clearly integral to a regional pattern based on the Trent and Humber river network, which apparently also reached north into Deira, up the Ouse to York.[167] A rare coin of Pippin III from Repton (Map 3, no. 7) is matched by another from the settlement site at Flixborough further down the Trent valley (Map 3, no. 9).[168] The Roman road north to York from the Humber crossing seems to have been another route by which Carolingian coins entered Deira; two coins of Charlemagne (one very early, another very late in his series) have been found close to this road (Map 3, nos 10 and 11).[169] In the later eighth and ninth

---

[165] D. M. Metcalf and J. P. Northover, 'Coinage Alloys from the Time of Offa and Charlemagne to c. 864', *Numismatic Chronicle*, 149 (1989), 101–20; and Chapter 6, above, 188–95.

[166] Metcalf, 'The Monetary Economy', 176; Ulmschneider, 'Settlement, Economy, and the "Productive" Site', 77; C. Loveluck, 'Wealth, Waste and Conspicuous Consumption: Flixborough and its Importance for Middle and Late Saxon Settlement Studies', in H. Hamerow and A. MacGregor (eds), *Image and Power in the Archaeology of Early Medieval Britain. Essays in Honour of Rosemary Cramp* (Oxford, 2001), 78–130.

[167] Two deniers, of Pippin III (Map 3, no. 7; *EMC* 1986.0392) and Louis the Pious (Map 3, no. 8; *EMC* 1986.0122), have been recovered at or near Repton; P. Grierson, 'A Denier of Pepin the Short (751–68)', in M. A. S. Blackburn (ed.), *Anglo-Saxon Monetary History* (Leicester, 1986), 127–30; M. A. S. Blackburn and M. Bonser, 'Single Finds of Anglo-Saxon and Norman Coins – 3', *BNJ*, 56 (1986), 64–101, no. 122. The northern zone is noted, but underplayed, by Metcalf who concentrates his analysis on the Southumbrian zone; Metcalf, 'The Monetary Economy', 176.

[168] The Flixborough coin is unpublished. I am grateful to K. Leahy for information regarding this important find.

[169] An early pre-reform denier (770–775, probably Mainz), from 'South Newbald'; J. Booth and I. Blowers, 'Finds of Sceattas and Stycas from Sancton', *Numismatic Circular*, 43 (1983), 139–45; J. Booth, 'Northumbrian Coinage: The Productive Site at South Newbald', *The Yorkshire*

centuries, when native Northumbrian coin was becoming increasingly debased, the import of Carolingian coins made of good-quality silver would have made an even greater impact on local users than in the south where Carolingian-style coin had been the norm since Offa's reforms. In this respect, the single finds are important corroboration of the hoard recovered from Coney Street, York in the eighteenth century, which seems to have comprised Carolingian coins, mostly of ninth-century date.[170]

Also impressive is the quantity and distribution of Carolingian coin in East Anglia. A large number of coins minted after Charles's reforms in 864 have been recovered from the area around Norwich, suggesting that, in the last quarter of the ninth century, significant quantities of coinage were passing into the hinterland of the town. This concurs with the excavation evidence from Norwich itself which shows a boom period for the town at this time, perhaps linked to the establishment of an Anglo-Scandinavian borough.[171] The Norwich zone contrasts with the pattern of coins found further south around Ipswich, which was an older Anglo-Saxon settlement and was the likely location of the eighth-century East Anglian mint.[172] Here, the number of Carolingian coins recovered is (currently) very much less than around Norwich. In this respect, the Ipswich pattern is reminiscent of Kent and London, where the other Anglo-Saxon mints were located and which seem to have been successful in collecting and preventing the dispersal of foreign coinage. In addition, the Ipswich distribution is more closely focused on the town itself, with very few coins recovered from the hinterland. Although the total number of coins is still relatively low, the East Anglian distribution pattern of Carolingian coins may reflect both the growth of Norwich in the later ninth century (possibly at the expense of Ipswich) and also, perhaps, an increasingly sub-urban use of money over time.

Another change is suggested by the distribution of Carolingian coins over time in Wessex. As already noted, it is striking that (with the exception of the Charlemagne denier from St Albans (Map 3, no. 12),[173] all single finds of Carolingian coins yet reported from London or the Thames valley were minted after Charles the Bald's reform of 864. In contrast, all along the south coast

---

Numismatist, 3 (1997), 15–38, at 26; (Map 3, no. 10; *EMC* 1983.0101). An imperial, portrait issue denier (812–14, palatine mint) was recovered in 1999 from near Market Weighton; C. Loveluck, personal communication.

[170] M. Dolley, 'New Light on the Pre-1760 Coney Street (York) Find of Coins of the Duurstede Mint', *Jaarboek Voor Munt- en Penningkunde*, 52/53 (1965–66), 1–6.

[171] A. Carter, 'The Anglo-Saxon Origins of Norwich', *ASE*, 7 (1978), 175–204; B. Ayres, 'How Norwich Began', *Current Archaeology*, 170 (2000), 48–51 and 54.

[172] Metcalf, 'The Monetary Economy', 175; J. Newman, 'Wics, Trade, and the Hinterland: The Ipswich Region', in M. Anderton (ed.), *Anglo-Saxon Trading Centres: Beyond the Emporia* (Glasgow, 1999), 32–46.

[173] R. H. M. Dolley and D. M. Metcalf, 'Two Stray Finds from St Albans of Coins of Offa and of Charlemagne', *BNJ*, 28 (1957), 459–66.

(with a focus on the excavated evidence from Southampton), the Carolingian coins recovered pre-date Charles' reforms. A change of this type could reflect changes in the control of the money supply in ninth-century Wessex and may suggest that, in the last quarter of the ninth century, imports of Carolingian coin into Wessex were centralized (as they had been at Canterbury and London in previous decades) and that fewer imported coins were able to escape the moneyers melting-pot – although it is not until the 890s that Winchester became a significant mint.[174] Alternatively, the pattern may imply that the mechanisms by which Carolingian coin had traditionally reached the south coast of Wessex were disrupted after *c.* 860 in favour of routes further east, focused on the Thames estuary and the east coast.

The coincidence of these changes in the decade or so after 864 with the crescendo of Viking activity in ninth-century England, inevitably focuses attention on the Vikings as the catalyst for change. However, the current absence of Carolingian coins from the East Midlands – an area heavily affected by Scandinavian activity in the last quarter of the ninth century – should make us wary of regarding the Vikings as the sole mechanism for transmission (and deposition) of such coins; the pattern is not homogenous and is just as likely to reflect changes in Anglo-Saxon minting practices and political priorities. Keynes's re-evaluation of Alfred's interests in Mercia in the 870s alongside the reassessment of the output of the London mint points decisively to the increasing importance of London in the West Saxon agenda in the last quarter of the ninth century, and this could be a factor behind the changing distribution pattern of Carolingian coins in southern England.[175]

Metcalf has argued that the use of Carolingian coinage in ninth-century England occurred in 'windows of opportunity' where no English mint was available locally or when royal control of the native money supply had lapsed.[176] The (current) absence of Carolingian coins from the East Midlands, which after the division of the kingdom in 877 is an area that fits this definition exactly, argues against this conclusion. Additionally, the incorporation of coins minted in the second half of the eighth century into Metcalf's data-set suggests that the patterns of use of Carolingian coinage was regionally consistent over a longer period than his analysis of the ninth-century material implies, and that the concentration of finds in the Danelaw may have a context which pre-dates Viking conquest and settlement. While the variation within regions apparent in the last quarter of the ninth century may well reflect changes in the use and supply of money brought about directly or indirectly through Viking activity,

---

[174] P. Grierson and M. A. S. Blackburn, *Medieval European Coinage, with a Catalogue of the Coins in the Fitzwilliam Museum, Cambridge. Vol. 1: The Early Middle Ages 5–10th Centuries* (Cambridge, 1986), 294–95, 314–15.

[175] Keynes, 'King Alfred and the Mercians', 1–46; M. A. S. Blackburn 'The London Mint in the Reign of Alfred', in Blackburn and Dumville, *Kings, Currency and Alliances*, 105–24.

[176] Metcalf, 'The Monetary Economy', 175–77.

overall, the regional consistency of the pattern of use and loss of Carolingian coin is striking. The quantity of Carolingian coin recovered in relationship to contemporary pennies suggests that, within the regions identified, Carolingian coinage was not an unusual feature of the Anglo-Saxon monetary economy.[177]

---

[177] Ibid.

Chapter 8

Conclusion

It is abundantly clear that the history of Anglo-Saxon England in this period has to be studied with a view to events and concerns on the Continent. The Vikings certainly did not discriminate between Carolingian and Anglo-Saxon targets; and English and Frankish chronicles track the hostile Viking armies back and forth across the Channel, recording their movement from one kingdom to another when pickings were richer and more easily obtained elsewhere. The defensive strategy of fortified bridges to block rivers was used in England from the early ninth century, and was a tactic deployed effectively in Francia by Charles the Bald, following, perhaps, the English example.[1] The threat of a mutual enemy gave common cause to the building of an alliance between the courts of Charles and Æthelwulf but, as we have seen, the foundations of that alliance were considerably older.

During the reign of Charles's grandfather and namesake, the relationship between the Anglo-Saxon kingdoms and Francia had taken on new dimensions. The older insular influence on the Frankish Church was maintained, but the centralizing tendencies of the Carolingian regime brought the focus of activities much closer to the king and his court. As such, the evidence of the later eighth century reveals a number of Anglo-Saxons in close proximity to the Frankish king. Alcuin was much the most prominent of these men and, for a time, was part of the inner circle of the king's advisers, but he was by no means the only representative of his *gens* at the Carolingian court. After his retirement to Tours, other compatriots took his place; his pupils, Candidus (from Lindisfarne) and Fridugisius (probably from York), were particularly favoured by the king. Candidus became an important envoy in the negotiations to resolve the crisis surrounding Pope Leo III, and Fridugisius became tutor to members of Charlemagne's family, abbot of St Martin's after Alcuin's death, and was a witness to Charlemagne's will.[2] In a letter to Charlemagne written from Tours, Alcuin revealed some resentment at being superseded by younger men, saying to the king, 'I grant that

---

[1] As mentioned in a Kentish charter of 811, S.1264, *BCS* 332; *AB* 862, 865; *ASChron.* A, 896; N. P. Brooks, 'The Development of Military Obligations in Eighth- and Ninth-century England', in P. Clemoes and K. Hughes (eds), *England Before the Conquest* (London, 1971), 69–84, reprinted in N. P. Brooks, *Communities and Warfare 700–1400* (London, 2000), 32–47.

[2] Einhard, *VK*, c. 33. On Candidus's links with Lindisfarne see, Alcuin, *Ep.* no. 24; *Alcuin of York c. A.D. 732 to 804: His Life and Letters*, trans. S. Allott (York, 1974), 30. Also, M. Garrison, 'The English and the Irish at the Court of Charlemagne', in P. L. Butzer et al. (eds), *Karl der Grosse und sein Nachwirken. 1200 Jahre Kultur und Wissenschaft in Europa. Vol. 1: Wissen und Weltbild* (Turnhout, 1997), 97–124, at 106, 114.

with your help and commands they are able to take up the sweat of my work, but I do not yet concede to them the remuneration which I was accustomed to receive frequently through your generosity'.[3]

Although these men were engaged in the business of the Carolingian king, their presence at the court undoubtedly helped to raise the profile of Anglo-Saxon affairs there. Famously, Alcuin offered to ask Charlemagne to help negotiate the release of young men taken prisoner in the Viking raid on Lindisfarne.[4] His access to the court also helped secure audiences with the king and safe passage through Francia for distinguished Anglo-Saxon visitors such as the archbishop of Canterbury and his entourage, en route to Rome in 801 to negotiate a solution for the dispute over the metropolitan see of Lichfield.[5] The archbishop and his companions were following a well-worn route to Rome through Frankish territory. Ever since the establishment of Christianity in Kent at the turn of the seventh century, Anglo-Saxons had felt a special link with the city that they considered the font of their faith, and many clerics and laymen had made the pilgrimage to the 'threshold of the apostles' for the sake of their souls (and careers, in the case of Bishop Wilfrid). The sheer numbers of Anglo-Saxon men and women travelling to Rome led to the growth of an English enclave (the *Schola Saxonum*) in Rome between St Peter's and the Tiber.[6] The less virtuous fell by the wayside; Boniface complained vociferously that almost every town on the route to Rome was served by Anglo-Saxon prostitutes.[7]

By the end of the eighth century the status of the Carolingian king had grown to such an extent that it is unlikely that any important Anglo-Saxon envoy would have travelled to Rome without taking in the Carolingian court wherever it was based. Yet, for some travellers, such as the exiled Kentish pretender Eadberht Præn or Eardwulf, the deposed king of Northumbria, Charlemagne seems to have offered more than just a sympathetic ear to their grievances. His interest in the cases of the Anglo-Saxon exiles was part psychology and part pragmatic politics. The arrival of such petitioners at his court, particularly exiled princes and kings, enhanced Charlemagne's sense of his own importance and centrality to the political world beyond the borders of his own realm, even more so after 800 when, with the encouragement of papal rhetoric, the notion of *imperium* developed an elasticity which could be stretched to include guardianship of the virtues of Christian kingship.

---

[3] Alcuin, *Ep.* no. 178; *Alcuin of York*, trans. Allott, no. 71.

[4] Alcuin, *Ep.* n. 20; *Alcuin of York*, trans. Allott, no. 26; *Historia regum* (*York Annals*), 793.

[5] Chapter 6 see above, 200–1.

[6] The gate nearby was similarly known as the *Porta Saxonum*; R. Krautheimer, *Rome: Profile of a City 312–1309* (Princeton, NJ, 1980), 82. See also W. J. Moore, *The Saxon Pilgrims to Rome and the Schola Saxonum* (Fribourg, 1937), and R. Schieffer, 'Charlemagne and Rome', in J. M. H. Smith (ed.), *Early Medieval Rome and the Christian West: Essays in Honour of D. A. Bullough*, (Leiden, 2000), 279–96, at 292.

[7] Boniface, *Ep. to Cuthbert*, 78; *The Letters of Saint Boniface*, trans. E. Emerton (New York, 1940), no. 62; and *The Anglo-Saxon Missionaries in Germany*, trans. C. H. Talbot (London, 1954), no. 35.

Early evidence of this is seen in the report written by Bishop George of Ostia and Amiens to Pope Hadrian following the councils held in Britain in the autumn of 786. The personnel involved indicate that there was a strong Carolingian interest in the mission. George held a Frankish and a Roman see in plurality, a situation which matched his twofold loyalty to Charlemagne and to Pope Hadrian, and his report should certainly be seen in that light. Embedded in his report are notions which fit closely with evolving Carolingian ideology and the practice of kingship, not least in the linkage of secular and ecclesiastical reform. Most clear are the references to the protected status of anointed kings. The subsequent 'hallowing' of Offa's son Ecgfrith at the Synod of Chelsea, a few months after the second Mercian council which ratified the legates' reform programme, makes a causal connection between the two events likely. Equally significant is the innovative form of the report and the capitulary embedded within it; the Legates' Capitulary, formulated in Northumbria and ratified in Mercia, is one of the earliest documents of its type, and can be regarded as an important witness in the development process of this definitively Carolingian form of legislative document. The legates' mission provided a forum for discussion with the leading churchmen and nobility of the kingdoms of Mercia, Northumbria, Kent and Wessex, as well as an opportunity for an injection of ideas current in Francia and Rome, not least the political theory which lies behind the final report. It was also an opportunity for high-placed men from the Carolingian and papal courts to obtain a close and detailed understanding of the personalities of Anglo-Saxon rulers and of the character of the kingdoms and regimes they controlled.

The mission was clearly a very prestigious occasion and, though unusually well documented, was not an isolated event. The chronicles' accounts of the mission come in the context of other links between England, Rome and Francia. Earlier in 786 Pope Hadrian seems to have taken it for granted that, when he ordered litanies to be sung to celebrate Frankish victories over the Saxons, that 'those regions across the sea' would be included within Charlemagne's instructions.[8] References to such connections increase after 786 reflecting, in part, the coincidence of timing with Alcuin's most prolific years. However, the increased quantity of evidence is probably not entirely deceptive; Alcuin's journeys to and from Francia in the decade from 786 coincide with the peak of Offa's power and with the fractious episode surrounding the marriage negotiations between his children and Charlemagne's. Partial though our evidence is for this episode, the fall-out from the failure of the negotiations demonstrates not only the prestige in which Offa's court was regarded by the Franks but also the importance of commercial interaction between Francia and England. Furthermore, the care with which relations were patched up before Offa's death in 796 shows that these issues remained important to Charlemagne's diplomacy.

Furthermore, the mission of 786, along with the decision to send the proceedings of the Second Council of Nicaea to Northumbria in 792, and with

---

[8] *Codex Carolinus*, 76: *Charlemagne, Translated Texts*, trans. P. D. King (Kendal, 1987), 294.

the presence of Alcuin at the Synod of Frankfurt in 794 (accompanied, perhaps by other Anglo-Saxon clerics) shows a concern to draw the Anglo-Saxon Church into the mainstream theological debates of the day, concerning image-worship and iconoclasm, and the heresy of adoptionism. The numerous journeys of Anglo-Saxon bishops through Francia and the evidence for monastic reform in the Canterbury sources of the early ninth century further support the suggestion that Anglo-Saxon ecclesiastical affairs could be informed and affected by developments abroad.

Writing of Carolingian diplomacy with Byzantium, Einhard cited a Greek proverb that cautioned against the pugnacious reputation of the Franks: 'Have a Frank as a friend, never as a neighbour.'[9] Anglo-Saxon England had a special relationship with Carolingian Francia; among Charlemagne's neighbours, it was only the kingdoms of England that never received the hostile attention of Frankish armies. Protected in part by the sea that separated the two kingdoms, Charlemagne's interest in Anglo-Saxon England developed differently to his concerns for other bordering kingdoms. The Christian heritage of the English was, as we have seen, of considerable importance to the development of Carolingian ambitions, first with the mission to the east and then within the *renovatio* of learning that Charlemagne encouraged and patronized at his court. Einhard understood the value of foreign diplomacy; Charlemagne 'increased the glory of his own kingdom by winning over kings and peoples by friendly means', and he names the kings of the Irish and the Asturians among those who were seriously impressed by Charlemagne's kingship.[10] The Anglo-Saxon kings and the *gens* they ruled were also part of this wider audience for Carolingian power, and it is important to bear this Francocentric perspective in mind when evaluating the evidence for Carolingian interaction with Anglo-Saxon England. Prestige at home was an important motivating factor behind the cultivation and maintenance of contacts with rulers of distant kingdoms – as much for Charlemagne as for the kings of the English. By looking at the better documented kingdom of the Franks, a historian can find much to illuminate the history of the Anglo-Saxons; the English have long been recognized as a vital element in the formula for *renovatio* in Carolingian Francia, but there can be little doubt that, by the end of Charlemagne's reign, the English kingdoms were viewed by some in Francia as an integral part of the Carolingian world.

---

[9] Einhard, *VK*, c. 16.
[10] Ibid.

Appendix

Evidence of Anointing in Eighth-Century England

Anglo-Saxon evidence for the practice of rituals of anointing in the eighth and ninth centuries has been widely discussed, with particular reference to emergent Carolingian practices. Nelson has argued that the Carolingians did not seem overly vexed by the need for episcopal anointing of incipient kings until Hincmar's interventions in the mid-ninth century, preferring (after 751) to make use of rituals performed by a pope when needs required.[1] This distinction between the use of papal and episcopal kingmaking rituals in the Carolingian realm, and the apparent preference there before 848 for papal rituals, draws the historian's eye to the scanty, but significant, evidence for episcopal kingmaking rituals in contemporary Anglo-Saxon practice – that is, in the later eighth and earlier ninth centuries.

An important, but hitherto neglected, piece of eighth-century evidence for Anglo-Saxon interest in the anointing of kings can be found on the first folio of a manuscript which is now kept in the National Library of Russia, St Petersburg, MS Q.v.XVI.1 (Figure A.1).[2] The recto of this folio, which acts as a flyleaf to the main text, bears two pen and ink drawings, one of which shows the Old Testament king David being anointed by the prophet Samuel; it is the earliest known depiction of this scene from Anglo-Saxon England. These drawings and the accompanying pen-trials are closely contemporary with the main body of the manuscript which contains six Latin poems in praise of St Felix written by Paulinus, the early fifth-century incumbent of the bishopric of Nola near Naples. This copy of the *carmina* was written out, unusually and rather archaically, in long lines rather than in short lines of metrical verse, and was copied in an Anglo-Saxon minuscule script that Lowe (and others) have considered likely to be Northumbrian work of the second half of the eighth century; the insular half-

---

[1] J. L. Nelson, 'Kingship, Law and Liturgy in the Political Thought of Hincmar of Rheims', *EHR*, 92 (1977), 241–79, reprinted in her *Politics and Ritual in Early Medieval Europe* (London, 1986), 133–72, at 137–38; *idem*, 'The Lord's Anointed and the People's Choice: Carolingian Royal Ritual', in D. Cannadine and S. Price (eds), *Rituals of Royalty: Power and Ceremonial in Traditional Societies* (Cambridge, 1987), 137–80, reprinted as Chapter 6 in her *The Frankish World, 750–900* (London and Rio Grand, 1996), 99–132, at 102, 110–114.

[2] J. J. G. Alexander, *Insular Manuscripts, 6th to 9th century* (London, 1978), no. 42, at 65–66 and illus. 179; M. W. Evans, *Medieval Drawings* (London and New York, 1969), 21, pl. 5; M. Kilpiö and L. Kahlas-Tarkka (eds), *Ex Insula Lux: Manuscripts and Hagiographical Material Connected with Medieval England* (Helsinki, 2001), 45–46, Pl. 13, 14.

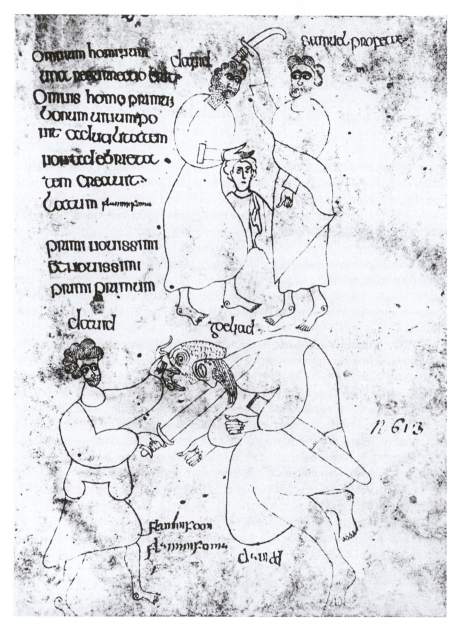

Fig. A.1 Russian National Library, St Petersburg, Cod. Lat. Q.v.XIV.1, fo. 1r

uncial pen-trials on the flyleaf he dated more generally, *saec*. VIII.[3] Julian Brown preferred an earlier date for the St Petersburg manuscript, placing it in the first half of the eighth century on the basis of comparison with another insular copy of Paulinus's poems, now kept in Rome (Biblioteca Apostolica Vaticana, MS Palatinus lat. 235), which he argued was a Northumbrian product from the first decade of the eighth century.[4]

At least five scribes contributed to the copying of the Rome manuscript, suggesting that it was made in a well-endowed scriptorium which contained several scribes able to write a competent minuscule script. The book is utilitarian in format and function, and glosses indicate that it may have been intended for teaching purposes; a single Old English gloss in hard-point on folio 24r indicates that it was used as such by an English speaker. Much of Julian Brown's seminal work on the chronology of insular texts was centred on the assumption that the Lindisfarne Gospels (London, British Library Cotton MS Nero D.iv) were written for St Cuthbert's translation in 698. However, Michelle Brown has recently questioned the association of the Gospels with this event, preferring to link them with the subsequent development of the cult of the saint in the first quarter of the eighth century. If correct, her hypothesis has a consequential impact on the dating of all manuscripts which Julian Brown dated by association with the Lindisfarne Gospels, including the Rome Paulinus which (in his opinion) post-dated the production of the great gospel books made in that location.[5]

The palaeographic similarities between these two copies of Paulinus's *carmina* are such that Lowe thought the two manuscripts may well have been written in the same 'English' scriptorium, a conclusion supported by Ganz who has argued that the St Petersburg Paulinus can be considered 'a doublet' of that

---

[3] E. A. Lowe, *CLA* XI, no. 1622, *s*.VIII[2]. See also A. Staerk, *Les Manuscrits Latins du Ve au XIIIe siècle conservés à la Bibliothèque Impériale de Saint Petersbourg* (St Petersburg, 1910), Vol. 1, no. 68, at 222–23. Alexander gives a date of '8th–9th century' in his *Insular Manuscripts*, 65; T. H. Ohlgren (ed.), *Insular and Anglo-Saxon Illuminated Manuscripts: An Iconographic Catalogue c. AD 625 to 1100* (New York and London, 1985), no. 42, at 39 dates the manuscript 'VIII[ex]'. Cf., now, H. Gneuss, *Handlist of Anglo-Saxon Manuscripts: A List of Manuscripts and Manuscript Fragments Written or Owned in England up to 1100* (Tempe, AZ, 2001), no. 847, s.VIII[1].

[4] *CLA* I, no. 87, s.VIII[ex]; T. J. Brown and T. W. Mackay, *Codex Vaticanus Palatinus Latinus 235, An Early Insular Manuscript of Paulinus of Nola 'Carmina'*, Armarium codicum insignium, 4 (Turnhout, 1988), 25–28, s.VIII[in]; L. Webster and J. Backhouse (eds), *The Making of England. Anglo-Saxon Art and Culture, AD 600–900* (London, 1991), no. 85, s.VIII[in]. Brown's re-dating is also followed by Gneuss, *Handlist*, no. 910 (contra the date given in his preliminary list in *ASE*, 9 (1981), 1–60 where he dated the manuscript s.VIII[ex]). On Brown's definition of Phase II Insular half-uncial see especially T. J. Brown, 'Tradition, Imitation and Invention in Insular Handwriting of the Seventh and Eighth Centuries', and 'The Irish Element in the Insular System of Scripts to c. AD 850', in J. Batley, M. P. Brown and J. Roberts (eds), *A Palaeographer's View. The Selected Writings of Julian Brown* (London, 1993), 179–200 and 201–220.

[5] M. P. Brown, *'In the beginning was the Word': Books and Faith in the Age of Bede*, Jarrow Lecture (Jarrow, 2000); Brown and Mackay, *Codex Vaticanus Palatinus Latinus 235*, 27.

in the Vatican, 'containing the same text copied in the same centre, though in a slightly more ornate script'.[6] On the basis of the decoration and particular form of cursive minuscule employed, both Brown and Mackay thought that a Bernician scriptorium, possibly Lindisfarne, may have been that centre. Furthermore, they noted that the version of the *carmina* represented by these two manuscripts was of the same type available to Bede in the early eighth century.[7] Alcuin was also familiar with Paulinus's poetry, quoting from it in his *York Poem* and referring to a copy of Paulinus's work in the library collected by his master Ælberht.[8] Indeed, it is probable that it was through this northern English route, and through manuscripts written in Northumbria such as those now preserved in Rome and St Petersburg, that Paulinus's work was reintroduced into the libraries of Charlemagne's Europe.[9]

The subsequent medieval provenance of the two manuscripts is, indeed, Frankish. The Rome copy shows signs of having been in a continental collection, possibly at Lorsch or Fulda, before the end of the eighth century. Likewise, the St Petersburg manuscript was known in Corbie, where it appears in a twelfth-century catalogue; from there it went to the Parisian house of St Germain-des-Prés where the flyleaf acquired a press-mark for the whole volume, N. 613.[10] In the aftermath of the French Revolution, an official at the Russian embassy in Paris, Peter Dubrovsky, acquired the manuscript (along with many other early books), and from his possession it eventually entered the Imperial library in St Petersburg.[11] The date at which the manuscript left Anglo-Saxon shores is unclear, although Caroline minuscule headings to the poems seem to be of early ninth-century date suggesting that the manuscript may have been taken to Francia not very many decades after it had been copied, and may well have been at

---

[6] D. Ganz, *Corbie in the Carolingian Renaissance*, Beihefte der Francia 20, (Sigmaringen, 1990), 41.

[7] Bede, *HE* V.24. C. D. Verey, T. J. Brown and E. Coatsworth, *The Durham Gospels*, EEMF 20 (Copenhagen, 1980), 49, n. 107; E. Chatelain, 'Notice sur les manuscrits des poésies de S. Paulin de nole suivie d'observations sur le texte', *Bibliothèque des Écoles Française d'Athènes et de Rome*, 14 (Paris, 1880), 1–98, at 41–42; T. W. Mackay, 'Bede's Hagiographical Methods: His Knowledge and Use of Paulinus of Nola', in G. Bonner (ed.), *Famulus Christi. Essays in Commemoration of the Thirteenth Centenary of the Birth of the Venerable Bede* (London, 1976), 77–92.

[8] *Alcuin: The Bishops, Kings and Saints of York*, ed. and trans. P. Godman (Oxford, 1983), lxx, 124–25 at line 1552; M. Lapidge. 'Latin Learning in Ninth-Century England', in *idem, Anglo-Latin Literature. Vol 1: 600–899* (London and Rio Grande, 1996), 409–45.

[9] R. McKitterick, 'The Diffusion of Insular Culture in England and on the Continent: The Manuscript Evidence, c. 650–c. 850', in H. Atsma and K.-F. Werner (eds), *La Neustrie: Le pays au nord de la Loire de 650 à 850*, Beihefte der Francia 16/1 (Sigmaringen, 1989), 395–431, at 401.

[10] Ganz, *Corbie in the Carolingian Renaissance*, 41, 130. The St Germain volume is now split between our manuscript and a ninth-century book in the same collection; St Petersburg MS Cl. Lat. F.v.7; Staerk, *Les Manuscrits Latins*, no. 47, at 127–28.

[11] P. Z. Thompson, 'Biography of a Library: The Western European Manuscript Collection of Peter P. Dubrovski in Leningrad', *The Journal of Library History*, 19 (1984). 477–503; M. Logutova; 'Insular Codices from Dubrovsky's Collection in the National Library of Russia, in Kilpiö and Kahlas-Tarkka, *Ex Insula Lux*, 93–98.

Corbie by *c*. 800.[12] Although it is difficult to be certain on codicological grounds, palaeographic and art-historical parallels (discussed below) strongly suggest that the flyleaf (which is a singleton and so is not attached to a folio containing the main text), with its illustrations, has had a long association with the accompanying manuscript; there is no apparent reason to doubt that the flyleaf and the copy of the poems of Paulinus of Nola with which it is bound are very distant in terms of date or place of origin[13] – that is, Northumbria in the middle decades of the eighth century.

The flyleaf bears two drawings. The upper drawing shows two figures placed centrally on the page and labelled in insular half-uncial script as *david* and *samuel profeta*. David stands on the left with his head meekly bent and right hand outstretched towards Samuel, who has his right hand raised over the head of David clutching an upturned horn. Thus the viewer sees a depiction of the very moment of the anointing of David as king over the people of Israel (I Sam. 16: 13). Between the two figures a later artist has sketched, freehand, the upper half of a third figure who watches the action; this figure is not part of the original composition.[14] Below this drawing is another of similar size, which depicts a different scene from the life of David, the slaying of Goliath (1 Sam. 17: 48–51; Ps. 143). Again, the two figures are labelled, by the same hand as in the upper drawing, *david* and *goeliad*. David is shown on the left, stepping forward he grabs, with his left hand, the crest of his opponent's helmet and, with his right hand grasping Goliath's sword, prepares to decapitate his enemy. Goliath falls to his knees in defeat, eyes shut, clutching an empty scabbard.

In a subsequent action, various *probationes pennae* which praise good wine and the resurrection have been added in a competent but heavy-handed insular half-uncial with some minuscule elements (those between David and Goliath are later still, mimicking words above). The pen used to write these notes is notably thicker and the script more bulbous than that used for the naming-labels associated with the drawings. These pen-trials respect the central placement of the drawings on the page and must therefore have been written after the drawings were done. The dating of the half-uncial pen-trials provides an associated *terminus ante quem* for the drawings.[15]

---

[12] McKitterick, 'The Diffusion of Insular Culture', 416; Ganz, *Corbie in the Carolingian Renaissance*, 41–42, 129–30.

[13] Brown and Mackay, *Codex Vaticanus Palatinus Latinus 235*, 19.

[14] Alexander likened this image to Anglo-Saxon work of the later tenth or eleventh century which, unless we suppose it to be the work of an itinerant English artist, would have implications for the date at which the flyleaf (and perhaps the manuscript) left England, but Brown considered the sketch to be continental work of the mid-ninth century; Alexander, *Insular Manuscripts*, 65. See also Brown and Mackay, *Codex Vaticanus Palatinus Latinus 235*, 19 n. 24.

[15] *CLA* IX, no. 1622. *Omnium hominum una resurrectio erit. Omnis homo primum bonum vinum ponit, ad utilitatem non ad ebrietatem creavit latum flammiforma. Primi novissimi et novissimi primi primum.*

Art historians have long recognized the importance of these drawings as early evidence for the presence in Anglo-Saxon England of formulaic cycles of illustrations of scenes from the life of David, well known from late antique and pre-iconoclastic Byzantine mobiliary art.[16] The composition of both scenes in our manuscript are very like those on two Byzantine silver dishes, part of a set of nine displaying scenes from the life of David which were made late in the reign of Heraclius (613–629/30). Closely comparable images are found in two Byzantine manuscripts of the tenth and eleventh centuries, now kept in Paris and in Rome. The similar composition of all these images is strongly suggestive of the widespread and long-term circulation of common models depicting scenes from the life of David, the Old Testament prefiguration of Christ.[17] Our drawings stand alongside the surviving illuminations from another early English manuscript, the Vespasian Psalter (s. VIII[2/4]) as evidence that such cycles were known to illuminators in eighth-century England. The Vespasian Psalter has two historiated initials showing David with Jonathan and another of David as the Good Shepherd rescuing a lamb from the lion, as well as the famous full-page illumination of David composing the psalms.[18] It does not, however, contain either of the two scenes depicted on the St Petersburg flyleaf, although the Vespasian Psalter as it survives today is fragmentary and the probability that it once had other illustrations is high. The fifteenth-century scholar of Canterbury, Thomas of Elmham, noted that the opening initial B of the first psalm in this manuscript, now missing, contained an image of Samuel – quite probably anointing David.[19] Indeed, scenes of this type (though

---

[16] Alexander, *Insular Manuscripts*, 65. On the nine silver plates from Cyprus bearing depictions of scenes from the life of David and stamped with the mark of the Emperor Heraclius (613–29/30) see O. M. Dalton, 'Second Silver Treasure from Cyprus', *Archaeologia*, 60 (1906), 1–24; and K. Weizmann (ed.), *The Age of Spirituality: Late Antique and Early Christian Art, Third to Seventh Centuries. Catalogue of the Exhibition at the Metropolitan Museum of Art, November 19, 1977 through February 12 1978* (New York, 1979), 475–83, cat. 425 and 431. Wander has argued that the set was made to celebrate the defeat in single combat of the Persian general Razatis by the Emperor Heraclius in 627, and an event recorded in the contemporary Chronicle of Fredegar as the achievement of a latter-day David; S. H. Wander, 'Cyprus Plates: The story of David and Goliath', *Metropolitan Museum Journal*, 8 (1973), 89–104; *idem*, 'The Cyprus Plates and the Chronicle of Fredegar', *Dumbarton Oaks Papers*, 29 (1975), 356–46, fig. 1.

[17] Paris, Bibliothèque Nationale, Cod. gr. 139 (s. X), fo. 3r (David anointed) and 4v (death of Goliath), and Rome, Biblioteca Apostolica Vaticana, Cod. gr. 333 (s. XI), fo. 22v (David anointed) and fo. 24v (death of Goliath). See also Weitzmann, *The Age of Spirituality*, 477, 483 where it is argued that Heraclius's silversmith used a manuscript as his model. See also K. van der Horst, W. Noel and W. C. M. Wüstefeld, (eds), *The Utrecht Psalter in Medieval Art: Picturing the Psalms of David* (Utrecht, 1996), 87–93; and O. Kurze, 'Ein insulares Munster-buchblatt und die byzantinische Psalterillustration', *Byzantinisch-neugriechische Jahrbücher*, 14 (1938), 84–93.

[18] London, British Library, Cotton MS Vespasian A.I fo. 30v, 31r and 53r; *CLA* II, no. 193; D. Wright (ed.), *The Vespasian Psalter*, EEMF 14 (Copenhagen, 1967); Alexander, *Insular Manuscripts*, no. 29; Ohlgren, *An Iconographic Catalogue*, no. 29; R. Gameson, 'The earliest books of Christian Kent', in *idem* (ed.), *St. Augustine and the Conversion of England* (Stroud, 1999), 313–73, at 330–36.

[19] Ibid., 334.

differently arranged) are known from four eleventh-century Anglo-Saxon psalters (as well as two Irish psalters of the ninth century), demonstrating that images of the anointing of David and the killing of Goliath were certainly part of the illustrative schema available to later Anglo-Saxon illuminators of the Psalms.[20] Undoubtedly, first-hand knowledge of just such a David-cycle also lies behind depictions of David killing the lion on contemporary Pictish sculpture, most especially on the sarcophagus from St Andrews which is not far in date from our manuscript.[21]

The St Petersburg illustrations, however, are unique in the surviving corpus of Anglo-Saxon manuscript depictions of David in that they are not associated with a text of the psalms. Furthermore, unlike the accomplished and highly decorative illuminations of the Vespasian Psalter, those on the St Petersburg flyleaf are stilted, mannered and clearly the work of an apprentice rather than an expert artisan. The overemphasis of the heads, hair and eyes of the four figures, as well as the artist's rather unsteady line are indicative of a novice at work (the artist also gave Goliath two right hands). However, the real value of these drawings lies in their very marginality; this type of practice-work survives only by chance and preserves rare evidence for the mode of transmission of late antique models, and something of the circumstances of their assimilation at a provincial level.[22] Inexperienced artists, less sure of their ability, will tend to stay closer to their exemplar,[23] but the rather rigid and stiff appearance of the figures in these drawings cannot belie the fluidity and movement of the underlying composition, and so preserve the drama, if not the quality, of the model.

Though not terribly accomplished, the artist of these drawings was not entirely without skill, and aspects of the composition and draftsmanship suggest that he was able to adapt certain elements of his model, helping to pinpoint still more accurately the date and place of origin of the drawings. A close examination of their structure shows that the curves which outline the figures were made by drawing around a template. For example, the upper bodies of Samuel and David in the top drawing are mirror images of the same oval-shape, as is the curve on David's robe around his left leg, the curve of Goliath's beard, and the curve of his left arm; in addition, the outer curve of Goliath's left leg is the same as that outlining his back. In this technical aspect, these drawings are comparable to the illustrations in an abbreviated version of Cassiodorus's commentary on the Psalms (now Durham, DCL MS B.II.30), a Northumbrian manuscript similarly dated to the mid-eighth century, which is often ascribed to Wearmouth

---

[20] Ohlgren, *An Iconographic Catalogue*, nos 73, 169, 171, 198, and 203; F. Wormald, *Collected Writings, 1, Studies in Medieval Art, 6th to 12th centuries*, ed. J. J. G. Alexander, T. J. Brown and J. Gibbs (London, 1984), 123–37.

[21] The sarcophagus is now dated *c.* 750–*c.* 850. See I. Henderson, 'Primus inter Pares: The St. Andrew's Sarcophagus and Pictish Sculpture', in S. M. Foster (ed.), *The St. Andrew's Sarcophagus*, (Dublin, 1998), 97–167, at 105–8, 118–34.

[22] Alexander, *Insular Manuscripts*, 65.

[23] Henderson, 'Primus inter Pares', 119.

Jarrow but which Lapidge and Gneuss have argued may be a rare survival from the York scriptorium.[24] As Bailey has demonstrated, the full-page frontal images of David the Psalmist and David/Christ trampling the beasts in the Durham Cassiodorus (fos 81v and 172v, respectively) were masterfully drawn with the aid of a template, which provided the artist with a series of standardized curves and lines around which to structure the form and composition of his figures. Although less skilful, the figures on the flyleaf were clearly constructed using a similar method, and this technical feature may help to localize and date the drawings further; David's tightly curled hair and lack of beard also recall the Cassiodorus illustrations, although his pubescent stubble is an innovation. And, like the St Petersburg drawings, those in the Durham Cassiodorus have naming labels in insular half-uncial. Another feature of the drawings which seems to come from the artist, rather than the model, is the characteristic curl on the heels of the figures, which recalls the curving delineation of joints on Pictish animal drawings (and on the Otho-Corpus eagle) although, curiously, the closest parallel for this feature and for the long and deeply incised fingers of the figures comes from Spanish manuscript illuminations of the tenth century, where these features are commonplace.[25]

The most significant local adaptation made by the artist is in the drawing of the helmet worn by Goliath.[26] In the later Paris Psalter, David grabs the Philistine warrior by his hair as he falls, Goliath's helmet having tumbled to the ground at David's feet. In the St Petersburg drawing, Goliath still wears his helmet and David grabs it by the crest. The helmet is very precisely drawn with careful detail; the spiral on the cap (like the curly heels) is an attempt to depict three-dimensional volume, and the scales covering it perhaps depict schematically linked plates or chainmail (as used on a contemporary helmet from York). The most diagnostic feature is the careful depiction here of a raised crest in the form of an animal. To Anglo-Saxonists this immediately recalls both the Benty Grange

---

[24] Some six scribes worked on this book; R. A. B. Mynors, *Durham Cathedral Manuscripts to the End of the Twelfth Century* (Durham, 1939), 21–22; Alexander, *Insular Manuscripts*, 46; R. Bailey, *The Durham Cassiodorus*, Jarrow Lecture (Jarrow, 1978); Alexander, *Insular Manuscripts*, no. 17; Webster and Backhouse, *The Making of England*, no. 89; D. A. Bullough, 'Alcuin and the Kingdom of Heaven: Liturgy, Theology and the Carolingian Age', in U.-R. Blumenthal (ed.), *Carolingian Essays* (Washington, DC, 1983), 1–69, at 18–22; Lapidge, 'Latin Learning', 427; Gneuss, *Handlist*, no. 237, s. viii$^{2/4}$, Northumbria (York?).

[25] C. Hicks, 'The Pictish Class I Animals', in R. M. Spearman and J. Higgitt (eds), *The Age of Migrating Ideas. Early Medieval Art in Northern Britain and Ireland* (Edinburgh, 1993), 196–202. Cambridge, Corpus Christie College MS 197B, fo. 1; Alexander, *Insular Manuscripts*, no. 12, Ill. 58; Webster and Backhouse, *The Making of England*, 83b; J. Williams, *The Illustrated Beatus. A Corpus of the Illustrations of the Commentary on the Apocalypse. Vol. 1: Introduction* (London, 1994) and *idem, Early Spanish Manuscript Illumination* (New York, 1977), esp. pl. 23 and 24 from Madrid, Academia de la Historia, Cod. Aemil. 33, fo. 68r and 92r.

[26] M. J. Swanton, 'The Manuscript Illumination of a Helmet of Benty Grange Type', *Journal of the Arms and Armour Society*, 10 (1980), 1–5; D. Tweddle, *The Anglian Helmet from 16–22 Coppergate*. The Archaeology of York, The Small Finds, 17/8 (York, 1992), 1100 and Fig. 534.

Fig. A.2   The Benty Grange helmet, showing boar-crest and nasal cross
Courtesy of Sheffield Galleries and Museum Trust

and Pioneer helmets, both of which have boar-crests (Figures A.2 and A.3).[27] It evokes also the famous reference in Beowulf to war-gear where 'Boar-figures shone over gold-plated cheek-guards, gleaming, fire-hardened; they guarded the lives of the grim battle-minded'.[28] In choosing an animal-crested helmet for Goliath, the artist of the flyleaf illustration was responding to a familiar, native type of armour, and one that had connotations of very high, and probably royal, rank. The Benty Grange and Pioneer helmets are two of only four helmets known from Anglo-Saxon England that are either complete or able to be reconstructed, the other two being from Sutton Hoo and York.[29] The extreme rarity of

[27] R. S. L. Bruce-Mitford and M. R. Luscombe, 'The Benty Grange Helmet and Some Other Supposed Anglo-Saxon Helmets', in R. S. L. Bruce-Mitford (ed.), *Aspects of Anglo-Saxon Archaeology* (London, 1974), 223–52; Webster and Backhouse, *The Making of England*, no. 46, with reference to the embossed panels on helmets from Vendel, Sweden. A preliminary report on the Pioneer helmet is to be found in, I. Meadows, 'The Pioneer Helmet', *Current Archaeology*, 154 (1997), 391–95; a fuller report by the same author is forthcoming.

[28] *Beowulf*, lines 303b–6a and see also lines 1148–54; *Beowulf, An edition*, ed. B. Mitchell and F. C. Robinson (Oxford, 1998), 58, 96; *Beowulf. A New Verse Translation* trans. R. M. Liuzza (Peterborough, Ontario, 2000), 62, 97–98.

[29] R. L. S. Bruce-Mitford, *The Sutton Hoo Ship Burial. Vol 2: Arms Armour and Regalia* (London, 1978), 138–231. Fragments of other helmets are suggested by remains from: Icklingham, Suffolk; Rempstone, Notts.; Caenby, Lincs.; Asthall, Oxon; Guilden Morden Cambs. On these see Bruce-Mitford and Luscombe, 'The Benty Grange Helmet', 223–52; J. Foster, 'A Boar Figurine

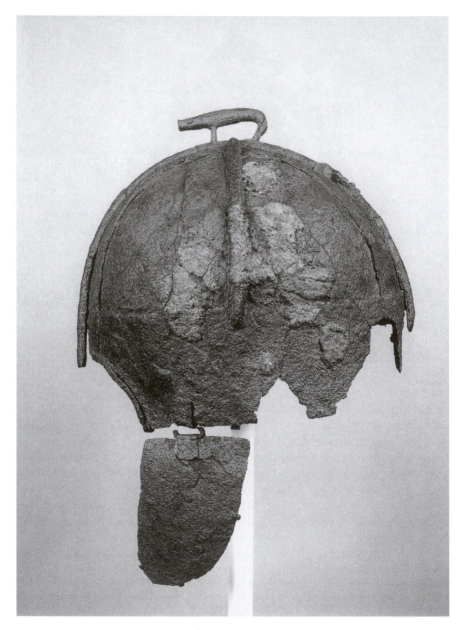

Fig. A.3   The 'Pioneer helmet' from Wollaston, Northamptonshire
Courtesy of Northamptonshire County Council

helmets recovered from Anglo-Saxon contexts and the value placed on them in later Anglo-Saxon wills and law-codes demonstrates the very high value attached to such armour, and implies that the wearer of a helmet was of the highest stratum of society.[30] The high-status context of the Sutton Hoo find needs no elaboration; the York helmet, although recovered from a well rather than an inhumation, bears a protective Christian inscription on behalf of a man with the aristocratic name, *Oshere*, who presumably had commissioned the helmet. The mixed uncial-'rune-like' script of the inscription, and art-historical parallels date the helmet to the eighth century, probably *c.* 750–775; the quality of the metalwork, the bold display of literacy and the *Os*-prefix of the name points to an owner of the highest rank in Northumbrian society.[31] The Pioneer helmet was found in 1997 in an isolated mound burial (with a hanging-bowl, pattern-welded sword and belt-fittings) alongside a Roman road at Wollaston, near Wellingborough, Northamptonshire, and is of a similar type to the York find with protective nose- and ear-pieces – a type derived ultimately from Roman paradehelmets. The Pioneer helmet has been dated provisionally to the third-quarter of the seventh century, certainly post-650 and broadly contemporary with the Benty Grange specimen which likewise was recovered from a burial mound close to a Roman road, south-east of Buxton in Derbyshire.[32] The two closest typological examples thus pre-date the flyleaf drawing by perhaps as much as a century, a factor which may account for the slightly elongated nose and tail of the boarcrest on the drawing; perhaps it was a type remembered, rather than witnessed, by the artist or his patron.

The drawing of the helmet on the St Petersburg flyleaf is thus a 'provincial', contemporary response to an antique model, in which the artist had sufficient skill to draw on local memory or personal experience to make a biblical scene resonate with contemporary idiom from his own world.[33] The question for historians for whom this image is unfamiliar is whether the scene in the upper

---

from Guilden Morden, Cambs', *Medieval Archaeology*, 21 (1977), 166–67; H. Steuer, 'Helm und Ringschwert. Prunkbewaffnung und Rangabzeichen germanischer Kreiger. Eine Übersicht', *Studien zur Sachsenforschung*, 6 (1987), 189–236, *Abb.* 1.192. On the helmet from York see Tweddle, *The Anglian Helmet*, 1083–86 and Fig. 525.

[30] N. P. Brooks, 'Arms, Status and Warfare in Late Saxon England', in D. A. Hill (ed.), *Ethelred the Unready: Papers to the Millennium Conference*, BAR Bri. Ser 69 (Oxford, 1978), 81–103, reprinted in Brooks, *Communities and Warfare, 700–1400* (London, 2000), 138–61, at 153–54.

[31] Tweddle, *The Anglian Helmet*, 1012–15, 1165–71; Webster and Backhouse, *The Making of England*, no 47.

[32] The Benty Grange helmet has a silver cross on the nose-piece as well as its 'protective' boar-crest, the implicit syncretism of which has led to the suggestion that it dates from a time of religious convergence in Mercia – that is, the mid-seventh century. See Webster and Backhouse, *The Making of England*, no. 46. The Pioneer helmet is dated by associated artefacts from the assemblage, particularly the narrow belt-buckles (I. Meadows, pers. comm.).

[33] A parallel example is the addition of a contemporary dagger to the image of David on the St Andrews sarcophagus, which Henderson believes otherwise to be a faithful facsimile of a late-antique ivory carving; Henderson, 'Primus inter Pares', 153, 161–65.

drawing of the anointing of a king likewise resonated with contemporary political ritual in the mind of the artist and viewers of his work. It is, admittedly, a
large step from the sketches of a trainee Anglo-Saxon artist to evidence for
anointing of kings in eighth-century England. The connection (if one exists) is
in the broad convergence of the dating of the image with the earliest secure
historical references to ecclesiastical kingmaking rituals in Anglo-Saxon England – a connection that is underlined by the coincidence of the historical,
archaeological and art-historical evidence in Northumbria and northern Mercia.
The cultural milieu in which these drawings were produced was shared by
Alcuin and the ecclesiastical secular elites who attended the legates' synods in
Northumbria and Mercia in 786. The capitulary produced at the Northumbrian
meeting and subsequently taken to Mercia discussed the generic status of kings
as 'The Lord's Anointed' and, the following year, Offa's son Ecgfrith was 'hallowed' to kingship at the 'contentious' Synod of Chelsea. At least one subsequent
Mercian king was the subject of a consecration ceremony; a charter of 822
records the *consecratio* of Ceolwulf of Mercia on 17 September that year.[34] No
record survives of any such ceremony for the intervening king, Coenwulf, although the dispute over the Lichfield Metropolitan and the exile of the archbishop
of Canterbury at the beginning of his reign may have made the timing and
recording of such a ceremony more than usually difficult. In Northumbria, too,
the importance of episcopal involvement in the ceremony which made Eardwulf
king on 26 May 796 is explicit in the contemporary accounts. The illustrations
on the St Petersburg flyleaf show that the Old Testament context was well
understood among the northern Anglian peoples in the eighth century, and the
Goliath illustration shows that the artist was able to adapt his late antique
models for contemporary viewers.

[34] S 186.

Bibliography

Primary sources

Acts of the Abbots of St Wandrille
Gesra sanctorum patrum fontanellensis coenobii, ed. F. Lohier and J. Laporte (Rouen and Paris, 1936).

Æthelwulf
Carmen de abbatibus, ed. A. Campbell, *Æthelwulf De Abbatibus* (Oxford, 1967).

Alcuin, *Letters*
Epistolae Alcuini, ed. E. Dümmler, MGH Epp. IV, Epistolae Karolini Aevi II (Berlin, 1895).
Alcuin of York c. A.D. 732 to 804: His Life and Letters, trans. S. Allott (York, 1974).

Alcuin, *Poems*
Alcuini Carmina, ed. E. Dümmler, MGH PLAC I (Berlin, 1881), 160–351.
Poetry of the Carolingian Renaissance, trans. P. Godman (London, 1985), 118–44 (partial translation).

Alcuin, *York Poem*
Versus de Patribus Regibus et Sanctis Euboricensis Ecclesiae, ed. E. Dümmler, MGH PLAC I (Berlin, 1881), no. 1, at 169–206.
Alcuin: The Bishops, Kings and Saints of York, ed. and trans. P. Godman (Oxford and New York, 1982).

Alcuin, *Life of St Richarius*
Vita S. Richarii, ed. B. Krusch, MGH SS rer. Merov. III (Berlin, 1896), 435–57.

Alcuin, *Life of Willibrord*
Vita Willibrordi, ed. W. Levison, MGH SS rer. Merov. VII (Berlin, 1920), 81–141.
The Anglo-Saxon Missionaries in Germany: being the lives of SS Willibrord, Boniface, Sturm, Leoba and Lebom, together with the Hodeporicon of St Willibald and a selection of the correspondence of St Boniface, trans. C. H. Talbot (London, 1954), 3–24.

Altfrid, *Life of St Liudger*
Vita Liutgeri, ed. G. H. Pertz, MGH SS II (Berlin, 1829).
Die Vitae sancti Liudgeri, ed. W. Diekamp, Die Geschichtsquellen des Bisthums Münster 4 (Münster, 1881), 3–53.
EHD 1, trans. D. Whitelock (London, 1979), no. 160 (partial translation).

***Anglo-Saxon Chronicle* MS A**
The Anglo-Saxon Chronicle, MS A. A Collaborative Edition 3, ed. J. Bately (Cambridge, 1986).
The Anglo-Saxon Chronicle, A Revised Translation, ed. and trans. D. Whitelock, D. C. Douglas and S. I. Tucker (London, 1961).

Anglo-Saxon Chronicle MS D
The Anglo-Saxon Chronicle, MS D. A Collaborative Edition 6, ed. G. P. Cubbin (Cambridge, 1996).
The Anglo-Saxon Chronicle. A Revised Translation, ed. and trans. D. Whitelock, D. C. Douglas and
    S. I. Tucker (London, 1961).

Anglo-Saxon Chronicle MS E
Two Saxon Chronicles Parallel, ed. J. Earle and C. Plummer, 2 vols (Oxford, 1892–99).
The Anglo-Saxon Chronicle. A Revised Translation, ed. and trans. D. Whitelock, D. C. Douglas and
    S. I. Tucker (London, 1961).

Anglo-Saxon Chronicle MS F
The Anglo-Saxon Chronicle: Facsimile of MS. F, the Domitian bilingual. A Collaborative Edition 1,
    ed. D. Dumville (Cambridge, 1995).
The Anglo-Saxon Chronicle, MS F. A Semi-diplomatic Edition. A Collaborative Edition 8 (ed. P. S.
    Baker (Cambridge, 2000).

Annals of Lindisfarne and Durham
W. Levison, 'Die *Annales Lindisfarneses et Dunelmenses*: kritisch Untersucht und neu
    Herausgegeben', *DA* 17 (1961), 447–506.

Annals of St Bertin
Annales Bertiniani, ed. G. Waitz, MGH SS rer. Germ. V (Hanover, 1883).
The Annals of St. Bertin, trans. J. L. Nelson, Ninth Century Histories 1 (Manchester, 1991).

Annals of St Neots
*The Annals of St. Neots with Vita Prima Sancti Neoti, The Anglo-Saxon Chronicle. A Collaborative
    Edition* 17, ed. D. Dumville and M. Lapidge (Cambridge, 1985).

Anon., *Acts of the Abbots of Fontanelle (St Wandrille)*
Gesta sanctorum patrum Fontanellensis coenobii, ed. F. Lohier and J. Laporte (Rouen and Paris,
    1936).
EHD 1, trans. D. Whitelock (London, 1979), no. 20 (partial translation).

Anon., *History of the abbots, or Life of the Abbot Ceolfrid*
Historia Abbatum auctore Anonymo, ed. C. Plummer, *Venerabilis Bedae Opera Historica*, 2 vols
    (Oxford, 1896), Vol. I, 388–404.
Life of Ceolfrid, abbot of the monastery of Wearmouth and Jarrow, by an *Unknown Author of the
    Eighth Century*, ed. and trans, D. S. Boutflower (Sunderland and Jarrow, 1912).

Anon., *Life of Alcuin*
Monumenta Alcuiniana. ed. P. Jaffé, W. Wattenbach and E. Dümmler, Bibliotheca rerum
    Germanicarum VI (Berlin, 1873), 1–34.
Vita Alcuini, ed. W. Arndt, MGH SS XV.i (Hanover, 1887), 182–97.

Anon., *Life of Bertila, Abbess of Chelles*
Vita Bertilae abbatissae Calensis, ed. W. Levison, MGH SS rer. Merov. VI (Hanover and Leipzig,
    1913), 95–109.

Anon., *Life of St Gertrude*
Vita Geretrudis, ed. B. Krusch, MGH SS rer. Merov. II (Hanover, 1888).
Late Merovingian France: History and Hagiography 640–720, trans. P. Fouracre and R. A. Gerberding
    (Manchester, 1996), 301–26.

Anon., *Life of Wulfram of Sens*
Vita Vulframni, ed. W. Levison, MGH SS rer. Merov. V (Hanover and Leipzig, 1910), 657–73.

Anon., *Works of Dagobert III, King of the Franks*
Gesta Dagoberti Regis Francorum, ed. B. Krusch, MGH SS rer. Merov. II (Hanover, 1888), 509–24.

Anskar, *Life of St Willehad*
Vita Willehadi, ed. G. H. Pertz, MGH SS II (Berlin, 1829), 378–90.

Asser, *Life of Alfred*
Asser's Life of King Alfred Together with the Annals of St. Neots Erroneously Ascribed to Asser, ed. W. H. Stevenson (rev. edn) (Oxford, 1959).
Alfred the Great: Asser's Life of King Alfred and other Contemporary sources, trans. S. Keynes and M. Lapidge (Harmondsworth, 1983), 67–110.

Astronomer, *Life of Louis the Pious*
Vita Hludovici Imperatoris, ed. E. Tremp, MGH SS rer. Germ. LXIV (Hanover, 1995).
Son of Charlemagne. A Contemporary Life of Louis the Pious, trans. A. Cabaniss (Syracuse, NY, 1961).

Bede, *Ecclesiastical History*
Venerabilis Baedae Opera Historica, ed. C. Plummer, 2 vols (Oxford, 1896), I, 5–360.
Bede's Ecclesiastical History of the English People, ed. and trans. R. A. B. Mynors and B. Colgrave (Oxford, 1969), 1–571.

Bede, *Lives of the Abbots of Wearmouth and Jarrow*
Venerabilis Baedae Opera Historica, ed. C. Plummer, 2 vols (Oxford, 1896), I, 364–85.
The Age of Bede, trans. J. F. Webb and D. H. Farmer (Harmondsworth, 1988), 185–210.

Beowulf
Beowulf. An Edition, ed. B. Mitchell and F. C. Robinson (Oxford, 1998).
Beowulf. A New Verse Translation, trans. R. M. Liuzza (Peterborough, Ontario, 2000).

Boniface, *Letters*
Die Briefe des heiligen Bonifatius und Lullus, ed. M. Tangl, MGH Epp. Sel. I (Berlin, 1916).
The Letters of Saint Boniface, trans. E. Emerton (New York, 1940).
The Anglo-Saxon Missionaries in Germany, trans. C. H. Talbot (London, 1954), 65–149 (partial translation).

Byrhtferth of Ramsey, *Enchiridion*
Byrhtferth's Enchiridion, ed. P. S. Baker and M. Lapidge, EETS SS 15 (Oxford, 1995).

Byrhtferth of Ramsey, *Historia regum*
See **Symeon of Durham** below.
M. Lapidge, 'Byrhtferth of Ramsey and the Early Sections of the *Historia regum* Attributed to Symeon of Durham', *ASE*, 10 (1982), 97–122, at 115–16, reprinted in M. Lapidge, *Anglo-Latin Literature. Vol. 2: 900–1066* (London and Rio Grande, OH, 1993), 317–42.

Capitulary of Herstal
MGH Capit. I, Legum Sectio II, ed. A. Boretius (Hanover, 1883), no. 20.
Charlemagne. Translated Texts, trans. P. D. King (Kendal, 1987), 203–5.

Capitulary of Mantua

MGH Capit. I, Legum Sectio II, ed. A. Boretius (Hanover, 1883), no. 90.

The Reign of Charlemagne, Documents of Medieval History 2 trans. H. R. Loyn and J. Percival (London, 1975), 49–51.

***Cathwulf*, Letter to Charlemagne**

Epistola ad Carolum, ed. E. Dümmler, MGH Epp. IV, Epistolae Variorum (Berlin, 1895), no 7, at 501–4.

Chronicle of Æthelweard

The Chronicle of Æthelweard, ed. and trans. A. Campbell (London and New York, 1962).

Clausula de unctione Pippini

Clausula de unctione Pippini, ed. B. Krusch, MGH SS rer. Merov. I (Hanover, 1885), 465–66.

Carolingian Civilization: A Reader, trans. P. E. Dutton (Peterborough, Ontario, 1993), 12.

Codex Carolinus

Codex Carolinus, ed. F. W. Gundlach, MGH Epp. III, Epistolae Karolini Aevi I (Berlin, 1892), 476–653.

Monumenta Carolina, ed. P. Jaffe (Berlin, 1867), 1–334.

Charlemagne, Translated Sources, trans. P. D. King (Kendal, 1987), selection translated.

Continuatio Bedae

Venerabilis Baedae Opera Historica, ed. C. Plummer, 2 vols (Oxford, 1896), I, 361–63.

Bede's Ecclesiastical History of the English People, ed. and trans. R. A. B. Mynors and B. Colgrave (Oxford, 1969), 572–77.

Earlier Metz Annals

Annales Mettenses Priores, ed. B. de Simson, MGH SS rer. Germ. X (Hanover and Leipzig, 1905).

Late Merovingian France: History and Hagiography 640–720, trans. P. Fouracre and R. A. Gerberding (Manchester, 1996), 330–70 (for AD 687–727).

Charlemagne. Translated Texts, trans. P. D. King (Kendal, 1987), nos 149–166 (for AD 771–805).

Eigil, Abbot of Fulda, *Life of St Sturm*

Vita Sturmi, ed. G. H. Pertz, MGH SS II (Berlin, 1829), 366–77.

The Anglo-Saxon Missionaries in Germany, trans. C. H. Talbot (London, 1954), 181–202.

Einhard, *Life of Charlemagne*

Vita Karoli Magni, ed. F. Kurze, MGH SS rer. Germ. XXV (Hanover, 1911).

Charlemagne's Courtier: The Complete Einhard, trans. P. E. Dutton (Peterborough, Ontario, 1998), no. 2.

Felix, *Life of St Guthlac*

Felix's Life of St. Guthlac, ed. and trans. B. Colgrave (Cambridge, 1956).

Fredegar, *Chronicle*

The Fourth Book of the Chronicle of Fredegar and its continuations, ed. and trans. J. M. Wallace-Hadrill (London, 1960).

George of Ostia, *Report to Hadrian*

Epistola ad Hadrianum, ed. E. Dümmler, MGH Epp. IV (Berlin, 1895), no. 3, at 20–29.

Magdeburg Centuriators, *Ecclesiastica historia, integram ecclesiae Christi ideam ... congesta per aliquot studiosos et pios viros in urbe Magdeburgica*, 13 vols (Basle, 1561–74), cent. 8, cap. ix, cols 574–87.

Councils and Ecclesiastical Documents, ed. A. W. Haddan and W. Stubbs, 3 vols (Oxford, 1871), III, 447–61 (partial edition).

EHD 1, trans. D. Whitelock (1979), no. 191 (partial translation).

Gregory the Great, *Letters*

Gregorii I Papae Registrum Epistolarum, ed. P. Ewald and L. M. Hartmann, MGH Epp. I, II (Berlin, 1891–99).

Gregory of Tours, *Ten Books of Histories*

Libri decem historiarum, ed. B. Krusch, MGH SS rer. Merov. I (Hanover, 1885).

The History of the Franks by Gregory of Tours, 2 vols, trans. O. M. Dalton (Oxford, 1927).

Hincmar of Rheims, *On the Ordinance of the Palace*

Hinkmar von Rheims, De Ordine palatii, ed. and trans. T. Gross and R. Schieffer, MGH *Fontes* (Hanover, 1990), 145.

Historia post Bedam

See, below, **Roger of Howden**, *Chronica*, Vol. 1, xxvi–vii, xxxi–xl.

Historia regum (York Annals)

See **Symeon of Durham**, below.

Isidore of Seville, *Etymologies*

Isidore Hispalensis Episcopi, Etymologiarum sive originum, Libri XX, 2 vols, ed. W. M. Lindsay (Oxford, 1911).

Iter Hierosolymitanum Caroli Magni

F. Castets, 'Iter Hierosolymitanum ou voyage de Charlemagne à Jérusalem et à Constantinople. Texte latin d'après le MS de Montpellier', *Revue des langues romanes*, 36 (1892), 417–74.

A Thirteenth-century Life of Charlemagne, trans. R. Levine, Garland Library of Medieval Literature, Series B, Vol. 80 (New York, 1991).

John of Worcester, *Chronica*

The Chronicle of John of Worcester, Vol. 2: 450 to 1066, ed. and trans. R. R. Darlington, P. McGurk and J. Bray (Oxford, 1995).

Leo III, *Letters*

Epistulae X, ed. K. Hampe, MGH Epp. V (Hanover, 1899), 87–104.

Liber Historiae Francorum

MGH SS rer. Merov. II, ed. B. Krusch (Hanover, 1888).

Late Merovingian France: History and Hagiography 640–720, trans. P. Fouracre and R. A. Gerberding (Manchester, 1996), 79–96.

Liber pontificalis

Liber Pontificalis. Texte, introduction et commentaire, ed. L. Duchesne, 3 vols. rev. edn (Paris, 1955).

The Lives of the Eighth-Century Popes, trans. R. Davis (Liverpool, 1992).

The Lives of the Ninth-Century Popes, trans. R. Davis (Liverpool, 1995).

Lorsch Annals (*Annales Laureshamenses*)
Annales Laureshamenses, ed. G. Pertz, MGH SS I (Berlin, 1826), 22–30.
Charlemagne. Translated Texts, trans. P. D. King (Kendal, 1987), 137–45.

Lupus of Ferrières, *Letters*
Loup de Ferrières: Correspondence, ed. L. Levillain, Les Classiques de l'Histoire de France au
   Moyen Âge, Vols 10 and 16 (Paris, 1927–35).
The Letters of Lupus of Ferrières, trans. G. W. Regenos (The Hague, 1966).

Nithard, *History of the Sons of Louis the Pious*
Nithard: Histoire des fils de Louis le Pieux, ed. P. Lauer, Les Classiques de l'Histoire de France au
   Moyen Âge, 7 (Paris, 1926).
Carolingian Chronicles, trans. B. Scholz (Ann Arbor, MI, 1970), 129–74.

Northumbrian (Durham) *Liber Vitae*
Liber Vitae Ecclesiae Dunelmensis, ed. J. Stevenson, Surtees Soc. 13 (London, 1841).
Liber vitae ecclesiae Dunelmensis, ed. A. H. Thompson, Surtees Soc. 136 (London, 1923).

Procopius of Caesarea
The Gothic War, ed. and trans. H. B. Dewing, *The History of the Wars*, Vol. 5, Loeb Classical
   Library, vol. 217 (London and New York, 1928).

Ramsey Annals
Oxford, St John's College MS 17, fos 139r–143v and London, BL Cotton MS Nero C vii, fos 80r–
   84v.
C. R. Hart, 'The Ramsey Computus', *EHR*, 85 (1970), 29–44.

Roger of Howden, *Chronica*
Chronica Magistri Rogeri de Houedene, ed. W. Stubbs, RS 51, 4 vols (London, 1868–71).

Roger of Wendover, *Chronica*
Rogeri de Wendover, Chronica sive Flores Historiarum, ed. H. O. Coxe, 4 vols (London, 1841–44).
*Roger of Wendover's Flowers of History, Comprising the History of England from the Descent of
   the Saxons to 1235*, trans. J. A. Giles, 2 vols (London, 1849).

Royal Frankish Annals, *Annales regni Francorum* and Revised version
*Annales regni Francorum inde ab a. 741 usque ad. a. 829 qui dicuntur Annales Laurissenses
   maiores et Einhard*, ed. F. Kurze, MGH SS rer. Germ. VI (Hanover, 1895).
Carolingian Chronicles, trans. B. Scholz (Ann Arbor, MI, 1970), 37–125.

Sedulius Scottus, *Liber de Rectoribus Christianis*
Quella und untersuchungen zur lateinischen Philologie, ed. S. Hellmann (Munich, 1906), 1–91.
On Christian Rulers and the Poems: Sedulius Scottus, ed. and trans. E. Doyle (Binghampton, NY,
   1983).

Stephanus, *Vita Wilfridi*
The Life of Bishop Wilfrid by Eddius Stephanus, ed. and trans. B. Colgrave (Cambridge, 1927).

Symeon of Durham, *Libellus Dunelmensis Ecclesiae*
*Symeon of Durham: Libellus de exordio atque procursu istius, hoc est Dunelmensis, ecclesiae.
   Tract on the Origins and Progress of this Church of Durham*, ed. and trans. D. W. Rollason
   (Oxford, 2000).

Symeon of Durham, *Historia Regum* **(attr.)**
Symeonis Dunelmensis Opera et Collectanea, ed. J. Hinde, Surtees Soc. 51 (London, 1868).
Symeonis Monachis Opera Omnia, ed. T. Arnold, RS 75, 2 vols (London, 1885) II, 3–283.
Simeon of Durham: A History of the Kings of England, trans. J. Stevenson (Lampeter, 1987).

Theodulf of Orléans, *On the Court*
Theodulfi carmina, ed. E. Dümmler, MGH PLAC I (Berlin, 1881), no. 25, at 483–89.
Poetry of the Carolingian Renaissance, trans. P. Godman (London, 1985), 150–63.

Willibald, *Life of Boniface*
Vita Bonifatii, ed. W. Levison, MGH SS rer. Germ. LVII (Hanover and Leipzig, 1905).
Briefe des Bonifatius: Willibalds Leben des Bonifatius, ed. R. Rau (Darmstadt, 1968).
The Anglo-Saxon Missionaries in Germany, trans. C. H. Talbot (London, 1954), 25–64.

William of Malmesbury, *History of the English Bishops*
Willelmi Malmesbiriensis monachi De gestis pontificum Anglorum libri quinque, ed. N. E. S. A.
Hamilton, RS 52 (London, 1964).

William of Malmesbury, *History of the English Kings*
William of Malmesbury: Gesta Regum Anglorum. The History of the English Kings, ed. and trans.
R. A. B. Mynors, R. M. Thomson and M. Winterbottom, 2 vols (Oxford, 1998–99).

Secondary sources

Abel, S. and B. Simson, *Jahrbücher des Fränkischen Reiches unter Karl dem Großen, 789–814*, 2
vols (Berlin, 1883, reprinted 1969).
Aird, W., *St. Cuthbert and the Normans* (Woodbridge, 1998).
Alexander, J. J. G., 'The Illustrated Manuscripts of the *Notitia Dignitatum*', in R. Goodman and P.
Bartholomew (eds), *Aspects of the Notitia Dignitatum*, BAR Suppl. Ser. 15 (Oxford, 1976),
11–25.
Alexander, J. J. G., *A Survey of Manuscripts Illuminated in the British Isles. Vol. 1: Insular
Manuscripts, 6th to 9th Century* (London, 1978).
Anderson, A. O. and M. O. Anderson (eds), *The Chronicle of Melrose AD 735–1270: From the
Cottonian Manuscript Faustina B ix in the British Museum* (London, 1936).
Andrews, P. (ed.), *The Coins and Pottery from Hamwic*, Southampton Finds Vol. 1 (Southampton,
1988).
Angenendt, A., 'The Conversion of the Anglo-Saxons Considered against the Background of the
Early Medieval Mission', in *Angli e Sassoni al di qua e al di là del mare*, Settimane di Studio
32 (Spoleto, 1986), 747–81.
Angenendt, A., D. Geuenich and U. Ludwig (eds), *Der Memorial- und Liturgiecodex von San
Salvatore/Santa Giulia in Brescia*, MGH *Libri memoriales et necrologia*, ns 4 (Hanover, 2000).
Anton, H. H., *Fürstenspiegel und Herrscherethos in der Karolingerzeit*, Bonner historische
Forschungen 32 (Bonn, 1968).
Archibald, M. M., 'The Coinage of Beonna in the Light of the Middle Harling Hoard', *BNJ*, 55
(1985), 10–54.
Archibald, M. M., 'A Sceat of Ethelbert I of East Anglia and Recent Finds of Coins of Beonna',
BNJ, 65 (1995), 1–19.
Atsma, H. and J. Vezin, 'Le dossier suspect des possessions de Saint-Denis en Angleterre revisité
(VIIIe–IXe siècles)', MGH *Schriften* 33.4, *Falschungen im Mittelalter* 4, *Diplomatische
Fälschungen* 2 (Hanover, 1988), 211–36.

Atsma, H. and K.-F. Werner (eds), *Neustrie: Le pays au nord de la Loire de 650 à 850. Colloque historique international*, Beihefte der Francia 16 (Sigmaringen, 1989).

Ayres, B., *The English Heritage Book of Norwich* (London, 1994).

Ayres, B., 'How Norwich Began', *Current Archaeology*, 170 (2000), 48–51.

Baker, D., 'Scissors and Paste: Corpus Christi, Cambridge MS 139 Again', in *SCH*, 11 (1975), 83–124.

Baker, P. S. and M. Lapidge (eds), *Byrhtferth's Enchiridion*, EETS ss 15 (Oxford, 1995).

Bailey, R., *The Durham Cassiodorus*, Jarrow Lecture (Jarrow, 1978).

Barrow, J., 'English Cathedral Communities in the Late Tenth and Eleventh Centuries', in Rollason et al (eds), *Anglo-Norman Durham 1093–1193* (Woodbridge, 1994), 25–39.

Barker, E. E., 'Sussex Anglo-Saxon Charters, Part 2', *Sussex Archaeological Collections*, 87 (1948), 112–63.

Barsocchini, D., *Memorie e documenti per servire all'istoria del ducato di Lucca*, Vol. 5.2 (Lucca, 1837).

Bassett, S., 'In Search of the Origins of Anglo-Saxon Kingdoms', in Bassett (ed.), *The Origins of the Anglo-Saxon Kingdoms* (London, 1989), 3–27.

Bassett, S. (ed.), *The Origins of the Anglo-Saxon Kingdoms* (London, 1989).

Bauer, F. A. and M. Heinzelmann, 'The Constantinian Bishop's Church at Ostia: Preliminary Report on the 1998 Season', *Journal of Roman Archaeology*, 12 (1999), 342–53.

Becher, H., 'Das königliche Frauenkloster San Salvatore/Santa Giulia in Brescia im Spiegel seiner Memorialüberlieferung', *Frühmittelalterlich Studien*, 17 (1983), 299–392.

Becher, M., 'Karl der Große und Papst Leo III', in Stiegmann and Wemhoff (eds), *799 Kunst und Kultur* (Mainz, 1999), I, 22–36.

Behr, C., 'The Origins of Kingship in Early Medieval Kent', *EME*, 9 (2000), 25–52.

Berger, P. C., *The Insignia of the Notitia Dignitatum* (London and New York, 1981).

Berndt, R. (ed.), *Das Frankfurter Konzil von 794*, Kristallisationspunkt karolingischer Kultur Akten zweier Symposien (vom 23 bis 27 Februar und vom 13 bis 15 Oktober 1994) anlässkich der 1200–Jahrfeier der Stadt Frankfurt am Main, *Vol. 1 Politik und Kirche; Vol. 2 Kultur und Theologie* (Mainz, 1997).

Best, W., R. Gensen and P. R. Hömberg, 'Burgenbau in einer Grenzregion', in Stiegmann and Wemhoff (eds), *779 Kunst und Kultur* (Mainz, 1999), III, 328–45.

Biddle M., et al., 'Coins of the Anglo-Saxon Period from Repton', in Blackburn (ed.), *Anglo-Saxon Monetary History* (1986), 111–32.

Biddle, M., C. Blunt, B. Kjølbye-Biddle, M. Metcalf and H. Pagan, 'Coins of the Anglo-Saxon Period from Repton, Derbyshire, II', *BNJ*, 56 (1986), 16–35.

Biddle, M. and B. Kjølbye-Biddle, 'Repton and the Vikings', *Antiquity*, 66 (1992), 36–51.

Bierbrauer, K., 'Der Einfluß insulare Handschriften auf die kontinentale Buchmalerei', in Stiegemann and Wemhoff (eds), *799, Kunst und Kultur* (Mainz, 1999), III, 465–81.

Bischoff, B., *Manuscripts and Libraries in the Age of Charlemagne*, trans. M. Gorman (Cambridge, 1994).

Bishop, M. C. and J. C. N. Coulston, *Roman Military Equipment from the Punic Wars to the Fall of Rome* (London, 1993).

Blackburn, M. A. S. (ed.), *Anglo-Saxon Monetary History: Essays in Memory of Michael Dolley* (Leicester, 1986).

Blackburn, M. A. S., 'Coin Circulation in Germany During the Early Middle Ages: The Evidence of the Single Finds', in B. Kluge (ed.), *Fernhandel und Geldwirtschaft: Beiträge zum deutschen Münzwesen in sächsischer und salischer Zeit. Ergebnisse des Danenberg-Kolloquiums 1990* (Sigmaringen, 1993), 37–54.

Blackburn, M. A. S., 'Money and Coinage', in *NCMH* 2 (1995), 538–59.

Blackburn, M. A. S., 'The London Mint in the Reign of Alfred', in Blackburn and Dumville (eds), *Kings, Currency and Alliances* (Woodbridge, 1998), 105–24.

Blackburn, M. A. S., 'Finds from the Anglo-Scandinavian Site of Torksey, Lincolnshire', in B.

Paszkiewicz (ed.), *Moneta Mediævalis: Studia numizmatyczne i historyczne ofiarowane Profesorowi Stanisławowi Suchodolskiemu w. 65 rocznice urodzin* (Warsaw, 2002), 89–101.

Blackburn, M. A. S., 'Gold in England during the Ninth and Tenth Centuries', in J. Graham-Campbell and G. Williams (eds), *Silver Economy in the Viking Age* (forthcoming).

Blackburn, M. A. S. and M. Bonser, 'Single Finds of Anglo-Saxon and Norman Coins – 3', *BNJ*, 56 (1986), 64–101.

Blackburn, M. A. S. and M. Bonser, 'A Carolingian Gold Coin Struck from a Die of Chartres and Found at Congham, Norfolk', *Numismatic Circular*, 92 (1990), 304–6.

Blackburn, M. A. S. and D. N. Dumville (eds), *Kings, Currency, and Alliances: History and Coinage of Southern England in the Ninth Century* (Woodbridge, 1998).

Blackmore, L., 'Aspects of Trade and Exchange Evidenced by Recent Work on Saxon and Medieval Pottery from London', *Transactions of the London and Middlesex Archaelogical Society*, 50 (1999), 38–54.

Blair, J., *Early Medieval Surrey: Landholding, Church and Settlement before 1300* (Stroud, 1991).

Blockley, K., *Canterbury Cathedral Nave: Archaeology, History, and Architecture*, The Archaeology of Canterbury, NS Vol. 1 (Canterbury, 1997).

Blunt, C. E., 'Ecclesiastical Coinage in England (Part 1 to the Norman Conquest)', *Numismatic Chronicle,* 20 (1960), i–xvii.

Blunt, C. E., 'The Coinage of Offa', in R. H. M. Dolley (ed.), *Anglo-Saxon Coins* (London, 1961), 39–62.

Blunt, C. E., 'Anglo-Saxon Coins Found in Italy', in Blackburn (ed.), *Anglo-Saxon Monetary History* (Leicester, 1986), 159–69.

Blunt, C. E. and G. Van der Meer, 'A New Type for Offa', *BNJ*, 38 (1969), 182–83.

Booth, J., 'Sceattas in Northumbria', in Hill and Metcalf (eds), *Sceattas in England and on the Continent* (Oxford, 1984) 71–111.

Booth, J., 'Coinage and Northumbrian History: *c.* 790–810', in D. M. Metcalf (ed.), *Coinage in Ninth-century Northumbria* (Oxford, 1987), 57–90.

Booth, J. and I. Blowers, 'Finds of Sceattas and Stycas from Sancton', *Numismatic Chronicle*, 143 (1983), 139–45.

Bonner G. (ed.), *Famulus Christi. Essays in Commemoration of the Thirteenth Centenary of the Birth of the Venerable Bede* (London, 1976).

Bonner, G., C. Stancliffe and D. Rollason (eds), *St. Cuthbert, his Cult and Community to A.D. 1200* (Woodbridge, 1989).

Bonser, M., 'Fifteen Years of Coin Finds from Productive Sites', *The Yorkshire Numismatist*, 3 (1997), 15–38.

Bonser, M., 'Single Finds of Ninth-century Coins from Southern England: A Listing', in Blackburn and Dumville (eds), *Kings, Currency, and Alliances* (Woodbridge, 1998).

Booth, J., 'Northumbrian Coinage: The Productive Site at South Newbald', *The Yorkshire Numismatist*, 3 (1997), 15–38.

Boppert, W., 'Die frühchristlichen Grabinschriften aus der Servatiuskirche in Maastricht', in C. G. De Dijn (ed.), *Sint-Servatius, bisschop van Tongren-Maastricht. Actes du Colloque à Alden Biesen* (Tongres and Maastricht, 1984), 64–96.

Borghini, G. (ed.), *Marmi Antichi* (Rome, 1998).

Borgolte, M., *Der Gesandtenaustausch der Karolinger mit den Abbasiden und mit den Patriarchen von Jerusalem* (Munich, 1976).

Botfield, B. (ed.), *Catalogi veteres librorum Ecclesiae Cathedralis Dunelm Catalogue of the Library of Durham Cathedral at various periods, from the Conquest to the dissolution, including catalogues of the library of the abbey of Hulne and of the MSS in the Library of Bishop Cosin at Durham*, Surtees Society 7 (London, 1838).

Brandon, P. (ed.), *The South Saxons* (London, 1978).

Braunfels, W. (ed.), *Karl der Große: Lebenswerk und Nachleben*, 5 vols (Düsseldorf, 1965–67).

Brisbane, M., 'Hamwic (Saxon Southampton): An Eighth-Century Port and Production Centre', in

Hobley and Hodges (eds), *The Rebirth of Towns in the West AD 400–1050* (London, 1988), 102–8.

Brooks, N. P., 'The Ecclesiastical Topography of Early Medieval Canterbury', in M. W. Barley (ed.), *European Towns: Their Archaeology and Early History* (London, 1977).

Brooks, N. P., *The Early History of the Church of Canterbury Christ Church from 597 to 1066* (Leicester, 1984).

Brooks, N. P., 'The Development of Military Obligations in Eighth- and Ninth-Century England', in P. Clemoes and K. Hughes (eds), *England Before the Conquest* (London, 1971), 69–84, reprinted in N. P. Brooks, *Communities and Warfare 700–1400* (London, 2000), 32–47.

Brooks, N. P., 'Arms, Status and Warfare in Late Saxon England', in D. Hill (ed.), *Ethelred the Unready: Papers to the Millennium Conference*, BAR Bri. Ser. 69 (Oxford, 1978), 81–103, reprinted in N. P. Brooks, *Communities and Warfare, 700–1400* (London, 2000), 138–61.

Brooks, N. P., 'England in the Ninth Century: The Crucible of Defeat', *TRHS*, 5th ser., 29 (1979), 1–20, reprinted in N. P. Brooks, *Communities and Warfare, 700–1400* (London, 2000), 48–68.

Brooks, N. P., 'The Formation of the Mercian Kingdom', in S. Bassett (ed.), *The Origins of Anglo-Saxon Kingdoms* (London, 1989), 159–70, reprinted in N. P. Brooks, *Anglo-Saxon Myths: State and Church, 400–1066* (London, 2000), 61–78.

Brooks, N. P., 'The Cathedral Community at Canterbury, 597–1070', in P. Collinson and N. Ramsay (eds), *The History of Canterbury Cathedral* (Oxford, 1995), 1–35, reprinted in N. P. Brooks, *Anglo-Saxon Myths: State and Church 400–1066* (London, 2000), 101–54.

Brooks, N. P., *Bede and the English,* Jarrow Lecture (Jarrow, 1999).

Brooks, N. P., 'Canterbury, Rome, and the Construction of English Identity', in J. M. H. Smith (ed.), *Early Medieval Rome and the Christian West: Essays in Honour of D. A. Bullough* (Leiden, 2000), 221–46.

Brooks, N. P. with J. Graham-Campbell, 'Reflections on the Viking-Age Silver Hoard from Croydon, Surrey', in Blackburn (ed.), *Anglo-Saxon Monetary History* (Leicester, 1986), 91–110.

Brown, G. H., 'The Preservation and Transmission of Northumbrian Culture on the Continent: Alcuin's Debt to Bede', in P. E. Szarmach and J. T. Rosenthal (eds), *The Preservation and Transmission of Anglo-Saxon Culture* (Kalamazoo, MI, 1997), 159–76.

Brown, M. P., 'Continental symptoms in Insular Codicology: Historical Perspective', in P. Rück (ed.), *Pergament: Geschichte, Struktur, Restaurierung, Herstellung* (Sigmaringen, 1991), 57–62.

Brown, M. P., *The Book of Cerne: Prayer, Patronage and Power in Ninth-century England* (London and Toronto, 1996).

Brown, M. P., *'In the beginning was the Word': Books and Faith in the Age of Bede*, Jarrow Lecture (Jarrow, 2000).

Brown, T. J., 'The Distribution and Significance of Membrane Prepared in the Insular Manner', *La Paléographie Hébraïque*, Colloques Internationaux du Centre National de la Recherche Scientifique 547 (Paris, 1972), 127–35, and reprinted in J. Batley, M. P. Brown and J. Roberts (eds), *A Palaeographer's View. The Selected Writings of Julian Brown* (London, 1993), 125–39.

Brown, T. J., 'Tradition, Imitation and Invention in Insular Handwriting of the Seventh and Eighth Centuries', in J. Batley, M. P. Brown and J. Roberts (eds), *A Palaeographer's View. The Selected Writings of Julian Brown* (London, 1993), 179–200.

Brown, T. J., 'The Irish Element in the Insular System of Scripts to c. AD 850', in H. Loewe (ed.), *Iren und Europa im früheren Mittelalter*, 2 vols (Stuttgart, 1982), I, 101–19, and reprinted in J. Batley, M. P. Brown and J. Roberts (eds), *A Palaeographer's View. The selected writings of Julian Brown* (London, 1993), 201–220.

Brown, T. J. and T. W. Mackay, *Codex Vaticanus Palatinus Latinus 235. An Early Insular Manuscript of Paulinus of Nola 'Carmina'*, Armarium codicum insignium, 4 (Turnhout, 1988).

Browne, G. F., *Alcuin of York* (London, 1908).

Brownrigg, L. L. (ed.), *The Making of the Medieval Book: Techniques of Production* (Los Altos, 1995).

Bruce-Mitford, R. S. L. (ed.), *The Sutton Hoo Ship Burial,* 3 vols (London, 1975–83).

Bruce-Mitford, R. S. L., 'The Sutton Hoo Ship Burial: Some Foreign Connections', in *Angli e Sassoni al di qua e al di là del mare*, Settimane di Studio 32 (Spoleto, 1986), 143–218.

Bruce-Mitford, R. S. L. and M. R. Luscombe, 'The Benty Grange Helmet and Some other Supposed Anglo-Saxon Helmets', in R. Bruce-Mitford (ed.), *Aspects of Anglo-Saxon Archaeology* (London, 1974), 223–52.

Brugmann, B., 'The Role of Continental Artefact-types in Sixth-Century Kentish Chronology', in Hines et al. (eds), *The Pace of Change* (Oxford, 1999), 65–79.

Buckler, F. W., *Harunu'l-Rashid and Charles the Great* (Cambridge, MA, 1931).

Bu'Lock, J. D., 'The Celtic, Saxon and Scandinavian Settlement at Meols in Wirral', *Transactions of the Historical Society of Lancashire and Cheshire*, 112 (1961), 1–28.

Bullough, D. A., 'Europae Pater: Charlemagne and his Achievement in the Light of Recent Scholarship', *EHR*, 85 (1970), 59–105.

Bullough, D. A., *The Age of Charlemagne* (London, 1973).

Bullough, D. A., 'Alcuin and the Kingdom of Heaven: Liturgy, Theology and the Carolingian Age', in U.-R. Blumenthal (ed.), *Carolingian* Essays (Washington, DC, 1983), 1–69, reprinted in Bullough, *Carolingian Renewal* (Manchester, 1991), 161–240.

Bullough, D. A., '*Albuinus deliciosus Karoli regis*. Alcuin of York and the Shaping of the Early Carolingian Court', in L. Fenske, W. Rösener and T. Zotz (eds), *Institutionen, Kultur und Gesellschaft im Mittelalter* (Sigmaringen, 1984), 73–92.

Bullough, D. A., '*Aula Renovata*: The Carolingian Court before the Aachen Palace', *Proceedings of the British Academy*, 71 (1985), 267–301, reprinted in Bullough, *Carolingian Renewal* (Manchester, 1991), 123–60.

Bullough, D. A., *Carolingian Renewal: Sources and Heritage* (Manchester, 1991).

Bullough, D. A., 'What has Ingeld to do with Lindisfarne', *ASE*, 22 (1993), 93–125.

Bullough, D. A., 'Reminiscence and Reality: Text Transmission and Testimony of an Alcuin Letter', *Journal of Medieval Latin*, 5 (1995), 174–201.

Bullough, D. A., 'Alcuin before Frankfort', in Berndt (ed.), *Das Frankforter Konzil von 794* (Mainz, 1997), 571–85.

Bullough, D. A., 'Alcuin's Cultural Influence: The Evidence of the Manuscripts', in L. A. J. R. Houwen and A. A. MacDonald (eds), *Alcuin of York. Scholar at the Carolingian Court*, Germania Latina 3 (Groningen, 1998), 1–26.

Burn, A. R., 'Procopius and the Island of Ghosts', *EHR*, 70 (1955), 258–61.

Burnell, S. and E. James, 'The Archaeology of Conversion on the Continent in the Sixth and Seventh Centuries', in Gameson (ed.), *St. Augustine and the Conversion of England* (Stroud, 1999), 83–106.

Cabaniss, A., 'Bodo-Eleazar: A Famous Jewish Convert', *Jewish Quarterly Review*, ns 43 (1952–53), 313–28.

Cameron, A., *Procopius and the Sixth Century* (London, 1985).

Campbell, A., *Old English Grammar* (Oxford, 1959).

Campbell, J., 'The First Century of Christianity', *Ampleforth Journal*, 76 (1971), 12–29, reprinted in Campbell, *Essays in Anglo-Saxon History* (London, 1986) 49–67.

Campbell, J., *Essays in Anglo-Saxon History* (London, 1986).

Carver, M. O. H., *Sutton Hoo: Burial Ground of Kings?* (London, 1998).

Casey, P. J. and R. Reece (eds), *Coins and the Archaeologist* (2nd edn) (London, 1988).

Castets, F., 'Iter Hierosolymitanum ou voyage de Charlemagne à Jérusalem et à Constantinople. Texte latin d'après le MS de Montpellier', *Revue des langues romanes*, 36 (1892), 417–74.

Celini, J., *Le vocabulaire politique et Social dans la Correspondance d'Alcuin*, Travaux et Mémoires, 12 (Aix-en-Provence, 1959).

Chaplais, P., 'The Origin and Authenticity of the Royal Anglo-Saxon Diploma', *Journal of the Society of Archivists*, 3.2 (1965), 48–61, reprinted in F. Ranger (ed.), *Prisca Munimenta* (London, 1973), 28–42.

Chaplais, P., 'The Letter from Bishop Waldhere of London to Archbishop Brihtwold of Canterbury: The Earliest Original "Letter Close"', in M. B. Parkes and A. G. Watson (eds), *Medieval*

Scribes, Manuscripts and Libraries (London, 1978), 3–24, at 9–10, reprinted in P. Chaplais, *Essays in Medieval Diplomacy and Administration* (London, 1981), 3–13.

Chaplais, P., 'The Anglo-Saxon Chancery: From the Diploma to the Writ', *Journal of the Society of Archivists*, 3 (1966), 160–76.

Chase, C. (ed.), *Two Alcuin Letter-Books*, Toronto Medieval Latin Texts 5 (Toronto, 1975).

Chatelain, E., 'Notice sur les manuscrits des poésies de S. Paulin de nole suivie d'observations sur le texte', *Bibliothèque des Écoles Française d'Athènes et de Rome*, 14 (Paris, 1880).

Cheney, R. (ed.), *Handbook of Dates for Students of English History*, Royal Historical Society Guides and Handbooks, No. 4, revised by M. Jones (Cambridge, 2000).

Chick, D., 'Towards a Chronology for Offa's Coinage: An Interim Study', *The Yorkshire Numismatist*, 3 (1997), 47–64.

Classen, P., 'Karl der Große, das Papsttum und Byzanz', in Braunfels (ed.), *Karl der Große* (1965), Vol. 1, 537–608.

Classen, P., *Karl de Große, das Papsttum und Byzanz, die Begründung des Karolingischen Kaisertums*, Beiträge sur Geschichte und Quellenkunde des Mittelalters 9, 2 vols (Sigmaringen, 1985–88).

Clemoes, P. and Hughes, D. (eds), *England before the Conquest: Studies in Primary Sources Presented to Dorothy Whitelock* (London, 1971).

Collins, R., *Early Medieval Spain* (London, 1983).

Collins, R., *Charlemagne* (Basingstoke, 1998).

Coupland, S., 'Dorestad in the Ninth Century: The Numismatic Evidence', *JMP*, 75 (1988), 5–26.

Coupland, S., 'Money and Coinage under Louis the Pious', *Francia*, 17 (1990), 23–54.

Coupland, S., 'The Early Coinage of Charles the Bald, 840–864', *Numismatic Chronicle*, 151 (1991), 121–58.

Coupland, S., 'The Vikings in Francia and Anglo-Saxon England to 911', in *NCMH* 2 (1995), 190–201.

Cramp, R. J., 'Schools of Mercian Sculpture', in Dornier (ed.), *Mercian Studies* (1977), 191–231.

Cramp, R. J., 'Wearmouth and Jarrow in their Continental Context', in K. Painter (ed.), *'Churches Built in Ancient Times': Recent Studies in Early Christian Archaeology* (London, 1994), 279–94.

Cubitt, C., *Anglo-Saxon Church Councils, c. 650–c.850* (London, 1995).

Cubitt, C., 'Finding the Forger: An Alleged Decree of the 679 Council of Hatfield', *EHR*, 114 (1999), 1217–48.

Cunliffe, B., *Wessex to AD 1000* (London, 1993).

Dalton, O. M., 'Second Silver Treasure from Cyprus', *Archæologia*, 60 (1906), 1–24.

Davis, C. R., 'Cultural Assimilation in the Anglo-Saxon Royal Genealogies', *ASE*, 21 (1992), 23–36.

Davis, R. H. C., 'Brixworth and Clofesho', *JBAA*, 25 (1962), 71.

Deanesley, M., *The Pre-Conquest Church in England* (London, 1963).

Déer, J., 'Das Untergang des Awarenreiches', in Braunfels (ed.), *Karl der Große* (1965), Vol. I, 719–91.

de Clercq, C. (ed.), *Conciliae Galliae, a 511–695*, CCSL 148A (Turnhout, 1963).

de Maillé, G. A., *Les Cryptes des Jouarre. Plans et relevés de P. Rousseau* (Paris, 1971).

De Rossi, J. B., 'L'Inscription du tombeau d'Hadrien I composée et gravée en France par ordre de Charlemagne', *École Française de Rome. Mélanges d'archéologie et d'histoire*, 8 (1888), 478–501.

Dolley, R. H. M., 'New Light on the Pre-1760 Coney Street (York) Find of Coins of the Duurstede Mint', *JMP*, 52/53 (1965–66), 1–6.

Dolley, R. H. M. and D. M. Metcalf, 'Two Stray Finds from St Albans of Coins of Offa and of Charlemagne', *BNJ*, 28 (1957), 459–66.

Dolley, R. H. M. and K. F. Morrison, 'Finds of Carolingian Coins from Great Britain and Ireland', *BNJ*, 32 (1963), 75–87.

Dornier, A. (ed.), *Mercian Studies* (Leicester, 1977).

Dornier, A., 'The Breedon Lion and its Associates: A Comparative Study of Anglo-Saxon and

Frankish Architectural Animal Panels', in J. Bourne (ed.), *Anglo-Saxon Landscapes in the East Midlands* (Leicester, 1996), 37–52.

Douglas, J., *Nenia Britannica: or, a sepuchral history of Great Britain, from the earliest period to its general conversion to Christianity* (London, 1793).

Drew, K. F. (trans.), *The Laws of the Salian Franks* (Philadelphia, 1991).

DuCange, C., *Glossarium mediae et infirmae Latinis*, 10 vols (Niort, 1883–87).

Duchesne, L., *Fastes épiscopaux de l'ancienne Gaul*, 3 vols (Paris, 1907–15).

Dümmler, E., 'Zur Lebensgeschichte Alchuins', *NA*, 18 (1893), 51–70.

Dumville, D. N., 'The Corpus Christi "Nennius"', *Bulletin of the Board of Celtic Studies*, 25 (1972–74), 369–74.

Dumville, D. N., 'The Anglian Collection of Royal Genealogies and Regnal Lists', *ASE*, 5 (1976), 23–50.

Dumville, D. N., 'Annalistic Writing at Canterbury', *Peritia*, 2 (1983), 23–57.

Dumville, D. N., 'The West Saxon Genealogical Regnal List and the Chronology of Early Wessex', *Peritia*, 4 (1985), 21–66.

Dumville, D. N., 'The West Saxon Genealogical Regnal list: Manuscripts and Texts', *Anglia*, 104 (1986), 1–32.

Dumville, D. N., 'Textual Archaeology and Northumbrian History Subsequent to Bede', in D. M. Metcalf (ed.), *Coinage in Ninth-century Northumbria*, BAR Bri. Ser. 180 (Oxford, 1987), 43–55.

Dumville, D. N., 'The Tribal Hidage: An Introduction to its Texts and their History', in Bassett (ed.), *The Origins of the Anglo-Saxon Kingdoms* (London, 1989), 225–30.

Dutton, P. E. (trans.), *Carolingian Civilization: A Reader* (Peterborough, Ontario, 1993).

Dutton, P. E., *The Politics of Dreaming in the Carolingian Empire* (Lincoln, NB, 1994).

Egan, G., 'Material from a Millennium: Detritus from a Developing City', *Transactions of the London and Middlesex Archaelogical Society*, 50 (1999), 29–37.

Ellmers, D., 'The Frisian Monopoly of Coastal Transport in the 6th–8th Centuries AD', in S. McGrail (ed.), *Maritime Celts, Frisians and Saxons*, CBA Res. Rpt., 71 (London, 1990), 91–92.

Emerton, E. (trans.), *The Letters of Saint Boniface* (New York, 1940).

Enright, M. J., 'Charles the Bald and Aethelwulf of Wessex: The Alliance of 856 and Strategies of Royal Succession', *JMH*, 5 (1979), 291–302.

Evans, M. W., *Medieval Drawings* (London and New York, 1969).

Evison, V. I., *The Fifth-Century Invasions South of the Thames* (London, 1965).

Evison, V. I., *Dover, Buckland Anglo-Saxon Cemetery*, Historic Buildings and Monuments Commission for England Archaeological Report, 3 (London, 1987).

Ewig, E., 'Milo et eiusmodi similes', in *Sankt Bonifatius. Gedenkgabe zum zwölfhundertsten Todestag* (Fulda, 1954), 412–40, reprinted in H. Atsma (ed.), *Spätantikes und Fränkisches Gallien*, Beihefte der Francia, 3 (Zurich and Munich, 1976).

Faussett, B., *Inventorium Sepulchrale: an account of some antiquities dug up at Gilston, Kingston, Sibertswold, Barfriston, Beakesbourne, Chartham and Crondale in the county of Kent, from AD 1757 to AD 1773* (London, 1856).

Favreau, R., *Épigraphie Médiévale*, L'Atelier du Médiéviste, Vol. 5 (Turnhout, 1997).

Fernie, E., *The Architecture of the Anglo-Saxons* (London, 1983).

Finberg, H. P. R., 'Princes of the Hwicce', in H. P. R. Finberg, *Early Charters of the West Midlands* (Leicester, 1964), 167–80.

Fichtenau, H., *Karl der Große und das Kaisertum*, Mittelungen des Instituts für Österreichische Geschichtsforschung 16 (Darmstadt, 1971).

Fletcher, E., 'The Influence of Merovingian Gaul on Northumbria in the Seventh Century', *Medieval Archaeology*, 20 (1980), 69–81.

Fletcher, R., *The Conversion of Europe: From Paganism to Christianity 371–1368 AD* (London, 1997).

Foester, H. (ed.), *Liber Diurnus romanorum pontificum* (Bern, 1958).

Forsyth, K., 'Evidence for a Lost Pictish Source in the *Historia regum Anglorum* of Symeon of Durham', in S. Taylor (ed.), *Kings, Clerics and Chronicles in Scotland, 500–1297* (Dublin, 2000), 19–34.

Foster, J., 'A Boar Figurine from Guilden Morden, Cambs', *Medieval Archaeology*, 21 (1977), 166–67.

Foster, S. M. (ed.), *The St Andrew's Sarcophagus: A Pictish masterpiece and its International Connections* (Dublin, 1998).

Fournier, P. and G. Le Bras, *Histoire des collections canoniques en Occident depuis les Fausses Décretals jusqu'au Décret de Gratien*, 2 vols (Paris, 1931).

Fouracre, P., *The Age of Charles Martel* (Harlow, 2000).

Fouracre, P. and R. A. Gerberding (trans.), *Late Merovingian France: History and Hagiography 640–720* (Manchester, 1996).

Fox, C., *Offa's Dyke: A Field Survey of the Western Frontier Works of Mercia in the Seventh and Eighth Centuries AD* (Oxford, 1955).

Freeman, A., 'Carolingian Orthodoxy and the Fate of the Libri Carolini', *Viator*, 16 (1985), 65–108.

Fryde, E. B., D. E. Greenway, S. Porter and I. Roy (eds), *Handbook of British Chronology*, Royal Historical Society Handbooks 2 (3rd edn) (London, 1986).

Gameson, R., 'The Earliest Books of Christian Kent', in Gameson (ed.), *St. Augustine* (Stroud, 1999), 313–73.

Gameson, R. (ed.), *St. Augustine and the Conversion of England* (Stroud, 1999).

Ganshof, F. L., *Recherches sur les Capitulaires* (Paris, 1958).

Ganshof, F. L., 'The Use of the Written word in Charlemagne's Administration', in *The Carolingians and the Frankish Monarchy. Studies in Carolingian History*, trans. J. Sondheimer (London, 1971), 125–42.

Ganshof, F. L., 'The Frankish Monarchy and its External Relations, from Pippin III to Louis the Pious', in *The Carolingians and the Frankish Monarchy. Studies in Carolingian History*, trans. J. Sondheimer (London, 1971), 161–204.

Ganz, D., *Corbie in the Carolingian Renaissance*, Beihefte der Francia 20 (Sigmaringen, 1990).

Gariel, E., *Les monnaies royales sous la race carolingienne*, 2 vols (Strasbourg, 1883–84).

Garrison, M., 'The English and the Irish at the Court of Charlemagne', in P. L. Butzer, M. Kerner and W. Oberschelp (eds), *Karl der Grosse und sein Nachwirken. 1200 Jahre Kultur und Wissenschaft in Europa. Vol. 1: Wissen und Weltbild* (Turnhout, 1997), 97–124.

Garrison, M., 'The Social world of Alcuin: Nicknames at York and at the Carolingian Court', in L. A. J. R. Houwen and A. A. MacDonald (eds), *Alcuin of York. Scholar at the Carolingian Court*, Germania Latina 3 (Groningen, 1998), 59–80.

Garrison, M., 'Letters to a King and Biblical Exempla: The Examples of Cathwulf and Clemens Peregrinus', *EME*, 7 (1998), 305–28.

Gaskoin, C. J. B., *Alcuin: His Life and Work* (London, 1904).

Gasparii, F. (ed. and trans.), *Suger: Œuvres, Vol. 1. Écrit sur la consécration de Saint-Denis; L'Œuvre administrative; Histoire de Louis VII* (Paris, 1996).

Gem, R., 'Architecture of the Anglo-Saxon Church, 735 to 870: From Archbishop Ecgberht to Archbishop Ceolnoth', *JBAA*, 146 (1993), 29–66.

Gerberding, R. A., *The Rise of the Carolingians and the Liber Historiae Francorum* (Oxford, 1987).

Gerberding, R. A., '716: A Crucial Year for Charles Martel', in J. Jarnut, U. Nonn and M. Richter (eds), *Karl Martell in seiner Zeit*, Beihefte der Francia, 37 (Sigmaringen, 1994), 205–16.

Gerchow, J., *Die Gedenküberlieferung der Angelsachsen*, Arbeiten sur Frümittelalterforschung, 20 (Berlin and New York, 1988).

Ghislain, J.-C., 'La production funéraire en pierre de Tournai à l'époque romaine. Des dalles funéraires sans décor aux oeuvres magistrales du 12e siècle', in *Les Grands-Siècles de Tournai*, Tournai Art et Histoire 7 (Louvain-la-Neuve, 1993), 115–208.

Godfrey, C. J., 'The Archbishopric of Lichfield', *Studies in Church History* I (1964), 145–53.

Godman, P., *Poetry of the Carolingian Renaissance* (London, 1985).

Goffart, W., 'Bede and the Ghost of Wilfrid', in *Narrators of Barbarian History (A.D. 550–800): Jordanes, Gregory of Tours, Bede, and Paul the Deacon* (Princeton, NJ, 1988), 235–328.

Gorman, M., 'The Encyclopedic Commentary on Genesis Prepared for Charlemagne by Wigbod', *Recherches Augustiniennes*, 17 (1982), 173–201.

Gorman, M., 'Wigbod and Biblical Studies under Charlemagne', *Revue Benedictine*, 107 (1997), 40–76.

Gneuss, H., *Handlist of Anglo-Saxon Manuscripts: A List of Manuscripts and Manuscript Fragments Written or Owned in England up to 1100* (Tempe, AZ, 2001).

Gnoli, R., *Marmora Romana* (Rome, 1971, reprinted 1988).

Godfrey, C. J., 'The Archbishopric of Lichfield', *Studies in Church History*, 1 (1964), 145–53.

Granger-Taylor, H., 'The Weft-patterned Silks and their Braid: The Remains of an Anglo-Saxon Dalmatic of *c.* 800?', in Bonner et al. (eds), *St. Cuthbert* (Woodbridge, 1989).

Gransden, A., *Historical Writing in England, c. 550 to c. 1307* (London, 1974).

Gransden, A., 'The Chronicles of Medieval England and Scotland, Part 1', *JMH*, 16 (1990), 129–50.

Gray, N., 'The Palaeography of Latin Inscriptions in the Eighth, Ninth and Tenth Centuries in Italy', *Papers of the British School at Rome* 16, ns 3 (1948), 38–162.

Greenhalgh, M., *The Survival of Roman Antiquities in the Middle Ages* (London, 1989).

Gretsch, M., 'Æthelwold's Translation of the Rule of St. Benedict and its Latin Exemplar', *ASE*, 3 (1974), 125–51.

Grierson, P., 'The Gold Solidus of Louis the Pious and its Imitations', *Jaarboek voor Munt- en Penningkunde*, 38 (1951), 1–41, reprinted with corrections as Ch. XXII in Grierson, *Dark Age Numismatics* (London, 1979).

Grierson, P., 'The Canterbury (St. Martin) Hoard of Frankish and Anglo-Saxon Coin-ornaments', *BNJ*, 27 (1952), 39–51.

Grierson, P., 'Chronologia delle riforme monetari di Carolo Magne', *Riuista Italiana di Numismatica*, 5th Ser. 56 (1954), 65–79, reprinted as Chapter XVII in Grierson, *Dark Age Numismatics* (London, 1979).

Grierson, P., 'Commerce in the Dark Ages: A Critique of the Evidence', *TRHS*, 5th series 9 (1959), 123–40.

Grierson, P., 'La date des monnaies d'or de Louis le Pieux', *Le Moyen Age*, 69 (1963), 67–74, at 72–73, reprinted as Ch. VIII in Grierson, *Dark Age Numismatics* (London, 1979).

Grierson, P., 'Money and Coinage under Charlemagne', in Braunfels (ed.), *Karl der Große* (Düsseldorf, 1965).

Grierson, P., *Catalogue of the Byzantine Coins in the Dumbarton Oaks Collection*, 5 vols (Washington, DC, 1966–73).

Grierson, P., *Dark Age Numismatics: Selected Studies* (London, 1979).

Grierson, P., 'A Denier of Pepin the Short (751–68)', in Blackburn (ed.), *Anglo-Saxon Monetary History* (1986), 127–30.

Grierson, P. and M. A. S. Blackburn, *Medieval European Coinage, with a catalogue of the coins in the Fitzwilliam Museum, Cambridge. Vol. 1: The Early Middle Ages, 5th–10th Centuries* (Cambridge, 1986).

Grierson, P., 'The *Gratia Dei Rex* Coinage of Charles the Bald', in M. Gibson and J. L. Nelson (eds), *Charles the Bald: Court and Kingdom* (2nd edn) (Aldershot, 1990), 52–64.

Griffiths, D., 'Trade and Production Centers in the Post-Roman North: The Irish Sea Perspective', in *The Archaeology of Gudme and Lundeborg. Papers Presented at Svendborg, October* 1991, Archæologiske Studier 10 (Copenhagen, 1994), 184–88.

Gullick, M., 'The Scribes of the Durham Cantor's Book (Durham, Dean and Chapter Library, MS B.IV.24) and the Durham Martyrology Scribe' in Rollason et al. (eds), *Anglo-Norman Durham* (Woodbridge, 1994), 93–109.

Gullick, M., 'The Hand of Symeon of Durham: Further Observations on the Durham Martyrology Scribe', in Rollason (ed.), *Symeon of Durham* (Stamford, 1998), 14–31.

Halbertsma, H., 'Dokkum', *Bulletin van de Koninklijke Nederlandse Ouheidkundige Bond*, 69 (1970), 33–52.

Halphen, L., *Études critiques sur l'Histoire de Charlemagne* (Paris, 1921).

Hamerow, H., 'Migration Theory and the Migration Period', in Vyner (ed.), *Building on the Past* (London, 1994), 164–77.

Hampe, K., 'Die Wiedereinsetzung des Königs Eardulf von Northumbrien durch Karl den Großen und Papst Leo III', *Deutsche Zeitschriften für Geschichtswissenschaft*, 9 (1894), 352–59.

Hannig, J., *Consensus Fidelium: Frühfeudale Interpretation des Verhältnisses von Königtum und Adel* (Stuttgart, 1983).

Harrison, K., *The Framework of Anglo-Saxon History to A.D. 900* (Cambridge, 1976), 38–42.

Hart, C. R., 'The Ramsey Computus', *EHR*, 85 (1970), 29–44.

Hart, C. R., *The Early Charters of Northern England* (Leicester, 1975).

Hart, C. R., 'Byrhtferth's Northumbrian Chronicle', *EHR*, 97 (1982), 558–82.

Hart, C. R., 'The Anglo-Saxon Chronicle at Ramsey', in J. Roberts, J. L. Nelson and M. Godden (eds), *Alfred the Wise: studies in honour of Janet Bately on the occasion of her sixty-fifth birthday* (Cambridge, 1997), 65–88.

Hartmann, W., *Die Synoden der Karolingerseit im Frankenreich und in Italien* (Paderborn, 1989).

Harvey, P. D. A. and A. McGuinness, *A Guide to British Medieval Seals* (London, 1996).

Hawkes, J., 'A Question of Judgement: The Iconographic Programme of Sandbach, Cheshire', in C. Bourke (ed.), *From the Isles of the North* (Belfast, 1995), 213–20.

Hawkes, J., 'Constructing Iconographies: Questions of Identity in Mercian Sculpture', in M. P. Brown and C. A. Farr (eds), *Mercia: An Anglo-Saxon Kingdom in Europe* (London, 2001), 230–45.

Hawkes, S. C., J. M. Merrick and D. M. Metcalf, 'X-ray Fluorescent Analysis of Some Dark Age Coins and Jewellery', *Archaeometry*, 9 (1966), 98–138.

Haywood, J., *Dark-Age Naval Power: A Reassessment of Frankish and Anglo-Saxon Seafaring Activity* (London, 1991).

Henderson, G., *From Durrow to Kells, the Insular Gospel-books, 650–800* (London, 1987).

Henderson, G., 'Emulation and Invention in Carolingian Art', in McKitterick (ed.), *Carolingian Culture* (Cambridge, 1994), 248–73.

Henderson, I., 'Primus inter Pares: The St. Andrew's Sarcophagus and Pictish Sculpture', in Foster (ed.), *The St. Andrew's Sarcophagus* (Dublin, 1998), 97–167.

Hennebicque-le Jan, R., 'Prosopographica Neustrica, les agents du roi en Neustrie de 639 à 840', in H. Atsma (ed.), *La Neustrie, le pays au nord de la Loire de 650 à 850*, Beihefte der Francia 16/11 (Sigmaringen, 1989), 231–70.

Hicks, C., The Pictish Class I Animals', in Higgitt and Spearman (eds), *The Age of Migrating Ideas* (Edinburgh, 1993), 196–202.

Higgitt, J. and R. M. Spearman (eds), *The Age of Migrating Ideas. Early Medieval Art in Britain and Ireland* (Edinburgh, 1993).

Higham, N. J., *An English Empire: Bede and the Early Anglo-Saxon Kings* (Manchester, 1995).

Hill, D., 'Offa's Dyke: Pattern and Purpose', *Antiquaries Journal*, 80 (2000), 195–206.

Hill, D. and D. M. Metcalf (eds), *Sceattas in England and on the Continent*, BAR Bri. Ser. 128 (Oxford, 1984).

Hines, J., 'The Becoming of the English: Identity, Material Culture and Language in Early Anglo-Saxon England', *ASSAH*, 7 (1994), 49–59.

Hines, J. (ed.), *The Anglo-Saxons from the Migration Period to the Eighth Century. An Ethnographic Perspective*, Studies in Historical Archaeoethnology 2 (San Marino, 1997).

Hines, J., K. Høilund Nielsen and F. Siegmund (eds), *The Pace of Change: Studies in Early Medieval Chronology* (Oxford, 1999).

Hobley, R. and R. Hodges (eds), *The Rebirth of Towns in the West, A.D. 400–1050*, CBA Res. Rpt 68 (London, 1988).

Hodges, R., *Dark Age Economics: The Origins of Towns and Trade A.D. 600–1000* (London, 1982).

Hodges, R., *The Anglo-Saxon Achievement: Archaeology and the Beginnings of English Society* (London, 1989).

Hodges, R., 'Trade and Market Origins in the Ninth Century: Relations between England and the Continent', in M. T. Gibson and J. L. Nelson (eds), *Charles the Bald: Court and Kingdom*, (2nd rev. edn) (Aldershot, 1990), 203–23.

Hodges, R., *Towns and Trade in the Age of Charlemagne* (London, 2000).

Hodgkin, R. H., *A History of the Anglo-Saxons* (Oxford, 1935).

Holher, C., 'Some Service Books of the Later Saxon Church', in D. Parsons (ed.), *Tenth-Century Studies: essays in commemoration of the millennium of the Council of Winchester and 'Regularis Concordia'* (London, 1975), 60–83.

Hooke, D., 'The Droitwich Salt Industry: An Examination of the West Midlands Charter Evidence', in *ASSAH*, 2, BAR Bri. Ser. 92 (Oxford, 1981), 123–69.

Hooke, D., *The Anglo-Saxon Landscape: The Kingdom of the Hwicce* (Manchester, 1985).

Huggett, J., 'Imported Grave Goods and the Early Anglo-Saxon Economy', *Medieval Archaeology*, 32 (1988), 63–96.

Hunter-Blair, P., 'The Moore Memoranda on Northumbrian History', in C. Fox and B. Dickins (eds), *The Early Cultures of North West Europe* (Cambridge, 1950), 245–57.

Hunter-Blair, P., *The Moore Bede, Cambridge University Library MS Kk.5.16*, EEMF 9 (Copenhagen, 1959).

Hunter-Blair, P., *An Introduction to Anglo-Saxon England* (Cambridge, 1959).

Hunter-Blair, P., 'Some Observations on the "Historia Regum" Attributed to Symeon of Durham', in N. K. Chadwick (ed.), *Celt and Saxon. Studies in the Early British Border* (Cambridge, 1963), 63–118.

Hunter-Blair, P., 'From Bede to Alcuin', in Bonner (ed.), *Famulus Christi* (London, 1976), 239–66, reprinted as Ch. XII in M. Lapidge and P. Hunter-Blair (eds), *Anglo-Saxon Northumbria* (London, 1984).

James, E., *The Origins of France, from Clovis to the Capetians, 500–1000* (London, 1982).

James, E., *The Franks* (Oxford, 1988).

James, E., 'Introduction Part 2: The Post Roman Period to AD 1069', in D. Phillips and B. Hayward (eds), *Excavations at York Minster: From Roman Fortress to Norman Cathedral* (London, 1995), 1, 9–15.

James, E., 'The Continental Context', in Foster (ed.), *The St. Andrews Sarcophagus* (1998).

James, M. R., *A Descriptive Catalogue of the Manuscripts of Corpus Christi College, Cambridge*, 2 vols (Cambridge, 1909–12).

Jarnut, J. (ed.), *Karl Martel in seiner Zeit*, Beihefte zu Francia 37 (Sigmaringen, 1994).

Jeanne-Rose, O., 'Trouvailles isolées de monnaies carolingiennes en Poitou', *Revue Numismatique*, 151 (1996), 241–84.

Jellema, D., 'Frisian Trade in the Dark Ages', *Speculum*, 30 (1955), 294–99.

Jenkins, F., 'St. Martin's Church at Canterbury', *Medieval Archaeology*, 9 (1965), 11–15.

Jewell, R., 'The Anglo-Saxon Friezes at Breedon-on-the-Hill', *Archæologia*, 108 (1986), 95–115.

John, E., *Orbis Britanniae and other Studies* (Leicester, 1966).

John, E., 'The Point of Woden', *ASSAH*, 5 (Oxford, 1992), 128–34.

John, E., *Reassessing Anglo-Saxon England* (Manchester, 1998).

Jones, C. W. (ed.), *Bedae Opera de Temporibus*, Mediaeval Academy of America Publications 41 (Cambridge, MA, 1943).

Käuper, S., 'Annales Laureshamenses (Lorscher Annalen)', in Stiegmann and Wemhoff (eds), *799 Kunst und Kultur* (1999), I, 38–40.

Keary, C. F., *A Catalogue of English Coins in the British Museum. Vol. 1: The Anglo-Saxon Series* (London, 1887).

Kelly, J. N. D., *The Oxford Dictionary of Popes* (Oxford, 1986).

Kelly, S. E., 'Anglo-Saxon Lay Society and the Written Word', in McKitterick (ed.), *The Uses of Literacy* (Cambridge, 1990), 36–62.

Kelly, S. E., 'Trading Privileges from Eighth-century England', *EME*, 1 (1992), 3–28.

Kelly, S. E., *Charters of Selsey*, Anglo-Saxon Charters 6 (Oxford, 1998).

Kemp, R., *Anglian Settlement at 46–54 Fishergate*, The Archaeology of York, Anglian York, Vol. 7.1 (York, 1996).

Kent, J. P. C., 'From Roman Britain to Saxon England', in R. H. M. Dolley (ed.), *Anglo-Saxon Coins. Studies Presented to F.M. Stenton on the Occasion of his 80th Birthday* (London, 1961), 1–22.

Ker, N. R., *Catalogue of Manuscripts Containing Anglo-Saxon* (Oxford, 1957).

Ker, N. R. and A. G. Watson (eds), *Medieval Libraries in Great Britain: A List of Surviving Books. Supplement to the Second Edition*, Royal Historical Society Guides and Handbooks 15 (London, 1987).

Keynes, S., *The Diplomas of King Æthelred the Unready, 978–1016: a study in their use as historical evidence* (Cambridge, 1980).

Keynes, S., 'Changing Faces: Offa, King of Mercia', *History Today*, 40 (1990), 14–19.

Keynes, S., 'The Control of Kent in the Ninth Century', *EME*, 2 (1993), 111–32.

Keynes, S., *The Councils of Clofesho*, University of Leicester Vaughan Paper, 38 (Leicester, 1994).

Keynes, S., 'England, 700–900', in McKitterick (ed.), *NCMH* 2 (1995), 17–42.

Keynes, S. (ed.), *The Liber Vitae of the Newminster and Hyde Abbey, Winchester*, EEMF 26 (Copenhagen, 1996).

Keynes, S., 'Anglo-Saxon Entries in the "Liber Vitae" of Brescia', in J. L. Nelson and M. Godden (eds), *Alfred the Wise* (Woodbridge, 1997), 99–119.

Keynes, S., 'King Alfred and the Mercians', in Blackburn and Dumville (eds), *Kings, Currency, and Alliances* (Woodbridge, 1998), 1–46.

Keynes, S., 'Rulers of the English, *c.* 450–1066', *The Blackwell Encyclopaedia of Anglo-Saxon England*, ed. M. Lapidge (1999).

Kilpiö, M. and L. Kahlas-Tarkka, *Ex Insula Lux: Manuscripts and Hagiographical Material Connected with Medieval England* (Helsinki, 2001).

King, P. D. (trans.), *Charlemagne: Translated Sources* (Kendal, 1987).

Kirby, D. P., 'Bede, Eddius Stephanus and the Life of Wilfrid', *EHR*, 98 (1983), 101–14.

Kirby, D. P., *The Earliest English Kings* (London, 1991).

Kirby, D. P., *Bede's Historia Ecclesiastica: Its Contemporary Setting*, Jarrow Lecture (Jarrow, 1992).

Knowles, D., et al., *Heads of Religious Houses, England and Wales 940–1216* (London, 1972).

Krautheimer, R., *Rome: Profile of a City 312–1309* (Princeton, NJ, 1980).

Krüger, K. H., *Königsgrabkirchen der Franken, Angelsachsen und Langobarden bis zur Mitte des 8. Jahrhunderts: Ein Historische Katalog,* Münster Mittelalter-schriften 4 (Munich, 1971).

Kurze, F., 'Ein insulares Munster-buchblatt und die byzantinische Psalterillustration', *Byzantinisch-neugriechische Jahrbücher*, 14 (1938), 84–93.

Lamb, G., 'Carolingian Orkney and its Transformation', in C. E. Batey, J. Jesch and C. D. Morris (eds), *The Viking Age in Caithness, Orkney and the North Atlantic* (Edinburgh, 1993), 260–71.

Lampen, A., 'Sachsenkriege, sächsischer Widerstand und Kooperation', in Stiegemann and Wemhoff (eds), *779 Kunst und Kultur* (Mainz, 1999), Vol. 1, 264–72.

Langefeld, B., '*Regula canonicorum* or *Regula monasterialis vitae?* The Rule of Chrodegang and Archbishop Wulfred's Reforms at Canterbury', *ASE*, 25 (1996), 21–36.

Lapidge, M., 'Byrhtferth of Ramsey and the Early Sections of the *Historia regum* attributed to Symeon of Durham', *ASE*, 10 (1982), 97–122, at 115–16, reprinted in Lapidge, *Anglo-Latin Literature. Vol. 2: 900–1066* (London and Rio Grande, OH, 1993), 317–42.

Lapidge, M., 'The School of Theodore and Hadrian', *ASE*, 15 (1986), 45–72.

Lapidge, M., 'Aediluuf and the School of York', in A. Lehner and W. Berschin (eds), *Lateinische Kultur im VIII. Jahrhundert: Traube-Gedenkschrift* (St Ottilien, 1990).

Lapidge, M., 'The Study of Greek in the School of Canterbury in the Seventh Century', in M. Herren (ed.), *The Sacred Nectar of the Greeks: The Study of Greek in the West in the Early Middle Ages*, King's College London, Medieval Studies 2 (London, 1992), 169–94.

Lapidge, M., 'The Career of Archbishop Theodore', *Settimane di studio del Centro Italiano di Studi sull'alto medioevo*, 39 (Spoleto, 1992), 137–91.

Lapidge, M., *Anglo-Latin Literature. Vol. 1: 600–899* (London and Rio Grande, OH, 1993).

Lapidge, M., 'Latin Learning in Ninth-Century England', in Lapidge, *Anglo-Latin Literature. Vol. 1: 600–899* (London and Rio Grande, OH, 1996), 409–54.

Lapidge, M., *Anglo-Latin Literature. Vol. 2: 900–1066* (London and Rio Grande, OH, 1996).

Lapidge, M., J. Blair, S. Keynes and D. Scragg (eds), *The Blackwell Encyclopaedia of Anglo-Saxon England* (Oxford, 1999).

Latham, R. E., *Revised Medieval Latin Word-List from British and Irish Sources* (London, 1965)

Latham, R. E. et al. (eds), *Dictionary of Medieval Latin from British Sources* (London, 1975–).

Lebecq, S., *Marchands et navigateurs frisons du haut moyen âge*, 2 vols (Lille, 1983).

Lebecq, S., 'Routes of Change: Production and Distribution in the West (5th–8th centuries)', in Webster and Brown (eds), *The Transformation of the Roman World* (London, 1997), 67–78.

Lebecq, S., 'England and the Continent in the Sixth and Seventh Centuries: The Question of Logistics', in Gameson (ed.), *St. Augustine* (Stroud, 1999), 50–67.

LeClercq, H., 'Hadrien I, (épitaph de)', in *Dictionnaire d'Archéologie Chrétienne et de liturgie*, ed. H. LeClercq, 15 vols (Paris, 1924–53), VI.ii, cols 1964–67.

Leeds, E. T., *The Archaeology of the Anglo-Saxon Settlements* (Oxford, 1913).

Leeds, E. T., *Early Anglo-Saxon Art and Archaeology Being the Rhind Lectures Delivered in Edinburgh, 1935* (Oxford, 1936).

Levison, W., 'St Willibrord and his Place in History', *The Durham University Journal*, 32 (1940), 23–41.

Levison, W., *England and the Continent in the Eighth Century* (Oxford, 1946).

Levison, W., *Wilhelm Levison, 1876–1947. A Bibliography* (Oxford, 1948).

Levison, W., 'Die "Annales Lindisfarnenses et Dunelmenses": kritisch Untersucht und neu Herausgegeben', *Deutsches Archiv für Erforschung des Mittelalters*, 17 (1961), 447–506.

Leyser, K., 'Early Medieval Canon Law and the beginnings of Knighthood', in L. Fenske et al. (eds), *Institutionen, Kultur und Gesselschaft im Mittelalter* (Sigmaringen, 1984), 549–66 reprinted in Leyser, *Communications and Power in Medieval Europe* (London, 1994), 51–73.

Leyser, K., 'Early Medieval Warfare', in J. Cooper (ed), *The Battle of Maldon: Fiction and Fact* (London and Rio Grande, OH, 1993), 87–108 reprinted in Leyser, *Communications and Power in Medieval Europe* (London, 1994), 29–50.

Leyser, K., *Communications and Power in Medieval Europe: The Carolingian and Ottonian Centuries*, ed. T. Reuter (London, 1994).

Liebermann, F. (ed.), *Die Gesetze der Angelsachsen. Vol. 1: Text und Übersetzung* (Halle, 1903).

Lobbey, U., J. Mitchell and P. Peduto, 'Inschriften', in Stiegmann and Wemhoff (eds), *799 Kunst und Kultur* (1999) 2, 570–74.

Logutova, M., 'Insular Codices from Dubrovsky's Collection in the National Library of Russia', in Kilpiö and Kahlas-Tarkka (eds), *Ex Insula Lux* (2001), 93–98.

Loveluck, C., 'A High-status Anglo-Saxon Settlement at Flixborough, Lincolnshire', *Antiquity*, 72 (1998), 146–61.

Loveluck, C., 'Wealth, Waste and Conspicuous Consumption: Flixborough and its Importance for Middle and Late Saxon Settlement Studies', in H. Hamerow and A. MacGregor (eds), *Image and Power in the Archaeology of Early Medieval Britain. Essays in Honour of Rosemary Cramp* (Oxford, 2001), 78–130.

Löwe, H., 'Eine Kölner Notiz zur Kaisertum Karl der Große', *Rheinische Vierteljahrsblätter*, 14 (1949), 7–34.

Löwe, H. (ed.), *Die Iren und Europa im früheren Mittelalter*, 2 vols (Stuttgart, 1982).

Loyn, H. R. and J. Percival (trans.), *The Reign of Charlemagne: Documents of Carolingian Government and Administration* (London, 1975).

Lyon, C. C. S., 'A Reappraisal of the sceatta and styca coinage of Northumbria', *BNJ*, 28 (1955–57), 227–42.

Lyon, C. C. S., 'Historical Problems of Anglo-Saxon Coinage – (1)', *BNJ*, 36 (1967), 215–21.

McCormick, M., 'The Liturgy of War in the Early Middle Ages: Crisis, Litanies, and the Carolingian Monarchy', *Viator*, 15 (1984), 1–23.

Mackay, T. W., 'Bede's Hagiographical Methods: His Knowledge and Use of Paulinus of Nola', in Bonner (ed.), *Famulus Christi* (London, 1976), 77–92.

McKitterick, R., *The Frankish Church and the Carolingian Reforms, 789–895* (London, 1977).

McKitterick, R., 'Some Carolingian Law books and their Function', in P. Linehan and B. Tierney (eds), *Authority and Power: Studies on Medieval Law and Government* (Cambridge, 1980), 13–27, reprinted as Chapter 2 in McKitterick, *Books, Scribes, and Learning* (Aldershot, 1994).

McKitterick, R., *The Frankish Kingdoms under the Carolingians 751–987* (London, 1983).

McKitterick, R., 'The Anglo-Saxon Missionaries in Germany: Reflections on the Manuscript Evidence', *Transactions of the Cambridge Bibliographical Society*, 9 (1989), 291–329.

McKitterick, R., *The Carolingians and the Written Word* (Cambridge, 1989).

McKitterick, R., 'Anglo-Saxon Missionaries in Germany: Personal Connections and Local Influences', Eighth Brixworth Lecture, Vaughan Papers, 36 (Leicester, 1990) reprinted in R. McKitterick, *Frankish Kings and Culture in the early Middle Ages* (Aldershot, 1995).

McKitterick, R. (ed.), *The Uses of Literacy in Early Mediaeval Europe* (Cambridge, 1990).

McKitterick, R., 'Nuns' scriptoria in England and Francia in the Early Middle Ages', *Francia*, 19 (1992), 1–35.

McKitterick, R., 'The Diffusion of Insular Culture in Neustria between 650 and 850: The Implications of the Manuscript Evidence', in Atsma and Werner (eds), *La Neustrie* (Sigmaringen, 1989), 395–432, reprinted as Chapter 3 in McKitterick, *Books, Scribes and Learning* (Aldershot, 1994).

McKitterick, R., *Carolingian Culture: Emulation and Innovation* (Cambridge, 1994).

McKitterick, R., *Books, Scribes, and Learning in the Frankish Kingdoms, 6th–9th Centuries* (Aldershot, 1994).

McKitterick, R., 'England and the Continent', in McKitterick (ed.), *NCMH* 2 (1995), 64–84.

McKitterick, R. (ed.), *The New Cambridge Medieval History*, Vol. 2 (Cambridge, 1995).

McKitterick, R., 'Constructing the Past in the Early Middle Ages: The Case of the Royal Frankish Annals', *TRHS*, 6th Ser., 7 (1997), 101–29.

McKitterick, R., 'The Illusion of Royal Power in the Carolingian Annals', *EHR*, 115 (2000), 1–20.

McKitterick, R., 'Social Memory, Commemoration and the Book', in S. J. Ridyard (ed.), *Reading and the Book in the Middle Ages*, Sewanee Medieval Studies 11 (Sewanee, TN), 5–26.

Mayr-Harting, H., *The Coming of Christianity to Anglo-Saxon England* (London, 1991).

Marenbon, J., *From the Circle of Alcuin to the School of Auxerre: Logic, Theology and Philosophy in the Early Middle Ages* (Cambridge, 1981).

Meadows, I., 'The Pioneer Helmet', *Current Archaeology*, 154 (1997), 391–95.

Meehan, B., 'A Reconsideration of the Historical Works Associated with Symeon of Durham: Manuscripts, Texts and Influences', unpublished PhD thesis, University of Edinburgh (1979).

Meehan, B., 'Durham Twelfth-century Manuscripts in Cistercian Houses', in Rollason et al. (eds), *Anglo-Norman Durham* (Woodbridge, 1994), 439–50.

Meens, R., 'A Background to Augustine's Mission to Anglo-Saxon England', *ASE*, 22 (1994), 5–17.

Metcalf, D. M., 'Fiufar or Arfiuf = Strasbourg', *Hamburgh Beiträge sur Numismatik*, 20 (1966), 380–84.

Metcalf, D. M., 'Artistic Borrowing, Imitation and Forgery in the Eighth Century', *Hamburger Beitrage sur Numismatik*, 20 (1966), 379–92.

Metcalf, D. M., 'The Prosperity of North-western Europe in the Eighth and Ninth Centuries', *EcHR*, 2nd ser. 20 (1967), 344–57.

Metcalf, D. M., 'Estimation of the Volume of Northumbrian Coinage, c. 738–88', in Hill and Metcalf (eds), *Sceattas in England and on the Continent* (Oxford, 1984), 113–16.

Metcalf, D. M. (ed.), *Coinage in Ninth-Century Northumbria. The Tenth Oxford Symposium on Coinage and Monetary History*, BAR Bri. Ser. 180 (Oxford, 1987).

Metcalf, D. M., 'Monetary Expansion and Recession: Interpreting the Distribution Pattern of

Seventh- and Eighth-Century Coins', in Casey and Reece (eds), *Coins and the Archaeologist* (London, 1988), 230–53.

Metcalf, D. M., 'The Monetary Economy of Ninth-Century England South of the Humber: A Topographical Analysis', in Blackburn and Dumville (eds), *Kings, Currency, and Alliances* (Woodbridge, 1998), 167–98.

Metcalf, D. M. and Miskimin, H. A., 'The Carolingian Pound: A Discussion', *Numismatic Circular*, 76 (1968), 296–98.

Metcalf, D. M. and Northover, J. P., 'Coinage Alloys from the Time of Offa and Charlemagne to *c.* 864', *Numismatic Chronicle*, 149 (1989), 101–20.

Metcalf, D. M., *Thrymsas and Sceattas in the Ashmolean Museum, Oxford*, 3 vols (London, 1993–94).

Metcalf, D. M., *An Atlas of Anglo-Saxon and Norman Coin Finds c. 973–1086* (London and Oxford, 1998).

Mitchell, J., 'Literacy Displayed: The Use of Inscriptions at the Monastery of San Vincenzo al Volturno in the Early Ninth Century', in McKitterick (ed.), *The Uses of Literacy in Early Mediaeval Europe* (Cambridge, 1990), 186–225.

Moesgaard, J. C., 'Stray Finds of Carolingian Coins in Upper Normandy, France', *Studia Numismatica. Festschrift Arkadi Molvogin*, 65 (Tallinn, 1995), 87–102.

Moisl, H., 'Anglo-Saxon Royal Genealogies and Germanic Oral Tradition', *JMH*, 7 (1981), 215–48.

Moore, W. J., *The Saxon Pilgrims to Rome and the Schola Saxonum* (Fribourg, 1937).

Mordek, H., 'Karolingische Kapitularien', in H. Mordek (ed.), *Überlieferung und Geltung normativer Texte des frühen und hohen Mittelalters* (Sigmaringen, 1986), 25–50.

Mordek, H., *Bibliotheca capitularium regum Francorum manuscripta*, MGH Hilfsmittel 15 (1995).

Morris, R. K., 'Alcuin, York and the *Alma Sophia*', in L. A. S. Butler and R. K. Morris (eds), *The Anglo-Saxon Church: Papers on History, Architecture and Archaeology in Honour of Dr H. M. Taylor*, CBA Res. Rpt., 60 (London, 1986), 80–89.

Morrish, J., 'King Alfred's Letter as a Source on Learning in England', in P. E. Szarmach (ed.), *Studies in Earlier Old English Prose* (Albany, NY, 1986), 87–107.

Morrish, J., 'Dated and Datable Manuscripts Copied in England during the Ninth Century: A Preliminary List', *Mediaeval Studies*, 50 (1988), 512–38.

Morison, S., *Politics and Script: aspects of authority and freedom in the development of Graeco-Latin script from the sixth century B.C. to the twentieth century A.D.* (Oxford, 1972).

Morrison, K. F., 'The Gold Medallions of Louis the Pious and Lothaire I and the Synod of Paris (825)', *Speculum*, 36 (1961), 592–99.

Mosse, W. E., J. Carlebach, G. Hirschfeld, A. Newman, A. Paucker and P. Pulzer, *Second Chance: Two Centuries of German-speaking Jews in the United Kingdom* (Tübingen, 1991).

Murray, A., *Suicide in the Middle Ages. Vol. 1: The Violent against Themselves* (Oxford, 1998).

Mütherich, F. and J. Gaede, *Carolingian Painting* (London, 1997).

Mynors, R. A. B., *Durham Cathedral Manuscripts to the End of the Twelfth Century* (Durham, 1939).

Nelson, J. L., 'National Synods, Kingship as Office, and Royal Anointing: An Early Medieval Syndrome', *Studies in Church History*, 7 (1971), 41–59.

Nelson, J. L., 'The Problem of King Alfred's Royal Anointing', *JEH*, 18 (1967), 145–63, reprinted in Nelson, *Politics and Ritual in Early Medieval Europe* (London, 1986), 309–28.

Nelson, J. L., 'Kingship, Law and Liturgy in the Political Thought of Hincmar of Rheims', in *EHR*, 92 (1977), 241–79, reprinted in Nelson, *Politics and Ritual in Early Medieval Europe* (London, 1986), 133–72.

Nelson, J. L., 'Queens as Jezebels: The Careers of Brunhild and Balthild in Merovingian History', in D. Baker (ed.), *Medieval Women: Essays Presented to Rosalind Hill*, SCH Subsidia 1 (Oxford, 1978), 31–77.

Nelson, J. L., 'The Earliest Surviving Royal Ordo: Some Liturgical and Historical Aspects', in B. Tierney and P. Linehan (eds), *Authority and Power: Studies in Medieval Law and Government*

Presented to W. Ullmann on his Seventieth Birthday (Cambridge, 1980), 29–48 reprinted in Nelson, *Politics and Ritual* (London, 1986), 341–60.

Nelson, J. L., 'Legislation and Consensus in the Reign of Charles the Bald', in Wormald et al. (eds), *Ideal and Reality in Frankish and Anglo-Saxon Society* (Oxford, 1983), 202–27, reprinted in Nelson, *Politics and Ritual*, 91–116.

Nelson, J. L., 'The Church's Military Service in the Ninth Century: A Comparative View?', *SCH*, 20 (1983), 15–30, reprinted in Nelson, *Politics and Ritual* (London, 1986), 117–32.

Nelson, J. L., 'Inauguration Rituals', in Nelson, *Politics and Ritual* (London, 1986).

Nelson, J. L., 'Charles the Bald and the Church in Town and Countryside', in Nelson, *Politics and Ritual* (London, 1986), 75–90.

Nelson, J. L., *Politics and Ritual in Early Medieval Europe* (London, 1986).

Nelson, J. L., 'The Lord's Anointed and the People's Choice: Carolingian Royal Ritual', in D. Cannadine and S. Price (eds), *Rituals of Royalty: Power and Ceremonial in Traditional Societies* (Cambridge, 1987), 137–80, reprinted in Nelson, *The Frankish World* (London and Rio Grande, OH, 1996), 99–132.

Nelson, J. L., 'Ninth-century Knighthood: The Evidence of Nithard', in C. Harper-Bill et al. (eds), *Studies in Medieval History Presented to R. Allen Brown* (Woodbridge, 1989), 255–66, reprinted in Nelson, *The Frankish World* (London and Rio Grande, OH, 1996), 75–87.

Nelson, J. L., 'The Annals of St. Bertin', in M. T. Gibson and J. L. Nelson (eds), *Charles the Bald: Court and Kingdom* (Aldershot, 1990), 23–40.

Nelson, J. L., 'The Last years of Louis the Pious', in P. Godman and R. Collins (eds), *Charlemagne's Heir* (Oxford, 1990), 147–60 reprinted in Nelson, *The Frankish World* (London and Rio Grande, OH, 1997), 37–50.

Nelson, J. L., 'Literacy in Carolingian Government', in McKitterick (ed.), *The Uses of Literacy in the Early Middle Ages* (Cambridge, 1990), 258–96.

Nelson, J. L., 'Reconstructing a Royal Family: Reflections on Alfred from Asser, Chapter 2', in I. N. Wood and N. Lund (eds), *People and Places in Northern Europe, 500–1600: Essays in Honour of Peter Hayes Sawyer* (Woodbridge, 1991), 47–66.

Nelson, J. L., *Charles the Bald* (London and New York, 1992).

Nelson, J. L., 'Women at the Court of Charlemagne: A Case of Monstrous Regiment?', in J. C. Parsons (ed.), *Medieval Queenship* (New York, 1993), 43–61, reprinted in Nelson, *The Frankish World* (London and Rio Grande, OH, 1996), 223–42.

Nelson, J. L., *The Frankish World 750–900* (London and Rio Grande, OH, 1996).

Nelson, J. L., 'The Frankish Kingdoms, 814–898: The West', in *NCMH* 2 (Cambridge, 1995), 110–41.

Nelson, J. L., 'England and the Franks in the Ninth Century Reconsidered', in P. E. Szarmach and J. T. Rosenthal (eds), *The Preservation and Transmission of Anglo-Saxon Culture* (Kalamazoo, 1997), 141–58, reprinted, as Chapter VI in Nelson, *Rulers and Ruling Families in Early Medieval Europe* (Aldershot, 1999).

Nelson, J. L., 'Early Medieval Rites of Queen-Making', in A. Duggan (ed.), *Queens and Queenship in Medieval Europe* (Woodbridge, 1997), 301–15.

Nelson, J., '"... Sicut olim gens Francorum ... nunc gens Anglorum": Fulk's Letter to Alfred Revisited', in J. Roberts, J. Nelson and M. Godden (eds), *Alfred the Wise* (Rochester, NY, and London, 1997), 135–44.

Nelson, J. L., 'Making a Difference in Eighth-Century Politics: The Daughters of Desiderius', in A. C. Murray (ed.), *After Rome's Fall. Studies in Honour of Walter Goffart* (Toronto, 1998), 171–90.

Nelson, J. L., *Rulers and Ruling Families in Early Medieval Europe: Alfred, Charles the Bald and Others* (Aldershot, 1999).

Newman, J., 'Wics, Trade and the Hinterland: The Ipswich Region', in M. Anderton (ed.), *Anglo-Saxon Trading Centres: Beyond the Emporia* (Glasgow, 1999), 32–46.

Noble, T. F. X., 'Louis the Pious and his Piety Re-reconsidered', *Revue belge de philologie et d'histoire*, 58 (1980), 297–316.

Noble, T. F. X., *The Republic of St. Peter: The Birth of the Papal State 680–825* (Philadelphia, 1984).

Noble, T. F. X., 'Louis the Pious and the Frontiers of the Frankish Realm', in P. Godman and R. Collins (eds), *Charlemagne's Heir* (Oxford, 1990), 333–47.

North, J. J., *English Hammered Coinage. Vol. 1: Early Anglo-Saxon to Henry III, c. 600–1272* (London, 1980).

Norton, C., 'History, Wisdom and Illumination', in Rollason (ed.), *Symeon of Durham* (Stamford, 1998), 61–105.

Ó Cróinín, D., 'Rath Melsigi, Wilibrord and the Earliest Echternach Manuscripts', *Peritia*, 3 (1984), 17–42.

Odegaard, C. E., *Vassi and Fideles in the Carolingian Empire* (Cambridge, MA, 1945).

O'Donovan, M. A., 'An Interim Revision of Episcopal Dates for the Province of Canterbury, 850–950, Part 1', *ASE*, 1 (1972), 23–44.

Offler, H. S., 'A Note on the Last Medieval Bishops of Hexham', *Archaeologia Aeliana*, 4th ser. 40 (1962), 163–69.

Ohlgren, T. H. (ed.), *Insular and Anglo-Saxon Illuminated Manuscripts: An Iconographic Catalogue c. A.D. 625 to 1100* (New York and London, 1985).

Ortenberg, V., *The English Church and the Continent in the Tenth and Eleventh Centuries: Cultural, Spiritual and Artistic Exchanges* (Oxford, 1992).

Pagan, H. E., 'Northumbrian Numismatic Chronology in the Ninth Century', *BNJ*, 38 (1969), 1–15.

Pagan, H. E., 'The Imitative Louis the Pious Solidus from Southampton and Finds of Other Related Coins in the British Isles', in Andrews (ed.), *The Coins and Pottery from Hamwic* (Southampton, 1988), Vol. 1, 71–72.

Page, R. I., 'Anglo-Saxon Episcopal Lists, Parts I and II', *Nottingham Medieval Studies*, 9 (1965), 71–95.

Page, R. I., 'Anglo-Saxon Episcopal Lists, Part III', *Nottingham Medieval Studies*, 10 (1966), 2–24.

Panhuysen, T., 'Maastricht, centre de production de sculptures gallo-romaines et d'inscriptions paléo-chrétiennes', in H.-J. Häßler and C. Lorren (eds), *Studien zur Sachsenforschung* 8, (Hildesheim, 1993), 83–96.

Parsons, D., 'Brixworth and its Monastery Church', in Dornier (ed.), *Mercian Studies* (1977), 173–90.

Parsons, D., 'England and the Low Countries at the Time of St Willibrord', in E. de Bièvre (ed.), *Utrecht, Britain and the Continent: Archaeology, Art and Architecture*, British Archaeological Association Conference Transactions 18 (London, 1996), 30–48.

Parsons, D., 'Before the Parish: The Church in Anglo-Saxon Leicestershire', in J. Bourne (ed.), *Anglo-Saxon Landscapes in the East Midlands* (Leicester, 1996), 11–36.

Parsons, M. P., 'Some Scribal Memoranda for Anglo-Saxon Charters of the Eighth and Ninth Centuries', *Mitteilungen des Österreichischen Instituts für Geschichtsforschung*, 14 (1939), 13–32.

Pauli, R., 'Karl de Große in northumbrischen Annalen', *Forschungen sur deutschen Geschichte*, 12 (1872), 137–66.

Peacock, D. P. S., 'Charlemagne's Black Stones: The re-use of Roman Columns in Early Medieval Europe', *Antiquity*, 71 (1997), 709–15.

Picard, J. M., 'Church and Politics in the Seventh Century: The Irish Exile of King Dagobert II', in Picard (ed.), *Ireland and Northern France, AD 600–850* (Dublin, 1991), 27–52.

Picard, J. M. (ed.), *Ireland and Northern France, AD 600–850* (Dublin, 1991).

Piper, A. J., 'The Libraries of the Monks of Durham', in M. B. Parkes and A. G. Watson (eds), *Medieval Scribes, Manuscripts and Libraries: Essays presented to N. R. Ker* (London, 1978), 213–49.

Piper, A. J., 'The Durham Cantor's Book (Durham, Dean and Chapter Library, MS B.IV.24', in Rollason et al. (eds), *Anglo-Norman Durham* (Woodbridge, 1994).

Piper, A. J., 'The Historical Interests of the Monks of Durham', in Rollason (ed.), *Symeon of Durham* (Stamford, 1998), 301–32.

Pirie, E. J., *Coins of the Kingdom of Northumbria c. 700–867 in the Yorkshire Collections: The Yorkshire Museum, York, The University of Leeds, the City Museum* (Llanfyllin, 1996).

Pirie, E. J., 'Earduulf: A Significant Addition to the Coinage of Northumbria', *BNJ*, 65 (1996), 20–31.

Plunkett, S. J., 'The Mercian Perspective', in S. M. Foster (ed.), *The St. Andrews Sarcophagus: A Pictish Masterpiece and its International Connections* (Dublin, 1998), 202–26.

Pohl, W., *Die Awaren: Ein Steppenvolk in Mitteleuropa, 567–822* (Munich, 1988).

Poole, R. L., 'St. Wilfrid and the See of Ripon', *EHR*, 34 (1919), 1–24.

Poole, R. L., *Studies in Chronology and History* (Oxford, 1934).

Prinz, J., *Der Corveyer Annalen* (Münster, 1982).

Prou, M., *Catalogue des monnaies française à la Bibliotheque Nationale. Les monnaies carolingiennes* (Paris, 1896).

Raabe, C., Büttner, H. and Hilpisch, S. (eds), *Sankt Bonifatius: Gedenkgabe zum zwölfhunhertsten Todestag* (Fulda, 1954).

Raine, J. (ed.), *The Historians of the Church of York and its Archbishops*, RS 71, 3 vols (London, 1879–94).

Raine, J. (ed.), *The Priory of Hexham: The History and Annals of the House*, Surtees Society, 44 (Durham, 1864)

Ramackers, J., 'Die Werkstattheimat der Grabplatte Papst Hadrians I', *Römische Quartalschrift*, 59 (1964), 36–78.

Reuter, T. (ed.), *The Greatest Englishman: Essays on St. Boniface and the Church at Crediton* (Exeter, 1980).

Reuter, T., 'Plunder and Tribute in the Carolingian Empire', *TRHS*, 5th ser. 35 (1985), 75–94.

Reuter, T., 'The End of Carolingian Military Expansion', in P. Godman and R. Collins (eds), *Charlemagne's Heir* (Oxford, 1990), 391–405.

Reuter, T., '"Kirchenreform" und "kirchenpolitik" im zeitalter Karl Martells: Beigriffe und Wirklichkeit', in Jarnut (ed.), *Karl Martel in seiner Zeit* (Sigmaringen, 1994), 51–58.

Reynolds, L. D. (ed.), *Texts and Transmission: A Survey of the Latin Classics* (Oxford, 1983).

Reynolds, S., *Fiefs and Vassals: The Medieval Evidence Reinterpreted* (Oxford, 1994).

Richards J. D., et al., 'Cottam: An Anglian and Anglo-Scandinavian Settlement on the Yorkshire Wolds', *Archaeological Journal*, 156 (1999), 1–110.

Rigold, S., 'The Sutton Hoo Coins in the Light of the Contemporary Background of Coinage in England', in Bruce-Mitford (ed.), *The Sutton Hoo Ship Burial* (London, 1975), I, 653–77.

Roberts, J., Nelson, J. L. and Godden, M. (eds), *Alfred the Wise: Studies in Honour of Janet Batley on the Occasion of Her Sixty-Fifth Birthday* (Rochester, NY, and Woodbridge, 1997).

Rollason, D. W., 'Lists of Saints' Resting Places in Anglo-Saxon England', *ASE*, 7 (1978), 61–93.

Rollason, D. W., *The Mildrith Legend: A Study in Early Medieval Hagiography in England* (Leicester, 1982).

Rollason, D. W., 'The Cults of Murdered Royal Saints in Anglo-Saxon England', *ASE*, 11 (1983), 1–22.

Rollason, D. W., *Sources for York History to AD 1100, The Archaeology of York, Vol. 1* (York, 1998).

Rollason, D. W. (ed.), *Symeon of Durham: Historian of Durham and the North* (Stamford, 1998).

Rollason, D. W., M. Harvey and M. Prestwich (eds), *Anglo-Norman Durham 1093–1193* (Woodbridge, 1994).

Rovelli, A., 'Some Consideration of the Carolingian Coinage of Lombard and Carolingian Italy', in I. L. Hansen and C. Wickham (eds), *The Long Eighth Century: Production, Distribution and Demand* (Leiden, 2000), 194–223.

Runciman, S., 'Charlemagne and Palestine', *EHR*, 50 (1935), 606–19.

Runciman, S., 'The Empress Irene the Athenian', in D. Baker (ed.), *Medieval Women: Essays presented to Rosalind Hill*, SCH Subsidia 1 (Oxford, 1978), 101–18.

Sawyer, P. H., *Anglo-Saxon Charters: An Annotated List and Bibliography*, Royal Historical Society Guides and Handbooks, No. 8 (London, 1968).

Sawyer, P. H., *The Age of the Vikings* (London, 1971).

Sawyer, P. H., 'Kings and Merchants', in Sawyer and Wood (eds), *Early Medieval Kingship* (Leeds, 1977), 139–58.

Sawyer, P. H., 'Some Sources for the History of Viking Northumbria', in R. A. Hall (ed.), *Viking Age York and the North*, CBA Res. Rpt 27 (London, 1978), 3–7.

Sawyer, P. H., *From Roman Britain to Norman England* (New York, 1978).

Sawyer, P. H., 'Fairs and Markets in Early Medieval England', in N. Skyum-Nielsen and N. Lund (eds), *Danish Medieval History: New Currents* (Copenhagen, 1981), 153–68.

Sawyer, P. H., 'Early Fairs and Markets in England and Scandinavia', in B. L. Anderson and A. J. H. Latham (eds), *The Market in History* (London, 1986), 59–78.

Sawyer, P. H., *Anglo-Saxon Lincolnshire*, History of Lincolnshire 3 (Lincoln, 1998).

Sawyer P. H. and I. N. Wood (eds), *Early Medieval Kingship* (Leeds, 1977).

Scharer, A., 'The Writing of History at King Alfred's Court', *EME*, 5 (1996), 177–206.

Scharer, A., 'The Gregorian Tradition in Early England', in Gameson (ed.), *St. Augustine* (Stroud, 1999), 187–201.

Scheiber, F.-C., 'Alcuin und die Admonitio Generalis', *DA*, 14 (1958), 221–29.

Scheiber, F.-C., 'Alcuin und die Briefe Karls des Grossen', *DA*, 15 (1959), 181–93.

Schieffer, T., *Winfrid-Bonifatius und die christliche Grundlegung Europas* (Freiburg, 1954).

Schieffer, T. (ed.), *In Memoriam Wilhelm Levison (1876–1947). Reden und Grußbotschaften bei der Gedenkfeier der Universität [Bonn] zum 100. Geburtstag am 31. Mai 1976* (Cologne and Bonn, 1977).

Schieffer, T., 'Charlemagne and Rome', in J. M. H. Smith (ed.), *Early Medieval Rome and the Christian West: Essays in Honour of D. A. Bullough* (Leiden, 2000).

Schoebe, G., 'The Chapters of Archbishop Oda (942/6) and the Canons of the Legatine Council of 786', *Bulletin of the Institute of Historical Research*, 35 (1962), 75–83.

Schove, D. J. and A. Fletcher, *Chronology of Eclipses and Comets AD 1–1000* (Woodbridge, 1984).

Schramm, P. E., *A History of the English Coronation* (Oxford, 1937).

Schramm, P. E., *Kaiser, Könige und Papst*, 4 vols (Stuttgart, 1968).

Scull, C. and A. Bayliss, 'Radiocarbon Dating and Anglo-Saxon Graves', in U. von Freeden, U. Koch and A. Wieczorek (eds), *Völker an Nord- und Ostsee und die Franken* (Bonn, 1999), 39–50.

Scull, C. and A. Bayliss, 'Dating Burials of the Seventh and Eighth Centuries: A Case Study from Ipswich, Suffolk', in Hines et al. (eds), *The Pace of Change* (Oxford, 1999), 80–92.

Semmler, J., 'Legislation Aquisgranensis', in K. Hallinger (ed.), *Corpus Consuetudinum Monasticorum* 1 (Sieburg, 1963).

Sharpe, R., *A Handlist of the Latin Writers of Great Britain and Ireland before 1540* (Turnhout, 1997).

Shepard, J., 'The Rhos Guests of Louis the Pious: Whence and Wherefore?' *EME*, 4 (1995), 41–60.

Simoons, F. J., *Eat not this Flesh: Food Avoidances from Prehistory to the Present* (2nd edn) (Madison, WI, 1994).

Sims-Williams, P., 'Continental Influence at Bath Monastery in the Seventh Century', *ASE*, 4 (1975), 1–10.

Sims-Williams, P., *Religion and Literature in Western England, 600–800*, Cambridge Studies in Anglo-Saxon England, 3 (Cambridge, 1990).

Simpson, L., 'The King Alfred/St Cuthbert episode in the *Historia de sancto Cuthberto*: Its Significance for Mid-tenth-century English History', in Bonner et al. (eds), *St. Cuthbert* (Woodbridge, 1989), 397–412.

Simson, B., *Jahrbücher des fränkischen Reichs unter Ludwig dem Frommen*, 2 vols (Leipzig, 1876).

Sisam, K., 'Anglo-Saxon Royal Genealogies', *Proceedings of the British Academy*, 39 (1953), 287–348.

Smith, J. M. H., *Province and Empire: Brittany and the Carolingians* (Cambridge, 1992).

Smith, J. M. H., '*Fines imperii*: The Marches', in McKitterick (ed.), *NCMH* 2 (1995), 169–89.

Smyth, A. P., *King Alfred the Great* (Oxford, 1995).

Somerville, R. and S. Kuttner, *Pope Urban II, the Collectio Britannica, and the Council of Melfi (1089)* (Oxford, 1996).

Springer, M., 'Geschichtsbilder Urteile und Vorurteile', in Stiegemann and Wemhoff (eds), *799 Kunst und Kultur* (Mainz, 1999), III, 224–32.

Staerk, A., *Les Manuscrits Latins du Vᵉ au XIIIᵉ siècle conservés à la Bibliothèque Impériale de Saint Petersbourg*, 2 vols (St Petersburg, 1910).

Stafford, P., 'The King's Wife in Wessex, 800–1066', *Past and Present*, 91 (1981), 3–27.

Stafford, P., 'Charles the Bald, Judith and England', in M. T. Gibson and J. L. Nelson (eds), *Charles the Bald: Court and Kingdom* (2nd edn) (Aldershot, 1990), 139–53.

Stancliffe, C., 'Kings who Opted Out', in Wormald et al. (eds), *Ideal and Reality in Frankish and Anglo-Saxon Society* (Oxford, 1983), 154–76.

Stenton, D. M. (ed.), *Preparatory to Anglo-Saxon England, Being the Collected Papers of Frank Merry Stenton* (Oxford, 1970).

Stenton, F. M., 'The Supremacy of the Mercian Kings', *EHR*, 33 (1918), 433–52, reprinted in Stenton (ed.), *Preparatory to Anglo-Saxon England* (Oxford, 1970), 48–66.

Stenton, F. M., 'Anglo-Saxon Coinage and the Historian', in Stenton (ed.), *Preparatory to Anglo-Saxon England* (Oxford, 1970), 371–82.

Stenton, F. M., *Anglo-Saxon England* (3rd edn) (Oxford, 1971).

Steuer, H., 'Helm und Ringschwert. Prunkbewaffnung und Rangabzeichen germanischer Kreiger. Eine Übersicht', *Studien zur Sachsenforschung*, 6 (1987), 189–236.

Stevens, W., *Bede's Scientific Achievement*, Jarrow Lecture (Jarrow, 1985).

Stevenson, W. H., *The Church Historians of England, III. Part ii: Containing the Historical Works of Symeon of Durham* (Lampeter, 1858, reprinted 1987).

Stewart, I., 'Anglo-Saxon Gold Coins', in R. A. G. Carson and C. M. Kraay (eds), *Scripta Nummaria Romana: Essays Presented to Humphrey Sutherland* (London, 1978), 143–72.

Stewart, I., 'The London Mint and the Coinage of Offa', in Blackburn (ed.), *Anglo-Saxon Monetary History* (1986), 27–44.

Stiegemann C. and M. Wemhoff (eds), *799 Kunst und Kultur der Karolingerzeit. Karl der Große und Papst Leo III in Paderborn,* 3 vols (Mainz, 1999).

Stoclet, A., 'La Clausula de unctione Pippini regis: mises au point et nouvelle hypothèses', *Francia*, 8 (1980), 1–42.

Story, J. E., 'Symeon as Annalist', in Rollason (ed.), *Symeon of Durham* (Stamford, 1998), 202–13.

Story, J. E., 'Cathwulf, Kingship, and the Royal Abbey of Saint-Denis', *Speculum*, 74 (1999), 1–20.

Suchodolski, S., 'Der Geldumlauf in der karolingischen Epoche', *Deutscher Numismatikertag München 1981* (Augsburg, 1983) 43–53.

Suchodolski, S., 'Remarques sur la circulation monétaire dans l'Europe du haut Moyen Age', *Quaderni Ticinesi di Numismatica e antichità classiche*, 22 (1993), 249–56.

Swanton, M. J., 'The Manuscript Illumination of a Helmet of Benty Grange Type', *Journal of the Arms and Armour Society*, 10 (1980), 1–5.

Taylor, H. M., 'St Wystan's Church, Repton, Derbyshire. A Reconstruction Essay', *Archaeological Journal*, 144 (1987), 205–45.

Taylor, H. M. and J. Taylor, *Anglo-Saxon Architecture*, 3 vols (Cambridge, 1965–78).

Thacker, A., 'Some Terms for Noblemen in Anglo-Saxon England, c. 650–900', in *ASSAH* 1, ed. D. Brown, BAR Bri. Ser. 92 (Oxford, 1981), 201–36.

Thompson, P. Z., 'Biography of a Library: The Western European Manuscript Collection of Peter P. Dubrovski in Leningrad', *The Journal of Library History*, 19 (1984), 477–503.

Thomson, R., *William of Malmesbury* (Woodbridge, 1987).

Thorpe, N., *The Glory of the Page: Medieval and Renaissance Illuminated Manuscripts from Glasgow University Library* (London, 1987).

Tonnochy, A. B., *Catalogue of British Seal-Dies in the British Museum* (London, 1952).

Tweddle, D., *The Anglian Helmet from Coppergate*, The Archaeology of York, The Small Finds 17.8 (York, 1992).

Ullmann, W., '"Nos si aliquid incompetenter ..." Some Observations on the Register of Fragments of Leo IV in the Collectio Britannica', *Ephemerides Iuris Canonici*, 9 (1953), 3–11, reprinted as c. 7 in W. Ullmann, *The Church and the Law in the Earlier Middle Ages* (London, 1975).

Ulmschneider, K., 'Settlement, Economy and the "Productive" Site: Middle Anglo-Saxon Lincolnshire AD 65–780', *Medieval Archaeology*, 44 (2000), 53–80.

Ulmschneider, K., *Markets, Minsters, and Metal-detectors: The Archaeology of Middle Saxon Lincolnshire and Hampshire Compared*, BAR Bri. Ser. 307 (Oxford, 2000).

Unterkircher, F., *Das Wiener Fragment der Lorscher Annalen*, Codices selecti phototypice impressi 15 (Graz, 1967).

Unterkircher, F. (ed.), *Sancti Bonifatii Epistolae*, Codices Selecti phototypice impressi 24 (Graz, 1971).

van der Horst, K., W. Noel, W. C. M. Wüstefeld (eds), *The Utrecht Psalter in Medieval Art: Picturing the Psalms of David* (Utrecht, 1996).

van Es, W. A., H. Sarfatij and P. J. Woltering (eds), *Archeologie in Nederland. Die rijkdom van het bodemarchief* (Amsterdam, 1988).

Verey, C. D., T. J. Brown and E. Coatsworth, *The Durham Gospels*, EEMF 20 (Copenhagen, 1980).

Vollrath, H., *Die Synoden Englands bis 1066,* Konziliengeschichte Reihe A, Darstellungen (Paderborn, 1985).

Vollrath, H., 'Die Landnahme der Angelsachsen nach dem Zeugnis de erzählenden Quellen', in M. Müller-Wille and R. Schneider (eds), *Ausgewählte Probleme der europäischen Landnahmen des Früh- und Hochmittelalters. Methodische Grundlagendiskussion im Grenzbereich zwischen Archäologie und Geschichte*, Vorträge und Forschungen 41 (Sigmaringen, 1993), 317–37.

von Daum Tholl, S. E., 'The Cutbercht Gospels and the Earliest Writing Centre at Salzburg', in L. L. Brownrigg (ed.), *The Making of the Medieval Book: Techniques of Production* (Los Altos, 1995), 17–33.

von Heinemann, O. (ed.), *Die Handschriften der Herzoglichen Bibliothek zu Wolfenbüttel, Vol. 1: Die Helmstedter Handschriften* (Wolfenbüttel, 1884, reprinted 1963).

Vyner, B. (ed.), *Building on the Past. Papers Celebrating 150 Years of the Royal Archaeological Institute* (London, 1994).

Wade, K., 'The Urbanization of East Anglia: The Ipswich Perspective', in J. Gardiner (ed.), *Flatlands and Wetlands: Current Themes in East Anglian Archaeology*, East Anglian Archaeology 50 (1993), 144–51.

Waddell, H. (trans.), *More Latin Lyrics from Vergil to Milton* (London, 1976).

Wallace-Hadrill, J. M., 'The Franks and the English in the Ninth Century: Some Common Historical Interests', *History*, 35 (1950), 202–18, reprinted Wallace-Hadrill, *Early Medieval History* (1975), 201–16.

Wallace-Hadrill, J. M., 'Charlemagne and England', in Braunfels (ed.), *Karl der Grosse* (Düsseldorf, 1965), Vol. 1 at 683–98, reprinted in Wallace-Hadrill, *Early Medieval History* (1975), 155–80.

Wallace-Hadrill, J. M., 'A Background to St. Boniface's Mission', in P. Clemoes and K. Hughes (eds), *England before the Conquest* (London, 1971), 35–48.

Wallace-Hadrill, J. M., 'Charlemagne and Offa', in Wallace-Hadrill, *Early Germanic Kingship* (Oxford, 1971), 98–123.

Wallace-Hadrill, J. M., *Early Germanic Kingship in England and on the Continent: The Ford Lectures Delivered in the University of Oxford in Hilary Term 1970* (Oxford, 1971).

Wallace-Hadrill, J. M., *Early Medieval History* (Oxford, 1975).

Wallace-Hadrill, J. M., *The Frankish Church* (Oxford, 1983).

Wallach, L., *Alcuin and Charlemagne: Studies in Carolingian History and Literature* (Ithaca, NY, 1959).

Wallis, F. (trans.), *Bede: The Reckoning of Time*, Translated Texts for Historians 29 (Liverpool, 1999).

Walpole, R. N., 'Charlemagne's Journey to the East: The French Translation of the Legend by Pierre of Beauvais', *University of California Publications on Semitic Philology*, 11 (1951), 433–52.

Wamers, E., 'Insular Art in Carolingian Europe – The Reception of Old ideas in a New Empire', in Higgitt and Spearman (eds), *The Age of Migrating Ideas* (Edinburgh, 1993), 35–44.

Wamers, E., 'Insulare Kunst im Reich Karls des Großen', in Stiegemann and Wemhoff (eds), *799, Kunst und Kultur* (Mainz, 1999), III, 452–64.

Wander, S. H., 'Cyprus Plates: The Story of David and Goliath', *Metropolitan Museum Journal*, 8 (1973), 89–104.

Wander, S. H., 'The Cyprus Plates and the Chronicle of Fredegar', *Dumbarton Oaks Papers*, 29 (1975), 356–46.

Wasserschleben, M., *Beiträge zur Geschichte der vorgratianischen Kirchenrechts quellen* (Leipzig, 1837).

Watts, W. (ed.), *Matthæi Paris Historia major. Juxta exemplar 1640 verbatim recusa. Accesserant duorum Offarum Merciorum regum, et viginti trium abbatum S. Albani Vitae. Una cum libro additamentorum* (London, 1684).

Watson, A. G., *Catalogue of the Dated and Datable Manuscripts c. 700–1600 in the Department of Manuscripts, the British Library* (London, 1979).

Wattenbach, W., W. Levison and H. Löwe, *Deutschlands Geschichtsquellen im Mittelalter. Vorzeit und Karolinger. Vol. 2: Die Karolinger vom Anfang des 8. Jahrhunderts bis zum Tode Karls des Großen* (Weimar, 1953).

Webster, L. and J. Backhouse (eds), *The Making of England: Anglo-Saxon Art and Culture, AD 600–900* (London, 1991).

Webster, L. and M. Brown (eds), *The Transformation of the Roman World AD 400–900* (London, 1997).

Weizmann, K. (ed.), *The Age of Spirituality: Late Antique and Early Christian Art, Third to Seventh Centuries. Catalogue of the Exhibition at the Metropolitan Museum of Art, November 19, 1977 through February 12 1978* (New York, 1979).

Welch, M., 'The Kingdom of the South Saxons: The Origins', in Bassett (ed.), *Origins of the Anglo-Saxon Kingdoms* (London, 1989), 75–96.

Welch, M., 'Contacts across the Channel between the Fifth and Seventh Century: A Review of the Archaeological Evidence', *Studien zur Sachsenforschung*, 7 (1991), 261–69.

Werner, K.-F., 'Le rôle d'aristocratie dans la christianisation du nord-est de la Gaule', *Revue de l'histoire de l'église de France*, 62 (1976), 45–74.

Werner, K.-F., 'Les rouages de l'administration', in P. Perin and L. Feffer (eds), *La Neustrie: Les pays au nord de la Loire de Dagobert à Charles le Chauve (vii–ix siècles)* (Créteil, 1985), 41–46.

Werner, M., 'The Luidhard Medalet', *ASE*, 20 (1991), 27–41.

Whitelock, D., *After Bede*, Jarrow Lecture (Jarrow, 1960).

Whitelock, D., *The Genuine Asser*, Stenton Lecture 1967 (Reading, 1968).

Whitelock D., et al. (eds), *Councils and Synods: with other Documents Relating to the English Church. Vol I: AD 871–1204* (Oxford, 1981).

Whitman, F. H., 'Aenigmata Tatwini', *Neuphilologische Mitteilungen*, 88 (1987), 8–17.

Whitting, P. D., 'The Byzantine Empire and the Coinage of the Anglo-Saxons', in R. H. M. Dolley (ed.), *Anglo-Saxon Coins: Studies Presented to F.M. Stenton on the Occasion of his 80th Birthday* (London, 1960), 23–38.

Williams, G., 'Mercian Coinage and Authority', in M. P. Brown and C. A. Farr (eds), *Mercia: An Anglo-Saxon Kingdom in Europe* (London, 2001), 210–28.

Williams, J., *Early Spanish Manuscript Illumination* (New York, 1977).

Williams, J., *The Illustrated Beatus. A Corpus of the Illustrations of the Commentary on the Apocalypse. Vol. 1: Introduction* (London, 1994).

Wilson, D. M., 'England and the Continent in the Eighth Century – An Archaeological Viewpoint', *Angli e Sassoni al di qua e al di là del mare*, Settimane di Studio 32 (Spoleto, 1986), 219–44.

Wilson, H. A. (ed.), *The Calendar of St Willibrord from MS Paris Lat. 10837: a facsimile with transcriptions, introduction and notes* (London, 1918).

Witney, K. P., *The Kingdom of Kent* (London, 1982).

Wood, I. N., *The Merovingian North Sea*, Occasional Papers on Medieval Topics 1 (Alingsås, 1983).

Wood, I. N., 'Ripon, Francia and the Franks' Casket in the Early Middle Ages', *Northern History*, 26 (1990), 1–19.

Wood, I. N., 'The Channel from the 4th to the 7th Centuries AD', in S. McGrail (ed.), *Maritime Celts, Frisians, and Saxons* CBA Research Report 71 (London, 1990), 93–97.

Wood, I. N., 'St. Wandrille and its Hagiography', in I. N. Wood and G. A. Loud (eds), *Church and Chronicle in the Middle Ages: Essays Presented to John Taylor* (Hambleton, 1991), 1–14.

Wood, I. N., 'Frankish Hegemony in England', in M. O. H. Carver (ed.), *The Age of Sutton Hoo: The Seventh Century and North-western Europe* (Woodbridge, 1992), 235–41.

Wood, I. N., 'The Mission of Augustine of Canterbury to the English', *Speculum*, 69 (1994), 1–17.

Wood, I. N., *The Merovingian Kingdoms 450–751* (London, 1994).

Wood, I. N., 'Before and after the Migration to Britain', in Hines (ed.), *The Anglo-Saxons from the Migration Period to the Eighth Century* (San Marino, 1997), 41–51.

Woolf, A., 'Pictish Matriliny Reconsidered', *Innes Review*, 49.2 (1998), 147–67.

Wormald, F., *Collected Writings. 1: Studies in Medieval Art, 6th to 12th Centuries*, ed. J. J. G. Alexander, T. J. Brown and J. Gibbs (London, 1984).

Wormald, P., 'Bede and Benedict Biscop', in Bonner (ed.), *Famulus Christi* (London, 1976), 141–69.

Wormald, P., '*Lex Scripta* and *Verbum Regis*: Legislation and Germanic Kingship from Euric to Cnut', in Sawyer and Wood (eds), *Early Medieval Kingship* (Leeds, 1977), 105–38.

Wormald, P., 'The Ninth Century', in J. Campbell (ed.), *The Anglo-Saxons* (Oxford, 1982), 132–57.

Wormald, P., 'The Age of Offa and Alcuin', in J. Campbell (ed.), *The Anglo-Saxons* (Oxford, 1982), 101–31.

Wormald, P., 'Bede, the Bretwaldas, and the Origins of the *Gens Anglorum*', in Wormald et al. (eds), *Ideal and Reality* (Oxford, 1983), 99–129.

Wormald, P., 'Æthelwold and his Continental Counterparts: Contacts, Comparison, Contrast', in Yorke (ed.), *Bishop Æthelwold* (Woodbridge, 1988), 13–42.

Wormald, P., 'In Search of King Offa's "Law Code"', in I. N. Wood and N. Lund (eds), *People and Places in Northern Europe, 500–1600. Essays in Honour of Peter Sawyer* (Woodbridge, 1991), 25–45.

Wormald, P., *The Making of English Law: King Alfred to the Twelfth Century* (Oxford, 1999).

Wormald, P., D. Bullough and R. Collins (eds), *Ideal and Reality in Frankish and Anglo-Saxon Society. Studies Presented to J.M. Wallace-Hadrill* (Oxford, 1983).

Wright, D., ed. *The Vespasian Psalter*, EEMF 14 (Copenhagen, 1967).

Yorke, B. A. E., 'The Kingdom of the East Saxons', *ASE*, 14 (1985), 1–36.

Yorke, B. A. E., *Kings and Kingdoms of Early Anglo-Saxon England* (London, 1990).

Yorke, B. A. E., *Wessex in the Early Middle Ages* (London and New York, 1995).

Yorke, B. A. E., 'The Reception of Christianity at the Anglo-Saxon Royal Courts', in Gameson (ed.), *St. Augustine* (Stroud, 1999), 152–73.

Yorke, B. A. E., ed. *Bishop Æthelwold: His Career and Influence* (Woodbridge, 1988).

Young, J. and P. H. Aitken (eds), *A Catalogue of the Manuscripts in the Hunterian Library of the University of Glasgow* (Glasgow, 1908).

Zipperer, S., 'Coins and Currency: Offa of Mercia and his Frankish Neighbours', in U. von Freeden, W. Koch and A. Wieczorek (eds), *Völker an Nord- und Ostsee und die Franken. Akten des 48. Sachsensymposiums in Mannheim vom 7 bis 11 September 1997* (Bonn, 1999), 121–28.

Index